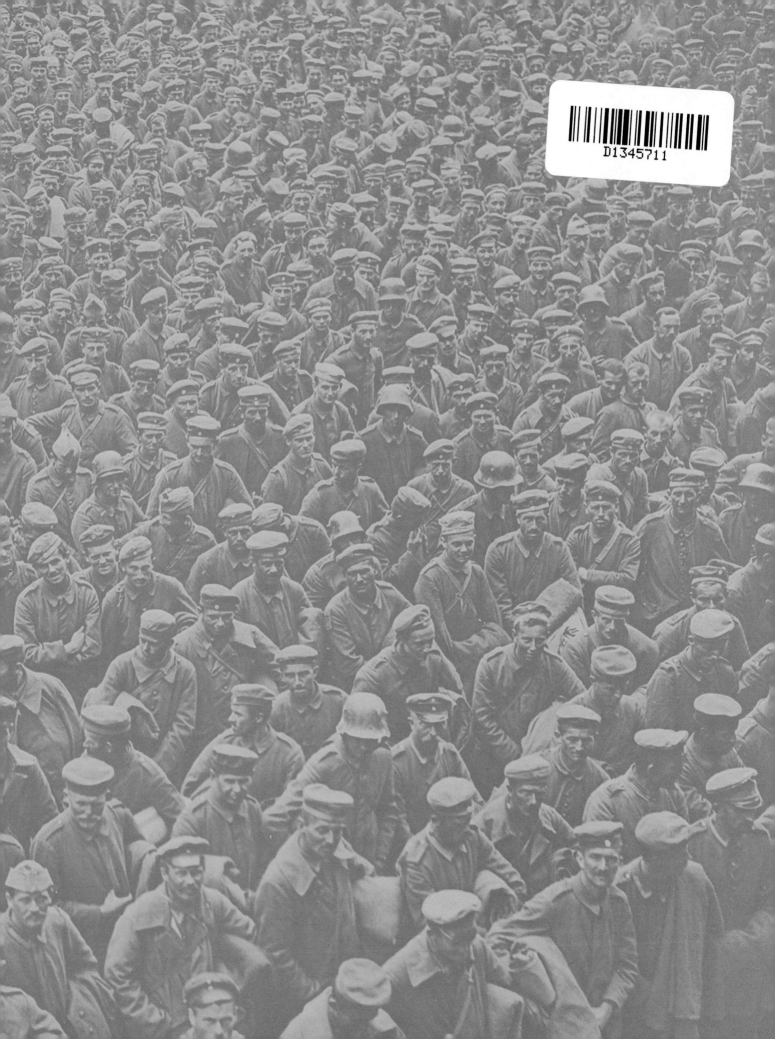

THE ART
OF WAR
Great Commanders
of the Modern World

THE ART OF WAR

Great Commanders of the Modern World

EDITED BY

Andrew Roberts

Quercus

CONTENTS

continued...

212
ULYSSES S. GRANT
John A. Barnes

220
WILLIAM T. SHERMAN
Richard J. Sommers

228
HELMUTH VON MOLTKE
John Lee

236
GARNET WOLSELEY
Ian Beckett

244
ERICH LUDENDORFF
John Lee

252
FERDINAND FOCH
Peter Hart

260
PHILIPPE PÉTAIN
Charles Williams

268
EDMUND ALLENBY
Jeremy Black

276
JOHN PERSHING
Carlo D'Este

284
KEMAL ATATÜRK
Ian Beckett

292
BASIL LIDDELL HART
Andrew Roberts

300
CARL GUSTAF MANNERHEIM
Allan Mallinson

308
GERD VON RUNDSTEDT
Michael Burleigh

316
ERICH VON MANSTEIN
Michael Burleigh

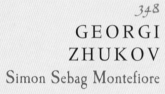

INTRODUCTION

This is the second of two volumes that seek to explore what the greatest military commanders of world history can tell us about the Art of War, from the very earliest moments of recorded history right up to the present day. The first volume covers the 3,000 years from the age of the warrior pharaoh Thutmose III to the dawn of the Age of Gunpowder; the second volume takes us from the dynastic wars of the early seventeenth and eighteenth centuries to the global conflicts of the twentieth century.

'Greatness is not universal,' thundered the military historian and theorist Major-General J. F. C. Fuller to Captain Basil Liddell Hart after reading his 1926 biography of Scipio Africanus, provocatively entitled *Greater Than Napoleon*. '"Who is the greatest?" is the question of a child stretching out its hand for the moon. To say that Homer is greater than Shakespeare, or Shakespeare than Goethe is absurd. Each may have been the great of his epoch. You may rightly say that Scipio was greater than Hannibal, but you cannot logically say that he was greater than Alexander or Napoleon or Frederick.'

We are not attempting to stretch out our hands for the moon in this work. Instead we are asking who were the greatest commanders in their own historical periods, which we have chronologically split

between the Ancient and Medieval, and the Modern worlds. Here, surrounded by contemporaries or near-contemporaries, it is easier to make a running order of those soldiers who must be included.

Of course there are omissions, as there have to be with a small finite number like one hundred across the two volumes of *The Art of War*. Why Nathanael Greene and not George Washington? Was not Ney a greater marshal than Davout? We have chosen solely on the grounds that our great commanders fulfil better than anyone else the ultimate criterion for successful military leadership, the one that the great Prussian military theorist Carl von Clausewitz returned to again and again in his seminal work *On War*: Genius.

The distribution of military genius is surprisingly widespread both chronologically and geographically. I was surprised that our list contained quite so many non-Europeans, since Europe has been the principal crucible of global warfare for the past half-millennium or so. It was not out of political correctness that warriors such as Shaka Zulu, Tomoyaki Yamashita and Vo Nguyen Giap forced themselves into these pages, but because great military attributes seem to know no racial or geographical boundaries.

Neither is there any definable connection between fighting well and fighting in a good cause. If there are a large number of generals in these pages who fought for barbarism and enslavement rather than civilization and liberty, that is because the righteousness of the ultimate

goal seems to be pretty immaterial when it comes to military genius. 'It is a piece of idle sentimentality', wrote John Stuart Mill, 'that truth, merely as truth, has any inherent power denied to error, of prevailing against the dungeon and the stake.' The same goes for the Panzer and the Stuka. This book reminds us how fortunate we are that despite the generally higher quality of the Wehrmacht to the Allied generals in the Second World War, the Führer himself was a strategic dunderhead who nonetheless reckoned himself 'the greatest warlord who ever lived'.

As to the question of whether great commanders are born great, achieve greatness or have greatness thrust upon them, the answer seems to be both all and none of the above. Although the more viscous social structures of early times militated towards regal and noble commanders until the end of the Age of Gunpowder, death and the fear of death was always democratic enough to ensure that soldiers of merit rose faster in war than in periods of peace, just as revolutions fling up the kind of leaders that would never emerge in tranquil times. Talent will always out, even in the most hidebound societies: Clive was a debt-ridden clerk, Napoleon a Corsican outsider, and so on.

We have – except in the debatable exception of Eisenhower – opted for hands-on tacticians and battlefield commanders, as opposed to chiefs of staff who decided grand strategy far behind the lines, or even in different countries altogether. Good arguments can be made for General George C. Marshall, General Sir Alan Brooke (later Lord Alanbrooke) and even for the 'Big Three' statesmen being included as great commanders for the way that they planned the victorious grand strategy of the Second World War at Tehran and Yalta, but they are not generally recognized as such, even though they probably had more overall say in how that war was won than the generals who fought such battles as El Alamein, Stalingrad and Kursk.

André Malraux once said that the purpose of war was to do the utmost to ensure that fragments of metal penetrated human flesh. It is a severe but essentially fair summation of the art of the great commander, at least once the period of pre-battle manoeuvre is over. On rare occasions manoeuvre alone is enough, and these are paid tribute to in this book.

So what are the attributes that distinguish history's greatest commanders? 'The power to command has never meant the power to remain mysterious,' wrote one of them, Marshal Foch, in his 1919 work *Precepts and Judgments*. The qualities are not secret but openly on display and have been remarkably unchanging over the centuries, and thus capable of analysis in this book. For all the revolutions in technology, the coming and departing of the Age of Gunpowder, the advent of the machine-gun and the rise of air power, the characteristics have remained astonishingly ageless. Heinz Guderian would have recognized the audacity of Joshau; Dwight Eisenhower would have admired the sheer, overawing *puissance* of Cyrus; Robert E. Lee would have applauded the attention to detail of Wellington, or for that matter the tactical aptitude of Alexander.

Fuller's correspondent – and sometime protagonist – Liddell Hart wrote in his *Thoughts on War* in 1944 that: 'The two qualities of mental initiative and strong personality, or determination, go a long way towards the power of command in war – they are, indeed, the hallmark of the Great Captains.' In these pages will be found much mental initiative and strong personality, certainly, but also a feel for the *coup d'œil*, the capacity for inspiring strangers, a remarkable sense of timing, an aptitude for observation, the ability to create surprise, a facility for public relations, the gift of interlocking strategy with tactics and vice versa, a faculty for predicting an opponent's likely behaviour, a capability for retaining the initiative, and as General Patton wrote in October 1944, a capacity for 'telling somebody who thinks he is beaten that he is not beaten'.

It will be noted that no soldier of our own times has merited inclusion in this volume. That is because although the Cold War overheated regionally on a number of occasions – Korea and Vietnam being the most obvious examples – the nuclear deterrent has kept the Great Powers formally at peace, while generalship has tended to become a more managerial, even technological, concept. Nor has the post-1989 world thrown up great commanders of the significance of those featured in this book. In time, the names of General Norman Schwarzkopf in the 1990/91 Gulf War and General David H. Petraeus in the insurgency phase of its successor conflict, the Iraq War, might be seen as justifying inclusion in a future volume, particularly the latter for his command of the 'surge' of five extra US brigades, numbering over 30,000 men, in 2007. At the time of writing in the summer of 2008, however, it is simply too early to make any such judgement.

ANDREW ROBERTS
August 2008

CONTRIBUTORS

John A. Barnes

A native New Yorker, John Barnes took a bachelor's degree in journalism from New York University in 1982 before embarking on a seventeen-year career as a reporter and editorial writer for columnists Rowland Evans and Robert Novak, the *Detroit News* and the *New York Post*. He joined Pfizer Inc. in 1999 as part of its corporate communications unit. He is the author of three books: *Irish-American Landmarks: A Traveler's Guide* (1995); *Ulysses S. Grant on Leadership: Executive Lessons from the Front Lines* (2001); and *John F. Kennedy on Leadership: The Lessons and Legacy of a President* (2005). He lives in Manhattan with his wife Mary and their two children.

Ian Beckett

Ian Beckett is Professor of History at the University of Northampton. Educated at Aylesbury Grammar School and the universities of Lancaster and London, he has been Major General Matthew C. Horner Professor of Military Theory at the US Marine Corps University, Professor of History at the University of Luton and Visiting Professor of Strategy at the US Naval War College, as well as Senior Lecturer in War Studies at the Royal Military Academy, Sandhurst. A Fellow of the Royal Historical Society, he is Chairman of the Army Records Society and Secretary to the Trustees of the Buckinghamshire Military Museum. His many publications on British military history and the First World War include *The Amateur Military Tradition, 1558–1945* (1991); *The Victorians at War* (2003); *Ypres: The First Battle, 1914* (2004); *The Great War 1914–1918* (2007); and *Territorials* (2008). He is currently working on the politics of command in the late Victorian army.

Jeremy Black

Graduating from Queens' College, Cambridge with a starred first, Jeremy Black studied at St John's College and Merton College, Oxford, before teaching at Durham and Exeter universities. He is a Fellow of the Royal Society for the Arts and a past Council member of the Royal Historical Society. His many books include *War and the World 1450–2000* (2000); *World War Two: A Military History* (2003); *The British Seaborne Empire* (2004) and, for Quercus, *Tools of War* (2007).

Stephen Brumwell

Dr Stephen Brumwell is a freelance writer and independent historian based in Amsterdam. Leaving school to work as a newspaper reporter, he subsequently attended the University of Leeds as a mature student. After gaining a First in History, Brumwell was awarded British Academy funding to research eighteenth-century North America. His doctoral dissertation was published by Cambridge University Press as *Redcoats: The British Soldier and War in the Americas, 1755–63* (2002). Drawing upon his research interests Brumwell has since published *White Devil: A True Story of War, Savagery and Vengeance in Colonial America* (2004); and *Paths of Glory: The Life and Death of General James Wolfe* (2006). All of Brumwell's books have been widely acclaimed for engaging general readers and specialists alike – what Canada's *Globe & Mail* characterized as a combination of 'first-rate, innovative scholarship, and page-turning readability'. He is currently writing a biography of George Washington for Quercus.

Michael Burleigh

Since 2001 Michael Burleigh has worked as an independent historian and writer after eighteen years as an academic: in Britain at New College, Oxford, LSE and the University of Cardiff, and in the United States at Rutgers University in New Jersey, at Washington & Lee University in Virginia, and as Kratter Visiting Professor at Stanford University, California. His recent books include *The Racial State: Germany 1933–1945* (1991); *Death and Deliverance: Euthanasia in Germany 1900–1945* (1994); *Ethics and Extermimation: Reflections on Nazi Genocide* (1997); *The Third Reich: A New History* (2001) which won the Samuel Johnson Prize for Non-Fiction; *Earthly Powers* and *Sacred Causes*, a two-volume study of politics and religion in Europe from the Enlightenment to Al-Qaeda (2005–6); and *Blood and Rage: A Cultural History of Terrorism* (2008). He is a regular commentator on international affairs for *The Times, Sunday Times* and *Daily Telegraph,* and he has made three award-winning television documentaries. He is married and lives in London.

John Childs

Educated at the University of Hull and King's College, London, John Childs is Professor of Military History and Director of the Centre for Military History in the University of Leeds. As well as publishing a pioneering investigation of the military use of land and co-authoring a *Dictionary of Military History*, he has written a number of books on European armies and warfare during the seventeenth and eighteenth centuries, principally a trilogy on the social and political history of the British army from 1660 to 1702, a study of the Nine Years War, and, most recently, *Warfare in the Seventeenth Century* (2001) and *The Williamite Wars in Ireland, 1688–1691* (2007). He is currently writing a history of the War of the Spanish Succession. A former trustee of the Royal Armouries, John Childs chairs the Royal Armouries Development Trust and the Battlefields Panel of English Heritage.

Martin van Creveld

Martin van Creveld, formerly of the Hebrew University, Jerusalem, is a leading expert on military history and strategy, with a special interest in the future of war. He is the author of twenty books, including *The Culture of War* (2008); *The Changing Face of War: Lessons of Combat from the Marne to Iraq* (2007); *The Transformation of War* (1991); *Command in War* (1985) and *Supplying War* (1978). Between them, these books have been translated into seventeen languages.

He has acted as consultant to defence establishments in several countries, and has taught or lectured at practically every institute of strategic studies from Canada to New Zealand and from Norway to South Africa. He has also appeared on numerous television and radio programmes as well as writing for, and being interviewed by, hundreds of newspapers and magazines around the world. He is married to Dvora Lewy, a painter, and lives in Mevasseret Zion near Jerusalem.

Saul David

Saul David is Visiting Professor of Military History at the University of Hull, and Professorial Research Fellow at the Humanities Research Centre of the University of Buckingham. His many books include *The Indian Mutiny: 1857* (2002); shortlisted for the Westminster Medal for Military Literature, *Zulu: the Heroism and Tragedy of the Zulu War of 1879* (2004, a Waterstone's Military History Book of the Year) and, most recently, *Victoria's Wars: The Rise of Empire* (2006). He has presented history programmes for most of the major TV channels, appeared as an expert on the BBC2 virtual battle series *Time Commanders*, and was the historical consultant for the BBC *Timewatch* documentary *Zulu: The True Story*.

Malcolm Deas

Malcolm Deas has been a Fellow of St Antony's College, Oxford since 1966, where he was one of the founders and subsequently the Director of the University's Latin American Centre. He has written extensively on the history and politics of Colombia and its neighbouring republics. For five years after the Falklands War he wrote leader columns on Latin American affairs for *The Times*, and he has contributed articles and reviews to the *TLS*, the *Spectator* and the *London Review of Books*. He has also worked as an adviser to the Colombian government.

Philip Dwyer

Philip Dwyer is Senior Lecturer in Modern European History at the University of Newcastle, Australia. His primary research interest is eighteenth-century Europe with particular emphasis on the Napoleonic Empire. His most recent publications include: *Napoleon and Europe*, ed. (2001); *The French Revolution and Napoleon. A Sourcebook*, with Peter McPhee (2002); *Talleyrand (Profiles in Power)* (2002); *Napoleon and His Empire: Europe, 1804–1814*, ed. with Alan Forrest (2007); and *Napoleon, 1769–1799: The Path to Power* (2007). He is currently writing the sequel.

Carlo D'Este

Carlo D'Este served in the US Army in Vietnam, Germany and Britain before retiring as a lieutenant-colonel in 1978. He received his MA from the University of Richmond and has now published six books that have won high praise both sides of the Atlantic: *Bitter Victory: The Battle for Sicily, 1943* (1989); *World War II in the Mediterranean 1942–1945* (1990); *Fatal Decision: Anzio and the Battle for Rome* (1991); *Patton: A Genius for War* (1995); *Decision in Normandy: The Real Story of Montgomery and the Allied Campaign* (2000); and *Eisenhower: Allied Supreme Commander* (2003). Acclaimed by Antony Beevor, John Keegan, Victor Davis Hanson, Martin Blumenson and Alan Clark, he is one of the greatest military biographers working today.

Antonia Fraser

Since 1969, Antonia Fraser has written many acclaimed historical works which have been international bestsellers, including *Mary Queen of Scots* (1969, James Tait Black Memorial Prize); *Cromwell: Our Chief of Men* (1973); *The Six Wives of Henry* VIII (1992) and *The Gunpowder Plot: Terror and Faith in 1605* (1996, St Louis Literary Award; CWA Non-Fiction Gold Dagger); and *Marie Antoinette* (2001). Antonia Fraser was made CBE in 1999, and awarded the Norton Medlicott Medal by the Historical Association in 2000. She is married to the playwright Harold Pinter and lives in London.

Peter Hart

Peter Hart was born in 1955. He went to Liverpool University before joining the Sound Archive at the Imperial War Museum in 1981. His many books include *Jutland, 1916* (2003); *Somme, 1916* (2005); *Bloody April* (2005); *Aces Falling: War above the Trenches, 1918* (2007); and *1918: A Very British Victory* (2008). He is now Oral Historian at the Imperial War Museum Archive.

Robert Harvey

Robert Harvey has been a columnist for the *Daily Telegraph*, assistant editor of *The Economist* and an MP. He is the author of many books, including a highly popular biography of Lord Cochrane. He is a former member of the House of Commons Foreign Affairs Committee, and foreign affairs leader writer for the *Daily Telegraph*. His books include *Portugal: Birth of a Democracy* (1978); *The Undefeated: The Rise, Fall and Rise of Modern Japan* (1994); *Liberators* (2000); and *Cochrane* (2000). Robert Harvey lives in Powys, Wales.

Alistair Horne

Alistair Horne was educated at Le Rosey, Switzerland, and Jesus College, Cambridge. He ended his war service with the rank of captain in the Coldstream Guards attached to MI5 in the Middle East. From 1952 to 1955 he worked as a foreign correspondent for the *Daily Telegraph*. In 1969 he founded the Alistair Horne research fellowship in modern history, St Antony's College, Oxford. His numerous books on history and politics have been translated into over ten languages, he was awarded the 1962 Hawthornden prize (for *The Price of Glory*) and the 1977 Wolfson prize (for *A Savage War of Peace*). In 1992 he was awarded the CBE; in 1993 he received the French Légion d'Honneur for his work on French history and a Litt.D. from Cambridge University. He was knighted in 2003 for services to Franco-British relations.

John Hughes-Wilson

John Hughes-Wilson is one of Britain's leading commentators and authors on intelligence, contemporary military developments and military history. With Professor Richard Holmes, he is President of the Guild of Battlefield Guides and has specialized in a number of First World War topics, from the mystery of Richthofen's death to British undercover intelligence operations. He is a frequent broadcaster for BBC television, and is the presenter of numerous television programmes, including the award-nominated BBC *What If?* television series. His non-fiction books include the best-selling *Military Intelligence Blunders* (1999) and *Blindfold and Alone* (2001); described by reviewers as 'the definitive work on the First World War executions'. *The Puppet Masters*, the secret history of intelligence, was published in 2004 to outstanding reviews and was shortlisted for the Westminster Gold Medal for military history. His latest book is *An American Coup: Who Really Killed JFK?* (2008). After initial service as an infantry officer with the Sherwood Foresters, during his twenty-five years in the Intelligence Corps he saw active service in the Falkland Islands, Cyprus, Arabia, and Northern Ireland as well as the political jungles of Whitehall and NATO. His family has grown up and he now lives and works in Cyprus.

John Lee

John Lee has MAs in War Studies and Social and Economic History. He is an Honorary Research Fellow of the Centre for First World War Studies, University of Birmingham, and a member of the British Commission for Military History, the Western Front Association, the Gallipoli Association, the Army Records Society and the International Churchill Society. He is the author of *A Soldier's Life: General Sir Ian Hamilton 1853–1947* (2001); *The Warlords: Hindenburg and Ludendorff* (2005); and, with his wife, Celia Lee, *Winston and Jack: The Churchill brothers* (2007) together with fifteen or more chapters in books of essays on the First World War. Retired from a life in bookselling and publishing, he is a battlefield guide for Holt's Tours, and a military lecturer and writer.

Giles MacDonogh

Giles MacDonogh went to school in London, and university in Oxford and Paris, where he first read and later undertook research into modern history. He is the author of twelve books, six of them on the history of Germany. He has written biographies of Frederick the Great (1999), the Kaiser and the resistance leader Adam von Trott. He has also published histories of Prussia and Berlin. His latest book, *After the Reich* (2007) looks at Germany and Austria at the end of the Second World War. He is currently working on a book on Germany in 1938 to be published in 2009. MacDonogh has written for the main British newspapers such as *The Times*, *Financial Times* and the *Guardian*. He has lectured at universities in France, Germany, Italy and Bulgaria. He also works as a translator from French and German and produced *The Hitler Book* for John Murray (2005) and *A Garden of Eden in Hell* for Macmillan (2007).

Allan Mallinson

Allan Mallinson was a professional soldier for thirty-five years, first in the infantry and then the cavalry. He commanded the 13th/18th Royal Hussars whose history, after their 1992 amalgamation with the 15th/19th King's Royal Hussars, he wrote: *Light Dragoons* (published by Leo Cooper); recently republished with an additional chapter covering the years since amalgamation. He is author of the Matthew Hervey series of novels, set in the Duke of Wellington's cavalry, the tenth of which – *Warrior* – was published by Transworld in June 2008. He is currently working on a history of the British Army. Allan Mallinson is a regular reviewer for *The Times*, the *Sunday Telegraph*, and the *Spectator*, and is the defence columnist of the *Daily Telegraph*. He lives on Salisbury Plain.

Simon Sebag Montefiore

Simon Sebag Montefiore was born 1965 and read history at Gonville and Caius College, Cambridge. *Catherine the Great and Potemkin* (2000) was shortlisted for the Samuel Johnson, Duff Cooper, and Marsh Biography Prizes. *Stalin: The Court of the Red Tsar* won the History Book of the Year Prize at the 2004 British Book Awards; its prequel, *Young Stalin*, was awarded the Costa Prize and the Los Angeles Times Book Prize in 2007, and was nominated for the James Tait Black Memorial Prize in 2008. Montefiore's books are worldwide bestsellers, published in thiry-four languages. *101 World Heroes* was published by Quercus in 2007 and has been translated into ten languages; its companion volume, *Monsters*, appeared in September 2008. A Fellow of the Royal Society of Literature, Montefiore lives in London with his wife, the novelist Santa Montefiore, and their two children. He is now writing *Jerusalem: The Biography*, a fresh history of the Middle East.

Richard Overy

Richard Overy is a best-selling historian. He specializes in the Hitler and Stalin dictatorships, the Second World War, air power in the twentieth century, and German history from 1900. He is the author of *Russia's War* (1997); *Interrogations: Inside the Mind of the Nazi Elite* (2002); *The Dictators: Hitler's Germany and Stalin's Russia* (2004); and *Chronicles of the Third Reich*, forthcoming from Quercus. Richard Overy is Professor of History at Exeter University.

Alan Palmer

Alan Palmer was Head of History at Highgate School, London, for eighteen years before retiring early to concentrate on historical writing and research. The author of more than three dozen narratives, biographies and reference books, he was elected a Fellow of the Royal Society of Literature in 1980. Subjects of his biographies include Tsar Alexander I, Marshal Bernadotte, Metternich, Bismarck, Kaiser William II, Emperor Francis Joseph, Frederick the Great, King George IV and Kemal Atatürk. His other books include *Napoleon in Russia* (1967); *Russia in War and Peace* (1973); *The Decline and Fall of the Ottoman Empire* (1993) and *Northern Shores, A History of the Baltic Sea and its Peoples* (2005). His most recent book was *The Salient, Ypres 1914–1918* (2007).

Geoffrey Perret

Geoffrey Perret was educated at Harvard and the University of California at Berkeley and served for three years in the US Army. He is the award-winning author of thirteen books, including *Old Soldiers Never Die: The Life of Douglas MacArthur* (1996); *Eisenhower* (2000); *Ulysses S. Grant: Soldier and President* (1997); and *Commander in Chief* (2007). Three of his works have received Notable Book of the Year awards from the *New York Times* and four have been nominated for the Pulitzer Prize in History. His work has appeared in the *New York Times*, the *Washington Post, American Heritage, Military History Quarterly, Civil War Book Review* and *GQ*. He is currently writing an account of the Vietnam War that focuses on William C. Westmoreland, Nguyen Cao Ky and Vo Nguyen Giap.

Andrew Roberts

Andrew Roberts took a first in modern history from Gonville & Caius College, Cambridge, from where he is an honorary senior scholar. His biography of Winston Churchill's foreign secretary Lord Halifax, entitled *The Holy Fox*, was published by Weidenfeld & Nicolson in 1991, followed by *Eminent Churchillians* (1994); *Salisbury: Victorian Titan*, which won the Wolfson Prize and the James Stern Silver Pen Award (1999); *Napoleon and Wellington* (2002); *Hitler and Churchill: Secrets of Leadership* (2003) and *Waterloo: Napoleon's Last Gamble* (2005).

He has also edited a collection of twelve counterfactual essays by historians entitled *What Might Have Been* (2004) as well as *The Correspondence of Benjamin Disraeli and Mrs Sarah Brydges Willyams* (2006). His *A History of the English-Speaking Peoples Since 1900* (2006) won the US Intercollegiate Studies Institute Book Award for 2007. Roberts is a Fellow of the Royal Society of Literature, an honorary Doctor of Humane Letters, and reviews history books for more than a dozen newspapers and periodicals. He has recently published *Masters and Commanders: How Churchill, Roosevelt, Alanbrooke and Marshall Won the War in the West, 1941–45*. His website can be found at www.andrew-roberts.net.

Lucy Riall

Lucy Riall is Professor of History at Birkbeck College, University of London, and the editor of *European History Quarterly*. She was educated at the London School of Economics and Cambridge University. She has held previous appointments at Cambridge and the University of Essex, and been a visiting professor at the Ecole Normale Supérieure, Paris, and the Freie Universität, Berlin. Her publications include *Risorgimento: The History of Italy from Napoleon to Nation-state* (2008); *Garibaldi: Invention of a Hero* (2007); *Sicily and the Unification of Italy: Liberal Policy and Local Power, 1859–1866* (1998) and the edited volume (with David Laven); *Napoleon's Legacy: Problems of Government in Restoration Europe* (2000).

Trevor Royle

Trevor Royle is an author and broadcaster specializing in the history of war and empire with over a score of books to his credit. His latest books are *Flowers of the Forest: Scotland and the First World War* (2006); *Civil War: The Wars of the Three Kingdoms, England, Ireland and Scotland, 1638–1660* (2004); and a study of General George S. Patton as a military commander. Other recent books include *Winds of Change: The End of Empire in Africa* (1996); *Crimea: The Great Crimean War 1854–1856* (1999); and a highly praised biography of the controversial Chindit leader Orde Wingate. He is currently writing concise histories of the pre-1968 Scottish infantry regiments. As a journalist he is an Associate Editor of the *Sunday Herald* and is a regular commentator on defence matters and international affairs for the BBC. He is a Fellow of the Royal Society of Edinburgh.

Hugo Slim

Dr Hugo Slim has worked for Save the Children UK and the United Nations in Sudan, Ethiopia, the Middle East and Bangladesh. He has been on the Council of Oxfam GB and an International Advisor to the British Red Cross. He was Reader in International Humanitarianism at Oxford Brookes University from 1994 to 2003 and most recently was Chief Scholar at the Centre for Humanitarian Dialogue in Geneva. He is currently a Director of Corporates for Crisis in London, advising international companies on their community relations in emerging markets. His latest book is *Killing Civilians: Method, Madness and Morality in War* (2007). He is a grandson of Field Marshal the Viscount Slim.

Richard J. Sommers

Richard J. Sommers was born in Hammond, Indiana, and raised in suburban Chicago. He earned his BA from Carleton College and his Ph.D from Rice University. His numerous publications on the American Civil War include *Richmond Redeemed: The Siege at Petersburg* (1980), which won the National Historical Society's Bell Wiley Prize as the best Civil War book of 1981–2. Since 1970, he has served as the US Army Military History Institute's Chief Archivist-Historian, Assistant Director for Archives, and Chief of Patron Services. In 2007 he held the General Harold Keith Johnson Chair of Military History at the Institute and the US Army War College. In 2008, he assumed his current position as the Institute's Senior Historian. He has served on the boards of the Society of Civil War Historians, the Jefferson Davis Association, the Richmond Battlefields Association, and the Harrisburg Civil War Round Table. He lives in Carlisle, Pennsylvania.

Charles Spencer

Charles Spencer was educated at Eton and at Magdalen College, Oxford, where he read Modern History. He was a reporter for seven years with the News Division of the American television network NBC. His books include *Althorp: The Story of an English House* (1998); *The Spencer Family* (1999); *Blenheim: Battle for Europe* (2004), which was shortlisted for History Book of the Year at the 2005 National Book Awards; and *Prince Rupert: The Last Cavalier* (2007). He is a book reviewer for the *Independent on Sunday*, and has written for the *Spectator*, the *Guardian* and many other newspapers and magazines in the UK and the USA. Charles Spencer has been the owner of Althorp, Northamptonshire, since 1992, and founded the Althorp Literary Festival. He is the father of six children.

Andrew Uffindell

Andrew Uffindell has written extensively on the Napoleonic period. His books include *Napoleon's Immortals* (2007), a major reassessment of the Imperial Guard; *Waterloo Commanders* (2007); *Great Generals of the Napoleonic Wars* (2007); *The Eagle's Last Triumph: Napoleon's Victory at Ligny* (1994); and (as a co-author) *On the Fields of Glory: The Battlefields of the 1815 Campaign* (1986). He has edited a collection of essays by the late Jac Weller, *On Wellington* (1998); and also wrote *The National Army Museum Book of Wellington's Armies* (2003), part of a series that collectively won the Royal United Services Institute's Duke of Westminster Medal for Military Literature (2004). His published articles include studies of the Franco-Austrian War of 1859 and friendly fire at Waterloo.

Alan Warren

Alan Warren is the author of *Waziristan: the Faqir of Ipi and the Indian Army* (2000); *Singapore 1942: Britain's Greatest Defeat* (2001); and *World War II: A Military History* (2008). He has been a Fellow of the State Library of Victoria and has taught at Monash University, Melbourne, Australia.

Charles Williams

Charles Williams, Lord Williams of Elvel CBE, is a Labour peer and political biographer. Educated at Westminster and Christ Church, Oxford, he did National Service in the King's Royal Rifle Corps and went on to a career in banking before becoming Chairman of the Price Commission in 1977. In 1985 he became a life peer and in 1989 was elected Deputy Leader of the Opposition in the House of Lords. His political biographies to date are of de Gaulle, Adenauer and Pétain, and he is currently working on a life of Harold Macmillan. As a former cricketer (he captained Oxford in 1955 and subsequently played for Essex in the County Championship) he thought that he had all the right credentials to write the life of Sir Donald Bradman, a book which Bradman himself said was the best of the many written about him. His wife Jane was Rab Butler's niece and one of Winston Churchill's devoted secretaries. They live in London and Wales.

'Nature brings forth some valiant men, but good order through industry makes more.' JUSTUS LIPSIUS, *SIX BOOKES OF POLITICKES OR CIVIL DOCTRINE* (1594)

MAURICE OF NASSAU
1567–1625

JOHN CHILDS

MAURICE OF NASSAU, the most admired soldier in Europe at the turn of the seventeenth century, saved the infant Dutch Republic from reconquest by Spain, leading to the truce that effectively recognized the state's legal right to exist. He also reformed the Dutch armed forces and in doing so established the basis for new tactical and organizational methods that spread widely across western Europe.

(Opposite) **Maurice of Nassau in full armour** in the early 1620s, painted by Michiel van Mierenveld. Despite his personal caution, Maurice oversaw military reforms that proved both effective and widely influential across Europe. Following his overthrow of Johan van Oldenbarneveldt, Landsadvocaat of Holland, in 1618, Maurice's political authority was unchallenged, although he was never to recover his confidence or vigour.

Maurice was born in Dillenburg Castle in the Duchy of Nassau, Germany, on 14 November 1567, the second son of William the Silent of Nassau, Prince of Orange, and his second wife Anna of Saxony. He became heir to his father's titles and estates before his first birthday, after his elder half-brother Philip William was abducted to Spain as a hostage in 1568. The same year, his father, stadholder (royal representative or governor) of the mainly Calvinist provinces of Holland, Zeeland and Utrecht, led the Dutch forces in open revolt against Spain, thus initiating a struggle for independence that was to continue for eighty years and to which Maurice was to devote his career.

The states of Holland and Zeeland funded Maurice's education at Heidelberg and then Leiden, where he was tutored by the mathematician and engineer Simon Stevin (1548–1620). After his father's assassination at the hands of a French Catholic in 1584, Holland and Zeeland invited the 16-year-old Maurice to succeed as stadholder – Utrecht, Gelderland and Overijssel following suit in 1587 – and, in 1586, conferred upon him the title Prince of Orange. In 1588, at the age of 21, he was appointed Admiral-General of the United Netherlands and Captain-General of the troops in Brabant and Flanders. His cousin William Louis (1560–1620) was chosen as stadholder of Friesland, Groningen and Drenthe.

Dour, taciturn, careful and slow to make decisions, Maurice was not a sovereign ruler but an appointee of the States General, the central representative institution and effective government of the nascent Dutch Republic, so his authority and independence were prescribed by the civil power. As admiral-general, he was answerable to five provincial admiralty boards, whilst a committee of the States General, the Council of State (Raad van State), coordinated military affairs and supervised field operations through civilian 'field deputies'. His own natural caution complemented the States

Maurice of Nassau

MILITARY REFORMS

MAURICE NEEDED TO WELD the Dutch army's ineffective and unreliable mixture of mercenaries and city militias into a professional army capable of resisting the Spanish forces. The programme, which he began in 1589, was largely achieved within ten years. Maurice's *more Romano* ('in the Roman style') combined contemporary practice with ideas and models derived from Classical authors, particularly Vitruvius, Caesar, Aelianus, Vegetius Renatus and the Byzantine Emperor Leo VI. He also owed much to the teaching of the philosopher Justus Lipsius, professor of history at Leiden from 1579 to 1590, whose treatises on the Roman army, *De Militia Romana* (1595), and siege warfare, *Poliorceticon* (1596), provided the underlying historical information.

Although pressed by Lipsius to create an army of citizen-soldiers, Maurice was forced to use mercenaries because the Dutch population only numbered about 1 million people, most of whom were engaged in the agricultural, commercial and maritime activities essential to provide the revenues for the continuation of the war. Thus, the majority of the rank-and-file in Maurice's army were English, Scots, French, German, Swiss and Danish, but quality and loyalty were enhanced through careful selection and the provision of comparatively attractive and extended periods of service. In return, these long-term

mercenaries came to accept enhanced standards of discipline and expectations of unit loyalty.

To foster instant obedience and cohesion, at the suggestion of William Louis the men were trained daily at routines partly devised from Aelianus and Leo, with the original Greek words of command translated into Dutch, French, English and German. Drills for handling pikes and reloading muskets were reduced to numerical sequences, chanted in unison. Prompt and uniform execution of the manual of arms developed combat effectiveness and became the obvious manifestation of discipline. Daily exercises allowed more precise evolutions, permitting improved coordination between shot (muskets) and pike, and increased the rate of infantry fire. The problem of

delivering a sufficient weight of shot from the inaccurate and unwieldy matchlock muskets was solved in 1594 by the introduction of the counter-march (based on Roman javelin drill), again at the recommendation of William Louis.

Constant training and the more independent combat role allotted to sub-units required more numerous and better-educated junior officers, preferably Dutch. However, the military expertise of foreigners remained indispensable because many native officers continued to owe their appointments to non-military factors: the publication of a table of ranks was delayed until 1618. Maurice began the gradual change in the ethos of the military profession from a foundation of noble birth, honour and chivalry to a publicly recognized authority derived from a commission issued by the state.

The field army was cut to a size that was financially and logistically supportable: before 1600, it rarely amounted to more than 12,000 men (2,000 mounted and 10,000 infantry), accompanied after 1595 by six field guns and a siege train of forty-two cannon. The effectiveness of the artillery was improved by establishing a gun foundry in The Hague in 1589 and, from 1590, limiting production to just three calibres: 12-, 24- and 48-pounders. In tune with the general European tendency to improve articulation by making infantry units smaller – Spanish *tercios* (the distinctive pike-and-musket infantry formations that formed the basis of Spanish triumphs on the battlefield in the sixteenth century) had been halved to 1,500 men in 1584 – Maurice trimmed his companies to 130, all ranks, raised the number of musketeers until there was one for every pikeman, and arrayed his men in ten ranks, later reduced to six. In 1592 William Louis organized the companies into 'half regiments', or battalions, of around 800 men, later slimmed to 580, which were arranged on the battlefield in a chequerboard formation reminiscent of the deployment of a Roman legion. Troops of cavalry protected the vulnerable battalion flanks.

In combat, Maurice's reforms achieved two objectives. First, the new battalions were more mobile and better suited to operating in the 'great bog of Europe'. Secondly, they were much handier than the larger tercios both in conducting sieges and defending field works and fixed fortifications. Maurice of Nassau was less concerned about performance in pitched battle, although the new system functioned effectively at Turnhout in 1597 and Nieuport in 1600.

Maurice of Nassau

General's watchful, methodical strategy, which sought to conduct military operations with minimum risk. However, the States General pursued neither military traditions nor aspirations and was usually content to leave martial business to the stadholders. Maurice lacked political ambitions of his own, so this arrangement worked satisfactorily.

The conduct of sieges

Siege warfare was particularly apposite to the situation: it decreased operational risk though at an increased financial cost which the United Provinces could afford through its burgeoning trade and commerce. Maurice developed the siege techniques established by the Spanish governors Alva and Parma. Target towns and cities would be blockaded and then enclosed within a double ring of redoubts (contravallation and circumvallation) which protected the besiegers' camp. First trenches then zigzagged saps (mines) were excavated towards the 'front' selected for attack, and the artillery installed in batteries. Lighter cannon destroyed breastworks and countered the garrison's artillery whilst the heavier guns concentrated on breaching the fortifications. When the defending fire had been substantially subdued, the

> '[The armed forces of the States General were] the military schools where most of the youth of Europe did learn their military exercises.'
>
> SIR JAMES TURNER, *PALLAS ARMATA*

besiegers sapped up the glacis (sloping earthwork rampart) to capture the counterscarp (the outer slope of the ditch in front of the main wall or scarp). The artillery was then advanced to begin battering the main ramparts, whilst the attacking infantry built a bridge or causeway over the wet ditch ready to assault the breach; occasionally hydraulic engineers had to be summoned to assist with drainage and diversion of watercourses.

Rather than rely upon gangs of unwilling, conscripted civilian labour, Maurice trained his soldiers to dig their own siege works and field fortifications, a reform that greatly increased the speed and effectiveness of siege operations. Shovels and hand-tools were routinely carried in the siege train.

Two treatises by Stevin, *Legermeting* (*The Marking Out of Army Camps*; 1617) and *Nieuwe maniere van Sterckebouw door spilsluysen* (*New Manner of Fortification by Means of Pivoted Sluice Locks*; 1617), provided the theoretical basis for Dutch fortification techniques. In 1600, he and Maurice established a course in surveying and military engineering at Leiden, in which the lectures were given in Dutch rather than the traditional Latin. Stevin did not confine himself to theory and by 1592 was serving as engineer and quartermaster to the army of the States General, designing entrenched camps and drawing up instructions and standing orders for men engaged in building fortifications and undertaking siege operations. He was often present at sieges, and indicated the mode of attack to be employed.

Stevin's prominence in military engineering supports the view that many of the military reforms developed by the Dutch were actually team efforts in which Maurice himself may not have played the leading role. In recruiting and financing the army, the political and moral support of Johan van Oldenbarneveldt (1547–1619), the Lands-advocaat of Holland, was central, as administration of the field forces rested with the Raad van State which he dominated; whilst in tactical and operational matters, Maurice was ably supported by his cousins William Louis and John VII, Count of Nassau-Siegen, who devised drill movements and supervised the publication of instruction manuals.

(Opposite) **Maurice's simplified military drill** allowed a polyglot army to follow orders quickly and efficiently. The key steps were shown in engravings such as these by Jakob de Gheyn, published in 1607, facilitating their take-up across Europe.

Maurice of Nassau

Dutch strategy

Oldenbarneveldt and Maurice appreciated that Dutch strategy had to concentrate upon defending the central provinces of Holland, Zeeland and Utrecht. This was best achieved by checking Spanish attempts at further reconquest whilst employing cautious, positional warfare to recapture fortified towns and cities to extend the outlying areas of the state, comprising the four 'land' provinces of Friesland, Groningen, Overijssel and Gelderland, which protected the three key provinces. Usually after very close consultation with Maurice, the States General decided upon targets to be besieged. Mostly he was content with this arrangement; indeed it strengthened his position, although the emphasis of the States General upon protecting the particular interests of the individual provinces and keeping costs to a minimum occasionally clashed with wider strategic priorities.

Maurice sought to avoid open battle: between 1589 and 1609, twenty-nine fortresses were recaptured, three sieges relieved but only two battles fought. Interior lines and the great rivers acted as force multipliers enabling the small Dutch army to move rapidly between the eastern and southern fronts. When obliged to use overland routes, as in an abortive campaign into Brabant in 1602, results were less impressive.

Keeping the Spaniards at bay

Alexander Farnese, Duke of Parma, who arrived in the Netherlands in 1578, successfully reduced the opposition to Spanish rule in the southern Netherlands, but the northern provinces continued to hold out. At the end of 1587, however, the Dutch Republic held only Holland, Zeeland and Utrecht, a few isolated outposts in Overijssel, Gelderland and Friesland, plus Ostend and Bergen-op-Zoom south of the great rivers. Parma was then called away to Dunkirk to provide troops for the Spanish Armada against England and, when ready to resume his offensive in 1589, was redirected into France to support the Catholic League against the Huguenots. These distractions provided Maurice with the opportunity to begin rebuilding the army, safe within the defences of the waterline in *Vesting Holland* ('Fortress Holland', with natural defensible borders formed by the rivers Rhine and Meuse to the south and west and the Ijsselmeer to the east), whilst the States General concentrated upon building fortifications. Maurice surprised Breda on 26 February 1590, the first major town to be captured since 1580, but when Parma departed for France in July, the States General was unprepared to exploit the occasion and could only authorize an excursion into Brabant which retook some small forts.

Confident that some of Parma's forces would again be deployed in France in 1591, the States General mounted a major campaign to secure the line of the River Ijssel and retake the northeastern towns seized during the 1580s. Commanding 10,000 men and

Maurice of Nassau's artillery breaches the walls of Steenwijk and his army pours through, 4 July 1592, in an anonymous engraving. Maurice's successful siege of Steenwijk was part of his strategy of protecting the Dutch heartland provinces of Holland, Zeeland and Utrecht (see map opposite) by extending his control over the surrounding areas through increasingly effective use of siege warfare.

a train of artillery, Maurice captured Zutphen on 30 May following a seven-day siege, and Deventer on 10 June. The next target was Nijmegen but, despite having to send 6,000 men to France and losing another 2,000 to a mutiny over pay, Parma parried Maurice's thrust. His health failing, in August Parma travelled to Spain for medical treatment but was back in Brussels by November, assembling 20,000 men for the French wars to relieve Henry of Navarre's siege of Rouen. Maurice moved his troops rapidly by barge and seized Hulst on 24 September. Then he doubled back to Dordrecht and marched overland to Nijmegen, which fell on 21 October after a siege lasting only six days. These results were achieved by rapid movement, swift siege operations and the offer of generous terms to enemy garrisons. Maurice continued to campaign in the northeast during 1592, taking Steenwijk and Coevorden, but further operations were compromised by the localist attitudes of the four 'land' provinces. Nevertheless, after a long siege during which Maurice and Stevin demonstrated the improved techniques, Gertruidenberg fell in June 1593, and on 23 July in the following year Maurice captured Groningen. Their principal objectives realized, the States General cut back military expenditure, obliging Maurice to suspend major operations; reform of the army continued, however, during the ensuing long pause in campaigning.

With 6,800 men, Maurice surprised a marching column of 5,000 Spanish troops near Turnhout on 24 January 1597, but the resulting Dutch victory had little impact on the overall situation. Later the same year, when Spain was again heavily committed in France, Maurice took Rheinberg and Groenlo, further securing the eastern borders. In 1598, however, peace between France and Spain altered the strategic balance. Reinforced, a Spanish army pushed north through Bommel across the river lines, but again the troops mutinied and all the captured towns and forts were regained by the Dutch in 1599, some purchased from the rebellious garrisons. Oldenbarneveldt ordered Maurice to exploit the opportunity and the inexperience of the new governor of the Spanish Netherlands, Archduke Albrecht of Austria, by advancing down the Flemish coast to link up with the isolated Dutch garrison at Ostend before moving against the Spanish privateer bases at Nieuport and Dunkirk. Maurice was reluctant, favouring a more cautious strategy, but was overruled by Oldenbarneveldt who was willing to accept the risk. On 2 July 1600, Maurice's 11,400 men defeated a hastily mustered Spanish army of 9,000 in the sand dunes outside Nieuport. However, it was only a tactical victory because the Dutch army was not strong enough to besiege either Nieuport or Dunkirk and had to be evacuated into Zeeland by sea. Archduke Albrecht then attacked Ostend. Leading 5,442 cavalry and around 19,000 infantry, Maurice invaded Brabant, intending to march into Flanders to lift the siege, but the thrust was abandoned because insufficient horse forage was available.

The States General ordered Maurice to stand on the defensive,

THE CONQUESTS OF
MAURICE OF NASSAU,
1590–1606.

Emden

FRIESLAND

Groningen
1594

Steenwijk
1592

Coevorden
1592

OVERIJSSEL

L. Ijsselmeer

R. Ijssel

Ootmarsum
1592–97

HOLLAND

Deventer
1591

Oldenzaal
1597–1605

UTRECHT

Zutphen
1591

Utrecht

Groenlo
1597–1606

Dordrecht

Gertruidenberg
1593

Nijmegen
1591

Grave
1602

Rheinberg
1597

Breda
1590

R. Rhine

Sluis
1604

Ostend
(Sp. in 1604)

ZEELAND

Bergen-op-Zoom

GELDERLAND

Bruges

Hulst
1591–95

Axel
1586

Turnhout

Nieuport 1600

Aardenburg
1604

Dunkirk 1600

Ghent

BRABANT

R. Yser

FLANDERS

R. Lys

R. Scheldt

R. Meuse

N

Base for Maurice's conquests

Area under Spanish occupation in 1607

Area conquered by Maurice

Linguistic boundary

0   50 km

0   50 miles

The Prices Battel: The Arch Dukes Batte

N

NORTH SEA

Dutch warships

Dutch transports
making for Ostend

Louis of
Nassau

Solms

Frisians

Dutch
Guards

Monroy

La
Barlotte

Hurchtenburch

Marquette

Horace
Vere

The
'Mutineer'
Regiments

Villar

The
Archduke

Bucquoy

Ghistelles

Prince
Maurice

PRINCE
MAURICE'S
FORCES

THE
ARCHDUKE'S
FORCES

Sapena

Bostock

Harbour
of
Nieuport

Dubois

Domerville

Francis
Vere

High water mark

Avila

Nassau

Swiss

Frisians

Infantry

Cavalry

Artillery

T H E   Frisians   D U N E S

**THE BATTLE
OF NIEUPORT,**
2 July 1600.

passing the initiative to the newly arrived Ambrogio Spinola, the best Spanish general
to serve during the Eighty Years War (1568–1648). While the siege of Ostend dragged
on for three years, the States General began the construction of a line of defensive
redoubts along the River Ijssel to improve the defences of the vulnerable eastern front.
Even so, when Spinola transferred his attention to the east in 1606, he made progress
into Overijssel and Gelderland before heavy rains prevented further advance. Aware
of Spain's catastrophic financial condition, Spinola now advocated an end to hostil-

Maurice of Nassau

ities and, following a ceasefire in 1607, a twelve-year truce came into effect in 1609, marking the end of the solitary struggle of the Dutch Republic: when fighting resumed in 1621, the conflict was subsumed within the larger Thirty Years War.

Maurice considered the truce to be a betrayal, as only military victory over Spain could guarantee the long-term viability of the Dutch state; his close working relationship with Oldenbarneveldt, the leading advocate of the truce, was irrevocably ruptured. Political differences were expressed in religious terms. Maurice was supported by the orthodox Calvinists of the Reformed Church, the Contra-Remonstrants, many of whom were exiles from the southern provinces that remained in Spanish hands, whilst the Arminians, or Remonstrants, favoured greater religious latitude and toleration and looked to Oldenbarneveldt for leadership. Maurice himself claimed little theological knowledge and once remarked that he did not know whether predestination was blue or green, but he was firmly committed to the Reformed Church and convinced that it formed the bedrock of the Dutch revolt against Spain: to attack the church was to imperil the state and therefore an act of treason. Although enjoying a more sophisticated understanding of the theological issues, Oldenbarneveldt differed sharply from the Contra-Remonstrants over the relationship of church to state. He upheld the state's right to determine church government and favoured keeping the doctrinal door wide open to admit all loyal and obedient subjects. To Oldenbarneveldt, the state was not the States General but the individual provinces, especially Holland. In 1618, on the authority of the States General, Maurice arrested Oldenbarneveldt for treason; he was tried and executed in 1619.

Demoralized, prematurely aged and badly damaged by the judicial murder of Oldenbarneveldt, on the resumption of the war in 1621 Maurice had lost the vigour and zest required to lead his troops to victory. When Spinola besieged Breda in 1624, Maurice was unable to effect a relief. His health collapsed and he asked the States General to commission a deputy commander. His brother, Frederick Henry, was appointed on 12 April, and eleven days later, on 23 April 1625, Maurice died.

Reputation

Maurice's reforms were enthusiastically imitated throughout Europe. In the Electorate of Brandenburg they were known as the *exercitia Mauritiana*. The French writer Louis de Montgomery, Siegneur de Corbouzon, devoted part of his book on tactics (1603) to '*les évolutions et les exercises, qui se font en la milice de Hollande avec les mots dont il faut user ...*' Another French author, Jeremias de Billon, wrote of '*ce grand Capitaine le Prince Maurice de Nassau*', whilst the English writer John Bingham added an appendix to his book *The Tactiks of Aelian* (1616) entitled 'The Exercises of the English in the Service of the high and mighty lords, the Lords of Estate in the United Provinces of the Low Countries'. The engraver Jakob de Gheyn translated Maurice's infantry drills into a series of pictorial representations, *Wapenhandling van roers, musquetten ended spiessen* (*The Exercise of Armes*; Amsterdam, 1607), quickly followed by English, German, French and Danish editions (see p. 22). Johann von Wallhausen taught only the Mauritian method at the *Kriegs und Ritterschule* in Siegen, 1616–23. Even the Swiss, master exponents of the pike square, switched to Dutch tactics during the 1620s. The 'Nassau Doctrine' was thus given the widest possible circulation across western Europe and directly informed the tactical methods of Gustavus Adolphus of Sweden.

(see p. 22).

(Opposite) **The Dutch heavy cavalry** charge the Habsburg army of Archduke Albrecht of Austria at Nieuport on 2 July 1600, as portrayed in a mid seventeenth-century drawing. Fought in the dunes close to the Spanish naval base of Nieuport (present-day Belgium), the battle was one of Maurice's rare victories in the field. The small and shallow 'half-regiments' of Dutch infantry, on the upper left, are clearly distinguishable from the larger, clumsier Spanish tercios facing them.

Maurice of Nassau

'The best and most valorous commander that ever any soldiers had.' ALEXANDER LESLIE, SCOTTISH MERCENARY

GUSTAVUS ADOLPHUS
1594–1632

STEPHEN BRUMWELL

HAILED AS A DAUNTLESS PROTESTANT CHAMPION, King Gustav II Adolph of Sweden (known elsewhere as Gustavus Adolphus) was a charismatic commander who propelled his kingdom from backwater to Great Power. His influential tactical innovations, which underpinned Sweden's dramatic intervention in the Thirty Years War (1618–48), exploited lessons learned during a decade of conflict in northeastern Europe.

Born in Stockholm in December 1594, Gustavus Adolphus was well prepared for his role as king, learning ancient and modern languages, law and Lutheran theology. But his real passions were history, particularly tales of Sweden's early warrior kings, and the art of war itself.

Gustavus grew up tall and burly, inclining to paunchiness, but of great strength and endurance. A keen sportsman and accomplished horseman, he was well suited to the rigours of campaign life. His golden-red mane of hair and small, pointed beard helped to inspire his nickname, 'the Lion of the North'. Proud and moody, he was nonetheless capable of deploying great charm when required. Gustavus shunned luxury and finery: his usual dress was the simple buff coat and broad-brimmed hat of the soldier, a plain ensemble relieved only by a scarlet sash. Yet Gustavus was no bluff swordsman but an astute statesman and a gifted commander. Both skills were honed through hard experience.

Prussian apprenticeship

At his accession in 1611, Gustavus was just 16. He inherited wars with Denmark and Muscovy (Russia), although by 1617 peace treaties had been concluded with both powers. Through the latter, Sweden acquired Estonia on the Baltic's southern shore, a development that sparked hostilities with Poland, which considered that territory part of Polish Livonia. Over the coming decade, the protracted Polish war would provide Gustavus with an intensive military apprenticeship.

In 1621 Gustavus invaded Livonia, swiftly capturing the vital port of Riga. This was his first significant victory. Over the next four years the Poles were pushed out of most of Livonia, and in 1626 Gustavus turned his attention to Polish East Prussia. The Swedish army won significant battles: at Mewe, on 1 October 1626 a picked corps of infantry and artillery stormed a strong Polish position, and at Dirschau, on 17 August 1627, the Swedish cavalry proved its worth, vanquishing the vaunted Polish hussars; a general action on the following day began well for the Swedes, only to be abandoned after Gustavus was shot through the shoulder.

On a tactical level, these small-scale engagements testified to the growing confidence of Swedish troops, itself a consequence of reforms initiated by Gustavus. In stra-tegic terms, however, the king overreached himself in Prussia. Although key ports were captured, the Swedes stalled in the face of fierce local resistance that hemmed them in within a band of territory along the shore of the Baltic Sea.

Events now turned against Gustavus. In August 1628, his bid to destroy the Polish commander Stanislas Koniecpolski, who was encamped around Mewe with 10,000 men, ended in fiasco. The canny Pole refused to risk a battlefield clash with Gustavus's 15,000 men, instead devastating the countryside and obliging the hungry Swedes to conduct an ignominious retreat to winter quarters.

Worse was to follow in 1629. Sigismund III of Poland was not only Gustavus's cousin but also the brother-in-law of the Holy Roman Emperor Ferdinand II, who loaned him 12,000 of his soldiers under Hans George von Arnim. Gustavus had 23,000 men in Prussia, but gar-rison commitments left him

Gustavus Adolphus wearing a traditional Polish delia coat, in a painting by Matthäus Merian, c. 1632. One of his military innovations was to introduce standard-coloured red, blue or yellow coats for his regiments.

with a field force of just 14,000 to pitch against the 26,000 Poles and Imperialists led by Koniecpolski and Arnim. Unable to confront his opponents before they could unite, Gustavus suffered a heavy defeat at Honigfelde on 27 June, barely escaping with his life.

At Altmark, in September 1629, Gustavus had no option but to sign a six-year truce with Poland. With his own kingdom exhausted, the relieved Sigismund conceded generous terms to Sweden, which not only retained Livonia and some of her Prussian conquests, but was also granted licences to collect lucrative tolls on shipping using Prussian and Polish ports, thus giving a vital boost to Sweden's war chest.

Military reform

Gustavus's punishing Polish war provided a valuable opportunity to learn from a formidable enemy, to identify weaknesses in his own army, and to overhaul its structure and tactics. The extent to which these reforms contributed to a 'military revolution' – a term which is likewise controversial – has been hotly debated. Yet whether 'revolutionary' or not, by 1630 Gustavus had implemented changes destined to have a profound impact upon the battlefields of western Europe.

The king's military reforms built upon his own long-standing interest in the theory of warfare, both past and present. He was the most dedicated – and influential – disciple of Maurice of Nassau, who had remodelled the Dutch army in the 1590s (see p. 22), placing an emphasis upon shallower and more flexible formations, improved drill and increased firepower.

At the outset, Gustavus inherited a national army, based upon a system of conscription (*utskrivning*) dating from 1544. In 1620, this was regulated, with one infantry conscript provided by every *rota*, or 'file', of ten men. By contrast, the Swedish cavalry were either foreign mercenaries or native-born volunteers. Throughout the 1620s there had been experiments to find the most effective administrative and tactical units. Both merged in the infantry regiment of two squadrons, each at 'battalion' strength of 480 men. By 1630, the infantry was employing the 'Swedish brigade' of 1,500–2,000 men, formed of three or four squadrons, or two regiments, arrayed in wedge or arrow-shaped formation, with one squadron held in reserve. An unusually high proportion of officers and non-commissioned officers ensured discipline and control.

Intensive drill permitted the Swedish infantry to adopt a far thinner formation

The Battle of Dirschau (17 August 1627), in a painting by an anonymous seventeeth-century artist. The battle was fought during the Polish–Swedish War, when Gustavus Adolphus and Stanislas Koniecpolski were contesting control of the region of Danzig (Gdansk). Despite initial successes for the Swedish cavalry, the battle ended indecisively with Gustavus wounded (bottom right). But it demonstrated the effectiveness of his developing tactics, which would prove their worth in the larger war in Germany.

than usual. At just six ranks deep, this was even shallower than Maurice's recommended ten, and only a fifth of the depth of the unwieldy blocks of infantry employed by most Western armies. By 1631, the Swedish musketeers were using the salvo, an innovation attributed to Gustavus himself. Here, the musketeers doubled up their ranks, so that they were only three deep, allowing them to deliver a concentrated, devastating volley, intended, in the words of the Scottish volunteer Sir James Turner, to 'pour as much lead in your enemies' bosom at one time'.

Each infantry squadron enjoyed the close support of two or three light 3-pounder guns. Mobile enough to be manhandled, they augmented the infantry's firepower with blasts of the newly introduced close-range projectile canister. Neither was cold steel neglected. While the proportion of pikemen to musketeers was typically declining elsewhere, Gustavus retained a higher than usual ratio, using the pike as an offensive, rather than a purely defensive, weapon.

In the cavalry, as with the infantry, formation depths were reduced. In contrast to many armies, where cavalry employed the 'caracole', a technique by which successive relays of troopers fired their pistols before peeling off to reload and repeat the process, the Swedes were trained to deliver their fire and then immediately charge home with the sword. The Swedish cavalry's effectiveness was increased by close support from parties of musketeers.

Gustavus's reforms forged a well-organized and highly disciplined army, capable of punching its weight through a fusion of close-range firepower and shock action. As events would demonstrate, this was a formidable combination.

Intervention in Germany

Peace with Poland freed Gustavus to turn towards Germany, where hostilities between the Catholic forces of Emperor Ferdinand and a loose alliance of Protestant princes had escalated since 1618. By 1630, the conflict – which would continue until 1648, thus becoming known as the Thirty Years War – was going badly for the Protestants. Gustavus was the devout leader of a staunchly Lutheran state, but he played down the ideological justification for intervention: despite his future reputation as champion of the beleaguered Protestant cause, this was no anti-Catholic 'crusade'; indeed, vital financial support for Sweden came from Catholic France, which was chiefly concerned with curbing Habsburg power. For Gustavus too, *Realpolitik* was the prime motivator: Ferdinand's military aid to Poland still rankled, but above all there were growing fears that Imperial ambitions threatened Sweden's security.

In 1627, after Christian IV of Denmark had rashly taken a direct hand in the war, Ferdinand retaliated by sending an army to the Baltic. The Imperialists invaded southern Denmark, and their defeat of Christian at Wolgast in September 1628 permitted the diversion of manpower into Prussia that led to Gustavus's stinging defeat at Honigfelde. It seemed clear that the Habsburgs aimed to extend their influence by creating a naval base on the shores of the 'Scandinavian Lake'. This so-called 'Baltic Design' angered Sweden and Denmark alike. Back in 1627, while still mired in his Prussian campaigns, Gustavus had informed his trusted chancellor Axel Oxenstierna that war with the emperor was already inevitable: the lapping waves of the 'Popish League', which had now inundated much of Denmark, must be stemmed in good time if they were not to swamp Sweden, too.

In June 1630, Gustavus told the *Riksdag*, or parliament, of his decision to intervene personally in Germany. He predicted a gruelling struggle in which all Swedes must be prepared to make sacrifices, not least himself: 'just as the pitcher taken often to the well would finally be broken, so he, who had on so many occasions risked his life for his realm, must surely lose it at last.'

On 27 June Gustavus sailed from Stockholm with 13,000 men, landing at Peenemünde in the Oder estuary on 6 July. A swift conquest of Usedom and Stettin forced the local ruler, the Duke of Pomerania, to grant the invaders a foothold from which to step onwards into Germany. But for the rest of 1630 the Swedes stayed in Pomerania, waiting for the North German princes to rally to them. Major figures such as Electors John George of Saxony and George William of Brandenburg proved wary of defying the emperor, but support came from others with less to lose and more to gain, notably the dispossessed Duke of Mecklenburg, and Margrave Christian William of Brandenburg, the former administrator of the archbishopric of Magdeburg, a strategically important city on the Elbe.

The Swedish bridgehead gradually expanded, and by February 1631, most of Mecklenburg had been occupied. Gustavus continued his methodical advance southwards into Brandenburg, taking Küstrin and Frankfurt-an-der-Oder. But he arrived too late to save his ally, Magdeburg. On 20 May, that Protestant bastion was stormed by the Imperialists under John 't Serclaes von Tilly, and sacked with a savagery that sent shock waves of horror across Europe (see p. 42). Prompted by Magdeburg's grim fate, George William of Brandenburg finally sided with Gustavus on 21 June 1631. This was a timely pact. By the Peace of Cherasco, ratified two days earlier, the Imperialist army in Northern Italy was freed to fight elsewhere. Encouraged by the prospect of reinforcement, Tilly vacated the smoking ruins of Magdeburg to tackle Gustavus.

With Swedes and Imperialists alike short of supplies, much now hinged on Saxony, the rich and hitherto unravaged territory between them. On 4 September, after the Elector, John George, refused his formal request to enter Saxony, Tilly invaded regardless, storming Merseburg and Leipzig. John George immediately joined forces with Gustavus, adding 18,000 raw Saxons to his own army of 23,000 veterans, by now a kernel of Swedes outnumbered by foreign mercenaries. Heading down the Elbe,

Gustavus encountered Tilly's 31,000 men on 17 September near Breitenfeld, a village amid gently rolling countryside north of Leipzig (see pp. 34, 35 and 43).

The virtual annihilation of Tilly's previously unstoppable army took Europe's rulers by surprise, not least because Gustavus was unknown outside the Baltic theatre. Indeed, the magnitude of his victory surprised Gustavus himself. His battle-hardened and proficient army handed the German Protestants a powerful new weapon, but as the king had already achieved his aim of pushing the Imperialists back from the Baltic's southern shore, a question mark remained over how next to wield it.

While Gustavus pondered his options, Tilly received a reprieve that allowed him to withdraw beyond the Saale and Weser, and begin rebuilding his shattered army. Meanwhile, Gustavus led his weary men southwest into the rich Catholic lands along the Rhine and Main. Despite Breitenfeld – the first major victory of the war for the Protestant cause – the Swedes were no more successful in attracting the support of substantial rulers. Some who would have preferred neutrality felt obliged to side with Gustavus as his hard-bitten horde drew ever closer to their territories. Such lukewarm 'allies' provided the supplies that sustained Gustavus's swollen army. While far from popular with Germany's Protestant rulers, elsewhere Gustavus enjoyed celebrity as the bulwark of his religion, fuelling a veritable industry of publications and artefacts commemorating his exploits.

'I seek not my own advantage in this war, nor any gain save for the security of my kingdom. I can look for nothing but expense, hard work, trouble and danger to life and limb.'
GUSTAVUS ADOLPHUS, JULY 1630

During the winter of 1631–2 the Imperialists regained their balance. In the northwest, Pappenheim raided Swedish communications, while Tilly shifted to Bavaria to raise forces for a fresh campaign. Now aged 73 and plagued by pessimism, in March 1632, Tilly precipitated events when he ejected the Swedes from Bamberg. Gustavus's response was brisk and brutally effective: within a month he moved south with a formidable army of 37,000 men to counter Tilly's 22,000. Covered by an intensive barrage from seventy-two heavy guns, on 5 April a pontoon bridge was constructed across the River Lech at Rain, enabling his troops to smash Tilly's Bavarian army. Tilly died of his wounds, Bavaria lay helpless and the Catholic cause seemed at its nadir. In this crisis situation, in April 1632, it was decided to reinstate Albrecht von Wallenstein, a lapsed Protestant whose cynicism and greed were remarkable even by the standards of seventeenth-century commanders, as the only man capable of raising and leading a viable Imperial army.

Acutely aware that the Imperial cause now depended upon the survival of his army, Wallenstein campaigned cautiously. In July 1632 he selected a heavily fortified position adjoining an old castle called the Alte Feste, just outside Nuremberg. On 24 August Gustavus instigated a bloody and futile effort to dislodge him, his determined assaults baffled by a tenacious defence and rugged terrain. Weakened by heavy casualties, disease and desertion, in October the Swedes finally withdrew towards the northwest. While his subordinates cleared Saxon forces from Bohemia and Silesia, Wallenstein personally overran Saxony itself. On 1 November, Leipzig once again fell to the Imperialists.

For two weeks Wallenstein kept his troops together. Then, on 14 November, he dispersed them to winter quarters. This was a costly decision. Next day, when intelligence reported that the Swedes were converging upon his headquarters at Lützen, he was

Gustavus Adolphus

THE BATTLE OF BREITENFELD

AT BREITENFELD NEAR LEIPZIG, the rival armies offered a striking contrast. The Imperial infantry were arrayed across Tilly's centre in seventeen tercios (mixed infantry formations of pikemen and musketeers), each fifty files wide and thirty ranks deep. Cavalry formed each wing, and all the guns were massed in the middle of the line. The Swedish–Saxon force was in reality composed of two separate armies: the untried Saxons took the left, the experienced Swedes held the centre and right. Each army was flanked by cavalry.

Unlike the Saxons, the Swedish infantry fought in its unique six-rank, 500-man battalions; every three of these were grouped into T-shaped brigades – at 1,500 men, equivalent in manpower to Tilly's dense tercios. Unlike their opponents, the Swedish infantry were formed in depth, so providing reserves. Detachments of musketeers were threaded between the Swedish cavalry squadrons. Each Swedish brigade was supported by at least six 3-pounder guns. In addition, Gustavus deployed fifty-one heavy field guns. With just twenty-seven artillery pieces, Tilly was not only heavily outnumbered, but also outgunned. Yet the Imperialists could deploy a powerful weapon of their own: the aura of invincibility.

The action commenced with the traditional artillery duel. Then Tilly's ponderous tercios lumbered forward, initially making for the centre of the allied line before veering towards the nervous Saxons. By now the cavalry on both flanks were in action. Gottfried Heinrich von Pappenheim led forward the Imperial horse of the left, riding at the head of his dreaded cuirassiers, all clad from crown to knee in sinister blackened armour. Under the personal command of Gustavus, and stiffened by the musketeers posted among them, the Swedish cavalry held its ground. On the Imperialist right, it was a very different story. Here, Egon von Fürstenberg's troopers

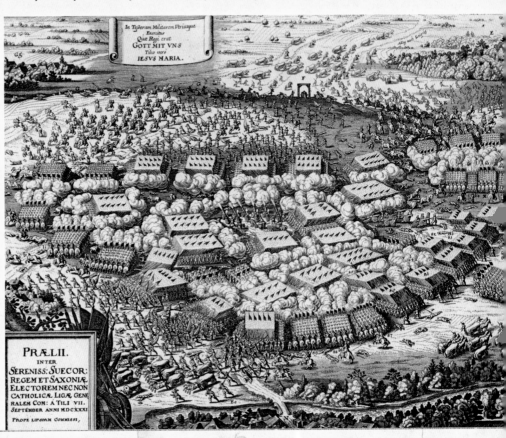

PRÆLII.
INTER
SERENISS: SUECOR:
REGEM ET SAXONIÆ
ELECTOREM NEC NON
CATHOLICÆ LIGÆ GENE
RALEM COM: A TILI VII.
SEPTEMBER ANNI MDCXXXI
PROPE LIPSIAM COMMISSI,

The Battle of Breitenfeld, 17 September 1631. The map opposite shows the initial dispositions of the opposing forces. In the print above, the Swedish and Saxon army is in the foreground; it shows the decisive moment towards the end of the battle when Gustavus's right wing broke through, and Imperial forces began to retreat to Leipzig (upper right).

unable to concentrate his detachments. Despite his summer losses, when Gustavus met Wallenstein on 16 November, their armies were evenly matched, with 19,000 men apiece. As Swedes and Imperialists alike employed the new formations that had triumphed at Breitenfeld, the battle degenerated into a brutal slugging match, fought under a masking mist until both armies were exhausted. That evening, after tallying his 6,000 casualties, the disheartened Wallenstein resolved to withdraw, not only abandoning his artillery and baggage, but relinquishing his Saxon conquests and retreating to Bohemia.

Although now technically the victors, the Swedes had little to celebrate: their losses were likewise heavy, and Gustavus himself had been killed. Spurring into the cavalry mêlée on his white charger Streiff, he had been shot in the arm and back, unhorsed and dragged along with one foot entangled in a stirrup. As he lay face down in the mud, a bullet in the head from some anonymous soldier finished him off.

Gustavus Adolphus

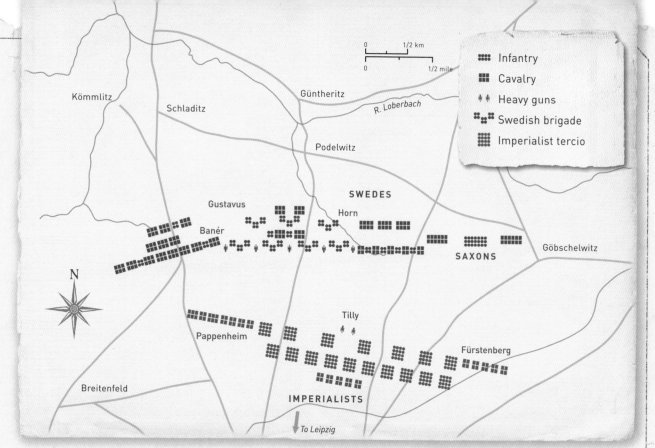

swiftly broke the Saxon cavalry, allowing Tilly's foot to grind its way through Elector John George's infantry. The Saxon army was eliminated, and another Imperial victory seemed assured.

The Swedish left – 4,000 men under General Gustav Horn – lay dangerously exposed. At this crisis, the flexibility of the Swedish battalion system proved its worth: Horn calmly formed a new front to cover his vulnerable flank, drew upon reserves, and then counter-attacked. He struck Tilly's tercios while they were still winded and disorganized from their clash with the Saxons. Meanwhile, a combination of cavalry charges and infantry firepower had finally rebuffed the persistent Pappenheim. Gustavus's triumphant right wing now wheeled inwards, captured Tilly's guns and turned them upon his own reeling infantry. This clinched the Swedish victory. The wounded Tilly withdrew northwest, the remnants of his army covered by the indefatigable Pappenheim.

Some 7,600 Imperialists were killed, with 9,000 wounded or taken prisoner, and another 4,000 deserters. Swedish casualties totalled 1,500, with Saxon losses at 3,000. Gustavus's triumph, which rested upon the effective integration of infantry, cavalry and artillery, was overwhelming.

Stripped by looters, the king's body was only identified after the fighting was over.

Reports of Gustavus's death were hard to credit. That December, courtiers in London were willing to wager £200 that the news was false. The loss of Gustavus, and Lützen's indecisive outcome, ended the spectacular upsurge of Protestant fortunes in Germany. The king's death left a vacuum; his heiress Queen Christina was just 6 years old, so affairs remained in the capable hands of Gustavus's trusted collaborator, Oxenstierna. His guidance, combined with the battlefield talents of commanders who had learned their trade in the Polish wars of the 1620s, ensured that Sweden maintained the prestigious new position won by the military prowess of Gustavus and his devoted soldiers: when the Thirty Years War ended at the Peace of Westphalia in 1648, their territorial conquests were confirmed, elevating Sweden to Great Power status.

COUNT TILLY

JOHN CHILDS

1559–1632

TILLY WAS AMONGST THE LAST of the great *condottieri* who combined managerial, political, financial and military acumen to raise and lead *ad hoc* armies on behalf of princes. Favouring well-established tactics rather than the innovative styles of his opponents, Tilly is renowned for his efforts on behalf of the Imperial and Catholic forces during the first half of the Thirty Years War. He knew that battle could deliver decisive results and would fight whenever the odds were favourable. His high reputation declined after the sack of Magdeburg and his defeat at Breitenfeld, where his antiquated approach failed before the new methods of Sweden's Gustavus Adolphus.

Born in February 1559 in the Château de Tilly, Brabant, about 30 miles southeast of Brussels, he was a younger son of Martin 't Serclaes, Count Tilly, and Dorothea von Schierstädt. During his youth he saw his homeland ravaged by Dutch Calvinists, and developed a hatred of Protestantism reinforced by attendance at the Jesuit seminary in Cologne. However, he did not take Holy Orders but turned instead to the profession of arms, the traditional alternative occupation for junior offspring of the aristocracy, joining the Walloon regiment in the army of Ernst von Bayern, Prince-Bishop of Liège, in 1574.

He served in Germany and the Netherlands, including the capture of Antwerp in 1585, and in France when the army of Flanders intervened in the Wars of Religion. Following transfer into the cuirassier regiment of Count Adolf von Schwarzenburg he was successively governor of Dun-sur-Meuse and Villefranche in Lorraine. In 1594 Tilly entered the Imperial army engaged in the 'Long War' against the Turks in Hungary (1593–1606), fighting at the capture of Stuhlweissenburg, 9–14 October 1601, and receiving promotion to major-general before purchasing the colonelcy of a Walloon regiment in 1602. For his role in the successful defence of Gran on the Danube in 1604 he was raised to the rank of general of cavalry. Elevation to Imperial field marshal followed in 1605.

As the religious and political compromise established in Germany in the 1550s deteriorated and princes looked to their defences, in 1605 Duke Maximilian I of Bavaria appointed Tilly lieutenant general at a monthly salary of 4,000 florins. Tilly led the

Bavarian forces, mostly mercenaries and militia, when they occupied the Imperial free city of Donauwörth on 17 December 1607. Bavaria founded the Catholic League in 1609 and the following year Tilly became commander of the League's army (effectively that of Bavaria). Although he spent much time training the Bavarian militia, there were few permanent troops apart from some garrisons and guards: in the event of war, the army had to be filled with trained officers and recruits. Here Tilly proved his worth in managing the military enterprisers, most pre-engaged to the Bavarian government, to produce a professional force. He subsequently grew rich through salary, commission, plunder, booty, contributions and the sale of protections.

Early successes in the Thirty Years War

When Protestant Bohemia rebelled against the Holy Roman Empire in 1618, the Catholic League pledged its support to the emperors Matthias (r. 1612–19) and Ferdinand II (r. 1619–37). Accompanied by the Imperial army under Charles de Longueval, Count of Bucquoy, Tilly led the League army through Austria into Bohemia. In less than an hour on the morning of 8 November 1620, across the slopes of the White Mountain outside Prague, Tilly and Bucquoy with 25,000 soldiers annihilated the 15,000-strong Bohemian army. While the army of Flanders attacked from the west, Tilly invaded the Rhenish territories of the Elector Palatine and now-deposed king of Bohemia, Frederick V, who was defenceless until another profes-sional soldier, Count Ernst von Mansfeld, his pockets stuffed with English and Dutch gold, reactivated the 21,000 troops

Johannes 't Serclaes, Count Tilly, in a painting by an unknown artist. Tilly was known as the 'Monk in Armour', a reference to his fierce anti-Protestantism and his personal devotion.

of the dissolved Protestant Union. Mansfeld withdrew towards Alsace to link up with another Protestant mercenary corps under George Frederick, Margrave of Baden-Durlach. They advanced north to prevent a junction between Tilly and 20,000 men from the army of Flanders under Gonzalo Fernández de Córdoba. This objective was achieved and they successfully repulsed an attack by Tilly on their rearguard south of Heidelberg on 27 April 1622. Mansfeld did not pursue and Tilly was able to combine with Córdoba. Mansfeld and Baden-Durlach sought to combine with the 12,000 troops of Duke Christian of Brunswick who was approaching the right bank of the River Neckar.

Mansfeld and Baden-Durlach separated their corps in the hope that Tilly and Córdoba would do likewise. Mansfeld crossed the Neckar near Heidelberg whilst Baden-Durlach marched eastwards along the Neckar intending to cross at Wimpfen. Tilly and Córdoba did not oblige by dividing their forces and pursued and overtook Baden-Durlach's 12,700 soldiers on 6 May near Wimpfen, on the left bank of the Neckar north of Heilbronn. Trusting that Mansfeld would march down the right bank, cross at Wimpfen and come to his aid, Baden-Durlach deployed defensively along a low, horseshoe-shaped ridge outside the village, his front covered by a wagon-laager (*wagenburg*). Tilly and Córdoba's 18,000 men made little impact on the wall of wagons until a cannon-ball hit a powder-cart which had been positioned too close to the front line. The resultant explosion ripped a hole in the defences and Baden-Durlach's army disintegrated under a general assault, only 3,000 escaping to reinforce Mansfeld.

Numerically inferior, Mansfeld was in a vulnerable position on the right bank and hurried to unite with Christian of Brunswick at Höchst on the River Main, a junction that Tilly and Córdoba intended to thwart. They intercepted Brunswick at Höchst on 20 June whilst he was bridging the Main. Although surprised and outnumbered by nearly two to one – 28,000 to 15,000 – Brunswick established a bridgehead which he successfully defended against heavy musketry and artillery fire. At a cost of 2,000 men and nearly all his baggage, Brunswick held off Tilly and linked up with Mansfeld. Tilly

The Battle of the White Mountain, fought outside Prague on November 1620, in a painting by Pieter Saayers (1592–1667). Tilly, commanding the Catholic League army, delivered a short sharp shock to the Bohemian army and drove the recently elected king Frederick V (henceforth known as the 'Winter King') out of the country. Tilly entered Prague and executed the remaining leaders of the anti-Imperial insurrection.

exploited his success by besieging Heidelberg, the capital of the Palatinate, which fell on 19 September following a siege of eleven weeks.

Having dismissed Mansfeld and Baden-Durlach on 13 July, Frederick of the Palatinate retired into exile at The Hague. After wintering in East Friesland, Christian of Brunswick, an arrogant, rash, one-armed adventurer of questionable judgement known as the 'mad Halberstadter', took 15,000 men into Lower Saxony through the Weser-Elbe corridor in March 1623. Deprived of Mansfeld's anticipated support, Christian found himself isolated deep in Catholic territory with no possibility of reinforcement. Tilly had learned of Brunswick's expedition and marched 25,000 men to intercept before he could reach shelter in the Dutch Republic. Encumbered by loot, Brunswick squandered a three-day lead and was forced to stand and fight on 6 August at Stadtlohn, 10 miles short of the Dutch border. Taking position on a low ridge, with his infantry deployed in Dutch-style battalions, Brunswick's 15,000 troops withstood several assaults from Tilly's four tercios, which went into action directly from column of march, until both wings of cavalry were swept away. Trapped between a bog on their left and the River Berkel in the rear, Brunswick's infantry lost 6,000 killed and 4,000 prisoners. Stadtlohn ended the Palatinate Phase of the Thirty Years War.

Tilly's successes of 1620–23, which had resulted in the suppression of the Bohemian revolt and conquered the Palatinate, were attributed to the quality of his army, which was better trained, drilled, commanded and organized than the hastily raised hordes of Mansfeld, Baden-Durlach and Christian of Brunswick. Tilly was raised to the status of Count of the Holy Roman Empire.

The war with Denmark

Tilly and the Bavarian army of the Catholic League had fought the lion's share of the Palatinate War, allowing Emperor Ferdinand's Austrian forces to operate in Hungary against Prince Bethlen Gabór of Transylvania. During the winter of 1624–5, Bavaria asked for Imperial assistance and the Catholic forces in Germany were reorganized. Already chafing at the political constraints imposed by his reliance upon Tilly's League army and anxious to possess his own German army, Emperor Ferdinand turned to Albrecht von Wallenstein (1583–1634) who quickly raised 24,000 men at his own expense in return for permission to 'recover' expenses and appoint his own officers.

> **'A bright musketeer but a ragged soldier.'**
> ANON.

Christian IV of Denmark, who hoped to acquire the bishoprics of Verden, Bremen and Osnabrück but saw that partial Spanish and Imperial occupation of northern Germany threatened his ambitions, now advanced across the Elbe in July 1625 with 17,000 men, a mixture of mercenaries and militia cavalry, heading for Hamelin on the Weser. Tilly, whose troops were cantoned in Westphalia, successfully parried the Danish advance in a series of minor actions before capturing Calenburg (3 November) and defeating a Danish relieving force at Seeze on the following day. However, at The Hague on 9 December 1625, Denmark, England, the Dutch Republic and Frederick of the Palatinate, supported by France, Bethlen Gabór and his suzerain, the Ottoman sultan Murad IV, formed a loose alliance against the Catholic League and Imperialists. Funded by the English and Dutch, Christian IV undertook to attack Lower Saxony; Christian of Brunswick agreed to assault Tilly in Westphalia and the lower Rhineland; and Mansfeld, the coalition's generalissimo, would engage Wallenstein and advance

LUTTER-AM-BARENBERG

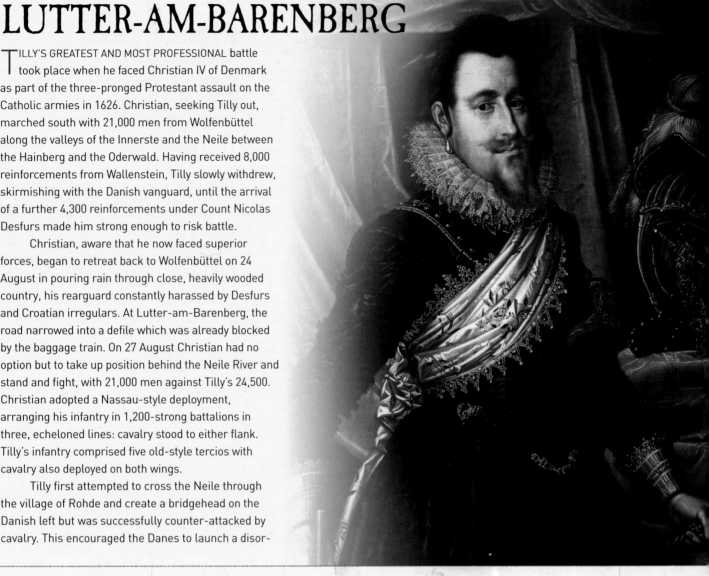

TILLY'S GREATEST AND MOST PROFESSIONAL battle took place when he faced Christian IV of Denmark as part of the three-pronged Protestant assault on the Catholic armies in 1626. Christian, seeking Tilly out, marched south with 21,000 men from Wolfenbüttel along the valleys of the Innerste and the Neile between the Hainberg and the Oderwald. Having received 8,000 reinforcements from Wallenstein, Tilly slowly withdrew, skirmishing with the Danish vanguard, until the arrival of a further 4,300 reinforcements under Count Nicolas Desfurs made him strong enough to risk battle.

Christian, aware that he now faced superior forces, began to retreat back to Wolfenbüttel on 24 August in pouring rain through close, heavily wooded country, his rearguard constantly harassed by Desfurs and Croatian irregulars. At Lutter-am-Barenberg, the road narrowed into a defile which was already blocked by the baggage train. On 27 August Christian had no option but to take up position behind the Neile River and stand and fight, with 21,000 men against Tilly's 24,500. Christian adopted a Nassau-style deployment, arranging his infantry in 1,200-strong battalions in three, echeloned lines: cavalry stood to either flank. Tilly's infantry comprised five old-style tercios with cavalry also deployed on both wings.

Tilly first attempted to cross the Neile through the village of Rohde and create a bridgehead on the Danish left but was successfully counter-attacked by cavalry. This encouraged the Danes to launch a disor-

Christian IV of Denmark, in a portrait (1612) by Pieter-Franz Isaaksz. His intervention in the Thirty Years War led to a devastating reverse at Lutter-am-Barenberg.

along the Elbe to ravage the Habsburg lands before combining with Gabór against Austria and Moravia.

The plan was both ludicrously complex and took insufficient account of Wallenstein's new Imperial army, and led to disaster for Christian. On 25 April 1626 Mansfeld was checked by Wallenstein at Dessau Bridge on the Elbe and lost one-third of his force, but after regrouping, on 30 June he marched southeast for Silesia with 10,000 men, pursued by Wallenstein with 30,000. Meanwhile Christian IV of Denmark, assuming that Tilly's Catholic League army – deployed far to the west in Westphalia – had been weakened by the need to quell a peasant revolt in Upper Austria, now sought him out. Tilly lured him to fight at Lutter on 17 August, and destroyed his army for good.

Tilly and Wallenstein swept through Saxony in 1627, occupied the Jutland peninsula and drove the Danes into the islands. Wallenstein defeated Christian's remaining forces at Wolgast on 24 August 1628, Tilly and Wallenstein were now estab-

Count Tilly

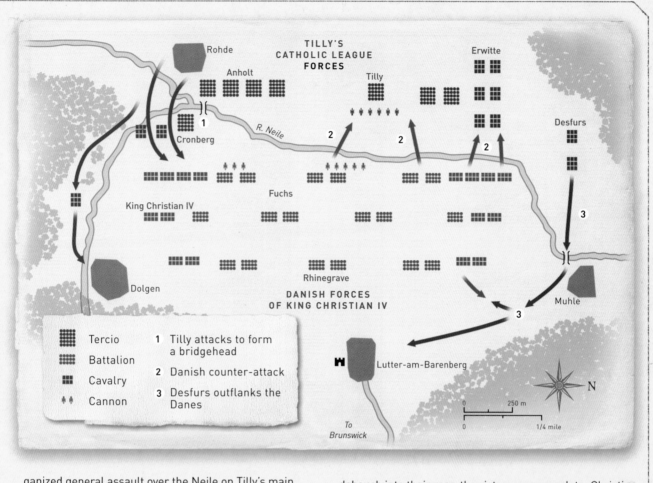

ganized general assault over the Neile on Tilly's main infantry position, but they were thrown back and cut to pieces by artillery fire and disciplined musketry from the tercios. When Desfurs finally brought his detachment forward through Muhle to outflank the Danish right and debouch into their rear, the victory was complete. Christian lost about 8,000 men whilst Tilly suffered only 700 casualties. The remains of the Danish army straggled north to form a defensive front along the Elbe.

lished along the Baltic coast and had reconquered Germany on behalf of the emperor and the Roman Catholic faith.

The Peace of Lübeck, on 22 May 1629, ended the Danish War. Christian of Denmark was restored to his possessions provided that he supported the Spanish and Imperial ambitions to control the Baltic through the creation of a navy based at Wismar, terms that he was happy to accept because they incommoded his principal enemy, Sweden.

War with Sweden

Emperor Ferdinand now dismissed Wallenstein, who was beginning to allow personal ambition to override his duty to the emperor, and when Gustavus Adolphus of Sweden landed with 13,000 men at the mouth of the Oder in 1630, the emperor appointed Tilly to command both the Imperial and Catholic League armies. The general was now over 70 years of age, increasingly prone to misjudgements and mistakes and unable to control his headstrong subordinates: in the opinion of Lieutenant General Count

Gottfried von Pappenheim, he was rapidly descending into senility. To contain Gustavus within his Pomeranian bridgehead, Tilly blockaded Magdeburg, Sweden's principal German ally, a key bridging point on the Elbe commanding the roads from Pomerania into Lower Saxony and Thuringia.

At the end of March 1631 Tilly upgraded the blockade of Magdeburg into a formal siege. In an unsuccessful attempt to draw Tilly away from Magdeburg, Gustavus struck southwards and seized Frankfurt-an-der-Oder on 13 April, but the bait was refused and Magdeburg was stormed, looted and burned on 20 May: only 5,000 out of 20,000 inhabitants and garrison survived.

Across Europe, the sack of Magdeburg was represented as a deliberate slaughter of Protestants by the Roman Catholic forces of the Holy Roman Empire. Tilly, who already had a considerable and justified reputation for permitting barbarities and atrocities against Protestants, explained that his soldiers had reacted to months of deprivation in flooded siege trenches, and that the unwritten laws of war permitted the pillage of towns that offered over-enthusiastic resistance and caused the attacker to suffer unnecessary casualties. In fact, neither Tilly nor Pappenheim personally sanctioned the massacre and they tried to intervene, but their men were beyond control. The impact was immense: the Lutheran and Calvinist states began to reconsider their tacit support for the emperor and support grew for the new Protestant hero and talisman Gustavus, the 'Lion of the North'.

Tilly moved northwards from Magdeburg but could make no impression on Swedish field fortifications at Werben. After losing a small cavalry engagement at Burgstall (27 July), he withdrew on 29 July. Tilly demanded that Elector John George of Saxony disband his army but when he refused Tilly, short of supplies, invaded Saxony, storming Merseburg and Leipzig in September. Gustavus concluded an agreement with John George on 2 September that added 18,000 Saxons to his 23,000 Swedes. Gustavus then pushed down the Elbe from Werben and encountered Tilly's twenty-seven field guns and 31,000 men on 17 September at Breitenfeld, a village on the northern edge of modern Leipzig (see also pp. 34–5). Gustavus's army comprised two separate forces: the Saxons on the left under Hans George von Arnim and the Swedes in the centre and right. The Imperial infantry deployed in twelve tercios, the Swedes and Saxons in 500-man battalions, six ranks deep. Tilly first attacked the Saxons and drove them from the field before turning on the exposed Swedish left. Exploiting the flexibility of the battalion organization, Johan Banér and Gustav Horn formed a new front to the left, ordered up reserves from the third line and launched a series of vigorous counter-attacks against Tilly's tercios which were tired and disorganized after their exertions against the Saxons. Once Pappenheim's cavalry on the right – he made a total of seven charges – had eventually been held and defeated by the Swedish horse, Horn and Banér crushed Tilly's tercios in a fury of musketry, cannon-fire and hand-to-hand combat.

Despite having moved some way towards the new Dutch methods during the 1620s by increasing the numbers of musketeers in the tercio and thinning the ranks of pikemen from thirty to fifteen, Tilly's outmoded deployments had been exposed. In response to Breitenfeld, Wallenstein experimented with shallower infantry formations, which he put into effect with some success at Lützen in 1632. However, Tilly's conservatism was based on sound practical considerations: the tercio allowed the military enterprisers to give lightly equipped, raw recruits a minimum of instruction before pushing them into the rear ranks, whereas the Dutch–Swedish systems required extensive drill. Similarly, Tilly's cavalry employed the 'caracole', an equally antiquated tactic of riding forward, firing pistols and then wheeling around and returning to the lines to reload, but one which could be performed adequately by relatively untrained troopers and horses.

Tilly now withdrew and scraped together reinforcements from amongst the Imperial garrisons in north Germany, incorporated the corps of Duke Charles IV of Lorraine and then retreated into northern Bavaria, taking winter quarters around Ingolstadt. Having captured half of Germany in the wake of Breitenfeld, in March 1632 Gustavus moved south with 37,000 men from Nuremberg to Donauwörth, intending to beat Tilly before advancing on Vienna. Elector Maximilian I of Bavaria brought reinforcements to Tilly at Ingolstadt, raising his forces to 22,000 men. Tilly entrenched behind the River Lech, close to the town of Rain, confident that Gustavus would be unable to force a crossing. On 5 April, a portion of the Swedish infantry, covered by an artillery barrage and the smoke from burning straw, threw a bridge of boats over the river and succeeded in establishing a bridgehead despite furious counter-attacks from Tilly's foot. In the interim, the Swedish cavalry moved 6 miles south of Tilly's position, crossed the Lech unopposed and was marching rapidly into the open left flank and rear of the Imperial League army when Tilly was badly wounded by a cannon shot. He was carried into Ingolstadt and his army rapidly withdrew, thus unintentionally thwarting the Swedish plan. Tilly lost 3,000 men and the Swedes about 2,000. He died in Ingolstadt on 30 April and was succeeded in command of the Bavarian/Catholic League army by Johann von Aldringen.

(Opposite) **The siege of Magdeburg,** begun by Tilly in March 1631, as depicted by Alexander Marshal (c. 1625–82). A strategically important site on the Elbe, Magdeburg had been a centre of Protestantism since the time of Luther. In May 1631 Tilly stormed the city and his army sacked it with great savagery.

Count Tilly

OLIVER CROMWELL
1599–1658

ANTONIA FRASER

OLIVER CROMWELL IS PROBABLY UNIQUE among the great commanders of the world in that he had no proper military training nor any military experience until he was well over 40. The most famous soldiers among his contemporaries – Gustavus Adolphus of Sweden, Marshal Turenne, the Prince de Condé, Rupert of the Rhine – were all vigorously engaged in warfare from their youth. Yet as a general Cromwell was in effect undefeated. Certainly the few minor reverses he did endure were very small in contrast to the swingeing victories that enabled him to charge at full gallop down the path of British history. And by these victories Cromwell undoubtedly changed the course of the nation.

During the two English Civil Wars – of 1642 and 1648 – to say nothing of Cromwell's campaigns in Ireland and Scotland, the Royalist side was well supplied with generals, many of them trained and experienced soldiers who had commanded troops in the wars which had raged across Europe since 1618. Militarily speaking, the odds were never loaded in favour of the Parliamentary side, rather the reverse, hence the inestimable value of Cromwell's personal contribution. It is no wonder that the twentieth-century paladin Field Marshal Montgomery called Cromwell one of the great 'captains' – his preferred term – of history. And the novelist John Buchan, a serious military writer and author of many campaign studies, called him 'the first great soldier of the new world' who would not be matched until Marlborough half a century later.

The making of a great leader

Oliver Cromwell was born in Huntingdon in 1599; he was thus two years older than the man who would succeed the first Stuart monarch James I as King Charles I in 1625. There was no princely magnificence in his own background: he came of a minor branch of the gentry, originally Welsh, and received the conventional upbringing of his class, a brief spell at Cambridge University followed by education in the law. By the time the king raised the standard at Nottingham in August 1642, Cromwell had enjoyed a career from which it would have taken a remarkable feat of prophecy to predict future greatness. He sat in parliament for his native Huntingdon in 1628 and

Oliver Cromwell

during the eleven years of the king's 'personal rule' retreated to Ely, becoming a convinced Puritan. When the issue of taxation obliged the king to call parliament once more, Cromwell was twice elected as MP for Cambridge in 1640, both in the Short Parliament and the Long Parliament which was still sitting at the outbreak of the war.

Military character

There were elements, however, in this apparently obscure life which were to be enormously influential in his future career as a soldier, even if it is easier to discern this with hindsight. First Cromwell had a passion, verging on an obsession, for horses. Later foreign ambassadors realized that horses as gifts to the Lord Protector were a sure way of gaining favour. This passion extended to days spent hunting and hawking, a kind of amateur military training of a sort – and the nearest Cromwell got to studying the elements of a cavalry charge. Cromwell's interest in the physical welfare of his horses (a novel idea, surprising as it may seem) would pay dividends for parliament, as the Royalists were originally so much better endowed with cavalry resources. And there was a human parallel in his local concerns for those small-scale peasant farmers in East Anglia whose livelihood was being destroyed by Fenland enclosures.

Thus by the arrival of war, Cromwell had an excellent territorial base of local support. The building of the army of the Eastern Association, as this territorial group became known, and later the New Model Army benefited from this cohesion between some of the local gentry and smaller landholders.

His instinct for leadership of men (and animals), together with an emphasis on the materials of war, was to prove vital almost at once in the battles in which Cromwell was involved. But it was a kind of leadership which deplored disorder, let alone anarchy. The inspirational, wild and wonderfully reckless courage of, for example, Cromwell's opponent Prince Rupert was in direct contrast to Cromwell's emphasis on discipline. He expected of his men not the freebooting style of the

Peter Lely's portrait of Oliver Cromwell, painted in 1650 and probably based on a miniature by Samuel Cooper. Dressed in his armour, Cromwell is presented as a man without airs or graces. When he became Lord Protector after 1653, his image became quasi-regal.

Oliver Cromwell

Cavaliers but the decent restraint of 'a russet-coated captain that knows what he fights for', as he once remarked. He rated military order with God's order: if the battle was won (as it nearly always was) then clearly God approved of the winners and their agenda. His battle cry was 'The Lord of Hosts' and his motto 'Seeking Peace Through War' (*Pax Quaeritur Bello*). So the man who became Cromwell the Commander combined from the start messianic fervour with a strong materialist grasp of the need for proper supplies and well-trained men. It was to prove a lethal combination.

Civil war leader of men

Cromwell fought as a captain at Edgehill on 23 October 1642. It was, however, at the Battle of Marston Moor in the Vale of York on the evening of 2 July 1644 that his outstanding quality was first displayed with results that turned a prospective defeat into something more like a victory (see feature below). Cromwell's disciplined use of cavalry was the single element that saved the day for the Parliamentary army, despite

MARSTON MOOR

THE PARLIAMENTARY FORCES were intending to besiege the northern Royalist fortress of York. Sir Thomas Fairfax was in overall command, Lord Manchester was in general charge of the cavalry, and Lord Leven led the large contingent of Scots. However, the arrival of the intrepid Prince Rupert to relieve York's commander, the Marquess of Newcastle, caused the Parliamentarians to draw back from the siege; the day of 2 July was spent in sporadic fighting. By the evening the prospective forces were drawn up facing each other, according to the custom of the time, ready for what would prove to be the largest battle ever fought on British soil. According to modern reckoning, about 22,000 allied (Parliamentarian and Scots) forces faced 18,000 Royalists.

Both armies consisted of cavalry, dragoons (mounted infantry) as well as foot soldiers and artillery.

As was customary, the foot were placed in the centre, flanked by the cavalry, including dragoons, on both wings. Close by Long Marston, on the Parliamentarian right, were Fairfax's forces, including 2,000 horse and a further reserve of Scottish cavalry. On the left were 3,000 cavalry of the Eastern Association under Cromwell's personal command, interspersed with platoons of infantry musketeers, some Scots dragoons and a further reserve of Scots cavalry under David Leslie.

Facing Fairfax was the bulk of the Royalist cavalry under Lord Goring; opposite Cromwell was drawn up the cavalry of Lord Byron. Both sides showed their mettle: the Parliamentarians with psalm-singing, the Royalists with banners which caricatured their opponents as little beagles yapping 'Pym, Pym, Pym' (the Parliamentarian political leader who had died in December).

At about six o'clock in the evening, as the Royalist commanders ate supper, the allies took the dramatic decision to attack. Cromwell with his loyal men of the Eastern Association charged on the left: this was a rapid but controlled exercise, the men riding short-reined and short-stirruped, close together at something like a fast trot rather than the modern gallop. The careful pace meant that they did not lose contact with their infantry firepower. The whole line moved forward 'like so many

Tockwith

N

york

Oliver Cromwell

the fact that Cromwell himself was at this point a mere cavalry leader not a strategist.

One year later – at Naseby in Northamptonshire on 15 June 1645 – Cromwell was able to lead the recently developed 22,000-strong New Model Army to a decisive victory over the king's forces (see p. 49); after this there was never any question of the Royalists winning the war. Marston Moor had done more than consolidate Cromwell's military reputation: it also called attention to his potential as a leader. In the intervening months the removal of the Parliamentarian aristocrats and Presbyterians from army command, in the so-called Self-Denying Ordinance, left the religiously 'Independent' Cromwell as the military strongman under Fairfax's command. Naseby was not won without a struggle, though the Parliamentarians enjoyed a huge numerical superiority of 11,000 to around 7,500 Royalists. At first Prince Rupert's brilliant, successful cavalry charge seemed to assure another of his daring victories, but then his troops scattered for pillaging, while Cromwell's men held firm. This allowed them to overwhelm the Royalist right flank as the army which the Royalists had derided as 'the New Noddle'

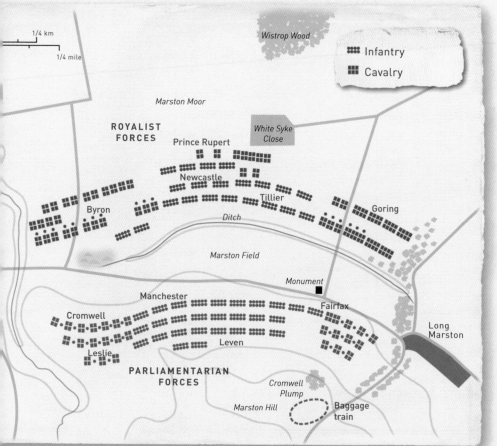

Two hours into the battle the situation was chaotic. Not only was Fairfax in trouble but Cromwell may have been lightly wounded, leaving David Leslie and his Scots cavalry to come to the rescue. There was at least the strong possibility of a Parliamentarian rout. It was at this point that the recovered Cromwell and his stalwart men of the Eastern Association, held 'close and firm together in a body', proved themselves to be the one coherent force left on the battlefield. Conventional wisdom of the time might have been to plunge on and strike at York. Instead, Cromwell used his 'lovely company' like a hammer, to assault the Royalist centre, and most surprising of all, strike from behind at Goring whose exhausted cavalry was not expecting an attack that evening and from that quarter. The Royalist cavalry scattered and at least 3,000 Royalists were killed with only 300 of the allies, although there were many wounded on both sides.

thick clouds', wrote Manchester's chaplain, an eye-witness. This ferocious yet disciplined charge 'in the bravest order and with the greatest resolution that ever was seen' went extremely well, scattering the enemy opposite them; the allies' infantry in the centre also fought doughtily. Unfortunately Fairfax on the right, with marshy ground to hamper him, was soon in trouble.

'Truly England and the Church of God hath had a great favour from the Lord in this great victory given unto us,' wrote Cromwell characteristically afterwards. It was true. Marston Moor cost the king his northern army and indeed the north. For those who sought a more human explanation, it was Cromwell's disciplined use of cavalry which was the single element which had saved the day.

Oliver Cromwell

(Opposite) **The Battle of Naseby**, 14 June 1645, in which Cromwell and Fairfax drew up their strong army on high ground to the north of Naseby in Northamptonshire. Rupert's initial charge broke Ireton on the Parliamentarian left wing, but the pursuit took his cavalry from the field, and after heavy infantry fighting in the centre Cromwell swung the day with a cavalry charge. Charles, who lost most of his artillery and infantry, never recovered.

showed its calibre. Even in success Cromwell did not allow his men the fatal indulgence of plunder that had effectively ruined the Royalist triumph earlier in the day. As a result Cromwell was full of 'holy glee,' according to contemporaries. That particular emotion, a kind of manic elation at God's apparent favour, might hold an ominous message for the future, in contrast to his usual emphasis on discipline both of himself and his troops. Cromwell's persistent references to his victory at Naseby led to rumours after his death that he had actually been buried on the battlefield.

Preston: Second Civil War

Cromwell passed – for the time being – into civilian and political life with the ending of the First Civil War. He was not seen in action again until the beginning of the Second Civil War in the spring of 1648. By this time the military defeat of the king had merely exposed crucial divisions between parliament and its army. This renewal of warfare, about which Cromwell felt extremely bitter – he called it 'a great mischief'– was the result of the collusion of English and Scottish Royalists. Nevertheless it included one of Cromwell's most spectacular victories. When 20,000 Scots under the Duke of Hamilton invaded northern England, the natural reaction of a competent commander would have been to fall back and protect the capital. Cromwell, however, decided on the risky gambler's throw of marching northwest himself – and then attacking the Scots from their own rear. His reasoning was that if he defeated the Scots in battle, he would rout them completely, leaving them no opportunity to withdraw to Scotland and regroup. After nine days of constant fighting in late August 1648, during which he covered 140 miles – a prodigious feat – Cromwell routed the Scots at Preston in Lancashire with 8,500

An early representation of a regimented uniform in a painting from 1672 of Randolph Egerton, an officer of the King's Troop of Horse Guards and a veteran of Edgehill in 1642. Many in both the Royalist and Parliamentarian armies had served in the Thirty Years War, and wealthier Royalist officers adopted the Continental practice of equipping their men in distinctive colours, as did the New Model Army.

Oliver Cromwell

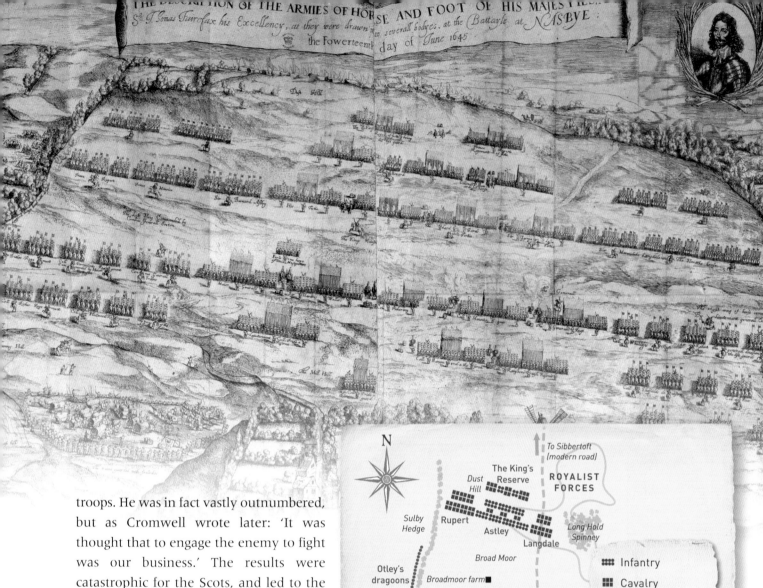

THE DESCRIPTION OF THE ARMIES OF HORSE AND FOOT OF HIS MAJES.

Sr Tomas Fairefax his Excellency, as they were drawn in severall bodies, at the Battayle at NASBYE:

the Fowerteenth day of June 1645

N

Dust Hill

The King's Reserve

To Sibbertoft (modern road)

ROYALIST FORCES

Sulby Hedge

Rupert

Astley

Langdale

Long Hold Spinney

Broad Moor

Otley's dragoons

Broadmoor farm ■

Infantry

Cavalry

Ireton

Skippon

Cromwell

Naseby Covert

Red Hill farm ■

Fairfax

The Spinney

To Clipstone (modern road)

Naseby Field

PARLIAMENTARIAN FORCES

■ Mill Hill farm

To Kelmarsh

Baggage train

Naseby

• Obelisk

0   1/2 km

0   1/2 mile

troops. He was in fact vastly outnumbered, but as Cromwell wrote later: 'It was thought that to engage the enemy to fight was our business.' The results were catastrophic for the Scots, and led to the end of the Second Civil War much as Naseby had led to the end of the First.

General in Ireland

During the various stages of political strife which now led up to the trial and execution of Charles I on 30 January 1649, Cromwell's position was at all points strengthened by his hold over and popularity with the army, especially when Fairfax withdrew from the judicial proceedings in disgust. It was thus Cromwell whom parliament, as the sole authority in the country after the death of the king, dispatched to Ireland in the summer of 1649: he was to blast the resistance of that intractable (and of course mainly Catholic) island. Opposition in Ireland, consisting of a number of disparate forces in favour of royal rule, could never be taken lightly given the geographical position which made it a convenient launching-pad for

England's foreign enemies. Nevertheless it was in Ireland that Cromwell irrevocably stained his reputation with the massacres of Drogheda and Wexford on 11 September and 11 October 1649 respectively.

How far is this staining justified? To estimate it, we must divide the military from the humanitarian. The seventeenth-century rules of warfare, as carried out all over Europe during the Thirty Years War and earlier, were indeed ruthless, even chilling. But they were generally recognized. The commander of a fortress had to make a decision, when officially 'summoned', whether to surrender or not. If he refused to do so, and the city was successfully stormed, then his soldiers and other combatants might be killed out of hand and the rest of the civilian population – women and children – would be subject to the unrestrained looting and rapacity of the besiegers. This provision was based on the harsh physical conditions of the attackers, in their camps, compared to the comparative ease of those within the town, endowed with shelter, water and provisions. It was naturally in the best interests of any fortress to procrastinate – unless there was a strong motive to do otherwise. Nor was Drogheda, where around 2,800 troops and several hundred priests and civilians were massacred, an easy target: as one saying had it, 'He who can take Drogheda can take Hell'.

But if Cromwell, desperate to pacify Ireland and to establish a solid armed presence before winter set in, had a military justification for the massacres which followed the sieges (they certainly presented a clear message to the rest of Ireland), the same cannot be said of his personal attitude to the native inhabitants. Here was a kind of scornful xenophobia, a sense of a holy crusade in which religion justified everything, singularly lacking from the disciplined Cromwell of England and Scotland. Once again but in a more marked form, 'holy glee' is evident in Cromwell's attitudes to these victories; furthermore at Wexford (where a similar number died as at Drogheda, though a higher

The Battle of Preston, the decisive battle of the Second Civil War, fought in sodden conditions on 17 August 1648, as depicted by Charles Cattermole, 1877. Cromwell had a major fight to capture the bridge over the Ribble before he could attack the main Royalist position, and the Royalist army retreated chaotically under cover of darkness.

proportion were civilians) his soldiers, encouraged no doubt by the rampaging atmosphere, even broke out and pillaged, something that was elsewhere expressly forbidden.

Dunbar and Worcester

We are on less controversial ground with Cromwell's two last fighting engagements. These were at Dunbar in Scotland against the Presbyterians under the young King Charles II on 3 September 1650 and at Worcester exactly a year later: in a letter to Parliament Cromwell called this the 'crowning mercy', since he had defeated Charles and thus brought the nine years of wars to a conclusive end. In both cases Cromwell showed himself a daring strategist and a cool calculator: no manic streak was visible here, illustrating the truth of Machiavelli's maxim: 'In war, discipline can do more than fury.' At the coastal town of Dunbar, apparently hemmed in, he lured the Scots, with twice his own numbers, down from their superior position on the hills. He was thus able to break their flank, and so drive them 'like turkeys'. There were 3,000 Scots' casualties to a few hundred English. Heading for Worcester, Cromwell showed an astonishing turn of speed, marching parallel with the young king as he attempted to raise English support. Not only that, but apart from planning a successful, two-pronged attack with his generals John Lambert and Charles Fleetwood, he led his own men in the assault, at the age of 52, with great personal courage. However, there is some evidence that Cromwell, normally eager for the sudden sally, actually delayed the action to coincide with the date of 3 September, his 'most auspicious day': it is always interesting to be reminded of the other semi-mystical side to 'Old Ironsides' (as he was nicknamed, just as his men were known as the Ironsides).

After that it was forward to what the poet John Milton, saluting Cromwell, called 'peace's victories'. Cromwell's career as Lord Protector (from 1653) meant that the man who had killed a king played a virtually royal role before his death in 1658, also on 3 September – another coincidence? His tortured attempts at a godly rule, unable to manage either with or without parliament, are another story. Nevertheless it is impossible to consider his political career realistically without the knowledge that he had gained this position in war – even if he had been seeking 'peace through war'. Cromwell had shown himself a military genius, a leader of men, and by that means had reached the highest position of state. It was the perfect example of another Machiavellian principle, by which war 'not only maintains those that are born Princes but many times raises men from a private fortune to that dignity'. Unfortunately the qualities which made him a great soldier – daring, the capacity to innovate, courage, a steely nerve – worked much less well in the complex world of politics, where his legacy is, to say the least, controversial. Lucy Hutchinson, whose husband John had been one of those who signed Charles I's death warrant in 1649, described Cromwell in her memoirs as having 'much natural greatness'. It is easier to agree with her unequivocally in the military rather than in the political sphere.

'At the battle of Dunbar ... Oliver was carried on with a Divine impulse; he did laugh so excessively as if he had been drunk; his eyes sparkled with spirits. He obtain'd a great victory; but the action was said to be contrary to human prudence.'

JOHN AUBREY, *MISCELLANIES*

Oliver Cromwell

> 'Il est mort aujourd' hui un homme qui faisait honneur à l'homme!'
> (Today a man died who brought honour to all mankind!)
>
> RAIMONDO MONTECUCCOLI, IMPERIAL GENERAL

VICOMTE DE TURENNE
1611–75

JOHN CHILDS

LOUIS XIV'S GENERAL TURENNE possessed one of the outstanding military minds of the seventeenth century. Always prepared to adapt and improvise, he became thoroughly expert in tactics, strategy and manoeuvre. Having served his apprenticeship during the Thirty Years War, he reached professional maturity in the 1650s and, following Louis's creation of a powerful French army in the 1660s, his most masterful campaigns occurred during the final two years of his life. Although an aristocrat, Turenne had the common touch, enjoying a close rapport with the soldiers whose lives he husbanded.

Initially trained in the military style of Nassau and Gustavus Adolphus, Turenne developed their techniques to such an extent that they became instrumental in the widespread adoption of linear tactics between 1660 and 1700. Unhindered by preconceptions, he learned from his mistakes, especially in his campaign against the Bavarians in 1645 in the final years of the Thirty Years War. A cautious, circumspect and calculating tactician, Turenne placed great emphasis upon accurate intelligence and could assess situations quickly before acting with despatch and decisiveness.

From 1667, leading an improved French army, he began to act more offensively. In order to reduce desertion and enable greater freedom of action he encouraged logistical planning, the magazine system and the creation of protected lines of communication and supply. Turenne always aimed to campaign in an opponent's territory both to inhibit the enemy's recruitment and logistics, and to reduce the costs of warfare to France: this was the old Swedish principle of making 'war pay for war'. Contrary to received wisdom, in order to maintain concentration of force he preferred to billet his men in the countryside rather than disperse them into garrisons, a technique that paid handsome dividends during the defence of Alsace against the Imperial forces in 1674–5, the campaign that brought his death.

Into the service of the French king

Henri de la Tour d'Auvergne was born on 11 September 1611, the second son of the Duke de Bouillon, ruler of the semi-independent principality of Sedan, by his second wife,

Elizabeth of Nassau, daughter of William the Silent. The family was Calvinist. A slow developer who enjoyed poor health, Turenne also suffered from a life-long speech impediment. As an aristocrat's younger son, he was destined for a career in either the church or the army and, in view of his physical frailty, the former seemed more likely; but his health improved with physical maturity and in 1625 he entered into a cadetship in the Dutch army commanded by his uncles, princes Maurice and Frederick of Nassau. After a year as a private soldier in Frederick's bodyguard, Turenne was commissioned captain in 1626. During the next four years he learned the modern art of war, the 'Nassau School', and experienced extensive action including the siege of 's-Hertogenbosch in 1629.

In 1623 his elder brother Frederic Maurice had succeeded as Duke de Bouillon, and the statesman Cardinal Richelieu, ever keen to strengthen the authority of the French state, began to seek to reduce the independence of the principality of Sedan. Elizabeth and Frederic resisted these overtures, but Turenne was withdrawn from the Dutch army in 1630 and sent to Paris as an unofficial hostage for Sedan's political loyalty. Richelieu formed a favourable impression of the young man and appointed him colonel of an infantry regiment. Turenne returned to the Dutch army for short secondments but after 1635 devoted his career wholly to the French monarchy.

Turenne in a portrait by Charles Le Brun, 1665. Napoleon was to describe him as history's greatest military leader.

Vicomte de Turenne

Apprenticeship

Whilst serving under a fellow Huguenot, Marshal Henri de la Force, at the siege of La Motte in Lorraine in 1634, Turenne's courage and determination during the final assault earned a field promotion to *maréchal de camp* (major-general). In 1635, Turenne fought under Cardinal de la Valette, raising the Imperial siege of Mainz on 8 August. For want of provisions, Valette had to retire to Metz. During the retreat, Turenne, in command of the rearguard, tangled with General Matthias Gallas. He was seriously wounded in the successful storming of Saverne in 1636, but returned to action in 1637. During 1638, under the command of Bernhard of Saxe-Weimar, he directed the siege of Alt-Breisach, which fell on 17 December. In 1639 he was transferred into the army of the Comte de Harcourt in northern Italy, where distinguished service resulted in promotion to lieutenant general in 1640. He commanded his own corps in Italy in 1641 and Roussillon during 1642.

Marshal of France

Politically suspect because of his Protestantism and family connections with the principality of Sedan, in 1642 Turenne's position was compromised by his brother's involvement in the conspiracy of the Marquis de Cinq Mars to bring down Richelieu. However, Turenne continued to demonstrate his personal loyalty to the French crown, whilst his increasing proficiency at his job guaranteed employment. In 1643, Richelieu entrusted him with an independent command in northern Italy under the direction of Prince Thomas of Carignano. At the end of the campaign he was promoted to Marshal of France on 9 December 1643 and appointed to Alsace to command the 'army of Weimar', the remnants of Bernhard of Saxe-Weimar's corps following its defeat at Tuttlingen a few weeks earlier. Turenne now campaigned in Alsace and Germany until the end of the Thirty Years War, but he enjoyed mixed fortunes: his military education was incomplete and the French army still compared unfavourably with the veteran formations available to the Imperialists, Swedes and Bavarians.

In June 1644, Turenne's army of Weimar joined a French detachment commanded by the Duc d'Enghien, the future Prince de Condé who, as a prince of the blood, assumed overall command. They defeated Franz von Mercy's Bavarian army at Freiburg-im-Breisgau, then harassed his retreat in a cavalry action, successes that resulted in the capture of Philippsburg (between 25 August and 12 September). The following spring, having received information that von Mercy's army had been weakened through sending reinforcements to the Imperialists to counter a Swedish offensive towards Vienna, Turenne crossed the Rhine. Mercy had, however, actually received substantial reinforcements. Turenne was enticed deep into Swabia, lost contact with his line of communications and was obliged to disperse his troops to find supplies. In this vulnerable position he was surprised and badly beaten by Mercy at Marienthal-Bad Mergentheim on 5 May. Enghien absorbed the remains of Turenne's corps and defeated the Bavarians at the second Battle of Nördlingen (Allerheim) on 3 August.

The following year Turenne, accompanied by a Swedish army under Karl Gustav Wrangel, separated the Bavarian army from the Imperialists, forcing Elector Maximilian I to conclude a separate peace in March 1647 (though this was annulled in September). In a final campaign against the recalcitrant Maximilian, Turenne and Wrangel heavily defeated an Imperial–Bavarian army under Count Jobst Maximilian von Gronsfeld and Count Peter Melander von Holzapfel at Zusmarshausen near

Augsburg on 17 May 1648, in one of the last battles of the long and bloody war.

Internal pressures and unrest in France led to the outbreak of civil war known as the 'Frondes' (between 1648 and 1653), and Turenne was central in securing the victory of the young King Louis XIV and his chief minister Cardinal Mazarin. In 1652 Condé, supporting the defeated rebellious French nobles, led a Spanish invasion of France. The resultant Franco-Spanish War, between 1653 and 1659, witnessed the flowering of Turenne's martial abilities as he led the French armies into the Spanish Netherlands and defeated the Habsburg forces at the Battle of the Dunes, near Dunkirk, on 14 June 1658.

Turenne had proved a most able and devoted servant of the French monarchy. He was created Marshal General of France when Louis XIV assumed his majority in 1661, but came under pressure to cement his loyalty by converting to Roman Catholicism. Perhaps understanding that the Catholic Church was one of the principal pillars of the French crown whilst the Huguenot faith encouraged division, localism and fragmentation, he finally renounced Protestantism in October 1668.

Franco-Dutch War, 1672–3

In the 1660s Louis, aided by Michel le Tellier and his son the Marquis de Louvois, both of whom served as secretary of state for war, built an army and navy capable of dominating the Habsburgs and the Dutch Republic. With it Turenne led 80,000 men

Turenne leading the charge against Spanish Habsburg forces under the Prince de Condé at the Battle of the Dunes, 14 June 1658, in a painting by Charles-Philippe Larivière (1798–1876). Cromwell had sent 6,000 English infantry to support Turenne, while the Duke of York, with a smaller Royalist contingent, was fighting on the Spanish side. Victory allowed the French to take Dunkirk.

Vicomte de Turenne

The French encirclement of Maastricht at the end of June 1673, just before the key Dutch fortress finally fell, as depicted by the contemporary French artist Jean Paul. Turenne had played a key role in preventing the allies from relieving the siege, while the siegeworks in preparation for the final assault were masterminded by the celebrated military engineer Sebastien Vauban.

across the border with the Spanish Netherlands on 24 May 1667. The resultant *'promenade militaire'* captured Bergues, Ath, Charleroi, Tournai, Oudenarde, Alost and Lille. Had the Dutch remained loyal to France rather than panicking at French success and joining the English and Swedes in a Triple Alliance in 1668, commented Turenne, the entire Spanish Netherlands would have fallen. Louis now determined to punish the Dutch and in 1672 Turenne advanced along the Sambre whilst Condé (rehabilitated and back in the service of the French crown) marched up the valley of the Meuse from Lorraine, the two forces joining at Visé in the Bishopric of Liège. They feinted towards Maastricht, causing the Dutch to denude their Rhineland garrisons to reinforce this key fortress, before turning away through the Electorate of Cologne, crossing the Rhine at Lobith and penning the Dutch army into Holland.

Leaving Condé to contain the Dutch within their 'Water Line', Turenne demonstrated before Maastricht, then on 31 August 1672 marched 15,000 men to the Rhine. He proceeded south to Koblenz before turning down the Moselle to take winter quarters in Lorraine. He allowed his men to plunder the Rhine and Moselle valleys in order to 'waste' the countryside and ensure that Imperial forces would be unable to operate in those areas during the next campaign, thus clearing the flank and rear of the French forces in Utrecht and Holland. The peasants removed themselves and their possessions into the afforested hills and skirmished fiercely with the starving soldiers.

The centrepiece of the campaign of 1673 was the siege of Maastricht. Turenne

Vicomte de Turenne

screened the preparations during February and March by threatening the Imperialists and Brandenburg forces along the Rhine whilst the besieging corps of 40,000 men assembled at Ghent. Once Maastricht had been enveloped, Turenne moved west and blockaded the suburb of Wyck on the right (east) bank of the Maas. Maastricht fell on 30 June but the position of the Dutch Republic soon improved following an alliance with Spain on 30 August 1673 and the termination of the war with England on 19 February 1674. What had begun as a short, limited campaign of conquest for Louis XIV had turned into a major conflict against a European coalition.

The defence of Alsace, 1674–5

During 1674, Turenne was charged with preventing a large German–Imperial army from interfering in either the Spanish Netherlands or Franche-Comté. Its general, Aeneas Caprara, had already crossed to the west bank of the Rhine and encamped near Strasbourg. He dispatched Duke Charles IV of Lorraine south along the right (east) bank of the Rhine to threaten Franche-Comté, but Turenne parried the thrust and forced Charles of Lorraine to return downstream. Turenne sought to subsist at the enemy's expense by operating on the right bank of the Rhine; his army contained 6,000 cavalry but only 1,500 infantry so that he could gather supplies from a wide area. In June, he left Hagenau, crossed to the east side of the Rhine on a bridge of boats near Philippsburg and set off to locate Caprara, who was known to be marching northwards to effect a junction

THE CAMPAIGNS OF TURENNE IN ALSACE AND THE RHINELAND, 1674–5.

with reinforcements approaching from Frankfurt-am-Main under the cautious Duke Alexander de Bournonville. Covering 100 miles in five days, Turenne overhauled Caprara's 7,000 horsemen and 2,000 infantry before they had contacted Bournonville, and brought them to battle at Sinzheim on 16 June.

Although Turenne's preponderance of cavalry had been ideal for rapid marching and widespread foraging, it severely circumscribed the conduct of battle. Caprara, whose army was similarly unbalanced, lined the hedges and gardens along the edge of the village with musketeers but Turenne deployed his foot and dismounted dragoons in small skirmishing parties that drove in Caprara's outposts and forced a passage over the River Elsatz into the village. Behind a fighting rearguard, Caprara withdrew and formed line of battle on the plateau above Sinzheim. The French now had to advance up a narrow defile knowing that the Imperial horse would pounce as they emerged on to the plateau. Turenne, however, took

Turenne's first campaign 1674
Second campaign of 1674
Third campaign of 1674
Fourth campaign of 1674–75

advantage of the new tactical capabilities of the French army by pushing his infantry and dismounted dragoons up the sides of the defile to line the numerous hedges along the edge of the plateau and occupy a castle on the left and a vineyard on the right. The flanks thus anchored, the cavalry moved up the defile and arranged itself in order of battle relatively unhindered. Turenne mingled groups of musketeers amongst the horsemen in the Swedish manner, to provide additional firepower, lengthen the front and disorder any Imperialist attacks. A premature advance by the French right nearly resulted in disaster, but well-aimed volleys from the infantry in the vineyard broke up the counter-attack. Turenne then ordered a general advance and, supported by musketry, the mounted troops steadily pushed the Imperialists back across the plateau. Exhausted and somewhat disorganized, Turenne's soldiers allowed the Imperialists to leave the field in good order. Both sides incurred about 2,000 casualties.

Lacking the strength to exploit his success, Turenne demonstrated towards Heidelberg before recrossing the Rhine to encamp at Neustadt. Early in July 1674, having taken in reinforcements, he returned to the right bank of the Rhine and marched towards the Imperial headquarters at Heidelberg, seeking to force Bournonville to battle. Bournonville, however, refused to be drawn and withdrew north of the River Main. Turenne's troops remained on the right bank, living off the country, commandeering, looting, plundering and levying contributions whilst the peasants retaliated by attacking isolated parties and murdering stragglers. This 'First Devastation of the Palatinate' continued until Bournonville took 30,000 men over the Rhine at Mainz towards the end of August, threatening Lorraine and northern Alsace. Turenne terminated his maraud and concentrated 25,000 men between Wissembourg and Landau, confident that Bournonville would be unable to feed his troops and have to retire. As anticipated, Bournonville withdrew to the right bank and marched south to attack Strasbourg with its valuable Rhine bridge, thus separating Turenne from supporting forces in Upper Alsace and Franche-Comté.

Bournonville's 36,000 men stood in the village of Enzheim, west of Strasbourg behind the River Breusch, awaiting the arrival of reinforcements under Frederick William von Hohenzollern, the 'Great Elector' of Brandenburg. Turenne knew that he would have to risk battle in order to reopen his communications with Upper Alsace and prevent a junction between Bournonville and Frederick William. Through an oversight, Bournonville had failed to block all the Breusch crossings and, on the night of 3/4 October, Turenne quietly moved his army over the river and drew up at Molsheim between Bournonville and Strasbourg and attacked at dawn. According to Bournonville, the Battle of Enzheim was 'one of the longest, most obstinate, and artilleryized that have [sic] ever been seen', the French firing 2,500 cannon balls. At the end of a day of crude frontal assaults, both Bournonville's flanks were in danger and he withdrew from the field having suffered around 3,500 casualties. Turenne lost about 3,000 men.

On 10 October Frederick William crossed to the west bank of the Rhine at Kehl with 20,000 soldiers and 33 cannon, passed through Strasbourg and joined Bournonville to create an army of 50,000. Greatly outnumbered, Turenne fell back to Deittweiler, between the fortresses of Saverne and Hagenau, where he received reinforcements suffi-

> 'Dieu est toujours pour les gros battaillons.'
> (God is always on the side of the big battalions.)
>
> TURENNE: ALSO ATTRIBUTED TO VOLTAIRE

cient to raise his strength to 33,000 men. Thinking that Turenne had gone into winter quarters, Bournonville and Frederick William settled their men into cantonments on the plain between the rivers Ill and Rhine. Early in December 1674, Turenne left nine battalions at Saverne and Hagenau to cover his rear and marched his troops in a series of small detachments first north and then west. Through snow and heavy frost he then turned south behind the screen of the Vosges before swinging east into the Belfort Gap. Having reassembled his army at Belfort, on 27 December Turenne debouched on to the plain of the Rhine, surprising the Imperialists who were scattered in garrisons and quarters. Bournonville threw forward his cavalry to delay the French whilst attempting to concentrate his forces on Colmar and the little town of Türkheim. Driving rapidly north, Turenne broke the Imperial horse at Mulhouse on 29 December and appeared before Türkheim on 4 January 1675. In the interim, Bournonville and Frederick William had assembled 30,000 men between Colmar and Türkheim but their front was over-extended and could not be held in strength along its entirety: Türkheim itself was under-garrisoned. Quick to spot these weaknesses, Turenne denied his opponents the opportunity to improve their deployment by ordering his 30,000 men into line of battle. The French advanced to pin the Imperial left and centre while making their main effort against Türkheim itself. Progress through the town was inter-rupted when Bournonville committed reserves, leading to heavy fighting in the outskirts.

As more and more French troops were sucked into the fighting around Türkheim, the pressure on Bournonville's left and centre eased, enabling him to swing his line round to face Türkheim and block any further advances. After dark, though, the Imperial army left Turenne in possession of the battlefield and withdrew through Strasbourg and over the Rhine.

Turenne's last campaign and death

For the 1675 campaign, Emperor Leopold I recalled the veteran Italian Raimondo Monte-cuccoli to command the Imperial forces on the Rhine. He decided to capture the bridge at Kehl-Strasbourg prior to invading Alsace. Leading 35,000 men directly on Strasbourg, he was thwarted by Turenne's 25,000. Next, Montecuccoli feinted before moving north to attempt a crossing at Speyer but again Turenne was able to gain position and block the attempt. True to his principle of operating on the right bank of the Rhine whenever possible, Turenne then passed the river and a campaign of manoeuvre followed during which each side felt for the other's supply lines and communications, seeking a fractional advantage. By the end of July, Montecuccoli had been manoeuvred into such a disad-vantageous position at Nieder Sasbach that he was compelled to offer battle on terms propitious to the French. Whilst reconnoitring an enemy artillery battery, however, Turenne was decapitated by a cannon-shot on 27 July.

He was buried in the Abbey of St Denis, the final resting place of the kings of France. The tomb was defaced during the French Revolution and his remains stored in the Jardin des Plantes until 1800 when Napoleon ordered their removal to Les Invalides church.

Turenne's tomb in Les Invalides, Paris. He had originally been buried in St Denis with the kings of France, but was moved during the Revolution. In 1800 Napoleon had Turenne, like Vauban, reinterred in Les Invalides, where he himself was eventually buried in 1861.

Vicomte de Turenne

DUKE OF MARLBOROUGH

1650–1722

CHARLES SPENCER

THERE HAS BEEN no more successful English soldier than John Churchill, 1st Duke of Marlborough. During the War of the Spanish Succession, he won all his battles, and triumphed at every siege. Moreover, Marlborough was simultaneously in charge of overall allied strategy and, as Ambassador-Extraordinary, of high diplomacy. The finer details of military administration, operations and logistics again fell to him. No other British general has ever been burdened with such all-pervading responsibilities.

The future duke came from gentry stock. His father, Sir Winston Churchill, had served as a Royalist cavalry captain in the Civil War, his ill-fated allegiance leading to a large fine that consigned his family to a life of poverty. After a sketchy education at St Paul's, John followed his sister Arabella to court. She became the Duke of York's favourite mistress, while John became his popular page-boy. Although a consummate courtier throughout his life, Churchill's primary ambitions were, from an early age, military.

Baptism of fire

In September 1667 the 17-year-old Churchill gained his first commission as an ensign in the King's Regiment of Foot Guards. He was sent to Tangier the following year, where he received his baptism of fire against the Moors. In 1670 he also saw his first action at sea, blockading the Barbary pirates in Algiers. Two years later Churchill fought aboard the English flagship, the *Royal Prince*, at the Battle of Sole Bay, off the Suffolk coast. The precise nature of his daring against the Dutch that day is unrecorded, but it resulted in a rare double promotion.

Captain Churchill next displayed his valour when fighting the Dutch on land, in the British unit serving as part of Louis XIV's army. During the storming of Maastricht, despite being wounded, he saved the life of the English commander, the Duke of Monmouth. Churchill raised the French standard over an outwork of the city just before it fell. Ironically, given his later stellar career at France's expense, after the taking of the city Churchill was singled out by the Sun King for praise.

Duke of Marlborough

The most significant part of Churchill's military apprenticeship now followed. From 1672 to 1675 he served under Marshal Turenne, perhaps Louis XIV's most able general (see pp. 52–9). The fighting was hard: at the Battle of Enzheim, half of Churchill's fellow English officers were killed or wounded. However, Turenne took a personal pride in the potential, spirit and accomplishments of his 'handsome Englishman'.

It was from Turenne that Churchill learnt the importance of infantry firepower; the effectiveness of employing artillery throughout a battle, rather than as a mere prelude; and the desirability of seeking decisive battle, rather than following convention and marching from siege to static siege.

Royal favourite

Churchill was entrusted with command of a new regiment of foot in 1678, and was promoted brigadier general. He had recently married Sarah Jenyns, the girlhood crush of the Duke of York's younger daughter, Anne. The two women's association was to have, in turn, happy and disastrous consequences for Churchill's military career. At this juncture John's links with York and Sarah's with Anne reaped dividends. In

John Churchill, Duke of Marlborough, painted by Adrien van der Werff in 1705. His close connections with the Dutch gave him exceptional political influence on top of his undoubted status as a great general capable of defeating the long-feared armies of Louis XIV.

Duke of Marlborough

QUEEN ♣

The Defeat of the Rebells
2,000 Slayn & their Canon taken

A playing card depicting the defeat of the Duke of Monmouth at Sedgemoor near Bridgwater, 6 July 1685. The defeat of the rebels was masterminded by Churchill as Royalist commander after the surprise night attack through the marshes by Monmouth's forces had been detected.

1682 John entered the Scottish peerage as Baron Churchill of Aymouth (Eyemouth), and the following year he became Colonel of the Royal Dragoons.

In 1685 the Duke of York succeeded to the throne as James II. That same year the Duke of Monmouth, an illegitimate son of Charles II, landed in the West Country in an attempt to seize the throne from his uncle. However, Churchill saw that Monmouth was never allowed to settle, snapping at his heels with his terrier force. Worn down, the rebels were eventually provoked into that most high risk of manoeuvres, a night-time attack, which ended in defeat at the Battle of Sedgemoor on 6 July. Although nominally only second in command, Churchill was the architect of victory, directing the royal troops with courage, flair and energy. He was upset not to have his contribution sufficiently recognized.

Fall from favour

When William of Orange landed in 1688, Churchill was again Lieutenant General of the English army. However, this time he sided with the invaders, putting his desertion down to James's increasingly dogmatic Catholicism. After the success of the 'Glorious Revolution', the newly crowned William III granted Churchill the earldom of Marlborough and confirmed him in his military rank, while charging him with the particular task of reforming and strengthening the English army in the wake of James II's defeat and exile; but with the titles came little trust. William's instinct was to rely on his Dutch compatriots, who were allowed to dominate the upper reaches of the English army, and he never forgot the surprising speed with which Marlborough had deserted his previous royal master.

In 1689 Marlborough was dispatched to command the 8,000 English soldiers serving with the Dutch in Flanders. He proved a tireless general, training his poorly regarded men until satisfied that they were fit to fight the French. That same year, Marlborough demonstrated the improvements he had instilled in his men at the Battle of Walcourt. His troops took the brunt of the French attack, before Marlborough led the Household Cavalry in a spirited counter-charge. The veteran allied commander, the Prince of Waldeck, reported to King William: 'Marlborough, in spite of his youth, had displayed in this one battle greater military capacity than do most generals after a long series of wars.'

Marlborough received his first independent command in 1690. In a combined operation by land and sea, he quickly captured the Irish strongholds of Cork and Kinsale from the Franco-Jacobite army. Despite these successes, his career came to a halt when he was among those suspected (correctly) of communicating with the exiled court of James II. Dismissed from all his posts in 1692, Marlborough was briefly imprisoned on false charges in the Tower of London. After his release, his career lay in the doldrums for several years. In 1694, he was suspected of giving information to the French about a secret English attack on Brest. However, the enemy already knew of the plan from other sources.

Redemption

Peace arrived in western Europe in 1697, but William III's distrust of Louis XIV made him think ahead to the inevitable next war. Aware that his own fragile health was on the wane, William identified Marlborough as the man to continue the fight against France during the next reign, and restored him to his army ranks. By the time of William's death and the accession of Queen Anne in 1702, the War of the Spanish Succession – in which the French Bourbon claim to the Spanish crown was challenged by Louis XIV's old enemies – had broken out. Marlborough, the new monarch's favourite, was appointed Captain-General of the English army, and Deputy Captain-General of that of the Dutch. Aged 52 (six years older than both Napoleon and Wellington at Waterloo), he was keen to establish the military reputation denied him in his prime.

Marlborough's aggressive intent was constrained by the constant interference of Dutch field deputies. These civilian representatives determinedly shielded their troops from the risk of open battle. On several occasions they refused Marlborough permission to attack the wrong-footed French, to his intense annoyance. Nevertheless, 1702 was a triumphant year for Marlborough: he swept the enemy out of the 'barrier fortresses' lying along the River Meuse, captured Liège, and was rewarded for an outstanding campaign with the dukedom of Marlborough.

The Blenheim campaign

The year 1703 was marked by further English exasperation at Dutch reluctance to fight. Marlborough decided on an astonishingly bold plan for the following year: he would march from the North Sea to the Danube, and rescue the Austrians from a Franco-Bavarian advance that threatened to knock the Habsburgs out of the war. This rescue mission could only be achieved if neither Louis XIV nor the field deputies guessed the duke's true intentions.

Marlborough's men covered the 250-mile trek, observed from a distance by a succession of mystified French marshals. Discipline on the march was excellent: supplies were paid for with gold provided by Marlborough's friend and ally, Sidney Godolphin, the English Lord Treasurer. The allied troops marched mainly before the sun was at its hottest, arriving at camps that were ready to welcome them with rest and food. At Frankfurt, every man received fresh boots. Marlborough's attention to his men's welfare led to the affectionate nickname 'Corporal John'.

The Battle of Schellenberg at Donauwörth, 2 July 1704, as depicted by August Querfurt in the 1730s. Marlborough won a costly victory for the allies against the Franco-Bavarian army to capture the fortress commanding the Danube river crossing. His success here opened the way to the great victory at Blenheim six weeks later.

(Opposite) **The Battle of Ramillies,** 23 May 1706, as depicted by an eighteenth-century French artist. Marlborough's defeat of Marshal Villeroi north of Namur enabled the allies to capture Antwerp, Ghent and Bruges. Both armies consisted of around 60,000 men; after Villeroi reacted to Marlborough's initial attack by sending reinforcements to his left flank, Marlborough concentrated his forces on the weakened French right and fought his way steadily into the village of Ramillies at the centre of the French position.

Arriving at the Bavarian frontier, Marlborough led a bloody assault on the Schellenberg, a fortified hill overlooking Donauwörth. Thirty-eight generals were among the 1,500 allies to die that July day. However, 12,000 of the Franco-Bavarian forces were killed, wounded or captured as the Schellenberg fell for only the second time in its 2,000-year history. Albeit at great cost, the allies had gained their crucial bridgehead across the Danube.

Marlborough now began his successful partnership with the hugely talented and charismatic Imperial field marshal, Prince Eugène of Savoy (see p. 68). Both commanders wanted to bring the enemy quickly to battle. Marlborough goaded the Elector of Bavaria to attack by torching his villages, but to no avail. Eventually, on 13 August, the allies launched a surprise dawn attack on the strong enemy position surrounding three villages, including Blindheim (named 'Blenheim' by the British). The French outnumbered the allies by 55,000 men to 50,000. Marlborough's masterstroke was to coop up the bulk of the French infantry inside Blenheim village, annulling the enemy's numerical advantage. The ensuing Battle of Blenheim (see map, p. 71) demonstrated what were to become the signature pieces of Marlborough's generalship: relentless pressure on the French line at a chosen point, which drew the enemy reserves to that sphere of the action, before delivering a body blow elsewhere. Blenheim also vindicated the methods that Marlborough had instilled in his men through rigorous training: allied infantry fire was delivered by platoon rather than in line, which led to more concentrated and controlled fusillades, which in turn led to greater enemy casualties.

Meanwhile Marlborough employed his artillery throughout the battle. When, at one point, the 'Wild Geese' (Irish troops serving Louis XIV) threatened to break through the allied centre, Marlborough hauled some of his guns through muddy marshland and raked grapeshot into the enemy ranks, to devastating effect. Blenheim also proved the superiority of Marlborough's cavalry tactics. He led the steady focused charge that swept the enemy from the field, relying on growing momentum and cold steel instead of the French method – firing pistols and carbines on horseback then retreating to reload.

Blenheim, Louis XIV's first taste of defeat in a reign of sixty years, stunned Europe. Marshal Tallard, the French commander, was among the prisoners: indeed, of the 4,500 Franco-Bavarian officers who fought at Blenheim, only 250 were not killed, wounded or captured. Marlborough's rewards included the principality of Mindelheim, and what was to become Blenheim Palace in Oxfordshire.

The Battle of Ramillies

Arguably Marlborough's greatest victory, the Battle of Ramillies took place in May 1706. Effectively invited by his opponents Marshal Villeroi and the Elector of Bavaria to fight on their chosen battleground, Marlborough eagerly accepted, even though he rated the large enemy army – its front measured 4 miles across – the best he had ever seen.

It was all over in two hours: Marlborough made a strong feint, with his English and Scottish troops, into the enemy's left flank, which Villeroi reinforced at great cost to the centre of his line. The allies pushed hard into the French right, while Marlborough led the cavalry in the centre. Here the fighting was intense, the elite *Maison du Roi* cavalry nearly breaking through. Marlborough himself had his horse shot from beneath him. He was nearly killed soon afterwards, a cannon ball passing

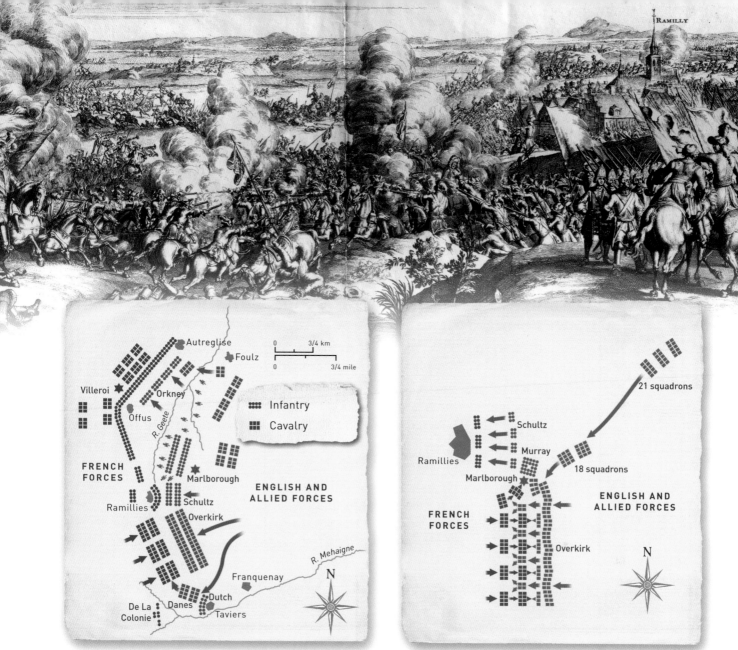

RAMILLY

| Infantry |
| Cavalry |

between his legs as he clambered on to a fresh mount. Under the steady pressure of increasing allied reinforcements, Villeroi's men buckled, before eventually breaking into a total rout when confronted by Marlborough's final cavalry charge. There were 22,000 Franco-Bavarian casualties, as opposed to Marlborough's 2,500. Total victory brought huge rewards: the enemy lost two-thirds of the Spanish Netherlands in a day, while the duke's reputation for military genius soared yet higher.

THE GENERAL ENGAGEMENT AT RAMILLIES, left, and Marlborough's intervention, right.

The Battle of Oudenarde

Reunited with Prince Eugène in 1708, Marlborough achieved his third great victory at Oudenarde to prevent a French invasion of the Dutch United Provinces. The allies ambushed the more numerous French, Marlborough marching his men 15 miles overnight to surprise a French army that had taken longer to cover just 6 miles. The French had to decide whether to fight the allies before them, or to retreat to Ghent. Marshal Vendôme urged caution, but the Duke of Burgundy, a prince of the blood, overruled his fellow commander.

Duke of Marlborough

Oudenarde was predominantly a running infantry battle between two armies of over 80,000 men, the French enjoying the advantage in numbers and terrain. Marlborough risked everything by urging his men to attack across the River Scheldt. It was the duke's cool command, assisted by Eugene's grit, as well as the dissent between the two enemy generals, that eventually led to gradual but total victory. The allies kept pushing more and more men on to the plain where the battle was decided. The result was the double encirclement of the enemy centre and right, and 16,400 French casualties – five times the allies' losses. Marlborough then oversaw the successful (but costly) siege of the supposedly impregnable city of Lille.

Pyrrhic victory

The year 1709 witnessed Marlborough and Eugène's third joint victory, Malplaquet, which Marlborough termed 'a very murdering battle'. Marshal Villars initiated the action, in an attempt to lift the siege of Mons. Some 110,000 allies attacked 80,000 French in woodland, where they were embedded in trenches and earth ramparts. The fighting was furious, and the Dutch advance on the allied left was subject to particularly terrible fire from well-placed French artillery. Marlborough and Eugène suffered 24,000 casualties, to Villars's 14,000, the worst losses in any European battle for more than a century. The day after the engagement, Mons was invested. It fell to Marlborough five weeks later. However, Marlborough and Eugène were later severely criticized for fighting the enemy unnecessarily, when the siege of Mons could have been pursued without such terrible bloodshed. The decision was apparently Eugène's, with Marlborough agreeing to it against his better judgement.

The Marlboroughs had risen through royal whim, and now their careers were crushed by the same capricious force. Sarah's outspokenness and hot temper had placed her increasingly at odds with the queen. Meanwhile the huge losses at Malplaquet had given the duke's enemies ammunition with which to attack him.

Aware of this, and worried by the Whig government's rejection of Louis's peace terms, Marlborough sought personal and career security. He asked the queen to make him Captain-General for life. This ill-judged request played into his detractors' hands: they had long sought to paint Marlborough as a self-interested parvenu. In October 1710, after the Whigs were swept away in a general election, the new Tory ministry conspired to undermine Marlborough's control of the army while fomenting suspicion at the duke's desire to see the war through to total French defeat. Weighed down by

The Battle of Malplaquet, 11 September 1709, painted by Louis Laguerre (1663–1721). This, Marlborough's last great battle in the War of the Spanish Succession, was by far the most costly. Attacking the French force that was seeking to raise the allied siege of Mons, Marlborough and Eugène repeatedly tested the French wings in the hope of weakening the centre, which was eventually broken by the allied cavalry.

the stress of it all, the duke seriously considered resigning his command, but was talked out of this decision by his friends at home and his military allies overseas.

Marlborough's military swansong was a brilliant manoeuvre in the summer of 1711. In early May he began to prod Villars's supposedly impenetrable 'Ne Plus Ultra' defensive lines which ran 160 miles from the English Channel to the Ardennes. The French were confident that, if they could avoid a major engagement with the duke, political developments in London would force his dismissal – a result to place above mere victory in battle.

Marlborough was equally keen to advance into France. In August he tricked Villars into suspecting a frontal attack in the west. The duke then led an electrifying night march that left the French in his wake, before piercing the lines at their centre, at Arleux. News of this success was greeted with astonishment across Europe. He then moved to Bouchain, despite being advised by nearly all his senior officers that this city was impossible to take. He dug 28 miles of earthworks and corridors round the French to assist supplies and attack the garrison, and Bouchain fell to him the following month. This was his last great achievement, in his tenth great campaign as England's Captain-General.

Unbeknown to Marlborough or to Britain's allies, the Tories had been secretly negotiating a peace with France. The duke was now in the way, and he was brought down by a series of attacks on his war expenditure: Marlborough's enemies were determined to have him branded an embezzler. In January 1712 he was dismissed his posts, by a cruel letter in Queen Anne's own hand. She claimed that she had not 'deserved the treatment I have met with' from Marlborough – an accusation that cut him deeply.

Unappreciated at home, he and Sarah spent increasing periods on the Continent. They returned in August 1714 to a new reign: Queen Anne had died that same day. George I's first signed state paper was the restoration

> '… Upon all occasions he concerted matters with so much judgement and forecast, that he never fought a battle, which he did not gain, nor laid siege to a town which he did not take.'
>
> CAPTAIN ROBERT PARKER, WHO SERVED IN ALL OF MARLBOROUGH'S CAMPAIGNS

of Marlborough to the Captain-Generalship. However, there were to be no more heroics: the ageing duke suffered a disabling stroke in 1716. He died six years later, aged 72. Buried in state at Westminster Abbey, his remains were later interred at Blenheim Palace.

Assessment

Cool-headed, resourceful and focused, Marlborough had a genius for soldiering. At Blenheim, he commanded a British-led army in its first Continental victory since Agincourt, three centuries earlier. The painstaking training of his men; the unison and expertise he demanded from infantry, cavalry and artillery; his meticulous logistics; his astonishing calm and decisiveness in battle; the ease of his relationship with Prince Eugène: all helped to forge some of the earliest battle honours of the British army. He also ended Louis XIV's six decades of victory and blocked the Sun King's chances of becoming emperor of Europe. Marlborough was greatly admired by a later French tyrant, Napoleon, who encouraged (and contributed to) the research and recording of the Duke's military accomplishments. If the duke's gifts are less celebrated today than they were, this is the fault of the teaching of history rather than of the man in question: Marlborough is the military colossus of a major war that is now almost forgotten.

PRINCE EUGÈNE OF SAVOY

1663–1736

CHARLES SPENCER

SMALL, SLIGHT, POCK-MARKED AND BUCK-TOOTHED – physically, Prince Eugène of Savoy (also known as Prinz Eugen) makes an unlikely martial hero. However, he was a military Titan who, in Napoleon's estimation, deserves to be ranked as one of the seven greatest generals of all time.

(Opposite) **The unprepossessing but bellicose Eugène** at the siege of Belgrade, 1717, as portrayed by an unidentified eighteenth-century artist. In later life Eugène became a great collector of paintings, prints and books.

It was France's tragedy that the extraordinary talents of Prince Eugène of Savoy, although home-grown, should be displayed with such dazzling effect against, rather than for, Louis XIV. Some of his successes against the Sun King were achieved when he was in sole command, others in tandem with the 1st Duke of Marlborough, with whom he formed one of the greatest military partnerships of history.

The other principal sufferers, as Eugène wielded his sword for the Holy Roman Empire through thirty-two campaigns, were the Ottoman Turks. Although frequently outnumbered, Eugène was never daunted. He knew his enemy, and made their numerical advantage irrelevant through careful exploitation of terrain, as well as superior discipline and weaponry. His sure touch during the key moments of an engagement, as well as his charismatic bravery, made him a leader of rare distinction. Eugène's Turkish victories, culminating in his delivery of Belgrade, ended the Ottoman threat to western Europe once and for all. It had taken the Holy Roman Empire a century and a half to unearth a soldier capable of such an achievement.

Drive and charisma

Eugène led the Habsburg armies at a time when Vienna was desperately short of money, and the war effort was further hamstrung by the machinations of ministers jealous of the prince. At times it was only the sheer force of Eugène's personality that kept the Imperial war machine functioning. The same could be said of his talismanic presence on the battlefield.

The prince would lead from the front, wearing his simple brown leather jacket with brass buttons. The dowdy clothing was misleading, for Eugène in battle was a blood-curdling sight. In the nineteenth century the English novelist William Thackeray described, from first-hand accounts, how the prince 'became possessed with a sort of warlike fury; his eyes lighted up; he rushed hither and thither, raging; he shrieked curses and encouragement, yelling and harking his bloody war-dogs on, and himself always at the end of the hunt'. His men worshipped him.

Royal roots

Eugène (full name François-Eugène de Savoie-Carignan) was a scion of the royal house of Savoy. His father was a brave but unspectacular soldier, his mother – a niece of Cardinal Mazarin – a scheming harridan. When she failed in her ambitions to become the queen of her childhood friend, Louis XIV, she resorted to increasingly bizarre tactics, including the use of magic spells, to try to remain in favour. She was eventually exiled, in disgrace, accused of witchcraft.

Eugène's early years were also scandalous. An ugly yet effeminate boy, with questionable sexuality and pitiful personal hygiene, he was known by malicious elements at court as 'Madame l'Ancienne'. Despite appearances, Eugène was passionate about soldiery. To prepare for his vocation, he strengthened his body through vigorous exercise, and improved his mind by devouring biographies of the ancient heroes, as well as mastering mathematics. However, when Eugène asked for a commission in the French army, he was insultingly rebuffed. Louis XIV, accustomed to his generals being cut from more obvious martial cloth, denied Eugène a commission, insisting that he instead join the priesthood. After a final plea to the king was rejected, and with his mother's humiliation still rankling, Eugène left France promising only to return with vengeful sword in hand.

Imperial service

In 1683 Eugène joined the army of Emperor Leopold. Here he would be known as 'Prinz Eugen'. The same year he received his baptism of fire, serving in the Duke of Lorraine's army which lifted the Turkish siege of Vienna. So brave was Eugène that day that Lorraine gave him a pair of golden spurs and command of a regiment. This was the beginning of a startlingly swift rise. A colonel of dragoons at 20, he was appointed major-general at 22, lieutenant general at 24, field marshal lieutenant at 25 and general of horse at 26.

Eugène's military exploits demanded attention. In 1687 he led the decisive cavalry charge that delivered Imperial victory over the Turks at the Battle of Mohács. The prince planted the Imperial Eagle in the vanquished enemy's camp, and carried off their standard, the Crescent. As a reward for his

The Battle of Zenta, 11 September 1697, by an anonymous Austrian artist. At Zenta Eugène destroyed a much larger Ottoman army, which he surprised as it was crossing the River Tisza (in modern Serbia). He allowed the cavalry to cross, then destroyed the bridge, isolating and annihilating the Turkish infantry.

valour, Eugène was given the honour of delivering news of the victory to the emperor.

After the outbreak of the War of the League of Augsburg in 1688 between France and the Grand Alliance, Eugène was active in Italy. His troops were a ramshackle mixture of Spaniards, Savoyards and Piedmontese, confronted by crack French troops with a record of invincibility stretching back half a century. It was Eugène's exceptional leadership, as well as his men's ruthlessness, that made this contest equal. (In 1690 he reported that they habitually castrated prisoners before dispatching them.) From 1694, Eugène was the supreme allied commander in Italy.

Victory at Zenta

In Vienna there was jealousy and resentment at Eugène's success. When in 1697 the Ottomans drove westwards, recapturing cities lost a decade earlier, Eugène was sent to meet them, though with instructions from the Imperial war council not to attack. Eugène, always a man of action, ignored such negativity. He appreciated that the Turks' huge numbers and bravery could not compensate for their often rudimentary weaponry, which included bows and arrows, and that Ottoman hopes of success depended on their ability to maintain forward momentum and strict formation. The prince was confident of exploiting these vulnerabilities.

Eugène attacked the Turks at Zenta on 11 September 1697, and 30,000 of the enemy were killed, including the grand vizier and four of his deputies. Among the booty were 60,000 camels and the Great Seal, the grand vizier's symbol of authority, which had never before been captured. Meanwhile Eugène lost just 300 men.

The prince's immediate reward for this astonishing victory was dismissal by the Imperial war council for disobeying orders. However, popular demand ensured that the emperor quickly restored him. Eugène only accepted his reinstatement on condition that he was given greater independence in future. Zenta eventually led to the conclusion of the war with the Turks.

Fighting the French

The Peace of Ryswick (20 September 1697) ended the conflict with France at much the same time. However, in 1701 the War of the Spanish Succession broke out, after Louis XIV championed his grandson's acceptance of the Spanish crown rather than allow it to go to the Austrian Habsburg claimant. Eugène returned to the Italian peninsula, keen to reverse early enemy strikes, and convinced that this would be the key sphere of the Franco-Austrian conflict. He advanced southwards with just 22,000 men, passing through neutral Venice before beginning a successful guerrilla campaign against Marshal Catinat's forces. Louis XIV castigated Catinat: 'I sent you to Italy to fight a young and inexperienced prince; he has flouted all the precepts of warfare. But you appear to be mesmerized, and let him do as he pleased.' Catinat was replaced by Marshal Villeroi.

Villeroi attacked Eugène and his army in the fort at Chiari. Outnumbered, Eugène was nonetheless confident of success: he had observed that the French were most effective in their initial charge, and tended to be much less successful in subsequent fighting. He ordered his men to lie on their stomachs, and only to stand and fire when the French were close, which caused them to flee in disarray. Villeroi lost 2,000 men, Eugène just 40.

In February 1702, before the beginning of the customary campaign season, Eugène launched an audacious strike. Finding Villeroi in winter quarters at Cremona, Eugène led his forces through an abandoned canal, up into the centre of the French position. Although unable to overrun the city, Eugène took Villeroi prisoner.

Now Louis XIV pitched Marshal Vendôme against Eugène. The Frenchman had 80,000 men, the prince 28,000. In August the two armies met at Luzzara, a bloody battle that ended in stalemate. Eugène's bosom friend, Prince Commercy, was killed during the engagement. After the fighting both armies stubbornly remained facing each other for eighty-two days, rather than withdraw in defeat. Thanks to his exploits and his tenacity, Eugène was now the foremost hero of the Grand Alliance. In 1703 the prince was appointed president of the Imperial war council in Vienna, the controller of the emperor's military affairs.

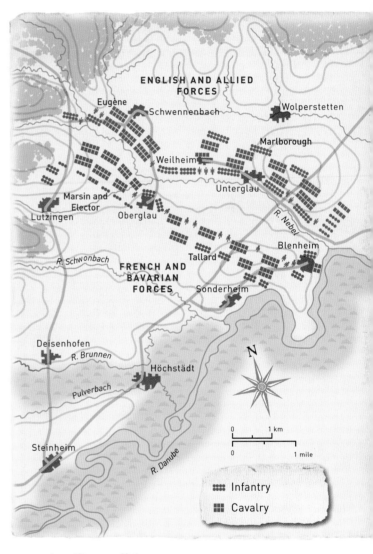

THE BATTLE OF BLENHEIM, 13 August 1704. Eugène commanded the right wing of the allied army, and his persistence despite heavy fighting held the line. He claimed afterwards that every member of his squadron attacked at least four times in the course of the day.

Comrades-in-arms

The next stage of Eugène's career was inextricably linked with that of the other great military genius of the era. John Churchill, Duke of Marlborough, met Prince Eugène in the summer of 1704, while leading his allied army towards the Danube, in a bid to save the Imperialists from a potentially devastating advance by the Franco-Bavarians. It was the beginning of an extraordinary military partnership.

The duo's first victory was at Blenheim, on 13 August 1704. Prince Eugène led the Imperialists on the right-hand wing of the Allied army, overcoming rough terrain and

Prince Eugène of Savoy

superior enemy numbers to contribute hugely to the victory. Eugène continued to lead his infantry and cavalry forward, despite repeated repulses. When he spied two of his men deserting, he rode them down and shot them both in the back.

Late in the afternoon, Marlborough led the cavalry charge that destroyed the main French army. Although the junior partner at Blenheim, Eugène's role had been crucial, as Louis XIV suffered his first major defeat on land, after sixty years on the throne (see also pp. 63–4).

Eugène of Savoy (on the bay) with the Duke of Marlborough at Blenheim in 1704, in a tapestry from Blenheim Palace, Oxfordshire. Marlborough had specifically asked for Eugène's presence, and the two men formed a close partnership in the weeks before the battle.

Triumph at Turin

In 1705 Eugène returned to Italy. He was attacked at Cassano, another bloody stalemate. In early 1706, his army was overwhelmed at Calcinato before he could reach it. The prince withdrew his forces to the Alps, and the Franco-Spanish thought they had seen the last of his interference in Italy. However, Eugène marched towards Turin, the allies' last major possession in Savoy, which was being besieged. Such was the effect of Eugène's reputation that the French army, poised to strike the city, seemed paralysed by news of his approach.

On 7 September Eugène led the attack outside Turin, capturing the enemy guns and turning them on the French. In the fierce fighting, the prince's page and servant fell beside him, and he himself had his horse shot from beneath him. Later in the day he was wounded in the head. While both sides suffered 3,000 dead and wounded, the French also forfeited 6,000 prisoners. Louis's dreams of Italian domination were over in a day, and Eugène's victory resulted in Austria, rather than Spain, being the dominant power in the peninsula over the next century and a half. Eugène's rewards from the emperor included the governorship of Milan.

Disaster in Provence

The year 1707 started promisingly, when the prince was promoted Imperial Field-Marshal. Meanwhile Peter the Great of Russia proposed Eugène to fill the vacant position of king of Poland. However, the emperor, anxious not to lose his ablest lieutenant, failed to support his candidacy. It was now decided that Eugène, under the nominal command of his cousin the Duke of Savoy, should attack the French naval base of Toulon, and so gain control of the Mediterranean for the alliance. This, it was hoped, would persuade the French to withdraw their forces from Spain.

The viability of the Toulon offensive relied on surprise. However, the Duke of Savoy wasted time waiting for supplies, and by the time Eugène's army, 35,000 strong, set off on 30 June, the French had established his true destination. The prince was now in a race with Marshal de Tessé's force of the same size, which the Frenchman won. Never optimistic about the Toulon campaign, Eugène now grew despondent. On 22 August he admitted defeat and lifted the siege.

Prince Eugène of Savoy

Partnership resumed

In 1708 Eugène was reunited with Marlborough. The action was in Flanders, where the Duke of Burgundy and Marshal Vendôme headed an army of 110,000 men, which quickly took Bruges and Ghent before heading for Oudenarde. In a bid to save the city the duke pushed his men to march 50 miles in two and a half days. Eugène, while unable to get his troops to link up with Marlborough's grand army in time, managed to join his colleague.

The Battle of Oudenarde began at 4 p.m. on 11 July. It was a fast-moving engagement, during which Eugène, commanding the allied right wing, was almost swamped by Vendôme. Timely reinforcements allowed Eugene to break Vendôme's first line, before the Dutch all but encircled the French. At nightfall the allies were ordered to cease fire, to prevent them from inflicting casualties on their own. Eugène was not finished, though. He ordered his drummers to sound the French army's retreat, and had his Huguenot officers shout false orders to trick their compatriots into following them. Those duped by the prince were among the 9,000 prisoners taken at Oudenarde. Meanwhile the allies suffered 3,000 casualties, against the French 6,000.

Eugène and Marlborough now tackled Lille, France's second city. With solid and intricate defences designed by Vauban, Louis XIV's great fortifier-in-chief, it was the toughest of propositions. Eugène invested the city on 17 August. Five weeks later, he was hit by a musket-ball when leading an attack. Eventually, on 9 December, Lille fell. Ghent and Bruges soon followed.

Eugène enters Milan at the head of the Austro-Piedmontese army on 9 September 1706, two days after defeating the French at Turin. His victory ensured that Austria would dominate Lombardy for the next 150 years. Eugène himself was appointed governor of Milan.

The following year, 1709, was more challenging. Eugène oversaw the main army, while Marlborough besieged and took Tournai. When marshals Villars and Boufflers divined that Mons was the next allied target, they dug in to woodland at Malplaquet, and invited attack. On 11 September, Eugène led the allied right wing at the Battle of Malplaquet. His troops were Imperialist, supported by Danish infantry and Dutch cavalry. He took the wood of Sart after vicious fighting, during which the prince was hit behind the ear by a musket-ball. He refused to leave the battlefield for treatment. After a terrible day's fighting, the French withdrew in defeat. They had lost around 14,000 men, but the allied victory was a Pyrrhic one, with 24,000 men killed or wounded. Malplaquet was the last battle in which Eugène and Marlborough would act in concert.

Victim of Villars

Towards the end of 1710, the British government began clandestine negotiations with the French. At the beginning of 1712, the Tory government gained Marlborough's dismissal, and then secretly forbade his replacement, the Duke of Ormonde, from taking part in military action against the French. Eugène was left in the dark and, unsurprisingly, these years of English treachery were the least successful of his military career.

In July 1712, Eugène captured Quesnoy. This initial success persuaded him to venture forward too far. Later in the month Villars, the most able marshal available to Louis for a generation, wrong-footed Eugène and trounced the Dutch at Denai. After this, the French took Douai. Soon afterwards, with the Dutch field deputies constraining him terribly, Eugène had to surrender Quesnoy, and then Bouchain. In three months the prince had lost a third of his forces and five of his strongholds.

While the rest of the alliance made peace with Louis XIV through the Treaty of Utrecht in April 1713, the emperor continued the struggle alone, sending Eugène to command the Imperial army on the Rhine. With morale low, and Villars in the ascendant, Eugène lost Landau and Freiburg. After this, the prince represented the Imperial interest at peace negotiations with Villars, which resulted in the Treaty of Rastadt (7 March 1714).

'After God, thanks for the successes must go to the intelligence, efficiency and boldness of Prince Eugène.'
THE DUTCH STATES-GENERAL, 1708

The Turks tamed

The Turks now marched westwards, sending an army of 120,000 men under the grand vizier to Peterwardein. Eugène defended this Austrian fortress with 60,000 men and on 5 August 1716 he attacked. The grand vizier headed the list of 6,000 Turkish who died that day. Eugène took as a prize the fallen enemy leader's silk and gold tent (so large it required 500 men to erect it) as well as its rich contents. Eugène followed up by taking the fortress of Temesvar. The Turks sued for peace, but Eugène persuaded the emperor to hold out for one more great victory. He had Belgrade in his sights.

The taking of Belgrade in 1717 was the high-point of Eugène's career, ending the Turkish threat to Austria. Peace followed in 1718. When, fifteen years later, the elective crown of Poland was disputed – by France on the one side, and the emperor, Russia and Prussia on the other – Eugène was recalled to high command. This was a war too far for the frail septuagenarian who had been wounded eleven times in battle. His chest was permanently infected, and his memory was on the wane.

Prince Eugène of Savoy

BELGRADE: EUGÈNE'S MILITARY MASTERPIECE

ELGRADE HAD BEEN IN TURKISH HANDS since the mid sixteenth century. Prince Eugène was eager to recapture it, and to deprive the Ottomans of their principal westward staging-post. He hoped to overrun Belgrade quickly, and then turn on whatever rescue force the Turks sent from Adrianople.

Mustapha Pasha and a garrison of 30,000 men defended the city bravely, their efforts helped by a summer cyclone that destroyed Eugène's bridges over the Danube. The garrison remained defiant, as nearly a quarter of a million men under Halil Pasha arrived to deliver them from the prince. Trapped between two Turkish armies, his army wilting from dysentery and the heat, Eugène resorted to his customary reflex and attacked.

His men advanced in the pre-dawn mist of 16 August 1717. The Ottomans missed an early chance to decide the battle, when they unwittingly isolated the Imperialist right wing. Eugène, alive to the threat, led his cavalry forward, with strong infantry support, then advanced with a disciplined tread, holding his men's fire until within 50 feet of the Turks.

The Imperialists now fell upon the Ottoman enemy with bayonets and swords, inflicting 20,000 casualties. Belgrade surrendered immediately. Western Europe, prepared for news that Eugène had been crushed between two Ottoman armies, learnt instead that the prince had delivered them from the Turkish threat for the first time in 150 years.

Confronted in 1734 by a French army that outnumbered his by five to one, Eugène looked for victory in Germany to compensate for early Habsburg losses in Italy. He was, however, no longer the confident leader of his prime, and his indecision allowed Philippsburg to fall. In 1735 Eugène undertook his final campaign. He was, by this stage, physically and mentally in tatters. It was a relief to the Imperialists when, that autumn, the Peace of Vienna concluded the War of the Polish Succession and the prince retired. He died in April 1736, aged 72. Despite his Franco-Italian extraction, he is remembered as Austria's greatest soldier.

Prince Eugène of Savoy

'[Charles XII] experienced the extremes of prosperity and adversity, without being softened by the one or in the least disturbed by the other.'

VOLTAIRE

CHARLES XII
1682–1718

STEPHEN BRUMWELL

CHARLES XII OF SWEDEN has always attracted extreme reactions. Was he a heroic warrior king or a berserker whose belligerence ruined his country? Like Gustavus Adolphus before him, Charles was a bold leader and an astute tactician. Yet as a commander, Charles faced the greater challenges: Gustavus's military career coincided with the rise of Sweden, Charles's with her decline. And while he ultimately failed to save the Swedish empire, Charles's remarkable campaigns were worthy of 'the Lion of the North' himself.

When Charles XI of Sweden died from stomach cancer in April 1697 his namesake son was just 14 years old. Eager to exploit the young king's inexperience, Sweden's enemies and rivals saw an opportunity to attack her Baltic empire, clawing back territories lost during the previous century. Between 1698 and 1700, a formidable anti-Swedish coalition formed, allying the king of Poland-Lithuania and Elector of Saxony, Augustus II, 'the Strong', with Peter the Great of Russia and Frederick IV of Denmark.

But Sweden's perceived vulnerability was deceptive. The allies underestimated both the resilience of the Swedish empire and the determination of its teenaged ruler. Charles's father had groomed him carefully for kingship, and by his accession he was already well schooled in the theory of diplomacy, strategy and tactics. Such training was mandatory: Swedish tradition decreed that the monarch should not only conduct foreign policy – in conjunction with the expert advisers of his itinerant 'field-chancery' – but also command his troops in person.

Thanks to his father's reforms, Charles XII inherited a formidable army. It was well trained and equipped, and founded upon a reliable system of territorial recruitment, with individual provinces contracted to raise and maintain regiments in peace and war alike. Under the allotment system of conscription, farmers shared the burden of supporting soldiers, who were provided with housing and pay and in return helped with the farm-work when not on military service. This yielded a permanent, native army of 11,000 cavalry and 30,000 infantry. Another 25,000 mercenaries garrisoned the overseas provinces. In the summer of 1700, the streamlined and highly professional Swedish army mobilized for war on three fronts.

The onset of the Great Northern War

The coalition's members did not anticipate a long conflict, particularly as they calculated upon exploiting anti-Swedish sentiment in the Baltic provinces of Livonia and Estonia. In fact, the bitter and bloody Great Northern War lasted for twenty-one years. The allies' first overconfident assaults were uncoordinated, the Swedish response brisk and devastatingly effective. By the time Peter declared war on 20 August 1700, and the Saxons began a siege of Riga in Livonia, Denmark had already been eliminated. On 25 July, in Charles's baptism of fire, a 10,000-strong Swedish army had landed on the Danish island of Zealand and marched against Copenhagen. Blockaded in his capital, Frederick soon caved in, signing the Treaty of Travendal on 18 August 1700.

Meanwhile, Augustus's siege of Riga was also foundering. Contrary to expectations, the Livonian nobles did not rally to the Saxons, and the disillusioned Augustus raised the siege on 29 September. The Russian army, at least 35,000 strong, began bombarding Narva, in Ingria, on 31 October 1700. Charles was already heading to its relief. On 30 November, in the Battle of Narva, the Swedes assaulted the Russian siege-works under cover of a snow-storm. Outnumbered three to one, they nonetheless broke through and routed the enemy. Including fugitives drowned in a frenzied flight, Peter lost 8,000 men. The stunning victory, which reminded commentators of Gustavus Adolphus's impressive debut at Breitenfeld in 1631, gave notice that the Swedes remained a force to be reckoned with.

Charles had played an important role at Narva, and shared in the campaign's planning. Over the next six years, as he gradually gained experience and confidence and took an ever-greater role in command, the young king seemed invincible. In 1701, Charles resolved to deal with Augustus. On 19 July he

Charles XII

forced his way across the Dvina into Courland (western Latvia). Crossing the 600-yard-wide river in open boats against determined Saxon resistance was a remarkable feat, aided by a feint to deflect the defenders' attention and a smoke-screen to mask their fire. Along with Lieutenant General Bernard von Liewen, Charles led the first wave of 6,000 infantry. Although the cavalry were unable to cross in time to maximize the victory, the episode demonstrated that the Swedes could prove as effective against the well-trained Saxons as against the less professional Russians.

Charles invaded Poland-Lithuania in January 1702. That July, he destroyed a Saxon–Polish army at Kliszów, southeast of Krakow. Regarded as his finest victory, it was a battle in which Charles himself took the decisive role.

Charles XII comes of age as a commander

The young Charles XII's victory in the battle for the crossing of the Dvina, 19 July 1701, demonstrated the increasing potency of the Swedish army. Charles's feat of leading his infantry from the Swedish stronghold of Riga across the wide river into Courland, in the face of strong Saxon resistance, is depicted here by an anonymous eighteenth-century Swedish artist.

Narva has been dismissed as an aberration, scored against an outmoded enemy under fluke conditions; it was a battle in which Charles XII was subordinate to his generals. No such qualifications can diminish his victory at Kliszów, a battle fought in perfect summer weather against a numerically superior and thoroughly modern force arrayed in a formidable defensive position (see p. 79). In the brief but hectic interim of campaigning, Charles had matured as a commander, learning on the job: at Kliszów it was the king, not his advisers, who orchestrated events – with striking results that devastated Augustus and the Saxon army.

In the wake of the Battle of Kliszów, Poland's leading cities fell to Charles, and in July 1704 he presided over the election of his own candidate as king of Poland-Lithuania, Stanisław Leszczyński. Following a crushing victory by his trusted general Karl Gustaf Rehnskiöld over a Saxon–Russian army at Fraustadt in February 1706, Charles invaded Saxony. That September he obliged the Saxon Estates to accept the Treaty of Altranstädt,

BATTLE OF KLISZÓW

LATE ON THE MORNING of 19 July 1702, Augustus II of Saxony received disconcerting news at his headquarters at Kliszów, south of Kielce. The Swedish army thought to be encamped some 3 miles away had suddenly emerged from the woods fronting his own camp. Augustus immediately drew up his army on rising ground to the north. An extensive swamp protected his left flank, while a stream running through the boggy valley that sep-arated the rival armies discouraged frontal attack. Charles was keen to engage – so eager that he had been prepared to march against Augustus without the 4,000 men under General Karl Gustav Mörner who had only arrived the previous evening. Yet even Charles was awed by the strength of the enemy's position. He was also outnumbered by almost two to one: his 8,000 infantry, 4,000 cavalry and four light 3-pounder cannon faced 9,000 Saxon horse and 7,500 Saxon foot, plus another 6,000 Polish cavalry and no fewer than 46 guns.

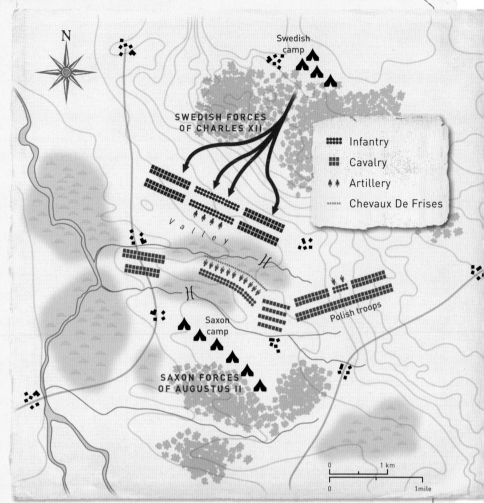

Despite the odds, Charles was undaunted. Examining the ground, he ordered an advance. As Augustus was most vulnerable on his right, Charles strengthened his own left wing for an enveloping attack there. After the initial Swedish assault was stymied, Charles's entire army stood on the defensive, withstanding charges by Hetman Lubomirski's Polish hussars on its left, and a Saxon thrust across the valley against the centre and right.

Decisively repulsed at last, Lubomirski withdrew, so exposing the Saxon right flank. Charles swiftly exploited this weakness: in personal command of his main left-wing force of mixed infantry and cavalry, he struck the Saxon flank, while the rest of his army advanced to its front. After hard fighting, the Saxons buckled under the mounting pressure, finally breaking in retreat across the marshes to their rear.

By late afternoon the battle was over. At a cost of about 900 killed and wounded, including Charles' brother-in-law, Frederick of Holstein-Gottorp, who was cut in half by a cannon ball, the Swedes had slain or captured some 4,000 Saxons. Kliszów vindicated Charles's opportunistic brand of personal leadership, and the potency of his army's equally aggressive tactics.

by which Augustus was to abdicate his Polish throne. Just a month later Augustus, at the head of a Saxon–Russian army, riposted with a victory of his own at Kalisz. However, Augustus had already ratified the Treaty of Altranstädt in secret, and when Charles publicized his duplicity, was shamed into complying with its terms. In November 1706 Augustus left for Saxony: Charles's second opponent had been knocked out of the war.

Charles XII stamped his character upon his army. His fatalistic piety – the belief that divine providence governed all things – was disseminated via the sermons of regimental chaplains, and encapsulated in the watchword, 'With God's help'. The king's frugal lifestyle, which likewise helped to forge a bond of comradeship with the rank and file, also attracted much comment. In an age when generals campaigned with extensive personal baggage, Charles's contemporaries were shocked and fascinated by a soldier-king who disdained such creature comforts, preferred weak beer or even water to wine, ate standing up and buttered his bread with his thumb.

Tall, slim-waisted and with a high, domed forehead, Charles rejected the full-bottomed wig universally worn by men of his class, instead sporting his own hair cropped short. His stark appearance was only heightened by a severely plain uniform of blue coat and elk-skin breeches, with a black taffeta scarf instead of a lace cravat. Charles's Spartan austerity was mocked by his enemies, but admired by many professional soldiers.

A 'Carolinian' way of war

Reflecting Charles' own inclinations and Swedish military traditions alike, his troops employed exceptionally aggressive tactics, calculated to dismay and overwhelm even the steadiest opponents. Such 'gå på' ('go on') techniques bucked conventional tactical trends, but proved remarkably successful. The Swedish infantry fought four deep, the musketeers reserving their fire until the enemy was just 40 yards away before pouring in volleys and rushing on with the bayonet and sword. At a time when other armies were abandoning the pike, the Swedish penchant for cold steel ensured that pikemen remained an important component of infantry battalions. Unlike their counterparts in most western European armies, the Swedish cavalry eschewed pistols and carbines, typically fired while advancing at a stately trot, instead maximizing shock value by charging home sword in hand.

'Hungry dogs bite best.'

CHARLES XII [IN RESPONSE TO SUGGESTIONS THAT TROOPS WHO HAD JUST ARRIVED IN CAMP SHOULD BE ALLOWED TO REST BEFORE ATTACKING THE ENEMY]

Such uncompromising battlefield tactics were matched by ruthlessness. At times, the Great Northern War was fought with a cold ferocity that prefigured the Eastern Front of the Second World War. The protagonists often proved themselves as unrelenting as the elements; combat was frequently savage, prisoners rarely taken. In Poland, where the Swedes were dogged by guerrilla resistance, brutal reprisals against civilians were common. The fighting between Swedes and Russians was especially pitiless, and included an ugly, racial element: the Russians were treated as sub-human, and as such, undeserving of mercy. After Rehnskiöld's victory at Fraustadt, while Saxon prisoners were spared, hundreds of captured Russians were butchered in cold blood.

Charles XII versus Peter the Great

While Charles was preoccupied with his convoluted Polish campaigns, Sweden's Baltic provinces suffered encroachment from a resurgent Russia. In 1703 Peter the Great seized Ingria, and began to build his new capital, St Petersburg; in the following year he took Dorpat, Narva and Ivangorod. Meanwhile Russian troops streamed into Poland-Lithuania to bolster factions opposed to Charles's puppet Leszczyński.

Whatever his merits as a tactician and battlefield commander, Charles's decision to intervene in Poland in 1701, instead of consolidating the outcome of Narva by marching directly against Peter, casts serious doubts upon his strategic judgement. The Polish interlude not only allowed Peter to make inroads upon Sweden's vulnerable Baltic posses-sions, but gave his own remodelled army a chance to acquire experience and confidence.

By 1707, however, Charles was resolved to settle matters with his last remaining enemy. He rejected Peter's offer of peace in exchange for the cession of Ingria, and marched his army – now rested and reinforced to about 35,000 men – eastwards in a full-scale invasion of Russia. With hindsight it is all too easy to point to the folly of such an undertaking, a perspective only underlined by the subsequent fates of Napoleon and Hitler. Yet Charles took a calculated gamble. Through a combination of circumstances, it went tragically wrong.

Peter's armies withdrew into Russia, scorching the earth behind them. Until mid 1708, Charles remained in Lithuania while General Adam Ludvig Lewenhaupt amassed supplies. On 14 July, at Hołowczyn – rated by Charles as the best of his battles – the Russians were beaten after an audacious crossing of the Vabich. In September 1708, without waiting for Lewenhaupt, Charles turned south to winter in the Ukraine, where he hoped to find fresh provisions and support from the rebel Cossack, Hetman Ivan Mazepa. This risky strategy proved disastrous. Peter pounced on Lewenhaupt's isolated corps at Lesnaia on 9 October, mauling his command and seizing the supply train. The Swedes suffered dreadfully in the bitter winter of 1708–9. Harried by the Russians, they died in their thousands from cold and disease. With Polish and Russian forces blocking Leszczyński from coming to his aid, Charles was trapped.

Disaster at Poltava

By late June 1709 Peter was ready to give battle outside the town of Poltava, which Charles had been besieging since April. The homesick Swedes were now running low on ammunition and morale. In addition, when the armies met on 27 June Charles

The Battle of Lesnaia,
9 October 1708, by Pierre-Denis Martin (1663–1742). Peter the Great's defeat of a Swedish army led by General Lewenhaupt took place while Charles XII himself was seeking reinforcements in the Ukraine. The victory bolstered the confidence of the Russians in the months before their decisive defeat of Charles XII at Poltava the following summer.

Charles XII

The end of Swedish ambitions: the Battle of Poltava in the Ukraine, fought in the early morning of 27 June 1709, and depicted here by Jean-Marc Nattier (1685–1766). With Charles XII unable to take personal command, the Swedish command was divided between Lewenhaupt and Rehnskiöld. The Swedes suffered massive casualties, and many of those taken prisoner were forced to work on building Peter's new capital at St Petersburg. Charles was forced to flee to Ottoman-controlled Moldavia, where he remained for five years.

was unable to take personal command: ten days earlier, he had been wounded in the foot by a Cossack rifle-ball. Relinquishing battlefield command to Field Marshal Rehnskiöld, the king was obliged to observe events from a litter.

Under these unpromising circumstances, Charles has been heavily criticized for accepting Peter's challenge. Yet the alternatives were scarcely attractive: withdrawing south to the Crimea or back towards Poland, in either case with the Russians snapping at his heels. By contrast, even if it failed to eliminate Peter's army, a victory would alleviate the Swedish supply crisis, strengthen Leszczyński's position, and hopefully persuade the Turks and Tartars to take the field against Russia.

Peter offered battle cautiously, under conditions calculated to blunt the edge of Charles's tactics. Not only were most of his green-clad infantry ensconced within a fortified camp, but the approach was defended by a T-shaped system of manned redoubts, its long 'arm' intended to act like a breakwater and dissipate the force of any assault. When the Swedish infantry attacked, the redoubts served their purpose; while some of Charles' bluecoats surged past towards the Russian camp, others became mired in a bloody and ultimately futile effort to capture them. Crucially, a six-battalion-strong force under Major-General Carl Gustaf Roos became isolated and was forced to surrender.

Meanwhile, Charles had, incredibly, come within grasp of victory: the Swedish cavalry routed their opponents, and the infantry deployed to assault Peter's camp. With Roos's men missing, it was decided to await them before attacking. This was a fatal error. Two hours were wasted – an interval in which the Swedes lost momentum and the Russians regained their composure. Buoyed up by news of Roos's fate, the Russians left their camp to fight in the open. They presented an awesome sight: no fewer than 22,000 infantry drawn up in two lines and supported by sixty-eight field guns. Ranged against them were the pitiful remnants of the Swedish foot. Now just 4,000 strong, and further winnowed by Russian artillery, they launched a last, desperate attack. This time Swedish aggression was not enough. A breakthrough on Peter's right went unsupported, and a counter-attack splintered Charles's army into a mass of fugitives.

Three days later, as the traumatized Charles and his personal escort crossed the Dnepr into Turkish-controlled territory, 17,000 demoralized Swedes surrendered at Perevolochna. Of the 23,000 made prisoner there and at Poltava, just 4,000 returned from captivity.

Exile and death

Charles spent the next five years languishing at Bender, in Moldavia, an increasingly restless and troublesome guest of the Ottoman Turks. During his exile, the coalition he had dismantled between 1700 and 1706 reformed. Within a month of Poltava, Augustus had returned to Poland with a formidable army of 11,000 Saxons; that

November, Danish troops invaded Scania, and Tsar Peter besieged Riga. In Charles's absence, the defence of Sweden was conducted by Count Magnus Stenbock. In February 1710 he defeated the over-confident Danes at Hälsingborg, but Sweden's prized Baltic provinces could not be saved. By September 1710, both Livonia and Estonia had fallen to Russia. The indomitable Charles now persuaded his reluctant Turkish hosts to confront the Russians. They defeated Peter at the Prut river in July 1711, but the wily tsar extracted his army by offering concessions. Although Peter reneged on these, subsequent Ottoman declarations of war were half-hearted. Two years later, the rivals signed a peace treaty.

Charles finally quit Moldavia in September 1714. For two months he travelled incognito across Eastern Europe, disguised under a wig and moustache and posing as 'Captain Peter Frisk'. When he arrived at Stralsund in Swedish Pomerania, instead of continuing his journey to Sweden Charles helped to defend the town against a Danish–Saxon–Prussian siege; wounded during a sortie, and aware that surrender was inevitable, he escaped in an open rowing boat on the very eve of the capitulation. In December 1715 Charles set foot in his kingdom once more. True to form, instead of contemplating peace he took the offensive, launching the first of two Norwegian campaigns calculated to knock Denmark out of the conflict. The second came to a sudden end on 30 November 1718, when Charles was shot through the head at the siege of Frederiksten.

Assessment

Like his life, Charles's death remains controversial. Was he slain by an 'honest enemy bullet' or by his own exasperated countrymen? The prime exhibit is Charles's embalmed skull, perforated from temple to temple. The left hole is much larger than the other and, by usual forensic criteria, should designate the 'exit' wound. This has been used to support the contention that Charles was shot from the right – from his own siege lines. A rival school maintains that because he was wearing his hat, with the brim folded up to the left, this double layer of felt would have minimized the exit wound: if this can be credited, the shot entered from the left – presumably from the besieged fortress. Here, as with so much else relating to this enigmatic figure, a conclusive verdict is unlikely.

By the time of Charles's death, Sweden's position had improved; war-weary and mutually suspicious, the coalition was disintegrating. Yet the verdict of the Great Northern War was unequivocal. When Sweden and Russia finally signed the Peace of Nystad on 30 August 1721, Peter's agreement to evacuate Finland gained him Estonia, Livonia and Ingria. Sweden's Baltic empire had been dismantled; her 'age of greatness' was over.

The extent to which Charles XII was personally responsible for Sweden's relegation from first- to third-rate power has generated intense debate, likewise his culpability for culling his countrymen in a succession of bloody campaigns. Modern research has acquitted him on the second count, although the first continues to provoke scholarly argument. Yet Charles XII deserves recognition as an inspirational battlefield commander, a soldier whose leadership propped up an overstretched empire long after it should have collapsed.

'I have been entertaining the hero of France, the Turenne of the age of Louis XV ... The Marshal should be the tutor of every general in Europe.' FREDERICK THE GREAT WRITING TO VOLTAIRE

MAURICE, COMTE DE SAXE
1696–1750

JOHN CHILDS

NOTWITHSTANDING HIS GERMAN BIRTH and Lutheran religion, Maurice de Saxe commanded the principal armies of France during much of the War of the Austrian Succession (1740–8). His victorious campaigns of 1744–8 constituted the high point of French military achievement between the death of Louis XIV and the Revolution. His reputation has subsequently diminished because his forte lay in strategy and manoeuvre rather than the conduct of battle – the victories at Fontenoy (1745), Roucoux (1746) and Laufeldt (1747) were 'half won' – and he faced either second-rate or inexperienced generals. He never lost a boyish adventurousness which suggested to many critics a greater suitability for subordinate rather than supreme command.

Maurice de Saxe was born on 28 October 1696 in the Imperial free city of Goslar, the result of a casual liaison between Frederick Augustus II, Elector of Saxony and king of Poland, and Countess Maria Aurora von Königsmarck. Aged 12, Saxe served in a Saxon corps in Flanders and witnessed action at the siege of Tournai and the Battle of Malplaquet in 1709 before returning to Dresden in 1711 to receive the title Count of Saxony. Between 1711 and 1715 he fought with the Saxon army against the Swedes in Pomerania and in Hungary under Prince Eugène of Savoy (1717). Bored, restless, dissolute and debauched – these were lifelong characteristics – in 1720 he travelled to Paris. Equipped with his father's money and the patronage of Elizabeth of the Rhine, dowager duchess of Orléans, on 9 August 1720 he was commissioned *maréchal de camp* (major-general) in the French army and purchased a regiment.

From colonel to lieutenant general

Abandoning some of the more adolescent aspects of his unruly personal conduct, Saxe applied himself to the military profession and the *Régiment Saxe* became an exemplar of administration and drill. Although a veteran of eleven campaigns, Saxe knew more about swinging a sabre than the science of war so he studied under the guidance of the leading military writer and theorist, Jean Charles de Folard. In 1725 he was proposed for the

Maurice, Comte de Saxe

vacant dukedom of Courland but his candidacy buckled under Russian pressure. By 1732 he had served in the French army for twelve years but remained only a colonel and *maréchal de camp*, his prospects hampered by his German birth and Protestantism.

The first indications of potential for higher command occurred during the War of the Polish Succession (1733–5). In 1734, the advance of Charles Louis Auguste Fouquet, Duc de Belle-Isle, along the Moselle was delayed at Traben-Trarbach by 20,000 Imperialists occupying Grevenburg castle and the ruined Vauban fortress of Mont Royal. Saxe led two unsuccessful assaults on 27 April before the position fell on 2 May. Saxe then joined the corps of Adrien-Maurice, Duc de Noailles, in front of the lines of Ettlingen. Leading fifteen companies of grenadiers in a night attack on 3 May, Saxe broke through the outpost zone but Noailles's caution prevented further progress. The remainder of the campaign was consumed by the French siege of the fortress of Philippsburg (7 June – 17 July) during which Saxe's direction of an assault on 14 July impressed both Noailles and Claude François Bidal, Marquis d'Asfeld. On 1 August, Saxe was promoted to lieutenant general. During the uneventful campaign of 1735, he guarded the Rhine above Mannheim.

War of the Austrian Succession

Another period of boredom and frustration ended when France declared war on Austria in 1741. In alliance with Elector Charles Albert of Bavaria, the French intended to march on Vienna to place him on the Imperial throne. Departing in late summer 1741 with Saxe leading the van, by mid October the Franco-Bavarian army had reached St Polten, only 30 miles from Vienna. At the insistence of the Elector, who wanted to annex Habsburg lands, they turned south into Bohemia, appearing before Prague early in November. Saxe thought the difficulties of siege warfare overrated and decided, with minimal reference to his superiors, to surprise Prague. He quickly assembled four companies of grenadiers supported by 2,000 infantry and 1,200 dragoons and, in a daring *coup de main*, during the night of 26 November 1741 seized the Charles Gate and forced the city to surrender. This feat made him famous throughout Europe, but greatly increased the animosity and jealousy felt towards him by many senior French officers. Nevertheless, François-Marie, Duc de Broglie, charged him with the task of besieging the Austrian fortress and magazine of Eger, which fell on 19 April 1742.

Prussia now deserted the alliance with France, leaving Broglie and Belle-Isle stranded in Prague. Saxe attempted a relief but was unable to make progress and Belle-Isle broke out on 16 December with 15,000 men, only half of whom reached the safety of Eger ten days later. France had been humiliated, and defeat by the Anglo-Hanoverian 'Pragmatic Army' at Dettingen, on 16 June 1743, raised the spectre of invasion. In the spring of 1743 Saxe assisted Broglie in Bavaria but envy and dislike led to his replacement by Louis-François I de Bourbon, Prince de Conti. However, the new minister of war, René-Louis de Voyer, Marquis d'Argenson, appreciated Saxe's qualities and appointed him to direct the corps at Speyer. Following the failure of his counter-offensive into Bavaria, Broglie withdrew into Alsace and handed over his entire army to Saxe.

The Austrian commander Prince Charles of Lorraine occupied Alt-Breisach and prepared to cross the Rhine; Saxe moved to Neuf-Breisach, the fortress on the opposite bank, and made clear his intention to fight. During the summer, Saxe blocked all Lorraine's attempts to force a crossing. The crisis past, Saxe was superseded by Marshal François Franquetot de Coigny and relegated to a subordinate command in Noailles's army. Nevertheless, when he returned to Paris in November 1743 he was fêted, welcomed to Versailles by Louis XV and offered grudging admiration by his French colleagues. His cousin and France's ally, Frederick the Great of Prussia, advised Versailles to make Saxe commander-in-chief.

Marshal of France

On 13 January 1744, Saxe was ordered to Dunkirk to prepare 10,000 men for an invasion of Great Britain in support of the anticipated landing of Prince Charles Edward Stuart (Bonnie Prince Charlie) but this enterprise was postponed indefinitely on 11 March. Saxe was promoted to marshal of France on 26 March and placed in command of the forces in Flanders. He determined that the best way to ease Austrian pressure along the middle and upper Rhine was by attacking the Austrian Netherlands, where a French advance into west Flanders would also separate Great Britain from its allies Austria, Hanover and Prussia; threaten the Channel ports endangering British supply lines; and overawe the Dutch Republic. Whilst Saxe directed the covering army, Noailles quickly reduced Menin and Ypres, menacing the key ports of Nieuport and Ostend. The commander of the allied army, George Wade, fell back behind the Scheldt and was looking over his shoulder towards Antwerp when news arrived that Charles of Lorraine had invaded Alsace. Louis XV and Noailles drew substantial reinforcements from Flanders and departed for Alsace, leaving Saxe with 55,000 men to face 22,000 British, 16,000 Hanoverians, 18,000 Austrians and 40,000 Dutch – 94,000 men in all. Wade remained encamped behind the Scheldt and the campaign concluded: Lorraine eventually withdrew to deal with an invasion of Bohemia by Frederick the Great, who had meanwhile concluded a secret alliance with France against Austria.

Fontenoy, 1745

Saxe's health deteriorated during the winter of 1744/5 – contemporaries described the condition as 'dropsy', probably oedema resulting from congestive heart failure – and he conducted the 1745 campaign from a padded chariot. By besieging Tournai, Saxe hoped to draw the allied commander, the inexperienced William Augustus, Duke of Cumberland, into battle early in the season before his forces had fully concentrated. Leaving Brussels on 23 April, Cumberland marched towards Tournai. Cumberland's slow progress across country and along bad roads allowed Saxe nearly two weeks to prepare the battlefield at Fontenoy, modelling his dispositions on those of Villars at Malplaquet and Charles XII at Poltava. Cumberland attacked on 11 May and his frontal assault was unexpectedly successful, driving the French centre towards the Scheldt, until finally halted by enfilade fire from flanking infantry and redoubts. At a cost of 7,000 French and 10,000 allied casualties, Saxe obliged Cumberland to withdraw, but it was not a resounding victory. Tournai fell on 22 May and Saxe sent his principal lieutenant, Marshal Ulrich Löwendahl, to seize Ghent by a *coup de main* on 11 July: Bruges, Oudenarde, Albert, Dendermonde, Nieuport and Ostend then succumbed in quick succession. Ath, in Hainault, surrendered to Saxe on 8 October. In three months Saxe had realized his strategic objectives in taking the major Channel ports and driving the British north and away from Germany and the Austrians.

Saxe remained in Ghent with his army during the winter of 1745/6. Whilst British attention was distracted by the advance of Charles Edward Stuart's Jacobite army to Derby and rumours of a French invasion force gathering at Calais, in January 1746

Saxe celebrating his success at Fontenoy, 11 May 1745, in a painting by Horace Vernet (1789–1863). His victory against the Anglo-Dutch-Hanoverian alliance was costly, but it allowed Saxe to seize control of much of Flanders. The defeat of the British army also encouraged Charles Edward Stuart to return to Scotland three months later and launch his challenge for the Scottish and English crowns.

Maurice, Comte de Saxe

Saxe drew 22,000 troops from their cantonments and marched for Brussels. Halle, Louvain, Malines and Vilvorde fell without a shot fired and on the night of 30 January the Brussels suburbs were occupied and the city surrounded. The governor Count Wenzel Anton Kaunitz had a garrison of 12,000 men, plentiful provisions and anticipated the arrival of a relief force from Antwerp. Instead of Brussels falling to a surprise attack, Saxe had to conduct a formal siege in the depths of winter. Losing hope of relief and with the French poised to storm, Kaunitz surrendered on 20 February. In just two campaigns, Saxe had overrun the Austrian Netherlands.

From Roucoux to Maastricht

Diplomatic progress towards peace caused Saxe to abandon the intended invasion of the Dutch Republic in 1746. Instead, the 200,000-strong French army further secured its recent gains by capturing Antwerp (May) and Mons (July). Anticipating that Saxe's next goal would be Namur, exposing Liège and Maastricht, the allied forces – comprising the British under General Sir John Ligonier, the Dutch under Karl August Friedrich, Prince de Waldeck, and the Austrians commanded by Charles of Lorraine – marched down the Maas in an effort to beat Saxe into Namur. Saxe, hampered by the open insubordination of Conti, increasing ill-health and the strategic limitations imposed by the French government, was slow to respond and lost the race. Although the allies' position was strong, their logistics were vulnerable and a series of French attacks on their lines of communication, culminating in the seizure of Huy on 29 August, obliged them to leave their powerful encampment and move north, enabling Saxe to capture Namur (6–19 September).

His next target was Liège. Lorraine tried to protect both Maastricht and Liège by throwing his 80,000 men across the roads from Tongres and St Trond, but Saxe executed a neat flank march and took up a position with 120,000 men between the two roads on 10 October. Liège, which anchored Lorraine's left flank, was betrayed to Saxe by its citizens on the night of 10/11 October, necessitating a rapid readjustment and weakening of the allies' position. A series of infantry frontal assaults levered the British out of the villages of Lier, Varoux and Roucoux (which gave the battle its name), while a flanking assault drove back the Dutch on their left. In good order, the allies left the field behind Ligonier's rearguard and retired across the Maas via the bridge at Visé. Saxe was promoted to marshal general of France in January 1747.

Saxe led 136,000 soldiers into the field at the end of April 1747: Cumberland commanded the 126,000-strong allied army assisted by Field Marshal Karl Batthyány and Waldeck. Saxe began by sending two detachments under Louis George Érasme, Marquis de Contades, and Löwendahl across the southern border of Zeeland to draw the allies away from Maastricht and threaten Cumberland's communications with Great Britain. Contades seized Fort Liefkenshoek, northwest of Antwerp, whilst Löwendahl took Sas-van-Ghent, Ijzendijke and Eeklo. Despite Cumberland's best efforts, Löwendahl then moved east to invest and capture Hulst and Axel. Both sides manoeuvred during May and June until Saxe sent a detachment under Louis de Bourbon-Condé, Comte de Clermont, forward to Tongres, 12 miles south of Maastricht. Sensing an opportunity to defeat Clermont's corps, Cumberland slipped south. Clermont was about to retreat rapidly when Saxe, who had anticipated and shadowed Cumberland's march, appeared in support. The armies met in early July at Laufeldt

'The Battle of Laufeldt was meant to enable us to besiege Maastricht. We made so many mistakes we had to draw back. The only thing we could do to justify this sorry outcome was to besiege Bergen-op-Zoom.'

MAURICE DE SAXE

where Saxe secured a technical victory (see pp. 90–91), but he was unable to follow up by taking Maastricht as he had intended.

Demonstrating greater skill in strategy and manoeuvre than in directing set-piece battles, Saxe launched Löwendahl from Tirlemont with 35,000 men against Bergen-op-Zoom, 63 miles distant. His intention was to draw Cumberland back to the north and thus uncover Maastricht. Furthermore, the capture of Bergen would close the entire length of the Scheldt to allied shipping and alarm the Dutch. On 16 September, following a long siege, Löwendahl stormed Bergen but lost control of his troops and a massacre ensued: overnight, Saxe and Löwendahl were transformed into mercenary Protestant barbarians. Strategically, too, the plan failed because Cumberland did not leave Maastricht.

Maastricht remained the target for 1748, the French needing both a major victory and an expensive bargaining counter to sell at the peace conference. Saxe left Brussels

Saxe disposes his forces at the Battle of Laufeldt, 2 July 1747, with Maastricht in the distance, in a painting by Pierre L'Enfant (1704–87). He did not capture the town until May the following year, in what was to be his last major success on the battlefield.

THE BATTLE OF LAUFELDT

ON 30 JUNE 1747 the Duke of Cumberland found himself facing Saxe and the full French army on a plain 2 miles west of Maastricht. Sir John Ligonier commanded the British cavalry standing against the River Geer (or Jaar) behind the villages of Wilre (Wolder) and Kesselt, while the Duke of Cumberland commanded the British infantry in Laufeldt and Vlijtingen; the Dutch, Hanoverians and Bavarians covered the swampy ground opposite Grote-Spaeven; and the Austrians occupied the right flank behind a ravine west of Kleine-Spaeven. Saxe was bound to attack the allies' left and centre to prise them away from Maastricht. Cumberland, whose line of battle was 4 miles long, initially intended to stand behind the line of villages, but was eventually persuaded by Ligonier to occupy them as redoubts to break up the French onslaught.

Cumberland's dithering – the villages were occupied, evacuated and reoccupied three times until they were finally garrisoned just one hour before the French attacked – convinced Saxe that he was about to withdraw across the Maas through Maastricht. Saxe decided to follow as closely and quickly as possible and sent forward Clermont's grenadiers, the heads of their columns masked by a host of light infantry and skirmishers, to take the supposedly deserted village of Laufeldt, only to be thrown back by musketry and enfilading artillery. Saxe then committed more infantry against both Laufeldt and Vlijtingen to force the Allies' centre. In a series of crude frontal assaults, French infantry charged down the slopes

from the Heights of Herderen: four times they took the rubble of the two villages and four times were forced out by the British and Germans under Landgrave Frederick II of Hesse-Cassel.

Saxe had to continue – he committed a total of forty battalions – or accept defeat whilst Cumberland was able to relieve and reinforce the garrisons from his second line and even bring nine battalions of Austrians around from behind the ravine. After four hours' fighting, Saxe led forward another twelve battalions which gained footholds in both Laufeldt and Vlijtingen. Saxe then charged towards Vlijtingen with his cavalry and Cumberland ordered the Dutch horse from the right to take them in the flank, but they turned and fled, riding down their own infantry. Cumberland's centre had been fractured, the garrisons of Laufeldt and Vlijtingen were isolated, and French infantry started to feed through the gap.

Saxe turned to Louis le Tellier, Comte d'Estrées, to lead 140 squadrons of cavalry down the road into Wilre to turn the allies' left and drive it into the fire of twenty field guns already positioned on either side of Laufeldt. Aware of the developing situation, Ligonier brought sixty British squadrons from behind Laufeldt and Vlijtingen and charged d'Estrées in the flank before his horsemen had gathered momentum. Ligonier's charge provided the defeated infantry with space to reorganize and leave the field in reasonable order. But he realized that if d'Estrées rallied, charged and broke through his shield, then the retreating infantry would be massacred. Ignoring

(Opposite) **Maurice de Saxe was buried in St Thomas,** the main Protestant church in Strasbourg. His monument by Jean-Baptiste Pigalle shows the marshal descending into his tomb, the symbols of the defeated Britain, Holland and the Empire to his right, and resplendent French standards to his left. Hercules weeps by the open tomb, while an inconsolable France guides Saxe into it.

on 20 March 1748 for Antwerp where he managed to persuade the allies that he was about to attack Breda. Meanwhile, Löwendahl had secretly assembled a second French army in six towns in southern Luxembourg before concentrating at Verviers. Saxe then turned the main army south and hurried for Maastricht whilst Löwendahl encircled the right bank suburb of Wyck. Maastricht fell on 10 May, in the last major engagement of the War of the Austrian Succession.

The war was formally concluded by the Peace of Aix-la-Chapelle on 18 October 1748. Saxe retired to the Château de Chambord on the Loire where he died on 30 November 1750 from a 'putrid fever', probably a stroke, following a long visit by several court beauties and various 'dancers'. He was buried in the Protestant city of Strasbourg on 8 February 1751.

Saxe's art of war

Saxe had recorded his thoughts on the art of war in 1732 when recovering from a serious lung infection, but *Mes Rêveries* was only published, posthumously and unedited, in 1757. *Mes Rêveries* was the work of an immature soldier who had yet to

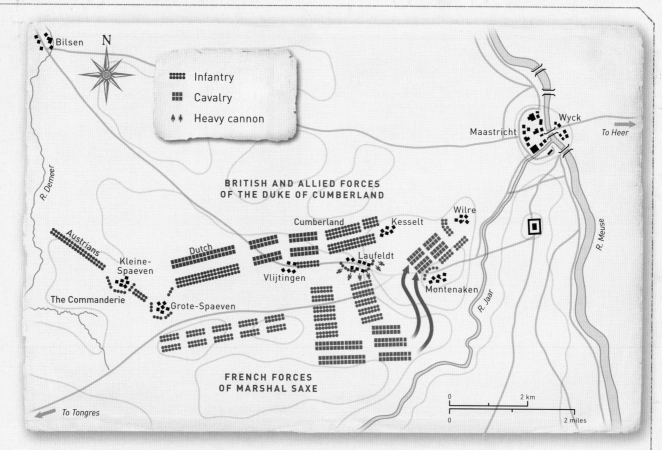

Infantry
Cavalry
Heavy cannon

BRITISH AND ALLIED FORCES
OF THE DUKE OF CUMBERLAND

Bilsen

N

R. Demeer

Austrians

Kleine-
Spaeven

The Commanderie

Dutch

Grote-Spaeven

Vlijtingen

Cumberland

Laufeldt

Kesselt

Wilre

Montenaken

Maastricht

Wyck

To Heer

R. Meuse

R. Jaar

FRENCH FORCES
OF MARSHAL SAXE

To Tongres

0   2 km
0   2 miles

Cumberland's order to disengage, he launched a second charge that was initially successful. He advanced too far, however, and his men were driven back by entrenched French musketeers and Ligonier himself was captured. By the time that Saxe had reorganized the French forces,

Batthyány had moved some Austrians to screen the retreating infantry. Saxe lost 14,000 killed and wounded: the Allies 6,000. Although Saxe was the technical victor, he had neither taken Maastricht nor destroyed the allied army.

experience high command and, during the War of the Austrian Succession, Saxe frequently failed to practise what he had earlier preached: for instance, although he said that he distrusted infantry fire and preferred cold steel, he ended his life an admirer of Frederick the Great's system of musketry, field artillery and drill. He argued for the vigorous pursuit of a beaten enemy, advocated the use of skirmishers at a time when they had temporarily gone out of fashion, and was the first to emphasize the importance of morale. He also suggested that all males between the ages of 20 and 30 should be conscripted for a period of five years because it was natural and just that men should participate in the defence of their state.

Maurice, Comte de Saxe

'I am in the position of a traveller who sees himself surrounded by a bunch of rogues, who are planning to murder him and divide the spoils up among themselves.' FREDERICK II, 1756

FREDERICK THE GREAT
1712–86

GILES MACDONOGH

FREDERICK II OF PRUSSIA'S CONTEMPORARIES dubbed him 'Frederick the Great' and the title went unchallenged until 1945. After the war, though, Frederick the Great was confined to the doghouse of history, and it has only been in the past twenty years that pen-portraits of him have been painted uncoloured by the notions of Prussian 'militarism' or Nazism. As a general, Frederick was very much a man of his time. His campaigns were short on strategy and big on politics. Campaigns were seasonal; during the Seven Years War, when the frosts melted and the spring flowers bloomed, Frederick knew it was time to fight. When the days grew short and snow covered the ground, he withdrew to winter quarters and wrote poetry.

(Opposite) **Frederick the Great** exercised an exceptional hold on later Prussian and German imagination for his supposed nationalism and militarism. Yet his interest in the arts and philosophy were at least equal to his interest in war: one of his closest friends was the French philosopher Voltaire. He is portrayed here in his prime by Johann Georg Ziesenis (1716–76).

Frederick was no militarist. He called his uniform a shroud. Wearing uniform was a tradition introduced by his father Frederick William I, who had created a great fighting machine and programmed his son to use it in Prussia's interests. At Frederick's accession as 'King in Prussia' in 1740, he may have appeared more interested in staffing his academy and opera house, but he was also adding to his regiments. The cue was to be provided by the death of the Holy Roman Emperor, Charles VI, in October 1740. He had no sons and in 1713 had made the German vassal states accept the 'Pragmatic Sanction', which allowed his eldest daughter, Maria Theresa, to inherit the Habsburg lands.

Frederick knew that Prussia had a claim to Habsburg Silesia, as Liegnitz, Brieg and Wohlau were meant to revert to Prussia on the death of the last of the Polish Piast princes, which had occurred in 1675. Unfortunately, Frederick William, the 'Great Elector' and Frederick's great-grandfather, had renounced his rights, but Frederick considered that re-asserting them would be acting in the interests of the Protestant majority in Lower Silesia; and it would be a fitting revenge for the way that the emperor had treated his father over the duchies of Jülich and Berg, which Frederick William believed were his by right but which his grandfather had renounced in exchange for Imperial approval of his adopting a royal title in 1701.

Frederick the Great

There was a further incentive: glory. This was what the young Frederick, as much as an intellectual as a warrior, hankered after most. It seems shocking now to risk subjects' lives for glory, but it was no less than he had read in the works of his favourite authors, the French neo-classical dramatists Corneille and Racine.

Reforming the balance of power in central Europe had long preyed on his mind. To his brother-in-law, Charles of Brunswick, he had said that the emperor's death 'will plunge Europe into bloody combat'. It was merely a question of 'putting those plans into action which I have been hatching so long in my head'.

There was also a nagging feeling that the Bavarians or the Saxons might move first. Maria Theresa's husband Francis Stephen was seen by many German princes as a French pawn, and undesirable as Holy Roman Emperor. Frederick could count on a certain amount of support in Protestant Germany, as well as Great Britain.

The First Silesian War

In 1740 Frederick began his occupation of Silesia, and its major towns and cities fell easily into his hands. It was not until 10 April 1741 that he had to prove his mettle. He surprised an Austrian force led by Graf Wilhelm von Neipperg at Mollwitz. Prussian morale broke when Neipperg's troops scattered their right flank and Frederick panicked. Taking advice from the Blenheim veteran Curt Christoph von Schwerin, he fled. It looked as if the Austrians would win, but Schwerin rallied his 'moving walls' – the Prussian infantry – and carried the day. Frederick was cowering in a mill and only heard of his first success the following morning.

It had been the Prussian cavalry that had failed at Mollwitz, and Frederick set about reforming it. He consolidated his power in Silesia while the Austrians, faced with a deep Bavarian incursion into their flank, tried to buy him off. Austria relinquished Lower Silesia and Neisse with the Treaty of Klein Schnellendorf of 9 October 1741, giving Maria Theresa time to deal with the French and Bavarians, whose Prince-Elector Charles Albert was elected Emperor Charles VII in February 1742. The Austrians, however, swiftly invaded Charles's electorate of Bavaria and deposed the new emperor, leaving them free to clamour for Silesia again.

The Battle of Chotusitz took place on 17 May 1742. Modern commentators have labelled it a draw, but politically it was carried by Frederick. It went badly at first, with the Prussian cavalry again failing to make its mark, but the infantry set to work and broke the Austrians, whose losses were marginally higher. At the Peace of Breslau in June, Frederick was confirmed in the possession of all Silesia barring a small pocket around Teschen.

The Second Silesian War

The Second Silesian War of 1744–5 was fought by Prussia to find a land for Frederick's ally, the ousted Emperor Charles VII. Frederick made for Bohemia where he hoped the new kingdom might be situated. He briefly took Prague, then abandoned it, exposing his army to terrible harassment on its retreat towards Silesia, which was already flooded with Hungarian soldiers.

On 20 January 1745 Charles died, leaving Frederick without a *casus belli* and Silesia threatened by its old Habsburg masters. It was not until 4 June that he was able to gain his first great victory, on the boggy ground of Hohenfriedberg. Hohenfriedberg is often compared to Leuthen (1757), Frederick's greatest triumph in the field. Continuing to observe the lessons from Mollwitz and Chotusitz, he had strengthened his cavalry, which was locked in a bitter fight at first until General Zieten found a ford that enabled him to bring up reinforcements and carry the day. It was the first time that Frederick attacked using an 'oblique order', concentrating the bulk of his forces on one flank of the enemy line yet spreading his troops all along it. Having prevailed at the point of attack, his armies could then 'roll up' the enemy from the chosen flank. On this occasion the attack did not go entirely according to plan, but Frederick showed admirable pragmatism on the field of battle. The Austrians and Saxons were routed. Unusually, enemy casualties were three times as great as his.

The Battle of Soor on 30 September was a blow to Frederick's self-esteem. The Prussians were caught in their blankets. The Austrian forces managed to take possession of a vital hill, but Frederick was able to rally his men. Once again it was the cavalry that carried the day, with considerable carnage. Soor counted as a victory for Frederick as the Austrians made their escape at midday, their casualties double the

Prussians'; even so, Frederick was disconsolate: he had lost not just men but his favourite dogs, flutes, snuff-boxes and ciphers.

After Soor, Frederick wondered whether he needed to 'box the Austrians' ears' yet again. The final drubbing was administered at Kesseldorf on 14 December, not by Frederick himself but by his general Leopold of Anhalt-Dessau, known as the *Alte Dessauer*. He made a 'ferocious frontal assault' against superior numbers, inflicting losses on the Austrians and Saxons of between a third and half their army. The peace was signed in Dresden on Christmas Day 1745. Frederick was confirmed as ruler of Silesia and he in turn recognized Francis Stephen as Holy Roman Emperor. The Prussians hailed their king as 'Frederick the Great'.

The Seven Years War: Prague to Kolin

More than a decade passed before Frederick went to war again, but he continued to think about ways of making his army even more effective. In 1748 he privately published his *Principes généraux de la guerre,* in which he made various plans to attack Saxony, combined with some musings on the philosophy of war that prefigured the more famous work by Carl von Clausewitz.

In his *Principes généraux,* Frederick showed that war needed to have an important political objective. Money was a problem for Prussia, and Frederick sought the best army at the lowest price. He reformed the hussars so that they would be a match for the fierce Austrian Pandurs (a force of irregular troops) and created a modern officer corps with promotion based on merit – he was prepared to sack even his brothers if they performed badly. Consequently, his generals were in the main first-rate, unlike some of their earlier Austrian counterparts.

Frederick understood the need for draconian discipline. Punishments were frequently meted out for pillaging or desertion. There were whippings and hangings as well as 'running the gauntlet' – where the miscreant was beaten with rods by other soldiers from his regiment. After the Seven Years War (1756–63) a number of cowardly generals were given short sentences of fortress detention, and one colonel was taken out to be shot, but was pardoned at the post. (It should be borne in mind, however, that the British shot Admiral Byng for losing a battle in 1757.)

Frederick knew Maria Theresa wanted Silesia back. With this in mind, in January 1756 he and his uncle, George II, King of Great Britain and Elector of Hanover, signed the Convention of Westminster, which drove the French, who had begun their colonial war with Britain the year before, back into the Austrian camp. Meanwhile the Austrians and their clever chancellor Wenzel Kaunitz set about raising fears of Prussia in St Petersburg: if they assisted Austria in retrieving Silesia, the Russians might help themselves to East Prussia. The marriage of Frederick's sister Ulrika to King Adolf Frederick of Sweden added to Russian anxiety, and it did not prove difficult to bring them round.

Frederick was now hemmed in. He was aware that he needed to make a pre-emptive strike in order to gain the advantage and to ensure that the fighting take place far from Prussia. In a much-quoted letter of 26 August 1756, Frederick wrote, 'I am innocent of this war. I have done what I could to avoid it. However great may be my love of peace, one may never sacrifice honour and security … now we must think only of the means of carrying out this war which removes the pleasure our enemies derive from disrupting the peace.'

Frederick divided his army into three and sent one part to face the Russians and another to tackle the French. He himself led the largest segment, against the Austrians. He planned to knock them out and then deal with the others. The attack he launched on Saxony on 29 August 1756 has become the prototype for all blitzkrieg. He had explained to the Saxon king that his territory needed to be violated to maintain supply lines to Bohemia. The Austrian coalition had already dangled the Duchy of Magdeburg before the Saxon king, which Frederick used as a justification for his aggression, but there is no denying he coveted Saxony: Frederick wanted to make sense of his otherwise straggling lands, which extended from the Lower Rhine to the Russian border. West Prussia was another fruit he hoped might fall into his lap. Like Lower Silesia, the vast majority of Saxony's population were Lutheran, and he could play that card once again, especially as the king was Catholic.

Frederick's first battle in the new war was fought at Lobositz in Bohemia. He decided on a direct attack on a well-defended position. It was a Pyrrhic victory, but the Prussian armies pursued their enemy to Prague; the Austrian army entered the city and closed the gates behind them. On 6 May 1757 Austria and Prussia met for battle. Frederick was suffering from food poisoning, and spent the day being sick. The Prussians made a number of errors: their cavalry was unsupported by the artillery, and the fearsome 'moving walls' were defeated by the marshy ground. Two of Frederick's best generals met their deaths: Winterfeldt and the 73-year-old Schwerin, who had rallied the scattered Prussians by tearing a flag out of a staff-captain's hand and crying, 'All brave fellows, follow me!' He was promptly hit in the head and chest. His example encouraged the men to charge with a cry of 'Revenge for Father Schwerin!' The tables were turned when the infantry found a gap in the Austrian line and poured twenty-two battalions through it. It was, however, General Hans Joachim von Zieten who won the day, scattering the enemy like 'straw in the wind'.

Despite his huge losses, his victory at Prague won Frederick European renown, but strategically it was not promising: it halted the Prussian advance and converted the king's campaign from an aggressive to a defensive one – from now on Frederick would be trying to prevent his enemies from coming together. Nineteenth-century critics pointed out that he had both failed to destroy his enemy and committed the error of not investing Prague. On 18 June the battle was followed by the bitter experience of his first major defeat, at Kolin. Frederick's decision to face a numerically superior enemy from a poorly chosen downhill position cost him dearly in terms of both bloodshed and reputation. He issued the command to attack too early. After the battle he said that he would have managed had he possessed four more infantry battalions. He had begun to believe too heavily in his winning streak. He would have lost more, had it not been for the amazing feats of the Prussian cavalry.

From Rossbach to Kunersdorf

Frederick was close to despair but he was determined to learn. The nineteenth-century Prussian General Staff officer Alfred von Schlieffen, who used to teach his students at that 'experience is useless unless it is studied', claimed that after Kolin Frederick immediately set about turning the defeat into the blueprint for the victory he would win at Leuthen. To Schlieffen, Leuthen was Frederick's Cannae, a battle of annihilation; this may have been stretching a point.

Frederick's enemies were closing in: the British ducked out of the Convention of Klosterzeven and the French were within an easy march of Berlin. Far worse, the Russians had arrived in East Prussia, and the Hungarian general Hadik had sacked Berlin.

Frederick badly needed a fillip, and he received it at Rossbach in Saxony. On 5 November 1757 a Prussian army of 21,000 faced a French and Imperial force of nearly twice that number. They walked straight into a trap of Frederick's making. The victory was decided in minutes. The cavalry general Friedrich Wilhelm von Seydlitz was the man of the match, nonchalantly tossing away his clay pipe as a signal to the cuirassiers to charge. When the Imperial units fought back, Seydlitz ordered up eighteen fresh squadrons. This occasioned a rout which ended when fleeing troops crashed into a sunken road. Frederick watched the enemy's confusion from the upper window of a house and ordered his artillery to cut up the advancing French regiments. More than 5,000 enemy troops were killed and the same number taken prisoner; Frederick lost 169 dead and 379 wounded. The French would not suffer as grave a defeat until Salamanca, over half a century later. Rossbach was the Agincourt of the German nation.

The cultural significance of Rossbach was immense, but Leuthen, fought in Silesia against heavy odds just a month later, was possibly Frederick's greatest victory, and according to the military historian General Sir David Fraser, 'one of the greatest battles of the century' (see p. 98). It was, though, the high point of the war for Frederick. For the next six years Frederick would be hounded by a numerically superior enemy while he sought to deliver short, sharp slaps to keep them at bay. The sheer doggedness of the Russians made them particularly hard to shake off. At Zorndorf in Brandenburg on 25 August 1758, Frederick only narrowly avoided defeat, and once again much of his success was down to Seydlitz. The

Frederick's commanders report their great victory over the French at Rossbach in 1757. It was a triumph of swift manoeuvring and surprise, as much as of arms. Frederick commented later: 'I won the battle of Rossbach with most of my infantry having their muskets shouldered.'

'The good fellows are leaving, let's let them go.'

AUSTRIAN COMMANDER CHARLES OF LORRAINE, DURING THE BATTLE OF LEUTHEN, 1757

THE BATTLE OF LEUTHEN

O N 3 DECEMBER 1757, Frederick summoned his commanders at Parchwitz in Silesia and issued a declaration: 'We must beat the enemy, or bury ourselves before his guns'. Two days later he gave battle: 39,000 men against the Austrian and Saxon army of 66,000, which was arrayed along a front some 4 miles long. Here he successfully used his favourite tactic of the oblique order, attacking the Austrian left after a feint towards the right which his enemy thought was a retreat, and which caused the Austrian commander Charles of Lorraine to make the disastrous decision of moving his cavalry to the right.

The Prussian manoeuvre, shielded by the cavalry and a line of small hills, only became evident once the well-drilled infantry had already outflanked the Austrians, which obliged the Austrians to turn their front and negated their superiority of numbers. Despite an attempt to reform the Austrian line (which took more than an hour, a result of the extremely extended original deployment), the Prussian infantry with artillery support continued a relentless advance through the village of Leuthen. In the three hours of the battle the Austrians lost 10,000 dead and wounded and a further 12,000 prisoners; Prussian casualties amounted to around a fifth of their army.

The Battle of Leuthen, 5 December 1757. 'Bear in mind, gentlemen, that we shall be fighting for our glory, the preservation of our homes, and for our wives and children': Frederick addresses his generals three days before the battle, as depicted in a lithograph based on a painting by Adolph Menzel.

Map

Legend:
- ▦ Infantry
- ▪ Cavalry

N

Nippern

Guckerwitz

Heidau

Borna

PRUSSIAN ARMY

Frobelwitz

Lissa

Sahra

AUSTRIAN AND SAXON ARMY

Rathen

Radaxdorff

Leuthen

Driesen

Lobetinz

Sagschütz

Gohlau

R. Schweidnitz

0   1 km

0   1 mile

Schriegwitz

Zieten

Frederick the Great

Prussians lost 12,800 men, the Russians a staggering 18,000. Zorndorf was to be the beginning of the backward slide: next came Hochkirch, in October. Once again a Prussian army of 30,000 men was caught napping by a hugely superior Austrian force. Frederick was now outnumbered two to one. He had lost half his officer corps since 1756.

The next blow, in August 1759, was Kunersdorf: the worst defeat of all. A combined force of Russians and Austrians numbering 64,000 men faced Frederick in the Brandenburg Neumark. Frederick had fewer than 50,000. Despite Frederick's personal bravery, his army was routed. He was again saved by the superior idiocy of the enemy: the Russians refused to advance, feeling their losses to be too great.

The rest of the war was an endurance test. Frederick won his battles: Liegnitz, Torgau, Bunzelwitz, Burkersdorf and Freiberg, each one demonstrating the pug-naciousness of the king. To some extent they washed away the stain of Kunersdorf. At the Peace of Hubertusburg of 15 February 1763, the Austrians, Prussians and Saxons agreed to return to the *status quo ante bellum*, and the Seven Years War came to an end.

Old age and assessment

As an old man, Frederick fought one last war, against Joseph of Austria who had become Emperor Joseph II in 1765. Fred-erick was able to pose as the defender of German liberties against the Austrians. Even the Saxons were on his side. There was no pre-emptive strike this time and no battle except a sad little skirmish at Habelschwerdt in January 1779. Most commentators agree that it was an old man's campaign. Frederick died peacefully at the summer palace of Sanssouci at Potsdam on 17 August 1786.

Throughout his career, Frederick craved territory, desiring wealth, power and men for his armies. Despite what Schlieffen thought, he had no wish to fight a Cannae, and never thought of annihilating his enemy. Frederick's tactics were Fabian: he fought to keep the upper hand, to hang on to his gains, to exhaust his enemy. His brother Henry helped by rupturing the lines of communication to starve out the lumbering armies that threatened Prussia's very existence.

He fought fifteen battles, winning twelve victories. Some, such as Hohenfriedberg and Leuthen, have gone down as some of the greatest battles in history. Frederick was no coward, and was always to be found where the fighting was hottest. He was unique as a modern soldier king. Napoleon paid him his greatest tribute when, after Prussia's catastrophic defeats at Auerstedt and Jena in 1806, he visited Frederick's tomb in the Potsdam Garrison Church. 'Gentlemen,' he said. 'Were he still alive, we would not be here.'

After the Battle of Leuthen, Frederick went to nearby Lissa Castle for the night; finding it full of defeated Austrian officers, he said, '*Bonsoir messieurs*. Is there room here for me?' This painting of the episode is by Adolph Menzel.

Frederick the Great

'By God, at this moment do I stand astonished by my own moderation.' ROBERT CLIVE DURING A PARLIAMENTARY CROSS-EXAMINATION, 1773

ROBERT CLIVE

ROBERT HARVEY

1725-74

ROBERT CLIVE – the clerk with the East India Company with no training as a soldier – was hailed as a 'heaven-born general' by William Pitt the Elder. As might be expected, his approach to warfare was unorthodox, based on sudden rapid marches and bold strikes where least expected, often taking on vastly superior odds; the formal eighteenth-century disciplines of lines of battle and standard manoeuvres were largely alien to him. The result was a succession of dazzling victories in southern India and Bengal, victories that resulted in the creation of British India. But Clive was much more than just a fighter. A strategic thinker, he was also a brilliant and decisive administrator and the ruler of millions of people, as well as a political intriguer, a lover of ostentation, an occasionally brutal governor, and, to his detractors, an ambitious and successful self-seeker.

(Opposite) **Robert Clive**, c. 1764, the man responsible for establishing British imperial rule in India, in a portrait by Thomas Gainsborough (1727–88).

Clive was born into a respectable gentry family on 29 September 1725 at Styche, near Moreton Saye in Shropshire. Something of a young tearaway, with few prospects in Britain, at the age of 17 he was sent off to make his fortune with the East India Company. Working as a clerk in the Company's headquarters in the prosperous British settlement of Madras, he was said to be so homesick and bored that he attempted to commit suicide, but his pistol twice failed to go off. When the French East India Company, under the formidable governor of Pondicherry, Joseph-François Dupleix, suddenly attacked and occupied Madras in 1746, the 21-year-old Clive and three companions escaped disguised as Indians, and made their way to Fort St David, 50 miles to the south.

Clive took part in defending the fort against French attack, and also participated in a failed attack on the French stronghold of Pondicherry; but in 1748 Madras was restored to the British under the Treaty of Aix-la-Chapelle. His first real command came when he was put in charge by a tough professional soldier, Major Stringer Lawrence, of thirty British troops and 700 Indians in an assault on Fort Devikottai; the fearlessness of his attack caused the hostile local Indian ruler to abandon the fort.

Robert Clive

The French meanwhile sought to gain control of most of southern India, and to this end, in 1751 some 800 French and 20,000 Indians besieged 60 English and 2,000 Indian troops inside the colourful citadel of Mohammed Ali, the Indian ruler of Trichinopoly. Clive was sent as an aide to an incompetent Swiss mercenary, Captain Rudolf de Guingens, who was in command of a relief force dispatched to Trichinopoly. Contemptuous of de Guingens and impatient for action, Clive persuaded his superiors in Madras to allow him to seize the fortress at Arcot, the stronghold of France's Indian allies, while most of their army was at Trichinopoly.

The siege of Arcot

Clive's modest force, which dwindled to 120 British troops and 2,000 Indians, marched through monsoon thunderstorms to seize the citadel at Arcot, which was abandoned on his approach. With his small force occupying the sprawling fortress, Clive held out against a besieging Indian army of some 15,000 men – many of them fervent Shi'ite Muslims – for seventy-five days.

On 13 November 1751 Clive's exhausted, parched and half-starved men, only two-thirds of them fighting fit, were subjected to a full-scale attack by their besiegers. Just before dawn a large number of men carrying ladders were seen running towards the walls. Behind them elephants with huge protective iron plates on their foreheads charged forward to batter down the gates. Further behind, as far as the eye could see, a torrent of enemy soldiers with muskets and spears surged towards the fort.

Clive, entirely cool in a crisis and apparently fearless, promptly gave orders for his men to shoot at the unprotected flanks of the elephants. The animals, maddened by the pain, reared up and then turned and stampeded into the soldiers following them. The gates remained secure. However, at the same time – spurred on 'with a mad kind of intrepidity' by their religious frenzy – the enemy was mounting attacks in the two major breaches caused by the guns brought up by the French to support the attackers.

Clive had organized his tiny force to fire their muskets and then hand them back to loaders who would promptly pass on another gun, thus making best use of both his active and inactive soldiers. This concentrated fire at last caused the attackers to waver. Meanwhile the defenders hurled grenades from the ramparts at the second line of enemy troops.

Two hours later a relentless barrage of musket and cannon-fire began. This was presumably a softening-up intended to deter his men from manning the ramparts. Clive embarked on his rounds once more, cheering up his men and cajoling them, checking on the defences. After more than four hours the relentless bombardment – which had set all of them on edge – ceased, and a small party arrived under a white flag requesting permission to carry off the dead, who were rapidly putrefying under the intense midday sun. The request was granted.

Two hours later the pounding began again. The exhausted garrison rested as best it could. The relentless bombardment continued for a full twelve hours; Clive imagined the enemy were seeking to exhaust the garrison mentally in preparation for the next assault. When the sun rose a second time there was no sign of the enemy, although their guns and baggage were strewn across the ground before the fort. They had left the city, and the bombardment had been a cover to allow them to retire in good order, in case the formidable enemy within the fort sallied out to attack them.

Two more hard-fought battles ensued, a set-piece encounter at Arni and an enemy ambush at Kaveripak, which Clive skilfully but narrowly won, before he returned to Trichinopoly, which was still under siege. Along with Lawrence, he carried the battle to the French, who were encamped on a narrow tongue of land behind a pagoda complex at Srirangam to the north, protected by the Cauvery and Coleroon rivers. Clive relentlessly bombarded the French and Indian forces while Lawrence closed the trap from the landward side, forcing a surrender. Clive's whirlwind of activity in his first tour of India ended with the decisive capture of two French forts, Covelong and Chingleput, before he returned in glory to Madras, where he married the redoubtable Margaret

The Fort at Trichinopoly, in what is now the Indian state of Tamil Nadu. It was in order to force a Franco-Indian force to raise their siege of Trichinopoly that Clive seized the fortress of Arcot in the late summer of 1751.

Maskelyne. Back in England, he enjoyed a hero's welcome. At the age of just 27, Clive was hailed as the man who had saved Britain's southern settlements in India.

In London Clive quickly squandered his new wealth, much of it on an expensive but unsuccessful attempt to enter the House of Commons, and in 1755 he was compelled to return to India to seek his fortune once again. On his journey back he took part in the successful storming of the pirate stronghold at Gheria, near Bombay, before taking up his new post as commander of Fort St David on 22 June 1756 – coincidentally just two days after the Black Hole of Calcutta, the much-exaggerated atrocity that followed the seizure of Fort William, the main British settlement in Bengal, which the governor, Roger Drake, had shamefully abandoned to its fate.

The invasion of Bengal

As soon as the news from Calcutta reached Madras, the British started to organize an expedition to regain the settlement, with Clive as one of three commanders. On 16 October one of the mightiest expeditionary forces ever assembled in the eighteenth century set sail. After a bombardment, the looted and largely destroyed Fort William was retaken. In revenge for the attack on Calcutta, Clive marched upriver and took the town of Hugli, which was also abandoned by the Bengalis. But this provoked the Nawab of Bengal, Siraj-ud-Daula, to march south back to Calcutta. Clive now faced his most formidable foe.

In February 1757 Clive bravely decided, as was his custom, on a pre-emptive attack on the nawab's camp at Dum Dum, outside Calcutta. But for once things went wrong: when a fog lifted he was left exposed to a far superior enemy force and he had to cut his way hurriedly through the Bengali camp to escape, inflicting some 1,500 casualties in the fighting. Siraj-ud-Daula nevertheless retreated further up the Hugli

Fort William, the site of the Black Hole of Calcutta, by an unknown artist. In 1756 over a hundred British soldiers were allegedly confined by the Nawab of Bengal in a small cell measuring 18 feet by 15 feet. According to their commander, less than a quarter of them survived, but modern historians have suggested that this figure is a significant exaggeration. Clive participated in the recapture of Fort William, which had been looted and largely destroyed, and later defeated the Nawab at Plassey.

Robert Clive

THE BATTLE OF PLASSEY

THE BATTLE OF PLASSEY was one of the greatest gambles in British history, a decisive turning point in which the very fate of British India was held in the balance. Clive, aged only 32 and with an army of only 3,000 men, had marched up the Hugli river to confront Siraj-ud-Daula. At this point, with the waters swollen by monsoon rains and still rising, he ordered his men to cross a tributary, aware that he was cutting off their line of retreat. On the wrong side of the river, they faced massacre if they lost. Clive took up position at the nawab's beautiful hunting lodge at Plassey; to the south there was an immense mango grove, to the west the river.

His position, although a good defensive one, was hardly a fort. He had only 3,000 men. Against him was an army of at least 35,000–50,000 disciplined infantry and 15,000 Pathans, fine fighters and riders from the northwest border. In addition, the nawab had more than fifty cannon, maintained and fired by fifty Frenchmen.

Clive ordered his men well beyond the shelter of the grove, to a position directly in front of the enemy line. He placed three of his small guns on either side, and hundreds of his soldiers in between. Sepoys guarded his flanks. A little further back he placed his two remaining 6-pound guns and howitzers protected by brick kilns. At 8 a.m. the first cannonade from the French guns began, and the British replied. The British fire ripped through Mir Madan's men; but the French had killed ten British soldiers and twenty Indians within half an hour. The two sides continued exchanging relentless fire for three hours. The monsoon clouds, which had been building up for hours, then broke; half an hour of torrential rain soaked every man to the skin. The British had hastily pulled tarpaulins over the ammunition as soon as the downpour started; the Bengali ammunition was drenched. British guns continued to fire throughout, while the enemy ones fell silent.

Siraj-ud-Daula was beginning to panic: Mir Jafar and the other senior commanders had so far taken no part in the fighting, although their flanking move had continued and they were now in a position to attack from the side, and very nearly from the back, cutting Clive off. The nawab sent repeatedly for Mir Jafar, who advised him to call off the attack.

Clive ordered his soldiers to advance to take the forward Bengali positions. Simultaneously, one of the enemy ammunition dumps blew up. Eyre Coote captured the little hill in front of Plassey House, while the French fled the redoubt from which their guns had kept the British pinned down for so long.

Siraj-ud-Daula, hearing that the British were attacking, jumped aboard a camel and fled back with 2,000 horsemen towards his capital at Murshidabad. His huge army now also fled, their panic becoming a rout. Around 500 of the enemy had been killed, compared to just 20 dead and 50 wounded on the British side.

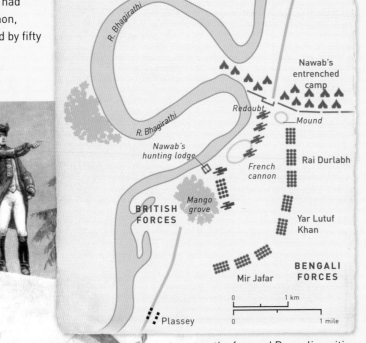

Map labels: N; R. Bhagirathi; Muncarra; Nawab's entrenched camp; Redoubt; Mound; Nawab's hunting lodge; French cannon; Rai Durlabh; BRITISH FORCES; Mango grove; Yar Lutuf Khan; Mir Jafar; BENGALI FORCES; Plassey; 0 1 km; 0 1 mile

river after this display of British determination, and forged an alliance with the nearby French settlement at Chandernagore. Clive promptly replied by bombarding and taking the French enclave.

Clive now set his sights on total victory over the nawab, and embarked on a policy of duplicity for which he was much criticized later, notably by Lord Macaulay. Yet it is hard to see what else he could have done, in view of the overwhelming force arrayed against him. A British merchant, William Watts, was sent to seek a secret agreement with Siraj-ud-Daula's chief general, Mir Jafar, to betray his master and attach his forces to the British side in any battle. This also involved double-crossing an untrustworthy go-between, the merchant Omichand, with a false treaty promising him huge rewards for his help. But by the time Watts secretly left the Bengali capital of Murshidabad, there was no certainty that Mir Jafar would come to the aid of the British.

In this climate of acute uncertainty, Clive marched upriver and took the enormous gamble of confronting the nawab's army at Plassey, a confrontation which he narrowly won, largely because Mir Jafar's forces stood aside from the battles (see p. 104). The consequences both for the British in India and Clive personally were momentous. The East India Company and Britain had acquired, at a stroke, effective control of the largest and wealthiest part of the subcontinent. Building on their superiority in the south, they now held nearly a third of its land area: only the central belt (divided between the Marathas and the French), the north (controlled by the Nawab of Oudh), and the wild northwest eluded them. Clive had effectively doubled the British area of occupation, and the Company was now indisputably the major power in India. The foundations for British rule had been laid, a rule that was to endure for two centuries.

Clive of India

Clive himself was in a position of power unparalleled by any Briton in history, before or since. He had a kingdom of 40 million people at his feet, more than six times the number of subjects of the British monarch. There was no effective control over his personal rule from the civilian authorities in Madras or Calcutta.

Clive entered in triumph into Murshidabad. After lengthy haggling, it was agreed that the nawab should pay half of what he owed the British immediately, two-thirds in bullion and one-third in jewels, plate and gold, and the rest in equal instalments over the next three years. Clive visited the treasury himself to satisfy his curiosity. From this was to derive his most famous remark before an inquiry of the House of Commons in 1773: 'When I recollect entering the nawab's treasury at Murshidabad, with heaps of gold and silver to the right and left, and these crowned with jewels, by God, at this moment do I stand astonished at my own moderation.'

Mir Jafar had Siraj-ud-Daula killed and became the new nawab, heavily dependent on the British. Clive, the real power in the land, consolidated the British hold on India, sending armies under Francis Forde and Stringer Lawrence to fend off a determined French attempt to take the Carnatic. Sir Eyre Coote routed the French at the Battle of Wandewash in 1760, and a year later took the French settlement at Pondicherry and razed it to the ground.

A further revolt threatened in northern India under the leadership of the Shahzada, the heir to the Mughal emperor. Clive himself marched forward and defeated the enemy, also indulging in uncharacteristic cruelty in destroying 300 villages

(Opposite) **Robert Clive, on the roof of Siraj-ud-Daula's hunting lodge,** examines the enemy lines at Plassey, 23 June 1757.

Robert Clive

in Pulwansing. After the triumph he extracted from Mir Jafar an annual payment of £27,000 – a staggering sum for those days – to be paid from the annual rent the East India Company was supposed to pay the nawab for the lands around Calcutta. Clive's many enemies in England complained of his becoming the recipient of the Company's rents. In the meantime, Mir Jafar – who had already shown his treachery once – was conspiring against the British with the Dutch at their settlement of Kasimbasar. The Dutch attacked the British downstream from Calcutta, but in a 'short, bloody and decisive action' were routed on the Plains of Badaw, with the Dutch losing 320 men for ten British dead.

In February 1760 the absolute ruler of much of India set sail for England, where he attempted to become a significant force in British politics. But this brilliant commander in the field and outwitter of the Indians proved no match for politicians such as the scheming prime minister, the Duke of Newcastle, and he also incurred the enmity of the chairman of the East India Company, Laurence Sulivan, and others jealous of his success. Meanwhile, conditions in India deteriorated steadily, with widespread allegations of corruption on the part of Company officials and their agents and the formation of military alliances among Indian princes against the British.

Clive's third tour

In June 1764 the seemingly indispensable Clive returned to India to restore order. On arrival he set out in a *budgerow*, a luxury houseboat, to Murshidabad, where he formally reduced the new nawab's status to that of puppet monarch. He then moved on to Allahabad, seat of the Mughal emperor and his old but prestigious foe, the Shahzada. Here, in August 1765, Clive forced Emperor Shah Alam II to award him the *diwani*, the right for the British to collect taxes in Bengal, Bihar and Orissa, thus in effect formally recognizing the British right to rule a huge swathe of India.

'Now I am satisfied you are British soldiers and not, as I was erroneously informed, assassins.'

CLIVE TO THE REBEL BRITISH OFFICERS AT MONGHYR

Clive now plunged into a whirlwind of administrative reform to establish the foundations of colonial government in India, including an anti-corruption drive – an ironic rebuttal of accusations of his own past profiteering. He also aimed to provide secure boundaries for British India, set up a Society of Trade to regulate commerce, proposed establishing a class of salaried civil servants – an idea only adopted under his successor, Warren Hastings – announced a crackdown on extortion, and introduced a new postal system and a land survey of Bengal.

Clive faced down intense local opposition, then a strike by company civil servants, and finally, most dangerously, a full-scale mutiny by his own British officers. Hastening up to the city of Monghyr, the centre of the mutiny, Clive walked into the garrison with only a single escort and ordered the rebels to lay down their weapons. When they did so he said, 'Now I am satisfied you are British soldiers and not, as I was erroneously informed, assassins.' The following year he left India for the last time at the still remarkably young age of 42.

Last years

Back in England, Clive used his own vast wealth to buy and improve a succession of large estates. But his enemies were gathering again, as news came that the warrior Hyder

Ali had launched a furious rebellion against the British in India, and that millions had perished in the 1769–70 Bengal famine, which was unfairly blamed on British maladministration. Clive defended himself manfully against these attacks, first in a House of Commons committee, then, in 1774, against a vote of censure on the floor, which he carried by 155 votes to 95. Clive could now be considered for the post of commander of British forces in the seemingly inevitable war with the American colonies.

In November the same year, however, Clive was found in the lavatory of his London home in Berkeley Square with his throat cut. That same night his body was hurried away for burial at the tiny church of Moreton Saye, his family's home in Shropshire. The secrecy surrounding his burial, as well as the fact that he was buried in an unmarked grave, suggested that Clive, often prone to depression and illness, had committed suicide. It was a huge shock, given that this was a man who had survived so many battles – it was as though Field Marshal Montgomery, for example, had taken his own life after the Second World War.

It also seems possible that he was murdered, or more likely sought in an emergency to cut his own throat to remove an obstruction, which was not uncommon in those days – a theory believed by at least one prominent surgeon today. The nation that had so often been grudging about his achievements belatedly granted him real recognition by awarding his eldest son, Ned, the earldom of Powys on the death of the 2nd Earl, whose daughter, Lady Henrietta Herbert, he had married. So perished, in tragic circumstances, one of the greatest British commanders of all time, a man whose qualities included decisiveness, speed, manic energy and a willingness to gamble against huge odds. In Clive there also died the only non-royal Englishman who can properly be described as having founded and run an empire.

In 1765 Clive pressured the Mughal emperor into granting the East India Company the responsibility of running the civil administration of a large part of India. Here, in Benjamin West's painting commissioned by the Company, Clive is seen receiving the right to the land revenues of Bengal, Bihar and Orissa.

> 'In war something must be allowed to chance and fortune, since it is in its nature hazardous.' JAMES WOLFE

JAMES WOLFE

STEPHEN BRUMWELL

1727–59

GENERAL JAMES WOLFE'S NAME will always be linked with one momentous event: the victory on the Plains of Abraham before Quebec in 1759 that cost him his life – and decided the fate of North America. Remarkably, Wolfe was just 32 years old when he was killed commanding that crucial campaign. Such precocious responsibility testified to the outstanding training and leadership skills that Wolfe had acquired during seventeen years as a British army officer.

The reputation of James Wolfe has undergone unusually dramatic fluctuations. In the wake of his death he was upheld as an iconic British hero, and this image held sway until the middle of the last century. As the man who won Canada for Britain, Wolfe was intimately associated with the British Empire, but when that institution crumbled after the Second World War, he too fell from grace. Since the bicentenary of Wolfe's death in 1959, both his character and military abilities have undergone assaults from debunking writers. Yet Wolfe was neither the saintly military genius lauded by his devotees, nor the vain, mediocre general vilified by his critics. Without doubt, however, James Wolfe was an unusually dedicated and determined professional soldier, a commander capable of inspiring his men to overcome the most daunting challenges.

Born for a soldier

For James Wolfe, who was born on 2 January 1727 at Westerham, Kent, wearing the red coat of the British soldier was a family tradition dating back to the days of Cromwell's New Model Army. James's father, grandfather and great-grandfather were all army officers, and he was destined to follow their example.

After Britain declared war on Spain in 1739 in what became known as the War of Jenkins' Ear, Wolfe's father, Edward, became colonel of a new regiment of marines. The following year, Wolfe's marines joined an expedition bound for the West Indies, and 13-year-old James accompanied his father as a 'volunteer', or officer cadet. But as the transport ships waited off the Isle of Wight, he sickened and was sent ashore. This was a lucky deliverance: when it reached the Caribbean the expedition met catastrophe. Wracked by inter-service rivalry and ravaged by tropical diseases, it achieved nothing.

James Wolfe

Originally commissioned in his father's marines, in March 1742 Wolfe transferred to a line infantry regiment, the 12th Foot, with the equivalent rank of ensign. The start of Wolfe's army career coincided with the escalation of the War of the Austrian Succession. Soon after, his battalion sailed to Flanders, and from there marched into Germany. On 27 June 1743, when a British–Austrian army defeated the French at Dettingen near Frankfurt, Wolfe underwent his baptism of fire. It was a bloody encounter, with Wolfe's regiment in the thick of the fighting, but the 16-year-old ensign behaved with distinction. By now Wolfe was already serving as regimental adjutant. This willingness to master the intricacies of his profession, allied to his father's cash and influence in army circles, swiftly brought promotion to lieutenant in the 12th Foot, and then captain in a senior regiment, the 4th, or 'King's Own'.

In 1745, with the outbreak of the Jacobite rebellion, Wolfe's regiment was recalled from Flanders. During the scrappy fight at Falkirk on 16 January 1746, when other units fled in blind panic, it stood steady against Bonnie Prince Charlie's Highlanders. Three months later, Wolfe served at Culloden. According to a famous anecdote, as the victorious British government forces ruthlessly scoured the battlefield, he reputedly spurned the order of William Augustus, Duke of Cumberland, to pistol a wounded Highlander.

With the Jacobite rebellion crushed, Wolfe was soon back fighting the French across the Channel. As a major of brigade, he was wounded at the Battle of Laufeldt outside Maastricht, on 2 July 1747. It was a British defeat, but the carnage left the victors eager for peace, which was brokered the following year.

James Wolfe in his early twenties, painted by Joseph Highmore. At this time Wolfe was stationed in Scotland as major of Lord George Sackville's 20th Foot.

The professional soldier

By 1748, James Wolfe had already served five arduous campaigns and survived four bloody pitched battles. It was a punishing apprenticeship: as he later confessed, those hard years 'stripped the bloom' from his youth. However, Wolfe's conscientiousness had brought steady promotion, and attracted powerful patrons. They included both Cumberland and the experienced soldier who ultimately succeeded him as commander-in-chief, Sir John Ligonier. Peace did nothing to halt Wolfe's rise: in 1749, aged just 22, he was appointed major to the 20th Foot in Scotland. A year later, he became its lieutenant colonel.

Wolfe thrived on action, and the ensuing eight years of peacetime service in Britain were characterized by frustration, boredom, thwarted romance, soul-searching and bouts of illness: from 1751 he was tormented by the 'gravel' – an agonizing bladder complaint that shortened his temper. Increasingly, Wolfe channeled his energies into professional perfectionism, transforming his regiment into one of the army's most efficient units. A tough disciplinarian, Wolfe balanced this stance with a genuine concern for his subordinates, officers and ordinary soldiers alike. Such paternalism earned him an enduring reputation as 'the officer's friend and soldier's father'.

> '[Wolfe had] activity, resolution and perseverance, qualities absolutely necessary for executing great plans of operations.'
>
> CHARLES MANNERS, MARQUESS OF GRANBY

Wolfe was an avid reader of military history, and the titles he recommended to a younger officer in 1756 are revealing: they embraced Thucydides and Xenophon, an account of the fifteenth-century Hussite leader Jan Zizka, and a 1754 essay on the art of war by the French officer Turpin de Crissé. Keen to keep abreast of the latest tactical thinking, Wolfe was among those officers who pioneered the adoption of the simplified firing drill used by the Prussians, even though this went against official British regulations. Most significantly, the fiercely patriotic Wolfe sought to inculcate an aggressive fighting spirit into his men, firmly grounded upon confidence in their own proficiency as soldiers.

The 1748 Peace of Aix-la-Chapelle was never more than an interval in the Anglo-French duel for global supremacy. Fighting had already flared in North America when hostilities officially resumed in 1756. In the opening rounds of what became known as the Seven Years War, Britain suffered jarring setbacks across the globe. In September 1757, it retaliated by raiding the French coast. A projected attack on the port of Rochefort in the Bay of Biscay resulted in humiliating withdrawal, but Wolfe, who served as the expedition's quartermaster general, was one of the few officers to urge an attack, and emerged from the débâcle with an enhanced reputation.

That autumn, the war ministry dominated by William Pitt, advised by the commander-in-chief Ligonier, sought fresh young officers capable of stemming the dismal tide of defeat: James Wolfe was among those named to serve in North America.

A transatlantic hero

With the temporary rank of brigadier general, in February 1758 Wolfe joined Major-General Jeffery Amherst's strike against the fortified port of Louisbourg, on Cape Breton. There, on 8 June, he commanded the hazardous amphibious assault that secured a vital toehold on the island. Conducted from open rowing boats in the teeth of heavy fire and pounding surf, this was a remarkable and unprecedented feat. During the siege that followed, Brigadier Wolfe was given a roving, independent command. He played an important role in forwarding the operations leading to the surrender of the fortress on 26 July 1758.

Louisbourg's conquest marked a turning point in a war hitherto dominated by depressing bulletins of defeat. Wolfe's courage and energy impressed his fellow officers, whose letters appeared in newspapers and made him a popular hero for Britons on both sides of the Atlantic. James Wolfe scarcely looked the part. Although 6 feet tall, he was scrawny, with narrow shoulders; red-haired and blue-eyed, his pale freckled features were dominated by a thin upturned nose. Yet Wolfe's unmilitary appearance was irrelevant to his men: they respected him as a fair and vigorous commander, ready to lead from the front.

In late August 1758, Amherst sent Wolfe north to the Bay of Gaspé, with orders to destroy fishing settlements that were vital to French Canada's economy. He fulfilled the task reluctantly, albeit efficiently, before sailing back to Britain with the fleet. Within weeks, he had been interviewed by Pitt and Ligonier. Wolfe was keen to fight again, preferably in Germany, although he was not averse to serving against the French in Canada. By December, Wolfe had been selected to command the most important campaign of the coming season, against Quebec. This was more than he had bargained for, but he felt duty bound to accept nonetheless. Still only a colonel in the army, Wolfe was given the rank of major-general for the expedition.

Detailed instructions made it clear that Wolfe's campaign and the other major offensive against Canada – which was to proceed via the Champlain valley under Amherst, Britain's commander-in-chief in North America – were to complement each other by dividing its defenders. Wolfe was promised an army of 12,000 men, and the support of three brigadiers: Robert Monckton, George Townshend and James Murray. All were older than Wolfe. And unlike their commanding officer, who came from a 'middling', if respectable, background, all were aristocrats. Both factors may have contributed to tensions that emerged during the campaign for Quebec.

The siege of Louisbourg in 1758, seen from the Lighthouse Battery established by Brigadier Wolfe. The French fleet is shown bottled up in the harbour, with the British fleet at anchor in the bay beyond the fortress.

The Quebec command

In February 1759, Wolfe sailed from Spithead with Vice Admiral Charles Saunders. He took with him a miniature of his fiancée, Katherine Lowther, plus another keepsake – a copy of Thomas Gray's *Elegy Written in a Country Churchyard*. During the tedious Atlantic crossing Wolfe annotated the book, underscoring the last line of one verse: 'The paths of glory lead but to the grave.'

Icy weather delayed the expedition's concentration at the designated departure point, Louisbourg, and it was early June – a month behind schedule – before it sailed for Quebec. The skill of Saunders' sailors made short work of the St Lawrence's navigational hazards, and by 27 June the task force was anchored off the Isle of Orléans, within 4 miles of Quebec.

Louis-Joseph, Marquis de Montcalm (1712–59), commander of French forces in Canada from 1756.

Wolfe had hoped to land on the low northern shore below Quebec then fight his way across the St Charles river to attack the city on its weak western side. This plan proved untenable: the whole Beauport shoreline from Quebec down to the Montmorency falls was heavily fortified. In addition, these defences sheltered a large army – no less than 14,000 men – under an experienced and capable officer, the 47-year-old Louis-Joseph, Marquis de Montcalm. Wolfe's own army was significantly smaller than promised, barely 9,000 strong. In a total reversal of military convention, Wolfe was heavily outnumbered by the force he was besieging. Unlike Montcalm's troops, however, Wolfe's were all veteran regular soldiers. If they could be brought face-to-face with the enemy, he was confident that their discipline and courage would prevail.

But how was Wolfe to achieve his objective? With barely three months before the onset of autumn there was no time to lose. In coming weeks, like a wrestler seeking to grapple a wily opponent, Wolfe tried a variety of moves. All were shrugged off. In early July, an attempt to land at St Michel, on the north shore above Quebec, was abandoned because naval support was inadequate. Indeed, while a powerful fleet had transported Wolfe's redcoats to Quebec, its subsequent usefulness was proscribed by broad shoals, a fierce ebb tide and prevailing westerly winds that left few chances to push into the upper river. A brief change in the wind allowed a handful of vessels to pass Quebec on 18–19 July, but they were not enough to change the strategic balance.

When a major British attack was finally launched on 31 July, on the Beauport lines below Quebec, it was decisively rebuffed. Anticipated support from Amherst's army failed to materialize, and by early August, the frustrated Wolfe had resorted to ravaging the countryside, in hopes of luring Montcalm from behind his trenches. But the marquis refused to budge.

Since arriving before Quebec, Wolfe had suffered poor health, with his gravel exacerbated by dysentery. But in late August a severe fever left him bedridden. On 27 August, while 'indisposed', he invited his increasingly truculent brigadiers to 'consult' together upon 'the best method of attacking the enemy'. Exploiting a sudden change in the wind that allowed more British ships to move upriver on the night of

27/28 August, they proposed transferring operations above Quebec. Their recommended landing zone stretched for some 12 miles beyond Cap Rouge bay, itself about 8 miles from the city.

Wolfe accepted his brigadiers' advice, although with little enthusiasm. On 5 September the British began moving upriver, and most of the army embarked aboard the fleet, now strong enough to mount a full-scale landing. Wolfe and his brigadiers approved an attack for the morning of 9 September, at an unspecified location 'a little below Pointe-aux-Trembles', but this was cancelled due to heavy rain. The same day, Wolfe made a lone reconnaissance downriver, then rejected the brigadiers' plan in favour of his own objective – the cliff-backed Anse au Foulon, a cove less than 2 miles from Quebec. The attack was scheduled to go in at about 4 a.m. on 13 September.

By landing so close to Quebec, Wolfe's critics argue, he added an unnecessary element of risk. But his plan had important advantages: it allowed him to strike between the enemy's two main forces, under Colonel Bougainville at Cap Rouge, and Montcalm at Beauport, and to concentrate all his available troops, including two battalions left downriver. Suggestions that Wolfe never expected his scheme to succeed, even that it was a face-saving 'suicide mission', do not withstand scrutiny. And although certainly risky, Wolfe's strategy was not reckless, but based on solid intelligence and meticulous planning. Above all, it was calculated to deliver what Wolfe had sought all summer – a stand-up fight with Montcalm's army. It achieved nothing less (see p. 114).

The Plains of Abraham

Montcalm had spent an anxious night watching the shore below Quebec. Rumours that British troops had landed at the Anse au Foulon reached him at about 6 a.m. Bougainville at Cap Rouge only heard the news at 9 a.m. An hour later, long before Bougainville could intervene, Montcalm attacked Wolfe at the head of 4,500 men.

The French advanced bravely enough but Wolfe's men, with exemplary discipline, held their fire until they were just 40 yards away. Their relentless volleys broke the assault within minutes. Fixing bayonets, the redcoats advanced to clinch their victory. Wolfe had shrugged off two flesh wounds early in the fight, but as he led forward his grenadiers, two more bullets slammed into his chest. Wolfe swiftly bled to death, living just long enough to learn that his men had beaten the enemy.

The dramatic scaling of the Heights of Abraham above Quebec, in the early hours of 13 September 1759. The advance guard was led by Colonel William Howe, who later commanded the British army in the early campaigns of the American War of Independence.

THE AMPHIBIOUS ASSAULT ON QUEBEC

WOLFE'S ASSAULT ON THE COVE OF ANSE AU FOULON involved a phased concentration of troops: the first wave, consisting of 1,700 men, was to be spearheaded by 400 crack light infantry, commanded by Colonel William Howe. They would be followed by the second division, another 1,900 infantry plus artillery and stores. Once these troops had disembarked, the empty boats were to row directly across the St Lawrence, where two more battalions would be waiting. Success would hinge upon clockwork timing, the professionalism of British soldiers and sailors alike – and a measure of luck. All three factors played a part in the coming operation.

Wolfe's troops began boarding their landing craft at about 9 p.m. on 12 September. Tense hours of waiting followed. Meanwhile, the British batteries at Pointe aux Pères bombarded Quebec. Crucially, around midnight, the boats of Saunders' warships below Quebec assembled off the Beauport shore, as if preparing for an assault there. This feint succeeded in fixing Montcalm's attention away from Wolfe's objective. Finally, at about 2 a.m. on 13 September, as the tide began to run swiftly past the anchorage, the signal to cast off was given.

Following the north shore in a long silent string, the boats of the first wave reached within a mile of their target without incident. Off Sillery they encountered a British sloop, HMS *Hunter*. Her crew gave timely intelligence, communi-cated just hours before by two French deserters: Quebec expected a provision convoy from Montreal that very night. When Wolfe's lead boats were soon after challenged by sentries on the shore, a quick-thinking Scottish officer, Captain Simon Fraser, fooled them by explaining that they were the convoy. Here, luck came to Wolfe's help: although the convoy had been cancelled, no news of this reached Quebec; and as no password had been agreed, Fraser's '*Vive le roi*' was sufficient.

Almost exactly on schedule, at just after 4 a.m., Wolfe's leading boats landed at the Anse au Foulon. They overshot slightly, beaching to the right of the path running up from the cove. Undaunted, Howe and his light infantry scaled the shale cliff that loomed directly in front of them. Gaining the summit, they dispersed the picket guarding the path. With the way cleared, the redcoat battalions swiftly disembarked, scrambling up the path and cliff. The ships of the second division arrived on cue; once they too had landed, the third wave of troops was ferried over from the south shore.

By about 8 a.m. a force of 4,500 redcoats, complete with artillery, had gained the heights and stood arrayed on the Plains of Abraham, within a mile of Quebec. Remarkably, all had gone precisely as Wolfe intended. It was a classic combined operation, a triumph of organization, discipline, improvisation – and leadership.

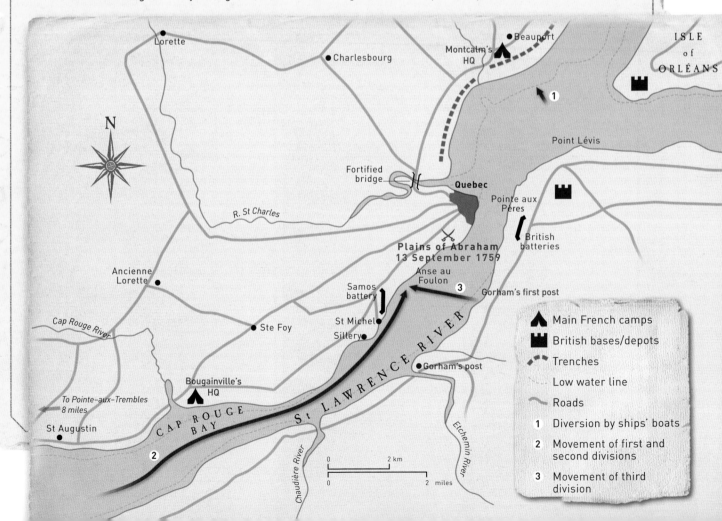

Plains of Abraham 13 September 1759

Legend:
- Main French camps
- British bases/depots
- Trenches
- Low water line
- Roads
- **1** Diversion by ships' boats
- **2** Movement of first and second divisions
- **3** Movement of third division

The clash was short but bloody: the British lost about 660, the French an estimated 1,500, with Montcalm and many of his senior officers slain. Although much of Montcalm's army escaped, the psychological blow was decisive: Quebec surrendered on 18 October 1759.

Apotheosis

Wolfe's final dispatch to Pitt, written on 2 September 1759 and received in London on 14 October, gave little cause to think that Quebec would fall that year. When, just two days later, tidings of victory arrived, they sparked an explosion of rejoicing, given added poignancy by news of Wolfe's death. For Britons still facing the prospect of French invasion, Wolfe epitomized a new mood of patriotic defiance, and a revival of national pride. His prominence in the *annus mirabilis* of 1759, which saw British victories on three continents, was only reinforced by the exploits of his old regiment, the 20th Foot, that August at the Battle of Minden in Germany.

The dramatic events at Quebec inspired outpourings of verse, mostly turgid, but it was the painters who really exploited them. Several had already tackled the theme of Wolfe's death before the young American Benjamin West created a sensation in 1771 with his epic version of the scene. Engraved in 1776, it became one of the era's most popular images, a largely fanciful depiction of martyrdom for king and country that fascinated the young Horatio Nelson.

Wolfe's conduct at Quebec will always generate debate among military historians. A single campaign, however important, is perhaps insufficient grounds upon which to decide whether or not a general merits the mantle of 'great commander'. Yet without Wolfe's determination and leadership, the siege of Quebec would undoubtedly have ended very differently. While James Wolfe's merits as a strategist remain open to question, his status as a fighting soldier and inspirational leader is beyond dispute.

The Death of General Wolfe, by the Anglo-American artist Benjamin West. Wolfe's demise at Quebec consolidated his heroic reputation, and West's much-reproduced painting of the scene, exhibited in 1771, depicted him as a martyr for British imperialism. His body was returned to England and buried in Greenwich.

James Wolfe

'We fight, get beat, rise and fight again.'
GENERAL NATHANAEL GREENE

NATHANAEL GREENE

STEPHEN BRUMWELL

1742-86

MAJOR GENERAL NATHANAEL GREENE was never victorious in battle. Yet his remarkable career throughout the American War of Independence provides striking proof that campaigns, not battles, decide wars. In the crucial Southern campaign of 1781, Greene's ability to grind down his enemies through harassment and evasion prefigured the guerrilla strategies of other revolutionary commanders obliged to pit largely irregular forces against the conventional armies of imperial powers.

(Opposite) **Nathanael Greene,** in a portrait by Charles Willson Peale, 1783. Greene personified the values of the American Revolution, fusing fierce patriotism with a realistic grasp of logistics. In January 1776 he predicted, 'An army unequipped will ever feel the want of spirit and courage but properly furnished [and] fighting in the best of causes will bid defiance to the united force of men and devils'.

For a general, Nathanael Greene's background was improbable. He was born near East Greenwich, Rhode Island, on 27 July 1742, into one of the colony's leading families of Quakers, a pacifist sect that eschewed formal education beyond the reading, writing and reckoning necessary for leading a godly existence and to make a living.

The self-taught soldier

The Greenes fared well enough, establishing a farm, sawmill and forge. But young Nathanael had wider interests. Hungry for knowledge, he devoured books, particularly military memoirs ranging the centuries from Julius Caesar to Frederick the Great. Despite his obsession with martial glory, Greene looked set for the unwarlike role of entrepreneur. As he entered his thirties, however, escalating tensions between Britain and her North American colonies intervened, transforming him into a dedicated opponent of British policy.

In 1774, as war loomed, Greene joined a local militia company. When this unit was embodied as the 'Kentish Guards', he assumed that his military knowledge and local prominence would ensure his election to officer. Instead, to his shame and chagrin, Greene's comrades spurned him because his slight limp – the result of a childhood accident – spoiled their parades. Greene soldiered on, and his persistence was soon rewarded: in May 1775, when Rhode Island responded to the outbreak of fighting in neighbouring Massachusetts by raising a 1,500-strong 'army of observation', he was invited to command it.

Within weeks, Greene and his men joined the American forces besieging General

Nathanael Greene

Thomas Gage and his redcoats in Boston. Greene missed the bloody clash at Bunker Hill in June, but absorbed its lessons: the British might have 'won' the battle, yet their horrific casualties made it a bitter victory. That month the Continental Congress in Philadelphia adopted the troops surrounding Boston as the 'Continental army', appointing George Washington its commander-in-chief. Greene, who had won notice for the efficiency of his Rhode Islanders, gained the rank of brigadier-general. At 33, he was the youngest general in the entire American army.

Washington and Greene first met at Cambridge, Massachusetts, on 4 July 1775. The Virginian planter and New England forge-master could not have been more different in background, yet they shared core ideals and beliefs, above all that American liberty could only be sustained by a professional, long-service army – not amateur militiamen. From the outset, Greene was devoted to Washington, serving him with an unswerving loyalty. Washington reciprocated by trusting Greene implicitly, and giving him ever-greater responsibility. In the grim years to come, they would form a formidable military partnership.

Precarious apprenticeship

The dreary siege of Boston dragged on until March 1776, when Gage's successor, General William Howe, withdrew to Halifax, Nova Scotia. It was clear the British would return, with New York their obvious destination. Washington ordered Greene there with a brigade, and when he arrived in April gave him command of Long Island. Heavily fortified, this was the key to the defence of New York and the strategically vital Hudson river. Greene's daunting responsibilities brought promotion to major general, but when the British assault finally came in August, he was too ill to meet it. As Greene battled a 'raging fever', Howe's army mauled Washington's outnumbered troops, forcing them to withdraw to Manhattan.

In early September, the recovered Greene advised Washington to burn and abandon New York. Congress baulked at torching the city, but the evacuation went ahead. On 16 September Greene faced combat for the first time at Harlem Heights, acquitting himself coolly. A question-mark remained over Fort Washington, above Harlem on the Hudson's east bank. Washington was inclined to evacuate its defenders,

Nathanael Greene

The Battle of Princeton, 3 January 1777, painted by William Mercer, c. 1786–90. George Washington's victory at Princeton, just a few days after he had turned the tide at Trenton, gave a huge boost to the morale of the dejected American revolutionaries. Nathanael Greene played a prominent role in both battles.

but Greene believed the fort could be held, and reinforced its garrison to 3,000. This was a fatal miscalculation. On 16 November, Howe stormed the fort, bagging the entire garrison. Greene's blunder drew heavy criticism, but Washington refused to dismiss him. His fortunes remained uncertain: just days later, while the evacuation of Fort Lee, New Jersey, was proceeding, news arrived that 5,000 British troops under Lord Charles Cornwallis had crossed the Hudson and were closing fast. Greene escaped, but it was not the last time he would find the determined Cornwallis snapping at his heels.

In the coming weeks Washington's dejected army retreated through New Jersey, enduring appalling weather. On 8 December 1776, it crossed the Delaware River into Pennsylvania. Although Washington had been bundled out of New Jersey, British garrisons there were dangerously isolated. Aware that many of his men's enlistments expired at New Year, Washington decided to take the offensive while he still could. A bold plan was agreed: three columns would cross the Delaware on Christmas Day to attack the 1,500 Hessian troops in Trenton. In icy darkness the complex plan swiftly unravelled, and only the main column, under Washington and Greene, reached its target, at 8 a.m. on 26 December. But surprise was total, and the Hessians were routed. An exultant Greene urged a vigorous pursuit. Reluctant to risk what he had won, Washington instead returned to Pennsylvania.

Trenton was a momentous victory, and Greene, who had spearheaded the attack, received a taste of the glory he craved. More was to come. Buoyed up by this timely success, Washington re-crossed the Delaware on 30 December. His reinvigorated army of 5,000 men, with Greene commanding a division, established defensive positions

Nathanael Greene

outside Trenton. Soon after, Cornwallis arrived at Princeton, some 12 miles off. Leaving three regiments to hold the college town, he went after Washington with his main force. But the wily Virginian gave Cornwallis the slip, using back roads to strike instead at the heavily outnumbered garrison of Princeton on 3 January 1777. Another victory followed, with Greene once more conspicuous for battlefield leadership.

Its morale restored, the Continental army went into winter quarters at Morristown, New Jersey. For Greene, no less than Washington, the Trenton–Princeton campaign was a turning point, reviving his self-esteem after the ignominious loss of Forts Washington and Lee.

Washington's right-hand man

In spring 1777 Washington sent Greene to Philadelphia as his representative in talks with Congress. The experience underlined the dichotomy between the Revolution's politicians and its soldiers, the talkers and the fighters: frustration with Congress would become a familiar theme in Greene's correspondence.

That summer, Howe's intentions remained unclear. Would he march up the Hudson, to join forces with General John Burgoyne, advancing south from Canada, or strike at Philadelphia? Howe eventually chose the second option, sailing to Maryland and advancing from there on 8 September. Washington prepared to stop him at Brandywine Creek, Pennsylvania. Greene was again given a key responsibility, holding the centre of the American line at Chadd's Ford. But when the British attacked, on 11 September, Howe virtually ignored Greene's position, opting instead for a flanking attack on Washington's right. Marching to the crisis point, Greene prevented retreat from escalating into rout.

Howe had beaten Washington yet failed to deliver a knockout blow. Naturally optimistic, Greene was undiscouraged by this setback. Brandywine underlined another Greene trait: eager for recognition and acutely sensitive of his personal reputation, he was disgruntled that Washington's report to Congress had not mentioned his services. On 26 September 1777, the British occupied Philadelphia. However, Washington's army remained in the field, and by 3 October was reinforced to 11,000 men – enough to take the offensive against Howe's 8,000. Greene and his colleagues urged an attack upon the main British encampment at Germantown. The plan followed that which had delivered victory at Trenton, with multiple columns mounting a surprise night assault. Greene played a pivotal role, heading three divisions. But the ambitious paper plan soon fell apart on the ground. Conditions were misty, and Greene's column momentarily lost its way. To add to Greene's problems, when he got back on track, one of his divisional commanders, the drunken Adam Stephen, opened fire on his fellows. Regaining their balance, the British counter-attacked, forcing Washington to retreat.

The Americans had been beaten once more but, as before, their performance had been far from despicable, and with a little luck the outcome might have been very different. Other revolutionaries, including leaders of Congress, took a bleaker view of Washington's campaign. Their criticisms of the commander-in-chief and his influential adviser Greene grew more strident when, just days after Germantown, news arrived that the Patriots' northern army under General Horatio Gates had decisively defeated Burgoyne at Saratoga. Perhaps the triumphant Gates and not the seemingly indecisive Washington should assume the chief command?

Nathanael Greene

Washington kept his place, but Congress's opinion of his confidante Greene was not improved when he voted against their proposal to eject Howe from Philadelphia. Instead, the Continental army broke camp and took up new winter quarters, north of Philadelphia, at Valley Forge.

Quartermaster general

During the winter of 1777–8, the Continental army faced other enemies than the British. A crisis of supply and transport demanded the attentions of a competent quartermaster. Washington pleaded with Greene to take the job. First and foremost a fighting soldier, Greene was loath to exchange his place in the line for such an inglorious and onerous role. He finally accepted the office – but solely from loyalty to Washington.

The Valley Forge winter was not wasted. While the Prussian officer Friedrich von Steuben overhauled the Continental army's drill, Greene placed its logistics on a firm footing, establishing strategically placed supply depots. Heartened by news that the French had signed a treaty of alliance with the fledgling United States, Washington's long-suffering soldiers faced the approaching campaigning season with renewed confidence.

Discredited by Burgoyne's fiasco, William Howe had been replaced by Sir Henry Clinton. With the French in the war, British strategists believed that the occupation of Philadelphia was no longer viable. In mid June, Clinton's army began a sluggish withdrawal into New Jersey, bound for New York. Washington's remodelled army pursued, its progress expedited by Greene's reforms.

Despite his administrative duties, Greene badgered Washington for a combat role – and a vigorous move against Clinton's rearguard. On the stiflingly hot 28 June 1778, 5,000 men under General Charles Lee attacked the British near Monmouth Courthouse. Lee was soon in trouble: Clinton's rearguard had been bolstered by elite troops led by the ubiquitous Cornwallis. Greene was ordered to support the first assault, but on learning of Lee's repulse fell back to reinforce Washington's main position. He buttressed the American right, facing and rebuffing his old rival, Cornwallis. Washington's line held, and the bloodied British continued on their way to New York.

In military terms, Monmouth Courthouse was a draw. Yet the psychological victory lay with the Americans, who gained a further fillip with the arrival of a French fleet off New Jersey, under Admiral Charles d'Estaing. The war's first Franco-American offensive, against British-held Newport, Rhode Island, was to be commanded by General John Sullivan. Greene, who orchestrated the operation's logistics, obtained leave to join the campaign in his home state. The attack was scheduled for August, but the allies soon fell out. When d'Estaing's fleet suffered storm damage that forced a refit in Boston, Sullivan raged at this 'betrayal'. Irate himself, Greene nonetheless knew the alliance was paramount, and worked to smooth ruffled French feathers.

By early summer 1779, the war's northern theatre was stalemated: the British held New York and Newport, while Washington's troops occupied Boston and Philadelphia. That autumn, however, the conflict's mainland axis shifted. In October, the British took Savannah, Georgia, rekindling hopes that the Lower South would host a victorious drive north through Virginia.

Clinton and Cornwallis sailed south to exploit the situation. By contrast, Washington and Greene stayed focused on the Hudson valley, fixing their winter quarters on familiar ground at Morristown. There, quartermaster general Greene kept

'He is vigilant, enterprising, and full of resources – there is but little hope of gaining an advantage over him.' GENERAL CHARLES CORNWALLIS

the kernel of the Continental army fed and clothed through an exceptionally severe winter. With money scarce, supplies ran perilously low. By May 1780 the famished troops were poised to mutiny. This crisis was only compounded by bleak tidings from the South: the 6,000-strong garrison of Charleston under General Benjamin Lincoln had fallen to Clinton's siege. This was Fort Washington writ large, the worst Patriot defeat of the war. Horatio Gates was sent south to take command. But the hero of Saratoga soon made a bad situation worse. On 16 August, at Camden, South Carolina, he rushed into battle with Cornwallis and was routed, losing both his army and his reputation.

As if these dire tidings were not enough, one of the Revolution's best fighters, Greene's close friend, Benedict Arnold, defected to the British. Luckily, Arnold's plot to betray the vital Hudson stronghold of West Point – in Greene's words 'treason of the blackest dye' – misfired when his British contact Major John André was captured. After a court martial presided over by Greene, André was hanged as a spy on 2 October. Less than two weeks later Greene, who had finally resigned as quartermaster general, was appointed Congress's new commander of the Southern Department.

Charles, Marquess Cornwallis, painted in 1792 by John Smart. Cornwallis earned a reputation as one of the most aggressive and determined British officers in North America, although his effectiveness was compromised by a poor relationship with his commander-in-chief, Sir Henry Clinton.

Commander in the south

Greene's first independent command seemed a poisoned chalice. Not only was he obliged to restore the morale of a demoralized army, but he must also browbeat the war-weary and apathetic southern states into recruiting, feeding, clothing and arming replacements for the men squandered at Charleston and Camden. Wary of sharing the fate of Gates, Greene resolved to avoid a battlefield confrontation with the aggressive Cornwallis, and instead to wear his opponent down by a rambling winter campaign across the south's punishing terrain, aided by Patriot partisans already seasoned in a vicious civil war with local Loyalists. He achieved this goal in masterly fashion: by spring 1781 the exasperated Cornwallis had turned north, bound for Virginia – and disaster.

Following his exhausting campaign and costly victory at Guilford Court House, Cornwallis' shattered little army limped off to Wilmington, and thence to Virginia, leaving British posts in South Carolina vulnerable to Greene's forces. While Patriot partisans ranged widely, Greene decided to confront Britain's next commander in South Carolina, Lord Francis Rawdon, who headed 1,500 men at Camden. On 25 April, at Hobkirk's Hill, Greene sustained another tactical defeat but once again scored a strategic victory, inflicting casualties that obliged Rawdon to retreat to

Nathanael Greene

Charleston. By July 1781, British forces in the Lower South were hemmed within a coastal band between that port and Savannah.

As crown influence waned, Greene sought battle with Rawdon's successor, Lieutenant Colonel Alexander Stewart. In a confused encounter at Eutaw Springs on 8 September, Greene was denied outright victory, although here, too, the British sustained losses they could ill afford. Thereafter the war wound down, with Greene's army watching Charleston and Savannah until the British evacuated in 1782. By then, the Revolutionary War had already been decided in Virginia. In July 1781, after two months of inconclusive manoeuvring, Cornwallis dug in at Yorktown. A British fleet failed to reach him, and the inexorable tightening of American–French siege lines forced his surrender on 19 October 1781.

Preoccupied elsewhere, Greene did not witness the culmination of his efforts.

(Below) **The Battle of Guilford Court House,** 1781, as depicted by H. Charles McBarron Jr (1902–92). The battle was technically a British victory yet its cost was high, allowing Greene to strengthen his control of much of the south.

THE CAMPAIGN IN THE LOWER SOUTH

ON 2 DECEMBER 1780, Greene assumed command at Charlotte, North Carolina. Two weeks later he boldly divided his army in the face of the enemy. Greene marched southeast, into South Carolina, camping near Cheraw Hill on the Pee Dee River. Meanwhile, a detachment of 600 men, under Brigadier General Daniel Morgan, moved southwest to distract Cornwallis's left flank. Morgan achieved much more: on 17 January 1781, at Cowpens, he eliminated a British force under the ruthless Colonel Banastre Tarleton.

Enraged, Cornwallis followed the retreating Morgan into North Carolina, determined to destroy both him and Greene. To speed his pursuit he jettisoned all excess baggage, including the soldiers' tents and even their cherished rum. Learning that Cornwallis had been reinforced to 2,500 men, Greene sought to reunite his own forces. The rendezvous was fixed at Salisbury, yet the pace of the chase forced a switch to Guilford Court House, deeper within North Carolina. Cornwallis was gaining swiftly, but unlike Greene, who was moving ever nearer to his supplies in Virginia, he was daily marching further from his own logistical base in South Carolina. Cornwallis nonetheless believed he had trapped Greene against the Yadkin river. But Greene's stint as quartermaster general had served him well: flatboats were waiting to ferry him over in the nick of time.

On 9 February 1781, Greene and Morgan linked up as planned. With just over 2,000 men, Greene had a choice: stand and fight, or retreat another 70 miles to the Dan, crossing that river into Virginia. North Carolina was conceded, but Greene still had to out-distance Cornwallis, now just 35 miles away. On 10 February, Greene again split his command, detaching 700 men under Colonel Otho Williams as a screening force. Cornwallis was convinced that Greene was heading for the Dan's upper fords. But Greene had boats waiting downriver, and Williams delayed Cornwallis long enough for him to reach them first. On St Valentine's Day 1781, Greene's army crossed the Dan, concluding a model strategic retreat.

Denied his prey, the frustrated Cornwallis marched his weary men 60 miles back to Hillsborough. There, he issued a victory proclamation. But the words rang hollow.

Re-supplied, rested and reinforced, Greene returned to North Carolina

Ironically, the self-taught soldier who had done so much to secure American liberty had scant opportunity to reap the rewards and recognition that he had earned from the new Republic, or to enjoy his young family. Mired in debt and hounded by creditors, Greene died suddenly at his Georgia plantation in June 1786, apparently from heatstroke. He was just 44 years old.

The decisive battlefield victory that Greene hankered after eluded him, yet his contribution to the winning of American independence was unquestionable, second only to that of the man to whom he was devoted. Indeed, of the American generals created at Boston in 1775, only Greene and Washington remained in service by the time of Yorktown. During those years, Greene learned his soldiering through hard experience, demonstrating flexibility, leadership, an instinct for guerrilla warfare, and, above all, an unrelenting belief in the ultimate victory of his cause.

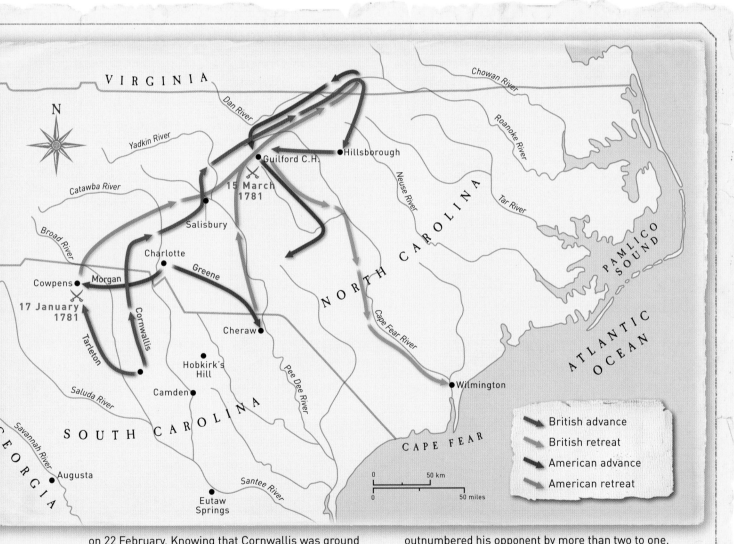

on 22 February. Knowing that Cornwallis was ground down by the futile 'race to the Dan', Greene determined to engage him in battle. Cornwallis eagerly accepted the challenge. They met on 15 March 1781, at Guilford Court House. With 4,400 Continentals and militia, Greene outnumbered his opponent by more than two to one. Undaunted, the bullish Cornwallis launched his veterans in a frontal assault. After savage fighting, the earl held the field, but with 25 per cent casualties, his was a Pyrrhic victory.

Nathanael Greene

'He crushed or thrust aside his enemies, without heed to anything other than the necessity or the interest of getting rid of them.'

PRINCE METTERNICH

NAPOLEON BONAPARTE
1769–1821

PHILIP DWYER

NAPOLEON HAS GONE DOWN IN HISTORY as one of the most successful generals of all time, and the reputation is, on the face of it, deserved. In the twenty-year period in which he commanded French revolutionary armies and then the imperial Grande Armée, he fought in eleven campaigns, personally conducted more than sixty battles (the vast majority of which he won) and defeated every major European power, except Britain. At the height of his power in 1807, at the age of 38, he ruled over a territory comparable to that of Charlemagne; that is, almost all of western Europe. Napoleon was much more than a general, however. He was also one of the most successful politicians of all time, combining a skilful use of propaganda and reform to create a legacy that is still felt today.

Born in Corsica on 15 August 1769, one year after the French occupation of the island, into a family of local notables, Napoleone di Buonaparte was the second surviving child of Carlo and Letizia (*née* Ramolino). He spent his youth on the island until, at the age of 9, he was sent to Brienne in the north of France to get a French military education. In 1784, at the age of 15, he was sent to the École Militaire in Paris, where he graduated the following year as a second lieutenant in the royal artillery.

Embarking on a military career

Napoleon's first posting was to La Fère Regiment in Valence, considered one of the best, if not the best, artillery regiment in France at the time. Over the next few years Napoleon would move between Corsica and France, torn between loyalty to his island and a career in the French army. With the coming of the French Revolution in 1789, Napoleon became deeply involved in Corsican politics. He and his brothers attempted to ingratiate themselves with the leading Corsican politician of the time, Napoleon's childhood hero, Pasquale Paoli. The Buonapartes also aligned themselves with the radical Jacobin faction in France. It was partly as a result of this, and partly as a result of the clan-based nature of Corsican politics, that the Buonapartes eventually fell out with the Paolist faction on the island. Things became so bad that the family was obliged to flee for their lives in 1793.

Napoleon Bonaparte

The Buonapartes landed as political refugees in the south of France in June 1793. Napoleon's fate would now be tied to that of France and the Revolution. His first big break came a few months later when he took part in the siege of Toulon, a port town that had been captured by the British (among other allies). It was there that Napoleon first came to the notice of some powerful men, including Augustin Robespierre, the brother of Maximilien Robespierre, the head of the Committee of Public Safety, and Paul Barras, a deputy to the Convention, who would go on to become the leading politician in France under the Directory. It was as a result of his performance at Toulon that Napoleon was promoted to brigadier general.

Nevertheless, in the mercurial world of French revolutionary politics, in the blink of an eye political leaders and incompetent generals could find themselves staring into

General Napoleon Bonaparte as Romantic hero, planting the French tricoleur on the bridge of Arcola, 17 November 1796, as depicted by Antoine-Jean Gros. It was as the 27-year-old commander of the Army of Italy in 1796 that Bonaparte first made his military reputation.

Napoleon Bonaparte

a basket waiting for the blade to drop. Thus Napoleon, after the arrest and execution of Robespierre in July 1794, briefly found himself in prison because of his Jacobin political associations. He was released, but 'purged' from the artillery and ordered to the west of France to take part in suppressing the revolts there. Napoleon baulked, staying in Paris in the hope that something better would turn up. It did, in the form of an uprising by royalist sympathizers in Paris known as the Coup of 13 Vendémiaire (5 October 1795), because of the revolutionary month in which it took place. Barras remembered Napoleon from Toulon and employed him to protect the Convention and to organize the artillery. It set the scene for the famous 'whiff of grapeshot' story that has Napoleon ordering cannon to fire on the crowds, but there is no proof that he either gave the order or was present – if indeed the event ever took place at all.

The rise to power

Nevertheless, as a reward for his role in suppressing the coup, Napoleon was promoted to general of division, and named commander-in-chief of the Army of the Interior, probably the most influential military position in the country. It was around this time, in October 1795, that Napoleon met Rose de Beauharnais, better known to history as Joséphine, and started courting her. They married on 9 March 1796. He was 27, she was 33. Two days later Napoleon rode off to take control of the Army of Italy. He had been harassing his political masters for an army command for some time, and they had finally relented.

Napoleon's military experience up to that point had been limited. He had helped put down a few riots, participated in a disastrous expedition to take Sardinia, taken part in the siege of Toulon and accompanied the revolutionary army into northern Italy in 1794, but that was the extent of it. Most of his military ideas came from books, not battlefield experience, and a good tactician does not always make for a good general. In Italy, Napoleon was to discover something that perhaps even he did not suspect: he was a brilliant strategist. In a series of battles fought throughout 1796 and into 1797 – Montenotte, Millesimo, Mondovi, Cherasco, Lodi, Castiglione, Arcola and Rivoli –

Napoleon defeated first the Piedmontese and then a number of Austrian armies. It was here that Napoleon put his ideas into practice, perfecting strategic ideas and battle techniques he had largely inherited from others. It was also during this period that he learned how to govern conquered peoples, creating a number of nominally independent sister republics that were in fact subordinated to France. Finally, he learned how to manipulate the media of the day to his own advantage. The military campaign was also a political campaign, which ended in October 1797 with the Treaty of Campo Formio. Britain was now the only power still at war with revolutionary France.

When Napoleon returned to France in December 1797 he briefly considered, but dropped, the possibility of an invasion of England. Instead, Napoleon and the then minister for foreign affairs, Charles-Maurice de Talleyrand, persuaded the French revolutionary government, the Directory, to consent to sending an expeditionary force to Egypt. It was justified as an indirect means of attacking Britain (possibly through India) as well as a scientific expedition that gave it the veneer of a 'civilizing mission'. Napoleon successfully evaded the British fleet under Nelson in the Mediterranean and landed in Egypt at the beginning of July 1798. After a painful march across the desert, the French made short shrift of the Mameluke army at the Battle of the Pyramids and entered Cairo. Nelson's victory over the French fleet at the Battle of the Nile (2 August) left Napoleon with a limited number of options, one of which was to pre-empt a Turkish counter-attack on Egypt by marching into Syria at the beginning of 1799. The most notable episode of this phase of the campaign was the massacre of Jaffa, not only of the townspeople but also of thousands of prisoners. The French advance was stalled at St Jean of Acre; lack of siege artillery and the presence of the plague did not help, but nor did the actions of Sir Sidney Smith, who helped organize if not galvanize the defence. Napoleon decided to return to Egypt in a retreat that resembled in many respects the long march from Moscow twelve years later. He returned in time to defeat a Turkish army that had landed at Aboukir Bay (25 July), almost one year to the day since he had entered Cairo. Shortly afterwards, Napoleon took the decision to leave (or abandon) the army in Egypt and return to France.

His landing in the south of France caused a sensation, coinciding as it did with news of the victory at Aboukir. He was soon approached by a number of conspirators, disaffected politicians who wanted to overthrow the notoriously corrupt government and to introduce a new constitution. They needed a 'sword' that would lend military support to the coup they intended carrying out. Napoleon, however, hijacked the whole process and imposed himself on the conspirators. On 9 November 1799 the coup of 18 Brumaire, as it became known, nominally brought Napoleon to power along with two other consuls, but it was evident from the start that only one consul counted.

The conquest of Europe

Napoleon quickly established his position both within France and without, firstly by introducing a series of reforms that consolidated the gains of the Revolution and which culminated in a concordat with the Catholic Church and the introduction of the Code Civil (commonly known as the Napoleonic Code), and secondly by quickly bringing the War of the Second Coalition to an end. Napoleon's second Italian campaign was marked by the closely fought Battle of Marengo (14 June 1800), which once again saw the Austrian army withdraw from Italy. The Treaty of Lunéville with Austria

(1801) and the Peace of Amiens with Britain (1802) reinforced Napoleon's reputation as a peacemaker. For the first time since the outbreak of war in 1792, France was at peace. It allowed Napoleon to conduct a plebiscite that named him consul for life in 1802, a major step on the path towards the foundation of a new dynasty and an empire. The Empire was duly proclaimed in May 1804, and in December Napoleon placed the imperial crown on his own head in Notre Dame de Paris.

The Peace of Amiens was, however, short lived. Within eighteen months a third coalition had formed against France, in part because of Napoleon's expansionist behaviour, and in part because neither Britain nor Russia could tolerate French hegemony on the Continent. Between the renewal of hostilities in 1803 and the actual resumption of land operations in 1805, Napoleon and the bulk of the French imperial army were camped in the environs of Boulogne on the French coast, poised to invade Britain. It was only after learning that an alliance between Alexander I of Russia and Francis I of Austria was forming against him, in association with Britain, that Napoleon decided to act. Rather than wait for the eastern powers to strike, Napoleon pre-empted them by marching east from the coast of France into southern Germany. This led to the

(Below) **Napoleon at Austerlitz,** 2 December 1805, as depicted by Gérard François Pascal Simon (1770–1837).

THE BATTLE OF
AUSTERLITZ

AUSTERLITZ IS RECOGNIZED as the ultimate Napoleonic battle, but myth and propaganda play just as much a role as the actual battle itself in establishing Napoleon's reputation as one of the greatest military commanders of all time. Much of the campaign that preceded the battle was improvised, and therein lay Napoleon's brilliance.

The battle, sometimes called the Battle of the Three Emperors because of the presence of Tsar Alexander I, Francis I of Austria and Napoleon himself, took place on the Pratzen Heights, about 15 miles east of Brünn (present-day Brno in the Czech Republic), on 2 December 1805 on the first anniversary of Napoleon's coronation. To the south of the heights were two shallow lakes. Prior to the battle, Napoleon abandoned the heights, thus giving

the impression that he had made a mistake. And not only did he not occupy the high ground, he was also clearly outnumbered – around 66,000 French troops and 139 cannon compared with 89,000 allied troops and 278 cannon – but a *corps d'armée* of about 6,000 men under Davout was on its way.

The plan was for the French right wing to feign retreat and to hold the bulk of the allied army, which would descend the Pratzen Heights in order to attack and thus leave its strong position. Most of the French cavalry, Oudinot's grenadiers, the Imperial Guard and Bernadotte's corps were concealed on the French left wing. At the right moment, Napoleon would give the order for the French left wing to attack and take the heights. The battle went according to plan. At about 7 a.m. the bulk of the allied army did indeed

Napoleon Bonaparte

battles of Ulm (20 October 1805) and Austerlitz (2 December) and the defeat of the Austro-Russian armies (see below). The Treaty of Pressburg (modern Bratislava) was imposed on Austria, while Russia, smarting from the loss, withdrew behind its borders. It left Napoleon master of central Europe, which he began to rearrange by putting an end to the Holy Roman Empire and by creating the Confederation of the Rhine out of a greatly reduced number of states.

Prussia, neutral since 1795, hesitated about joining the coalition against France in 1805, and pulled out at the last minute. With the defeat of its allies, it too was obliged to enter into a humiliating treaty that forced it to occupy Hanover (of which George III of the United Kingdom was prince-elector) and place a blockade on British shipping. The very next year, however, amid rumours of a deal between France and Britain involving Hanover, Prussia delivered an ultimatum to the French to withdraw behind the Rhine. Rather than wait for the arrival of Russian troops, the Prussians acted precipitously and

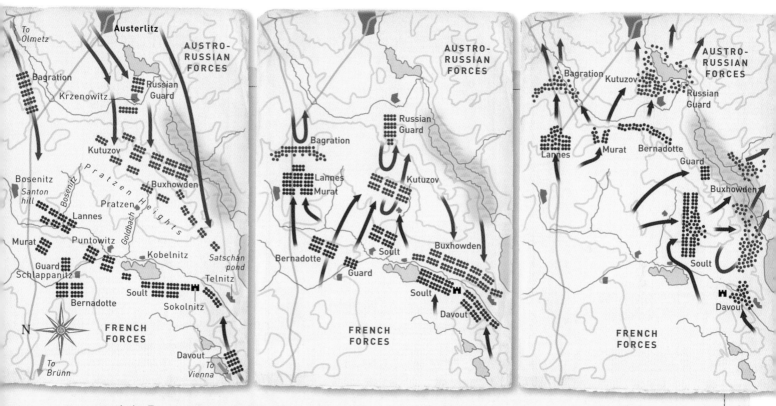

attack the French right, and were held off, although with difficulty, strengthened by the arrival of Davout. By 9 a.m. Napoleon, correctly thinking that the heights had been abandoned by all allied troops, ordered his centre and left wing to attack. By 3.30 p.m. the French had occupied the heights and were firing on the enemy below, now sandwiched between two French forces. An attempt to extricate the allied troops turned into a rout. Some troops tried to escape across an icy lake, but it broke under a French bombardment. As many as 2,000 died in this way.

Napoleon's strategy at Austerlitz was a calculated risk that could have just as easily not worked. If the battle had been fought only a day earlier, Davout and Bernadotte would

not yet have arrived, and the Grande Armée would have faced even bigger odds than it did. A detailed reading of Austerlitz makes it clear that, although an impressive victory for Napoleon, it was a much more difficult battle than is normally described in the history books. Allied casualties were high, some 15,000–16,000 killed and wounded and another 11,000–12,000 taken prisoner, or a third of the allied forces. The French losses were considerably less, some 7,800 killed and wounded and another 500 missing. The next day Francis sued for peace and within a month had signed the Treaty of Pressburg. The Russian forces withdrew into their own territory, leaving Britain the only remaining great power fighting the French.

engaged the French at Jena and Auerstädt (14 October 1806; see pp. 144–5). The Prussian army was not what it had been under Frederick the Great; it collapsed, and within weeks French forces had occupied most of the kingdom. Napoleon entered the Prussian capital, whence he issued the Berlin Decrees (21 November), prohibiting all commerce between Britain and the Continent.

The king of Prussia, Frederick William III, was down but not entirely out. His 'friend' and ally Alexander I of Russia lent his support, and Prussian but mostly Russian troops fought two further battles, at Eylau (7–8 February 1807) and Friedland (14 June 1807). After these two defeats, Russia (and Prussia) sued for peace. The resulting Treaty of Tilsit (7 July 1807), signed by Tsar Alexander and Emperor Napoleon on a raft in the middle of the Niemen (with a pitiful Frederick William III waiting to hear the fate of his kingdom on the banks of the river), led to a re-division of the map of Europe: Prussia was reduced to half its size; part of Prussian territory was incorporated into a new Kingdom of Westphalia (ruled by Napoleon's brother Jérôme), and another part became the Duchy of Warsaw. Furthermore, Russia agreed to join France in declaring war on Britain and blockading its goods from mainland Europe (a blockade known as the Continental System).

Downfall and exile

Tilsit is regarded as the zenith of Napoleon's power. He now ruled over a territory that stretched from the River Oder in the east to the Atlantic Ocean in the west, and from the Baltic Sea in the north to Sicily in the south. However, a series of errors in which Napoleon overplayed his hand, beginning with the Continental System – which led, as tradition would have it, to Napoleon's intervention in the Iberian Peninsula from 1807, the invasion of the Papal States in 1808 and even the invasion of Russia in 1812 – ultimately led to his downfall. In Spain, Napoleon overthrew the Spanish branch of the House of Bourbon and placed his brother Joseph on the throne, but soon faced a full-scale revolt. The combination of guerrilla fighters and the landing of a British army to help the Spanish regulars would tie down 200,000–400,000 troops per year and cost almost a quarter of a million casualties. Napoleon briefly intervened in Spain personally, but was distracted when in 1809 a recalcitrant Austria, financed (as was now usually the case) by British money, once more went to war with France. In the campaign that followed, Napoleon suffered his first real loss, at the Battle of Aspern-Essling, against Archduke Charles (May 1809). However, Charles made the mistake of not following up his advantage quickly enough and he was defeated the following month at Wagram. In 1810 Napoleon sealed an alliance with Austria by marrying the 16-year-old princess, Archduchess Marie-Louise, having divorced the childless Joséphine earlier that year.

'The art of war is a simple art. There is nothing vague in it, everything is common sense; ideology does not enter into it.'

NAPOLEON

If relations between France and Austria had been mended, relations with Russia went from good, after Tilsit, to bad (at Erfurt where the two emperors met in 1808), to very bad. Much of this was Napoleon's fault. By 1810 both sides were moving towards war. It nevertheless took another two years before Napoleon crossed the Oder in June 1812 with one of the largest land armies yet seen in Europe. The ensuing campaign was a disaster from beginning to end. Contrary to popular belief, Napoleon lost most of his men to desertion, disease, battle (Smolensk, Borodino; see pp. 152–3) and the Russian heat well before the Grande Armée reached Moscow. It is debatable whether the Russians deliberately drew Napoleon ever deeper into their heartland, thus extending the lines of supply, but the wisdom of retreating from Moscow back along the same route over which they had come was questionable (see pp. 154–5). Figures vary greatly, but it is likely that Napoleon lost about 400,000 troops, of which less than a quarter would have actually died in battle. As few as 20,000 men survived the ordeal.

The defeat showed just how precarious was Napoleon's empire. He was now forced to fight a rearguard action throughout 1813 in order to hold on to central Europe, a feat that was hampered by a dire lack of cavalry after the Russian fiasco. Even though Napoleon was able to fend off the combined Russo-Prussian armies with a number of victories before June – at Lützen (2 May 1813) and Bautzen (20–21 May) – they were Pyrrhic victories that cost the French twice as many men as their opponents. The entry of Austria into the war in July 1813 shifted the balance of strength in the allies' favour. With that, to paraphrase the historian Peter Paret, Napoleon was suddenly reduced to being just another competent general. The decisive battle came at Leipzig (sometimes known as the Battle of Nations). In the largest land battle to date, raging for four days, 177,000–195,000 French troops fought 320,000–365,000 allied troops. In the end, Napoleon could not hold out against such overwhelming odds and was forced to abandon central Europe. Leipzig was thus a turning point in much the same way that Blenheim was for Louis XIV, or Stalingrad was for Hitler.

The first few months of 1814 saw Napoleon desperately trying to stave off defeat against an allied army that brought all the great powers together for the first time in the history of the wars against France. Despite some brilliant tactical successes, Napoleon could not prevent the allies from entering Paris. The rest is a footnote in history: a first abdication in April 1814 that led to exile on Elba; his return less than a year later; the Hundred Days that ended at Waterloo on 18 June 1815 (a battle that Wellington described as 'the nearest run thing'; see pp. 137–9); the second abdication later that month. Napoleon passed the last years of his life in exile on St Helena, a remote island in the South Atlantic, where, on 5 May 1821 he died of cancer of the stomach.

Napoleon and his staff (marshals Ney and Berthier and generals Drouot, Bourgaud and Flahault) on the retreat as the allied armies enter France early in 1814, in a painting by Ernest Meissonier (1864). Napoleon's first abdication – and exile to Elba – followed in April.

> 'I never took so much trouble about any battle, and was never was so near being beat.' WELLINGTON ON WATERLOO

DUKE OF WELLINGTON
1769–1852

ANDREW ROBERTS

ARTHUR WELLESLEY, 1ST DUKE OF WELLINGTON, was – along with Marlborough – Britain's greatest military commander. He was also one of its worst prime ministers. While his premiership was fortunately only short-lived, it was more than made up for by the splendour of a wartime career in which he fought sixty-two battles and never lost one, at a time of peril when his country most desperately needed victories.

(Opposite) **The Duke of Wellington** as conquering hero, astride his beloved horse Copenhagen, painted by Sir Thomas Lawrence (1769–1830). After Waterloo he wrote, 'I hope to God that I have fought my last battle'. He had a less distinguished career when high political office beckoned.

Born in Dublin, the fourth son of the 1st Earl of Mornington, Wellesley hailed from the Anglo-Irish aristocratic 'Protestant Ascendancy' that ruled Ireland from Elizabethan times until the partition of the island in 1922. Educated firstly at Eton, where he learned little except perhaps how to use his fists, and then – probably due to a lack of funds at his father's early death – in Brussels, Wellesley entered the Angers Military Academy in 1786. Although his mother decried the idea of a military career for him, believing him to have no aptitude for soldiering, he was commissioned as a lieutenant in an infantry regiment in 1787 and became a captain of dragoons five years later.

In the meantime he was elected to a seat in the Irish parliament, but took as little interest in politics as he initially did in soldiering, preferring to idle life away socializing and playing the violin. Indeed he might have spent his life as a wallflower attending the picnics of the Irish Lord-Lieutenant as an aide-de-camp had not the French executed their king in 1793, prompting Wellesley suddenly to take his life and career seriously. He burnt his violin in the grate and became a colonel of the 33rd Foot Regiment, in which capacity he saw action against the French at Boxtel in the Netherlands campaign in 1794 and then again at Geldermalsen the following year.

The campaign, which had been intended to culminate in an invasion of France, was short-lived and disastrous, though no blame attached to Wellesley who performed well, and the incompetence of the British officers prompted him to take up closer study of the military arts. When his elder brother Richard became governor-general of India in 1797, Wellesley took the 33rd Foot out there and founded a great reputation for himself as a brilliant but also painstaking commander. His victories in Mysore and

HANC
ARTHURI DUCIS DE WELLINGTON

The storming of the fortress of Seringa-patam on 4 May 1799, as depicted in an engraving by Thomas Sutherland. Tipu Sultan, ruler of Mysore, was killed in the battle for the fortress. The British victory resulted in Wellesley's appointment as governor of the town, a post he retained until 1802, when he was given command of the army in the Second Maratha War.

Seringapatam against the sultan of Mysore and over the mercenary king Dhoondiah Waugh won him promotion to major-general.

Fighting next the Marathas, Wellesley won the famous victory of Assaye in south-central India in September 1803, which he personally considered strategically the finest of his battles. He was knighted the following year and in 1805 returned home, stopping off on the way on the remote island of St Helena in the South Atlantic Ocean. From commanding thousands and subduing sub-continents, he was given the command of a lowly battalion in Hastings in 1806, and the same year was elected MP for the Sussex town.

This time around Wellesley took politics seriously, and became Chief Secretary for Ireland in 1807, largely as the result of the influence of his ambitious and influential family, who were prominent Tory politicians. He also found time the same year to take part in the brief Copenhagen campaign, which was not quite as disastrous as earlier British incursions on Napoleon's continent of Europe had been.

The Peninsular War, 1808–14

In 1808, by then a lieutenant general, Wellesley was at last given an opportunity for genuine glory, when he was – albeit too briefly – given command of the British expeditionary force destined for Portugal. He told a friend that he would not be chased off the Continent as so many other similar forces had been, because he had made a study of French tactics and would not be at any kind of psychological disadvantage to the enemy.

'They may overwhelm me but I don't think they will out-manoeuvre me,' he said. 'First, because I am not afraid of them, as everybody else seems to be; and secondly, because if what I hear of their system of manoeuvre is true, I think it a false one against steady troops. I suspect that all the continental armies were more than half beaten before the battle was begun. I, at least, will not be frightened beforehand.'

It was a brave boast, but fully justified by events.

The Peninsular campaign started off well with victories at Roliça and Vimeiro in August, but soon afterwards Wellesley was superseded in command by two generals, Sir Harry Burrard and Sir Hew Dalrymple, who signed the Convention of Cintra (30 August), an armistice with the French that allowed the defeated enemy safe passage back to France with all their arms, baggage and booty, and even transportation in Royal Navy vessels. Back in Britain there was outrage at the terms of the Convention and an 'Inquiry' (which was effectively a court-martial) was heard in the Great Hall of the Royal Hospital at Chelsea. Wellesley, Burrard and Dalrymple were all summoned to it, but after several weeks Wellesley was finally acquitted.

Reassuming command in Portugal in 1809, Wellesley – hugely aided at all times by the Portuguese army and the Spanish guerrillas – proceeded to spend the next five years expelling the French from the Iberian peninsula. He took not one day's leave as he campaigned to and fro across Portugal and Spain, occasionally being forced to retreat because of the pressure of numbers opposing him, but never losing a battle or even so much as a single cannon. He was almost always outnumbered by the huge French forces that were occupying Spain in the name of Napoleon's brother, King Joseph. The leadership Wellesley showed in the Peninsular campaign was exemplary; he won a reputation of expecting the best, and being a harsh disciplinarian when he did not get it. Yet his troops also knew he never risked their lives unnecessarily.

The Battle of Vittoria, 21 June 1813, in an aquatint after a painting by William Heath. Following this, Wellington's great final victory in the Peninsular War, Joseph I retreated to France, abandoning his guns, ammunition, baggage and a vast amount of money. The looting of the latter by the British army caused Wellington to remark, 'We have in the service the scum of the earth as common soldiers'.

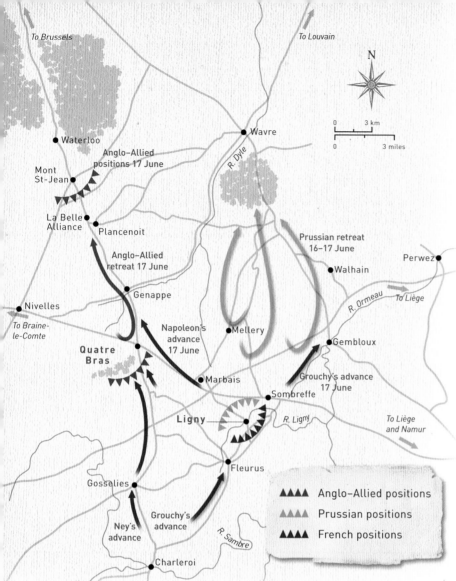

To Brussels

To Louvain

N

0   3 km
0   3 miles

Waterloo

Anglo–Allied
positions 17 June

Mont
St-Jean

R. Dyle

Wavre

Prussian retreat
16–17 June

Perwez

Walhain

La Belle
Alliance

Plancenoit

Anglo–Allied
retreat 17 June

Genappe

R. Ormeau   To Liège

Nivelles

To Braine-
le-Comte

Napoleon's
advance
17 June

Mellery

Gembloux

Quatre
Bras

Grouchy's advance
17 June

Marbais

Sombreffe

To Liège
and Namur

Ligny

R. Ligny

▲▲▲▲ Anglo–Allied positions

▲▲▲▲ Prussian positions

Fleurus

▲▲▲▲ French positions

Gosselies

Ney's
advance

Grouchy's
advance

R. Sambre

Charleroi

**THE WATERLOO
CAMPAIGN**, June 1815.

Waterloo and beyond

Wellesley – who had been elevated to the dukedom of Wellington in 1814 – had crossed the Pyrenees into France just before Napoleon abdicated, after which he become ambassador to Paris. He was then appointed British pleni-potentiary to the Congress of Vienna, which is where he was when, in March 1815, the news arrived that the ex-emperor had escaped from his exile on the island of Elba. Pausing only to declare Napoleon an international outlaw, Wellington went to take up command of the Anglo-Allied army in Brussels. He defeated Napoleon in the only battle the two men fought against one another – Waterloo (see pp. 137–9) – and one month later the emperor abdicated and surrendered to the British, who exiled him to the remote island of St Helena in the South Atlantic Ocean.

Wellington was covered in hon-ours both from Britain and all the European powers, but instead of retiring he entered the Cabinet in 1818, staying there as Master-General of Ordinance until 1827. The following year he be-came prime minister, and, despite being a reactionary Tory he passed Catholic Emanci-pation in 1829 with the help of Sir Robert Peel, albeit against his private inclinations. He resigned in 1830 when it became clear that he could not prevent parliamentary reform being enacted.

As commander-in-chief of the British Army from 1827 to 1828 and from 1842 to 1852, Wellington was a force for conservatism, and it has been argued that the lack of reforms in his time led to British ill-preparedness for the Crimean War. Yet even if his political and administrative careers were rather less impressive than his military and diplomatic ones, nothing can detract from his untarnishable glory as the conqueror of Napoleon and, along with Marlborough, as one of the two finest commanders Britain has ever produced.

'Judging by Wellington's actions, his despatches and above all his conduct towards Ney, I should pronounce him to be a man of little spirit, no generosity and without grandeur of soul.'

NAPOLEON BONAPARTE, 1817

THE BATTLE OF
WATERLOO

IF GENIUS IS IN PART THE ABILITY to take infinite care over details, then Wellington showed genius at Waterloo on Sunday, 18 June 1815. A master of topography, he personally sited every battalion in his large, polyglot army of 68,000 men, an ungainly mélange of different British, Dutch, Belgian and German formations, a large proportion of which were raw recruits. It was far removed from the seasoned army Wellington had moulded into a crack fighting force during the Peninsular War.

On 12 June Napoleon had suddenly left Paris and marched north into present-day Belgium, making for Brussels. The speed with which he gathered his force of 120,000 men, crossed the Sambre and Meuse rivers and simultaneously attacked the Anglo-Allied army at Quatre Bras and the Prussian army under Field Marshal Prince von Blücher at Ligny on 16 June, suggested that he was back on the form he had shown in the brilliant campaigns of spring 1814. He defeated the Prussians at Ligny and only bad staff work by his Chief of Staff, Marshal Soult, prevented him from utterly routing them.

Wellington was forced to retreat on 17 June to the defensible slopes of Mont St-Jean, 3 miles south of his headquarters at the village of Waterloo. Only 3½ miles wide, the battlefield was protected by woods and villages on both flanks and two well-defended farmhouses – Hougoumont and La Haie Sainte – in the centre. As in so many of his victorious battles in the Peninsular War, Wellington had chosen his ground with an expert eye. Napoleon, meanwhile, made a cardinal error in splitting off a large proportion of his troops under Marshal Grouchy, with orders to prevent the Prussians joining up with Wellington's Anglo-Allied force.

Heavy rainfall on 17 June meant that Napoleon had to wait until about 11.30 a.m. the next day for the muddy ground to firm up enough for his Grand Battery of eighty-four guns to be deployed and begin cannonading Wellington's line. This loss of time proved crucial because, unbeknownst to him, the Prussian army had evaded Grouchy and was marching in force upon his right flank.

Wellington meanwhile ordered some of those regiments in the direct line of fire of the French cannons to lie down behind the ridge, thus minimizing casualties. He used to say that soldiering was largely about guessing accurately what was 'on the other side of the hill', and his seasoned feel for the unusual ground of Waterloo – with its dips, folds and minor escarpments – served him well.

Wellington had invested Hougoumont with some of his best troops – including the light companies of the Foot Guards – because he knew that the loss of that strategic point would allow Napoleon to operate one of the extravagant flanking manoeuvres at which he was expert. The struggle for the farmhouse became a battle-within-a-battle, lasting all day and sucking in some 9,000 French troops, but although a small number of them did enter the courtyard at one point, and the roof caught fire at another, its 3,000 defenders nonetheless held out.

The next great assault on Wellington's position came at 1.30 p.m. when General Comte D'Erlon's huge corps of 16,000 men marched against Wellington's centre-left, in an attempt to punch through Wellington's force, split it in two, and roll each side up on itself. They were at first held back by the accurate musketry of the Anglo-Allied regiments facing them, and then put to flight by a bayonet charge led by Lieutenant General Sir Thomas Picton, who was killed just after it began.

At just the right psychological moment, a cavalry charge of the Union and Household Brigades under the overall command of Wellington's second-in-command, Lord Uxbridge, then turned D'Erlon's fighting retreat into a rout. Two of the four French eagle standards captured that day were taken then. In one of the few tactical errors made on the Anglo-Allied side, much of the cavalry went too far, and were badly mauled by Marshal Ney's lancers. Wellington severely admonished Uxbridge for this.

No-one knows to this day why (or even if) Marshal Ney ordered his huge cavalry assault against the centre-right of Wellington's line at 4 p.m., and there are even indications that it was entirely accidental. It was launched without the infantry and horse artillery support that might have led to its success. Wellington

The victorious generals of Waterloo, Wellington and Blücher, commemorated on a snuffbox.

continued...

ordered his infantry to form thirteen or so squares, none of which was penetrated by the French cuirassiers. Instead the cavalry rode round and round them, churning up the already muddy fields and exhausting itself, but not finding any way into the self-protective formations of infantrymen bristling with bayonets. Wellington himself took refuge inside one of the squares during this part of the battle.

It is estimated that the duke rode 20 miles that day on his horse Copenhagen, and he was always directing the most important part of the battle at great personal danger. Almost every member of his immediate staff was either killed or wounded during the battle, so far forward in the line were they at times. Wellington kept a very close and immediate control of every aspect of the struggle against the determined assaults of a veteran, homogeneous French army of 72,000 men.

At about 4.30 p.m. Prussian units of General von Bülow's corps began debouching on to the battlefield from the east, in accordance with a promise that Blücher had made Wellington early that morning. Having successfully evaded Grouchy, they began arriving in ever greater numbers, staving in Napoleon's right flank and forcing him as the battle progressed to divert more and more troops – including parts of his elite Imperial Guard – away from attacking Wellington and towards defending his exposed positions. The question as to whether Wellington would have won the battle without Blücher is an illegitimate one, since he would not even have fought had he thought that no reinforcements were arriving. (Grouchy, by contrast, ignored the cannon-fire to his west and continued to obey the emperor's by then woefully out-of-date orders.)

The crisis came at about 6.30 p.m. when, after much heavy fighting, the farmhouse of La Haie Sainte finally fell to Marshal Ney. The King's German Legion which had been courageously defending it – 90 per cent casualties were incurred within its high walls – finally ran out of ammunition and so had to concede the building to the French besiegers. Wellington later nobly accepted the blame for not having had a hole cut in the back of the farmhouse wall for ammunition to be passed through.

With La Haie Sainte – which commanded the Charleroi–Brussels road – now in French hands, the whole of Wellington's centre was threatened. Ney brought up horse artillery which poured fire into the Anglo-Allied line at short range. Regiments like the 27th Inniskillings which had formed squares took terrible casualties, but somehow held together. 'Ah,' said Wellington after the battle, 'they saved the centre of my line.'

Ney was unable to exploit this significant but temporary success. After D'Erlon's attack and his own cavalry débâcle, and troops being siphoned off to meet the Prussian threat to the west, and with Hougoumont still under siege, there was simply a dearth of troops available to him. Had Grouchy marched to the sound of guns as soon as he heard the Grand Battery open up before noon, it might have been a different matter.

Wellington, meanwhile, brought up reserves to plug holes in the line, occasionally placing British cavalry regiments behind foreign units that looked on the point of breaking. Putting himself at the head of solid Brunswick troops to close a gap between two British brigades, Wellington showed great bravery. As the contemporary historian General Sir James Shaw Kennedy recorded: 'He was necessarily under a close and very destructive infantry fire at a very short distance; at no other period of

the day were his great qualities as commander so strongly brought out, for it was the moment of his greatest peril as to the result of the action.' The line held.

The time had come at about 7 p.m. for Napoleon to unleash his eleven elite grenadier and chasseur battalions of the Old and Middle Guard in a final desperate attempt placed his reserve cavalry brigades under Major-General Sir Richard Vivian and Major-General Sir John Vandeleur in the best tactical position to deal with any breakthroughs. 'A black mass of the grenadiers of the Imperial Guard,' wrote a British observer, 'with music playing … came rolling onward from the farm of la Belle Alliance.'

The Anglo-Allied line held against three separate and furious assaults by the Imperial Guard, which nonetheless almost managed to reach the crest of the ridge that formed Wellington's line (it is invisible today owing to the subsequent building of the commemorative 130-foot-high Lion Mound). 'The ground was completely covered with those brave men,' recorded a Briton of the dead and dying grenadiers and chasseurs, 'who lay in various positions, mutilated in every conceivable way.'

Crying 'Up, Guards, ready!', Wellington ordered the 1st Regiment of Foot Guards to rise up from the shoulder-height corn and fire a musket volley at virtually point-blank range into the French ranks. Lieutenant Harry Powell later recorded how, 'Whether it was from the sudden and unexpected appearance of a Corps so near them, which must have seemed as starting out of the ground, or the tremendously heavy fire we poured into them, La Garde, which had never before failed in an attack, suddenly stopped.' Once the momentum had drained out of the attack, it was a matter of time before the superior Anglo-Allied musketry and artillery firepower of the line prevailed over the columns of French. A brilliant flanking movement by Sir John Colborne's 52nd Regiment against the chasseurs of the Guard completed the rout.

Snapping his telescope shut and riding to the crest of the ridge, Wellington then waved his cocked hat, the signal for a general advance across his whole line, crying: 'Go forward, boys, and secure your victory!' The cries from the French, first of 'La Garde recule!' and then 'Sauve qui peut!' and 'Nous sommes trahis!' indicated that Wellington had won his greatest victory of a long and distinguished military career.

Map

To Waterloo and Brussels · Mont St-Jean · **To Louvain** · Mont St-Jean Farm · **To Wavre**

ANGLO-ALLIED FORCES · Household brigade · Union brigade

Braine l'Alleud · **To Hal** · Picton · Bylandt

La Haie Sainte · Hougoumont

La Belle Alliance · FRENCH FORCES · Lobau · Plancenoit · Guard · Le Caillou

To Nivelles

To Quatre Bras and Charleroi

N

0   1/2 km
0   1/2 miles

Legend:

- Infantry
- Cavalry
- French gun battery
1. 11.30 Reille and Jérôme attack Hougoumont
2. 1.30 D'Erlon attacks Anglo-Allied centre
3. 4.00 Ney's cavalry charges begin
4. 4.30 Prussians under Bülow attack
5. 6.30 Ney attacks and takes La Haie Sainte
6. 7.00 Prussians under Zieten arrive
7. 7.30 Old Guard's final attack

to break through Wellington's line. As he later observed, Wellington was fighting with the dense Forest of Soignies to his rear, with only one road through it, so any retreat would inevitably have turned into a monstrous rout. The French Imperial Guard had provided the *coup de grâce* several times in battles of the past; now was the chance to exploit Wellington's paucity of reserves, spot a weak point in the line and pour through to snatch victory.

Wellington had about a quarter of an hour to meet this challenge and he used it to reorganize his defences, taking care not to allow units to fall back in such a way that might be misinterpreted as a retreat by other hard-pressed troops further down the line. Thirty cannon loaded with double-grapeshot were manoeuvred into position and he

The Battle of Waterloo, one of a series of paintings of the subject by the naval and military artist Denis Dighton (1792–1827). Wellington looks on as French hussars and Polish lancers fight the British infantry. The farmhouse of Hougoumont is in the background on the far right.

> 'He is one of the purest glories of France.'
> NAPOLEON

LOUIS-NICOLAS DAVOUT

ANDREW UFFINDELL

1770–1823

LOUIS-NICOLAS DAVOUT was not the most charismatic of Napoleon's famous twenty-six marshals, for that distinction lay with more colourful but mercurial colleagues, men such as Lannes, Murat and Ney. Where Davout shone was as a consistently professional, competent and just soldier, and as one of the most intelligent and educated of the marshals. He was more than just a heroic combat soldier, and performed some of his most outstanding services off the battlefield. A capable organizer, administrator, logistician and trainer of troops, he was also adept at collecting and evaluating intelligence. The rigour with which he did his duty and his strictness, even harshness, in upholding standards won him respect and resentment in equal measure.

(Opposite) **Louis-Nicolas Davout, Duke of Auerstädt,** Prince of Eckmühl, and Marshal of the French Empire, painted by Tito Marzocchi de Belluci, c.1852.

Davout was born on 10 May 1770 in Burgundy in eastern France, and came from an old noble family with a tradition of military service. 'When a d'Avout is born,' it was said locally, 'a sword springs from the scabbard.' After a good education at a royal military school at Auxerre and then at the École Militaire in Paris, Davout joined the Royal-Champagne cavalry regiment in February 1788 as a sub-lieutenant. His outspokenness and fervent support for the Revolution that broke out the following year contributed to a turbulent period of service and six weeks in a military prison. He then took extended leave, and used the opportunity to study and improve his understanding of his profession.

A military apprenticeship

Davout remained inactive for less than a year. In September 1791 he was elected junior lieutenant colonel of a local battalion of volunteers, and in 1792 saw action against the Austrians in northern France and Belgium. In April 1793 he had his men fire on his own commander-in-chief, Lieutenant General Charles-François Dumouriez, in an unsuccessful attempt to prevent him from deserting to the Austrians.

Despite such notable actions, Davout repeatedly had to overcome setbacks in the early stages of his career. He was promoted to general of brigade in July 1793, but as a former noble he had to resign from the army the following month as the Revolution became more extreme. He and his mother were both arrested and were in danger of being executed until a coup toppled the radical Jacobin faction and ended the Reign of Terror. The episode helps to explain Davout's subsequent support for Napoleon as a strongman who could maintain order and stability. Davout resumed his army service in September 1794, but was captured a year later when the city of Mannheim surrendered to the Austrians. He was exchanged in 1796, and then served in the Rhine theatre until hostilities with Austria ended in April 1797.

During this time, Davout found an influential friend and mentor in General Louis-Charles-Antoine Desaix de Veygoux. It was through Desaix that Davout met Napoleon for the first time and secured a place in his expedition to Egypt in 1798. He repeatedly saw action, particularly when he was detached with Desaix's force to pacify Upper Egypt, and he further distinguished himself during the fighting at Aboukir on the Mediterranean coast in July and August 1799. At one stage he found himself trapped inside a house with about fifteen men, while Ottoman Turks tried to break in. Davout had his men fire through the closed door, killing several assailants, and then, taking advantage of the surprise, broke out with fixed bayonets and reached safety.

Davout returned to France in May 1800 and was promoted to general of division in July. Meanwhile, Napoleon had seized power in a *coup d'état*, and by February 1801 he had secured a peace on the continent of Europe that would last for four years. Davout, who had divorced his first wife in 1794, made a happier marriage with Louise-Aimée-Julie Leclerc in November 1801. Since Aimée was the sister of Napoleon's brother-in-law, Davout became one of the extended Bonaparte clan, and this was undoubtedly one reason for his appointment that same month as commander of the crack *Grenadiers à pied* of the Guard.

When Napoleon established the Empire three years later, Davout was one of eighteen generals to be made marshals. Some commentators have expressed surprise at his selection, not least as he was only 34 years old and the youngest of this first creation. But Napoleon could hardly do otherwise than elevate all four of the Imperial Guard's most senior generals, including Davout, to the marshalate, in order to enhance the Guard's prestige and avoid destructive jealousies among its component units. Napoleon also knew Davout's ability as a soldier, disciplinarian and administrator, and recognized his potential to develop as he assumed higher responsibilities.

Emergence of a great commander

It was Napoleon's campaigns of 1805–9 in central and eastern Europe that saw Davout emerge as a great battlefield commander. He had already proved himself as a brave and capable subordinate, and had a mixture of experience in both the infantry and cavalry, but had yet to make a name for himself in a large combat command. He was entrusted with the Grande Armée's superb III Corps, a unit he had spent two years training and disciplining in a camp at Bruges, and one that he himself compared with Julius Caesar's renowned Tenth Legion.

On 2 December 1805 Davout played a key role in Napoleon's most famous victory, the Battle of Austerlitz. Summoned northwards from Vienna as Napoleon concentrated his forces for a masterly counter-stroke against the Austro-Russian army, Davout's leading division marched 70 miles in 46 hours. His arrival checked the allied attempt to outflank Napoleon, and made possible the destruction of the allied southern wing (see pp. 128–9).

Louis-Nicolas Davout

When hostilities broke out with Prussia in October 1806, Davout helped crush its army with his brilliant but costly victory at Auerstädt (see pp. 144–5), and then took part in a bitter winter campaign against the Russians in Poland and East Prussia. On 8 February 1807 Napoleon was saved from defeat at the bloody Battle of Eylau when Davout arrived with his corps from the south.

Following the conclusion of peace with Russia and Prussia at Tilsit in July, Napoleon entrusted Davout with the role of governor-general of the Duchy of Warsaw, a satellite state created from Polish territory previously held by Prussia. Davout was one of the few marshals equal to such important administrative and political roles.

Davout added to his reputation in the 1809 campaign against Austria. He played a key role in the initial phase, the defeat of the Austrian invasion of Bavaria, Napoleon's ally in southern Germany. This culminated in the Battle of Eckmühl on 22 April, where Davout with just 20,000 troops contained the Austrian army under Archduke Charles until Napoleon could arrive and fall on its southern flank. Davout was made Prince of Eckmühl in recognition of his conduct, and he won further laurels in a massive and costly battle at Wagram near Vienna on 5–6 July. As so often, his corps was once again on the right of the line, traditionally the place of honour, and after hard fighting in which he had a horse shot beneath him, Davout drove back the Austrian left wing and contributed to a victory that induced the Austrians to make peace.

'The brave will die gloriously here – only the cowards will visit the waste- lands of Siberia.'
DAVOUT EXHORTS HIS MEN AT THE BATTLE OF EYLAU

The Battle of Wagram 5–6 July 1809, in an aquatint by Louis François Mariage. More than 80,000 men were killed or injured in one of the largest and bloodiest battles of the Napoleonic Wars.

THE BATTLE OF AUERSTÄDT

AUERSTÄDT WAS DAVOUT'S FINEST ACHIEVEMENT as a commander and the victory from which he took his title when made a duke in 1808. It was a battle won in his own right as an independent commander, without Napoleon's direct supervision.

When war broke out with Prussia in the autumn of 1806, Napoleon advanced northeastwards from southern Germany on Berlin, with his army so disposed that it could turn in any direction and swiftly concentrate once it encountered the enemy.

The Prussians belatedly began to retreat northwards, but were attacked on 14 October in the twin actions of Jena and Auerstädt. Napoleon himself crushed part of the Prussian forces on the heights above the town of Jena, but was unaware that the bulk, 63,500 troops, were in fact 12 miles to the north at Auerstädt, where they faced the 26,000 men of Davout's III Corps.

Auerstädt was an encounter battle, in which both sides unexpectedly ran into each other in thick fog. The fighting developed as Davout's three infantry divisions came into action one after the other, between 7 and 10.30 a.m. For their part, the Prussians generally fought bravely, but failed to exploit their numerical superiority, partly because congestion delayed the arrival of their reinforcements. Even after the fog lifted, they launched a series of disjointed attacks instead of coordi-

nating a general onslaught. Nonetheless, Davout was repeatedly on the brink of defeat, until the arrival of another division enabled him to restore the situation and deliver a further blow.

The confusion on the Prussian side was increased by the dislocation of their high command. The commander-in-chief, Karl Wilhelm Ferdinand, Duke of Brunswick, was mortally wounded, and there was a delay before King Frederick William III could be informed. The king failed to get a grip on the battle and, not realizing that he faced only one corps, decided to retreat. Davout launched a general offensive that overcame heavy resistance and by the end of the day had turned the Prussian withdrawal into a rout.

(Above) **Napoleon leads his army** – headed by Davout's III Corps – through the Brandenburg Gate in Berlin, following Davout's victory at Auerstädt against a Prussian force more than twice the size of his own, October 1806. This painting is by Charles Meynier, 1810.

The invasion of Russia

It was nearly three years before Davout fought in another campaign. As relations with Tsar Alexander I deteriorated, Napoleon prepared to invade Russia and entrusted Davout with a leading role in assembling an army of over half a million troops. For the actual invasion in June 1812, Davout commanded I Corps, comprising 70,000 men, by far the largest corps and one widely recognized, with its discipline and meticulously organized logistics, as the finest formation in the Grande Armée after the Imperial Guard.

Napoleon failed to trap the Russian armies in the opening weeks of his onslaught, and was instead drawn deeper into the interior as they retreated. It was during these early stages that Davout fought a skilful defensive battle at Mogilev on 23 July, in which he checked a numerically superior Russian army under General Prince Peter Bagration. But it was at Borodino on 7 September that Davout saw the heaviest

Louis-Nicolas Davout

Napoleon gave III Corps the honour of leading the Grande Armée's entry into Berlin on 25 October. Auerstädt had been a triumph of superior discipline, training, experience and flexible tactics, but, above all, of better generalship. Davout had kept tight control of his corps, skilfully assessed the terrain and the timing of his moves, and personally inspired his men with his coolness under fire. The ability and professionalism of Davout and his famous trio of divisional commanders (Gudin, Friant and Morand) formed a stark contrast to the fumblings of the Prussian generals as they reacted to the French moves. But the cost was high: Davout had lost one in every four of his men.

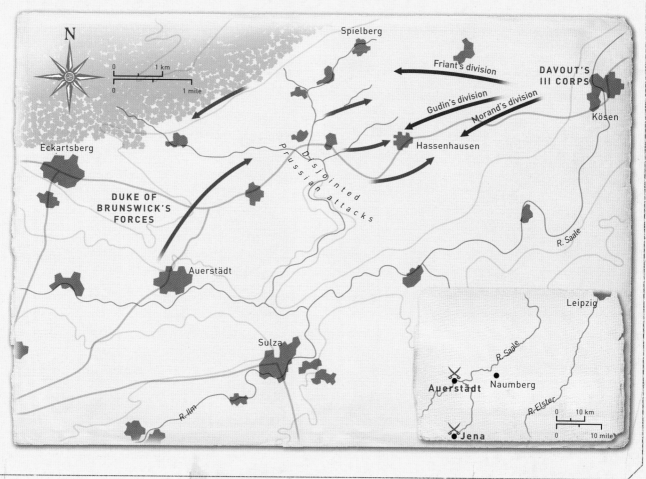

fighting. Napoleon attacked the Russians head on, and both sides suffered appalling losses. Davout himself was unhorsed, knocked unconscious and wounded in the belly, but refused to leave his command (see also pp. 152–3).

Napoleon occupied Moscow a week later, but found that Alexander I refused to sue for peace. Five weeks after his arrival, Napoleon abandoned the city and was soon in full retreat. Undermined by relentless marching, exhaustion, indiscipline, inadequate supplies and spells of snow and bitter cold, the Grande Armée became increasingly demoralized and began to disintegrate. Davout's corps initially formed the rearguard, but was relieved after being temporarily cut off and mauled on 3 November. A fortnight later, as Napoleon continued the retreat westwards from Smolensk, the Russians again tried to sever the rearmost corps at Krasnoe. Davout was widely blamed when Ney, the popular hero of the retreat, was cut off and given up for lost until he unexpectedly reappeared with just 900 survivors. In fact, Davout could not have done

The future Marshal Ney as a young sub-lieutenant of the 4th Hussar Regiment in 1792, in a portrait by Adolphe Brune. Dubbed the 'bravest of the brave' by Napoleon, Ney ended his life in front of a firing-squad in Paris in December 1815, Davout's words in defence of his fellow marshal having fallen on deaf ears.

more to support Ney without destroying his own corps, but he had made influential enemies, not least Marshals Berthier and Murat, while his professional and realistic outlook was often seen by more head-strong men as a lack of dynamism and an unwill-ingness to cooperate.

Hamburg

In the wake of the disastrous invasion of Russia, Napoleon raised a new army in the first months of 1813 with which to defend his empire in central Europe. But he was faced with a coalition that by the middle of August included all the major European powers, and he was short of reliable subordinates whom he could entrust with detached commands. When Cossacks occupied Hamburg in March, Napoleon sent Davout to retake the city, for it was of vital strategic and commercial importance. Davout then used Hamburg as a base for semi-independent operations in northern Germany.

After a massive defeat at Leipzig in October, Napoleon retreated across the Rhine and prepared to defend Paris in the face of an allied invasion of France. This left Davout isolated in Hamburg, and by December 1813 he found himself besieged by an army at least twice his own strength. Despite the numerical odds, he repelled several major assaults. To ensure the city held out, he had to take harsh actions, including the demolition of suburbs to clear his fields of fire and the expulsion of 25,000 civilians who were unable to feed themselves. He was subsequently accused of brutal and arbitrary acts, but was able to demonstrate that he had acted justly – in fact, he had moderated the measures that Napoleon had ordered him to take. He also enforced strict discipline on his troops to try to prevent looting. Not until the end of May 1814, seven weeks after Napoleon's abdication and six months after being isolated inside the city, did the French troops evacuate Hamburg and they returned to France with their weapons and baggage.

Final years

Exiled to the Mediterranean island of Elba, Napoleon escaped in February 1815 and swiftly regained power from King Louis XVIII, but faced the prospect of renewed war against a European coalition. Davout, who had remained unemployed under the restored Bourbon monarchy, now became Napoleon's minister of war and governor of Paris. He would have preferred a field command, and the outcome of the Waterloo campaign might have been different had his wish been granted. But Napoleon needed a strong, feared and capable soldier-administrator to rebuild the French army and control the politically unstable capital.

By 22 June Napoleon had suffered a decisive defeat at Waterloo and abdicated for the second and final time. Davout prepared to defend Paris to enable a provisional

Louis-Nicolas Davout

146

government to negotiate the best possible terms with the invading allied armies. He did not want to waste lives in a pitched battle, but was prepared to fight smaller-scale actions to strengthen the French negotiating position.

After an armistice was agreed on 3 July, Davout resigned as minister of war and took command of the French army, which withdrew south of the Loire. By giving the army's submission to Louis XVIII, Davout helped to avert the risk of civil war. He also did his best to help officers who found themselves at risk of being arrested for having supported Napoleon. When the most prominent victim, Marshal Ney, was put on trial, Davout spoke vainly in his defence.

By the end of 1815 Davout was once again a private citizen, and remained out of favour for the next two years. He then returned to public life, but died from consumption on 1 June 1823 at the age of 53.

The iron marshal

Davout was ruthless, ambitious and sometimes brutally sarcastic. Often taciturn, he lacked the charm and easy manner of some of his peers; he was also physically unimpressive, being bald, bespectacled and careless of his appearance. But Davout was brave and incorruptible, and as outspoken with high-ranking colleagues as with his juniors. On one occasion he apologized publicly to a subordinate he had unfairly berated, and he made firm friends as well as bitter enemies. When one of his divisional commanders, Charles-Étienne Gudin de la Sablonnière, was mortally wounded in 1812, he broke down and wept.

Many accounts that portray Davout in a hostile light were in fact written by unreliable witnesses, notably Louis-Antoine Fauvelet de Bourienne and the Duchesse d'Abrantès, who were mentally unstable, intent on making a fortune or keen to win favour from the restored Bourbons. In contrast, soldiers who actually served under Davout often had more positive views. One brigade commander frankly admitted:

> I, too, had arguments with the Prince of Eckmühl, and I asked the minister of war to permit me to leave his army corps before the Russian campaign. I am well aware that he was not always amiable, but I will always be proud of having served under him, of having learned much from him, and if we had to make war again, I would not ask for better than to serve once more under his orders. Those who serve zealously are sure to obtain his approval. You know that with him you will be well commanded, which is something, and minor disagreements are compensated for by big advantages.

Davout was a lucky general. He did not have to fight in the Iberian Peninsula or face Wellington in battle; nor did he share in Napoleon's final defeats, for he successfully defended Hamburg during the 1813 and 1814 campaigns and served in Paris in 1815. Only in the invasion of Russia did Davout experience disaster, and the damage to his reputation was temporary.

The secret of Davout's success lay in his combination of intelligence, education and strength of character. Dubbed 'the just', 'the terrible' and 'the iron marshal', Davout was not the most flamboyant of Napoleon's marshals, but for sheer competence, moral courage and consistent reliability, he eclipsed them all.

MIKHAIL KUTUZOV

1745–1813

ALAN PALMER

AMONG EUROPE'S OUTSTANDING COMMANDERS Mikhail Illarionovich Kutuzov, 'saviour of the Fatherland in the Patriotic War', is unique in two respects. Although he cracked the legend of Napoleon's invincibility at Borodino, he was never credited with victory in any major battle; and he owes his enduring fame, not to military historians, but to his pride of place in a great novel, Tolstoy's *War and Peace*, where he epitomizes the Russian people's spirit of resistance to the invader.

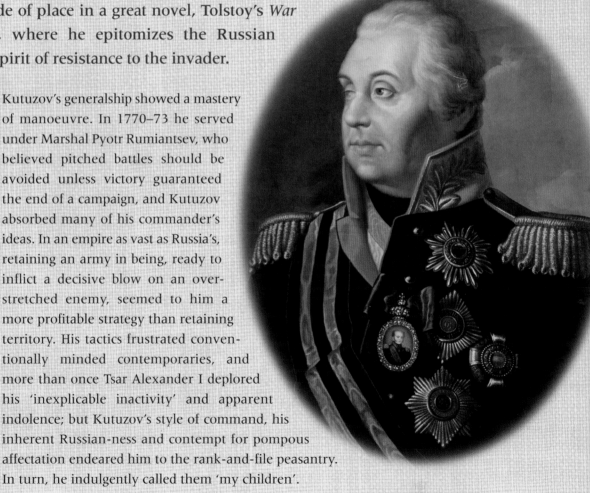

Prince Mikhail Kutuzov, the man credited with saving Russia from Napoleon, in a copy of a portrait by R. M. Volkov, 1813.

Kutuzov's generalship showed a mastery of manoeuvre. In 1770–73 he served under Marshal Pyotr Rumiantsev, who believed pitched battles should be avoided unless victory guaranteed the end of a campaign, and Kutuzov absorbed many of his commander's ideas. In an empire as vast as Russia's, retaining an army in being, ready to inflict a decisive blow on an over-stretched enemy, seemed to him a more profitable strategy than retaining territory. His tactics frustrated conventionally minded contemporaries, and more than once Tsar Alexander I deplored his 'inexplicable inactivity' and apparent indolence; but Kutuzov's style of command, his inherent Russian-ness and contempt for pompous affectation endeared him to the rank-and-file peasantry. In turn, he indulgently called them 'my children'.

Mikhail Kutuzov

From cadet to governor-general

Kutuzov was born in St Petersburg on 6 September 1745, the son of a general with thirty years service in the Corps of Engineers behind him. Almost inevitably the boy followed his father's career. At the age of 12 he entered the military engineering school as a cadet private, working his way through the ranks while showing outstanding intelligence in his studies. He was commissioned in 1761. By the following spring he was in the Volga delta, serving as a captain in an infantry regiment under Colonel Alexei Suvorov, whose empathy with the peasant soldiery had already made him a legendary commander.

In later campaigns Kutuzov became Suvorov's partner against the Turks, but their first acquaintance was brief. Kutuzov went on to serve three years in Estonia as aide to the military governor, and then helped to crush a Polish rebellion in a clash of arms near Warsaw. But in Catherine the Great's reign (1762–96) reputations were made around the Black Sea, and in 1770 Major Kutuzov went south to Moldavia to join Rumiantsev's army in pushing the Turks out of what is now Romania. Three years later he was wounded leading an assault on Alushta, on the southeast coast of the Crimea. A musket ball penetrated the temple, weakening his right eye; recuperation was slow.

A two-year truce in the Russo-Turkish conflict enabled Kutuzov to tour widely. He met Frederick the Great in Potsdam, received eye treatment at Leyden in the Netherlands and visited London and Vienna. But by 1776 he was again in the Crimea, serving Suvorov with such intrepidity that in 1782 he rose to command the crack Corps of Chasseurs. 'He's crafty and shrewd, that one!' commented Suvorov, 'No one will fool him.'

For more than a year (1788–9) Kutuzov led sorties during the siege of Ochakov, the citadel commanding the Bug–Dniester estuary. Again he was wounded in the temple, completely losing the sight of his right eye, but he was back in the field within weeks. The campaign reached a climax with a bloody assault on the fortress of Ismail. 'General Kutuzov commanded my left flank, but he was my right arm,' a triumphant Suvorov reported to St Petersburg.

Under the allegedly 'mad Tsar' Paul I (reigned 1796–1801) Kutuzov saw little fighting. Instead, he proved an able ambassador in Constantinople and Berlin. He therefore missed the famous 1799 campaign in Italy, when Suvorov defeated the French before subsequently extricating his men from a trap in Switzerland by skilfully retreating through the Alpine valleys.

By then Kutuzov was governor-general in Vilna (Vilnius in Lithuania), achieving such success that he was given similar responsibilities in St Petersburg. He was among Tsar Paul's dinner guests a few hours before his murder by officers in a conspiracy that brought his 23-year-old son Alexander to the throne. Kutuzov soon learnt that Alexander, his companion at table, had approved the plot, though on the understanding his father would not be killed. Memory of that night engendered lasting mistrust between Kutuzov and Alexander.

The War of the Third Coalition

War came in September 1805, with Alexander joining Britain and Austria in the Third Coalition against Napoleon. Kutuzov received command of an army to support an Austrian advance into Bavaria, while Alexander (yet to experience his baptism of fire) mobilized a more powerful army to join his ally in Moravia. Kutuzov's vanguard reached the River Inn too late to save Austria's General Mack from humiliating capitulation at Ulm, and with hopes of invading Bavaria dashed he put into practice his modified Rumiantsev doctrine. On 24 October the army began a retreat down the Danube and into Moravia.

The French pursuit was hampered by wintry weather, Kutuzov's cunning, and running battles in which the Georgian general, Prince Bagration, commanded the rearguard with courage and enterprise. Marshal Murat, commanding Napoleon's cavalry reserve, was deliberately tempted to turn aside for what his emperor angrily called 'the petty triumph of entering Vienna'. Bagration won valuable time by a delaying action at Schöngraben (16 November). Three days later Kutuzov's troops joined the Russo-Austrian army in Moravia at Brünn (Brno, in what is now the Czech Republic).

Kutuzov urged Alexander and the Austrian emperor, Francis, to continue the retreat into Galicia. Winter would play havoc with the invaders, he argued, and it was then that the allies should fall on them in a decisive battle. Both emperors rejected this advice, preferring the conventional strategy of Francis's chief of staff, Weyrother, who wished to envelop the French and recover Vienna. Kutuzov was ordered to prepare for battle above Austerlitz, 15 miles east of Brünn, on a snow-covered plateau pitted with frozen lakes. He obeyed, but suspected that Weyrother was playing into Napoleon's hands by proposing an initial outflanking assault that would expose the centre to French counter-attack. (For the Battle of Austerlitz, see pp. 128–9.)

'It was as though some kind of power emanated from the venerable commander, inspiring those around him.'

AN OFFICER NAMED MITAREVSKI RECALLS KUTUZOV AT BORODINO

Kutuzov's fears were justified. He could do little to avert disaster. When he sought to delay General Miloradovich's corps from supporting Weyrother's advance, Alexander ordered him to send the troops forward. Within minutes the Russians received the full impact of the French cavalry, and Kutuzov was wounded on the cheek by a glancing shot. He remained in command, alerting Bagration on the left flank to form defensive squares and check the French thrust. After five hours of battle the tsar's brother, Constantine, led a cavalry charge on his own initiative, without orders from Kutuzov. It incurred such heavy casualties that coordinated counter-attack was impossible. The broken Russian troops trudged eastwards while Austria made a separate peace.

Back in St Petersburg no attempt was made to brand Kutuzov a scapegoat; blame was assigned to Weyrother and the Austrians. But with Alexander preferring non-Russian generals such as the Hanoverian Bennigsen and Barclay de Tolly (a Latvian of Scottish descent), Kutuzov was sent to Kiev as military commander and missed the grim campaign of 1806–7, when Napoleon defeated Bennigsen at Eylau and Friedland.

Defeating the Turks, 1811–12

After another term as governor in Vilna, in 1811 Kutuzov received command of the Army of the Danube with orders to bring final victory in the long-running Turkish wars. This task he accomplished within a year by a campaign planned with characteristic cunning. The Turks were lured across the lower Danube near Rustchuk (modern Ruse in Bulgaria) and advanced towards Bucharest. Kutuzov avoided battle in the summer heat, but in September re-crossed the river upstream, surrounding the Turks on the south bank. Rather than incur heavy casualties in a frontal assault, he settled down to a winter siege. In St Petersburg Alexander fumed at 'General Dawdler's' hesitancy and the slowness of peace talks preceding

(Opposite) **Prince Mikhail Barclay de Tolly,** a Latvian of Scottish descent who commanded the Russian First Army at Borodino, depicted here by George Dawe, 1829.

Mikhail Kutuzov

150

the Treaty of Bucharest (May 1812). But Kutuzov's military and diplomatic skills kept Turkey from alliance with France and enabled the Army of Moravia to move north and tighten the grip on Napoleon in the great retreat later that year.

Commander-in-chief

Napoleon's invasion of Russia on 24 June 1812 found Kutuzov on his estate, in poor health, obese and crippled with rheumatism. It seemed improbable he would see active service again. But as the Grande Armée drew nearer Moscow popular clamour for a 'true Russian' leader to check the invaders induced Alexander to appoint Kutuzov commander-in-chief in suc-cession to Barclay. On 29 August he reached field head-quarters near Vyasma; his arrival boosted morale in a weary army.

Relentlessly hot weather took a heavy toll on Napoleon's men, and in ten days he lost one-third of his troops, either through sickness or desertion. Kutuzov realized Napoleon's predic-ament and prepared for an early clash of arms. He selected a formidable defensive position at Borodino, 20 miles east of Vyasma, where on 7 September the French and Russian armies fought each other to a stalemate at a cost of some 75,000 casualties on both sides (see pp. 152–3). Having dealt a critical, though not decisive, blow to the Grande Armée, Kutozov and his forces slipped away to the east.

At first St Petersburg and Moscow celebrated Borodino as a victory. The tsar sent Kutuzov 100,000 silver roubles and a marshal's baton. But on 12 September the Muscovites realized the truth, and in fear began to flee eastwards. Next morning at Fili, 5 miles from the Kremlin, Kutuzov convened a council of war in a peasant's cottage. Three generals urged a battle to save Moscow; three backed their marshal's strategy of continued retreat. 'Napoleon is a torrent which as yet we are unable to stem,' Kutuzov explained. 'Moscow will be the sponge that sucks him dry.' That night the Russian army filed through des-erted streets and overflowed into the emptiness of the steppe. The Grande Armée entered Moscow

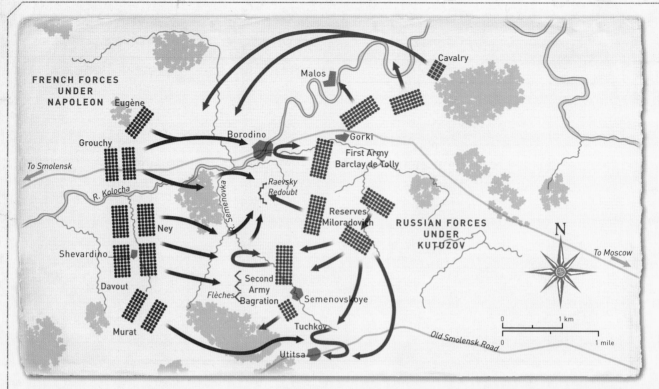

FRENCH FORCES
UNDER
NAPOLEON   Eugène

Grouchy

To Smolensk

R. Kolocha

Ney

Shevardino

Davout

Murat

Malos

Cavalry

Borodino

Gorki

First Army
Barclay de Tolly

R. Semenovka

Raevsky
Redoubt

Reserves
Miloradovich

RUSSIAN FORCES
UNDER
KUTUZOV

N

To Moscow

Flèches

Second
Army
Bagration

Semenovskoye

Tuchkov

Utitsa

Old Smolensk Road

0   1 km

0   1 mile

THE BATTLE OF
BORODINO

KUTUZOV'S CHOSEN GROUND to take
on Napoleon's Grande Armée in
the late summer of 1812 lay 75 miles
west of Moscow around four villages –
Borodino itself, Gorki, Semenovskoye and Utitsa. A
tributary of the River Moskva, the Kolocha, protected his
northern flank. He placed the First Army, under the
command of Barclay de Tolly, on the Kolocha's steep south
bank, covering Gorki and centred on a redoubt named
after its commander, Raevsky. High ground, broken by a
rivulet leading to Semenovskoye, extended southwards for
3 miles and was held by Bagration's Second Army. South

of the stream *flèches* (fortified earthworks) were dug. Miloradovich's corps
formed a reserve, while General
Tuchkov covered the birch forest
in front of Utitsa in the south. In all, Kutuzov deployed
120,000 men and 640 cannon in a convex 5-mile curve;
Napoleon compressed 133,000 men and 590 cannon
along 4 miles of front.

A sharp engagement on Saturday 5 September
gained Murat an outlying redoubt at Shevardino, 3 miles
southwest of Borodino. There followed a lull for regrouping
on Sunday, Kutuzov's 67th birthday. The main battle began

on 14–15 September to find the city in flames – a massive act of defiant arson had denied
the invaders food and fodder. Napoleon expected Alexander to sue for peace, and over the
following month sent three conciliatory messages to him, but without response.

The 'old fox' was elusive. He fell back not towards St Petersburg as expected but
southeast, later veering west and setting up a fortified camp near Tarutino, 55 miles
south of Moscow. There he remained for four weeks, refitting and re-clothing his men.
'I will play for time, lull Napoleon and not disturb him in Moscow,' Kutuzov told an
aide. But at the same time he completed a comprehensive grand design, which was sent
to Alexander and finally approved, in amended form, on 23 October. Kutuzov
proposed a classic pincer movement: he would trail a retreating Napoleon while
Admiral Chichagov's Army of Moravia headed northwest to intercept the French
between Smolensk and Minsk and General Wittgenstein's First Army Corps swept
southwest from St Petersburg to Podolsk and on to rendezvous with Chichagov.

Mikhail Kutuzov

at 6 a.m. on Monday 7 September, with 100 French cannon bombarding the centre. Italians in Eugène Beauharnais's corps speedily captured Borodino village and Poniatowski's Polish corps took Utitsa, but the key positions around the Raevsky redoubt withstood wave after wave of assault for three hours. Although concentrated fire from 300 cannon halted a French thrust on Semenovskoye, Murat's cavalry swept forward against the *flèches*, which were taken after Bagration fell mortally wounded, to the dismay and demoralization of his men. By noon Kutuzov had rallied the Second Army, which he regrouped on neighbouring heights. At 2 p.m. Beauharnais threw three divisions of infantry supported by guns and cavalry against the Raevsky redoubt, and after an hour's onslaught it fell; exhaustion prevented the French exploiting their success. A last Russian counter-attack was thwarted by Napoleon's reserve artillery.

Around 5 p.m. the fighting died away inconclusively. The French had suffered 33,000 casualties in gaining a mile of hillocks above ruined villages. Kutuzov lost 44,000 men, but his troops were ensconced on a plateau 1,000 yards to the east, well placed to renew battle the next day. They did not; for though Kutuzov had inflicted a grievous blow on the French he had not routed them. To fulfil his strategic doctrine he needed to keep his army in good order and draw Napoleon even deeper into Russia before striking a second time at the increasingly exhausted invaders. Through rising mist at dawn next day Napoleon perceived 'the old fox' had slipped away overnight.

Borodino was the second bloodiest battle of the Napoleonic Wars, surpassed only by the four-day Battle of Leipzig. 'The most terrible of all my battles,' Napoleon was to recall in exile on St Helena. 'The French showed themselves worthy of victory, the Russians of being invincible.'

Kutuzov remained convinced Napoleon would soon find his position in Moscow untenable. On 18 October he ordered a surprise descent on Murat's cavalry screen near Winkovo. It was little more than a skirmish, but came as a warning to the French. So too did a light snowfall. Napoleon saw the need to evacuate Moscow before Russian horsemen and the onset of winter cut links with his empire. On 19 October he left the city.

Napoleon turned southwest at first, seeking sustenance from the fertile lands around Kaluga, but at Maloyaroslavets (24 October) General Docturov's corps intercepted his vanguard, Beauharnais's Italians. The town changed hands seven times before the main armies arrived. Neither Kutuzov nor Napoleon was ready to risk an impromptu major battle. Next morning Napoleon was fortunate to avoid capture by a Cossack patrol while reconnoitring the position. A few hours later he took the momentous decision to abandon the march on Kaluga in preference for Mozhaisk and the battle-ravaged road to the west.

(Above) **The Battle of Borodino,** in a painting by Peter von Hess (1792–1878). Fought on 7 September 1812, Borodino is said to have been the greatest battle in history up to that date, involving as it did as many as a quarter of a million men.

Mikhail Kutuzov

Trailing the great retreat

Kutuzov gave chase next day. He headed across country for Vyazma, hoping to outstrip Napoleon, who was shadowed by Miloradovich's corps and Cossacks under their hetman (leader), Matvei Platov. But Kutuzov made slow progress in the open country. When Napoleon reached Vyazma, Kutuzov was still 50 miles away. It was left to Miloradovich and Platov to maul the French rearguard.

On 4 November heavy snow fell. Blizzards enveloped both armies two days later. The French suffered appallingly, neither men nor horses being prepared for such conditions. Kutuzov's troops were better clothed and their horses better shod, able to cover 16 miles a day. But the snow left armies isolated. During the following week Kutuzov came closer to Napoleon's headquarters than he realized, just 2 miles away on 15 November. Next day Chichagov captured Minsk, and Wittgenstein's First Army Corps already held Vitebsk, but Kutuzov had no knowledge of their respective positions. He was still determined to preserve the army for a *coup de grâce*, probably along the main north–south divide, the River Berezina. For this reason he failed to exploit early gains in a three-day encounter with the French near Krasnoe, and on 17 November was surprised by the Imperial Guard and forced to retreat.

Ironically, his caution at Krasnoe robbed Kutuzov of participation in the decisive battle he sought. He was more than 40 miles short of the French rearguard when on 25 November Napoleon approached the Berezina, where three divisions of Chichagov's army already held the west bank and had destroyed the bridges. A feint by Marshal Oudinot drew Chichagov south from Studienka, the one fordable point where Napoleon's engineers hastened to construct pontoon bridges. Fighting continued around Studienka throughout two days. The French fought off the returning Chichagov and countered thrusts by Wittgenstein from the northeast. In crossing the Berezina the French lost 25,000 soldiers and some 28,000 non-combatants, but

The Burning of Moscow in 1812, by Jean Charles Langlois, 1854. On the night of 13/14 September 1812 Kutuzov withdrew his army from Moscow – but not before it was set alight, thus denying the advancing French both food and fodder. Just over a month later Napoleon gave the order to retreat from Moscow.

most deaths were caused by the collapse of the pontoons and their eventual firing.

Kutuzov finally reached the Berezina on the night of 29/30 November. The temperature fell dramatically in the first week of December. 'General Winter' caused more French casualties than any Russian army, with weary half-frozen stragglers robbed and killed by Cossack marauders. Napoleon left his troops on 5 December, hurrying back to Paris. The last fighting soldier of the once Grand Armée, Marshal Ney, crossed the Niemen out of Russia on 14 December, the day after Kutuzov and the main body of his army entered Vilna.

The death of Kutuzov

Tsar Alexander, who rejoined his army on 23 December, lavished praise on Kutuzov, creating him Prince of Smolensk and bestowing high decorations on him. But behind the façade of mutual respect lay deep divisions in temperament and policy. Kutuzov thought the fighting over, now the invaders were expelled from Russia; Alexander believed he had a divine mission to liberate Europe.

Reluctantly Kutuzov remained commander-in-chief. Weary, worn out and fearful of what would happen once Napoleon raised a new army, he accompanied the tsar when he entered Prussian Poland in mid January. Looking ahead he predicted, 'We can cross the Elbe easily enough, but we shall soon re-cross it with a bloody nose.' He was right, but he did not live to see the setback, nor the final victory, at Leipzig. Kutuzov collapsed with exhaustion in the spring of 1813 and died at Bautzen in Silesia on 28 April.

Marshal Ney Supporting the Rearguard during the Retreat from Moscow, by Adolphe Yvon, 1856. The retreat of the Grande Armée was dogged by skirmishes with the pursuing Russians. The French were ill-equipped for the Russian winter, while Kutuzov's troops were better clothed and their horses better shod.

Mikhail Kutuzov

> 'The maximum use of force is in no way incompatible with the simultaneous use of the intellect.'
> CLAUSEWITZ, *ON WAR*

CARL VON CLAUSEWITZ
1780–1831

ANDREW ROBERTS

CARL VON CLAUSEWITZ, a middle-ranking Prussian general who helped drive Napoleon from his country, wrote a single book that was unfinished at the time of his death but through it he can lay claim to have influenced – for both good and ill – the conduct of warfare more deeply and for longer than any other military theorist in history.

Born in Magdeburg in 1780, the fourth son of a retired lieutenant and minor tax official, Carl von Clausewitz came from a family of theologians and professors. His father had served under Frederick the Great in the Seven Years War, and Carl entered the Prussian army in 1792, going off to fight in the French Revolutionary War the following year aged only 13. He rose rapidly in the ranks owing to his courage and intelligence, becoming a major at 30, a colonel at 34 and a general by 38.

In 1801 Clausewitz received his only formal education when he joined the Military Academy in Berlin. It was there that he met and came under the influence of the charismatic Gerhard von Scharnhorst, Prussia's greatest general since Frederick. Scharnhorst, who fought against Napoleon at Flanders, Jena, Eylau and in the war of liberation of 1813–14 became a 'spiritual father', mentor and hero to Clausewitz.

After graduating top of his class in 1803, Clausewitz became adjutant to Prince Augustus of Prussia and the following year penned his first notes on military strategy. In 1805 he wrote a 100-page history of Gustavus Adolphus of Sweden during the Thirty Years War, and can claim to have been as much an historian as a military theoretician, at least in terms of his literary output.

Clausewitz and Napoleon

It was, as with all Prussians of his generation, the catastrophic defeat of his country at the hands of Napoleon in 1806 that was to focus, energize and radicalize Clausewitz, and the thirst to avenge the humiliation was to give his life meaning. He fought with a grenadier battalion during that disastrous campaign and was forced to surrender, going into French captivity with Prince Augustus.

Carl von Clausewitz

The total defeat of the Prussian army at Jena-Auerstädt in October 1806 (see pp. 144–5) was followed by widespread French rapine and pillage in Prussia, and although the monarchy and government were forced to accept Napoleon's humiliating peace terms, Prussian nationalists, patriots and especially the army from then on lived and worked solely for eventual revenge. Clausewitz wrote that the Prussian army was ruined 'more completely than any army has ever been ruined on the battlefield' at Jena. He refused to recognize the Napoleon-dictated armistice, writing to his beloved wife Marie: 'I shall never accept the peace which brings submission. If I cannot live in a free and respected state and enjoy the golden fruits of peace in your arms, then let peace depart forever from my heart.'

Prussia's Reform movement, which looked forward to a coming 'war of liberation', was intended to create a state that could one day turn the tables on Napoleon. The coming war against the French empire, the Reformers vowed, would see a very different Prussia in the field, a nation in arms.

After his release from France in the spring of 1808, Clausewitz rejoined Scharnhorst – who had been wounded at Auerstädt – and served as his private secretary. In that capacity he drafted many of the Reformers' papers, and became involved in every aspect of the movement. He also got to know (and hugely admire) Graf August von Gneisenau, a key military figure in it.

Military education was an important aspect of the Reform programme, and in 1810–11 Clausewitz taught guerrilla warfare at the War Academy. From 1810 to 1812 he also tutored the crown prince in military affairs. In the spring of 1812, when the Prussian government

Carl von Clausewitz, in a lithograph after a painting by Wilhelm Wach, *c.* 1820. His posthumously published *On War* begins: 'Just as many plants only bear fruit when they do not shoot too high, so in the practical arts the theoretical leaves and flowers must not be made to sprout too far, but kept near to experience, which is their proper soil. It is, perhaps, not impossible to write a systematic theory of war full of spirit and substance, but ours, hitherto, have been very much the reverse. This author has preferred to give in small ingots of fine metal his impressions and convictions, the result of many years' reflection on war, and of much personal experience.'

agreed to supply Napoleon with a Prussian army corps to fight against Russia, Clausewitz decided to leave the service of the king and join the Russian army as a staff officer. It was a hard decision for a proud Prussian patriot to take, but he justified himself thus:

> *Formerly … war was waged in the way that a pair of duellists carried out their pedantic struggle. One battled with moderation and consideration, according to the conventional proprieties … There is no more talk of this sort of war, and one would have to be blind not to be able to perceive the difference with our wars, that is to say the wars that our age and our conditions require … The war of the present time is a war of all against all.*

Or at least all against Napoleon, and if King Frederick Wilhelm and his 'dishonoured' government would not fight it, then Clausewitz would.

It was in the capacity of a staff officer – although more of an observer since he spoke no Russian – that Clausewitz took part in the war of 1812. In the last days of that fateful year, Clausewitz acted as intermediary when General Hans David Yorck, commanding 30,000 Prussians, changed sides from the French to the Russians.

During the ensuing war of liberation that began in 1813, Clausewitz devised a plan for organizing the East Prussian militia. He also advised both Scharnhorst and Gneisenau. Although Scharnhorst died in 1813 of a wound received at the Battle of

The Battle of Jena, in an engraving after a painting by Jacques Swebach. The double battles of Jena and Auerstädt (14 October 1806) were the greatest disasters for Prussian arms of the century, and resulted in the loss of over 45,000 Prussian troops (either dead, wounded or captured). Clausewitz, Scharnhorst and Gneisenau, future leaders of the Prussian Reform movement, were all present.

Grossgörschen, Gneisenau appointed Clausewitz – who showed great bravery in 1814 – as chief of staff of one of the Prussian corps that fought in the Waterloo campaign. After fighting at the Battle of Ligny in June 1815, Clausewitz was present at the vital rearguard engagement at Wavre two days later that prevented Marshal Grouchy from arriving to aid Napoleon at Waterloo (a battle that Clausewitz always called 'Belle-Alliance').

After Napoleon

The following year Clausewitz became chief of staff to Gneisenau, and from 1818 to 1830 he held the important post of Superintendent (administrative director) of the War Academy, which gave him time to develop his theories and write his masterpiece, *Vom Kriege* (*On War*). When the Bourbons were overthrown in France in 1830, Gneisenau became army commander-in-chief and again chose Clausewitz as his chief of staff, but the sense of national danger proved a false alarm after the Orléanist Louis-Philippe was crowned king of France and settled down to a generally pacific foreign policy, at least in Europe.

Gerhard von Scharnhorst (1755–1813), painted by Friedrich Bury. Scharnhorst taught Clausewitz at the Military Academy in Berlin, before leading the movement to create a truly national army for Prussia, a project with which Clausewitz identified strongly.

In August 1831 Gneisenau succumbed to the cholera epidemic that was sweeping through Eastern Europe, and then on 16 November Clausewitz himself, weakened by mild cholera, died of a heart attack. At the time of his death, Clausewitz was thought of as a respectable Prussian general of intellectual leanings who had been a conscientious if middle-ranking figure in the Reform movement that had revolutionized Prussia in time for the war of liberation. He was certainly not considered then, as he generally is today, the most important military theorist who ever lived.

On War

The year after his death, Clausewitz's widow Marie published his masterpiece *On War*, which sold fewer than fifteen hundred copies in its first twenty years. It was 1867 before the third edition came out. He had not wanted the book published in his lifetime, and was very substantially rewriting and revising the theory at the time that he died. Its many internal contradictions might have been ironed out had he not succumbed to his heart attack, but they should not detract from what is a monumental work of history, scholarship, military theory and occasionally philosophy.

Although he published little between hard covers, Clausewitz wrote extensively on education, politics and art and had a large, wide and varied correspondence. *On War* represents a distillation of thoughts over a lifetime of fighting, teaching and writing, and is presented in the direct, no-nonsense style one might expect from a Prussian general of the Napoleonic Wars. Much of it is very much of its time, with limited application to later ages using very different weapons under very different circumstances. Nonetheless, there are some generalizations that Clausewitz makes – particularly in the fields of morale, genius and chance – that still hold good today.

Although Clausewitz himself dismissed *On War* as a 'shapeless mass of ideas' in its

Carl von Clausewitz

early drafts – and there are undoubtedly many banalities and contradictions to be found in its pages – it is still the greatest work of military theory ever written, and therefore justifies its author's inclusion in a survey of history's great commanders, even though Clausewitz himself never exercised significant independent command.

His two central themes are firstly that war cannot be disentangled from the greater political issues that cause it – hence the well-known formulation 'War is nothing but the continuation of policy with other means' – and secondly that Total War (such as the Napoleonic Wars) constitutes a very different beast from the kind of limited dynastic or territorial wars that had constituted the European norm before the French Revolution.

Yet as well as those two major themes, Clausewitz had a great deal to say about how his country's greatest enemy, Napoleon, managed to impose his will on so much of Europe for so long. Annihilation of the enemy's main force, willingness to accept high levels of casualties, concentration of effort at the decisive point – the *Hauptschlacht* (major battle) which was 'the true centre of gravity of the war' – these were some of the messages Clausewitz imparted.

> 'The conduct of war resembles the workings of an intricate machine with tremendous friction, so that combinations which are easily planned on paper can be executed only with great effort.'
>
> CLAUSEWITZ, *ON WAR*

As one would expect from a long-serving superintendent of one of the world's greatest military academies, Clausewitz prized leadership above all else. In his editor and translator Sir Michael Howard's words, Clausewitz placed great 'emphasis on the creative power of the individual', concentrating in particular on the role and nature of genius in military affairs. Commanders needed to show freedom of thought, initiative, self-reliance. Of course Clausewitz's principal source of inspiration was the genius of Napoleon, whom he hated and sharply criticized but nevertheless called 'the god of war'.

In the Clausewitzian universe, military leaders were not intended to control state policy, since military strategy needed to be subordinated to greater political desiderata. Having personally witnessed Napoleon's nemesis in the retreat from Moscow, Clausewitz appreciated that ultimate success depended on knowing when and how to stop fighting. It was a message that his admirers in the Prussian High Command were to ignore during the First World War. Everything in war is political, Clausewitz argued, even strategy and tactics.

Having taken part in many campaigns in the French revolutionary and imperial wars over twenty-two years, Clausewitz also well understood the role that unquantifiable factors such as chance could play. Although he looked to history for examples of what happened in battle, he did not believe history was subject to patterns that could therefore lead to anything being predictable. Because of the crucial role of chance, there could be no dogmatic, universal right or wrong way to go about warfare. In explaining how and why smaller forces sometimes overcame larger ones, he dwelled on the importance of moral and psychological factors such as fear, morale and courage.

Clausewitz's uncompromising theories about Total War led to him being called 'the Mahdi of mass and mutual massacre' by Sir Basil Liddell Hart. Certainly Clausewitz did believe, unlike other contemporary thinkers such as Baron Henri Jomini, that extreme

Carl von Clausewitz

violence, rather than merely manoeuvre, was the very essence of war. Total War, such as the one Prussia fought against Napoleon in 1813–15, could only be conducted successfully through the supreme effort of the whole state, as the Reformers had insisted upon ever since the debacle at Jena. Since blood must be shed to break utterly the enemy's power and will to resist, Clausewitz was in a sense the link between the Total War that ended in 1815 and the one that started almost exactly a century later.

One of the many aspects of Clausewitzian thought that his German followers ignored in 1914–15 was his emphasis on defence rather than offence. By 1916–17 his lessons about the strategy of attrition, *Ermattungsstrategie*, versus that of annihilation,

Carl von Clausewitz

Prussian troops parade on the Champs-Elysées in January 1871, after their successful war with France and immediately prior to the declaration of the German empire. While the Franco-Prussian War represented the triumphant culmination of Bismarck's plans to consolidate Prussian power in Europe through lightning wars, those plans had been brought to fruition by the Prussian chief of staff Moltke, who placed particularly high value on Clausewitz's book *On War*.

Vernichtungsstrategie, had to be relearned by Hindenberg and Ludendorff. Equally, Clausewitz's almost total lack of interest in both sea-power and economics limited his relevance for his countrymen in a war in which both played important parts.

On War was of its (Napoleonic) time and place, and not particularly applicable to the warfare of the nuclear and terrorist age. That is the way that Clausewitz himself would have wanted it, being a man who decried attempts to codify strict, immutable laws and principles of warfare. Since it is impossible to know how the enemy will react in any given situation, and since a battle is a constant movement of interlocking action and reaction, abstract laws cannot, he argued, be applied to the battlefield.

Clausewitz's legacy

Field Marshal Helmuth von Moltke, Prussian army chief of staff from 1858 to 1888, used to say that, along with the Bible and Homer, *On War* was the only really seminal work that ever influenced him. Although Clausewitz's thought was known to only a small number of people by the early 1860s, Otto von Bismarck's three quick victories against Denmark in 1863–4, Austria in 1866, and France in 1870–71 suddenly placed Clausewitz in the Prussian pantheon, because these stunning conquests were popularly believed to have been won on Clausewitzian principles.

Count Alfred von Schlieffen, the German chief of staff, was another great admirer, and he wrote the 1905 preface to the fifth edition of *On War*, at the same time that he was drawing up his notorious Plan to invade France via neutral Belgium. The First World War was in a sense a Clausewitzian struggle on both sides, involving, as Michael Howard lists them, his views concerning 'the scepticism for strategic manoeuvre; the accumulation of maximum force at the decisive point in order to defeat the enemy main force in battle; the conduct of operations so as to inflict the greatest possible number of losses on the enemy and compel him to use up his reserves at a greater rate than one was expending one's own; the dogged refusal to be put off by heavy casualties'.

There was nothing Clausewitzian about fighting a war on two fronts, however, or about politicians being subordinated to the army High Command, or about building a high seas fleet and invading a neutral country, thereby bringing the British Empire into the war against Germany.

Marshal Foch took Clausewitz's strictures about the superiority of defensive over offensive fighting to heart, and Clausewitz's military thought was also debated throughout the 1920s and 1930s in France, Britain and America, as well as in Germany. 'In the realm of war,' wrote Basil Liddell Hart in 1932, 'which has covered so great a part of human activity, and has affected so greatly human life and history, the name of Clausewitz stands out more and is better known to soldiers ... than any of the generals of the nineteenth century, save perhaps Lee and Moltke.'

The Nazis eagerly embraced Clausewitz, even though he had died over a century before Hitler's rise to power. His call for a vigorous, inspired, flexible yet resolute commander who showed willpower and understood the power of the daring *coup d'oeil* seemed to presage the leadership of their Führer, and they were only encouraged by the knowledge that it had originally alluded to Napoleon. Clausewitz was also put to use by the Soviets; in November 1941 the Soviet air force dropped leaflets on the Wehrmacht quoting *On War*'s injunction that: 'It is impossible either to hold or to conquer Russia.'

Clausewitz's principles also deeply imbued American military thinking in the 1920s, especially his injunction to attack the main body of the enemy with as much force as possible to win the *Hauptschlacht*, 'the true centre of gravity of the war'. This was taken to heart by General George C. Marshall, US Army chief of staff 1939–45, who insisted that only an early second front in the West could defeat the Wehrmacht, and who consequently pressed for an invasion of northwestern France long before the British were finally persuaded to consent to D-Day taking place in June 1944.

With *On War* still on the syllabus at the Sandhurst, West Point, St Cyr and Voroshilov military academies, Clausewitz's day is not over yet.

> 'If nature opposes us we will fight her and make her obey.'
> SIMÓN BOLÍVAR

SIMÓN BOLÍVAR
1783–1830

MALCOLM DEAS

IN A DECADE AND A HALF of struggle Simón Bolívar freed much of South America from Spanish rule, achieving the independence of what are now six countries: Venezuela, Colombia, Panama, Ecuador, Peru and Bolivia – the last named in honour of Bolívar himself, the man who became known as the Liberator. Bolívar's operations ranged from the mouth of the Orinoco on the Atlantic to Peru and Bolivia in the south, a vast, geographically diverse crescent embracing many different societies, from the Indian communities of the high Andes to black slave plantations on the Caribbean coast.

In comparison with the size of the forces in the North American War of Independence, let alone those involved in the Napoleonic Wars, the armies Bolívar commanded in the field were minuscule: as he said himself, 'Here every trio is an orchestra.' In the early years of the struggle he suffered a number of severe reverses, and those campaigns gained him only what he called 'fruitless laurels'. His strategic sense took some time to develop, and none of his battles was of the sort to win a place in texts on the military art. His great achievement has to be measured against the difficulties posed by time and place: only then can one see behind the formal gold-embroidered uniform an extraordinary improviser of armies and resources, a pioneer of national liberation and a great commander. Without question, Bolívar stands above his rivals as the greatest figure in the emancipation of South America.

Bolívar was born in Caracas on 24 July 1783, a child of the local creole aristocracy. His family was one of the richest in the colony, but both his parents died when he was young. At 15 he was made a sub-lieutenant in the local militia, a social rather than a military distinction, and he had little formal military training. From 1799 he was in Spain and France, remaining until 1802 when he married and returned to Venezuela. His wife died early the next year. He swore never to marry again, and returned to Europe, living there until 1806 when he sailed again for Venezuela via the United States. He had been in Paris when Napoleon proclaimed himself emperor, and in Italy he had witnessed one of the emperor's grand military reviews, a sight he never forgot.

Simón Bolívar

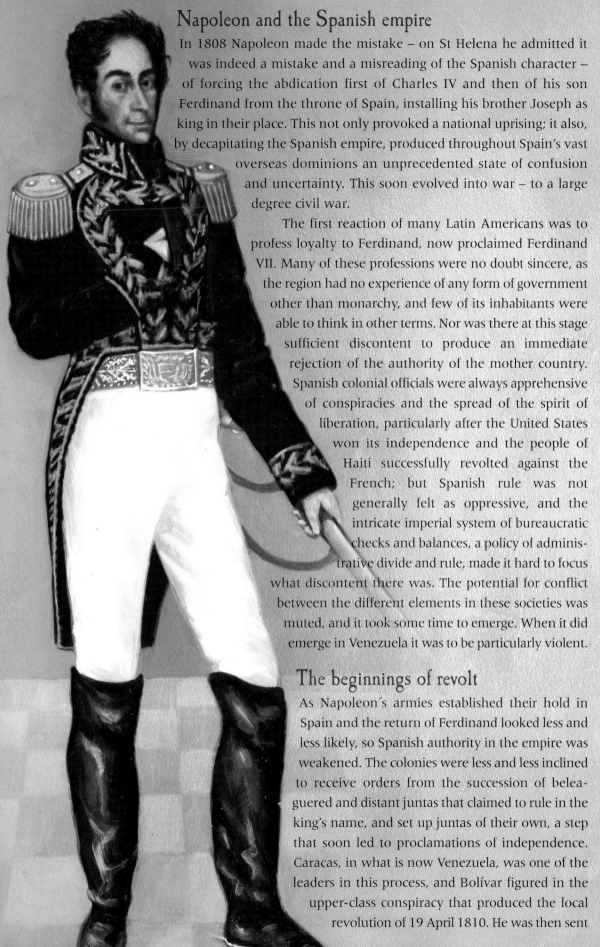

Napoleon and the Spanish empire

In 1808 Napoleon made the mistake – on St Helena he admitted it was indeed a mistake and a misreading of the Spanish character – of forcing the abdication first of Charles IV and then of his son Ferdinand from the throne of Spain, installing his brother Joseph as king in their place. This not only provoked a national uprising; it also, by decapitating the Spanish empire, produced throughout Spain's vast overseas dominions an unprecedented state of confusion and uncertainty. This soon evolved into war – to a large degree civil war.

The first reaction of many Latin Americans was to profess loyalty to Ferdinand, now proclaimed Ferdinand VII. Many of these professions were no doubt sincere, as the region had no experience of any form of government other than monarchy, and few of its inhabitants were able to think in other terms. Nor was there at this stage sufficient discontent to produce an immediate rejection of the authority of the mother country. Spanish colonial officials were always apprehensive of conspiracies and the spread of the spirit of liberation, particularly after the United States won its independence and the people of Haiti successfully revolted against the French; but Spanish rule was not generally felt as oppressive, and the intricate imperial system of bureaucratic checks and balances, a policy of administrative divide and rule, made it hard to focus what discontent there was. The potential for conflict between the different elements in these societies was muted, and it took some time to emerge. When it did emerge in Venezuela it was to be particularly violent.

The beginnings of revolt

As Napoleon´s armies established their hold in Spain and the return of Ferdinand looked less and less likely, so Spanish authority in the empire was weakened. The colonies were less and less inclined to receive orders from the succession of beleaguered and distant juntas that claimed to rule in the king's name, and set up juntas of their own, a step that soon led to proclamations of independence. Caracas, in what is now Venezuela, was one of the leaders in this process, and Bolívar figured in the upper-class conspiracy that produced the local revolution of 19 April 1810. He was then sent

The portrait of Simón Bolívar that hangs in the Federal Palace of Venezuela. Bolívar, hailed as the Liberator, freed much of South America from Spanish rule, and the country of Bolivia is named in his honour.

Simón Bolívar

on a diplomatic mission to London, where he met Francisco de Miranda, an early advocate of independence who had led an unsuccessful small-scale invasion of Venezuela in 1806. They both returned to serve the now independent republic.

Peace did not last long. The claim of Caracas to be the capital was contested by other cities, and strong royalist sentiments persisted. Many elements in society – blacks, mulattos, mestizos, poor whites – felt little deference towards Bolívar's class, and the new rulers had little experience of government, and even less tact. When desultory fighting began, as Caracas sought to impose its authority, it also soon became apparent that neither of the new rulers possessed any relevant military experience. Miranda, who was given command, had been a general in the armies of the French Revolution, and had acquitted himself well in 1793 – his name is on the Arc de Triomphe – but he had no idea how to lead the raw levies of a militarily innocent country.

'Bolívar in defeat is more dangerous than Bolívar victorious.'
A CONTEMPORARY SPANISH ASSESSMENT

Bolívar's active military career began with disaster and humiliation. Miranda failed to resist the advance on Caracas of small but disciplined local Spanish forces under Domingo de Monteverde. In March 1812 Caracas was reduced to ruins by an earthquake, and the effect on patriot morale was devastating – though it gave Bolívar the opportunity of announcing to the world from atop a pile of rubble that 'If nature opposes us we will fight her and make her obey' (this sounds too good to be true, but the witness is a contemporary royalist). Placed in command of the key fortress of Puerto Cabello, Bolívar failed to prevent its betrayal to the enemy. He and some of his fellow officers then vented their frustration by handing Miranda over to the victors, hardly an honourable act. Bolívar was then permitted to leave the country.

The struggles for Caracas

Bolívar went to Cartagena, the Caribbean fortress port of the neighbouring Viceroyalty of New Granada, and within a year showed the qualities that led the Spanish to conclude that 'Bolívar in defeat is more dangerous than Bolívar victorious'. He was given a minor command by the patriots of Cartagena, and ordered to conduct operations against royalist detachments along the River Magdalena. Through a combination of élan and persuasiveness he was able in May 1813 to turn this limited mission into an invasion of Venezuela from the west, with around a thousand men and a few pieces of artillery; opposing him, Monteverde commanded royalist forces of around 6,000 or 7,000 in the west and centre of the country. In June Bolívar issued his notorious decree of *Guerra a muerte* ('war to the death'), which promised to guarantee the lives of the native-born and to put to death all Spaniards who did not positively embrace the patriot cause. On 6 August he entered Caracas in triumph, and was proclaimed Liberator, a title that remained his alone.

This remarkable campaign showed Bolívar's talents for rapid movement and improvisation of resources; his declaration of 'war to the death' also showed his ruthlessness and decisiveness, and his taste for heightened, dramatic language. But it did not produce lasting success. From 1813, the year of this campaign, until 1819 Bolívar was obsessed by taking – or retaking – Caracas, and it took him a long time to realize that his native city was not the strategic key to undoing Spanish power.

Monteverde had lost Caracas, but he still held Puerto Cabello, and elsewhere the royalist reaction was not long in coming. It took the form of a rising led by a Spanish-born sailor and smuggler called José Tomás Boves, who now embraced war to the death on the royalist side with an enthusiasm that made Bolívar's proclamaton look insipid. Boves roused the lower classes – the masterless cattlemen of the plains of the interior (who proved to be natural lancers), the numerous poor immigrants from the Canary Islands, the free blacks and coloureds, and many slaves. Bolívar's small forces could not hold territory, and Boves inflicted a severe defeat on the patriots in the First Battle of La Puerta. This caused panic in Caracas, and Bolívar took the precaution of executing 800 Spanish prisoners. Boves's hosts continued to grow – they are said to have reached as many as 8,000 – and in the Second Battle of La Puerta he annihilated what was left of the patriot army under Bolívar's command. Bolívar and a tragic column of refugees fled Caracas to the east, and on 8 September 1814 he embarked again for Cartagena.

The wilderness years

Boves died of a wound in December 1814, but the following year, with the defeat of Napoleon in Europe, Spain was able to send to Venezuela and New Granada some

Francisco Urdaneta, colonel of dragoons, served under Bolívar in his campaigns of 1817–20. In this painting by a contemporary Colombian artist, Urdaneta's horse wears a fringe of string or leather to keep the flies away from its nose and eyes.

10,000 veterans under the command of Pablo Morillo. Bolívar had once again been employed in New Granada, and had taken part in the internal conflicts that still divided that country despite the manifest threat of Spanish reconquest. Morillo proved irresistible, and Bolívar had to seek refuge first in Jamaica and then in Haiti.

The desire to retake Caracas and to fight Morillo in Venezuela continued to dominate Bolívar's thinking for the next two years, resulting in little success and much frustration. He had to beg meagre assistance from speculators in Jamaica and Haiti, and the odds on his winning must have looked long. Early in 1816 he landed on the Venezuelan coast from Haiti with some 250 men, but failed to establish a footing. His authority was by no means unchallenged within the scattered patriot remnants, and some other commanders – Mariño, Piar, Páez, Monagas – held sway over solid local fiefs of a sort Bolívar never enjoyed.

It was a time of indecisive defeats and victories for the diminutive, ill-supplied and insecurely disciplined patriot forces. The war to the death seesawed in its intensity; prisoners and deserters were dispatched with a knife or lined up in twos

OVER THE ANDES TO VICTORY AT BOYACÁ

FROM HIS BASE AT ANGOSTURA, in 1819 Bolívar abandoned his long-sought aim of retaking Caracas. Instead, he attacked the Spanish forces in New Granada by crossing the Eastern Cordillera of the Andes from the plains of Casanare. The obstacles to this plan looked insuperable, and though Morillo, the skilful and experienced royalist commander, saw that it might be attempted, the Spanish in New Granada thought it impossible: it was the rainy season and the plains were flooded; the passes were few and narrow, the men from the plains would suffer too much from cold and mountain sickness, and would desert or die; the horses' hooves would not withstand the change of ground from the soft plains to the rocks; surprise would not be attained.

These obstacles were all real enough, but they were overcome. Not all the forces painfully assembled in Casanare obeyed the order at the end of June to leave the plains, and José Antonio Páez disobeyed his instructions to make a feint towards Cúcuta. Men were lost, as well as horses and equipment, but 900 or so under Bolívar and his second-in-command Francisco de Paula Santander reached the highlands to the northeast of Tunja without meeting significant opposition. Bolívar more than made up for his losses in men by rapidly recruiting replacements, announcing that anyone not answering the call was to be shot.

The first battle with the disconcerted Spanish at Pantano de Vargas was not much more than a draw, but a draw in Bolívar's favour. Morale and momentum were on his side, and his opponent Barreiro was subsequently out-manoeuvred, exhausting his troops in attempting to cut off Bolívar's advance on Bogotá, the capital of New Granada. The two armies met again on 7 August south of Tunja at Boyacá, where Bolívar won his most decisive victory.

By European standards it was a small and unsophisticated engagement – some 2,850 patriots against 2,700 royalists, a cavalry and infantry affair lasting only two hours, and in which (according to one account) Barreiro's artillery managed to get off only three shots. Before long, Barreiro had surrendered, with nearly all his officers and 1,600 men. The viceroy, his officials and numerous Spaniards and royalists fled from the capital, and its small remaining garrison withdrew to the south before Bolívar entered the city ahead of his army on 10 August.

Although it lasted only two hours, and involved fewer than 6,000 men, the Battle of Boyacá, fought on 7 August 1819, proved to be Bolívar's most decisive victory, leading to independence for Colombia.

Simón Bolívar

or threes to be economically shot with a single bullet. Nevertheless, despite the strategic confusion, some clarity began to emerge. Bolívar was back again in Venezuela at the end of 1816, this time for good, and he gradually reasserted his authority – crucially by executing the mulatto General Piar, who was reluctant to obey his orders and threatened vaguely racial mutiny. Bolívar found a base in the Orinoco delta town of Angostura: the region had good natural defences, and from there he could gather resources and import arms through the trade with Trinidad. He could also bring to Angostura British and other foreign mercenaries, many of whom were useless, but some had valuable military talents: the British were to fight conspicuously well at Boyacá and Carabobo. They were also loyal to Bolívar personally, and less liable to faction than his fellow countrymen. Bolívar could also pretend to be a government, and early in 1819 at Angostura he called together his first congress. That year also saw Bolívar's greatest strategic feat – leading his men over the Andes to defeat the royalists decisively at Boyacá (see opposite).

From victory to victory

After Boyacá, Bolívar's military career was by no means over, but whereas before that decisive victory he had lost as many battles as he had won, his armies were henceforth to be consistently victorious. New Granada gave him a base the Spanish could never retake, together with resources to tax and a substantial reserve of infantry. Leaving Santander to run the civil government of the new republic of Colombia – Venezuela and New Granada united – Bolívar turned east to deal with the royalist remnant in Venezuela. The Liberal revolution of 1820 in Spain now ended any hope Morillo had for reinforcements. After making a truce with Bolívar that formally ended the war to the death, he departed. In June 1821, after the truce had ended, Bolívar defeated Morillo's successor

Bolívar and his second-in-command, Francisco de Paula Santander, advancing on Bogotá, the capital of New Granada, after their victory at Boyacá, in a painting by Francisco de Paula Alvarez. When they arrived on 10 August 1819 they found the Spanish viceroy and his officials and soldiers had all fled.

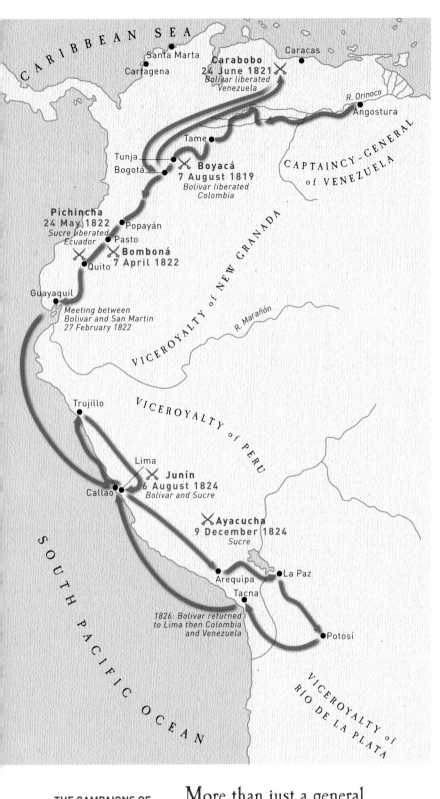

at Carabobo, which effectively ended Spanish rule in Venezuela.

Bolívar then turned south. What is now Ecuador was freed by the victory of Bolívar's favourite general, Antonio José de Sucre, at the Battle of Pichincha, fought in the hills around Quito on 24 May 1822. At the time Bolívar himself was bogged down by tenacious royalist resistance around Pasto in the south of New Granada, where the Battle of Bomboná on 7 April was not one of his greatest successes. With superior forces at his back, Bolívar met the Argentine José de San Martín, his only real rival in stature in the emancipation of South America, at a famous and still mysterious interview in Guayaquil. San Martín had been the liberator of Chile, and had half freed Peru, the grand viceroyalty where enthusiasm for independence had been most decidedly muted and Spanish resistance most effective. He now left the field to Bolívar and retired to Europe. Not without difficulty, Bolívar completed the task. On 6 August 1824, now in command of an army of some 9,000, he won the short and silent cavalry action of Junín – one hour long and not a shot fired – and on 9 December that same year Sucre won the Battle of Ayacucho, which finally decided the independence of Peru and Bolivia.

That can be said to mark the end of Bolívar's military career. His political career did not effectively end until his death from tuberculosis at Santa Marta on 23 December 1830, in an atmosphere of profound pessimism and *après moi le déluge*.

THE CAMPAIGNS OF SIMÓN BOLÍVAR, 1819–26.

More than just a general

One of the best summaries of Bolívar's greatness as a commander was written by the English mining engineer Joseph Andrews, who met the Liberator in Potosí in October 1825:

> *As a man, in my view, he had achieved more than Washington. He freed his country without foreign help and with all possible disadvantages. No France offered her assistance in armies and treasure. No Franklin, Henry or Jefferson was at his right*

Simón Bolívar

hand, nor the inflexible and austere character of New England. The ignorance and complete lack of experience of those around him, in civil and military matters, threw all on to his genius: he dared nobly and he succeeded. His talent in battle and invincible perseverance in despite of all obstacles were matched by his capacity for raising the resources of war and impressing on his countrymen confidence in his ability and respect for his authority as leader of his people.

Bolívar had to be more than just a general; he had to be the civil and military chief, the diplomat, and, above all, the visionary. He also had to create his forces out of scant and recalcitrant materials. In old age his fellow commander, José Antonio Páez, set himself to translate Napoleon´s *Maxims*, and found an 'incontrovertible truth' in number LVII: 'It is very difficult to create an army in a nation that has no military establishments or system.' Bolívar's comments on the societies and politics of his time – his letters are vivid and acute, he was a master of military eloquence and his formal political writing is never dull – show great sociological penetration, and sharp appreciation of the strengths and weaknesses of his subordinates: he alone could fit their awkward shapes together to achieve his ends. None came near him in overall vision,

and from his early travels and his reading – he always travelled with books – he had an unrivalled knowledge of the larger world and an aristocratic confidence in dealing with it.

Bolívar was physically brave, described as 'perhaps too fond of combat' and as 'a bold but not a graceful rider' (he was certainly a tireless one, given the vast distances he had to travel). He loved dancing, and marked his progress with fiestas. He shared all hardships, and did not care for wealth, giving away most of his fortune. He could be moved, but had duly hardened himself: 'Good God,' he once exclaimed, 'were I to weep for every friend I have lost, in future I would be called General Jeremiah not General Bolívar.' As well as possessing the appetite for glory that was part of the spirit of the age, the Liberator had a sardonic wit, a romantic sense of irony that would have appealed to Byron, who named his yacht after him. Here is the generous verdict of San Martín: '… the most astonishing man South America has produced … hardened by difficulties and never defeated by them, however great the dangers against which he hurled his burning spirit.'

Nada prefirió mas que la Libertad de su Patria.

Simón Bolívar

171

> 'Looking at the scope of Shaka's conquests, it becomes impossible to deny that he possessed military and political genius of a very high order.'
> DANIEL COHEN, AUTHOR OF *SHAKA: KING OF THE ZULUS* (1973)

SHAKA ZULU
1787–1828
SAUL DAVID

SHAKA KASENZANGAKONA, KING OF THE ZULUS, was arguably the finest black African commander in history. In just ten years his military and political genius transformed his small tribe into 'the most politically sophisticated, administratively integrated and militarily powerful' black state in sub-Saharan Africa. He achieved this by revolutionizing the tactics and weapons of war, and by fighting campaigns of annihilation that enabled him to absorb the survivors into his military system. Like all the great soldier-rulers – Alexander, Julius Caesar and Napoleon – he was a master of all aspects of command: tactics, strategy, and even diplomacy.

'Chaka King of the Zoolus', from *Travels and Adventures in Eastern Africa* (1836) by Nathaniel Isaacs. In 1824 Isaacs had actually visited Shaka's royal kraal, and in his book he gives a valuable account of the Zulus before they came under European influence.

Shaka was the eldest son of a minor Nguni chief whose clan numbered fewer than 1,500 people (the Nguni were a sub-division of the Bantu people, several hundred clans strong, which slowly spread across southeast Africa in the sixteenth and seventeenth centuries). Shaka was never recognized as his father's heir because he was born out of wedlock – hence his name, which is a sarcastic reference to the intestinal beetle, or *ishaka*, which the Zulu elders used as an excuse for his mother Nandi's inopportune pregnancy. The stigma of his ill-timed birth led to the 7-year-old Shaka and his headstrong mother being sent to live with her tribe, the eLangeni.

Early years as an outcast

Shaka did not stay long with the eLangeni. A well-developed boy with more than his share of his mother's aggression, he clashed with the chief's son and was packed off to a sub-clan of the Mthethwa, the dominant local tribe whose subordinate clans included the Zulu and the eLangeni.

Shaka Zulu

This disgrace rankled deep within Shaka's breast, as did the harsh treatment of his mother by her own people and his own social ostracism at the hands of his peers. He responded with the single-minded determination of the outcast, practising relentlessly at all martial activities: he became so proficient with the throwing spear, for example, that he could hit a small tuft of grass at thirty paces; and he was unbeatable at stick-fighting, directing his forces in mass combat with the same skill and innovation he would display in actual war.

Revolutionizing tribal warfare

Shaka's martial abilities brought him to the notice of Jobe, the paramount chief of the Mthethwa and, after Jobe's death in 1807, to his successor Dingiswayo. For nine years Shaka served in Dingiswayo's army as it subdued tribe after tribe. It was during his time with the Mthethwa that he devised the ruthless political and military strategy that would transform the fortunes of his father's clan.

Previously, tribal conflict had been little more than a ritual show of force with spears thrown from a distance and few casualties, leaving the 'defeated' clan to restart hostilities at a later date. Shaka changed all this by introducing the *iklwa*, a short stabbing spear with a broad, heavy blade that could only be used at close quarters; its name represents the sucking sound the spear made as it was withdrawn from flesh. He turned the traditional cowhide shield into an offensive weapon by instructing his men to hook its left edge behind the shield of their opponent; a powerful backhand sweep would then expose the left side of the enemy to a spear thrust. And, crucially, he introduced the tactics of envelopment by dividing his regiment (and later army) into three parts: a central column to pin down an opposing force, and two flanking parties to surround it.

As Zulu king he would refine these tactics further into the classic double envelopment formation known as *izimpondo zenkomo* (the 'horns of the buffalo'): a 'chest' to close with the enemy and hold it fast; two 'horns' to race either side of the enemy and, having met, to fight their way back to the 'chest'; and the 'loins', or reserve, which was placed behind the 'chest' and deployed as the situation demanded. Further refinements included the abandonment of cumbersome sandals, giving his men added mobility, and an increase in the size of his warriors' shields from 4 to 6 feet to protect them from top to toe.

In an uncanny echo of history, Shaka's new method of fighting was strikingly similar to that used by the legionaries of ancient Rome. They too would close with the enemy in tight formation, then use their shields to unbalance their opponents and their short swords, the *gladii*, to dispatch them. Shaka, of course, had no knowledge of classical warfare and yet applied the same methods to tribal conflict. An early indication that his innovations were working was when his regiment, the isiChwe, played a key role in putting to flight the army of the Ndwandwe paramountcy, the Mthethwa's main rivals for control of the Phongolo-Tugela region. Dingiswayo took note of this and marked Shaka out for rapid promotion. In 1814 he was appointed commander-in-chief and a member of Dingiswayo's inner council.

King of the Zulus

Two years later, on the death of his father Senzangakona, Shaka used Dingiswayo's support to seize the Zulu chieftainship. His half-brother, the designated heir, was quietly murdered and Shaka installed in his place. He was now master of a tiny polity that covered just 10 square miles, with an army of fewer than 500 men.

Shaka knew he had to expand his lands to survive, and within a month of becoming chief he had called up all Zulu men who could bear arms and organized them into three regiments, according to age: 30–40-year-olds, 25–30-year-olds and 18–25-year-olds. All three regiments were trained in the fighting tactics he had developed for the isiChwe, and they were armed with the new heavy-bladed *iklwa*, Shaka having instructed his blacksmiths to convert all existing spears and to forge new ones from raw iron ore.

Tribe after neighbouring tribe either submitted to or was destroyed by Shaka's war machine, his mother's eLangeni clan being the first to cave in. All those clan members who had tormented him or his mother were impaled on stakes from the cattle enclosure. Perhaps mindful of this, the powerful Buthelezi tribe chose not to submit, and the ensuing battle gave Shaka the first opportunity to deploy his *izimpondo zenkomo* formation. It was a resounding success, and not a single Buthelezi warrior was spared. Their homesteads were burned and their women, children and cattle taken back to the Zulu heartland. Shaka's new concept of total war, *impi embomvu* (literally 'war red with blood'), had had its first demonstration.

Defeating the Ndwandwe

In under a year the Zulu lands had quadrupled in size. But Shaka was still technically Dingiswayo's vassal and had to tread carefully. This all changed in 1817 when Dingiswayo, on the eve of battle with the Ndwandwe, was captured and beheaded. The leaderless Mthethwa army melted away and Shaka, aware that a reckoning with the Ndwandwe was imminent, returned to his capital of kwaBulawayo to build up his army, recruiting many former Mthethwa warriors, including the entire isiChwe regiment.

When the Ndwandwe invaded Zulu lands in early 1818, Shaka was ready and waiting. Like Wellington at Waterloo three years earlier, he carefully chose a site for battle, selecting the gentle slopes of kwaGqokli Hill, which he believed would afford his army the greatest chance of a defensive victory. Through clever planning and superior tactics, he was able to defeat the numerically superior Ndwandwe army, though it was a close run thing (see opposite). So serious were his casualties, and so severe the damage inflicted by the retreating Ndwande army to Zulu homesteads and crops, that Shaka had to move for a time nearer to the coast to build up his army and supplies. His victory was crucial to the survival of the fledgling Zulu state, though he knew it to be no more than round one in an ongoing struggle.

THE BATTLE OF KWAGQOKLI HILL

NONE OF SHAKA'S MANY VICTORIES illustrates the full panoply of his military talents better than this early success (1818) against his great foe, the Ndwandwe. Heavily outnumbered by more than two to one, Shaka knew he would have to use every trick at his disposal to come out on top.

His plan involved leaving part of his force of 4,000 warriors at fords across the swollen White Mfolozi river with orders to hold out for as long as possible, and then to fall back to kwaGqokli Hill, 2 miles to the south of the river, where the bulk of his warriors were in position. A low-lying, rounded hill that rises only a few hundred yards above the surrounding countryside, kwaGqokli could have been a death trap for a less capable commander. But Shaka knew the importance of surprise and was a master of deception. He deployed a portion of his men in a series of rings around the hill and hid the rest, as a reserve, in a shallow depression behind the southern summit. There, in case of a lengthy siege, he also stockpiled food and water, oxen for slaughter, and firewood. And to deprive the enemy of sustenance he denuded the area of food and shelter.

His masterstroke, however, was to use his herdsmen as a decoy on the emThonjaneni Heights, a few miles to the southeast of kwaGqokli Hill, in the hope that the Ndwandwe commander, Nomo-hlanjana, would send part of his army in pursuit. The herdsmen were to use smoke signals to indicate the position of the detached force.

For a time, Shaka's plan went like clockwork. The defenders at the river held the Ndwandwe back for more than a day, inflicting severe casualties, before withdrawing to the hill with the enemy hard on their heels. As he advanced, Nomo-hlonjana noticed the herdsmen and fell for Shaka's ruse by detaching part of his force to engage what he thought was a second Zulu *impi* (war band). With the bulk of his troops, around 7,000 warriors, he formed a semicircle round the base of kwaGqokli and opened the battle by advancing towards the first line of defenders, 1,500 strong. But, on Shaka's orders, the Zulus attacked first and, using their superior close-quarter fighting skills, hacked great gaps in the tightly packed Ndwandwe ranks.

When the Ndwandwe withdrew, Shaka took advantage of the lull to replace his frontline soldiers with men from his reserve, and at no time was his enemy aware exactly how many warriors he had at his disposal. Again the Ndwandwe attacked, this time round the whole base of the hill, and again were repulsed with heavy casualties, three Ndwandwe warriors dying for every Zulu. Nomohlonjana now tried a ruse of his own, instructing his men to feign a panicked retreat, but the sandal-less Zulus were able to avoid the trap by outrunning the Ndwandwe reserve.

Assuming the Zulus were on the point of collapse, Nomohlonjana formed his remaining men into a huge column, 200 yards wide, and sent it up the hill. This gave Shaka the opportunity to deploy his reserve in his favourite 'horns of the buffalo' formation, stopping the Ndwandwe column with his 'chest' and sending the two 'horns' to outflank it on either side. Nomohlanjana and four of his brothers were killed in the carnage, as were 4,000–5,000 of their men. It was a victory to rival Hannibal's at Cannae, though so battered was Shaka's army that he chose not to pursue the beaten Ndwandwe, preferring to withdraw to his capital at kwaBulawayo to re-gather his strength for the battles that lay ahead.

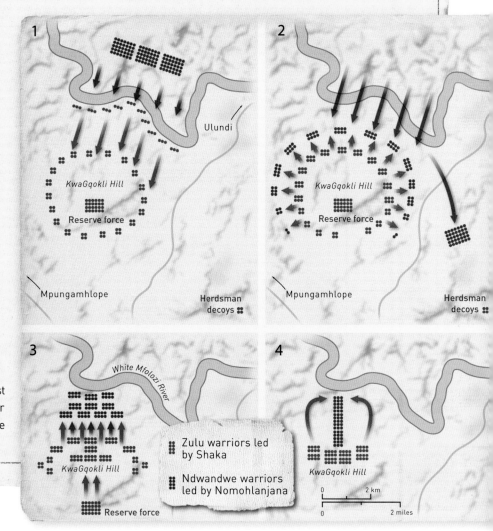

1

Ulundi

KwaGqokli Hill

Reserve force

Mpungamhlope

Herdsman decoys ⠶

2

KwaGqokli Hill

Reserve force

Mpungamhlope

Herdsman decoys ⠶

3

White Mfolozi River

KwaGqokli Hill

Reserve force

⠶ Zulu warriors led by Shaka

⠶ Ndwandwe warriors led by Nomohlanjana

4

KwaGqokli Hill

0 ___ 2 km
0 ___ 2 miles

Shaka redoubled his efforts to increase the size of his army, and by 1819, through a combination of clever diplomacy and brutal conquest, he had brought all the tribes between the White Mfolozi and Tugela rivers under his control. This augmentation of force enabled him to rout the Ndwandwe again in 1819, forcing the tribe to move its power base north of the Phongolo into what is now southern Swaziland.

Shaka's military system

As Shaka's authority increased, so did the size of his army, with military conscription compulsory for all adult males. For three years, from the age of 14, boys lived in *amakhanda* (military kraals), where they herded cattle, tended crops and received military instruction. They were then formed into *amabutho*, or age-grade regiments, and spent another eight months together before returning to their homes where, for a quarter of the year, they served as reserves in the district *amakhanda*. Only for national festivals and in times of war would they remobilize as a regiment. Shaka even brought girls into the military system by grouping them in *amabutho* for the purpose of marriage. Not only did they have to wait for Shaka's permission to wed, they also had to choose their partners from those male *amabutho* who had been given leave to wear the *isicoco* (a fibre circlet sewn into the hair, coated with gum and then greased and polished), a privilege rarely granted before the age of 35. The award of the *isicoco* marked the attainment of adulthood, full acceptance into the village community and the right to marry and set up home. By withholding it until a relatively late age, Shaka was trying to keep young Zulu men more firmly under the authority of their tribal elders and, by extension, their king.

A young Zulu warrior photographed *c.* 1900. He carries an *iklwa*, the short stabbing spear introduced by Shaka.

Within a few years Shaka's army had increased from its original nucleus of 500 to 20,000 men; his territory from 10 to 11,500 square miles. The many tribes he subdued even began to refer to themselves as Zulus, so that the original clan of 3,000 had soon swelled to a nation of a quarter of a million. Shaka was no longer fighting wars of survival but of conquest, and the Zulus, a pastoral people who measured their wealth in terms of cattle, grew rich on the huge herds they looted from their victims. By 1824 the Zulus had laid waste much of modern Natal and, in the process, had set off a stampede to the south that consumed clan after clan until it petered out on the borders of Britain's Cape Colony. This stampede was known as the *mfecane*, the 'crushing' (though in its widest sense the term applies to *all* the wars and migrations caused by rival emergent states north of the Tugela, and not just Zulu aggression).

The final showdown

One implacable foe had not gone away, however. Since retreating north of the Phongolo, the Ndwandwe had used the intervening years to re-gather their strength and build a new army. In the autumn of 1826, under the command of their young Chief Sikhunyana, they crossed the Phongolo into Zulu territory. Shaka responded by calling up his entire army, 20,000

warriors, and marching it north in a massive column, which, according to an early British settler called Henry Fynn, created huge clouds of dust. Fynn observed how each regiment was accompanied by *izimbongi* (praise singers) who hailed Shaka's heroic achievements. The warriors carried their own weapons, with their shields rolled up and strapped to their backs, and iron rations of maize grains and cooked cow's liver. Younger boys carried sleeping mats and drove the herds of cattle that provided the army with the bulk of its food.

After marching for ten days, the Zulu army rested on a sandstone ridge near to the battlefield of Kambula where, fifty-three years later, the Zulus would be defeated by British troops armed with breech-loading rifles and cannon. From here Shaka sent out scouts and advance guards to gather intelligence and tempt the enemy into an attack. These spies revealed that Sikhunyana, in a mirror image of the Battle of kwaGqokli Hill, had concentrated the majority of his warriors just below the rocky summit of a peak in the izinDolowane Hills. Above them he had placed their cattle and, higher still, their women and children.

Given the confines of the battlefield, Shaka could not use his favourite tactic of envelopment. Instead his only option was a frontal attack that would, if all went well, pierce the Ndwandwe ranks and enable the Zulus to surround and destroy the broken remnants, a tactic known to Western generals as defeating in detail. As well as his peerless generalship, Shaka had one further advantage over the Ndwandwe: the firepower of Fynn and a small group of British settlers who had agreed to fight on his behalf.

Their opening volley of bullets into the tightly packed Ndwandwe ranks was the signal for the Zulu warriors to mount the first of a series of charges, which Shaka

Zulu warriors at a kraal on the Tugela river during the Zulu war with Britain, 1879. Under Shaka's military system, for three years from the age of 14 all males lived in amakhanda, special kraals where, in addition to tending cattle and crops, they trained as warriors. Men were rarely given permission to marry until they were in their mid thirties.

Shaka Zulu

177

likened to waves striking the shore. As the third 'wave' swept into the Ndwandwe position, Shaka noticed from his vantage point on a nearby knoll that the enemy was beginning to waver; he took this as the cue to throw in his reserves. Like Alexander at Gaugamela, and Napoleon at Austerlitz, he had recognized the decisive moment in the battle and acted accordingly.

For a short time the Ndwandwe held their ground, but then a tiny gap appeared in their centre through which the Zulu reserves poured. Attacked from front and rear, the Ndwandwe broke and ran. Most were caught by their barefoot pursuers and killed, as were all the women and children. Among the handful of survivors was Chief Sikhunyana, who hid in a pit to avoid capture.

With this victory, Shaka finally removed the most dangerous and persistent threat to his power. In just ten years, thanks to his unequalled genius for war, he had created a huge empire that extended from Delagoa Bay in the north to the Mthamvuna river in the south, from the Indian Ocean to the Drakensberg Mountains. But he did not rule for much longer.

'This new way of fighting, unknown to the neighbouring nations, and Shaka's conquest to such a degree that in the twelve years of his reign

ADULPHE DELEGORGUE, A FRENCH NATURALIST WHO VISITED NATAL IN THE 1830s

Shaka Zulu

A tyrant's death

Shaka's people had grown tired of ceaseless war and their ruler's penchant for random executions (he once had an attendant brained for sneezing while he was eating). The final straw was his hysterical reaction to the death of his mother, Nandi, in October 1827. Thousands of mourners were bludgeoned to death, and for a year, on Shaka's orders, no women were to get pregnant, no crops to be planted and no milk drunk. After three months Shaka came to his senses and revoked the edicts; but the damage to his prestige had been done.

His assassins were his half-brothers Dingane and Mhlangana. On 24 September 1828, while the army was away campaigning and Shaka virtually unprotected, they launched their attack. As Shaka was stabbed by each brother in turn, he pleaded with them: 'What is the matter, children of my father?' They ignored his cries for mercy and finished him off in a flurry of thrusts from the weapon he had invented. He was 41 years old.

which seemed to speak of something desperate, facilitated he succeeded in destroying more than a million men, women and children.'

Shaka Zulu

'Soldiers ... this is what awaits you ... no pay but toil and danger, no roof, no rest, but absolute poverty, exhausting vigils, extreme marches, and fighting ... Who loves Italy follow me!'

GARIBALDI TO HIS TROOPS, ROME, 2 JULY 1849

GARIBALDI

1807–82

LUCY RIALL

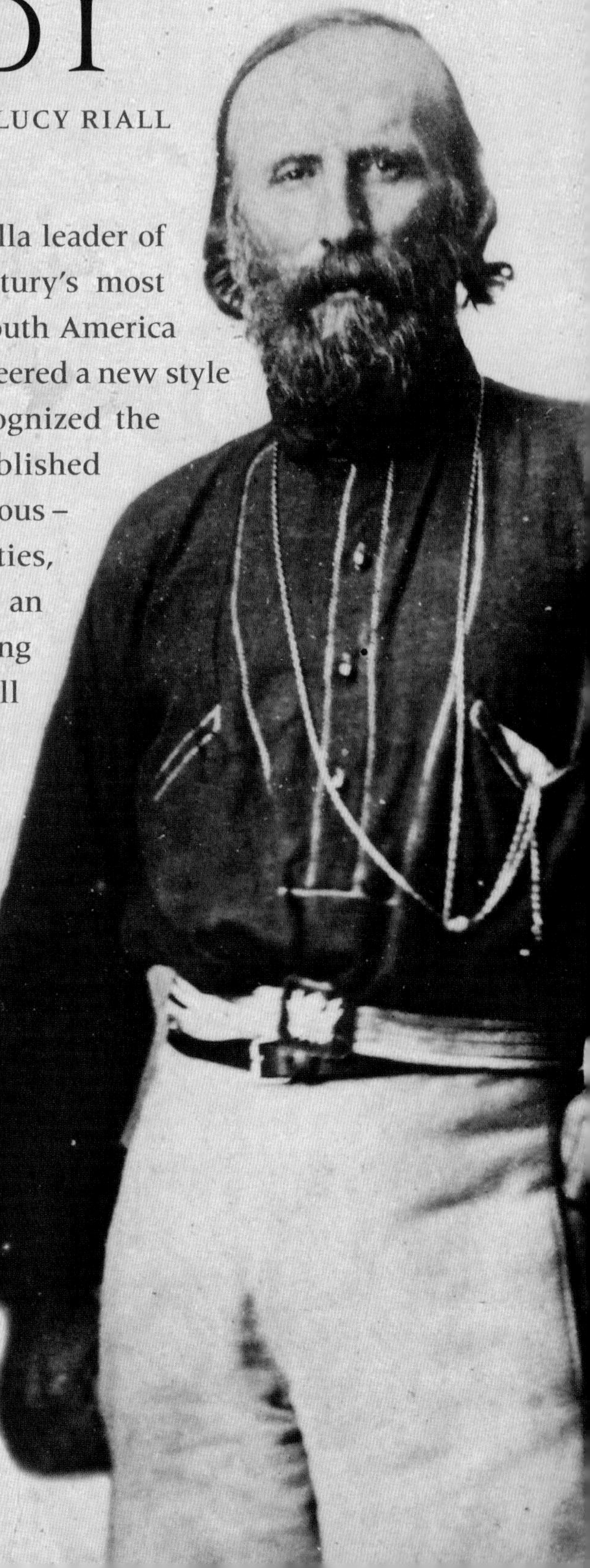

GIUSEPPE GARIBALDI was the greatest guerrilla leader of the nineteenth century, and possibly the century's most popular hero. His career spanned Europe and South America and, from these experiences, he adapted and pioneered a new style of warfare. A convinced revolutionary, he recognized the weakness of his forces relative to those of established regimes; and the tactics for which he became famous – commanding untrained men of varied capacities, using passion and courage as a weapon against an enemy superior in number and resources, relying on mobility and surprise to get ahead – were all designed to overcome this disadvantage.

Giuseppe Garibaldi – dashing guerrilla leader, radical republican and a great popular hero far beyond his native Italy.

Garibaldi's successes were still more important for the challenge they posed to perceptions of Italian decadence and cowardice. Before Garibaldi, all revolutionary uprisings against Italy's rulers ended in humiliating defeat, and had reinforced stereotypes of Italian military weakness associated with the peninsula's political decline. 'Italians don't know how to fight,' proclaimed General Oudinot, heading the army sent to Rome in 1849 to crush the short-lived revolutionary Roman Republic. Garibaldi's victory on that famous occasion tied his name for ever to a vision of Italian military resurgence – the *Risorgimento*.

Garibaldi's feats on the battlefield captivated the liberal public. Good-looking, brave

and charming, he led an adventurous life that became the stuff of popular legend. In his self, he defied all military convention. His image was that of the radical soldier-hero, the embodiment of romantic rebellion, his long hair, exotic clothes and overt sexuality representing a drastic departure from the traditional, austere military type. Garibaldi's international fame also had a direct impact on his military successes. It guaranteed a steady supply of volunteers and money for his cause, while his fearsome reputation served to intimidate his adversaries, and often helped him gain the upper hand. Yet his extremism caused problems with the established authorities. Tensions with the regular military hierarchy tarnished the wars of Italian unification, and Garibaldi remained until his death a controversial figure, as disliked by conservative Europe as he was loved by radicals, outsiders and the poor.

Character and early career

Garibaldi's military career is inseparable from his belief in liberty and independence. As a young man in 1834, he deserted his post in the Piedmontese navy and was sentenced to death for his part in a nationalist conspiracy against the Piedmontese government. In 1835 he left for a new life as a merchant seaman in Brazil. There he became convinced of what he called a 'greater destiny', and abandoned commercial life to become a corsair for the Río Grande government, engaged in a war for independence from Brazil.

After four tough years of fighting at sea and on land, and as the war petered out into a bloody civil conflict, Garibaldi moved to Montevideo in Uruguay, where war had broken out between Uruguay and the Argentine confederation over control of the Río de la Plata region. He was to remain in Uruguay from 1841 until early 1848, first as a naval officer, then as the commander of the Uruguayan fleet, and finally as the head of the Italian Legion of Montevideo, organized to defend the city against the Argentine siege.

According to the liberal historian G. M. Trevelyan, Garibaldi's education at sea and on the plateaux of South America sheltered him 'from every influence which might have turned him into an ordinary man or an ordinary soldier'. His experiences there had a lasting impact on his political beliefs, and were especially crucial from a military point of view. In Brazil, Garibaldi learnt the art of guerrilla warfare and how to ride a horse; in Uruguay, he perfected these skills and discovered in himself the outstanding talents of a naval and military leader. Although doubts have always been cast on Garibaldi's achievements (there were rumours of piracy and plunder, and he was accused of insubordination), the skill with which he helped put together a fighting force from the Italian community in Montevideo seems harder to dispute. Here, as elsewhere during his career, Garibaldi's personal qualities played a vital role. With his officers, Garibaldi led from the front and by example. They moved fast and light, and defeated the enemy in surprise attacks; and when trapped or outnumbered, as in the celebrated battle of San Antonio del Salto in 1846, used the tactics of frontal assault to break out and scatter their adversaries.

The Italian legionaries of Montevideo wore red shirts, in an explicit reference to the colours of the French Revolution. In other aspects of their eclectic dress, and in their manners and relationships, they copied the gaucho militias of South America; Garibaldi, in the words of a British naval officer who observed him at this time, resembled 'altogether the beau ideal of a chief of irregular troops'. They attracted publicity, and this publicity was used in the parallel propaganda war being waged against Argentina. The Legion itself, and specifically its public commitment to the liberty of Uruguay against the tyranny of Buenos Aires, embodied a spirit of combatant cosmopolitanism. Personal courage, flamboyant dress and international solidarity: all these were to prove lasting motifs for Garibaldi and his followers.

The Revolution of 1848–9

When Garibaldi returned to Italy in the spring of 1848 he was already a well-known figure. But his efforts to join the Piedmontese army, and to support Charles Albert of Piedmont-Sardinia in his self-proclaimed nationalist war against the Austrian empire, were rejected by the king. Garibaldi's first Italian operation, conducting guerrilla action against the Austrian army in the Lake Maggiore area during August 1848, was also not a success.

All this changed at Rome in 1849. French military intervention at the end of April to restore the pope, who had fled the city following revolutionary disturbances there, should have spelt the immediate end to the isolated and largely undefended Roman Republic that had been proclaimed in February. But in one of the most spectacular episodes in his career, Garibaldi and his volunteer army met the French forces on the Janiculum Hill and led a massive bayonet charge on horseback that put the French to flight. He followed this up with two further victories, at the battles of Palestrina and Velletri.

The small Roman Republic was indeed doomed, especially after Garibaldi was tricked by the French, who broke a military truce and seized and held on to the vital strategic heights around Villa Corsini in early June. However, it is for these early, heroic victories in Rome that the Republic is most remembered.

At the time, and later, Garibaldi was criticized by other nationalist leaders both for disobeying orders and for suicidal attacks on unassailable positions (his attempt to retake Villa Corsini resulted in terrible casualties). That said, Garibaldi showed how to snatch moral victory out of certain defeat. Helped by able propagandists, the defence of Rome made front-page news in the international press, and made a villain of the pope and a hero of Garibaldi. Events thereafter – Garibaldi's departure from Rome in July, his march north across the mountains in an attempt to defend Venice from Austrian siege, and the death en route of Anita, his pregnant Brazilian wife – all turned him into a legend. Moreover, the spread and popularity of the volunteer movement, and their victories in the early summer, seemed to create a template for military success.

Exile and independence

After 1849 Garibaldi spent four years away, first in New York and then as a merchant seaman in the Pacific Ocean. Only in 1854 did he return to Europe. There, in a changing political climate, he seemed to abandon his republican convictions and to move closer to the moderate liberalism then being experimented with by the Savoy monarchy in Piedmont. When the 'National Society' was formed in 1857 to press for national unifi-cation in Italy under the leadership of Piedmont, Garibaldi was one of its first members.

Garibaldi's rapprochement with the new Piedmontese king, Victor Emmanuel II, and with Cavour, his prime minister, led to their alliance during the war of 1859. This war was the product of a secret agreement between France and Piedmont, and its purpose was to drive Austria out of northern Italy. Cavour made a number of promises in return for French military assistance, the most important of which was the cession of two provinces, Savoy and Nice, to France, and he also undertook to provoke Austria into declaring war on Piedmont. Garibaldi became a pawn in this plan of provocation: specifically, his name was used to encourage men to join volunteer militias, and his fame became part of the anti-Austrian agitation in the months leading up to the war.

The reality was that Garibaldi's role in the planned war with Austria was far from clear, and both the French and Piedmontese high command had severe misgivings about using him and the volunteers. In the end, however, they bowed to nationalist pressure, and Garibaldi was made a major-general in the army and allowed to organize three volunteer corps (the *Cacciatori delle Alpi*). Yet at the outbreak of war, he was given the oldest and least trained men and sent away from the main army into the mountains. Still Garibaldi won some notable victories over the Austrian forces there: first at Varese and then at San Fermo and Como.

The 1859 war ended with the compromise Peace of Villafranca, by which Austria held on to Venetia; this infuriated moderates and revolutionaries alike. Just as the French, by negotiating a separate peace with Austria, had reneged on the deal with Cavour, so had official Piedmontese obstruction hampered Garibaldi's progress during the 1859 war. Nevertheless, Garibaldi's skill as a guerrilla commander and in Alpine warfare was much in evidence in 1859, as was the population's enthusiastic support for both he himself and his cause. Garibaldi, commented one observer, 'did not seem to be a general as much as the leader of a new religion, followed by a fanatical rabble'. During the events of 1860 this popular fervour intensified still further.

> '**Garibaldi has done Italy the greatest service ... he has proved ... that Italians can fight and die in battle to reconquer a fatherland. Everybody recognizes this.**'
>
> COUNT CAMILLO BENSO DI CAVOUR, 9 AUGUST 1860

'The Thousand'

In the spring of 1860, amid international condemnation, Piedmont ceded Savoy and Nice to France. For Garibaldi it represented a personal defeat. During the previous winter he had sought to continue the nationalist struggle against Austria by organizing a volunteer army 'made up of every man able to carry a firearm', along with a popular subscription to buy a million rifles. Blocked by Piedmontese officialdom, he had been forced to abandon these plans. The handover of Nice was even more of a blow. The town was Garibaldi's birthplace, and its cession cemented both his political frustration and sense of betrayal by Cavour: 'Thirty years of service for the cause of popular freedom,' he exclaimed, '[and] I will have won only the servitude of my poor land!'

In this mood, Garibaldi let himself be talked into leading a military expedition to Sicily, where the Bourbon government was said to be facing a serious insurrection. But the news from Sicily was vague, and when the expedition left Quarto, near Genoa, in early May, it comprised just over a thousand poorly armed volunteers (their rifles had been seized by the Piedmontese government). The men were crammed into two

Count Camillo Benso di Cavour, prime minister of Piedmont 1852–9, who in 1860 became the first prime minister of the newly formed Kingdom of Italy. Alongside Garibaldi, Cavour was the other great figure in Italian unification, but the two men had very different political agendas.

Giuseppe Garibaldi

boats seized in Genoa, and they lacked a clear idea, or even maps, of their destination. What the volunteers did possess, however, was patriotic enthusiasm. Passion and bravery, disorganization and good fortune: these elements lay behind the story of 'the Thousand' and lent a miraculous quality to all that ensued.

The volunteers landed at Marsala in western Sicily, and quickly pressed into the interior. In the hill town of Salemi they joined forces with Sicilian revolutionaries, notably with some peasant irregulars (or *picciotti*). From here, against all odds, they overcame the enemy on a hillside at Calatafimi (see p. 186). Then, in a masterstroke of guerrilla strategy, Garibaldi decided not to descend immediately into Palermo from the west but to remain hidden in the mountains, join up with more peasants, and enter the city from its most vulnerable point on the southeast side. The wounded were sent south on the Corleone road so that the Bourbons would believe that the *Garibaldini* were retreating, and send troops from Palermo to pursue them.

On the morning of 27 May Garibaldi and his men climbed silently down the mountain path from Gibilrossa to Palermo's Porta Termini, where only a temporary gate stood between them and the city. They took the troops guarding the city by surprise ('total surprise', one volunteer wrote in his diary), and under heavy fire charged into one of the main markets, the Piazza Fieravecchia, where they were greeted with enthusiasm. Garibaldi then went on to seize the municipal government building and the adjacent crossroads in the centre of town. There followed three days of street fighting during which Bourbon warships in the port opened fire on the city, while Garibaldi made a great show of his indifference, giving orders out in the open while the shells crashed around him. On 30 May the Bourbon government requested

GARIBALDI'S CAMPAIGNS IN SICILY, May 1860.

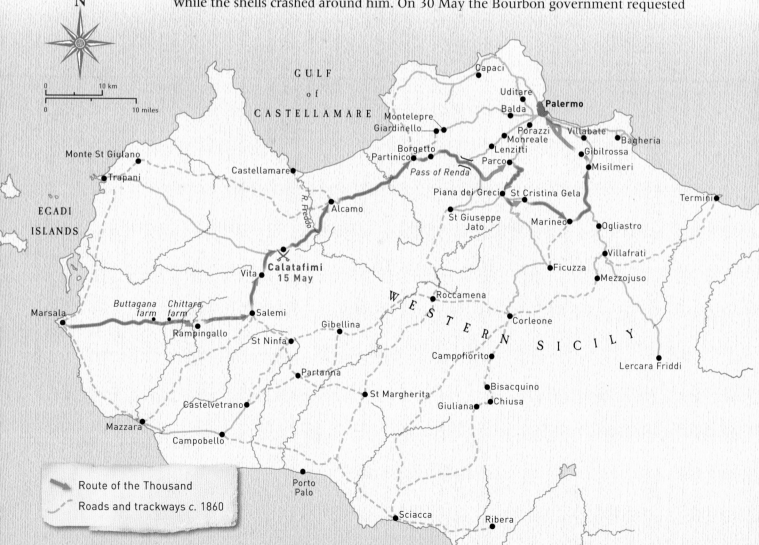

a truce, which was negotiated by a British naval commander in Palermo; the truce was extended until 6 June when the government capitulated entirely and agreed to withdraw all 20,000 troops from the city.

Sicily was Garibaldi's moment, on which much of his status as a great commander rests. To this day, there remains something astonishing about what he achieved. In less than a month, a handful of poorly armed civilians had challenged and overthrown a regular army, relying on little more than daring, local knowledge and luck. Although the weakened state of Bourbon bureaucracy played a role in its army's defeat, much of the credit must go to Garibaldi. Apart from his ability to continually wrong-foot the enemy, perhaps the most important element in explaining his success was his use of the volunteers. As Calatafimi showed, their courage and self-motivation could make the difference in close-combat situations using the bayonet. 'It was not long shots that imposed on the well-armed Neapolitans [Bourbons]', Garibaldi told his men in 1860, 'but a determined rush in advance.'

These same tactics worked at the Battle of Milazzo in July, and in his army's rapid sweep through Calabria and the southern mainland towards Naples in August. When Garibaldi arrived in Salerno, south of Naples, in early September he was moving so fast that he had left most of his army behind. His progress so disheartened the enemy that, according to one observer, 'Garibaldi ... [had] gradually assumed the nature and the form of Fate.' On 7 September Garibaldi took a train from Salerno to Naples and entered the capital to a vociferous public welcome. The Bourbon king, Francis II, had abandoned the city days before and had retreated to the fortress of Capua some miles to the north.

Garibaldi and the Thousand at Quarto, near Genoa, in early May 1860, embarking on their long voyage to Sicily and glory, as depicted by Gerolamo Induno (1825–90). Their red shirts symbolized the spirit of the French Revolution, republican fervour and international solidarity.

Giuseppe Garibaldi

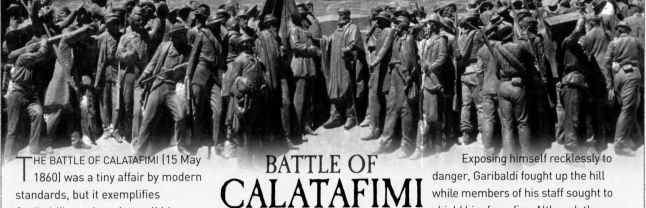

BATTLE OF CALATAFIMI

THE BATTLE OF CALATAFIMI (15 May 1860) was a tiny affair by modern standards, but it exemplifies Garibaldi's tactics, above all his capacity to surprise and improvise. The disadvantages he faced were evident from the outset. He was outnumbered (around 2,000 men against 1,200) and entirely outgunned. The Bourbon army had better and more rifles, and much more ammunition; they also occupied a defensive position on the top of a steep hill (the Pianto dei Romani) on which they placed two cannons.

Undaunted, Garibaldi relied on two elements to make his advance up the precipitous slope. The first was the intermittent, partly overgrown, terraces constructed on the hillside, which provided some cover from view. The second element was the fearless courage of his officers. It was Garibaldi himself who led the first rush up the hill, drawing his sword and shouting to his men to follow him. As one of the volunteers recounted: 'We thousand attacked, with the General in the lead: every last soldier was used without pause, without care, and without reservation because on that day rested the outcome of the whole expedition.'

Exposing himself recklessly to danger, Garibaldi fought up the hill while members of his staff sought to shield him from fire. Although the outcome of the battle was doubtful until the very last minute, the 'Thousand' kept up a relentless pressure on the enemy throughout the long, hot afternoon. At last, they stood on the final terrace before the summit. Garibaldi rallied his men for one more rush ('Italians, here we must die,' he reportedly told them), and, leaping over the bank in one final bayonet charge, they managed to scare the Bourbon soldiers into a full-blown retreat across the countryside.

Victory at Calatafimi changed everything. Its price was some thirty killed and over a hundred wounded, but it opened the road to Palermo and made the conquest of Sicily possible. The victorious leader, Garibaldi, acquired an aura of invincibility. The battle also began the process of demoralization that was to play a significant part in the defeat and collapse of the Bourbon kingdom in 1860.

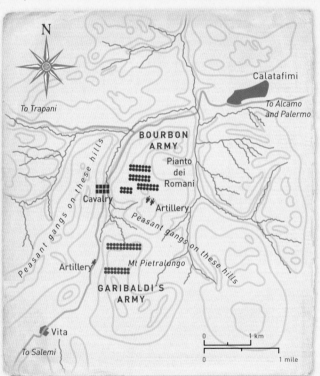

(Above) **The monument erected in 1892** near Calatafimi, Sicily, the site of one of Garibaldi's greatest victories, in which his volunteers, heavily outgunned and outnumbered, successfully stormed the enemy's strong hilltop position.

Unification

After Naples, Garibaldi won one more battle, on 1 October on the River Volturno against a Bourbon counter-attack with 50,000 men (Garibaldi's army was now some 20,000 strong). The battle lasted two days, and Garibaldi proved a master at maintaining offensive–defensive tactics along the whole line of attack. The point is worth stressing because, in the same period, he also allowed himself to be politically

Giuseppe Garibaldi

outmanoeuvred by the Piedmontese. During the summer Cavour had become alarmed at Garibaldi's progress, and came under international pressure to protect Rome and the pope from his threatened invasion. Accordingly, Cavour sent an army through the Papal States towards Naples and, at the end of October, Garibaldi met King Victor Emmanuel II and quietly handed power over to him.

The story of Italian unification was beset by rivalries within the nationalist movement, and 1860 was no exception. By giving the Bourbon kingdom to the king of Piedmont, Garibaldi abandoned the hope, long-cherished by republicans, that Italy would be united by the people. Until his death in 1882 he continued to campaign tirelessly for radical reform in the new liberal state, but the political defeat suffered in Naples put a halt to his heroic progress and overshadowed the rest of his career.

Garibaldi was involved in four military campaigns between 1860 and 1882, and they reflect his awkward position in a united Italy. In 1866 he fought with the king against Austria, and saw Venetia absorbed into the kingdom of Italy. Twice during the 1860s – in 1862 and 1867 – he led attempts to march on Rome and seize the city from the pope, but the first time he was stopped by Italian troops at Aspromonte (and badly wounded in the foot), and on the second occasion he was defeated by the French at Mentana. The French forces were equipped with the chassepot rifle, which allowed for fast reloading, and Garibaldi's tactics of rushing forward with the bayonet were no match for this weapon. Despite defeat at Mentana, in 1870 Garibaldi left for France to help defend the newly formed Third Republic against Prussian invasion. He was now old and ill, and the campaign was ineffective. However, Garibaldi's actions in France affirmed the principle of international solidarity; they were a reminder of his glory days in Brazil and Uruguay fighting for the freedom of oppressed peoples.

Revolutionary precursor

By the end of his life Garibaldi had become an uncomfortable presence, his skills supplanted by innovations in military technology. Still he represents much more than a parenthesis between the land battles of the Napoleonic period and the trench warfare of 1914–18. He was a precursor of the revolutionary militias of the twentieth century, and was the first to bring guerrilla tactics from America to Europe. He was a leading tactician of the volunteer movement, a crucial organization in the mid-nineteenth-century world. He was an exceptionally versatile commander, equally at home on land and at sea, and able to command field armies as well as guerrilla bands. Garibaldi may make us nostalgic for a time when courage could make the difference in battle. Yet his military victories were also modern, linked to the uses of publicity, fame and the press, and these tactics were not lost on the generations that followed.

Garibaldi before Capua, in a painting by Domenico Induno (1815–78). The Bourbon king, Francis II, had fled to the Campanian city after Garibaldi and his Red Shirts entered Naples to great popular rejoicing on 7 September 1860.

'To be a good soldier, you must love the army. To be a good commander, you must be willing to order the death of the thing you love.' ROBERT E. LEE

ROBERT E. LEE

1807–70

JOHN A. BARNES

ROBERT E. LEE was the most successful Confederate general in the American Civil War. His leadership is widely credited with preventing Union forces from overcoming the Confederate government in Richmond, Virginia, for nearly three years. Given the encrustation of political and historical agendas that attached to his name in the decades after the war and his own death, however, an objective assessment of his military reputation has proved difficult. Only in recent years has more scholarship in this area been undertaken, work that has revealed Lee as a bold tactician, but a deeply flawed strategist.

The family into which Robert Edward Lee was born on 19 January 1807 was one of the most distinguished in America. Lee's father, Revolutionary War hero Henry 'Light Horse Harry' Lee, served as a governor of Virginia and a US congressman, but he nevertheless disgraced the family name by his profligate spending and was twice imprisoned for debt. Young Robert and his siblings grew up in homes borrowed from wealthy relatives.

Lee's desire to erase this disgrace has been cited by biographers, notably Emory Thomas, as the source of his fabled rectitude, his drive to succeed and his devotion to what he saw as his duty. When he graduated second in his class from the US Military Academy at West Point in 1829, he was one of only a handful of cadets in the history of that institution to complete the course without incurring a single demerit.

Early career and Mexican War experience

Commissioned into the elite Army Corps of Engineers, Lee spent the first decade and a half of his military career working on various engineering projects in Virginia, New York, Maryland, Georgia and Missouri. In 1831 he married Mary Anne Randolph Custis, the daughter of George Washington's adopted son, which brought him the Custis mansion in Arlington, overlooking Washington DC.

Like his future antagonist Ulysses S. Grant, Lee's major pre-Civil War experience was the Mexican War. Attached to the staff of Major General Winfield Scott, Lee demonstrated his personal bravery on several occasions, distinguishing himself at the

Robert E. Lee

battles of Cerro Gordo, Contreras and Churubusco, and the final, war-winning assault on Chapultepec.

The war gained Lee valuable combat experience, though some historians (notably Edward H. Bonekemper III) think that Lee might well have drawn erroneous conclusions from that war about the value of audacious tactics and the efficacy of frontal assaults. While frequently successful against poorly trained and led Mexican infantry equipped with smoothbore muskets, such tactics would be far more problematic fifteen years later against Union soldiers firing rifled muskets.

The Civil War: early frustrations

Lee returned to garrison life following the Mexican War, serving for several years as superintendent (commanding officer) of the US Military Academy at West Point. In 1856 he accepted appointment as lieutenant colonel and executive officer of the 2nd US Cavalry Regiment in Texas.

A dramatic side-event of these years was Lee's capture of the anti-slavery zealot John Brown in October 1859, after Brown seized the federal arsenal at Harper's Ferry, Virginia, in an abortive effort to provoke a slave uprising in the South. The efficiency of Lee's operation further enhanced his reputation in Washington circles.

On the recommendation of Winfield Scott, Lee was offered overall command of US forces after the commencement of the Civil War in April 1861. Lee declined, however, since his native state of Virginia had chosen to secede and Lee resigned his commission. He was almost immediately commissioned a major general in the Virginia militia, and later a full general in the new Confederate States Army. He was also named military adviser to President Jefferson Davis.

The immediate problem facing the new Confederate government was the north-western counties of Virginia, where there were few slaves and the bulk of the population opposed secession. Union troops swiftly occupied most of this area (the future state of West Virginia).

Davis dispatched Lee on 22 July 1861 with vague orders to 'inspect' and 'consult' on the campaign. Once on the scene, Lee declined to bring order out of the chaos, sticking instead to the letter of his instructions to act merely as an observer. Later in the summer and autumn, he took a more active role, becoming de facto commanding officer, but this did little to salvage the situation. Although his forces actually outnumbered those of his Union opponents, the campaign ended in a complete rout for the Confederates.

For the next eight months Lee would operate under the cloud of this disaster. On 6 November he was dispatched to South Carolina to supervise the construction of defences in that region, a posting that earned him the nickname 'the King of Spades' from his soldiers as they dug in. For Lee, it was a backwater posting. He remained in the southeast until early March 1862, when he was recalled to Richmond to resume his post as Davis's chief military adviser.

The Seven Days Battle and the emergence of Lee

On 31 May 1862 General Joseph E. Johnston, who was commanding Confederate forces defending Richmond against the approach of Union Major General George McClellan's huge force on the Virginia Peninsula, was wounded at the Battle of Seven Pines. Davis named Lee as Johnston's successor, changing the character of the war entirely.

Lee succeeded in pushing the Union forces back from the gates of Richmond in the conclusion of the Battle of Seven Pines. Later in June he embarked on what became known as the Seven Days Battle, employing what came to be seen as the hallmark of his style: seizing the initiative with highly complex plans that involved aggressive attacks on Union forces; however, while these plans often resulted in tactical victory, it was only at the expense of high casualties to his own forces.

It was during this campaign that Lee began his famed partnership with an intense western Virginian named Thomas Jonathan Jackson (see pp. 196–203). The nickname of 'Stonewall' that Jackson earned at the First Battle of Manassas (also known as the First Battle of Bull Run) might indicate a preference for defensive tactics, but this was in no way true. Jackson turned out to be virtually the only one of Robert E. Lee's immediate subordinates who thrived under Lee's habit of issuing discretionary orders.

Commander of the Army of Northern Virginia

Having removed the threat to Richmond by mid July 1862, Lee wasn't about to rest on his laurels. With Union forces reorganizing in northern Virginia, Lee struck in that direction. With the audacious 'Stonewall' Jackson at his side, Lee routed Union forces under John Pope at the Second Battle of Manassas (also known as the Second Battle of Bull Run). Within two months Lee had moved the seat of battle from the gates of the Confederate capital of Richmond to the gates of the Union capital of Washington. At the same time, his popularity with the Southern people soared. Talk of 'the King of Spades' was gone.

At the same time, however, these victories were costing Lee in treasure he could not afford: manpower. Of the 95,000 men he had inherited on 1 June 1862, 30,000 had become casualties less than two months later. Union losses were also high, but less so in proportional terms, as the Union had a far larger population base on which to draw. Lee was demonstrating that he was all too willing to order the death of that which he loved: his army.

At least in part because of these losses, Lee promptly planned another offensive, this time north of the Potomac river into Maryland. The latter was a slave-holding state, but one that had been kept in the Union by the Lincoln administration through

a combination of force and subterfuge. Lee believed that if his victorious army entered the state, pro-Confederate Marylanders would flock to fill its depleted ranks.

It was not to be. On 3 September Lee's army crossed the Potomac into the western part of the state, led by a band playing the pro-Confederate anthem, 'Maryland, My Maryland'. Unfortunately for Lee, this portion of the state was pro-Union and unlikely to be susceptible to secessionist appeals. The new recruits on which Lee premised the campaign stayed away in droves.

On the Union side, although it was as slow-moving as usual, McClellan's Army of the Potomac was not idle. While moving to intercept Lee, a group of Union soldiers from an Indiana regiment discovered, under a tree and wrapped around three cigars, a copy of Lee's orders. These revealed that Lee had divided his forces in the face of the enemy, as he often did, to create the impression he had a much larger army than was actually the case. How the famous 'Lost Order' came to be lost remains a mystery – although one of Lee's shortcomings as a commander was that his staff was far too small for the tasks assigned to it, and in retrospect it is amazing that more crucial orders did not go astray.

Such an intelligence bonanza should have resulted in a crushing victory for any general but George McClellan. Instead, the result was the bloody but inconclusive Battle of Antietam on 17 September 1862. Outnumbered more than two to one and with its back to the Potomac river, Lee's army came to the brink of defeat several times. Each time, however, through a combination of luck, daring and Union ineptitude, Lee staved it off.

Tactically, Antietam ranks as one of Lee's great battles. Strategically, however, the campaign was a disaster for Lee and the Confederacy. Not only had the hoped-for recruits failed to materialize, but Lee had suffered a terrible 11,700 casualties, nearly a quarter of his men. Worse, Lee's retreat in the wake of the battle across the Potomac

Antietam Bridge, Maryland, site of the bloodiest single day's fighting of the Civil War, 17 September 1862. Although Lee managed to stave off defeat at the hands of an opposing force more than twice the size of his own, the battle proved to be a strategic victory for the Union.

back into Virginia looked ignominious. A few days later, Abraham Lincoln felt sufficiently confident to issue his preliminary Emancipation Proclamation, declaring that unless the Confederate states abandoned the war and returned to the Union by 31 December, all the South's slaves would be 'henceforth and forever free'. Given the battle's outcome and the issuance of the Proclamation, the prospect of British and French intervention – always the Confederacy's most realistic hope for independence – dimmed considerably.

Lincoln sacked McClellan a few months after Antietam, replacing him with Ambrose Burnside, who had won some minor victories early in the war. Burnside proved no saviour. In a grim preview of the Western Front in the First World War, on 13 December 1862 he sent wave after wave of Union infantrymen against Lee's solidly entrenched army at Fredericksburg, Virginia. The result was Lee's most lopsided victory, incurring only 4,700 casualties to nearly 11,000 for the Union.

Lee wrote frequently of his desire to inflict a 'Cannae' on the Union army, referring to Hannibal's victory of 216 BC in which his forces killed an estimated 50,000 Romans. Lee probably missed his best chance at Fredericksburg by failing to follow up his tactical success on 13 December with an attack late that day or early the next. Fredericksburg illustrates the key flaw in Lee's generalship: although his tactical gambles won him successes, he proved unable to cash in these successes for strategic victory.

The road to Gettysburg

As 1863 dawned, the Union Army of the Potomac received yet another commander, Major General Joseph Hooker, who replaced the hapless Burnside. Hooker made a good start with a decent plan that caught Lee napping on 27 April 1863, when the 130,000-strong Union force crossed the Rappahannock river to face Lee's army, which was only half as strong. The result was the Battle of Chancellorsville, Lee's greatest military success (see opposite).

The most consequential result of Chancellorsville was the death of 'Stonewall' Jackson. 'He has lost his left arm, but I have lost my right,' lamented Lee upon hearing

The Battle of Fredericksburg, 13 December 1862, in a contemporary oil painting. The solidly entrenched Confederate forces inflicted appalling casualties on wave after wave of attacking Union troops, commanded by the inept Ambrose Burnside. Lee's victory ended the Union campaign to capture the Confederate capital of Richmond, Virginia.

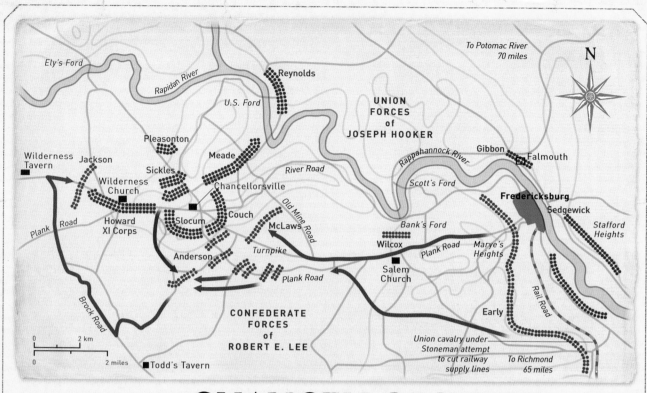

On the map (clockwise and by region):

To Potomac River 70 miles

N

Ely's Ford
Rapidan River
U.S. Ford
Reynolds
Pleasonton
Meade
Wilderness Tavern
Jackson
Wilderness Church
Sickles
River Road
Chancellorsville
UNION FORCES of JOSEPH HOOKER
Rappahannock River
Gibbon
Falmouth
Scott's Ford
Fredericksburg
Sedgewick
Stafford Heights
Howard XI Corps
Slocum
Couch
Old Mine Road
McLaws
Bank's Ford
Wilcox
Plank Road
Marye's Heights
Plank Road
Anderson
Turnpike
Plank Road
Salem Church
Early
Rail Road
Brock Road
CONFEDERATE FORCES of ROBERT E. LEE
Union cavalry under Stoneman attempt to cut railway supply lines
To Richmond 65 miles

0   2 km
0   2 miles
Todd's Tavern

THE BATTLE OF **CHANCELLORSVILLE**

THE CHANCELLORSVILLE CAMPAIGN promised to be a virtual Union walkover. With more than 130,000 well-rested and supplied troops at his disposal, Army of the Potomac commander Major General Joseph Hooker outnumbered Robert E. Lee's ragged, often barefoot Army of Northern Virginia by better than two to one.

Worse, from the Confederate point of view, Hooker had devised a bold plan, using four corps to slip past Lee's left flank and into his rear, interposing themselves between Lee and his capital of Richmond. The remaining corps would occupy Lee by feinting through Fredericksburg on his right. Meanwhile, some 7,500 cavalry under Major General George Stoneman would raid deep into the Confederate rear, cutting Lee's lines of communication and supply.

But having seized the initiative, Hooker failed to hold it. Instead, he abruptly halted, hunkered down on the south side of the river, and dared Lee to attack his superior force. Lee and Jackson took the gamble, with Lee agreeing to divide his already greatly outnumbered army further and to allow Jackson to take the bulk of it on a roundabout march around Hooker's unsecured right flank.

For the plan to work, everything had to go perfectly from the Confederate point of view. Incredibly, everything did. 'Stonewall' Jackson achieved total surprise in his flank attack late of the afternoon of 2 May, routing the Union XI Corps. The blow was not fatal, however.

Hooker's huge force could have absorbed it and bounced back, but the commander was psychologically shattered. He withdrew across the Potomac river.

Lee's tactical victory at Chancellorsville, so unlikely in almost every respect, seems to have bred an arrogance of its own in both Lee and his soldiers. The latter came to believe in their general as a god-like miracle-worker, while the former seemed to believe he could ask anything of his men and they would loyally deliver. It was to prove a fatal combination at Gettysburg two months later.

Wounded soldiers after the battle of Chancellorsville, May 1863.

that Jackson had been accidentally wounded by his own men at the climax of the battle. This led to complications, and Jackson died of pneumonia a week later. Thus was Lee deprived of his most reliably aggressive commander.

Despite this crushing loss, Lee planned his most ambitious campaign: a second invasion of the North, this time into Pennsylvania. The precise reasons for this adventure Lee never adequately articulated. He was apparently hoping that a major victory won on Northern soil would persuade the North to sue for peace or, failing that, convince the European powers to enter the war on the Confederacy's side. As the Germans were to discover at Verdun in 1916, a vague hope of breaking your enemy psychologically is a thin reed on which to rest a major campaign.

Lee never intended to fight at Gettysburg. As usual, he had divided his army, and only hastily decided to concentrate it in the small Pennsylvania town after he learnt, to his surprise, that the Army of the Potomac was closing rapidly on his position. This unwelcome news was a result of Lee having lost contact with his cavalry commander, Major General J. E. B. Stuart. The latter, following vague and contradictory orders from Lee, had ridden off on an independent operation, leaving Lee 'blind'.

The entire campaign was plagued by such errors, most of them traceable to Lee himself. Thanks once more to vague orders, on the first day of the battle, 1 July, an opportunity was missed to capture a commanding hill. On the second day Lee insisted on attacking the Union forces in their strong position on Cemetery Ridge, against the advice of such trusted subordinates as Lieutenant General James Longstreet, who favoured waiting for the Union forces to attack, as they had at Fredericksburg. Lee compounded his error on the third and final day when he launched the near-suicidal 'Pickett's Charge', in which some 12,500 Confederate troops advanced across a mile of open ground swept by artillery and musket fire from defenders ensconced on high ground behind a stone wall.

Gettysburg exposed all of Lee's major weaknesses as a commander: an excess of aggression, overly complex battle-plans, a tendency to issue vague orders vulnerable to interpretation, and a curious refusal to take determined charge of the battlefield. As Lee's army began the inevitable retreat to Virginia on 4 July in driving rain, it was with staggering casualties: 22,600 out of 75,000 men engaged in the battle (see also pp. 208–9).

On the same day, Major General Ulysses S. Grant captured Vicksburg, Mississippi, cutting the Confederacy in two (see p. 217). Lee had refused to send any of his troops west to Vicksburg, insisting they would be better employed in Pennsylvania. Now Vicksburg was lost, and the Pennsylvanian campaign had ended in failure. Lee's lack of strategic vision was starkly revealed.

Lee vs Grant

Such losses dictated the cessation of any further major Confederate offensives. Not unlike Napoleon's Grande Armée in 1813–14, the Army of Northern Virginia remained tactically dangerous, but its strategic circumstances were dire. As the spring campaigning season approached in 1864, Lee's only real hope was to inflict such punishment on the Army of the Potomac that a war-weary Northern public would vote out the Lincoln administration in the November elections.

It was Lincoln who first realized that the manpower of the Army of Northern Virginia was fatally depleted, and his appointment of Grant as commanding general of all Union forces in March 1864 reflected this. Grant's grand strategy was to attack simultaneously all along the front, putting maximum pressure on both Lee and the Western theatre in Tennessee and Georgia, preventing one part of the front from reinforcing another. Eventually, the thinning grey line would crack.

It wasn't that simple, of course, and Lee's resourcefulness and legendary luck – not to mention some incompetence on the part of Grant's subordinate generals – combined to make it a very close-run thing. Ultimately, however, Grant's theory proved correct. The Confederate line did indeed crack, but in Georgia, not Virginia. William T. Sherman's spectacular capture of Atlanta in September 1864 saved Lincoln's re-election two months later. Lee's short-sighted focus on Virginia and his neglect of the Western theatre of operations proved his own – and his cause's – undoing.

Assessment

Lee is the only general in the English-speaking world to become the object of a personality cult. Embittered white American Southerners – the only English-speakers ever to experience defeat in a total war – elevated him to near god-like status in an attempt to make sense of their own suffering. Lee, and, by implication, all Southerners, were undone exclusively by the North's superior resources and numbers of men.

Decades of such thinking prevented a realistic appraisal of Lee's qualities as an army commander, at least by American historians. By contrast, British historians, notably J. F. C. Fuller and Basil Liddell Hart, penned far more critical portraits. Fuller described Lee as 'in several respects … one of the most incapable Generals-in-Chief in history'.

'He was a Caesar without his ambition; Frederick without his tyranny; Napoleon without his selfishness; and Washington without his reward.'

SENATOR BENJAMIN HILL OF GEORGIA, 18 FEBRUARY 1874

Looking at the totality of Lee's record, that conclusion seems hard to escape. Not only did Lee never devise a strategy for winning the war – and history is replete with examples of weaker powers defeating stronger ones – his audacious, costly attacks and stubborn insistence on having his own way served to undermine whatever strategy the Confederacy possessed.

What then, of Lee the tactician? It must be pointed out that, with the sole exception of Grant, Lee's direct Union opponents were mediocre commanders at best. The likes of John Pope and Ambrose Burnside are hardly yardsticks against which greatness is measured. Nor can the 'Jackson effect' be discounted. Lee won every single one of his victories with 'Stonewall' Jackson at his side. Once Jackson was gone – the one general who thrived under Lee's 'hands-off' style of leadership – the thunder and lightning went out of the Army of Northern Virginia. It never again won another major victory.

A test of a great commander is his legacy to the future. Ulysses S. Grant bequeathed not only a united country poised on the cusp of world-power status, but a strategy and approach to war-fighting that remain the basic doctrine of the US Army to this day. 'Stonewall' Jackson's 1862 'Valley Campaign' is still studied as an example of how a smaller, weaker army can have an impact out of all proportion to its actual size.

Lee's strategy and tactics, by contrast, have less to offer today's commanders. His iconic status, therefore, owes more to the political needs of the post-war South than to the actual value of his military record.

Robert E. Lee

'STONEWALL' JACKSON

RICHARD J. SOMMERS

1824-63

THE LEGENDARY 'STONEWALL' JACKSON was the second greatest Confederate general in the American Civil War. He proved equally effective as battle brigadier, small-army strategist and big-army executive officer. His death in the middle of the war leaves unanswered the question as to how the conflict might have developed had he lived.

Thomas Jonathan Jackson was born in Clarksburg in what is now West Virginia on 21 January 1824. He graduated from West Point, seventeenth of fifty-nine, in 1846. His classmates included twenty-four future Civil War generals, among them the Union commander George B. McClellan and the Southerner George E. Pickett.

Early career

The Mexican War was already raging when Jackson graduated from West Point. Brevetted second lieutenant and posted to Company K/1st US Artillery, he served with that company, acting as infantry, at Vera Cruz and Cerro Gordo. Promoted second lieutenant on 3 March 1847, he soon transferred to Light Battery G/1st US Artillery under Captain (later Confederate Major General) John B. Magruder. With that famous fighting formation, Jackson earned promotion to first lieutenant, plus brevets as captain and major for his 'gallant and meritorious conduct' at Contreras, Churubusco and Chapultepec.

Back in Company K, Jackson left Mexico for New York harbour in 1848. In 1850 he was detailed to Company E in Florida during the Seminole troubles. There he clashed with company commander Captain (later Union Major General) William H. French, whose drunken, libertine behaviour offended the dour, devout Presbyterian Jackson. Jackson left Florida in May 1851 and resigned his commission on 29 February 1852.

That resignation proved anti-climactic. Since August 1851 Jackson had been professor of natural philosophy and artillery tactics at the Virginia Military Institute (VMI) in Lexington. Both happiness and sadness awaited him there. He married Elinor Junkin in 1853, but the following year she died in childbirth. He married again in 1857; his second wife, Anna Morrison, was the sister-in-law of future Confederate Lieutenant General Harvey Hill. Hill was an engaging, if argumentative, professor, but

'Stonewall' Jackson

Jackson proved an uninspiring pedagogue, whose eccentricities were derided by the cadets. Indeed, had he not become famous, even these oddities would probably have remained unrecorded.

The coming conflict

The growing sectional strife between North and South was to transform Jackson's prospects. John Brown captured the federal arsenal at Harper's Ferry on 16–17 October 1859, hoping to spark a slave insurrection. Instead, counter-attacking US regulars and state militia suppressed his abortive rebellion. Convicted of treason against Virginia, Brown was hanged on 2 December; at the execution, Jackson commanded the VMI artillery to prevent any attempts to release the condemned man.

Brown's uprising was over, but a bigger conflict was about to start. After the Civil War erupted on 12 April 1861, Jackson, as a VMI professor and Virginia militia officer, became an officer of the commonwealth's army and of the Confederacy. He initially, on 20–22 April, led the VMI cadets to Richmond to train volunteers. He himself remained only until 28 April. Now a major in the Virginia army, he took charge of militia at Harper's Ferry. In his first – but not last – show of aggressiveness, he crossed the Potomac to occupy the commanding Maryland Heights, but was soon withdrawn lest Maryland take umbrage.

Less than a fortnight later, Brigadier General Joseph E. Johnston superseded Jackson as commander at Harper's Ferry. As senior subordinate, Jackson commanded the 1st Brigade of Johnston's army: the 2nd, 4th, 5th, 27th, and 33rd Virginia Infantry Regiments, soon to be immortalized as 'the Stonewall Brigade'. A Confederate brigadier general himself as of 17 June, Jackson repelled a Union incursion across the Potomac at Falling Waters on 2 July.

A much bigger victory came on 21 July at the First Battle of Manassas (also known as the First Battle of Bull Run), where Johnston's army had been transferred. As the Northerners overran the Confederate left, one of Jackson's fellow generals spotted Jackson's soldiers atop Henry House Hill. 'There is Jackson standing like a stone wall,' he shouted; 'let us determine to die here, and we will conquer.' Despite a severe wound in his left hand, Jackson stood firm and repulsed the Union forces, leading to a great Confederate victory. Henceforth, the general and his brigade were nicknamed 'Stonewall'.

'Stonewall' Jackson – 'Old Jack' to his men – cared little for personal comfort. On 1–4 January 1862 his iron will compelled his brigade to march through wind-driven sleet and snow over two icy mountains, often without rations, to capture strategic Bath and Romney, (West) Virginia.

Independent command

This victory earned Jackson promotion on 7 October to major general (backdated to 7 August), and command of one of Johnston's four divisions. Even greater responsibility came on 5 November, when he took charge of the Valley District – the Shenandoah Valley west to the Allegheny Mountains. Although still subordinate to Johnston, Jackson was now detached from the main army with his own semi-independent command.

The new command involved a large territory and considerable responsibility – but few troops, even after the Stonewall Brigade joined him; his other forces consisted of inexperienced militia brigades and undisciplined cavalry companies. The arrival of William Loring's veteran division in December brought more men and more headaches. Loring, formerly a US army colonel, resented being subordinated to pre-war 'Lieutenant' Jackson. Isolated in icy Romney, Loring protested to Secretary of War Judah Benjamin, who recalled his division to the Shenandoah Valley. Outraged, Jackson resigned, and was persuaded to stay in service only with great difficulty. Instead, it was Loring and two brigades who departed. The remaining two joined Jackson's 'Army of the Valley', now a division of four brigades – three infantry and one cavalry.

The move to Romney plus earlier strikes toward the Potomac aimed to cut coal supplies via the Baltimore and Ohio Railroad and the Chesapeake and Ohio Canal. Jackson also sought to mask his weakness with activity, and to keep the Union forces so busy defending they could not attack. He even began planning to carry the war into the North. These operations thus foreshadowed his great Valley Campaign of 1862 (see pp. 200–201).

Surprises strategic and psychological

The Valley Campaign of March–June 1862 was Jackson's greatest success. But before June ended, he suffered his greatest failure: the Seven Days Battle. At first the Confederate strategists considered sending Jackson's victorious veterans to invade Pennsylvania, but they decided instead to bring them east to relieve beleaguered Richmond. Jackson's force, now increased to nine infantry brigades grouped into three divisions, moving by rail and road, was to surprise and envelop the right-rear of three Union divisions isolated north of the Chickahominy river. Three other Confederate divisions would simultaneously attack their front. General Robert E. Lee, Johnston's successor as commander of the Army of Northern Virginia, hoped thereby to crush the Union V Corps and raise the siege of Richmond.

With his brigades in transit, on 23 June Jackson rode ahead to confer with Lee, the first meeting of the two greatest Confederate commanders. Since Jackson's force had to travel farthest, he was allowed to set the attack date. He confidently picked 25 June; at James Longstreet's suggestion, 26 June was chosen instead. Even that later date proved over-optimistic. The primitive logistical infrastructure of the Confederacy, plus poor staff work and Jackson's own neglect, made him miss that mark. Unthreatened from their right-rear, the Federals repulsed Lee's frontal assaults at Mechanicsville. Now alert to the danger, V Corps withdrew overnight to Gaines' Mill, where, on 27 June, it once more parried Lee's thrusts. Again Jackson was slow in striking, finally engaging in mid afternoon. Several hours later, two of his brigades pierced the Union centre to gain the one clear-cut Confederate tactical victory of the Seven Days Battle.

Though driven from the field, the Federals escaped south of the Chickahominy. Both sides spent the following day manoeuvring. When fighting resumed on 29 June, Jackson took no part in it. The crisis came on 30 June. While three Confederate divisions attacked retreating Union forces south of White Oak Swamp, Jackson's four divisions were to fight their way across the swamp into the Union rear. Other than desultory skirmishing and shelling, however, Jackson did nothing. With their rear unthreatened, the Federals repelled the other attacks. They then escaped to Malvern Hill, where, on 1 July, they repulsed repeated onslaughts, including six from Jackson's brigades. The Federals then safely withdrew to the James river. Richmond had been saved, but the Union army had not been crippled or destroyed, largely due to Jackson's failures.

Jackson's uncharacteristic performance in the Seven Days Battle is mystifying. Blaming either his supposed reluctance to fight on Sundays (sometimes offered as an explanation of his inaction on 29 June) or his alleged unwillingness to be subordinated is unfair. He fought on Sundays when necessary, and he later became a model subordinate. A better explanation is the Valley Campaign itself. Its rapid marches and sterling successes had made him overconfident, while its fatiguing operations had left him and his men physically exhausted. Psychological exhaustion further sapped his energy to press the enemy.

Spearhead of success

Relative rest restored Jackson's resolve and his soldiers' strength. By August, they were facing John Pope's new army in central Virginia. One of Pope's corps attacked Jackson at Cedar Mountain on 9 August, and actually made early progress. Confederate counter-attacks, however, secured the field.

Both Lee and Pope sparred along the Rapidan and upper Rappahannock rivers. Then in a bold surprise turning movement, Lee sent Jackson's three divisions north through Loudoun Valley, then east across Bull Run Mountains into Pope's rear. On 26 August Jackson captured the main Union forward supply base at Manassas Junction and crushed a brigade at Bull Run Bridge.

Union troops from Major General John Pope's army stand amidst the ruined supply base after Jackson's troops had sacked Manassas Junction. The ensuing Second Battle of Manassas (also known as the Second Battle of Bull Run) in August 1862 was a notable Confederate victory.

THE SHENANDOAH VALLEY CAMPAIGN OF 1862

MARCH 1862 WITNESSED MASSIVE MOVEMENTS by Northern forces in Virginia: George McClellan's main army against Manassas, Nathaniel P. Banks's three divisions up the Shenandoah Valley, and John C. Frémont's three brigades eastward from what is now West Virginia toward the Shenandoah Valley. The Confederate forces in those sectors – respectively under Joseph E. Johnston, Jackson and Edward Johnson – retreated before this onslaught.

Instead of pursuing, McClellan sent one division to Frémont and moved his main army by water to Fort Monroe to attack Richmond from the east. One of Banks's divisions joined that transfer toward Richmond; another began marching east from the Shenandoah Valley into the Piedmont. Johnston correspondingly moved his army from the Rappahannock river to the Peninsula. He left only Richard S. Ewell's division in the Piedmont and a brigade at Fredericksburg.

Jackson, too, abandoned Winchester. Rather than yield the entire Shenandoah Valley, however, on 23 March his small division pounced on a supposedly isolated detachment at Kernstown – which proved to be a strong division under James Shields that beat Jackson badly. Tactically, First Kernstown was a handsome Federal victory.

Strategically, it was a striking success. That Jackson felt strong enough to attack so alarmed President Lincoln and Secretary of War Edwin Stanton that they left Banks's two remaining divisions in the Shenandoah Valley. Even more significantly, they retained McClellan's largest corps in the Piedmont as an independent command under Irvin McDowell.

Banks moved southward far up the Shenandoah Valley before withdrawing to Strasburg. He then sent Shields east to McDowell at Fredericksburg. McDowell's strengthened force was to move southward against Richmond, which McClellan threatened from the east.

Jackson, who had withdrawn all the way to Swift Run Gap, did not remain idle but challenged the Yankees for the strategic initiative. He brought Ewell west to hold the gap, then moved his own Stonewall Division westward to join Johnson. At the battle of McDowell on 8 May they beat Frémont's vanguard, which retreated northward. Jackson then moved down the Shenandoah Valley and the parallel Luray Valley with ten brigades – his own, Johnson's and Ewell's. They captured a regiment at Front Royal on 23 May, then routed Banks's three brigades at First Winchester two days later. As the Federals fled across the upper Potomac, Jackson threatened Harper's Ferry.

Activity behind the Union lines at the Battle of Cross Keys in the Shenandoah Valley, 8 June 1862. Cross Keys proved to be one of the decisive Confederate victories in Jackson's Valley Campaign.

Tactical success, strategic surprise and supply windfall were Jackson's means of implementing Lee's seizure of the strategic initiative. Yet Jackson in Pope's rear was a vulnerable target until Lee's main body rejoined him. Bagging Jackson was not easy, however. On 27 August he held back his pursuers at First Bristoe Station, and the next day at Groveton fought a stand-up battle to a standstill. The Groveton fighting alerted Pope to Jackson's location, and over the next two days Jackson and his men came under massive assaults; but Jackson firmly held his ground along a railroad

'Stonewall' Jackson

The government in Washington exaggerated this thrust into a threat against the capital itself. New York militia mobilized, raw volunteer regiments rushed to Harper's Ferry, and Frémont's six brigades were ordered to enter the Shenandoah Valley near Strasburg to cut off Jackson. Even worse, McDowell's drive on Richmond was cancelled. He was directed to take two divisions westward to Front Royal to intercept Jackson.

Theoretically, uniting Frémont and McDowell in Jackson's rear might have proved the latter's undoing. But as it happened, coordinating two distant columns in rainy, mountainous country proved impossible. Jackson's hard-marching 'foot cavalry' escaped the trap, smacked Frémont's van at Strasburg on 1 June and withdrew up the Shenandoah Valley. Frémont followed. McDowell's leading division under Shields moved south in a parallel route up the Luray Valley.

On 6 June Jackson lost his inspiring if undisciplined cavalry commander, General Turner Ashby, in bloodying Frémont's pursuit at Harrisonburg. Two days later Ewell defeated Frémont's entire army at Cross Keys, and on 9 June Jackson thrashed Shields's two leading brigades at Port Republic. Frémont and Shields retreated down their respective valleys. At this point the victorious Jackson even considered invading Pennsylvania, but he was transferred east to save Richmond and to try to destroy McClellan.

The eight battles of the Valley Campaign, including seven Confederate victories, are fascinating in themselves. The campaign's inherent importance, however, lies in its strategic impact. With sometimes only four brigades and never more than ten, Jackson challenged seemingly overwhelming Federal forces of thirty brigades intent on overrunning the Shenandoah Valley and central Virginia, then joining McClellan at Richmond. Rather than let them concentrate, Jackson, with swift, bold strokes reminiscent

of Frederick the Great's a century earlier, beat some of the Union forces and diverted the rest, leaving the planners in Washington distracted and distraught, and disrupting their entire campaign plan. Jackson succeeded in delaying eight brigades from joining McClellan, and prevented the other twenty-two altogether. He thus changed the course of the campaign and thereby the war. In late March 1862, Union victory in Virginia had seemed certain. Three months later, thanks to Jackson, Washington's plans lay in ruins, and the Confederacy appeared ascendant.

embankment. Longstreet's arrival led to a great counter-attack on 30 August, which made the Second Battle of Manassas Lee's first great victory. Jackson's effort to exploit that success at Chantilly on 1 September produced only limited gains, however.

Pope's ensuing retreat into the defences around Washington virtually cleared Virginia of Union forces. Lee then carried the war across the Potomac in the hope of liberating Maryland and crippling the Northern war effort, long one of Jackson's goals. Jackson led the advance, which began on 4 September. Two days later his new horse injured him, but he resumed command within days. He then led his three divisions westward to isolate Harper's Ferry, while three other divisions helped surround the town itself. His and their successful attacks on 14 September doomed the Union position. The capitulation of its 12,400 defenders the following day was the largest US surrender until Bataan in the Philippines in 1942.

Such a triumph proved risky, however. Lee had boldly scattered his army from Harper's Ferry almost to Pennsylvania. When his dispersal order fell into Federal hands, Union commander George McClellan had a great opportunity to beat the Confederates in detail. McClellan secured South Mountain, but failed to exploit his advantage. Jackson's capture of Harper's Ferry emboldened Lee to remain north of the Potomac. Jackson joined him at Sharpsburg on 16 September, and the following day, at Antietam, held the Confederate left. The first Federal onslaught inflicted terrible losses on Jackson, but reinforcements restored his lines. Antietam proved the bloodiest day of the Civil War. Lee finally withdrew into Virginia, on 18/19 September.

Promotion and promising prospects

Lee's battered army spent October in the Shenandoah Valley, resting and refitting. While there, his two senior subordinates, Longstreet and Jackson, were promoted to the newly created rank of lieutenant general (Jackson ranking from 10 October). On 6 November their 'wings' were officially designated the I and II Corps of the Army of Northern Virginia. Jackson's II Corps contained the three divisions that had served under him since August, plus Harvey Hill's division.

This respite ended in late October as McClellan's final campaign drew both armies east of the Blue Ridge. McClellan's successor, Ambrose E. Burnside, advanced further southeast to Falmouth. Lee countered by moving Longstreet to Fredericksburg and shifting Jackson further downstream towards Port Royal. Burnside crossed the Rappahannock river at Fredericksburg on 11 December. Two days later, he frontally assaulted Lee's position. On the Confederate left, Longstreet repulsed successive Union attacks, but on the right Jackson, who had returned from Port Royal, was having a harder time defending his position. A Union division under George G. Meade actually penetrated a gap in the Light Division, which was holding Jackson's front, but Jackson's counter-attacks restored his line. Not content with such defensive success, Jackson wanted to drive the defeated and demoralized Union troops into the Rappahannock, but he was thwarted by the early December dusk and by Federal artillery fire from the left bank. On the night of 14/15 December the Union forces withdrew across the river.

'He has lost his left arm; but I have lost my right arm.'

ROBERT E. LEE, 7 MAY 1863, ON THE WOUNDING OF JACKSON AT CHANCELLORSVILLE

By the end of January the opposing armies had gone into winter quarters. The fighting resumed in late April, when the new Union commander, Joseph Hooker, sent eight divisions upstream to envelop Lee's left-rear. By then, three of Longstreet's divisions had gone south, and Lee had only six infantry divisions to meet this threat. Jackson left one division to confront eight Union divisions at Fredericksburg, and formed the remaining five divisions facing west to meet the turning movement. Jackson's bold show of strength and combative counter-jabs on 1 May punctured Hooker's pretensions to power, and the formerly aggressive Union general withdrew into the Wilderness to defensive positions around Chancellorsville plantation.

With audacity born of confidence in his troops and in his executive officer, Lee again divided his forces. He kept one division at Fredericksburg and two facing Hooker's thirteen divisions at Chancellorsville. On 2 May Jackson boldly marched the remaining three divisions westward, across the entire front of the Yankee army, from its far left to its far right. The Wilderness concealed him, and the closed minds of the Union commanders, who also suffered from overconfidence and lack of initiative, failed to comprehend that Jackson would undertake such a move. His own great ability enabled

him to carry it out. In the late afternoon of 2 May Jackson routed the Union right flank west of Chancellorsville, crushing XI Corps. The resulting victory proved to be Lee and Jackson's greatest battlefield success (see also p. 193).

For Jackson, it also proved to be his last. As he reconnoitred in the darkness that evening for ways to exploit his initial success, his own men fired on him in error, seriously wounding his right hand and left arm, which was subsequently amputated just below the shoulder. He appeared to recover, but died of complications eight days later. He is buried in Lexington.

Assessment

From First Manassas to Chancellorsville, 'Stonewall' Jackson was the great popular hero of the Confederacy. Such adulation left him untouched. His stern Calvinism led him to attribute his successes to God's will. Moreover, he understood that, to be meaningful, battlefield victories must translate into strategic success. His Valley Campaign of 1862 best represents such strategic success. Other instances are Second Manassas, which not only drove the Federals from the field but from Virginia, and Harper's Ferry, which netted numerous prisoners. Chancellorsville, unquestionably a masterful tactical triumph, might have become a strategic victory had Jackson lived. Even the follow-up at Fredericksburg and the Romney campaign represent unfulfilled quests for strategic victory. Such major strategic gains more than offset the disappointing Seven Days and precarious Antietam. They mark Jackson as the best executive officer of the American Civil War.

The last meeting of Lee and Jackson, Chancellorsville, May 1863, in a painting (1868) by Everett B. D. F. Julio, now housed in the Museum of the Confederacy in Richmond, Virginia.

> 'I am tired of this playing war without risks. We must encounter risks if we fight, and we cannot carry on war without fighting.'
> GEORGE MEADE TO HIS WIFE, 2 JANUARY 1863

GEORGE MEADE
1815–72

RICHARD J. SOMMERS

GEORGE MEADE was a competent professional soldier who earned promotion after promotion during the American Civil War, until, during the greatest crisis of that war, he was unexpectedly given command of an entire army. Rising to his new responsibilities, he won a great victory at Gettysburg, repelling a Confederate invasion of the North, and thus affecting the entire outcome of the war.

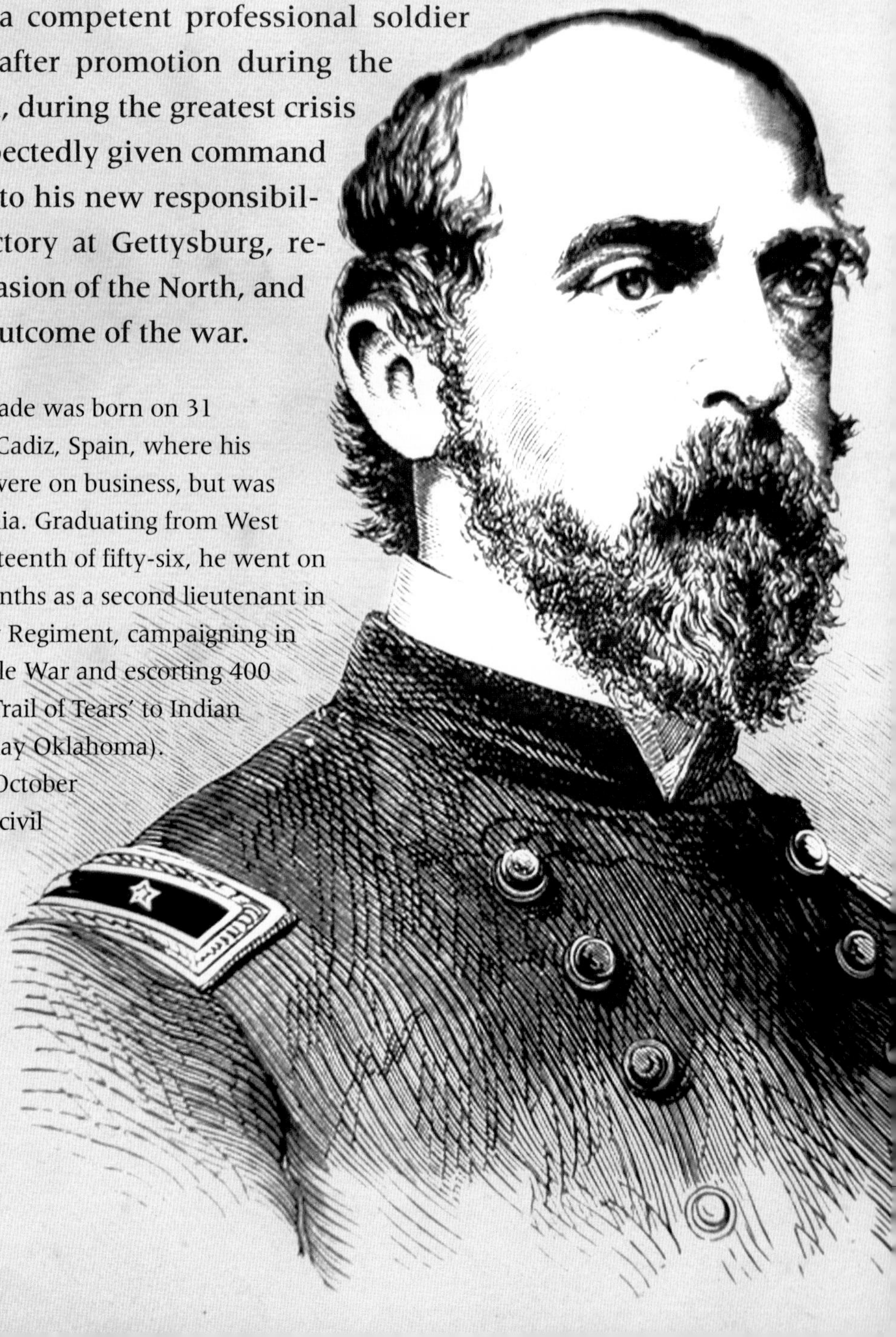

General George Meade, victor of Gettysburg, the largest, bloodiest, most strategically decisive battle of the American Civil War. Though a sound and capable commander, this consummate professional soldier does not rank with Grant and Sherman among the most effective Federal generals.

George Gordon Meade was born on 31 December 1815 in Cadiz, Spain, where his American parents were on business, but was raised in Philadelphia. Graduating from West Point in 1835, nineteenth of fifty-six, he went on to serve sixteen months as a second lieutenant in the 3rd US Artillery Regiment, campaigning in the Second Seminole War and escorting 400 Seminoles on the 'Trail of Tears' to Indian Territory (present-day Oklahoma). He resigned on 26 October 1836 and practised civil engineering.

George Meade

In May 1842, seventeen months after marrying Margaretta Sergeant in Philadelphia, Meade re-entered service as a second lieutenant in the Topographical Engineers. For nineteen years thereafter he made maps and designed, built and maintained lighthouses from Florida to New Jersey and Michigan. During the Mexican War he undertook topographical surveys from Palo Alto to Vera Cruz, and then he honourably returned to Washington in March 1847, before the drive to Mexico City was launched. Promoted to captain in 1856, he was engaged in lake survey work in Detroit when the Civil War broke out.

The battling brigadier

Many officers in the Corps of Engineers and the Topographical Engineers, largely upper graduates at West Point, immediately received high command on the outbreak of hostilities in April 1861. Perhaps because Meade had middling standing at the Military Academy and became a 'Topog' only indirectly, he initially languished in Detroit, despite desiring active service. Probably thanks to his wife's politically influential family, however, he was commissioned brigadier general of volunteers on 31 August.

On 16 September Meade assumed command of the 2nd Brigade of the Pennsylvania Reserve Division, which was among only a few Federal divisions entirely from one state. He and his first two fellow generals of brigade rose to great eminence. John F. Reynolds was a wing commander when killed at Gettysburg. Both Meade and Edward Ord commanded armies at Appomattox. Like most of George B. McClellan's army, the Pennsylvania Reserves spent seven months training, first north of the Potomac and from October onwards in Virginia. The following March they participated in the meaningless move to Manassas. As part of Irvin McDowell's I Corps, they remained in northern Virginia when McClellan's main body transferred to Fort Monroe to attack Richmond from the east.

McDowell occupied Fredericksburg and intended continuing south against Richmond. He was, however, ordered westward in a vain effort to trap 'Stonewall' Jackson. During that chase the Pennsylvania Reserve Division, commanded by George A. McCall, remained around Fredericksburg until 9 June, when it sailed to join McClellan. By 18 June the Reserves held McClellan's far right, north of the Chicka-hominy river just northeast of Richmond.

There they lay exposed to Robert E. Lee's great strategic counter-attack, the Seven Days Battle, which reversed the course of the war in the east. However, numerous Confederate errors cost Lee a victory of annihilation. Those shortcomings cannot eclipse the valour of the Reserves and the skill of their generals in resisting Confederate attacks throughout that prolonged battle. On 26 June, the Pennsylvanians repeatedly repulsed Confederate onslaughts at Mechanicsville. Meade, originally in reserve, fed his forces forward to bolster the front. Overnight the Federals withdrew to Gaines' Mill, where a bigger battle erupted the next day. McCall initially remained in reserve (Meade on the left, Reynolds on the right, 3rd Brigade further back). As the Union position progressively deteriorated, the Pennsylvania regiments reinforced the front or resisted breakthroughs piecemeal. When the whole Union position collapsed, Meade used his topographical skills to lead survivors safely south of the Chickahominy.

The weary V Corps, including McCall, was spared fighting for two days as McClellan's army shifted southward toward the James river. The crisis of the campaign came on 30 June, as Lee intercepted that lateral march at Glendale. Charles City Crossroads proved key. Meade, reconnoitring southwestward from there, alerted McCall to the danger. The 2nd Brigade held McCall's right. In the heaviest fighting of the Seven Days Battle, the Pennsylvanians blunted the Confederates' blow. Although yielding some ground, McCall secured the crossroads and assured the five divisions behind him safe passage to the James river. At the height of the battle Meade was severely wounded in the right arm and possibly the right kidney. He tried to ride away but grew faint from bleeding and had to be carried off. He was among the 2nd Brigade's 1,400 casualties in the Seven Days Battle, which accounted for almost half of McCall's 3,100 casualties. McCall and Reynolds had been captured; another brigadier was killed. Only one general remained with the division when it finally reached the James.

On 17 August Meade resumed command; by then his brigade (now redesignated the '1st') was back near Fredericksburg. In the ensuing Second Battle of Manassas (Bull Run) on 30 August Meade helped secure Henry House Hill against James Longstreet's great counter-attack, thus preventing defeat from becoming disaster. Meade lost 185 men in the battle.

Division and corps command

Prior to late June 1862 Meade had not led even a platoon in combat, but over the ensuing two months his prudence, skill and inspiration commanding a brigade in battle earned him promotion. It came on 12 September, when he succeeded Reynolds as commander of the Pennsylvania Reserve Division.

Two days later Meade delivered the decisive charge that drove the Confederates from South Mountain. Two days after that, he and John B. Hood tangled in the East Woods at Antietam. Then, on 17 September, Meade's devastating charge through Miller's cornfield nearly wrecked Jackson's wing. Meade again penetrated Jackson's centre at Fredericksburg on 13 December, the one bright spot in that dismal Union defeat. At both Antietam and Fredericksburg, Meade, left unsupported, was eventually driven out, but he demonstrated continued competence as a battle leader at this higher level of command. His casualties on 14 and 16–17 September and on 13 December were 393, 573 and 1,853 respectively.

> **'Gen. Meade is one of our truest men and ablest officers ...'**
>
> ULYSSES S. GRANT, 23 JANUARY 1865, REQUESTING CONFIRMATION OF MEADE'S PROMOTION TO MAJOR GENERAL, US ARMY

His service earned him higher rank. As of 29 November he became a major general of volunteers, and on 26 December he took command of V Corps. At Chancellorsville in the spring of 1863 (see p. 193) his corps spearheaded the drive into the Confederate left-rear. On 1 May, however, Jackson's stiffening resistance caused the Union army commander, Joseph Hooker, to go on the defensive. He thereby forfeited the initiative to Lee and Jackson, who won their greatest victory. Guarding the Union left, Meade saw little action in the decisive fighting of 2–3 May, suffering only 700 casualties in the entire battle.

In June Lee seized the strategic initiative and moved down the Shenandoah Valley into Pennsylvania. As Hooker repositioned his forces in reaction to Lee's strike, Meade's corps supported heavy cavalry fighting east of the Blue Ridge Mountains. Meade then crossed the Potomac and bivouacked near Frederick, Maryland, on 27 June.

Battles great and small

That night a War Department staff officer roused Meade from sleep. The general, who was among many senior subordinates openly critical of Hooker, feared he was being arrested. Instead he received command of the Army of the Potomac. In less than a week he led that army to victory at Gettysburg (see pp. 208–9). His victory ended the Southern invasion of the North, and the Confederates withdrew to central Virginia.

After resting, refitting and sending troops north to suppress draft riots, Meade resumed his advance on 13 September. He crossed the Rappahannock, easily overran Culpeper County and reached the Rapidan river. He had already detached one division to South Carolina; the requirement now to send four more to Tennessee stalled his advance. Lee, despite having sent off three divisions himself, took the initiative and tried to cut off the Union forces in Culpeper. Meade skilfully withdrew across the Rappahannock and Bull Run on to the fortified Centreville Heights, beating back the Confederates at Second Bristoe on 14 October.

Lee then withdrew behind the Rappahannock, but on 7 November Meade's victories at Rappahannock Station and Kelly's Ford again brought Culpeper County under Federal control. Late that month he crossed the Rapidan to turn Lee's right. Fighting flared at Payne's Farm on 27 November, but Meade thought assaulting fortifications along Mine Run too risky. The Unionists withdrew into Culpeper a few days

At the bloody Battle of Antietam, 17 September 1862, Meade led his Pennsylvania Reserves across Miller's corn-field in a devastating charge that almost destroyed 'Stonewall' Jackson's wing.

George Meade

GETTYSBURG

ON 28 JUNE 1863 MEADE was unexpectedly elevated to the command of the Army of the Potomac at Frederick, Maryland. All that month the army had manoeuvred defensively, shielding Washington and Baltimore. Lee, invading Pennsylvania, controlled the strategic initiative. Meade immediately changed that. Prudently but boldly, he advanced into Pennsylvania on 29–30 June, to challenge Lee. Meade thereby won the strategic duel. No longer could Lee advance unimpeded. He had to re-concentrate and respond to Meade. Thereafter each side sought victory on the battlefield, where the superior numbers and equipment of the North would count – if well led.

Meade provided that good leadership. He massed his largest force under his best subordinate, Reynolds, in the most threatened sector, the westerly left wing. The battle opened on Wednesday 1 July, when Confederate troops encountered that wing at Gettysburg, and attacked and defeated it. Despite this setback, Meade accepted Reynolds's and Hancock's recommendations that Gettysburg was the place to fight, and moved his remaining forces there.

Meade perceptively understood that Lee's offensive strategy mandated offensive tactics. To meet those attacks, Meade made excellent use of terrain. His 'fishhook' formation gave him interior lines, which allowed ready reinforcement of threatened sectors. Lee, in contrast, suffered from exterior lines.

Such reinforcements first saved the Union left, which Longstreet overran on Thursday afternoon. They similarly secured Meade's centre and right through Thursday night and Friday morning. Meade resolved to keep fighting on 3 July. That afternoon Hancock repulsed Lee's last great onslaught, Pickett's Charge.

During the night of 4/5 July Lee withdrew. Meade had won the battle. Now he tried reaping its fruits. Only two divisions chased the Confederates, while his main army rushed to Maryland, thence westward to intercept their retreat. Meade found them unable to cross the flooded Potomac, but fortified on defensible ground; he judged his own battered army too weak to attack. On the night of 13/14 July Lee escaped across the river.

Meade immediately continued southward across the Potomac east of the Blue Ridge. Again he did not chase

later, and went into winter quarters. Critics branded this operation 'the Mine Run Fiasco'. Actually, Meade deserves credit for his moral courage in refusing to squander his men in senseless slaughter.

Winning the war

Few fights flickered along that front during the winter of 1863/4. Spring saw the arrival of new General-in-Chief Ulysses S. Grant, who (unlike his predecessor, the desk-bound Henry W. Halleck) established headquarters 'in the field' in Virginia, operating directly

George Meade

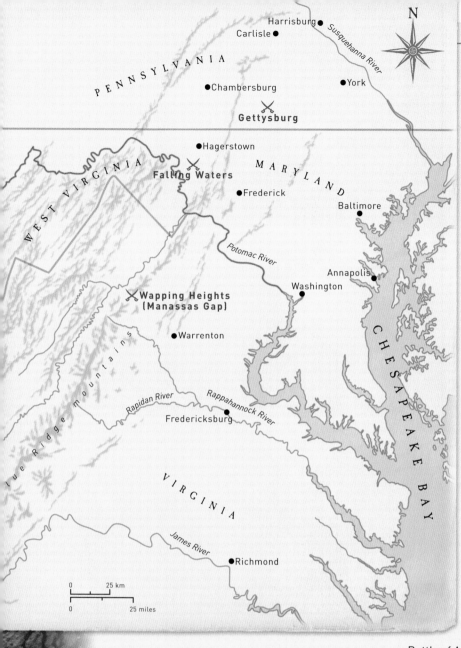

the Confederates from behind but sought to confine them west of the mountains. His slow vanguard, however, was repulsed at Wapping Heights on 23 July, and the Confederates crossed the mountains farther south. The Gettysburg campaign ended on 1 August, as both exhausted armies rested near Warrenton.

How fared Meade in his first five weeks of army command? Strategically, he immediately seized control of the campaign and forced Lee to react to him. Tactically, he took excellent advantage of terrain and skilfully deployed and redeployed troops to contain or repel attacks. Unquestionably, the Confederates made many mistakes. Equally clearly, Meade took advantage of them. One measure of a good general is how well he fights a flawed foe.

Nor should Meade be blamed for not counter-attacking at Gettysburg on 3–4 July, or for not assaulting on the Potomac on 13 July. So costly and close-run a victory as Gettysburg, with its terrible losses of soldiers and leaders (23,000 Northerners, 28,000 Southerners), left Meade too crippled to attack tactically. His decision not to attack is thus justifiable, and critics (including President Lincoln) who have said otherwise are being unfair. Indeed, Meade deserves credit for his aggressive strategic pursuit, from Gettysburg to Warrenton, with such a battered army. Contrast him with McClellan, stalled in Maryland for six weeks after the Battle of Antietam.

Gettysburg was the largest battle ever fought in the Americas. It did not end the war, nor could it have. The war, however, did change there. Meade deserves great credit for winning so tactically important and strategically significant a victory.

(Left) **Pickett's Charge,** the Confederates' last desperate effort on the third day of the Battle of Gettysburg. At 2 p.m. eleven Confederate brigades, including three under General George Pickett, attacked across three-quarters of a mile of open ground, exposed to the fire of over 100 Union guns and thousands of riflemen. Their attack failed, with casualties exceeding 55 per cent.

against Lee. Meade magnanimously offered to step aside, so Grant could take immediate command or install some preferred replacement. However, Grant left Meade in charge, while himself assuming the role, to use a modern term, of 'army group' commander, overseeing both Meade's Army of the Potomac and the independent IX Corps and later the Army of the James.

Grant wisely sought to work with and through the generals under his command, not around or without them. Over the ensuing twelve months, moreover, many of them earned his respect. Grant already knew of Meade by reputation; Gettysburg, after

George Meade

all, occurred at the same time as Grant's greatest victory, Vicksburg. Meade now confirmed that reputation. On 23 January 1865 Grant affirmed that 'Gen. Meade is one of our truest men and ablest officers … I defy any one to name a commander who could do more than he has done with the same chances.' Grant thereby assured Senate confirmation of Meade as major general of regulars, as of 18 August 1864. (Meade had, after Gettysburg, already been promoted to brigadier general of regulars.)

Grant's professional respect for Meade is unmistakable. Yet they were not friends (Grant was closer to Ord, William T. Sherman and, increasingly, Philip H. Sheridan), nor was their relationship harmonious. Proud, patrician, sensitive and well-connected, Meade, the hero of Gettysburg, chafed and seethed, imagining slights where Grant intended none. Too good a soldier to erupt against his superior, Meade lashed out at subordinates, including such old friends as Gouverneur K. Warren, Horatio G. Wright and even Winfield Scott Hancock. Meade particularly resented the growing prominence and influence of Sheridan, the coarse cavalry commander, one of the few outsiders whom Grant installed in the Army of the Potomac. The long, hot, dry summer of unfulfilled operations worsened frustration and tension among all parties. Already called 'Old Snapping Turtle', the acerbic Meade confirmed his nickname that summer.

Beyond personalities, the new institutional arrangements increased Meade's frustration. Previously he had made the fundamental decisions on starting, conducting and ending campaigns. Those decisions now rested with Grant, who functioned not only as grand strategist for the Union war effort but also as strategist for the eastern theatre and 'army group' strategist. Though nominally still army commander, Meade was, in effect, reduced to operations officer, responsible simply for troops and tactics to implement Grant's strategy. Grant respected Meade, and frequently deferred to his recommendations on operations. Yet they remained just recommendations. The final say was now with Grant.

Despite such institutional and personal problems, these two consummate professionals worked together to win the war in the east. Grant, through Meade, fought a series of bloody field battles in May and June 1864 – Wilderness, Spotsylvania, North Anna, Cold Harbor – which forced the Confederates from the Rapidan to Richmond. From the middle of June Grant waged the prolonged siege of Petersburg on both sides of the James river. Both Petersburg and Richmond fell on 3 April 1865. Six days later, Lee surrendered at Appomattox.

Meade (seated centre facing camera) and staff at the headquarters of the Army of the Potomac, Cold Harbor, Virginia, photographed by Mathew B. Brady on 12 June 1864. Meade received the command of the Army of the Potomac on 28 June 1863, and in less than a week led it to victory at Gettysburg.

Throughout those eleven months, Meade remained directly under Grant. When a new field army was created in August 1864 to conquer the Shenandoah Valley, Sheridan, not Meade, received that quasi-independent command. The latter general was considered for that post in October, but only because Sheridan, the junior officer, might be needed in Missouri. However, Sheridan remained in the Valley, and Meade remained at Petersburg. Even at Appomattox, Sheridan and Ord, who had blocked Lee's escape, were present for his surrender; but Meade, who had battled Lee for twenty-two months and was in hot pursuit of the Southerners on 9 April, was not invited. Grant did not mean to slight his subordinate, but Meade took offence, nonetheless.

Post-war career

The Army of the Potomac conducted its grand review in Washington on 23 May 1865. Five weeks later it ceased to exist. Meade immediately took command of the Military Division of the Atlantic, a position he held until 1868 and again from 1869 to 1872. Within that division he also headed the Department of the East, from 1866 to 1868. In 1868–9 he commanded the Third Reconstruction District, later the Department of the South. During his sojourn in the South he sought reconciliation in Georgia, Florida and Alabama (later in the Carolinas, too), and was spared most of the odium associated with Reconstruction. Nor did he fight Native Americans. His one post-war military operation involved intercepting a Fenian invasion of Canada in 1866.

Active service fighting Native Americans went to Grant's favourites, Sherman and Sheridan. When Grant became president on 4 March 1869, Sherman succeeded him as general-in-chief. That promotion vacated the one lieutenant-generalcy. The three contenders for that coveted third star were George H. Thomas, long Grant's enemy; Meade, Grant's proven subordinate; and Sheridan, Grant's favourite. Unsurprisingly, it was Sheridan who was promoted. Being again overlooked broke Meade's heart. He died on 6 November 1872, aged only 56, and is buried in Philadelphia.

Meade excelled commanding a brigade or a division in battle. His understanding of terrain, tactics and troops enabled him to maximize effectiveness offensively and defensively. Chancellorsville suggests he would have done well as a corps commander, too.

Yet army command is where Meade must be evaluated. That record is mixed. Genius he lacked. Other hallmarks of great captains – boldness, strategic insight, tenacity – Meade possessed only to a limited degree. Two years of army command show him a sound, competent, capable leader, well above average for the Union army but hardly in the front rank, either in the American Civil War or in other eras. If left in charge in the east without Grant, Meade was capable enough not to lose the war but not good enough to win it.

What entitles Meade to his place in this book is not his entire career but his greatest victory. Less than one week into army command, he defeated the best Confederate army under the best Confederate general (who really was a military genius). He thereby saved the North from invasion and reversed the course of the campaign. More than that, Gettysburg – together with major Union victories in the west in early July 1863 – changed the entire course of the American Civil War. Only rarely thereafter did the Confederates regain the strategic initiative. Never again did they mount a major invasion of the North (managing only two sizable raids into Maryland and Missouri in 1864). His victory at Gettysburg rightly ranks Meade among the great commanders of history.

'The art of war is simple enough. Find out where your enemy is. Get at him as soon as you can. Strike him as hard as you can, as often as you can, and keep moving on.' ULYSSES S. GRANT

ULYSSES S. GRANT

JOHN A. BARNES

1822–85

ULYSSES S. GRANT was the most successful military commander in American history, and was primarily responsible for the Union victory in the American Civil War. Undefeated on the battlefield, he forced the surrender of three enemy armies, including the most important, Robert E. Lee's Army of Northern Virginia. Every Union victory of any significance in the war, with the sole exception of Gettysburg, was won either by Grant personally, or under his overall direction. His legacy as a strategist influences the US and other armies to this day.

Grant's rise is also one of the most meteoric in military and political history. A clerk in his father's leather-goods store in the tiny town of Galena, Illinois, at the outbreak of the war in April 1861, he would become, within three years, the first American to hold the permanent rank of lieutenant general since George Washington. In less than eight, he would take office as president of the United States.

A soldier made, not born

The men who become professional soldiers and who grow into great military commanders seem to choose this career path very early in life, often as a result of having military ancestry. Robert E. Lee and George S. Patton, for example, were both descended from war heroes and settled on military careers while quite young. Ulysses S. Grant does not fit this pattern.

Hiram Ulysses Grant (the name Ulysses Simpson Grant was a result of an army clerical error at West Point) was born on 27 April 1822 to a prosperous local businessman in Point Pleasant, Ohio. If Grant had any thoughts of a military career as a young man, he kept them well to himself; his appointment to the West Point class of 1843 was arranged by his father without his knowledge. The young man baulked at first, according to his own account, giving in only when his father insisted.

Again, according to his own account, Grant did not enjoy his four years at the military academy. Nevertheless, he did quite well there, finishing twenty-first in a class of thirty-nine graduates. (Thirty-six cadets who entered with Grant in 1839 failed to graduate at all.) In addition to doing well in mathematics (which was also Napoleon's best subject), he was excellent at drawing (which improves the eye for topography) and served as president of the cadet literary society, thus displaying an interesting (and rare) blend of the precise and the artistic. He was also a superb horseman, setting a jumping record that stood at the academy for decades following his graduation.

Experience in the Mexican War

The United States declared war on Mexico on 13 May 1846; at the time Grant was a young lieutenant with the 4th US Infantry stationed near St Louis, Missouri. He was still ambivalent about his choice of a military career, admitting later that, as he faced his first action, 'I felt sorry I had enlisted.'

Grant had been appointed his regiment's quartermaster, a highly responsible position that meant he was in charge of providing everything the soldiers might need (except food, which was the responsibility of the commissary). In theory, this staff position should have kept him out of action, but Grant soon discovered that exposure to enemy fire did not 'un-man' him, and he sought out opportunities to engage the Mexicans. On one occasion he put his exceptional skills as a horseman to work by clambering atop a horse and riding pell-mell through a hail of enemy fire to bring back a re-supply of ammunition. The critical importance of this particular commodity was not lost on him, and in his later career he would ensure that adequate ammunition was always available.

Grant's other major experience in the war was in serving under both of its major commanders, Winfield Scott and Zachary Taylor. While both were excellent generals, Scott was a military showman, wearing, it was said, every inch of gold braid the regulations permitted, while Taylor tended towards extreme simplicity of dress and manner. Grant emulated Taylor, who was elected president of the United States in 1848. Grant also saw what could be achieved when commanders were sufficiently bold and daring.

Civilian life

Assigned to garrison duty in California after the war, Grant was quickly bored. He also missed his wife Julia and new family (including a son he had never seen), who had remained behind in St Louis. This was the period when he probably acquired his reputation for heavy drinking, although contemporaneous evidence for it is lacking. Seeing no other way to reunite his family, Grant resigned from the army in 1854, just after receiving his promotion to the rank of captain.

Ulysses S. Grant, Union commander, during the latter stages of the American Civil War, painted in 1844 by George Peter Alexander Healy.

Returning to St Louis, Grant took to farming the land that his father-in-law had given to him and his wife as a wedding present. With his restless mind and wanderlust, however, a man with less aptitude for the settled life of a farmer than Grant would have been hard to imagine. While he did well enough for the first few years, the economic depression that struck in 1857 hit him hard. Thus began his period of working as a debt collector, firewood salesman, and, when he had no other options, as a clerk in his father's leather-goods business.

Return to military service

The fall of Fort Sumter to Confederate forces on 14 April 1861 ignited the Civil War. Attending a public meeting in Galena, Grant resolved to return to the service. Getting back into the army, however, proved far more difficult than leaving it.

A surplus of serving and former officers, as well as a preference for commissioning officers who could raise regiments on their own, kept Grant from winning the colonelcy to which he believed his training and experience entitled him. (This was not a case of inflated ego; George McClellan, who had also left the army as a captain three years after Grant, was commissioned a major general in 1861.)

It took two months and some good luck, but in June 1861 Grant won a colonel's commission and command of the 21st Illinois Volunteer Regiment. At almost the same time, he got another piece of good news. Through the efforts in Washington of Elihu B. Washburn, Grant's congressman and a friend of Lincoln's who had taken positive notice of the leather-store clerk back in Galena, he was commissioned a brigadier general.

Even in these very early days, Grant displayed the major characteristic of his generalship: aggressively seeking out the enemy and endeavouring to bring him to battle. Approaching a small Confederate force encamped near the Salt river in Missouri, Grant apprehensively deployed the 21st Illinois for what he assumed would be its first engagement. But as he approached the site of the enemy camp, Grant found it hastily abandoned. The Confederate commander, Grant realized, 'had been as afraid of me as I had been of him'. It was a lesson Grant did not forget.

Early victories

The Mississippi river bisects the North American continent, with major tributaries such as the Missouri and Ohio cutting far to the east and west. Grant early realized the vital necessity to the Union war effort of controlling this waterway, and set about securing it while politicians in Washington and lesser generals obsessed over capturing the Confederate capital of Richmond, Virginia.

Belmont, Missouri, is a small town overlooking the Mississippi, directly across from the town of Columbus, Kentucky. Both towns were occupied by Confederate forces in early November 1861, and were being used to blockade the river to Union traffic. On 7 November Grant decided to see if he could scare the Confederates out of Belmont.

Assembling what would today be called a combined-operations task force, Grant loaded 12,000 men, along with supporting cavalry and artillery, aboard naval vessels at Cairo, Illinois, and sailed downstream to Belmont, landing 3 miles north of the Confederate encampment. Completely surprised, the Confederates scattered.

But the effect was only momentary, as the Confederates soon regrouped and counter-attacked, seeking to cut the Union troops off from their transport. Thanks to the artillery and cavalry Grant had brought along, these efforts failed, and the Union troops returned safely to Cairo.

Belmont wasn't much more than a big raid, but it was victory enough for a Northern public already growing wearily familiar with bad news from the front. The battle was also significant in that it featured what would later become Grant's trademarks of speed and surprise, and it was the first major use of what would later be called amphibious warfare.

Grant's successful cooperation with the navy – daring and innovative for the time – continued with his next major operation, against the Confederate strongholds of Fort Henry on the Tennessee river and Fort Donelson on the Cumberland river.

The movement against the two forts – made much against the will of Grant's superior, Major General Henry Halleck – illustrates Grant's innovative approach to waging war. While other Union generals were thinking in European terms of capturing cities – notably the Confederate capital of Richmond – or taking territory and holding it, Grant was thinking in terms of North American geography.

The Mississippi, Tennessee and Cumberland rivers all bit deep into the Confederacy. Unlike railroads, the rivers couldn't be severed by Confederate cavalry raiders. Using them as highways to move far inside the South, Union forces could cut the Confederate forces off from their sources of food and war materials. The cities and territories those armies were defending would then fall as ripe fruit from a tree.

The fall of the two forts, on 6 February and 16 February 1862 respectively, was the first significant Union victory of the war. Their capture made Grant a national hero, earning him the nickname, based on his initials, of 'Unconditional Surrender' Grant.

Shiloh: victory into defeat

Grant was a hero, but that fact also excited jealousy and envy among his fellow officers, particularly the scheming Henry Halleck. Incredibly, in the weeks following the fall of the two forts, Halleck plotted to have Grant removed. The only result of all this backstage manoeuvring was to yield the initiative to the Confederates.

In early April 1862 Grant's Army of the Tennessee was encamped near a country church called Shiloh, awaiting reinforcement from Brigadier General Don Carlos

Grant surveys the battlefield at Fort Donelson, the Confederate stronghold on the Cumberland river, in a painting by Paul Philippoteaux (1846–1923). Grant's capture of Fort Donelson on 16 February 1862, after a combined operation with the navy, made him a national hero.

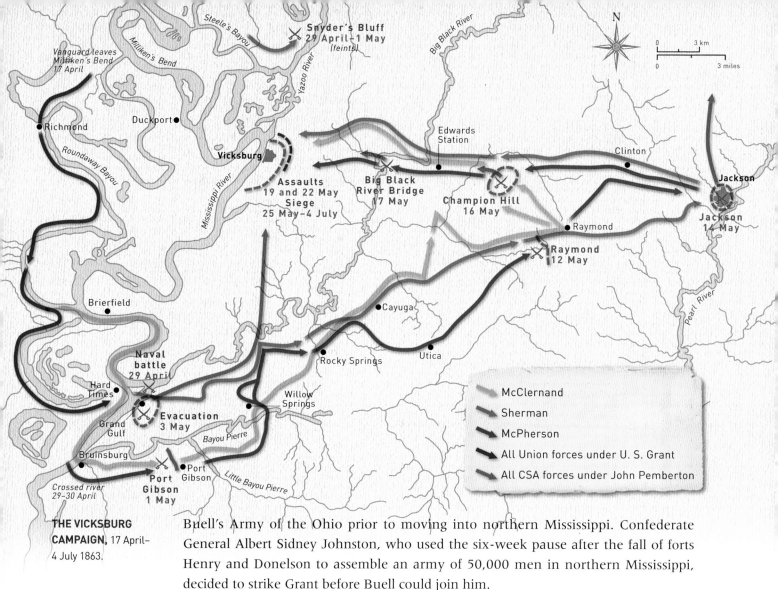

THE VICKSBURG CAMPAIGN, 17 April–4 July 1863.

Naval battle 29 April

Snyder's Bluff 29 April–1 May (feints)

Assaults 19 and 22 May Siege 25 May–4 July

Big Black River Bridge 17 May

Champion Hill 16 May

Raymond 12 May

Jackson 14 May

Evacuation 3 May

Port Gibson 1 May

Vanguard leaves Milliken's Bend 17 April

Crossed river 29–30 April

Legend:
- McClernand
- Sherman
- McPherson
- All Union forces under U. S. Grant
- All CSA forces under John Pemberton

(Opposite) **Grant (bottom right)** at the siege of Vicksburg (18 May–4 July 1863), as depicted in a colour lithograph of 1888. Grant's campaign at Vicksburg is regarded as the first example of blitzkrieg warfare, and became the model for the 1991 Gulf War campaign.

Buell's Army of the Ohio prior to moving into northern Mississippi. Confederate General Albert Sidney Johnston, who used the six-week pause after the fall of forts Henry and Donelson to assemble an army of 50,000 men in northern Mississippi, decided to strike Grant before Buell could join him.

The Battle of Shiloh, which began on the morning of 6 April 1862, was not merely the bloodiest battle of the war to that point, but its 24,000 total casualties exceeded those of all previous American wars combined. Grant had chosen his ground carefully, however, and the Confederates never came close to overrunning his position. Buell's troops joined him on the night of 6/7 April and Grant counter-attacked the next day, driving the Confederates from the field. The Union also achieved the grim bonus of the death of Johnston.

But the size of the butcher's bill stunned the Northern public. There was some wildly irresponsible reporting of the engagement, and the people who had lauded Grant only a few weeks earlier now turned viciously against him. Faced with demands for Grant's dismissal from influential members of Congress, President Lincoln is supposed to have replied, 'I cannot spare this man; he fights.' In his memoirs, Grant states that Shiloh was the battle that convinced him definitively that the war would be a long and costly one.

Wrapping up the west

Operating under this cloud, Grant nevertheless undertook his next objective: reducing the Confederate fortress of Vicksburg, on the Mississippi river (see p. 217). Following Vicksburg, it had been Grant's intent to strike against the port of Mobile, Alabama, and

THE ESSENCE OF WHAT CAME TO BE
KNOWN in the Second World War as
'blitzkrieg' or 'lightning war' was the
winning of a great strategic prize at
high speed and at relatively low cost in
men and matériel. The first modern practitioner of this
form of 'shock and awe' warfare was Ulysses S. Grant in
his campaign to take Vicksburg, Mississippi, between May
and July 1863.

Dubbed the 'Gibraltar of the West' by Confederate
President Jefferson Davis, the town of Vicksburg stands
on a high bluff overlooking a hairpin bend in the Mississippi river, making it a natural fortress. In Confederate
hands, it blocked the flow of Union commerce on the river,
cutting off the vast interior heartland of the Union from
access to the port of New Orleans (Union-held since April
1862). 'Vicksburg is the key,' Abraham Lincoln told his
advisers. 'The war cannot be brought to a close until the
key is in our pocket.'

Grant began manoeuvring against Vicksburg in the
autumn of 1862, trying a variety of plans to invest and take
the city, all without success. His movements, however, succeeded in thoroughly confusing Confederate Lieutenant
General John C. Pemberton, the commander of Vicksburg.

THE VICKSBURG CAMPAIGN: THE FIRST BLITZKRIEG

In April 1863 an increasingly demoralized Pemberton sent a telegram to
his superiors: 'Enemy is constantly in
motion in all directions.'

Grant now set in motion what he
later said was the only plan in which he really had confidence. He would come at the city through the 'back door' –
its lightly guarded southern approaches. Marching his army
south along the western bank of the river opposite
Vicksburg, Grant transported it across the river via steam-
boats and transports that had run the gauntlet of the city's
guns in a nerve-wracking operation on the night of 16 April
1863. (Army–navy cooperation is a much-overlooked hallmark of Grant's campaigns, just as air–ground cooperation
marked the German blitzkrieg campaigns of 1939–41.)

The stage was set for the main action of the
campaign. Between the time Grant's army landed on the
eastern bank of the river below Vicksburg on 30 April and
the start of the siege of the town on 18 May 1863, it
would march over 200 miles, take and burn the Mississippi state capital of Jackson, and fight and win five
battles, before locking Pemberton's army inside
Vicksburg, where it languished without hope of relief
until its surrender on 4 July. All the while, Grant's army
lived off the land, without a supply line. Grant thus
pocketed Lincoln's 'key' at a cost of fewer than 10,000
men killed, wounded, captured and missing.

'That man will fight us every day and every hour till the end of the war.'

CONFEDERATE LIEUTENANT GENERAL JAMES
LONGSTREET, UPON LEARNING OF GRANT'S
APPOINTMENT AS GENERAL-IN-CHIEF OF
THE UNION ARMIES

Ulysses S. Grant

then north to the southern railhead of Atlanta, Georgia. Combined with simultaneous thrusts from Tennessee and Mississippi, the Confederate armies in the field would be deprived of the men and supplies they needed to operate. Their choice would then be surrender or starvation, as at Vicksburg. Other considerations intervened, however. French intervention in Mexico in 1862 tied down Union forces in Louisiana, and Union forces in Tennessee were decisively beaten at the Battle of Chickamauga in September 1863 and forced back on Chattanooga, where the Confederates besieged them.

The need to lift the siege became paramount, and Lincoln placed Grant in command of all Union forces west of the Appalachian mountain chain. When Grant arrived at Chattanooga he found plans in place for breaking the siege, but Union General William Rosecrans apparently lacked the will to implement them. Grant did not. Between 23 and 25 November 1863, Grant's forces defeated those of Confederate General Braxton Bragg, driving them back in the direction of Atlanta.

Lincoln had seen enough. In March 1864 he took the obvious (in retrospect) course of naming Grant commander-in-chief of all Union forces, with responsibility for finding a way to win the war.

Grant vs Lee

Grant was still in favour of the Mobile operation and several simultaneous thrusts into the heart of the Confederacy, but by the spring of 1864 there was no longer time. Lincoln was facing a difficult re-election campaign that November; a direct confrontation with Confederate General Robert E. Lee on his home ground of northern Virginia was no longer avoidable.

Ulysses S. Grant, with his horse Cincinnati at Cold Harbor, Virginia, June 1864. An expert and fearless horseman, Grant developed his consummate equestrian skills as a cadet at West Point between 1839 and 1843.

Grant understood the strategic problem of confronting a foe who enjoyed the advantage of interior lines of communication. Until then the Confederacy was able to cope with widely separated Union thrusts by shuttling troops from one threatened sector to another – much as the Germans tried to do in both world wars. Grant prevented this in the same way that Eisenhower and Zhukov prevented it eighty years later: he launched simultaneous offensives in both the Virginian and western theatres. The latter would be commanded by William T. Sherman, while Grant would personally superintend the former.

Grant's aim was simple: he would grab hold of Lee's Army of Northern Virginia and refuse to let it go, denying Lee the initiative. From the opening of the Overland campaign on 4 May 1864 until the final surrender at Appomattox on 9 April 1865, the two armies would never be out of contact (except for a few days in mid June 1864).

Grant has been accused of wantonly squandering the lives of his men during this campaign. While his losses were indeed high (around 50,000 in May and June 1864), recent scholarship has shown that, proportionally, Lee's losses were even higher. The casualty list might also have been shorter had Grant been able to get better service out of the Army of the Potomac's officer corps, which was never able to entirely shake off its lethargic habits, nor its terror of Robert E. Lee.

Lee's only real hope during this period was to inflict such

Ulysses S. Grant

punishment on the Union armies that the Northern public would revolt and turn out the Lincoln administration. Had the Confederacy's western armies been able somehow to defeat Sherman, this strategy might have succeeded. But since the Confederates were outnumbered two to one, and even more inferior in terms of supplies, there was little hope of that. Lincoln's re-election in November 1864 and the thrashing of the Confederacy's western armies at the Battle of Nashville on 15 December 1864 essentially ended the war. All that remained was for Lee to recognize that fact, which he did at Appomattox.

Post-war career

The Appomattox campaign was Grant's last. Following Lee's surrender, he spent three years as general-in-chief of the US army, based in Washington DC. Concerned that the election of a Democratic candidate in the 1868 election would rob the nation of 'the fruits of victory', he reluctantly agreed to run for president as the Republican candidate, and was elected. He spent much of his time in the White House trying to protect the rights of newly freed blacks in the South, a policy that became increasingly unpopular as time went on, and which was abandoned when he left office in 1877.

Grant died of throat cancer at Mount McGregor, New York, on 23 July 1885. His memoirs, published after his death, sold more than 300,000 copies.

Assessment

Grant deserves to be ranked among the great captains of history. He skilfully handled huge armies that were separated by thousands of miles. Unlike Napoleon or Frederick the Great, who each tasted the bitterness of defeat more than once, Grant never lost a battle, whether facing mediocre opponents or highly talented ones.

Defying the Peter Principle, Grant never rose to a level of military incompetence. Whether a junior officer in Mexico or the highest-ranked since George Washington, he moved into each new role – which called for different skills and abilities – with seeming ease. In all these respects, he very closely parallels Wellington.

Grant also competently employed radical new military technologies with which no previous commander had had to cope : the telegraph, the rifled musket, the railroad and the steamship. He used all of these to their fullest advantage at the time, something none of his opponents managed, and only Sherman came close to matching.

Grant's legacy is still felt in today's US army, which combines a devotion to logistic mastery with speed, surprise and unmatched firepower. The 1991 Gulf War campaign was modelled closely on Grant's Vicksburg campaign.

In the light of these facts, the reality of Grant's genius emerges. His success set a very high standard for his successors.

Grant (seated centre left in front of the trees) holds a council of war outside Massaponax Church, Spotsylvania County, Virginia, in May 1864, using the church pews as benches. Those present include Assistant Secretary of War Charles A. Dana (to Grant's left) and General George Meade, the victor of Gettysburg (top of pew at far left).

Ulysses S. Grant

219

'War is cruelty and you cannot refine it ... You might as well appeal against the thunderstorm as against these terrible hardships of war.' WILLIAM T. SHERMAN TO THE MAYOR AND COUNCIL OF ATLANTA, 12 SEPTEMBER 1864

WILLIAM T. SHERMAN
1820–91

RICHARD J. SOMMERS

SHERMAN WAS THE SECOND BEST Union commander of the American Civil War. His keen intellect perceived the interrelationship between the fighting front and the home front, and by crippling the will of Southern civilians to continue waging war, he undercut Confederate military power and thereby contributed decisively to the Union victory.

(Opposite) **William Tecumseh Sherman,** c. 1864, photographed by Mathew B. Brady. In 1864–5 Sherman brought the Civil War to the Confederate home front in Georgia and the Carolinas, and thus anticipated the total warfare of the twentieth century.

William Tecumseh Sherman was born in Lancaster, Ohio, on 8 February 1820. Orphaned nine years later, he was raised by US Senator Thomas Ewing, an influential Whig, and married the senator's daughter Ellen in 1850. Ewing secured Sherman a place at West Point, where he graduated sixth of forty-two in the class of 1840.

Early career

Commissioned as a second lieutenant in the 3rd US Artillery Regiment in 1840 and promoted first lieutenant in 1841, Sherman helped garrison Charleston, South Carolina, where he came to appreciate antebellum Southern society. In the Mexican War he accompanied his regiment on its fourteen-week trip around Cape Horn to California, but by the time he got there it was already under US control, and the war was virtually over. Unlike many senior Civil War commanders, Sherman saw no combat in the Mexican War, and all that remained was garrisoning California. He performed staff duty at San Francisco headquarters and was promoted to captain (Commissary of Subsistence) on 27 September 1850.

The Gold Rush of 1849 lured many soldiers to desert, but Sherman faithfully remained on duty for four more years. On 6 September 1853 he resigned and went into banking in San Francisco. The panic of 1857 doomed the bank, and for the next two years he practised law in Leavenworth, Kansas Territory, with two of his brothers-in-law, Hugh and Thomas Ewing (both future Union generals). From 1859 to 1861 he served as first superintendent of the new Louisiana Military Academy in Pineville (forerunner of Louisiana State University).

William T. Sherman

Early years of the Civil War

Abraham Lincoln's election as president caused seven Southern states to secede, including Louisiana on 26 January 1861. Even before officially leaving the Union, Louisiana occupied some Federal installations, and the state's military school and its superintendent were expected to support these actions. Unlike some Northerners living in the South who fought for the Confederacy, Sherman never wavered. Despite his deep and genuine admiration, respect, even affection for the South and its people, he remained loyal to the Union. He promptly resigned and moved to St Louis, Missouri, where, ironically, he was almost killed on 10 May during street riots in that torn city following the Camp Jackson affair.

Sherman was still a civilian at this point, but within days he would be back in uniform, beginning four years of tumultuous military service – years full of anxiety and uncertainty, confidence and insight, tactical defeat and strategic success. Sherman would emerge from those four years as one of the foremost Northern generals, and one of the great commanders of military history.

On 14 May 1861 Sherman was appointed colonel of the 13th US Infantry, one of eleven new regiments in the regular US army. Almost all other colonels of new regiments had distinguished records fighting Mexicans and Indians. Sherman, by contrast, had never been under fire until, as a civilian, he had been caught up in the St Louis riots. His selection is unmistakably attributable to political and family connections: his father-in-law was now an elder statesman in the new Republican Party, while his brother John was a US senator, and it was their political influence that landed him the coveted appointment. This is not to say Sherman was a 'political general'. Indeed, he disdained politics and explicitly refused to exploit military service for political advantage. Yet his selection underscores the reality that in mid nineteenth-century America, even quintessential career regulars like Sherman benefited from patronage (his future friend Ulysses S. Grant comparably had a political sponsor). For Sherman, both political and family connections served him well.

Tactical defeat, strategic doubt

Such connections secured Sherman further promotion on 3 August 1861, as brigadier general of volunteers, backdated to 17 May, and he served briefly on General-in-Chief Winfield Scott's staff. On 30 June he took command of the 3rd Brigade, 1st Division, Army of Northeast Virginia, and three weeks later he took part in heavy fighting and in the ensuing Union defeat and rout at the First Battle of Manassas (Bull Run). Then in August he had to suppress a near mutiny among some of his troops, who mistakenly thought their service had expired.

Despite this inauspicious beginning, Sherman was appointed in late August by his Old Army friend Robert Anderson (the hero of Fort Sumter) as his senior subordinate in the new Department of the Cumberland (Kentucky and Tennessee). Both North and South strove to secure the strategic state of Kentucky, and in the end it was junior Federal officers who turned the tide for the Union. Anderson himself deserves little credit: overburdened by weighty responsibilities, he could not act vigorously. On 8 October he was gently shelved, and Sherman succeeded him.

Sherman, although younger and more energetic than Anderson, fared no better. His keen insight recognized the magnitude of the Civil War and of the force needed to win it: not content with the 20,000 soldiers on hand, he called for an army of 200,000. In retrospect, he appears far-sighted, but at the time he seemed unrealistic and alarmist. Unquestionably, he exaggerated Confederate strength and capabilities, and their supposed threat vexed him to distraction. The Federal government feared he would suffer a nervous breakdown, and on 9 November it engineered the department out from under him by transferring its areas of responsibility to other departments. Left without a command, Sherman went home to Ohio and then St Louis.

Bloody redemption

St Louis, fortunately, was headquarters of another Old Army friend, General Henry W. Halleck. Halleck, recognizing Sherman's abilities, gave him time to rest and then on 14 February 1862 restored him to command by putting him in charge of the District of Cairo. Sherman's new responsibility involved forwarding troops to support Grant's decisive breakthrough of the main Confederate line across Kentucky and Tennessee. On 1 March Sherman formed some reinforcements into what would gain immortality as the 5th Division, Army of West Tennessee (the future Army of the Tennessee). A week later he led that division up the Tennessee river to northern Mississippi, where flooding prevented him from landing to cut a key railroad. He then dropped downriver and went ashore on the left bank at Pittsburg Landing, Tennessee, near a country church called Shiloh.

Four of Grant's five other divisions soon joined him there. The Federals drilled, massed and prepared to move against the Southern stronghold of Corinth, Mississippi. But they did not fortify their own position, and they did not guard against the contingency that the Confederates might strike first. Yet on 6 April, the Confederates did attack. Ever afterwards, Grant and Sherman denied they were caught off guard. Tactically Shiloh was not a surprise, but strategically it was. For eleven weeks everything in the western theatre had gone the Union's way. Southern resistance seemed near collapse. Union planners – Sherman, Grant, Halleck – did not consider that the Confederates might counter-attack. Yet when they did, Sherman's tactical skills blunted the blow and extracted a heavy price, before he was obliged to yield his advance ground.

William T. Sherman

He thus bought time for reinforcements to bolster the defence, then to counter-attack on 7 April. Shiloh was the bloodiest battle in American history up to then. This potential disaster turned into strategic success forged a friendship between Grant and Sherman that lasted the rest of their lives.

Vicksburg and Chattanooga

Promoted major general of volunteers, Sherman participated throughout May 1862 in the First Corinth campaign. His greatest service in that summer of stagnation was keeping the despondent Grant from resigning. Sherman's responsibilities progressively increased, and on 21 July he was given command of Memphis. From there in November he led three divisions into northern Mississippi during Grant's first drive against Vicksburg. Concern that the political Union general John A. McClernand might take that stronghold led Grant to rush Sherman's four divisions down the Mississippi to capture that city first. Sherman, however, was repulsed at the end of December at Chickasaw Bayou. McClernand then arrived, assumed command (with Sherman subordinated to corps command) and, on 11 January 1863, captured Arkansas Post.

Grant shifted most divisions to the Mississippi and absorbed McClernand's force. Within that expanded army, Sherman's command (the 5th, 8th and 11th Divisions) became XV Corps. In March he led that corps to rescue the US navy trapped up Steele's Bayou, then in May helped to capture Jackson (the Mississippi state capital), and shared in Grant's repulses at Vicksburg (see p. 217). As the siege continued, Sherman took charge of the rear line facing east against Joseph E. Johnston's relieving army. Once Vicksburg surrendered on 4 July, Sherman led IX, XIII and XV Corps against Johnston and reoccupied Jackson on 21 July.

Victory at Vicksburg earned Grant promotion to command the new Military Division of the Mississippi, encompassing the entire western theatre, and on 24 October Sherman (now brigadier general of regulars) succeeded him in command of the Army of the Tennessee. Sherman was fortunate to be available then, because only a couple of weeks earlier he had narrowly evaded capture, perhaps death, near Colliersville, Tennessee, while isolated from his forces.

William Tecumseh Sherman (seated, centre). He succeeded Grant as commander of the Military Division of the Mississippi in the spring of 1864. Here he appears with his generals a year later.

Sherman went on to lead four divisions to help relieve Chattanooga. Grant gave him the main attack, turning the Confederate right, but on 25 November his charges were repeatedly repulsed. However, his West Point classmate George H. Thomas, now commanding the Army of the Cumberland, stormed Missionary Ridge to win a great victory. Sherman then led IV, XI and XV Corps to relieve Knoxville in early December. He returned to Vicksburg in January 1864, and the following month led XVI and XVII Corps eastward to capture Meridian, Mississippi. The Meridian campaign entailed little fighting, but it

William T. Sherman

confirmed the lesson Grant had demonstrated the previous May: Federal forces could cut loose from supply lines, penetrate deeply into the Confederacy and live off the land. Before 1864 ended, Sherman would apply this lesson with devastating effect (see pp. 226–7).

Advance to Atlanta

Saving Chattanooga earned Grant promotion to general-in-chief in March 1864. He chose to operate in Virginia against the greatest Confederate commander, Robert E. Lee. On 26 March Sherman succeeded him in command of the western theatre, centred on Chattanooga. Near there he massed 100,000 men in twenty-two divisions, grouped into seven corps and three armies. (Three more divisions, comprising an additional 13,000 men, arrived in June and July.)

Pursuant to Grant's grand strategy to advance simultaneously on major fronts, on 7 May Sherman moved against Johnston's army in northwestern Georgia. They battled at Rocky Face Ridge on 8–11 May. Sherman sent his former Army of the Tennessee, now under James B. McPherson, through Snake Creek Gap into Johnston's left-rear at Resaca. McPherson failed to press his advantage, however, and withdrew into the gap. Alerted to the danger, Johnston retreated to Resaca, where Sherman fought him on 13–15 May. The Confederates fell back across the Oostenaula river and then across the Etowah. Light fighting flared at Cassville and Kingston, and then in late May and June heavy combat erupted around Dallas, Gilgal Church and Kolb's Farm. Sherman's massive frontal assault on Kennesaw Mountain on 27 June proved a bloody failure. Despite such repeated tactical setbacks, Sherman enjoyed strategic success, pressing ever more deeply into Georgia to the Chattahoochee river.

Beyond the Chattahoochee lay Atlanta – and a more combative Confederate commander, John B. Hood. Sherman crossed the river unopposed, but was then attacked by Hood in late July at Peach Tree Creek, Decatur Road and Ezra Church. The Federals withstood such blows and throughout August tightened their siege of Atlanta. Late that month most of Sherman's army swung southwest, cutting the final two railroads into Atlanta. The Confederates failed to stop him at Jonesborough (31 August – 1 September), and that night Hood abandoned Atlanta. Northern troops occupied the city the next day – a strategic success that brightened a dreary summer and helped to re-elect President Lincoln.

Decisive blows

Sherman's victorious armies rested around Atlanta for a month. In October they actually re-crossed the Chattahoochee to protect the tenuous railroad to Chattanooga from Hood's attacks. Chasing the Confederates through northwestern Georgia into Alabama proved pointless. Sherman detached eight divisions under Thomas to handle Hood, while his main body returned to Atlanta to await the election results. Lincoln's overwhelming re-election on 8 November confirmed the North's commitment to win the war. One week later, Sherman burned Atlanta, plunged into Georgia and marched to the sea. He captured Savannah on 21 December.

Again his forces rested a month. He persuaded Grant not to transfer them to Virginia by water but allow them instead to march there, devastating the Carolinas en route. Sherman started on 1 February, and reached Columbia, South Carolina, on 17 February and Goldsboro, North Carolina, on 23–24 March. There he joined three corps moving inland from the coast. His reinforced army occupied Raleigh on 11 April, and received Johnston's surrender at Durham later that month. Together with Lee's surrender on 9 April, this virtually ended the American Civil War.

> 'A sagacious and resolute leader.'
>
> JOSEPH E. JOHNSTON DESCRIBES SHERMAN IN HIS POST-WAR MEMOIRS

Bitter aftermath

Johnston surrendered twice, on both 18 and 26 April, because Sherman's first terms were so generous they were called the 'Sherman–Johnston Treaty.' Sherman thought them consistent with Lincoln's intent to hasten reconciliation. By then, however, Lincoln was dead. Anger over his assassination caused Washington scornfully to repudiate Sherman's offer and to compel him to insist on the same terms Grant accorded Lee. Such abuse of a victorious commander at the height of success embittered Sherman and estranged him from Halleck. At the grand review of his troops in Washington on 24 May, Sherman publicly refused to shake hands with Secretary of War Edwin M. Stanton, whom he blamed for such mistreatment.

The three grand reviews were triumphal marches symbolizing the Union victory. On 27 June the great volunteer armies that won the Civil War were discontinued, and the US army began shifting to a peacetime footing. By then Sherman had been a major general of regulars for some ten months, and when Grant was promoted to full general on 25 July 1866 Sherman succeeded him as lieutenant general of the army. Then when Grant became president, on 4 March 1869, Sherman received a fourth star and became general-in-chief. First as commander of the Military Division of the Missouri, 1865–9, and then as commanding general of the army, Sherman remained discontented with political interference in the military – somewhat ironically, since he had re-entered service in 1861 through his political connections. To help immunize the army from such influences and heighten its capabilities, he enhanced its school system – the military dimension of the increased professionalization of American society in the Gilded Age. He adamantly refused to run for president himself.

Sherman stepped down as general-in-chief on 1 November 1883, and retired three months later. He died on 14 February 1891 and is buried in St Louis.

William T. Sherman

Assessment

Sherman was a strategist, not a tactician. Although he fought well defensively at Shiloh, most of his tactical attacks failed, from Chickasaw Bayou to Missionary Ridge, from Kennesaw Mountain to Bentonville.

The realm of strategy was where he excelled. His brilliant mind recognized key strategic objectives and how to attain them. Even more crucially, he understood that in a republic at war, civilian support for the war effort is essential. To cripple that support is to cripple the enemy, no matter how brave and well led are the enemy armies. Through his 'March to the Sea' and his Carolinas campaign, he won the war

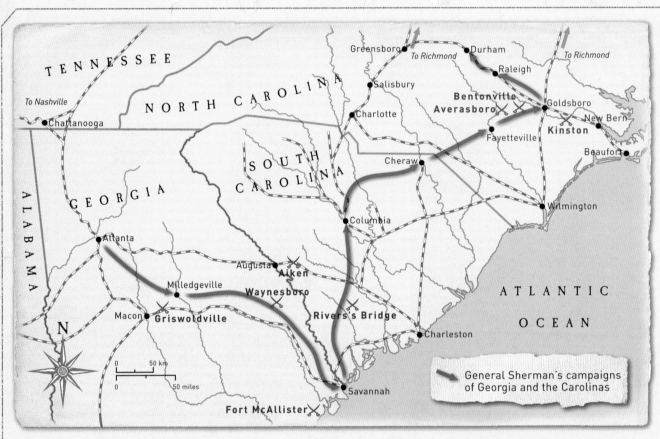

THE GREAT MARCH

IN MID NOVEMBER 1864 Sherman massed fourteen divisions (thirteen infantry and one cavalry) in Atlanta, divided into Oliver O. Howard's right wing (the Army of the Tennessee) and Henry W. Slocum's left wing (the Army of Georgia). These 60,000 veterans struck devastatingly deep into the Confederacy.

Sherman cut loose from his supply line to Chattanooga, burned Atlanta, and on 15 November began his 'March to the Sea', living off the land. He could have headed south for the Gulf of Mexico or east for Charleston. Instead, he advanced southeast toward Savannah. Uncertain of his destination, Southern commanders dispersed their forces. He compounded their confusion by demonstrating with his right against Macon and with his left against Augusta. Then he penetrated the unguarded centre and captured Milledgeville, at that time Georgia's state capital, unopposed on 22 November. He continued southeastward and on 13 December stormed Fort McAllister, thereby making contact with the US navy. Savannah fell on 21 December, but its garrison escaped.

These elegant manoeuvres demonstrate Sherman's deftness as a strategist. Yet they also reflect the reality that he faced minimal opposition. He could not have operated so boldly or broadly if Hood's army had still confronted him. But Hood had gone to Tennessee – and annihilation at Nashville on 15–16 December.

William T. Sherman

on the home front – and thereby won the war. In so doing, he did not revive the horrors of the Thirty Years War, which the genteel dynastic wars of eighteenth-century Europe had striven to avoid. Nevertheless, by re-introducing the home front into the equation of war, he foreshadowed the total wars of the twentieth century.

Thus, not only in the American Civil War but also in the continuity of command from Gustavus Adolphus and Tilly through Marshal Saxe and Frederick the Great to Yamashita and Zhukov, William T. Sherman holds an important place among the great commanders of history.

The strategic success of Sherman's march might have been minimized, even nullified, save for George H. Thomas's great battlefield victory there.

Both generals accomplished their missions. Sherman's success lay in demonstrating Federal ability to penetrate the South, unimpeded. The Confederacy could not protect its citizens. It was not through wanton plunder but through systematic strategic devastation of the home front that Sherman 'made Georgia howl'. He thereby crippled civilian commitment to the war and undercut the Confederate soldiers' morale.

A worse fate awaited South Carolina, the 'Cradle of Secession', beginning in February 1865. Sherman again feinted leftwards toward Augusta and rightwards toward Charleston, then swooped through the unguarded centre and took South Carolina's state capital, Columbia, which was burned on the night of 17/18 February. Sherman convincingly claimed he did not order its destruction, but destroyed it was. Its fall, moreover, doomed Charleston, which was abandoned on the same dates.

Sherman followed Charleston's fleeing garrison into North Carolina and took the arsenal city of Fayetteville on 11 March. The Charleston garrison gave Slocum a good fight at Averasboro on 15–16 March. Then at Bentonville on 19 March Johnston (restored to command) delivered a heavy counter-attack with local divisions and Nashville survivors. Slocum withstood this blow, and two days later Sherman almost severed Johnston's escape route, but the Southerner was too experienced in retreating to be intercepted.

Sherman reached Goldsboro on 23–24 March, where John M. Schofield's Army of the Ohio awaited him. He rested for seventeen days, met Lincoln and Grant in Virginia, then resumed advancing on 10 April. For reasons of both strategy and policy (to allow eastern armies to win the eastern war), Sherman no longer headed north toward Virginia. He turned west, occupied Raleigh on 11 April, and received Johnston's surrender at Durham.

From Atlanta to Durham via Savannah, Columbia, Goldsboro and Raleigh, Sherman marched virtually a thousand miles. He devastated the interior of the South, destroyed its already limited logistical infrastructure, demoralized its populace and depleted the determination of its defenders to sustain the struggle. Strategically, he caved the western front almost into the rear of the eastern front; psychologically, he destroyed the enemy's will to wage war. He became the decisive element in Grant's grand strategy of devouring the rest of the Confederacy while Grant pinned Lee in Virginia. Together, these two great commanders, who had become fast friends at Shiloh, won the American Civil War.

Sherman's forces burn McPherson-ville, South Carolina, on 1 February 1865. By such acts Sherman sought to demoralize the South by demonstrating that the Confederate government could not protect its own civilians.

William T. Sherman

HELMUTH VON MOLTKE

1800–91

JOHN LEE

HELMUTH VON MOLTKE, called 'the Elder' to distinguish him from his less distinguished nephew of the same name, brought the Prussian army to a level of machine-like efficiency that saw complete victory in three wars in seven years. In so doing, Moltke played a crucial part in the creation of the modern state of Germany. He also perfected a staff system and military organization that became the model for most armies in most countries of the world today.

Like many a great 'Prussian' general, Helmuth Karl Bernard von Moltke was born outside the kingdom, in Mecklenburg, into a family that had long served in the Prussian army. Because his father owned property in Denmark, Moltke's first military service was in the Danish army. He entered the military academy in Copenhagen in 1811 and graduated fourth in his class in 1819. After duty with two Danish infantry regiments he made a visit to Berlin, where the career prospects in the Prussian army so impressed him that he resigned his commission and applied to join the Prussian service.

The brightest and the best

In 1822 Moltke passed the stiff Prussian army entrance examinations, supervised by the great Gneisenau himself, and became a second lieutenant in the 8th Infantry Regiment. Such was the intensity of his study of the military art that, within a year, he passed into the War School in Berlin, then directed by Carl von Clausewitz. He earned a reputation as a 'library rat', working long and hard at his studies and excelling in modern languages (his mother had been an accomplished linguist). In 1826 he passed his final examinations, and was marked out as a young man of great promise. Rejoining his regiment, he ran a school for cadet officers and impressed all his superiors. From 1828 to 1831 he served in the Topographical Survey directed by the General Staff, doing important detailed work, as well as commencing deep studies of historical campaigns. He also wrote a number of literary essays, and contracted to translate the twelve volumes of Gibbon's *Decline and Fall of the Roman Empire* into German, only to see the publisher fail as he reached volume eleven. Years of work yielded a fee of only £25.

In 1832 Moltke was appointed to the General Staff in Berlin; his promotion to captain in 1834 was four years ahead of his contemporaries. In 1835, on leave of absence to tour Turkey, he was introduced to the chief adviser to the sultan, to whom he explained the idea of war games (*Kriegspiel*) so effectively that the Turkish Porte officially requested his services as a military advisor to their army. For four years he helped to reorganize the army along Prussian lines, conducted survey work and the planning of fortifications, and saw a little active service against the forces of the rebel, Mehmet Ali. In 1839 his sound advice was ignored and he saw the Turkish army defeated at Nisib. He returned to Berlin with his reputation enhanced by the detailed reports he posted.

In 1842 Moltke married Marie Burt, the English stepdaughter of his sister Augusta. She was twenty-five years younger than he was and, though childless, they were intensely happy together. The following year he invested all his savings in the new Hamburg–Berlin railway, and wrote an important essay on the principles of running a railway. Moltke was instantly aware of the huge importance this new technology would have, not just on a nation's economy, but on its capacity to mobilize for, and prosecute, war. In 1845 he was briefly the personal aide-de-camp to the aged and dying Prince Henry of Prussia, which brought him more closely to the attention of the royal family.

By 1848 Moltke had served on the staff of VIII Corps and became chief of staff to IV Corps. He had a busy and contented life, keeping his troops at a peak of efficiency, studying, writing and looking forward to retirement. The wave of revolutions that swept Europe that year saw the Prussian army stand firmly behind their king as he resisted the demand for reform from his citizens. In the wake of the 1848 Revolutions, Prussia had to stand by as Austria asserted her dominant role in German affairs, and this humiliation was deeply felt. In 1855 Moltke became the first adjutant to Prince Frederick William, and for two years toured with him through England, Russia and France. In 1857 the prince's father, acting as prince regent for his dying brother, temporarily appointed Moltke as chief of staff to the Prussian army and confirmed him in that post the next year.

(Opposite) **Helmuth von Moltke,** here seen wearing the famous Prussian *Pickelhaube* ('pointed hat'), was the joint architect, with Otto von Bismarck, of a united Germany. The latter provided the political cunning, while Moltke delivered the military machine to back it up.

Helmuth von Moltke

Chief of the General Staff

After the catastrophe of 1806 – the defeats by Napoleon at Jena and Auerstädt and the collapse of the Prussian state – a coterie of reforming geniuses comprising Scharnhorst, Gneisenau and Clausewitz came together to lay the basis for a new sense of professionalism in the army (see pp. 158–9). Under this new system the best young officers were singled out for intensive training in staff procedures, and they could thus be depended upon, regardless of which commanders they served, to act in a uniform manner according to sound military principles. The permanent General Staff in Berlin studied all military questions of the day, and rotated their officers through service with the army in the field, so that their methods were spread throughout the army.

Moltke inherited this well-defined system and brought to it a new intensity based on his own studious approach to life and work. Of the 120 candidates a year for the Berlin War Academy, 40 were accepted, and the 12 top graduates were selected for General Staff duties. Even these were only on probation until Moltke personally approved their work. Thus it was not long before he built up a corps of staff officers all completely in tune with his thought and methods. All staff officers were rotated through line units between promotions, and their ethos thus permeated the army. Many brigade and division commanders were trained by Moltke, and every general had a General Staff-trained officer as his chief of staff. It was this uniformity of doctrine and purpose that enabled Moltke to direct the movement of armies larger than Napoleon's with a sure confidence.

The General Staff studied all possible military contingencies that might affect the Prussian state. They drew up war-plans for most eventualities, and planned mobilizations accordingly. It was Moltke's personal view that 'a mistake in the original concentration of the army can hardly be made good in the entire course of the campaign'. His lifelong interest in railway development transformed the capacity of the army to mobilize quickly and effectively for war. After studying the problem in test mobilizations, he decentralized the whole process down to the corps districts into which the army was organized, and made them liaise with local railways to speed up and perfect the process. No new railway was built in Prussia without integrating it into military planning. A special Lines of Communication Department of the General Staff was created to work with a civilian–military Central Commission of Railways, and one of Moltke's three principal assistants was solely responsible for railway timetables and transportation.

Conscription, and the creation of large trained reserves, saw armies swell in size. Together with the increased lethality of firearms, Moltke saw that the ideal of seeking the enemy's flank on the battlefield was no longer possible. Instead he devised the scheme of conducting strategic developments over huge distances by a continuous operational sequence of mobilization, concentration, movement and battle.

Besides war-planning and mobilization, Moltke developed the educational role of the General Staff, through a deep and intense study of military history (one of the earliest special departments of the General Staff) and the use of war games and staff rides to allow officers to develop their skills in appreciating terrain and issuing orders under pressure without being actually involved in fighting.

In 1864 Prussia and Austria waged war on Denmark over the right to rule the provinces of Schleswig and Holstein. Moltke was not greatly involved in the early stages of the campaign, and watched from the sidelines as some reactionary old

Helmuth von Moltke

generals, who openly despised the 'pampered' staff officers, failed miserably to bring the Danes to heel. At this point the king appointed his nephew, Prince Frederick Charles, to command the army, and made Moltke his chief of staff in the field. By dint of careful planning and the proper concentration of troops at the decisive point, the war was brought to a rapid and successful conclusion. The General Staff, having won the confidence of the king, received an important boost to its reputation.

The Seven Weeks War

It was clear that Prussia would soon challenge Austria for supremacy in Germany. The crunch came in 1866, when Otto von Bismarck, the Prussian chief minister, sought a promise of French neutrality and an Italian alliance. Austria saw the threat and began mobilizing her army. The war against 'German brothers', was not popular, and the king delayed the decision to mobilize his army beyond the expected date. Moltke had to adapt his war-plan to cover Prussia from possible Austrian attack, and to deal with Austria's several allies among the many disunited states of Germany.

Moltke employed the principal railways to deploy three armies towards Austria and her Saxon ally. These armies would advance separately and be brought together in the decisive theatre of operations once it had been ascertained where that was going to be. Though the Austrians had mobilized weeks ahead of Prussia, Moltke was not dismayed: he felt he had a deep understanding of the Austrian army and its commanders, and was confident in the ability of the Prussian army and its generals. In a study of the Franco-Austrian War of 1859 he had written against the name of Benedek, the current Austrian commander: 'No commander-in-chief or strategist: will want a deal of assistance in running an army.'

From Berlin, on 15 June, at the end of lines of telegraphic communication, Moltke directed three armies south, while keeping in touch with three smaller armies dealing with Prussia's enemies within Germany. Even when one of these armies was defeated by the Hanoverians, Moltke did not allow himself to be distracted from his main objective: the defeat of Austria. (The Hanoverians, in fact, had fired off all their ammunition and surrendered two days later.) A complete breakdown of the telegraph left Moltke in a void for a day, and the poor performance of the Prussian cavalry in obtaining information about enemy movements often led to contact being lost with the Austrians.

> 'The triumphs of 1866 and 1870 ... were the coping-stone of a career of close professional study ... put to brilliant use.'
> LIEUTENANT COLONEL F. E. WHITTON

Moltke took calculated risks based on his solid knowledge of his own army and that of the enemy. He knew that the Austrians were deploying forward into Bohemia in a central mass. He knew that an active and resourceful commander might try to defeat the separate Prussian armies in sequence. But he also knew that his armies were drawing together, so denying the enemy the room to manoeuvre, and he knew that Benedek was indecisive and would need weeks to organize offensive operations.

Despite the slow progress of one army, and the short-term defeat of part of another, the Prussians ground forward relentlessly, inflicting a series of small tactical defeats on the Austrians and destroying what remained of their commander's will to win. When the Austrians made their stand at Königgrätz (see p. 232), with the River Elbe at their back, the stage was set for victory.

Helmuth von Moltke

THE BATTLE OF KÖNIGGRÄTZ

WHEN PRINCE FREDERICK CHARLES'S FIRST ARMY determined to attack the Austrians, he simply asked the Prussian crown prince's Second Army to lend him some assistance on his left. Moltke, now present with the army, immediately ordered the whole of the Second Army to march with all speed to close in on the Austrian flank as the First Army and the Army of the Elbe engaged them in battle. He was entirely clear in his intentions, and his orders were brief and to the point.

Having been lacklustre in advance, Frederick Charles impetuously launched his 75,000 infantry at 180,000 Austrians deployed in strong positions. There were anxious moments on the morning of 3 July as the Austrians made good use of their local superiority. At a critical moment Moltke turned to the king and said, 'Your Majesty will win today not only a battle but a campaign.' By 2 p.m. the Second Army had arrived on the field of battle; by 3.30 all three Prussian armies were advancing; by 6.30 the victory was complete. The gamble of uniting three armies on the field of battle had succeeded.

The Prussians allowed the Austrians to escape. They were not seeking to humiliate their enemy, and brought hostilities to a rapid conclusion, before other European powers, especially France, could intervene.

(Below) **Prussian artillery advancing against the Austrians** at the Battle of Königgrätz, fought near Hradec Králové (now in the Czech Republic) on 3 July 1866. The battle, which led to Prussia replacing Austria as the dominant power in Germany, is sometimes referred to as Sadowa, after the village (modern Sadová) around which the fighting took place.

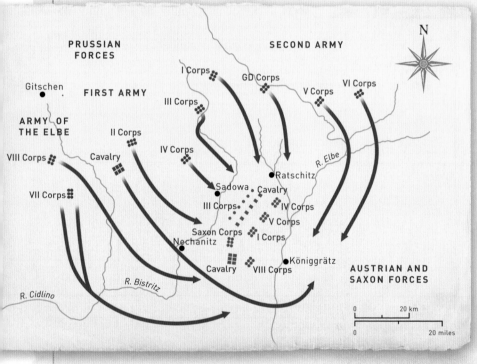

Helmuth von Moltke

After his stunning masterstroke against the Austrians, Moltke returned to Berlin, saying: 'I hate all fulsome praise … I but did my duty.' He now integrated all the armies of the northern German states into the Prussian system, and obliged the armies of southern Germany to conform. Almost at once contingency plans began to be laid for a future war with France, with Moltke and his staff drawing up the most intricate arrangements for mobilization by railway. His aim was to deliver over a million men to the Franco-German frontier.

The Franco-Prussian War

Moltke personally held France accountable for 200 years of war in Europe. War with France was not only inevitable but desirable, he believed. Once again his profound knowledge of the capabilities of all the armies involved led him to plan boldly for complete and early victory: 'Our object,' he said, 'is to seek out the main enemy mass and to attack it wherever found.' Needing to strike before Austria could intervene, he wanted 500,000 troops to be instantly available to meet a maximum of 300,000 French at the outbreak of war. Once again he would direct three armies to move quite separately towards the frontier and use one to pin the French army in place while the other two manoeuvred against the enemy flanks.

Prussia's – and Moltke's – opportunity came in 1870, when a dispute arose over a Spanish request for a Hohenzollern prince – a member of Prussia's ruling dynasty – to ascend their throne. When the French objected strenuously, the Prussian king was willing to let the matter drop. When the French rudely insisted that he promise never to support such an idea again, Bismarck and Moltke conspired to edit his reply to give maximum offence to the Emperor Napoleon III. The French then mobilized their army, placing them in the role of aggressor. At this point the Prussian war-plan swung into action. For two weeks, from 15 to 31 July, Moltke had little to do but read novels as half a million Prussian troops moved into position according to his carefully laid plan.

The French mobilization was chaotic, and their military organization all but collapsed under the strain. They rashly launched an offensive into Germany and briefly occupied Saarbrücken. Moltke quickly had to redraw his plans, and tried to secure an early crushing victory. But here the aggressive response of the Prussian commanders in the field was too prompt. Both First and Third Armies launched frontal assaults on the first enemy they encountered, at Spicheren and Worth respectively. The well-armed French inflicted heavy casualties, but could do nothing to stop the Prussians crowding forward, seeking their flanks and turning them out of strong positions. While nearby French forces waited for orders, all the Prussian units marched to the sound of the guns and fought the enemy where they found them. These two early defeats had a profound effect on French morale and on the minds of their commanders.

Emperor Napoleon III, whom Bismarck and Moltke deliberately provoked into mobilizing for war in 1870. Napoleon was taken prisoner at Sedan, and subsequently went into exile in England. This portrait, dating from 1862, is by Hippolyte Flandrin.

Helmuth von Moltke

Moltke set his armies marching towards the west. He considered whether the French might mass against any one of them but concluded that 'such a vigorous decision is hardly in keeping with the attitude they have shown up till now'. The French were in full retreat and threw themselves into the fortress zone of Metz as a safe haven. Moltke simply bypassed Metz and directed his armies across the French line of retreat. He ordered the Second Army and most of the First Army to close in on the French from the south. On 16 August two corps of the Second Army, thinking they were engaging a rearguard, bumped into the entire French army at Vionville. Only the excellent Prussian artillery, vastly improved since 1866, saved them from serious defeat in the morning. More and more Prussian troops were fed into the battle until it seemed to end in a bloody stalemate at about 7 p.m. The late arrival of still more Prussian formations saw the French driven from the field in disorder.

The next major battle (Gravelotte, 18 August) saw the Prussian First and Second Armies with their backs to Paris facing east, as the French tried to escape westwards. Once again impetuous Prussian generals attacked the enemy too vigorously, before the whole army had deployed for a united effort. After hard fighting and grievous losses, they could claim the terrible day as a victory. The French army retreated into Metz and was besieged there.

Moltke then directed fresh forces steadily westwards until contact was made with a new French army supposedly trying to relieve Metz. By 31 August the French had gone into camp on the Meuse at Sedan. There they were completely surrounded and bombarded into submission. On 1 September 104,000 French troops – along with their emperor – passed into captivity. The road to Paris was open.

Paris was duly besieged. Across France the government of the recently declared Third Republic organized new armies, but these were defeated one after another. Metz surrendered and, after an armistice in January 1871, the war came to end in March.

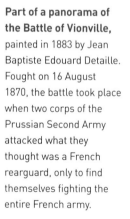

Part of a panorama of the Battle of Vionville, painted in 1883 by Jean Baptiste Edouard Detaille. Fought on 16 August 1870, the battle took place when two corps of the Prussian Second Army attacked what they thought was a French rearguard, only to find themselves fighting the entire French army.

Helmuth von Moltke

Moltke's legacy

The German empire was declared at Versailles in January 1871. Moltke would continue to serve as chief of the General Staff until 1888, having had a request to retire in 1880 refused. Constantly aware that the French might seek to revenge their defeat at any moment, he planned for every eventuality of war with France and any combination of her allies. Conscious of the dangers of a war on two fronts, he perfected his doctrine of the strategic offensive (carrying the war into the enemy's own territory) and the tactical defensive (using the power of the defence to break the enemy's attacking army before delivering a counter-attack at the decisive moment).

Moltke's legacy is that of the perfect professional, so deeply imbued with knowledge of military history and modern technology that, while never having personally commanded troops in battle, he could execute his plans with an icy calmness, with an intellect that coped with any emergency, and with a clarity of purpose that carried him to victory again and again. The 'Great Silent One', as the German people called him, died in 1891.

French and Prussian representatives negotiate the surrender terms at Sedan on the night of 1/2 September 1870, in a painting by Anton von Werner (1843–1915). Moltke stands on the right side of the table, with Bismarck seated beside him. Sedan proved to be the decisive victory in the Franco-Prussian War.

Helmuth von Moltke

'I always seem to be condemned to command in expeditions which must be accomplished before a certain season of the year begins.'

WOLSELEY TO HIS WIFE, 16 DECEMBER 1873

GARNET WOLSELEY
1833–1913

IAN BECKETT

WHEN GEORGE GROSSMITH performed the role of the Major-General in Gilbert and Sullivan's *The Pirates of Penzance* for the first time at the Opéra Comique on 3 April 1880 no member of the audience would have doubted for a moment that the 'very model of a modern Major-General' was meant to be Garnet Wolseley. Already known to the Victorian public as 'Our Only General', Wolseley had won his reputation on the Red River expedition in the Canadian northwest in 1870, the Ashanti (Asante) War of 1873–4 and, most recently, in bringing the Zulu War to a successful conclusion in 1879. Indeed, Wolseley remained in South Africa overseeing the post-war settlement until returning to England to become quartermaster general at the War Office in July 1880. Yet, his greatest military triumph was yet to come for, in September 1882, his victory at Tel-el-Kebir secured British control over Egypt and the Suez Canal.

Subsequently, there was also to be failure, for two years later, when the Mahdist revolt broke out in the Sudan, Wolseley was despatched belatedly to relieve Charles Gordon, besieged in Khartoum: his troops reached the city just two days too late. Unfortunately, Wolseley's health was declining by the time he became commander-in-chief of the British army in 1895, and he had inherited a post stripped of its former powers. Rapid mobilization at the start of the South African War in 1899 owed much to Wolseley, even if subsequent early defeats illustrated how much more military reform was yet required. Nonetheless, he had done much to define national military policy, and laid the foundations for further professionalism.

Born in Dublin on 4 June 1833, Garnet Joseph Wolseley was the eldest of seven children. His father, an impoverished major in the 25th Foot, had left the army shortly after his marriage and died when Wolseley was just 7 years old. The family was left in straitened circumstances, and Wolseley's first commission as ensign in the 12th Foot on 12 March 1852 was secured through his mother seeking a direct nomination from the commander-in-chief, the Duke of Wellington, on the strength of his father's service. At a time when many commissions were still purchased, Wolseley was to advance without

Garnet Wolseley

benefit of money through sheer courage and determination, a conviction that his destiny was willed by God having been imbued in the young Wolseley by his mother's deeply held Irish Protestant religious faith. In the Second Burma War (1852–3) Wolseley received a thigh wound that troubled him all his life. In the Crimean War (1854–6) he lost the sight of his left eye. After further service in the Indian Mutiny (1857–8) and the Third China War (1860–61), Wolseley emerged a brevet lieutenant colonel after just eight years service.

The 'Wolseley Ring'

Stationed in Canada, Wolseley visited the Confederacy in 1862, writing memorably of his impressions of leading Confederate commanders such as Robert E. Lee and 'Stonewall' Jackson. He also consolidated his reputation as a military reformer in 1869 with a practical manual, *The Soldier's Pocket Book*, aimed at improving tactical efficiency. The manual demonstrated Wolseley's instinctive understanding of logistics, knowledge immediately required when he was chosen to quell a rebellion by French-speaking *métis* in the Canadian northwest in 1870. Wolseley forged through 600 miles of wilderness with a force of 1,200 regulars and militia to re-occupy Fort Garry on the Red River and to return before the lakes froze. As it happened, the *métis* fled before Wolseley reached Fort Garry, but it had been a triumph of minutely supervised organization. Wolseley received a knighthood and was brought back to the War Office as assistant adjutant general in May 1871.

The reforms of the army instituted by Edward Cardwell as secretary of state for war were mostly completed before Wolseley returned to Britain, but he fully supported their aims, such as the introduction of short service. He was then selected by Cardwell in August 1873 to lead the expedition to repel an Ashanti incursion into the Gold Coast, and to punish the Ashanti by advancing on their capital at Kumasi. Once more it was a question of overcoming climate and terrain: Wolseley had to get British troops

Garnet Wolseley, affectionately satirized by W. S. Gilbert as the 'very model of a modern Major-General', eventually rose to be commander-in-chief of the entire British army.

to Kumasi and back before the onset of the rains and before tropical diseases took their toll. In Canada Wolseley had begun to make note of able young officers such as Redvers Buller and William Butler, and he now summoned them to join him on the Gold Coast. This was effectively the beginning of what was to become known, with the addition of others such as Evelyn Wood, George Colley, Frederick Maurice and Henry Brackenbury, as the 'Wolseley Ring' (or the 'Ashanti Ring').

Wolseley did not always have a free choice of staff on his campaigns, but he preferred those familiar with his working methods and in whom he had confidence. Ultimately, he did become something of a prisoner of the initial success of the 'Ring' system, often employing the same men in case it was felt his rejection of them would reflect on his initial choices. Moreover, Wolseley's ability to manage a campaign decreased in proportion to the increasing scale of the operations with which he was tasked, with many of his chosen subordinates proving unable to act on their own initiative. To rivals, the 'Ring' was the 'Mutual Admiration Society', but it was one of several such networks within the army, reflecting the absence of a properly formed general staff.

The outcome of the Ashanti War was taken to be proof of the success of the Cardwell reforms, although the regulars involved were soldiers enlisted under the old long-service system. Certainly, it was a model campaign and one extensively reported in the press. Wolseley arriving at the Gold Coast in October 1873, using locally raised forces to push the Ashanti back across the River Pra, and making extensive preparations for the arrival of his British troops. Crossing the Pra in January, Wolseley fought two sharp actions, took and burned Kumasi, and was back on the coast by 19 February 1874. Among other rewards, Wolseley was promoted to major-general.

The War Office and reform

In 1875 Wolseley was sent to administer Natal, and then in 1878 to occupy Cyprus, awarded to Britain by the Treaty of Berlin as a potential base should the Russians attempt to control the Dardanelles. Had a major war broken out against Russia, Wolseley would have been chief of staff to the proposed British expeditionary force. In June 1879 Wolseley and his adherents were dispatched to retrieve the situation in Zululand following early British defeats, though the Zulus were defeated before Wolseley reached the front. Completing the subjugation of the Zulus, Wolseley became successively quartermaster general at the War Office in July 1880 and adjutant general in March 1882, despite the opposition of military conservatives, who resented Wolseley's public championship of reform and their exclusion from his now well-publicized campaigns. Indeed, he had earned the particular enmity of the army's long-serving commander-in-chief (and cousin to Queen Victoria), the Duke of Cambridge. The duke resented Wolseley's flouting of command and staff selection by seniority, and believed that long service was essential to discipline, that discipline and drill were the key to military efficiency, and that reform would generally undermine regimental tradition. Wolseley had hopes for the chief command in India, but the duke steadfastly resisted this, while the queen also opposed granting Wolseley a peerage.

'It is quite true that Wolseley is an egotist and a braggart. So was Nelson.'

BENJAMIN DISRAELI TO QUEEN VICTORIA, 24 AUGUST 1879

Garnet Wolseley

In his two successive appointments at the War Office between 1880 and 1890, therefore, Wolseley found it difficult to achieve progress. He did, however, oversee the modernization of the infantry drill book, the introduction of mounted infantry, better tactical training and improvements to the suitability of campaign dress. The most significant development was the extension of the intelligence department of the War Office and the preparation of proper mobilization plans for the home army. Wolseley, indeed, embraced what became known as the 'imperial school' of British strategic thought, placing the priority on home defence and envisaging any potential war against Russia as being waged primarily through amphibious operations. By contrast, the 'Indian school', most often represented by Wolseley's most prominent military rival, Frederick Roberts, feared the Russian threat to India and, therefore, saw operations on the Northwest Frontier as the empire's first priority in war. In the process of his advocacy of proper military planning, Wolseley secured a definitive statement of the purposes for which the army existed and of the relative priorities to be accorded them through the so-called Stanhope Memorandum of 1888.

Egypt and the Sudan

Wolseley's tenure as adjutant general was twice interrupted by further field command. When Arabi Pasha's nationalist revolt in Egypt threatened the Suez Canal in June 1882, Wolseley was appointed to command the expedition to suppress it and restore the authority of the khedive. It was to be the largest expedition mounted by the British army between the end of the Crimean War in 1856 and the beginning of the South African War in 1899, Wolseley commanding a total force of 35,000 men.

Wolseley receives the surrender of the Zulu chiefs at the conclusion of the Zulu War in 1879. Wolseley had been dispatched to Zululand to replace Lord Chelmsford as commander, following early disasters such as that at Isandlwana. However, Chelmsford managed to defeat the Zulus at Ulundi before Wolseley arrived.

Garnet Wolseley

TEL-EL-KEBIR AND THE EGYPTIAN CAMPAIGN

THE GROWING POWER OF AHMED ARABI and anti-European riots in Alexandria in June 1882 persuaded Gladstone's government that the security of the Suez Canal and European investment in Egypt was imperilled. The British and French fleets, lying off Alexandria in a demonstration of force, were then threatened by the construction of new Egyptian shore batteries. Exceeding his instructions, Admiral Seymour bombarded the batteries on 11 July. With the khedive taking refuge on Seymour's ships, Arabi seized power.

Wolseley, given command on 4 August, had already drawn up a plan for securing the Suez Canal and Ismailia, and advancing on Cairo from the east, using the Ismailia-to-Cairo railway and the Sweetwater Canal to build up supplies before the final advance. The extensive logistic preparations began at once, including the provision of locomotives and wagons to bypass any need to rely on Egyptian rolling stock, and the purchase of horses and mules. Wolseley did not get all his own way on appointments, since the principal commands were taken by those already designated to act in the forthcoming autumn manoeuvres. He also found it politic to accept the queen's son, the Duke of Connaught, as a brigade commander.

Before his arrival at Alexandria, Wolseley, fearing that the Egyptians might block the Suez Canal, ordered a series of feints by the troops that had already landed, in order to persuade Arabi that he would advance upon Cairo from the

(Above) **The Highland Brigade attacks** the Egyptian trenches at Tel-el-Kebir early in the morning of 13 September 1882. Initially they met with fierce resistance, but within an hour the Egyptians were put to flight.

Appointed on 4 August, Wolseley arrived at Alexandria on 15 August, the first elements of his force having already been sent there in another highly organized logistic feat, with troops being dispatched not only from Britain, but also from Mediterranean garrisons and even India. Misleading the Egyptians as to his real intentions, Wolseley swiftly transferred his field force to Port Said and down the Suez Canal to Ismailia on 20 August. Wolseley advanced to Kassassin, bringing his force up to fortified Egyptian lines at Tel-el-Kebir. In a dawn attack on the lines on 13 September, Wolseley routed Arabi's army (see above). He received promotion to full general and, at last, the coveted peerage as Baron Wolseley of Cairo and Wolseley.

Though Britain controlled Egypt, the restored khedive still nominally governed. The khedival government had been struggling against the Mahdi's rebellion in the

Garnet Wolseley

west. On 19 August the field force embarked, seemingly to land at Aboukir in the west but, under cover of darkness, instead steamed east to Port Said, where marines and seamen had occupied key points. Having secured the canal, Wolseley advanced towards Kassassin to clear the line of the railway and the Sweetwater Canal on 24 August. Arabi entrenched at Tel-el-Kebir, an Egyptian sortie on 28 August being disrupted by a celebrated 'moonlit' charge by the Household Cavalry. A further Egyptian advance was also pushed back on 8 September.

Wolseley had some 16,000 men, while Arabi had perhaps 20,000 men and 75 guns behind entrenchments. Accordingly, Wolseley resolved upon a daring night march across the desert. Having carefully estimated the distance to be covered before dawn, Wolseley started his men out at 1.30 a.m. on 13 September in strictly enforced silence and guided by a naval officer using the stars as reference. The Highland Brigade was spotted coming up to the Egyptian trenches at about 4.55 a.m. In places there was fierce resistance to the Highlanders' charge, but by 6 a.m. the Egyptians were in flight. Wolseley unleashed his cavalry, which entered Cairo on 14 September, Arabi surrendering that night. The British suffered only fifty-seven killed, forty-five of them Highlanders.

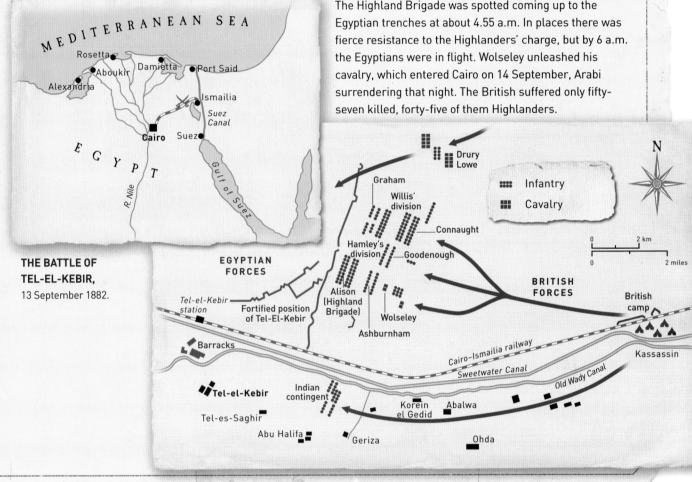

THE BATTLE OF TEL-EL-KEBIR, 13 September 1882.

Sudan even before Wolseley's victory at Tel-el-Kebir. Failure to contain the revolt, not least the destruction of an Egyptian army commanded by a former British officer, William Hicks, in November 1883, led the British government to resolve to abandon the Sudan. Sent to evacuate the Egyptian garrisons in January 1884, Charles Gordon chose to hold Khartoum instead. Wolseley, who had seen Gordon off on his mission, urged a relief expedition. It was not until September, however, that he was appointed to command such an expedition.

Influenced by the Red River experience, Wolseley chose to advance down the Nile from the Egyptian frontier rather than crossing the desert from Suakin on the Red Sea coast to the Nile at Berber, as most advised. Indeed, he brought over Canadian *voyageurs* (boatmen) to handle the 800 special boats he intended to construct. This

Garnet Wolseley

The Battle of Abu Klea, 17 January 1885, in which a British column advancing through Sudan defeated attacking Mahdist forces, as depicted by the late Victorian battle artist William Barnes Wollen (1857–1936). Wolseley had been given the task of relieving General Gordon, besieged in Khartoum, but the relief force arrived two days too late.

time, however, the logistic problems were even more formidable than in his previous campaigns, since there were 1,600 miles between Cairo and Khartoum. Refused permission by the government to go as far forward as he felt necessary, Wolseley had to rely more upon his chosen subordinates, now grown in seniority and status and riven by mutual animosities. Precious days were lost, especially when the able Herbert Stewart, commanding the 'river column', was mortally wounded. Stewart's successor reached Khartoum on 28 January 1885, two days too late to save Gordon, a particular hero for Wolseley, for whom Gordon's death was a bitter blow. It was little consolation that he was elevated to a viscountcy in August 1885.

Commander-in-chief

Approaching the end of his appointment as adjutant general, Wolseley was finally being considered for command in India – but, as there seemed less likelihood now of war with Russia and as Wolseley's daughter was coming out that season, he declined. Instead, he took up the Irish command in October 1890 and, with increased leisure time began to write more, penning a book on Napoleon and completing two volumes of what was to be an uncompleted life of Marlborough. He was promoted to field marshal in May 1894.

Ambition, however, remained, and it was clear that Cambridge would soon retire as commander-in-chief. Ironically, it was now Buller, his old colleague in the 'Ring', rather than Roberts who was Wolseley's greatest rival for the appointment, especially as the Liberal government favoured Buller. Wolseley regarded Buller's apparent

Garnet Wolseley

willingness to accept the appointment as something of a betrayal. In the event, a fortuitous change of government saw Wolseley secure the prize, and he became commander-in-chief in November 1895.

Wolseley's period as commander-in-chief, however, was overshadowed. Firstly, five years previously the Hartington Commission had recommended abolition of the post altogether and its replacement by a Continental-style chief of the general staff. The proposal had died with the opposition of the Duke of Cambridge and the queen, but the powers of the commander-in-chief had been reduced earlier in 1895 so that other departmental heads within the War Office would now sit on an army board with the commander-in-chief and have equal access to the secretary of state for war. Wolseley had no success in trying to restore the supreme authority of his post, describing the new situation as being like the 'fifth wheel on a coach'. He also enjoyed a poor relationship with the secretary of state, Lord Lansdowne, who was a friend and supporter of Roberts. Secondly, Wolseley's health began to fail: a serious illness in 1897, from which he never fully recovered, impaired his memory.

Nevertheless, Wolseley was able to take pride in the efficiency and speed with which the army was mobilized for war with the Boers in October 1899, despite the government's failure to heed his advice to mobilize much earlier. Yet the lack of empathy with Lansdowne had impaired strategic decision-making, and Wolseley's achievement was soon undermined by the early defeats suffered by Buller's field army in the 'Black Week' of December 1899. As a result, Wolseley was not consulted when Roberts was appointed to supersede Buller in South Africa. Wolseley was persuaded to remain at his post by the queen, finally retiring in November 1900 and, to his chagrin, being succeeded by his rival, Roberts. He died at Menton in France on 20 March 1913.

Assessment

Wolseley was a complex character, respected rather than liked by his subordinates. He was not as radical as opponents believed, and was certainly no liberal. Fiercely patriotic, he was utterly contemptuous of politicians and made little secret of his belief that party politics was 'the curse of modern England'. Some saw him, indeed, as a man of Caesarist tendencies, but, in reality, he fully understood the restricted constitutional parameters in which the army existed. That did not prevent him from manipulating the press he affected to despise and playing politics himself through that manipulation. He could be charming when he wished, but could also appear egotistical and snobbish.

Though Wolseley's reputation was to be eclipsed through the subsequent prominence of Roberts and the way in which memories of colonial warfare were forgotten amid the greater impact of the First World War, he did lay important foundations for a more professional army. Sadly, however, it was an unfulfilled career for the leading soldier of his generation. Through no fault of his own, he never exercised the supreme test of command against an equal adversary in the field.

ERICH LUDENDORFF
1865–1937

JOHN LEE

ERICH LUDENDORFF, inseparably linked to the name of Field Marshal Paul von Hindenburg, achieved fame by a string of victories on the Eastern Front between 1914 and 1916. He then brought his formidable energy to the task of organizing Germany for total war and, in 1918, carried his nation to the very brink of victory, before leading her to catastrophic defeat.

The great strength of the Prussian military system was that it harnessed the brightest and the best of its non-noble citizens into an elite dominated by the Junkers – the aristocratic class that had served their kings loyally and well in a unique social contract since the seventeenth century.

The consummate staff officer

Erich Ludendorff, the third of six children, was born on 9 April 1865 at Kruschevnia in the Prussian province of Posen (now part of Poland). His father was descended from Pomeranian merchants and was a landowner of small means, holding a commission in the reserve cavalry; his mother was from an impoverished noble family. He was described as a lonely boy at school, where his obsessive cleanliness separated him from the other boys, and where he displayed a marked talent for mathematics. His father greatly approved of his decision to embark on a military career. In 1877, aged 12, he passed the examinations for a cadet school with distinction, thanks to his excellent mathematics paper, and was placed in a class two years ahead of his actual age. Foregoing the temptations of the sports field and gymnasium, he studied hard and performed well. In 1880, still only 15, he entered the military academy at Lichterfelde, near Berlin, and forged ahead academically. His devotion to study and hard work intensified, driven by iron self-discipline, and he was consistently first in his class. In 1885 he was commissioned into the 57th Infantry Regiment at Wesel.

Eight years of regimental duty followed, first in the infantry, then in the 2nd Marine Battalion, and finally with the 8th Grenadier Guards. Ludendorff was singled out for praise by all his commanding officers. When he was selected for the War Academy in 1893 he flourished in its intense atmosphere. Though marked down for

Erich Ludendorff

service on the General Staff, he was first posted as a captain commanding a company of infantry at Thorn in 1895, then to other troop staff postings, with 9th Division at Glogau and V Corps at Posen. He was a major by 1900, and served at V Corps headquarters as a senior staff officer from 1902 to 1904.

In 1905 Ludendorff was called by the new Chief of the General Staff, Count Alfred von Schlieffen, to serve in the Second Section, responsible for the mobilization and concentration of all the German armies in the event of war. He loved this painstaking, meticulous work, and by 1908 he was appointed head of the section, and in this role was intimately involved in perfecting the details of what would become known as the Schlieffen Plan. There were many variations of Germany's war-plans, to cover as many eventualities as could be envisaged. The basic problem was how to face war on two fronts, against France in the west and her Russian ally in the east. Calculating that the Russian mobilization would be much slower, the Germans gambled on covering East Prussia with relatively light forces and throwing the vast majority of their army against France, to force a speedy decision on that front, before switching back to the east to settle matters there. They placed their faith in the perfection of their rapid mobilization and deployment of an overwhelming force before their enemy would be fully ready. It was Ludendorff's railway timetables that delivered these troops.

Ludendorff was a full colonel by 1911, acting well above his rank, and so completely in the confidence of Schlieffen's successor, Helmuth von Moltke 'the Younger', that he was widely tipped to become his chief of operations once the 'inevitable' war broke out. Instead he got involved in the political lobbying of the Reichstag for an increase in the size of the army and, in January 1913, was punished by being removed from the General Staff and put in command of an infantry regiment. By April 1914 his natural talent saw him commanding a brigade, with the rank of major-general.

A photograph of Erich Ludendorff probably taken in 1914, the year that he and Hindenburg, commander of the German Eighth Army, became the subject of popular adulation after the German victories at Tannenberg and the Masurian Lakes.

Erich Ludendorff

Under fire

On the outbreak of war in August 1914 Ludendorff was, because of his intimate knowledge of the unfolding of the war-plan, posted to Bülow's Second Army, to oversee the vital capture of the Belgian forts at Liège. Though having never been in action before, he performed remarkably well. He led troops forward under fire and personally penetrated to the city's citadel and demanded the surrender of the astonished garrison.

Soon afterwards, news came of Russian successes and some German panic in East Prussia. The high command there was to be replaced and Ludendorff was appointed the new chief of staff to the Eighth Army. On the train to the east he collected his new commander, Paul von Hindenburg. Such was the uniformity of staff thinking in the German army that, by consulting maps at a distance, Ludendorff came up with a plan to save the day which was almost exactly the same as that already being embarked upon by the more vigorous members of the Eighth Army's staff. The result was the Battle of Tannenberg, fought between 23 August and 2 September 1914, which resulted in the annihilation of the Russian Second Army, and the rapid retreat of the First (see opposite).

After his victory at the Battle of Tannenberg, the skilled use of the railway system to move troops between threatened points enabled Ludendorff to defeat further Russian offensives in Poland. As the commanders in the east clamoured for more men and matériel to complete their victories, they clashed repeatedly with the new chief of the General Staff, Erich von Falkenhayn. When he did release reinforcements for the Eastern Front Falkenhayn directed them to commanders other than Hindenburg and Ludendorff. Ludendorff argued, with some validity, that these attacks merely drove the Russians back into their limitless country, whereas he planned great turning movements aimed at surrounding and destroying their armies in the field.

This bickering at the highest levels went on into 1916. By then Falkenhayn's reputation had been damaged by his lack of success at Verdun and his failure to allow for Romania's entry into the war. When the Kaiser asked Hindenburg and Ludendorff for their advice, Falkenhayn resigned.

Ludendorff (right) confers with the Kaiser (centre) and Hindenburg (left). From 1916 Ludendorff and Hindenburg began to sideline democratically elected politicians in Germany as they mobilized the country for total war.

Erich Ludendorff

246

THE BATTLE OF
TANNENBERG

GREAT OBJECTIVES often require great risks. With calculated boldness based on confidence in their own troops and railway engineers, and an understanding of the strengths and weaknesses of their enemy, the Germans left a very thin screen of cavalry and Landwehr reservists to watch the slowest of the Russian armies (the Russian First Army under Paul von Rennenkampf). The bulk of their forces were swung south, by rail and road, to descend upon the unfortunate Samsonov's Second Army.

Local East Prussian troops, defending their homes, soaked up the Russian offensive while German formations moved into place on each flank. The German field commanders, used to being allowed to conduct their own operations within the wider plan, frequently disobeyed orders from above, but usually to good advantage, as they knew the local conditions. Ludendorff, occasionally prey to bouts of nervous tension as he awaited developments, gave his field commanders freedom of action so long as their fighting contributed to

the success of the overall plan. The Russian Second Army was driven to complete destruction in the dark forests of East Prussia by 30 August.

Having received reinforcements from the west, Ludendorff immediately reversed the process and swung the German troops north behind the Masurian Lakes to destroy Rennenkampf's First Army. By 14 September only the speed of the Russian retreat saved them from Samsonov's fate. Delivering the historic province of East Prussia from 'the Cossacks' made Hindenburg and Ludendorff heroes throughout Germany, at a time when heroes were badly needed.

(Above) **As they retreated after their defeat at Tannenberg** in August 1914, Russian troops left a swathe of destruction in their wake. This photograph, probably taken the following winter, shows the ruins of the East Prussian town of Gerdauen (now Zheleznodorozhny in the Russian Federation).

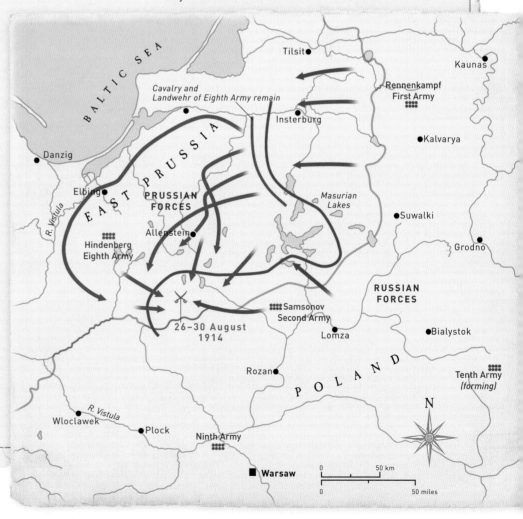

A German U-boat attacks an Allied ship. Ludendorff was a strong advocate of the extension of submarine warfare to neutral shipping, a strategy that backfired badly when it helped to bring the USA into the war.

The call to supreme command

On 29 August 1916 Hindenburg became Chief of the General Staff, and Ludendorff, as first quartermaster general, became Hindenburg's deputy and effectively his executive chief of operations. Having been completely absorbed in the complexities of war on the Eastern Front, the two men now had to view the struggle in its entirety. Ludendorff toured the army commands in the west and quickly realized the enormity of the problem that Germany faced. While the battles raged all summer along the Somme, he authorized the construction of massive defences in the rear (the Hindenburg Line), to which he authorized a retreat early in 1917. Proud of his claim to be an infantry officer above all things, he had a special interest in the development of the tactics of the attack and the defence. He oversaw the learning of lessons from the recent fighting, and the drawing up of new training doctrines for a more flexible defence, aimed at first disorganizing the attackers and then defeating them with heavy counter-attacks. This was achieved by inaugurating a debate amongst the staff and combat officers of the armies in the west, and distilling their practical and theoretical wisdom into new instruction manuals for conducting the defence in depth. The old Prussian tradition of studying operations in great detail, to draw lessons and improvements for future practice, was put to good use.

The next great task was the mobilization of the whole nation for war. The General Staff became intricately involved in the organization of the war industries, manpower, the press and, increasingly, domestic politics. Ludendorff's insatiable appetite for work drew one colleague to say that 'Too much rests on Ludendorff: all domestic and foreign

Erich Ludendorff

248

policy, economic questions, the matter of food supply, etc.' The army High Command encouraged the imperial navy to begin unrestricted submarine warfare, despite the danger of bringing the United States into the war against them. When the chancellor, Theobald von Bethmann-Hollweg, protested, they engineered his dismissal and had him replaced by a nonentity, more subservient to their will. The German military increasingly intervened in domestic politics to insist on its own viewpoint, and several more leading politicians fell victim to this drive for a united war effort.

1917 was a year to restore German confidence in victory. Their forces so completely defeated a French offensive on the Aisne that the French army became mutinous. The cumulative strain of defeat on the Eastern Front forced Russia into revolution and peace negotiations. Ludendorff's skilful use of the railway to move his reserves about saw a surprise offensive at Caporetto drive Italy to the brink of catastrophe (October–November). The abiding problem was the relentless offensive power of the British Expeditionary Force (BEF) under Sir Douglas Haig. Though Germany managed to contain British attacks at Arras in April, Messines in June, Ypres for three and a half months that autumn and Cambrai in November, the appalling drain on German resources was intolerable. Despite finessing their defensive tactics, Ludendorff could do little to stop the violently destructive nature of the British assaults. The submarine war failed to cripple the British war effort, and the Americans entered the war against Germany in April 1917. The longer the war lasted, the stronger the Allies would become, and the weaker the German home front, suffering terrible deprivation because of the Allied blockade.

The final gamble

Ludendorff determined to force a decision in the west, bringing the Allies to the peace table from a position of strength, before the American army could deploy its full capacity. Able to draw troops away from the Eastern Front, he planned a series of powerful offensives aimed at defeating his most implacable foe, the British. His most remarkable achievement was to reconfigure completely the western German armies for offensive warfare after years of defensive fighting. Having been impressed with the specially trained 'storm troop' battalions in service on the Western Front, with their skills at infiltrating enemy positions to great depth, he arranged for their techniques to be taught to the divisions selected

> '*Ludendorff ... personified the restless energy and surging power of the German empire; he also personified its ugliness, its crudity and its fatal unwisdom.*'
>
> CORRELLI BARNETT

for the upcoming offensive. In the attack divisions, men over 35 were replaced by younger soldiers, and Germany's best weapons and equipment were provided. In particular, Ludendorff selected for army command those generals who had shown their skill at conducting counter-attacks or offensives in France, Russia and Italy. Finally, he brought in Germany's greatest artilleryman, Georg Brüchmuller, who had perfected devastating bombardment programmes that had produced spectacular results in the east.

Although this was to be a final attempt to force the Allies to the peace table, Ludendorff was not able to bring as many new troops to the west as he might have liked. The High Command had so completely taken over the function of the civilian government, running the economy, social organization and foreign policy, that it was distracted by the possibilities of building on its successes in the east. Many German

Erich Ludendorff

troops were heavily embroiled in fighting in Finland, the Baltic states and the Ukraine, when everything should have been concentrated for the great effort in the west.

When the attack, Operation Michael, was launched on 21 March 1918 the immediate plan was to drive a wedge between the British and French armies, and turn north and drive the British back through their base camps to the Channel coast and 'into the sea'. Since this was their last chance, the Germans concentrated more guns, attack divisions and aircraft than had ever been used in one sustained attack on the Western Front. The intricately designed bombardment was of an unparalleled intensity, with heavy reliance on gas shells to neutralize the defences without ploughing up the ground with high explosive. Striking the British Fifth Army, the most thinly spread and least prepared in the BEF, the Germans gained more ground in three or four days than any offensive in the west to date. The problem was that, while capturing ground and prisoners did much for German morale, the BEF did not break decisively, and the French rushed to its aid and maintained contact throughout. The second phase of the offensive, Operation Mars, launched on 28 March, was meant to crack open the British lines at Arras and start the process of rolling up their defences from south to north. It was a massive tactical failure and, soon afterwards, Operation Mars was wound down.

Another powerful attack was launched across the Lys on 9 April, finding a weak spot manned by Portuguese troops. The fighting was so desperate that the imperturbable Haig issued a 'Backs to the Wall' message, calling on his troops to fight to the last man and the last bullet. As this attack ran out of steam, Ludendorff rethought his plan and, in an effort to draw reserves away from the British front, launched a series of attacks against the French. When these threatened Paris itself, it looked as if some great and decisive result must soon be his.

But the effort had worn out the German armies. Ludendorff had let each attack run its course, without concentrating on the original aim of turning the flank of the BEF and driving it to the north. The dogged resistance of the BEF and the nurturing of the French back to an offensive capability, together with the arrival of large numbers of American troops, had frustrated the great hopes of the 'peace offensives' of the spring of 1918.

German troops in action during the spring offensives of 1918. These were initially hugely successful, gaining more ground than any other offensive on the Western Front since 1914. But they failed in their intention of defeating the Allies before the Americans could deploy in large numbers.

Defeat and after

Despite the enormous conquests in the east, and advances in the west unheard of since 1914, the Germans now found themselves assailed by powerful and resurgent Allied armies on the Western Front. The proven skill of the German soldiery in defence was not enough to prevent the relentless Allied advance towards the German frontier. Ludendorff's great effort to mobilize the whole nation for total war, to bring the Allies to the peace table, had failed. He suffered greatly from the strain and was ordered by doctors to give up much of his astonishing workload. He offered his resignation once too often to the Kaiser, who accepted it on 26 October. As Germany slid towards defeat and revolution at home, Ludendorff quietly slipped out of the country.

From Sweden he wrote his war memoirs, dedicated to 'The Heroes who Fell Believing in Germany's Greatness', justifying his efforts to galvanize the nation to ever greater efforts to win the war. On his return to Germany he flirted with the new right-wing political movement led by Adolf Hitler. Although he went on to serve as a National Socialist deputy in the Reichstag, he had distanced himself from the Nazis by the time of his death in 1937.

If his life's work ended in catastrophic failure, Ludendorff deserves to be assessed as the product of the most efficient military General Staff the world had seen to date. At every stage in the Great War, Germany, facing a sea of enemies and linked to relatively weak allies, was hugely outnumbered. She defended large gains in France and Belgium for four years, conquered Serbia and Romania, hammered the Russian armies into a state where socialist agitators were able to seize power and take Russia out of the war, inflicted meaningful defeats on France and Italy, and launched an offensive in 1918 that overshadowed anything that had gone before. The trade blockade imposed by the Allies brought ruin to German agriculture, and her mighty industry had to perform miracles of improvisation to maintain the war effort. But shortages turned into real starvation, and the General Staff found itself doing the job of Germany's weak parliamentary democracy, running the country while trying to run the war. It was too much, even for a man with Ludendorff's Herculean appetite for unremitting hard work.

> 'In order to reach its end – which is the imposing of our will on the enemy – modern war uses but one means: the destruction of the organised forces of the enemy.' FERDINAND FOCH, *THE PRINCIPLES OF WAR* (1901)

FERDINAND FOCH

PETER HART

1851–1929

FERDINAND FOCH was a famed academic tactician who had the mental strength cheerfully to abandon his own theories when they proved inappropriate to real life. Although often caricatured as an archetypal individualistic Frenchman, Foch proved a brilliantly successful Allied supreme commander able to form and maintain solid working relationships with his various subordinates, to overcome petty nationalistic disputes, and to drive them on to victory in the final series of battles that secured victory for the Allies in 1918.

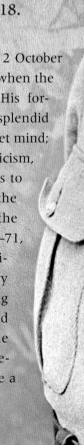

Ferdinand Foch, generalissimo of Allied forces on the Western Front from March 1918. Having resisted the great German spring offensives of that year, he went on to direct the French, British and American armies to victory.

Ferdinand Foch was born on 2 October 1851, and so was already 62 when the Great War began in 1914. His formative influences were a splendid education, which fed his gimlet mind; a staunch traditional Catholicism, which gave him a willingness to believe the impossible; and the trauma of French defeat in the Franco-Prussian War of 1870–71, which cemented his deep patriotism. The whole of his military life was devoted to countering the threat from Germany and in seeking revenge for the humiliating loss of Alsace-Lorraine. Foch did not pursue a

Ferdinand Foch

career serving in the French colonies, as did many of his contemporaries. Minor colonial wars were a mere distraction from the real challenge of defeating Germany.

Theoretical master

In 1885 Foch attended the staff course at the prestigious École Supérieure de Guerre in Paris. His studies convinced him that the only way to counter the perceived German superiority in numbers and matériel was to establish a culture of mental superiority in the French soldier that could overcome physically superior forces by dint of sheer élan in battle. After a tour of duty, Foch returned to the École Supérieure de Guerre, where he was an instructor from 1895 to 1901. Here his vibrant lectures created a sensation amongst a whole generation of French staff officers. Unfortunately, alongside much valuable material on the principles of war, Foch included elements that were demonstrably nonsense. As he had no practical combat experience, he failed to appreciate the coruscating power of modern weapons. He believed in the 'superiority' of the French national character, the power of 'faith' and the 'supremacy' of the offensive in its ability to seize the initiative and thereby dominate a passive enemy, who could do nothing but endure. His arguments were difficult to counter without suggesting, for instance, that the French character was not superior – a cleft stick for even the most recalcitrant of his students. In the event few dissented. Foch offered them hope, a way of succeeding against the hated Germans.

Foch's military career stalled owing to his staunch Catholicism, and also because of widespread suspicions that he was anti-republican. However, he managed to impress the secular, indeed downright anti-clerical, prime minister, Georges Clemenceau, who approved his appointment in 1907 as commandant of the École Supérieure de Guerre, a post he held until 1911. Now Foch's influence began to really permeate the French High Command. This was to have unfortunate consequences. The desire for a more aggressive approach to the conduct of war led them to into dangerous waters with the emergence of 'Plan XVII', which envisioned a ferocious French assault straight into the 'lost' province of Lorraine. This was certainly aggressive enough, but it offered far too many hostages to fortune, by ignoring many of the more sensible principles of war hammered out by Foch in his lectures. As a result, Foch himself harboured reservations over the plan, in particular the assumption that the Germans would respect Belgian neutrality, which thereby exposed the French to the threat of a comprehensive strategic surprise if the Germans attacked through Flanders. Foch was also worried that the French would not have a sufficient numerical supremacy to make success likely against their well-armed German counterparts.

The real thing: August–September 1914

When the war began in August 1914, Foch was the commander of XX Corps, based at Nancy. He was in his element at last, for despite his doubts over Plan XVII he was more than ready to launch the assault – finally to test himself and his theories on the field of battle. Foch was as caught up in the emotion of the moment as anyone else and, although he had recognized the risk of the Germans attacking through the Low Countries, he failed to think it through. As the French army lunged to the east they fell straight into the German trap. The Germans wheeled through Belgium into northern France and headed straight for Paris. Foch's part in the French offensive was initially

Ferdinand Foch

successful, but the awakening was to be brutal. XX Corps became isolated, and when the Germans launched a counter-attack on 20 August, the result was a disaster. For a while, Foch's whole reputation and career as a general hung in the balance. Had it not been for the wholesale cull of incompetent French generals and the personal backing of the commander-in-chief, Joseph Joffre, he might well have lost his command.

Thanks to the enduring confidence of Joffre, Foch was appointed to command a scattered mélange of units that would eventually form the Ninth Army in the area south of the River Marne, not far to the east of Paris. As he reorganized his units, Foch had a new priority, one forged in adversity: 'Infantry was to be economized, artillery freely used and every foot of ground taken was to be organised for defence.' Morale was important, but to secure enduring success an attack had to be backed up by overwhelming firepower, have a decent numerical superiority and the troops had to be ready to resist the inevitable German counter-attacks.

The crunch came as the Germans' wheeling attack began to move in ready to attack Paris from the east. The battle that resulted, on 6 September 1914, was a huge sprawling affair, but as part of the greater scheme devised by the French commander-in-chief, Joseph Joffre, Foch was ordered by to attack the flank of the German advance, feeling for the gaps between the German First and Second Armies. The fighting was desperate, and at one point it appeared that Foch's Ninth Army was about to be overrun. His response in adversity has become a legend: 'My centre is giving way, my right is in retreat. Situation excellent. I attack.' This superficially seems to hark back to his old theories, but this time Foch's apparent folly was underpinned by the knowledge that if his defence was crumbling and retreat was impossible, then in such a decisive battle there was nothing left to do but to attack. He had to do something to derail the German plans, and he had the inner steel and conviction to order his men forward come what may. In the end it was a close-run thing, but Joffre's plans came to fruition and the exhausted Germans were forced into the retreat. France had suffered grievous losses and so too had Foch, whose own son had been killed in the fighting. His reaction was typical of the man: 'I can do nothing more for him. Perhaps I can still do something for France.'

> 'My centre is giving way, my right is in retreat. Situation excellent. I attack.'
>
> FERDINAND FOCH, 8 SEPTEMBER 1914, DURING THE FIRST BATTLE OF THE MARNE

Hero of Ypres

After the Marne, Foch was appointed as assistant chief of staff and given command of the Northern Army Group. Both sides were trying to outflank each other, in what would become known as the 'Race to the Sea'. Here Foch had to learn the difficult business of alliance warfare, for he was responsible for the front also occupied by the British Expeditionary Force (BEF) and the Belgian army. Unlike many of his contemporaries, Foch recognized that diplomacy and an element of compromise were essential for success in such circumstances. He soon obtained the cooperation of Field Marshal Sir John French, commander of the BEF, and funnelled in the French reinforcements needed to help the struggling British hold the line at Ypres. Foch realized that further retreat was impossible, since the vital Channel ports lay just a few more miles behind Ypres. The BEF had to hold and Foch made sure that they did. His interventions were crucial as he prevented a split developing between the French army and the BEF.

Ferdinand Foch

The putative line around Ypres contracted as the Germans battered away, but it managed to hold. By the end of November the Western Front stretched from Switzerland to the North Sea. The Germans would launch one more offensive on the Ypres Salient on 22 April 1915, this time backed by the release of clouds of chlorine gas. Once again the Allied lines held, and from then on the German army was committed to defending the great strip of France and Belgium they had gained.

A brick wall: 1915–16

By this time Foch had grasped that attacks on German infantry dug in and supported by machine-guns and artillery would not usually succeed. This was even more the case when the original shallow-dug ditches mutated into multi-layered trench systems. Yet if they did not attack then the Germans would remain in situ, and that too was unacceptable. The Allied generals found themselves unable to overcome these problems with the weapons and resources at their disposal in 1915–16. They tried to use artillery power as a bludgeon to smash their way through, but it was impossible to amass the numbers of guns, shells and trained gunners required. In truth, new concepts and new weapons were required before it would be feasible to break through. Faced with these intractable problems Foch fared no better than any of his contemporaries – they all struggled to master the new language of war. The May 1915 attacks made by Foch's armies in Artois were dreadfully expensive in lives and had negligible results. The Allies again tried attacking in the Artois, Loos and Champagne areas in September. Again they got nowhere very slowly. Allied offensive tactics were simply not working in 1915.

In February 1916 the German army launched an offensive on Verdun with the murderous intent of sucking French reserves into the maw of a German mincing-machine of massed artillery. The French could never surrender the historic and deeply symbolic fortress of Verdun, and the darkest attritional battle of the Great War began (see pp. 264–5). For once the Germans had miscalculated, for they too were sucked into the mêlée and they too suffered excessive casualties. The battle would drag on for eleven months.

Foch was not involved in the Battle of Verdun, but he was responsible for

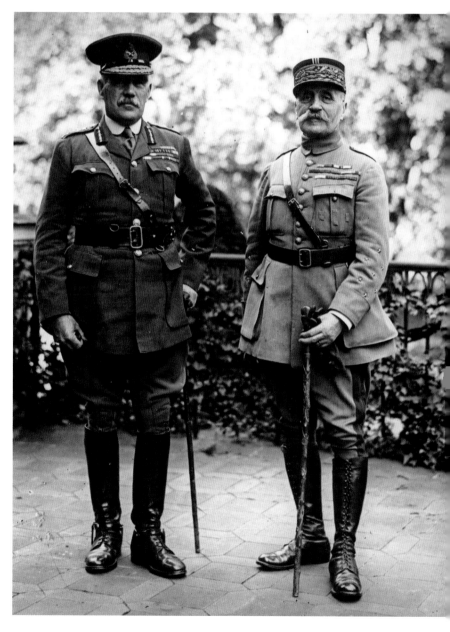

Foch with General Sir William Robertson, chief of staff to Sir John French before becoming chief of the Imperial General Staff. Foch's ability to work well with France's British allies was a key to his success.

Ferdinand Foch

FOCH'S PLAN FOR THE ALLIED OFFENSIVE, 24 July 1918.

French participation in the offensive to be launched alongside the British in the Somme area on 1 July 1916. This was originally designed to achieve breakthrough, but became, at least in part, a campaign to alleviate the German pressure on Verdun. By now Foch's reliance on artillery rather than élan was explicit. Victory now depended on 'a series of successive acts, each one necessitating a great deal of artillery and very little infantry'. Yet the Allies still did not have enough heavy guns, or the artillery techniques to secure tactical surprise. Most significantly, they still did not understand that it was far more efficient to suppress the ability of defenders to fire back during the moments of assault than to try to destroy them. The Somme offensive proved a disaster for the British; but the French started off reasonably well, only to get bogged down in yet more attritional fighting.

By this time the French politicians had had enough of the huge national sacrifices demanded by Joffre: he had more than exhausted the credit he had earned on the Marne in 1914. When Joffre fell, Foch fell with him.

The all-arms battle

While Foch's star was temporarily eclipsed, it was others who slowly, painfully, felt their way to the solution of the problems of successfully attacking on the Western Front. Munitions workers sweated to produce the requisite guns and ammunition; new technologies allowed the gunners to identify the position of their targets exactly and to open fire accurately without the prior registration that surrendered surprise; gas shells could saturate German batteries to suppress any return fire; the new tanks could crush the German wire under their tracks and take out German machine-gun posts; aircraft sped low over the battlefield, attacking targets

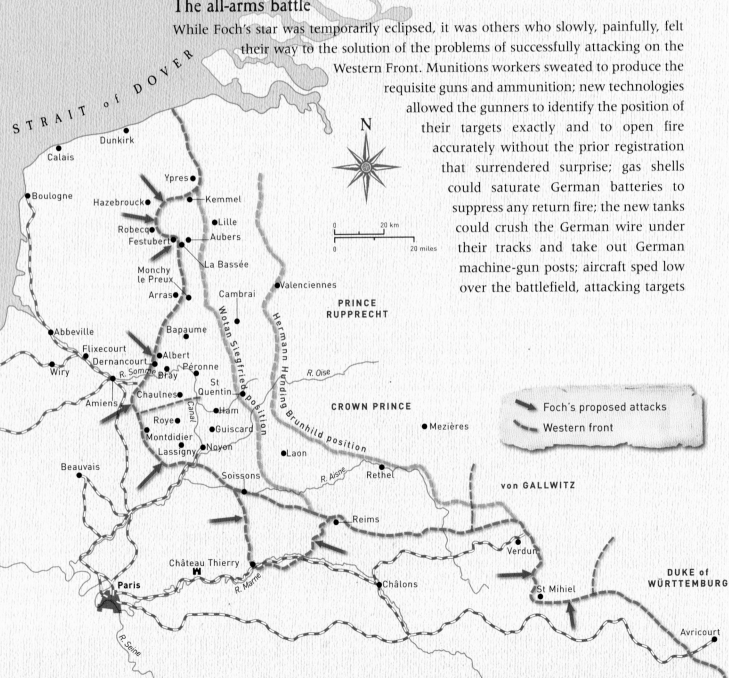

of opportunity. Above all, the infantry had learnt that discretion must temper natural élan. They now felt their way forward covered by additional firepower generated by light machine-guns, mortars and showers of hand grenades. This was the 'all-arms battle', in which flesh and blood was replaced with machines. Firepower was the key.

Foch returns

In 1917 the collapse of the Russians on the Eastern Front allowed the Germans to concentrate their forces for a last attempt in the spring of 1918 to break the strategic deadlock in the west. Their window of opportunity was short, for the American army was slowly gathering its strength ready to intervene on the Western Front in midsummer. Foch had been brought back as chief of staff of the French army, serving alongside the new French commander-in-chief, General Philippe Pétain. Foch's role was crucial, not only in rebuilding the shattered morale of the French army broken in the Champagne battles of April 1917, but also in putting into place the huge stockpiles of munitions that he knew would be needed for a successful offensive. He was also increasingly involved in Allied grand strategy, and indeed was beginning to be mooted as a possible future supreme commander. As a first step he was placed in charge of the theoretical general reserve set up by the Allied Supreme War Council.

Foch takes command

On 21 March 1918 the Germans hurled themselves forward, striking hard at the British in the Somme area. The badly outnumbered British fell back, and for a while it seemed that the Germans would succeed in driving between the British and French armies. Both Pétain and Douglas Haig, the commander of the BEF, were mutually suspicious that the other was about to revert to selfish nationalistic interests: the French to fall back and cover Paris; the British to cover their retreat to the Channel ports. At an emergency Allied conference convened at Doullens on 26 March, Foch was widely acclaimed as the perfect man to coordinate the desperate defence. He had done it before on the Marne and at Ypres – he could do it again. And he did. His stubborn determination stiffened resolve, and strategic priorities were firmly reasserted. He controlled the Allied reserves with impartial severity, doling them out only as absolutely necessary and generally husbanding them for use when the tide should turn – as he knew it would. With increasing desperation the Germans launched more massive offensives, each time gaining ground, but failing to break the integrity of the Allied line. Soon they were left with a collection of tumescent bulges pointing the way to nowhere. The German army was exhausted and it was plain that these ungainly salients were all too vulnerable to counter-attack.

Advance to victory

When he was appointed as Supreme Allied Commander-in-Chief, Foch immediately pulled the Allies together. He was almost alone in seeing the armies fighting on the Western Front as one force, to be directed in a single plan. By the end-phase of the Great War he was operating at the level of grand strategy, moving his armies across the western European battlefield in giant sweeps, with tactical geographical considerations almost irrelevant to his greater design – the total destruction of the military capacity of imperial Germany (see map opposite).

Ferdinand Foch

After the failure of the last German offensive in July 1918, Foch knew that the Germans were exhausted – and he knew that this was the moment for his old theories of the offensive to be dusted off. He responded by launching a sustained onslaught that matches anything else in military history. His most intuitive skill as a master of alliance warfare was to apply the right army to the task in hand: the French army was still teetering on the brink of exhaustion and the Americans were numerous but far too raw and inexperienced. So it was that Foch clearly perceived that Haig's BEF would have to be his main strike force. After painfully learning the grim trade of war, the British had fully grasped the concept of the all-arms battle, and it is to Foch's credit that he did not shrink from giving them the lead role in the 'Hundred Days' series of offensives between 8 August and 11 November. He ordered the British forward, time and time again, until their battalions were worn down to the bare bones. At the same time he skilfully wove in renewed assaults by the French army and launched forward the new American armies.

Foch drove his own generals as hard as he drove the Germans. He never stopped badgering them, always asking for more and demanding they take risks that would once have been considered suicidal. By switching focus from one end of the front to the other he never gave the German High Command a moment's peace to sit back and properly

Ferdinand Foch

reorganize their defences. German morale wavered and collapsed, and the result was an utterly comprehensive Allied victory. At every level the German war machine was beaten: their leaders were utterly demoralized, the much-vaunted storm troopers ground to dust, the elemental power of the German artillery quelled and the final victory secured over the solid phalanx of infantry divisions that had borne the brunt of the fighting and had at times nearly – but not quite – won the war for Germany. This, then, marked the final triumph for which Foch had striven all his adult life.

Armistice and after

When it came to the Armistice negotiations, Foch remained true to his beliefs. To ensure that the Allies could impose their collective will on the Germans, he sought conditions of such severity that the German armed services on the ground, at sea and in the air were stripped naked before their enemies. There was no way that the Germans could feasibly resume the war.

Foch was determined to hammer the Germans down into their coffin, and became estranged from the French politicians who sought to draw a line under the Great War. He was, however, acclaimed on both sides of the Channel as one of the key Allied architects of victory, and was made a British field marshal in recognition of his services. He died on 20 March 1929.

Foch (second from right), photographed in 1918 at Beauquesoie with (from left to right) Marshal Joseph Joffre, President Raymond Poincaré, King George V and Field Marshal Douglas Haig.

Ferdinand Foch

'Courage! On les aura!' (Courage! We'll have them!)

PÉTAIN AT VERDUN

PHILIPPE PÉTAIN

CHARLES WILLIAMS

1856–1951

MARSHAL PHILIPPE PÉTAIN was one of the greatest – and least appreciated – masters of warfare in the First World War. Alone among the generals on all sides, he quickly understood the battlefield effects of heavy artillery, barbed wire and machine-gun. As a consequence, he developed, as early as the autumn of 1914 and, more potently, at Verdun in 1916, tactics designed, above all, to mitigate the resulting casualty rate. It was this concern for the men under his command that allowed him to settle the mutinies of 1917 and, in the end, to bring the French army to the point where it was the finest fighting force of its time.

Pétain's reputation, even as a general, has been blackened by his acceptance of defeat in 1940, by his record as the leader of the collaborationist Vichy government, and by his subsequent conviction for treason (in a travesty of a trial) in July 1945. Nevertheless, whatever the negatives, he is still known as the 'Victor of Verdun'. True, his supporters cannot claim that he possessed the speed of thought of a Napoleon Bonaparte or the fierce determination of a Wellington, but in the understanding of the human element of warfare, and also in tactical intelligence, he ranks not far below them.

The son of my sorrow

Henri Philippe Bénoni Omer Pétain was born on 24 April 1856 into a peasant family in the northern French department of Pas-de-Calais. When he was 18 months old, his mother died (it was she who had called him 'Bénoni', meaning the 'son of my sorrow'), and on his father's remarriage he was farmed out to his grandparents. More attractive, however, was the home of his uncle, the priestly incumbent of the neighbouring village of Bomy. There Pétain was able to listen to extravagant military tales from his great-uncle, by then also in holy orders, who had fought in Napoleon's army in Italy. When it came for him to choose a future career, between peasant farming, the Church or the army, there was simply no contest. It would be the 'glorious' French army (in fact, only just recovering from its disastrous defeat in the Franco-Prussian War of 1870–71).

Philippe Pétain

The long apprenticeship

The decision taken, his clerical uncle was clear on one matter: the boy should not just go into the ranks but should join as an officer. Accordingly, the young Pétain went through the educational steps necessary to take him to the École Spéciale Militaire (Saint-Cyr) at Versailles. But he did not do well there, ranking, on merit, 229 out of 386. The cavalry, his original ambition, could no longer be a target. That left the infantry, where the choice was between the colonial army and the domestic army. Although he knew that promotion was quicker in the colonial army (officers were killed at a greater rate), he opted for the domestic army, and was posted to a battalion of the Chasseurs Alpins stationed in the Mediterranean fishing port, as it then was, of Villefranche-sur-Mer.

There was not much to do there, apart from seducing the wives of local dignitaries (at which the good-looking Pétain became an expert). Nor, for that matter, was there much else to do as he slowly crawled up the ladder of peacetime promotion; Besançon in 1883, where he made an unconvincing effort to get married, only to be refused by his prospective parents-in-law on the grounds of his peasant background; the École Supérieure de Guerre (better known as the École de Guerre) in Paris in 1888; a position as staff officer in Marseille in 1890; the command of an infantry battalion at Vincennes in 1893; and then back to Paris in 1895 on the staff of the military governor, carefully avoiding there any involvement in the topic of the day – the Dreyfus affair.

Pétain's lectures

One of the advantages of being an officer on the staff of the military governor of Paris was the possibility of an introduction to the higher-ranking officers in the capital's military establishment. Thanks to just such an introduction, Pétain was invited in 1901 to lecture at the École de Guerre. Yet it was not until he returned as a full professor in 1908 that his lectures provoked serious controversy, particularly in 1910, when he found himself at odds with Lieutenant Colonel Louis de Grandmaison, who was loud in advocating the doctrine of *offensif sans arrière pensée* ('offensive without second

An official portrait photograph of Philippe Pétain, c.1941.

thoughts'). Petain was more cautious, arguing for intensive preparation of the ground by artillery and machine-gun firepower – then, and only then, to be followed by infantry attack.

Where Pétain ran into trouble was in the presentation of his views. He seemed to be advocating a pause before serious engagement. Grandmaison countered that any pause would allow the enemy to regroup. But although much was made at the time of the supposed clash of opinion between Pétain and Grandmaison, there was, in fact, no great clash. Grandmaison was dealing with the deployment of whole armies, while Pétain was dealing with infantry tactics in localized battles. Nevertheless, in the popular mind – there was much debate on the matter in the Parisian press – Pétain was tarred with the brush of 'defensive' while Grandmaison was lauded as 'offensive'. As a result, Pétain was told – informally, of course – that he had reached the end of his military career and could expect no further promotion.

1914: retirement postponed

Pétain duly planned his retirement. He would, after all, be 60 in 1916, the retiring age for brigadiers. He found a plot of land in the Pas-de-Calais, and even bought a pair of secateurs with which, as an old retired bachelor, he would cultivate his garden. In April 1914 he left the command of the 33rd Infantry Regiment – where he had welcomed the arrival of one of his greatest admirers, the tall young sous-lieutenant Charles de Gaulle – to take over the 4th Infantry Brigade, headquartered at Arras. Its parade at Arras on Bastille Day, 14 July 1914, was meant to be his last showpiece. He rode on a white horse on to the parade ground at a brisk trot, inspected his brigade, turned his horse round and went off at the gallop.

> '*Le Maréchal est un grand homme ... qui est mort en 1925.*' (The Marshal is a great man ... who died in 1925.)
>
> CHARLES DE GAULLE ON PÉTAIN

One month later, of course, retirement was indefinitely postponed. Pétain then led his brigade into battle. During the Battle of the Frontiers in late August and early September 1914 he and his troops went on a series of forced marches into Belgium and back again, ending up, after a series of bruising engagements, on the River Marne, fighting to halt the German advance. There Pétain caught the attention of the French commander-in-chief, General Joseph Joffre. In fact, Pétain was one of the survivors, and indeed one of the beneficiaries, of Joffre's subsequent purge of obviously incompetent generals, and in October found himself in command of the 33rd Army Corps at the northern end of the French line of battle, in front of the city of Arras.

The battles of Artois, Champagne and Verdun

Pétain hardly had time to settle in before he was called on to repel a German attack aimed at Arras itself. By the time he took up his command, German advance units were within 2 miles of the outskirts of the city. After some desperate fighting the enemy attack was halted and an (unsuccessful) counter-attack launched. The pattern repeated itself for several weeks, but, as time and casualties wore on, Pétain realized that the tactics were mistaken. A strong defensive first line and a relatively weak second line, the official doctrine of the day, was the wrong way round. Much better was a weak first

line and a strong second line out of the range of heavy artillery. Moreover, even in the first line it was no good to have men just standing waiting to be shot. Pétain put the emphasis on camouflage and concealment, with centres of resistance, for instance in farm buildings, rather than on a line of poorly protected men on open ground. Trenches in the second line were dug deeper and machine-guns more carefully hidden. It was only when the enemy attack had been absorbed and weakened by the second line that a counter-attack could take place.

Pétain's tactic worked. Successful defence ensured that the Battle of Artois ground to a stalemate. All this, of course, was duly reported to Joffre. Joffre, however, insisted on an all-out offensive in the spring of 1915. Dutifully obeying orders, but with reluctance, Pétain launched the offensive on 9 May. At first, all went well. By mid afternoon his infantry had advanced to capture the commanding feature of Vimy Ridge. There was much congrat-ulation (Pétain was made a commander of the Légion d'Honneur in Joffre's orders of the day), but, in fact, the Germans had adopted Pétain's own tactics and had moved their reserve divisions into a

French *poilus* (infantrymen) in action during the Champagne offensive of autumn 1915, during which the French suffered 200,000 casualties. Pétain concluded that such general attacks were a waste of men and ammunition.

strong second defensive line. The French attack stalled and was then beaten back. By late June, when Joffre finally called off the offensive, no ground had been made and the French had lost 100,000 men.

By then, Pétain had been promoted again, to command the French Second Army, holding an extended line north of Châlons-sur-Marne in the Champagne. There again, after some bizarre tricks to try to keep his arrival a surprise for the Germans (his reputation had gone before him), the order came from Joffre to launch an offensive in the autumn to coincide with a British attack in the north on the village of Loos. Again, with reluctance, this was done.

In the event, all the attacks failed. The Germans had fully learnt the lesson of a strong defensive second line (particularly if invisible to the attackers on a reverse slope) and, true to Pétain's own doctrine, had absorbed the French attack at the second line and regained the ground lost in the initial assault. By the time the Champagne

(Below) **The ravine at the foot of Fort Douaumont** at Verdun, known as *le Ravin de la Dame* – but referred to by French soldiers as *le Ravin de la Mort*.

VERDUN

BY THE END OF 1914, with the stabilization of the Western Front, the Verdun salient had become the lynchpin of a defensive line stretching from the Channel to the Swiss frontier. The city itself, standing astride the River Meuse, was at the neck of the salient, protected by a ring of forts (although denuded of their heavy guns). Late in 1915 the German High Command decided to pre-empt an expected Franco-British assault in the northwest on the Somme by attacking Verdun. The German tactical build-up during January and February 1916 was massive. Ten new railway lines were constructed. Some 1,400 guns, 2.5 million shells, 168 aircraft and 400,000 men were delivered to the front. To cap it all, the Germans had a terrifying new weapon – the flamethrower.

On 21 February the German heavy artillery opened up with a barrage aimed at the French positions on the eastern, or right, bank of the Meuse. This was followed, just as the winter dusk was falling, by groups of German storm troopers, not in the customary waves but in zigzagging, crouching runs. The flamethrowers wrought terrible and fearsome havoc. In spite of localized and fierce French resistance, in the first week the fort at Douaumont fell, and the Germans advanced 5 miles into open ground – only 2.5 miles from the last line of defence in front of the city itself.

Pétain was brought in to assume command of the French defence on 26 February. He immediately ordered a tactical change: the defence would now consist of a forward line designed to blunt an attack but not to be held at all costs, a principal 'line of resistance' to be held at all costs, and a third line from which counter-attacks would be launched. He also organized the 'millwheel', a system of constant replacement of units in the front line with fresh units. (Fresh troops and ammunition were carried along a supply route between Bar-le-Duc and Verdun that came to be known as *La Voie Sacrée* – 'the sacred way' – and which has found its place in the canon of French military heroism.) Halted by these tactics on the right bank, Crown Prince Wilhelm, the German field commander, attacked at the beginning of April on the left bank of the Meuse, but after more prolonged fighting this too was held.

Philippe Pétain

264

offensive was called off by Joffre at the end of October 1915 the official French losses were nearly 200,000 men.

Yet again, Pétain reported that such general attacks were a waste of men and ammunition. The answer, he argued, was a tactic of limited strikes at the weak enemy front line and a quick retreat – in the hope of provoking him into a hasty counter-attack. In response, an irritated Joffre posted Pétain to direct the training of four army corps of reservists ready for another major spring offensive in 1916. Thus relieved of his command, Pétain took up his new post in the relative tranquillity of Noailles, just outside Paris. It was frustrating, but there was good food and wine, and many assignations with his mistress in the Hôtel Terminus at the Gare du Nord in Paris. Such were the pleasures of this life away from the front that it came as little more than an irritation to hear that on the morning of 21 February 1916 the German heavy guns had at first light begun their barrage at Verdun.

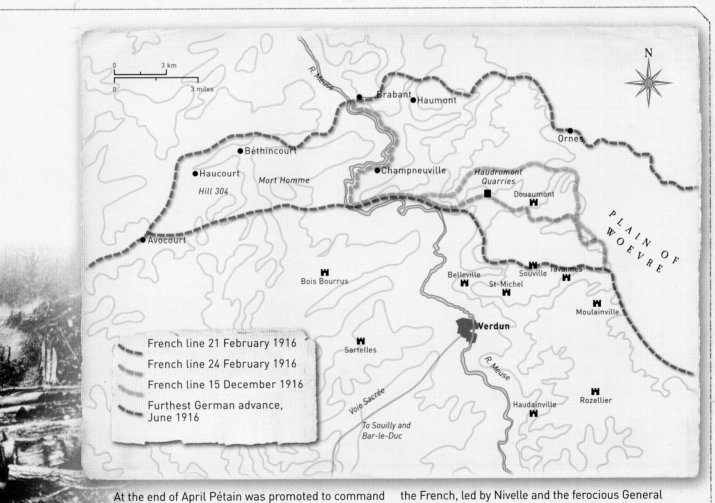

French line 21 February 1916

French line 24 February 1916

French line 15 December 1916

Furthest German advance, June 1916

At the end of April Pétain was promoted to command of the army group in the Verdun sector, while General Robert Nivelle took the immediate field command – although Pétain made daily visits to his headquarters. A further German offensive in June threatened again to break through but was stopped in front of the fort at Souville. It was to be the final German effort. In October the French, led by Nivelle and the ferocious General Charles Mangin, counter-attacked. By December they had recovered virtually all the ground lost. The whole exercise had turned out to be fruitless. By way of footnote, French casualties during the dreadful ten months of the battle were estimated at 550,000, German casualties at 434,000.

Philippe Pétain

Almost immediately Pétain was summoned by Joffre from one of his assignations at the Hôtel Terminus to take command of the defence of the Verdun salient. By a series of imaginative tactical moves he managed to save a situation that appeared to be lost and turn it into a platform for attack (see pp. 264–5). In the end, however, he was promoted to command the Centre Army Group covering the whole of the Verdun area, and the final attack in October was led by General Robert Nivelle. Much to Pétain's disgust, Nivelle then jumped above him to become commander-in-chief of the French army.

The 1917 mutinies

Nivelle's 1917 spring offensive was a disaster, as Pétain had predicted. Not only did it fail in all its objectives but it destroyed the morale of the French army. Mutinies broke out along the line in April and gathered pace in May. In a panic the French government sent for Pétain to replace Nivelle as commander-in-chief and to settle the mutinies. Pétain agreed, but only if he could do it in his own way and in his own time.

Unlike other generals before him Pétain visited every unit in the front line to hear the men's grievances at first hand. The main problem, as he found out, was that the soldiers had lost contact with their families, since they had not had any leave. Pétain immediately ordered that seven days leave every four months should be mandatory, at the same time arranging for extra trains and seeing to it that reception arrangements at Paris terminals were improved, with the French Red Cross providing canteens for arriving soldiers. He also demanded an improvement in the quality of men's rations in the front line. By July the mutineers had decided that they had made their point. (Not that Pétain was soft: some 49 men were shot and nearly 1,400 sentenced to deportation or forced labour.)

The offensives of 1918

Pétain then set about rebuilding the French army. A series of successful limited engagements in the autumn helped morale. So did the arrival of General John Pershing and the advance units of the American army (see p. 281). It was by then obvious that it was only a matter of time before the Americans would appear in force. Everybody knew that – not least General Erich von Ludendorff. In March 1918, in an attempt to finish the war before the Americans arrived, Ludendorff launched his last offensive. It was almost a complete success (see p. 249–50). The Germans broke the British Fifth Army and threatened a breakthrough to the Channel. The British commander-in-chief, Sir Douglas Haig, appealed to Pétain for help. Pétain immediately sent fifteen French divisions to seal off the breach in the British line in front of Amiens and promised twenty-five more when they could be mustered. But in doing so he weakened his own

defensive positions to the south. Ludendorff then diverted his attack there in late May, to open up the way to Paris. Pétain retreated – and went on retreating until he could be sure that the German supply lines were over-stretched. On 18 July he ordered the counter-attack. The German offensive had been halted – and Paris was safe.

That done, in October 1918 Pétain hatched a further plan. Starting from the northeast of Nancy in Lorraine, he and Pershing would strike eastwards into Germany beyond the River Saar, turn south and envelop the remaining German army on the Western Front, forcing a humiliating surrender. But the plan came too late. An armistice had been decided. On hearing the news, Pétain, as he said himself, was in tears. The opportunity to destroy the German army once and for all had been lost.

From Verdun to Vichy

Pétain lived for the rest of his long life in the shadow of his successes of 1914–18. Awarded the marshal's baton in December 1918, he outlived the other six marshals of the war. His last military command was in Morocco in 1925, where he met the Spanish Falangist leader Primo de Rivera and, like many generals before and since, became more and more authoritarian in his views. The result was Vichy, conviction for treason and a death sentence, commuted to life imprisonment. He died in prison in 1951.

But that was not altogether the end. Successive French presidents, from de Gaulle in 1968 until Jacques Chirac in 1998, arranged for a single red rose to be placed on his grave each year on 11 November – the anniversary of the 1918 Armistice. In spite of the shame of Vichy, the 'Victor of Verdun' had not been entirely forgotten.

Pétain in court on 30 July 1945, facing charges of collaboration with the Nazis and the sabotage of French democracy. At the conclusion of the trial he was sentenced to death, although this was commuted to life imprisonment.

Philippe Pétain

EDMUND ALLENBY
1861–1936

JEREMY BLACK

THE FIRST WORLD WAR is not noted for successful offensive operations, particularly on the part of the Entente Powers, but Edmund Allenby achieved two such. The first, in late 1917, led to the capture of Jerusalem from the Ottoman empire, while the Battle of Megiddo in late 1918 overthrew the Turkish position in Palestine and Syria and brought the war in the Middle East to an end. Subsequent difficulties in campaigning in the region have highlighted Allenby's achievements. They brought him fame and fortune and established Britain as a land power in the Middle East. Allenby's success contrasted with the inability of General Archibald Murray, his predecessor as commander of the Egyptian Expeditionary Force, to defeat the Turks.

(Opposite) **Allenby in London in 1916.** His career up to this point had given little indication of the successes that he was to achieve in Palestine over the next two years.

The eldest son of a wealthy British landowner, Edmund Henry Hynman Allenby was educated at Haileybury and sought a career with the Indian Civil Service. Failure twice in the entrance exams led him to turn, instead, to the army, and he passed out of the military academy at Sandhurst in 1881. A keen countryman, Allenby then took a decision that was to be very important in his military career: he joined the cavalry.

His regiment, the 6th (Inniskilling) Dragoons, was based in South Africa, and he joined it there in 1882. Aside from a two-year break, from 1886, at the cavalry depot in Canterbury, Allenby served in South Africa until the regiment returned to Britain in 1890. This service did not entail fighting, as he arrived too late for the Zulu War of 1879, but Allenby, eventually as adjutant, became an experienced officer, well able to execute tasks and take responsibility. However, he also became a somewhat harsh figure, focused on discipline, and this was to remain a characteristic of his command style.

In 1896, the year of his marriage, Allenby entered the Staff College at Camberley, where his class included Douglas Haig, the British commander on the Western Front from 1915 until 1918. Competent, not brilliant, at Staff College, Allenby benefited from his stint by becoming first a major (1897) and then adjutant to the 3rd Cavalry Brigade (1898).

Edmund Allenby

The Boer War and after

Not a triumph for Britain, the Boer War with the Afrikaners of the Transvaal and the Orange Free State in southern Africa (1899–1902) nevertheless made some reputations as well as destroying others. Allenby benefited from his ability to act as an effective cavalry commander in the campaigns to drive the Boer opponents from the veldt. He spent many hours in the saddle and his physical fitness was crucial to his ability to fulfil his command responsibilities. After being given temporary command of his regiment in 1900, he became a lieutenant colonel.

Following the war, Allenby continued his steady rise, appointed brigadier general (1905), major general (1909), and then inspector general of cavalry (1910). The last brought out his capacity to act as a martinet. He was certainly not associated with any particular insights as a military thinker.

The Western Front

The outbreak of war in 1914 brought command, first of the Cavalry Division and then of the Cavalry Corps. Like his colleagues, Allenby struggled to respond to the massive German attack. His defensive role in the First Battle of Ypres (1914) was effective in helping anchor the British front, and, in 1915, he was promoted to command, first of 5th Corps and then of the Third Army.

In the latter capacity, Allenby directed the unsuccessful Gommecourt diversionary attack at the northern end of the Somme offensive in July 1916. The following April, his reputation was seriously compromised in the attack at Arras. This became an attritional offensive, in which Allenby failed to show the necessary flexibility in command, leading to complaints from three divisional commanders. In the face of such complaints, he could no longer remain in command in France. This was the background for his dispatch to the Middle East.

The problem at Arras, as with other battles in 1917, was the inability of the British to break into the full depth of the German defences, consolidate and press home any advantage that arose, so that break-in could be converted to break-through. German counter-attacks had to be neutralized, but artillery and trench mortar tactics had yet to become sufficiently developed at interdiction, although Arras, in its turn, helped provide the lessons from which better tactics developed. The inability to exploit success was as much a problem of communication and control as it was one of planning, stamina and reinforcement.

Allenby came in for criticism twice over Arras: first, for wanting too short a preliminary bombardment, and later for not ending his assault when it had clearly ground to a halt. Whether the latter was due to his lack of awareness of the true situation because of poor communications, his stubbornness or a genuine belief that he could achieve his objective if he kept pushing, is not clear. He had an aversion to heeding what he thought was bad advice. His performance at Arras seems to have been used as a reason to get rid of him, but he was no worse than Hubert Gough who commanded the Fifth Army. Moreover, the success of the Canadians at Vimy, which coincided with the start of the Arras offensive, had overshadowed Allenby's initial achievement there.

In the Middle East, 1917–18

Allenby regarded his dispatch to replace the dismissed commander of the Egyptian Expeditionary Force (over which he assumed command on 28 June) as a mark of disfavour; but he transformed the situation there. His diligent oversight of his new command exuded vigour and raised morale. Moving his headquarters closer to the front was important both in practical terms and as a morale-boasting move.

Allenby, however, faced the serious problem of coping with very different expectations from his superiors. David Lloyd George, the hyperactive prime minister, wanted bold offensive thrusts and the capture of Jerusalem to help morale; while William Robertson, the Chief of the Imperial General Staff, favoured a more cautious approach. Recent failures at the hands of the Turks in Mesopotamia (Iraq) and at Gallipoli served as stark warnings of the dangers of boldness.

Allenby's Boer War experience of working with Australian troops served him in particularly good stead, as his new command was very much that over an army of the British Empire. Having revived the army, which he strengthened with troops, heavy artillery and aircraft, Allenby decided to implement the plan for a new offensive that had been already prepared by his new staff, particularly Lieutenant General Sir Philip Chetwode.

The resulting Third Battle of Gaza led to a shift in the axis of attack, away from Gaza and the coast (the axis in the costly first two battles in the spring of 1917), towards

Edmund Allenby

> 'Allenby and Howell of Cavalry Corps seem to be despondent regarding the possibilities of cavalry action in future. MacAndrew thinks that if these two had their way, cavalry would cease to exist as such. In their opinion, the war will continue and end in trenches.'
>
> DOUGLAS HAIG, *DIARY*, 11 APRIL 1915

the eastern end of the Turkish positions near Beersheba 30 miles inland. This was captured by the Australians on 31 October after a long advance across terrain with very little water, an advance that required intelligence, reconnaissance and engineering work. This was a surprise attack launched without a prior bombardment, and the Turks were unable to destroy the town's water wells as expected. Cavalry helped provide the British with the necessary mobility, but flexibility of mind was also required to vary the direction of attack. Near Gaza, moreover, where the attack began on 27 October, Allenby's forces used tactical lessons from the conflict on the Western Front to help break through the Turkish positions.

Victory was exploited with the capture of undefended Jerusalem on 9 December. Earlier, there had been tough fighting in the hills of Judea, and the British suffered 18,000 casualties in the campaign. The outnumbered Turks suffered heavier losses. The fall of Jerusalem helped to catapult Allenby into prominence. On 11 December, he publicly entered Jerusalem in a carefully scripted display. Rather than riding in, as

Desert reconnaissance in Egypt, during Allenby's campaign of 1917–18. In the foreground are soldiers of the 1st Hertfordshire Yeomanry, and behind them troops of the Bikaner Camel Corps, an Indian unit that fought for the Allies in both world wars.

Allenby formally enters Jerusalem's Jaffa Gate on foot on 11 December 1917. He read a proclamation of martial law and left again. Back home, he was lauded as a latter-day Richard the Lionheart.

Kaiser Wilhelm II had arrogantly done in 1898, Allenby dismounted and entered on foot. In a season without good news for the British public, Allenby's success was very welcome to the government, which therefore devoted considerable attention to it. The Turks, however, who had not been crushed, regrouped on a new defensive line to the north of Jerusalem. Their ability to do so has been ascribed by some critics to overly cautious generalship on the part of Allenby, but this was in keeping with his preference for methodical warfare, a preference towards which strong logistical pressures powerfully contributed. There was not enough water for the cavalry, while the strength of the opposing rear-guard was also a factor. Moreover, the prospects for campaigning were affected by the winter rains. The Cabinet wanted Allenby to press on for Damascus, but he urged the need to wait until the necessary infrastructure, including a double-tracked coastal railway, was ready.

Allenby, nevertheless, pressed forward to attack the Turks, capturing Jericho as part of an advance into the Jordan Valley, which put pressure on the Turkish flank. However, he was held back by the extent to which his army was used to provide reinforcements for the British forces in France, which were under heavy pressure from

Edmund Allenby

the German offensive in the spring of 1918. Fifty-four battalions were transferred. Their poorly trained Indian replacements took a while to adapt, and Allenby was concerned about Turkish attempts to woo Muslim sentiment in their ranks.

In the spring of 1918, Allenby launched two unsuccessful operations to the east of the Jordan. They were designed to cut the Hejaz railway from Syria to Medina and Mecca, and thus to support the Arab revolt, both by hitting Turkish communications and by creating a supply route for the Arabs from Palestine, so that they could advance into Syria. The first raid, however, was affected by the winter rains, which made it difficult to move the artillery. As a result, Amman was not captured. A threatened Turkish counter-attack led to the abandonment of the second raid.

The summer provided a welcome opportunity to develop the army, through the introduction of improved weaponry and the creation of a better logistical structure. A Turkish attack at Abu Tulul was defeated in July, and in September Allenby won a decisive victory at Megiddo (see pp. 274–5). A rapid advance on two axes then further exploited the situation. Along the coast, troops advanced to capture Tyre, Sidon and, on 2 October, Beirut. The previous day, Australian cavalry that had advanced from the Sea of Galilee joined Arab forces (advised by T. E. Lawrence) in taking Damascus. Syria was rapidly conquered, with Aleppo falling on 25 October. Five days later, an armistice signed at Mudros ended the conflict.

Allenby was helped by the range of Turkish commitments, as well as by the extent to which Turkish planners were more interested in exploiting the Russian Revolution of the previous year to make gains in the Caucasus, where they thus concentrated their forces. As a result, the Turks in Palestine were short of men and equipment and could not match the British, who outnumbered them and had air superiority. The demoralized Turks, their coherence fractured by the rapid British advance, readily surrendered, although some units mounted rearguard actions.

Allenby's victory helped ensure that Britain became the key power in the Middle East, which was seen as an important imperial goal. In the short term, this gave the British a strong negotiating hand in the post-war Paris peace talks, not least since the French wished to become the colonial power in Syria and Lebanon.

Assessment

As a general, Allenby was at his best when he was allowed to plan and fight without interference from above. At Arras, he had to satisfy Haig, whereas in Palestine he was more his own boss, albeit still answerable to meddlesome political and military oversight from London.

Allenby had several qualities that suggest that his generalship was sound. He was concerned for the men under his command, and well aware of the importance of good morale. He was meticulous. When he saw opportunities, he tried to take them. His use of cavalry was always good. He always wanted to fight on terms that he dictated to the enemy. His use of air power was very good. However, against these qualities, he had an

Allenby (right) with Arab leader Abdullah ibn Hussein (later Emir of Transjordan) and T. E. Lawrence in Palestine in 1917. The Arabs, directed by Lawrence, played a supportive role to Allenby during the battles of Gaza and Megiddo.

Edmund Allenby

explosive temper which suggests that he expected full compliance with his instructions and would not listen to subordinates. The implication is that he was less willing to let others have their way or use their initiative. He also had a reputation for being a martinet, which cannot have endeared him to his men.

Palestine allowed broad sweeping movements by mobile forces. Nevertheless, Allenby played to his strengths and minimized his weaknesses by not attacking in the spring and summer of 1918 when his experienced troops had been sent to France because of the German offensives.

After the war

The end of the war brought prestige, with Allenby becoming 1st Viscount Allenby of Megiddo and Felixstowe (the title linking the decisive battle and the Allenby family home), as well as a field marshal. He was also voted £50,000 by Parliament.

THE BATTLE OF
MEGIDDO

ON 20 SEPTEMBER 1918, Allenby launched the final offensive (with 69,000 troops and 550 pieces of artillery) against the Turkish forces (34,000 and 400 pieces) in Palestine. This battle was called Megiddo as Allenby's troops advanced by this ancient mound, the alleged site of the final battle (Armageddon) mentioned in the biblical Book of Revelation. Tanks, aircraft and cavalry were all vital, although, as on the Western Front in 1918, an effective artillery–infantry coordination was important in breaking through the opposing lines. Furthermore, Allenby's skilful strategy kept the Turks guessing about the direction of attack. He began by raiding the eastern end of the Turkish line, creating the impression that he would repeat his 1917 plan; but, in the event, did the opposite.

Allenby attacked with his left near the coast. The breakthrough with infantry and artillery provided an opportunity for the British cavalry to exploit as the cavalry had not been exhausted in the initial assault. They swung to the east, cutting the line of Turkish retreat. At the same time, other cavalry units advanced along the coast, capturing both Haifa and Acre on 23 September.

This dramatic success, in which 75,000 prisoners were taken for 5,666 casualties, was a triumph for mobility. Megiddo is widely seen as the last great cavalry battle. The Australian Light Horse used cavalry charges as well as acting as mounted infantry. Other weaponry, however, was also crucial. For example, armoured cars provided significant mobility. British forces in this context should, throughout, be understood to include imperial troops, in large numbers, particularly from Australia, India and New Zealand. Allenby's use of subterfuge to mislead the Turks and his planning at Megiddo show that

he was open to unconventional ideas and that he did not underestimate the Turkish forces, even though they were under-strength and badly equipped. It is interesting that this kind of misdirection was again used successfully in the Second World War, particularly by Montgomery at El Alamein in 1942, and prior to D-Day in 1944, both meticulously planned operations.

Allenby's use of air power in Palestine was also highly effective. Only air supremacy (as opposed to air superiority) could prevent the German air contingent

Edmund Allenby

Allenby himself continued to be linked to the Middle East. From 1919 until 1925, he served as special high commissioner for Egypt, a key posting for imperial security. As such, he had to use troops to suppress the Egyptian rising of 1919. He had greater success than his counterparts in Iraq, let alone those responsible for the unsuccessful British intervention in the Russian Civil War, and did not use the heavy repression shown by the French in Syria in the mid 1920s. Alongside his role in counter-insurgency, Allenby sought to consolidate the British position by appropriate policies. He recommended the end of the protectorate that had been declared in 1914, and in 1922 Egypt was given a greater degree of independence, although with Britain retaining control over security and foreign policy as well as a large garrison in the Suez Canal. After retiring in 1925, he focused on bird-watching, fishing, travelling, and his presidency of the British National Cadet Force. He died suddenly in London, on 14 May 1936.

supporting the Turks from flying reconnaissance sorties. Allenby, though, had an accurate picture of the Turkish position. Air supremacy also prevented interception of the RAF's bombers which were used to bomb telephone exchanges and rail junctions to disrupt communications and to destroy the Turkish forces when they retreated. (Air power was used in Normandy in the same way in 1944.) There was even naval support from two destroyers at Megiddo.

Allenby's mobile forces included 12,000 cavalry, Prince Faisal's Arabs, and armoured cars, all of which he used very effectively to break through, encircle and trap the Turkish forces. Their destruction with the aid of air power presaged the same tactic over northwest Europe in 1944 by the Second Tactical Air Force. It is noteworthy that the artillery bombardment at Megiddo only lasted 15 minutes, showing that Allenby knew the value of neutralization and shock. He was able to master the factor of time.

Damascus, the capital of Syria, fell on 1 October 1918 during the battle of Megiddo; as at Jerusalem, Allenby was sensitive to local sensibilities, and allowed the Arab forces to formally enter the city first. Here Emir Faisal ibn Hussein, who was briefly king of Syria in 1920, and later king of Iraq, leaves the Hotel Victoria after a meeting with Allenby.

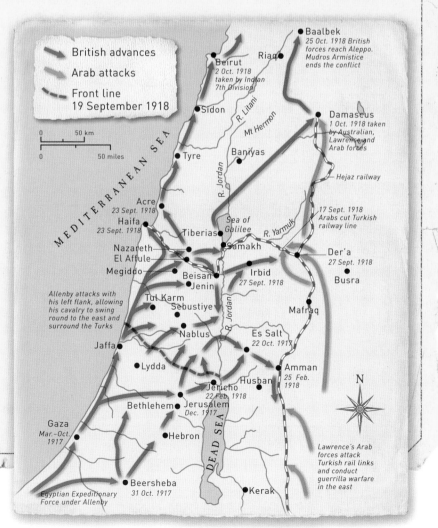

JOHN PERSHING

CARLO D'ESTE

1860–1948

GENERAL JOHN JOSEPH 'BLACK JACK' PERSHING was the most famous American soldier of his era. During a lifetime of soldiering, he rose to become the only officer ever to be accorded the title of General of the Armies. As the foremost American officer of his time, during the First World War Pershing commanded the American Expeditionary Force (AEF). Pershing's earlier colourful and star-studded career had taken him from the western plains during the Indian Wars, to the Spanish–American War as a Rough Rider under Teddy Roosevelt, where he won a Silver Star at San Juan Hill, and from fighting insurgents in the Philippines to a hunt for Pancho Villa in Mexico in 1916.

Pershing's family was of Alsatian origin and once spelled their name as Pfoershing. He was born on 13 September 1860 in Laclede, Missouri, the son of a railway section foreman for the Hannibal and St Joseph Railway and later the proprietor of a general store. Johnny, as he was known as a child, grew up in the shadow of the Civil War. His first memories were as a young child witnessing his home town being raided and his father and other local merchants robbed by a lawless band of Confederate partisans.

Although his father later became a prosperous businessman, the family suffered in the great depression of 1873. While working on a family farm, Pershing also managed to obtain enough education to secure a teaching position at a local school. Like a later young man in rural Kansas named Dwight Eisenhower, Pershing was determined to gain the benefit of a college education. To help make family ends meet, young Pershing attained a teaching position in 1878. The first example of his legendary reputation for no nonsense and stern discipline occurred when he faced down a rowdy group of students, one of whom had openly challenged his authority. Although his first teaching experience was short lived, it imbued the young man with a renewed desire for more education.

Pershing had no ambition for a military career but, when opportunity knocked, he took a competitive examination for West Point and finished first out of sixteen candidates. After several months of tutoring, Pershing entered the United States Military Academy in June 1882. He was not an especially notable student, had considerable trouble with French and ranked only thirtieth of seventy-seven in the class of

John Pershing

1886. Surprisingly for an officer who would later achieve a reputation as the army's sternest martinet, Pershing accumulated over 200 demerits, but nevertheless achieved the greatest honour bestowed on a cadet when he was appointed first captain of the corps of cadets. In this capacity he commanded the corps when the funeral train of General Ulysses S. Grant, a man Pershing deeply admired, slowly passed by West Point.

As first captain, Pershing was a disciplinarian – an early indication of what he would be as a future army officer and what his official biographer has described as his 'undoubting certainty of duty combined with a glacial self-possession'. A cadet a year ahead of Pershing who later served as an army commander under him in the First World War once remarked that, while Pershing had earned their respect, he never attained their affection – a trait that characterized his entire life.

Early army career

Pershing was commissioned a cavalry officer and assigned to the 6th Cavalry, based at Fort Bayard in what was then the New Mexico Territory. His first years as a cavalryman were marked by participation in various Indian campaigns in the West, which earned him citations for bravery. One was the notorious incident at Wounded Knee, South Dakota, on 29 December 1890, in which the 7th Cavalry massacred some 300 men, women and children of the Lakota Sioux tribe.

Pershing's reflections on Wounded Knee – in which his regiment played only a peripheral role – revealed an unsympathetic attitude towards Native Americans in general and a belief that the US army had through its actions averted more costly and protracted warfare with them.

General John 'Black Jack' Pershing, who was appointed to the high rank of General of the Armies in 1919. The rank was created for him; the only other recipient, George Washington, was awarded it posthumously, in 1976.

During this period, Pershing earned recognition as one of the army's best marksmen with both a rifle and pistol. While assigned as the professor of military science and tactics at the University of Nebraska-Lincoln, 1890–95, he organized a military drill company that eventually was renamed the Pershing Rifles in his honour. To this day, the prestigious Pershing Rifles drill teams exist at a number of American universities and among its distinguished alumni are James Earl Jones and generals Colin Powell and Curtis LeMay. Though he never practised, while at the university Pershing also studied law and became a graduate of the class of 1893.

He remained on the lowest rung of the officer corps' ladder as a second lieutenant until 1895. In 1897, Pershing returned to West Point as a tactical officer. His unbending, iron-fisted insistence on adherence to the letter of the regulations bordered on arrogance and left him with the dubious distinction of being the Academy's most unpopular tactical officer. Even worse, the cadets so disliked Pershing that he was once accorded the silent treatment, whereby the corps ostracized him by refusing to acknowledge his presence in the mess and refusing to eat as long as he remained. Pershing had just returned from an assignment in Montana in which he served as a white officer in the African-American 10th Cavalry, one of the now famous Buffalo Soldier regiments. The West Point cadets tagged him with the blatantly racist label of 'Nigger Jack', a denunciation that over time softened into 'Black Jack', the nickname by which Pershing was known for the rest of his life.

The Spanish–American and Philippine–American wars

The advent of war with Spain over Cuba in 1898 saw Pershing back with the 10th Cavalry as its quartermaster and with a brevet commission as a major in the all-volunteer force organized to fight the Spanish. On 1 July, moments before organizing and leading his black troops in an assault on both San Juan and Kettle Hills, Pershing barely escaped death after he stopped to salute the commander of the US cavalry, the dashing Lieutenant General 'Fighting Joe' Wheeler. Wheeler was on his horse in the middle of a creek when a shell exploded so close it soaked both officers.

When the Spanish were routed on San Juan Hill by Lieutenant Colonel Theodore ('Teddy') Roosevelt's Rough Riders and Pershing's cavalrymen, he emerged from the war not only having gained the favourable attention of Roosevelt but also with a well-earned reputation for bravery. In 1919, a year after it was created, he was awarded the Silver Citation Star, the precursor to the Silver Star, the nation's third highest award for gallantry. In 1932, the army retroactively awarded Pershing the Silver Star for his actions in 1898 in Cuba.

Pershing contracted malaria in Cuba and spent a brief period of service in the War Department in Washington DC until reassigned to the Philippines in August 1899. There, he became deeply involved in suppressing the Moro uprisings. To better understand the problems of pacifying the indigenous Muslim insurrectionists, Pershing diligently studied their culture and language, including the Koran, and formed close ties with some of their tribal leaders. His superior work in expeditions to eradicate a Moro stronghold earned him both a citation for bravery and notice in Washington, where Secretary of War Elihu Root observed to one of his West Point classmates that: 'If your friend Pershing doesn't look out, he will find himself in the brigadier general class very soon.'

In 1901, Pershing returned to the regular army after his Spanish–American War brevet commission was terminated and was promoted to captain. Reassigned to the 15th Cavalry, he served as an intelligence officer and participated in further action against the Moros at Lake Lanao, Mindanao, at one point temporarily filling the post of camp commander. With a combination of carrot and stick, Pershing opted for persuasion whenever possible, and when that failed, ferociously attacked and over-whelmed the Moros.

Pershing was posted to Washington in June 1903, his reputation so burnished by his accomplishments in the Philippines that Roosevelt, now president, singled him out by name in a speech to Congress. Roosevelt wanted Pershing promoted to the rank of brigadier general, but his petition to the army General Staff was summarily rejected and, to the president's dismay, he remained a captain.

It was while in Washington that Pershing met and married Francis Warren, the daughter of a wealthy and influential Republican senator from Wyoming. They were married in 1905 in a ceremony attended by Roosevelt. Days later, Pershing and his bride departed for Japan, where he took up the post of American military attaché. In this capacity he became an observer in Manchuria of the Russo-Japanese War of 1905.

In 1906, Roosevelt finally achieved a measure of payback over the army by having Pershing promoted from captain to brigadier general over the heads of 800 more senior

Brigadier General Pershing at his headquarters near Casas Grandes in March 1916, during the abortive punitive expedition to Mexico to track down Pancho Villa who had recently raided across the border in New Mexico.

officers. Pershing was never popular with his fellow officers, and his promotion resulted in cries of favouritism and the start of a smear campaign that endured for some years. Nevertheless, Pershing became the first example of Roosevelt's insistence that promotions be made on the basis of merit.

In 1908, after once again serving as a military observer, this time in the increasingly unstable Balkans, Pershing returned to the Philippines as the military governor of the Moro province in Mindanao, and until 1913 used a combination of diplomacy whenever possible and military force when necessary to control the ongoing unrest. His Philippines' service earned him the Distinguished Service Cross.

The punitive expedition to Mexico

In January 1914, Pershing assumed command of an infantry brigade at the Presidio of San Francisco. Relations with Mexico had gravely deteriorated and by 1913 America's southern neighbour was beset by revolution and anarchy. In January 1914, his brigade was re-assigned to Fort Bliss, Texas, where it assumed responsibility for the security of the US–Mexican border.

John Pershing

Disaster struck in August 1915 when Pershing's family quarters at the Presidio were destroyed by a raging fire that took the lives of his wife and his three daughters. Only Warren, his 6-year-old son, survived. Those closest to him believed Pershing never recovered from the anguish of losing his beloved wife and daughters in such a manner.

In March 1916, the Mexican rebel Francisco 'Pancho' Villa raided the border town of Columbus, New Mexico, killing a number of American soldiers and civilians and triggering an immediate response from President Woodrow Wilson. Pershing was ordered to form a 10,000-man punitive expedition to Mexico to track down and capture Villa.

The expedition penetrated deep into the wastelands of northern Mexico and, although the force engaged in minor skirmishes, the search for Villa proved fruitless and the rebel leader was never captured. The expedition was ill-prepared and badly equipped for an extended foray into the Mexican wilderness and received little cooperation from the Mexican government, while the US government placed restrictions on Pershing; it ended in failure in January 1917. The only event of note was that Julio Cárdenas, Villa's chief bodyguard, was killed in a shoot-out by one of Pershing's aides, a young cavalry officer named George S. Patton.

US troops of the American Expeditionary Force cross the Atlantic in 1917. The Americans were greeted enthusiastically by the French and British Allies on their arrival in France in mid June. Pershing, however, did not consider the force sufficiently trained to see action until October.

The First World War

The United States entered the war in April 1917, with the promise of an expeditionary force, as an ally of Britain and France. The decision to create an American Expeditionary Force (AEF) to send to France required the ablest officer to be its commander-in-chief. When the only other candidate, General Frederick Funston, died in February 1917, Major General John J. Pershing was appointed by Wilson and promoted to the rank of four-star general.

The new AEF commander was given virtual carte blanche by Wilson and Secretary of War Newton D. Baker. The task of creating and training an army for war was one of the most daunting ever faced by an American military commander. A force had to be formed, armed and trained for battle. The US army of 1917 was rife with bureaucracy and duplication, woefully untrained and barely exceeded 100,000 men. It lacked even the rudimentary tools of war, possessing a mere 285,000 Springfield rifles, just over 500 field guns and only enough ammunition for a nine-hour bombardment. Pershing carried out his mandate with ruthless efficiency, cutting through red tape to create a force that by war's end numbered over 2 million men.

When he arrived in Paris in the summer of 1917, huge crowds greeted Pershing with near-euphoria as a conquering hero. France was at a low point of the war; its men were being squandered in futile battles for a few yards of useless terrain at places like the Somme, Ypres and Verdun, which became ghastly monuments to the folly of trench warfare.

Pershing came under unrelenting pressure from the French government and French and British generals to place American forces under their command, but steadfastly refused to bend. The AEF, he declared, would remain independent and would only fight under American command. Pershing's legendary resolve prevailed despite attempts in 1918 by the Allied Supreme Commander, French Marshal Ferdinand Foch, to marginalize the American role in the war. 'While our army will fight wherever you may decide, it will not fight except as an independent American army,' he told Foch. The French president Clemenceau once called Pershing 'the stubbornest man I ever met'.

However, a larger problem loomed. Before the AEF could fight it had to be trained for battle. The troops arriving in France were raw recruits. Having seen for himself the appalling conditions at the front and a French army in such disarray that it had mutinied, in October 1917 Pershing announced, 'The standards for the American army will be those of West Point', a worthy ideal but one impossible to obtain with a largely

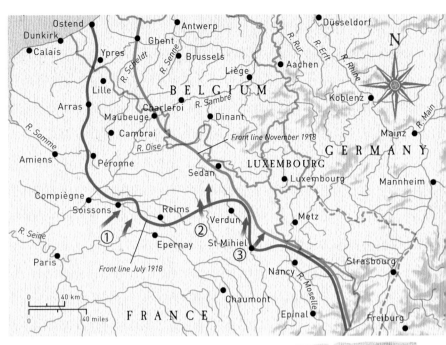

US offensives

① 18 July–6 August 1918
Aisne–Marne

② 12–16 September 1918
St Mihiel

③ 26 September–
11 November 1918
Meuse–Argonne

US OFFENSIVES ON THE WESTERN FRONT,
July–November 1918.

'I shall give you only two orders. One to go and one to return.'

SECRETARY OF WAR NEWTON D. BAKER TO PERSHING, 1917

John Pershing

conscript army. Nevertheless, he was determined to make the AEF the best fighting force in the war. Few escaped his stern presence; one of the few who did was a captain named George C. Marshall, who daringly challenged Pershing's criticism of the 1st Division. Most thought Marshall's career over, but instead Pershing promoted him to play a key role in the AEF.

Pershing established his headquarters far from Paris, at Chaumont, instituted a series of battle schools to train officers and men in every aspect of warfare, and tapped Patton to form and train an American tank force that fought for the first time in the Battle of Saint-Mihiel in September 1918.

The AEF soon came to bear Pershing's unmistakable stamp and by the autumn of 1918 consisted of two field armies. Pershing and the AEF won the admiration of its once-sceptical allies. Although his generalship in France was not without its flaws, it is to his eternal credit that he refused to permit American soldiers to become the same cannon fodder in the trenches as those of his British and French allies.

In recognition of his achievements in the war Pershing was promoted in September 1919 to General of the Armies, the highest rank ever accorded an American soldier. His popularity was so high that he was considered a possible Republican candidate for president in 1920, but Pershing declined to campaign and the nomination instead went to Warren G. Harding, who won the presidency.

Later years and legacy

Pershing served as chief of staff of the army from 1921 until he retired from active service in 1924 at the age of 64, a revered figure in both the nation and as the army's grand old man. Less well known is his service from 1923 to the time of his death as chairman of the American Battle Monuments Commission (ABMC), created that year to oversee the operation and maintenance of American military cemeteries overseas. One of the junior officers who served under Pershing in the ABMC was Major Dwight Eisenhower, who authored the manual on American memorials in France.

Pershing's years of retirement were private and unremarkable. He wrote his memoirs, which won the Pulitzer prize for history in 1932, and maintained his stature as America's most senior and respected general. In later life his health deteriorated and in the four years prior to his death he was a patient at Walter Reed Army Hospital where a regular stream of visitors came to pay their respects.

'Black Jack' Pershing died in Washington on 15 July 1948 and was buried in Arlington National Cemetery near the men of the AEF he had commanded. Despite his elevated rank, Pershing's plain white cross is the same as that of every soldier, sailor and airmen. Basil Liddell Hart later said of Pershing: 'There was perhaps no other man who would, or could, have built the American army on the scale he planned,

Pershing inspects African-American soldiers of the 2nd Battalion in 1917. His nickname 'Black Jack' derived from West Point in the 1890s, when he commanded a troop of Black soldiers in the 10th Cavalry Regiment.

John Pershing

and without that army the war could hardly have been saved and could not have been won.' Charles Dawes, his close friend and chief of supply in the AEF, and later vice-president under Calvin Coolidge, may have summed up the plain-spoken Pershing's legacy when he noted that: 'John Pershing, like Lincoln, recognized no superior on the face of the earth.'

His reputation as one of America's foremost and most resolute soldiers endures. As his official biographer notes: 'For two-score years he had soldiered; his career shaped the army and sustained his nation.' To this day, John J. Pershing remains a symbol of perseverance and iron will.

Pershing leads a parade down the Champs-Elysées after the Armistice. The AEF had played an important role in Meuse–Argonne offensive of September–November 1918, and Pershing claimed that the US breakout at Argonne in November 1918 was a decisive factor in the collapse of Germany and the armistice of 11 November 1918.

John Pershing

'I do not order you to attack, I order you to die.'

MUSTAFA KEMAL, 25 APRIL 1915

KEMAL ATATÜRK

IAN BECKETT

1881–1938

STATUES OF MUSTAFA KEMAL, known since 1934 as Atatürk ('Father of the Turks'), can be seen everywhere in modern Turkey. Inevitably, there are mythic elements in the heroic version of his life, but there is no doubt that, out of the disintegration of the Ottoman empire, he forged a Westernized and secular state that has endured for over eighty years. That he was able to do so rested on a military reputation first made at Gallipoli in April 1915, and upon his subsequent victories in the Greco-Turkish War of 1920–22.

Atatürk was born some time in 1881 in the Macedonian city of Salonika (now Thessaloniki in northeast Greece, then under Turkish rule). Initially he was simply called Mustafa, but at his military secondary school he was given the name Kemal ('Perfect') to distinguish him from other Mustafas. Despite opposition from his mother, he settled on a military career at an early age, passing through the War College to graduate as a lieutenant in 1902. Although of medium height and light build, Atatürk was nonetheless an imposing figure, and, with his fair hair, blue-green eyes and light complexion, by no means obviously Turkish: the sultan once referred to him as a 'Macedonian revolutionary of unknown origin', though it is more likely that he had Albanian antecedents. Atatürk was undoubtedly intelligent and shrewd, though also vain, cynical, domineering and unscrupulous. He drank heavily, played poker incessantly and had a prodigious sexual appetite.

The Young Turks

Atatürk's father, who died when Atatürk was 7 or 8, had been liberal-minded, and Atatürk was also influenced by the progressive liberal nationalism then popular among younger army officers. Indeed, he was arrested shortly after graduation from the Staff College in 1905 for being in possession of banned books – although, because of his youth, he was simply posted to a remote region in Syria. Atatürk was involved on the peripheries of subsequent military conspiracies that led to a coup staged by the army-based Committee of Union and Progress (CUP), popularly know as the Young Turks, in July 1908. This forced Sultan Abdul Hamid II to restore the liberal constitution that

Kemal Atatürk

had been suspended in 1877. However, Atatürk was not directly involved in the suppression of a counter-revolution by the Young Turks in April 1909, after which they forced the sultan's abdication in favour of his younger brother, Mehmet V. Nor did he play a role in the coup orchestrated by the minister of war, Mehmet Enver Pasha, in January 1913, by which the Young Turks seized total power.

The final straw for Enver and his colleagues had been Turkey's humiliation in the Italo-Turkish War of 1911–12 and the First Balkan War of 1912. Atatürk himself served against the Italians in Libya and in the Second Balkan War in 1913. The Young Turks had ambitions to revive Ottoman power and overthrow the settlement reached at the conclusion of the Balkan Wars. The remaining Turkish frontiers in Europe were now vulnerable to the territorial ambitions of Greece and Bulgaria, while Russia clearly retained its interest in the Dardanelles and the Bosphorus. Some Young Turks, therefore, favoured alliance with one of the great powers, while others wished to reach an accommodation with all the powers as a means of securing Turkey's future. From Enver's perspective, Germany had no apparent territorial ambitions on Turkish territory. By contrast, Britain and France seemed indifferent to Turkish sensitivities and were aligned with Russia.

Accordingly, with war breaking out in Europe, on 2 August 1914 Enver secured a secret treaty of alliance with Germany. Anxious to bring Turkey into the war, the Germans accepted Enver's invitation to give safe refuge in Turkish waters to two warships, *Goeben* and *Breslau*, which were being pursued by the Royal Navy in the Mediterranean. Their passage of the Dardanelles straits on 10 August violated international law, though the Turks claimed they had purchased the ships. Enver increased pressure on his colleagues by securing a German financial loan and then, on 29 October, by authorizing *Goeben* and *Breslau* to commence raids on Russian shipping and coastal towns on the Black Sea. Russia declared war on Turkey on 2 November, followed by Britain and France on 5 November; the Turkish counter-declaration was issued on 11 November 1914.

Mustafa Kemal as a young army officer. His subsequent achievements in preserving Turkey's territorial integrity and in forging a modernized secular state earned him the honorific name Atatürk, meaning 'Father of the Turks'.

The First World War

The Dardanelles were the most obvious place for Britain and France to attack in support of Russia and, in February 1915, Atatürk, though still only a lieutenant colonel, was appointed to command the Turkish 19th Division on the Gallipoli peninsula guarding the north side of the straits. A British and French naval operation to force the straits began on 19 February but, when it faltered on 18 March, the Allies resolved to land at Gallipoli. It so happened that Atatürk had planned an anti-invasion exercise for his command on the very day, 25 April 1915, on which the British and French landings

ANZAC COVE

THE INITIAL LANDINGS of General Sir Ian Hamilton's Mediterranean Expeditionary Force on the Gallipoli peninsula took place on 25 April 1915 at five beaches at Cape Helles in the south, and, 12 miles to the northwest, at what became known as Anzac Cove. It had been intended to land the Anzacs (the men of the Australian and New Zealand Army Corps) adjacent to the Gaba Tepe headland. In the pre-dawn darkness, however, the current swept the boats to a narrow beach under steep cliffs about a mile and half further north, between 'Hell Spit' and Ari Burnu.

There was little initial resistance, but confusion and the difficult terrain meant that it proved all but impossible to move inland quickly, though small parties began to climb the cliffs. Atatürk's division held the high ground at Chunuk Bair and Sari Bair. Getting no answer when he reported the landing to his superiors, Atatürk ordered an immediate counter-attack on his own initiative. Rushing to the front with just one junior officer, he found some of his men withdrawing. When they said they

had no ammunition, he ordered them to use the bayonet instead, and by the sheer force of his personality forced them to take up new positions. As more of his force arrived so he pushed them forward, famously saying, 'I do not order you to attack, I order you to die. By the time we die, we will be replaced by other troops and commanders.'

Atatürk's vigorous counter-attack amid the scrub-covered gullies and valleys that characterized the terrain behind the cliffs prevented any further exploitation by the Anzacs. Indeed, men began to struggle back down to the beach and to take shelter there, and most of the artillery landed was taken off again as the situation deteriorated. By midnight the position seemed so critical that the Anzac corps commander, Sir William Birdwood, and his two divisional commanders, Major-Generals Bridges and Godfrey, urged withdrawal. They were

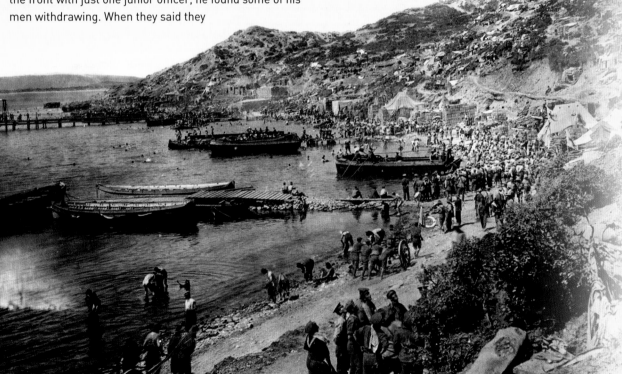

Kemal Atatürk

commenced. Atatürk's hastily improvised defence opposite the Australian and New Zealand Army Corps (Anzac) at 'Anzac Cove' halted their advance inland to the Sari Bair heights (see below). Atatürk led another successful defence when fresh British forces landed at Suvla Bay on 6 August, by which time he was commanding the Turkish XVI Corps. At one point, he was hit by a shrapnel fragment, but the watch in his breast pocket, which was shattered in the impact, saved his life. Atatürk contributed significantly to the Allied defeat at Gallipoli, although the repeated massed counter-attacks he ordered were extremely costly.

overruled by Hamilton, who ordered them to 'Dig, dig, dig until you are safe.'

The campaign now effectively became a struggle for command of the high ground. From the Allied perspective, too much was asked of troops with inadequate artillery support, arising not so much from a lack of guns but from the technical limitations of artillery faced with the steep elevations and with few means of accurately locating Turkish guns. The Turkish defenders, too, suffered from the technical limitations of artillery, and had relatively few machine-guns, but Atatürk continued to inspire the defence, reminding his command in May 1915, 'Every soldier struggling here along with me should know that to carry the honourable task given to us not one step backwards will be taken.' His counter-attacks were repulsed with heavy losses, but he always had sufficient forces and supplies to reproduce the stalemate already encountered on the Western Front.

(Left) **The landings at Anzac Cove,** 25 April 1915. By chance, Atatürk had planned an anti-invasion exercise on 25 April, the first day of the Allied operation.

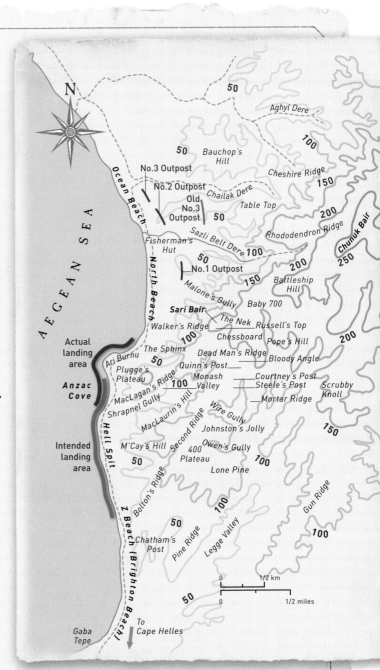

(Above left) **Australian infantrymen** heading for the beaches at Gallipoli. The stiff resistance mounted by Atatürk, combined with the difficult terrain, prevented the Allies from penetrating far inland.

Kemal Atatürk

A British naval division in action near Achi Baba, Gallipoli. One British staff officer had opined that 'The Turk is an enemy who has never shown himself as good a fighter as the white man.' Atatürk was to prove him wrong.

Following the final evacuation of the Allies from Gallipoli in January 1916, Atatürk served in the Caucasus, Syria and Arabia, ending the war in command of an army group in Syria, though still only a brigadier general. Atatürk had become increasingly critical of the CUP leadership, particularly Enver, who he believed had blocked his promotion. Enver, however, fled Constantinople as British forces entered Damascus and Aleppo in October 1918 and advanced towards Mosul. An armistice was concluded on 30 October 1918, the Allies occupying the Dardanelles and the Bosphorus.

The revolt against the sultan

Sultan Mehmet VI, who had succeeded his brother in July 1918, received the peace terms as the Treaty of Sèvres on 10 August 1920. They reflected Britain and France's wish to preserve some kind of Turkish state, though dividing much of the Ottoman empire between them and giving independence to Armenia and autonomy to the Kurds. Controversially, the treaty rewarded the Greek prime minister, Eleutherios Venizelos, for his wartime support of the Allies by awarding Greece most of the Aegean islands, the Gallipoli peninsula, Smyrna (Izmir) and Thrace. Indeed, in May 1919, with the Italians absenting themselves from the Paris Peace Conference during a dispute over their own irredentist claims in the Adriatic, Venizelos was invited to occupy Smyrna in order to forestall any Italian intervention, the Italians having landed troops

Kemal Atatürk

at Adalia (Antalya) in March 1919. The Greek landing at Smyrna on 15 May 1919 was the catalyst for Atatürk's nationalist revolt.

Between December 1918 and March 1919 a national resistance movement emerged in the Turkish army, which had been drawn back into Anatolia at the armistice. Atatürk was inspector general of the Ninth (later renamed the Third) Army with the task of restoring order on the Black Sea coast when the Greeks landed at Smyrna. Ostensibly, his appointment was to reassure the Allies that there would be no massacres of Greeks or other Christians. In reality, Atatürk's appointment was always intended to further the establishment of the new national movement away from Constantinople. It was the first time he had secured a position of real authority, and he began contacting army commanders and provincial governors. On 22 June 1919 he issued a declaration at Amasya, calling on Turks to resist foreign domination and to forge a new central national body free of outside influence and control. In the declaration he also summoned a national congress at Sivas, although this was pre-empted by a proposed national congress of the Defence of Rights Associations at Erzurum. Atatürk agreed to attend, resigning from the army on 8 July 1919 when his intended presence led the sultan to order his recall and arrest.

All the principal army commanders had agreed to follow Atatürk's orders, and at the Erzurum and Sivas congresses the national movement effectively pledged itself to maintain the integrity of the Turkish state and to elect a national assembly to mandate a government capable of negotiating a satisfactory peace agreement with the Allied powers. Following negotiations with the government, elections were held and a new assembly convened in Constantinople in January 1920. Though this assembly passed the National Pact on 28 January, by which it was agreed to seek an independent Turkish state within secure frontiers, the deputies were not prepared to consent to the formation of the single national party that Atatürk had asked for. In the event, a serious clash between Turkish and French troops in Cilicia on the borders of Turkey and Syria, and the accompanying slaughter of an estimated 20,000 Christians, led to the Allies occupying Constantinople on 16 March 1920. Then, with Allied backing, the sultan established a gendarmerie called the Army of the Caliphate to suppress the nationalists. Atatürk was condemned to death in absentia for treason. His response was to summon a national assembly in Ankara on 23 April, which elected him provisional head of state by a single vote. In June the sultan accepted the Treaty of Sèvres, at the very moment when the Turkish army was beginning to prevail against the untrained gendarmerie.

The British and French had only limited forces available. Consequently, they responded to Atatürk's advance by asking the Greeks to launch offensives in Anatolia and Thrace. Throwing some 150,000 men into the offensives, the Greeks enjoyed considerable success, since Atatürk had at best 70,000 men available. At this point, on 2 October 1920, King Alexander of Greece was bitten on the leg by one of his pet monkeys, which he was trying to separate from his spaniel. Blood poisoning set in, and the king died on 25 October.

Alexander's young wife was expecting a child, but it had been a morganatic marriage. Venizelos tried to get Alexander's younger brother Paul to accept the throne, but he refused unless the Greek people rejected both his father, the exiled King Constantine, and his older brother, former Crown Prince George. Opposed to Greek entry into the war and considered pro-German, Constantine had in 1917 been forced by Allied pressure to abdicate in favour of Alexander. Now, in the face of Prince Paul's conditions, Venizelos consented to an election in the belief that he would win it, but lost. On 19 December 1920 Constantine duly returned to the throne; incensed by this unexpected development, the Allies cut off all financial and military assistance, and withdrew their political support for the Greek action in Anatolia. Though he had opposed Greece entering the war against Turkey, Constantine decided not only to follow the Venizelist policy but also to step up the scale of a war that was relatively popular with the Greek public.

The Greco-Turkish War

Capitalizing on his good fortune, Atatürk appeared conciliatory towards Britain and France, while also reaching an accommodation with the Bolsheviks in Russia. Faced with problems in Syria and Lebanon, the French reached a secret understanding with Atatürk in October 1920 and withdrew from Cilicia; by June 1921 the Italians had also withdrawn their small force from southwest Anatolia. Meanwhile, Atatürk's army gave ground to the Greeks at Eskisehir in January 1921, but checked the Greek advance in the First and Second Battles of Inönü (6–10 January and 23 March – 1 April respectively), largely under the direction of Atatürk's chief of staff, Ismet Pasha. Now under Constantine's personal command, the Greeks advanced again, and in July 1921 forced the Turks back to the River Sakarya, only 50 miles from Ankara. Atatürk was much criticized for authorizing the retreat, but it was undoubtedly the right decision. Launching what they hoped to be a decisive offensive, the Greeks advanced again across the arid steppe of central Anatolia, but in a grim, attritional 22-day battle on the Sakarya, from 23 August to 13 September 1921, the Greeks were forced to retire with their supplies exhausted.

The burning of the Aegean port of Smyrna (now Izmir), 14 September 1922. The capture of the city by Turkish forces effectively ended the Greco-Turkish War and led to a mass exodus of Greeks from Anatolia.

The initiative was now in the hands of Atatürk, who, elevated to field marshal and *Ghazni* ('warrior for the faith'), had become commander-in-chief in August 1921. Atatürk implemented total mobilization, putting some 78,000 men into the field, and on 26 August 1922 he launched his own offensive, feinting in the north and attacking in the south at Afyon Karahisar and Dumlupinar. Caught by surprise, the Greek army collapsed. The Turks re-entered Smyrna on 9 September 1922, as the Allies evacuated over 213,000 people from the burning city.

With the Greeks now expelled, there remained the British occupation forces at Chanak on the Dardanelles. After Turkish forces appeared opposite them on 23 September 1922, Lloyd George's government instructed the British commander at Constantinople, General Sir Charles 'Tim' Harington, to issue an ultimatum demanding an immediate Turkish withdrawal, while at the same time also seeking the support of the other Allied powers, and the dominions. The French and the Italians had no intention of becoming entangled in a war with the Turks and, among the dominions, only New Zealand and Newfoundland were prepared to stand by Britain. In any case, Harington declined to pass on the ultimatum to Atatürk, stressing the likely dangers for the Christian population in Constantinople if he had to draw his forces out of the city as immediate reinforcements for Chanak. Harington also believed Atatürk had no real wish to fight and would negotiate. Indeed, Harington, who had already made tentative approaches to Atatürk, negotiated an armistice with Ismet on 11 October 1922 by which it was agreed to withdraw all remaining Allied and Greek forces from Turkish soil once a new peace treaty had been concluded. The conference began at Lausanne on 20 November. In the meantime, Lloyd George's coalition government had collapsed.

> ## 'The man of the century.'
> DAVID LLOYD GEORGE ON ATATÜRK

'Father of the Turks'

Atatürk's victories enabled him to move to abolish the sultanate on 1 November 1922, and less than a week later Mehmet VI had taken refuge on a British warship. The new treaty signed at Lausanne on 24 July 1923 revised the Sèvres terms to Turkey's advantage, with the restoration of Armenia, eastern Thrace, Smyrna and all of Anatolia. In the short term, the Treaty of Lausanne led to a mass exchange of Greek and Turkish populations; in the longer term, as the only peace treaty after the Great War that was negotiated rather than imposed, Lausanne was the only one to endure. The Dardanelles straits remained demilitarized, but were restored to Turkey in 1936. Ankara became the capital on 9 October 1923 and Atatürk became president of the new republic on 29 October 1923. Religion and state were then separated by the abolition of the caliphate in March 1924.

Thus, Atatürk was poised to effect what he had spoken of in June 1918 as a revolution in social life, but in many ways the programme he now embarked on – to secularize, modernize and Westernize Turkey, with the aim not of imitating the West but of participating with it as an equal – merely completed the liberal reform programme of the Young Turks. In the event, secularism has often proved divisive, and there was no room in Atatürk's Turkey for ethnic diversity. Nonetheless, it was not inappropriate that Mustafa Kemal should assume the name of Atatürk in November 1934, for he had certainly secured Turkey's continued independence. Characteristically perhaps for a larger-than-life figure, he died in November 1938 of cirrhosis of the liver.

Kemal Atatürk

BASIL LIDDELL HART

1895–1970

ANDREW ROBERTS

'THE CAPTAIN WHO TAUGHT GENERALS' was the soubriquet commonly used of Sir Basil Liddell Hart, the most famous and influential military historian and journalist of the twentieth century. There are others who can lay claim to have invented the ideas behind mechanized warfare between the two World Wars, but it was Captain Liddell Hart who popularized, politicized and propagandized these vital concepts. Since his theories of armoured warfare and the 'expanding torrent' were to play important roles during the Second World War and beyond, Liddell Hart deserves his place alongside Clausewitz in this book although, like the celebrated Prussian, he was more a great teacher than a great commander.

Basil Liddell Hart, veteran of the Somme and passionate and tireless advocate of the development of air power and mechanized warfare, photographed in 1952.

Born in 1895, the son of a Wesleyan Methodist clergyman based in Paris, Basil Liddell Hart was descended from Gloucestershire yeoman farmers. Despite his delicate health he formed a fascination for warfare from childhood; when playing with toy soldiers he would manoeuvre them strategically rather than simply knocking them down as other children might. He attended St Paul's School from 1911 to 1913, and then Corpus Christi, Cambridge, where he read History without much distinction. Despite having bad enough eyesight to exempt him from military service in the Great War if he so chose, he begged his parents' permission to join up and was commissioned into the King's Own Yorkshire Light Infantry (KOYLI) in December 1914, aged only 19.

Experience of the trenches

As well as fighting at Ypres in November 1915, Liddell Hart saw action on the first day of the Somme offensive, escaping unscathed because he was placed in the reserve. No fewer than 450 men in his 800-strong battalion were lost between 1 and 3 July 1916 in that engagement. 'All the KOYLI have suffered badly,' he wrote home, 'two other service battalions having lost all their officers without exception, and nearly all their men. I have never lost so many friends before, all my friends in the various battalions which I know having been wiped out.' After a week of recuperation he was sent back to the line for a renewed offensive.

Basil Liddell Hart

Between 16 and 18 July 1916, Liddell Hart disappeared in Mametz Wood, the scene of some of the most vicious fighting of the entire war. It is unclear to this day precisely what happened to him, and there are some slight indications from his writings that he might have suffered from a panic attack there, but when he emerged he was certainly suffering from the effects of phosgene gas. 'He abhorred war,' writes his biographer Alex Danchev. 'He abhorred its irrationality, its lumpishness, its contagion, its waste.' Liddell Hart himself described it as 'a farcical futility'.

The evangelist of the tank

The gas attack left Liddell Hart with a 'disordered action of the heart', but despite that he stayed in the army until 1924, before finally leaving to become assistant military correspondent of the *Morning Post*, which later became the *Daily Telegraph*. The following year he became its chief military correspondent and later stated: 'I decided to make it a platform for the mechanization of the army.' He stayed at the *Telegraph* until 1935, becoming easily the most influential military commentator in the history of journalism.

Of course in a sense armies had been mechanizing ever since the invention of the machine-gun in the mid nineteenth century, a weapon that by 1914 had made cavalry obsolete. The best way to attack enemy command and control posts across country was the constant concern of military theorists of the interwar years, such as generals J. F. C. Fuller, Giffard Martel, Percy Hobart as well as Liddell Hart, and their unanimous answer was the tank, which had, after all, been used in warfare ever since its first

effective use during the Battle of Cambrai in 1917. Nonetheless this was still highly controversial since in the early 1920s tanks still had no radio communications, were incredibly slow, often broke down, had limited firepower and relatively little cross-country capability.

'Soldiers are sentimentalists,' wrote Liddell Hart, 'not scientists.' His relationship with the War Office started off well, and he received leaks from the pro-mechanization lobby on the Army Council, invitations to manoeuvres, letters from successive chiefs of the Imperial General Staff and occasionally classified documents were passed to him if they put the army in a good light. Yet by the late 1920s it was clear to the High Command that he put his journalistic career before his popularity with them, and his harsh criticisms of their perceived military conservatism began to rankle.

As a Somme veteran, Liddell Hart had the necessary *locus standi* in inter-war Britain to seem to speak for those who had lost their family, their limbs or their youth to what he denounced as 'progressive butchery, politely called attrition', the strategy he accused Haig and others of having pursued on the Western Front. He wrote no fewer than thirty books expounding his theories, occasionally falling foul of the (hardly cardinal) sin of self-plagiarism and, as Danchev states with commendable under-statement: 'He did not suffer from modesty.'

Basil Liddell Hart

Liddell Hart and the Second World War

The outbreak of the Second World War gave Liddell Hart the opportunity to say 'I told you so' on a very regular basis for six years. As the very method of air-supported, tank-led, highly mobile warfare that he had been advocating for two decades – blitzkrieg – flashed over Poland, Norway, France, Belgium and Holland like the lightning it was named after, his theories were proved right.

The only problem was that it was the Germans rather than the Allies who were putting them into ostentatiously good practice. At 4 p.m. on 9 March 1943, General Heinz Guderian – along with Rommel the apostle of blitzkrieg – addressed Hitler and virtually the entire German Army High Command (OKW) in what developed into a hard-fought, four-hour meeting. In order to ram home his points about the capabilities of highly mobile mechanized forces on the Eastern Front, Guderian read out an article by Liddell Hart on the organization of armed forces, past and future.

The following year, 1944, Liddell Hart deduced the exact timing and place of the D-Day landings, not, as MI5 feared, because of leaks from his army contacts, but from a deep study of the geography and tidal flows of northwest France. In the latter part of the war he opposed the Allied area-bombing strategy against Germany, and in 1945 denounced the use of the atomic bombs against Japan. After the war he campaigned against nuclear weapons, and shortly before his death in 1970 described himself as a pacifist.

The strategy of the 'expanding torrent'

In November 1920, only two years after the armistice that ended the Great War, Liddell Hart expounded his 'Strategy of the Expanding Torrent' to an audience at the Royal United Services Institute (RUSI), by which an army 'would ensure that the momentum of the attack was maintained right through the whole of the enemy's system of defence, which might be miles deep'. By the following year he accepted that, to achieve this, the tank was the weapon of the future. He was persuaded in this by his mentor 'Boney' Fuller, its first major advocate, with whom Liddell Hart was to have a strange intellectual love-hate relationship over the coming decades.

'The development of mechanical firepower has negatived the hitting power of cavalry against a properly equipped enemy,' Liddell Hart was to write in his 1927 work, *The Remaking of Modern Armies*. 'But on land the armoured caterpillar car or light tank appears the natural heir of the Mongol horseman, for the "caterpillars" are essentially mechanical cavalry. Reflection suggests that we might well regain the Mongol mobility and offensive power by reverting to the simplicity of a single highly mobile arm.' Although Liddell Hart probably never actually sat in a moving tank, he spotted their potential early on and hailed every advance in firepower and motorization that made them more efficient.

'We learn from history that after any long war the survivors are apt to reach common agreement that there has been no real victor but only common losers. War is profitable only if victory is quickly gained. Only an aggressor can hope to gain a quick victory.' BASIL LIDDELL HART

Basil Liddell Hart

In retrospect it seems incredible that there was so much official scepticism over the likely future combat role of the tank. Yet in the 1920s, mechanization was considered 'that fearful fate which hung like a shadow of doom over all cavalry regiments at that period'. Today it is hard to see how anyone could have held out against full-scale mechanization, considering how tanks had been used to good effect at the Battle of Cambrai in 1917 and since, yet it was so.

As late as 1936 Alfred Duff Cooper, then Secretary of State for War, admitted to the eight cavalry regiments that were about to be mechanized: 'It is like asking a great musical performer to throw away his violin and devote himself in future to the gramophone.' Cooper's sole foray into fiction, the superb 1950 novel *Operation Heartbreak*, features an argument between two British officers on the prospect of mechanization a quarter of a century earlier:

> *'I'd as soon be a chauffeur,' exclaimed Willie passionately one evening, 'as have to drive a dirty tank about and dress like a navvy.' 'Of course,' replied Hamilton blandly, 'if all you care about is wearing fancy dress, playing games on horseback, and occasionally showing off at the Military Tournament, you're perfectly right to take that view; but if you're interested in war, or even hoped to take part in one, you'd be praying that your regiment might be mechanised before the next war comes.'*

MPs watch tank manoeuvres on Salisbury Plain in 1928. Throughout the 1920s Liddell Hart used his position at the *Daily Telegraph* to excoriate the army High Command for its slowness to take a positive attitude to the mechanization of warfare.

In the War Office and Westminster there were those who for an inordinately long time agreed with Rudyard Kipling, who had described the 1930 Salisbury Plain mechanized manoeuvres as 'smelling like a garage and looking like a circus'. Liddell Hart recalled how when Percy Hobart gave a demonstration of tank warfare on Salisbury Plain four years later, 'orthodox soldiers retorted that such a method would not work in war'. The

New Zealand cartoonist David Low even claimed to have overheard one cavalry officer telling another in a Turkish bath in the 1920s that if mechanization came, cavalry uniforms should nonetheless stay the same, right down to the spurs. (That moment proved the inspiration for his cartoon character Colonel Blimp.)

Yet the tank offered a way out of the slow stalemate of the trenches. For one who had fought at Ypres and the Somme, it was unsurprising that Liddell Hart considered speed as of the essence in any future conflict. 'Of all qualities in war it is speed which is dominant,' he wrote in a book that arose from lectures he had delivered at RUSI in 1922,

speed both of mind and movement, without which hitting-power is valueless and with which it is multiplied, as the greatest of all commanders [i.e. Napoleon] realised in his dictum that force in war is mass, or as we should better interpret it under modern conditions, firepower, multiplied by speed. This speed, only to be obtained by the full development of scientific inventions, will transform the battle-fields of the future from squalid labyrinths into arenas wherein manoeuvre, the essence of surprise, will reign again.

His hatred of trench warfare, which he called, with typical regard for alliteration, 'mausoleums of mud', was evident.

Along with the tank, Liddell Hart was an exponent of air power, as he had been ever since seeing a Zeppelin raid on Hull in 1915. 'One could see the gleam of light each time a trapdoor opened to drop a bomb,' he later recalled. To coordinate air power – specifically the dive-bomber – with tank and infantry support would, so Liddell Hart preached, be to effect the expanding torrent theory on a future battlefield, and this would be the key to victory.

The strategy of the indirect approach

What Liddell Hart called the 'Strategy of the Indirect Approach' was developed in 1928–9, and was followed up by his related book *The British Way in Warfare* three years later. It effectively argued that British grand strategy was best served not by huge direct Continental commitments – such as he had experienced on the Somme – but by wearing the enemy down by blockade, bombing and attacks on the periphery. (Less convincingly, Liddell Hart also believed that his theory could be applied to practical philosophy, religious disputation, the art of salesmanship and was even 'fundamental to sex life'.)

'Throughout the ages,' wrote Liddell Hart, 'effective results in war have rarely been attained unless the approach has had such indirectness as to ensure the opponent's unreadiness to meet it. The indirectness has usually been physical, and always psychological.' This was a paean to 'the art of outflanking' (which was the title his friend Robert Graves suggested for it). 'In strategy,' summarized Liddell Hart, 'the longest way round is often the shortest way home.'

Danchev believes that the book *Strategy: The Indirect Approach* (1941) was 'as near as Liddell Hart ever got to a treatise, an *essai général*, of his own'. Liddell Hart cited Cromwell at the battles of Dunbar and Worcester, and Marlborough's intensive marches and counter-marches, as examples of British attempts to turn flanks and, if possible, cut the enemy's lines of communication and retreat.

Basil Liddell Hart

297

Sir Alan Brooke (later Viscount Alanbrooke) in 1939. His appreciation of the value of mechanized warfare had developed rapidly through the 1930s.

(Opposite) **German commander and advocate of blitzkrieg, Heinz Guderian** on exercises in France in 1944; Liddell Hart and Guderian formed a mutual admiration society.

The British way

'This much is certain,' Liddell Hart said at RUSI in 1931, unveiling his 'British Way in Warfare' concept, 'he that commands the sea is at great liberty, and may take as much or as little of the war as he will. Whereas those that be strongest by land are many times nevertheless in dire straits.' Britain should, he argued, fight by exercising naval power, financing allies ('lending sovereigns to sovereigns'), shoring up trade, making minor amphibious landings, but essentially letting other powers fight the huge land engagements.

Yet as Sir Michael Howard has pointed out, such a strategy was usually forced on Britain through *force majeure*, and while it might have allowed Britain to survive, 'it never enabled us to win'. What allowed Britain to win historically, Howard argued convincingly, was instead 'a commitment of support to a Continental ally in the nearest available theatre, on the largest scale that contemporary resources could afford'. Blenheim, Waterloo and D-Day were all fought under those circumstances. Even Winston Churchill and Field Marshal Sir Alan Brooke, who both followed the 'British Way in Warfare' as long as they could during the 'Indirect Approach' part of the Second World War between 1939 and June 1944, nonetheless had to accept that Hitler could not be defeated except by landing on the Continent a British army 'on the largest scale that contemporary resources could afford'. There was indeed a British way of warfare, but it was not the one that Liddell Hart prescribed, and it was not based on the indirect approach, at least not in the last analysis.

Yet today the philosophy of the Indirect Approach – principally, of course, through the medium of international terrorism – is suddenly central to modern warfare, in ways Liddell Hart could not have predicted in 1941. As Danchev pointed out in 1998, 'Contemporary military doctrine is suffused with the indirect approach'. And that was even before 9/11.

Liddell Hart on the Great Commanders

In a book the subtitle of which contains the words *Great Commanders*, it is worthwhile repeating Liddell Hart's estimation of what he called 'the qualities that distinguished the Great Captains of history'. These included:

> coup d'œil, *a blend of acute observation and swift-sure intuition; the ability to create surprise and throw the opponent off balance; the speed of thought and action that allows an opponent no chance of recovery; the combination of strategic and tactical sense; the power to win the devotion of troops, and get the utmost out of them.*

Because this checklist has not materially changed for centuries, and is unlikely to do so in the foreseeable future, the 'Captain Who Taught Generals' still has much to teach us.

LIDDELL HART ON BLITZKRIEG

ON READING THE GERMAN GENERAL Heinz Guderian's account of the 1940 blitzkrieg campaign, Liddell Hart wrote of how it almost felt as if one were riding in a tank beside the general himself, and: 'For me it was like the repetition of a dream, as it was just the way that in pre-war years I had pictured such a force by a leader who grasped the new idea – only to be told, then, that the picture was unbelievable.'

In his 1950 autobiography, *Panzer Leader*, Guderian was unambiguous:

> *It was Liddell Hart who emphasized the use of armoured forces for long-range strokes, operations against the opposing army's communications, and also proposed a type of armoured division combining panzer and panzer-infantry units. Deeply impressed by these ideas I tried to develop them in a sense practicable for our own army. So I owe many suggestions of our further development to Captain Liddell Hart.*

Guderian later told Liddell Hart he had first read his articles in 1923–4, and that in the 1924 manoeuvres, he had been told by the inspector regarding tanks:

'To hell with combat! They're supposed to carry flour!'

Liddell Hart wrote a Foreword to Guderian's book. It was nominally about Guderian, but it could equally be read more autobiographically. Of blitzkrieg, Liddell Hart wrote of how the great Panzer commander shaped history 'by means of a new idea ... a new idea of which he was both the exponent and executant'. Guderian, he believed, personified 'the quintessence of the craftsman in the way he devoted himself to the progress of a technique ... To understand him one must be capable of understanding the passion of pure craftsmanship'.

Similarly, there might have been more than a trace of self-reference (and self-regard) in Liddell Hart's estimation of Guderian:

> *Most of the recognized masters of the art of war have been content to use the familiar tools and techniques of their time. Only a few set out to provide themselves with new means and methods ... Developments in tactics have usually been due to some original military thinker and his gradually-spreading influence on progressive-minded officers of the rising generation.*

Basil Liddell Hart

CARL GUSTAF MANNERHEIM
1867–1951

ALLAN MALLINSON

MANNERHEIM'S GENIUS, like Napoleon's, lay in his grasp of the complete art of war. The great Finnish marshal practised that art, with conspicuous success, at every level, from the tactical to the grand strategic. He practised statecraft, indeed, and in a fashion that would have brought plaudits from Machiavelli and Clausewitz. In doing so he earned the respect of friends and enemies alike. And whereas the bitter northern snows were Napoleon's nemesis, 'General Winter' was Mannerheim's ally in his greatest trial: war with Stalin's Russia.

But while those snows seem still to bear the footprints of the Grande Armée – and later those of the Wehrmacht, which tried in vain to reach Moscow – they have largely covered those of the Finns who fought in that early chapter of the Second World War, the 'Winter War' of 1939–40, and again in what became known as the 'Continuation War' of 1941–4. Mannerheim steered both Finland's armed forces, and the nation itself, to an outcome that none but a commander of the greatest integrity, foresight and skill could have achieved: the Finns fought the Russians to a standstill, twice, and with German help, yet in 1945 remained a free nation, unoccupied by the Red Army. Mannerheim is an exemplar – arguably one of the finest – of Clausewitz's concept of military genius, in particular its two indispensable components: 'first, an intellect that, even in the darkest hour, retains some glimmerings of the inner light that leads to truth; and second, the courage to follow this faint light wherever it may lead'.

Early years

Carl Gustaf Emil Mannerheim was born in Askainen, southwest Finland, on 4 June 1867, the third child of Count Carl Robert Mannerheim and his wife, Helena von Julin. The Mannerheim family's origins were Dutch, or possibly German, from the merchant families of Hamburg. The Marheins, as they were then called, emigrated to Sweden in the seventeenth century, and were later ennobled. Finland was a Swedish possession until 1809, when it became an autonomous grand duchy within the Russian empire. Like most of the Finnish nobility, the young Carl Gustaf's first language was Swedish, and all his life he spoke Finnish imperfectly and with a pronounced 'foreign' accent.

Carl Gustaf Mannerheim

His upbringing, though the family was by then in straitened circumstances, was idyllic: sledging, swimming, horses. Already exceptionally tall, at 13 he was sent to the Military Cadet School in the old fortress city of Hamina, on the southeast coast of Finland. Young Carl Gustaf neither enjoyed the school, nor did he excel, except at games. But he persevered, until one night, when he was 18, he decided that the cadet curfew was too restrictive, put a dummy in his bed, and slipped out of barracks. The offence brought instant dismissal.

It turned out to be the making of him, however. He polished his school-room Russian, and a year later was admitted to the Nikolaevsky Cavalry School in St Petersburg. Here he did well, and in 1889 was commissioned in the Alexandrijski Dragoons, quartered in Poland. But he knew that, for an ambitious Finn especially, he must get himself into a Guards regiment, which in 1891 he was able to do, joining the Chevalier Guards of the Empress in St Petersburg.

Regimental and court soldiering suited Mannerheim; he learned social and diplomatic skills, mastered several languages (by the end of his life, in addition to Swedish, Finnish and Russian, he spoke English, French, German, Portuguese and some Mandarin Chinese), and cut quite a dash. Contemporaries record that 'he was energetic, correct over money matters, a good sportsman, an excellent rider, and lived soberly'. Of the coronation procession of Tsar Nicholas II in 1896, one artist wrote 'Gustaf Mannerheim walked before the emperor's baldaquin with drawn sabre and looked very handsome – truly imposing.'

Not surprisingly, he made a 'good' marriage – to Anastasia Arapova, the daughter of a former Guards general and an heiress. They had two daughters, but after ten years the marriage fell apart. For the rest of his life Mannerheim lived as a bachelor, later with some asceticism.

Active service

Guards soldiering in St Petersburg was agreeable, but it wasn't real soldiering. War with Japan, in 1904–5, gave Major Mannerheim his opportunity. 'I am 37 years old,' he wrote home. 'Serious campaigns do not often occur, and if I do not take part in this one, there is every chance that I shall become an armchair soldier, who will have to keep silent while more experienced comrades make the most of their wartime impressions.' Promoted lieutenant colonel of the Nezhin Dragoons in Manchuria, Mannerheim sought – and saw – a good deal of action, much of it chaotic. Rather like the young Arthur Wellesley in Flanders, he learned how not to do things. He, personally, distinguished himself, however, and was promoted colonel.

When the war ended the following year, the General Staff sent the promising young colonel of cavalry on a

Carl Gustaf Mannerheim, photographed *c.* 1942. Not only a great general but also a great statesman, Mannerheim became a national hero in Finland following his successful resistance to Soviet aggression.

singular commission: a survey, on horseback, from Russian Turkestan to what was then Peking – a distance of almost 9,000 miles. It took two years, but his reports were well received. Colonel Mannerheim had proved himself a fine staff officer as well as a brave and capable commander. His star was in the ascendant: within five years he was promoted major-general and given command of the Emperor's Uhlans of the Guard in Warsaw.

The Great War

In August 1914 Major-General Mannerheim's brigade formed part of the scratch covering force for the mobilization of the Imperial Russian army. They were soon in action against the Austrians advancing into Galicia. At the Battle of Krasnik, 150 miles south of Warsaw, Mannerheim displayed such a mastery of initiative and manoeuvre that his brigade imposed a strategic check on the enemy – gaining four crucial days for the mobilizing army – for which he received his first decoration for gallantry, the Sword of St George. He was soon commanding a division.

Mannerheim's diaries and letters from this time show more than mere tactical flare, however. Rather, they reveal foresight and a rare grasp of the strategic and geo-political situation – not least an awareness of the ambivalence towards the war felt in Finland, where a pro-German sentiment had emerged out of opposition to Russian imperialism. Mannerheim was on leave in St Petersburg when in March 1917 the first shots of the Russian Revolution were fired, and had to flee his hotel in borrowed clothes – a useful taste of what might come in Helsinki if the revolutionaries seized power there.

In July Mannerheim was promoted lieutenant general to command VI Cavalry Corps in Romania, but the corps saw no action in the disastrous Russian offensive that summer. During sick leave in Odessa, he decided there was no future with any military integrity in Russian service, and set off back for Finland. Soon after, Lenin seized power.

The Bolshevik Revolution

'The White General' – as Mannerheim became known – managed, not without more close shaves, to get to Helsinki in December, where the new Finnish government at once made him commander-in-chief. Lenin had conceded independence to the Finns, under the terms of the Brest-Litovsk peace treaty with Germany, but in the expectation that the Finnish proletariat would overthrow the bourgeoisie and reunite with the new Soviet Russia.

Mannerheim had few forces with which to defeat the Finnish 'Red Guards' and eject the 40,000 Russian troops still in the country, most of them loyal to Lenin's provisional government. His masterstroke was in moving out of Helsinki, to Vaasa in the west, with its open lines of communication to Sweden. He had seen in Russia how a metropolitan senate and headquarters would inevitably be overthrown by the concentration of revolutionary forces, and that the fight back would then be against the odds. Away from Helsinki he would, at least, have balance.

At Vaasa he was able to build up an army based on the Civil Guards, and after three months of civil war, with the help of German troops, he defeated the Red forces. But it had been a fractious time, with Mannerheim at loggerheads with the pro-German elements of the government. He was exasperated, too, with Sweden, from whom little support materialized; indeed, Sweden's occupation of the Åland Islands was a lesson in the hazard of placing hope in Nordic solidarity.

After the conclusion of the civil war Mannerheim resigned, but when Germany finally collapsed in November 1918 he was recalled as regent. He stood in Finland's first presidential election the following summer, but was defeated by compromise voting among the centre parties, who were fearful of a split over his support for intervention in the Russian counter-revolution. He retired to private life, working for the Red Cross in Finland and for the League for Child Welfare, which he founded.

The gathering storm

In 1931 General Mannerheim was recalled once more – to be chairman of the new Defence Council, with the designation 'commander-in-chief in time of war'. Two years later he was made field marshal, and for the next five years he pressed for greater defence spending and rearmament. He was largely unsuccessful, but he did reorganize the army's mobilization, training and defence plans. Perhaps surprisingly for a cavalryman, he argued against the army high command's preference for a war of manoeuvre in the Karelian isthmus (the direct route from Leningrad to Helsinki), pressing instead for a line of fixed defences, the so-called Mannerheim Line.

Mannerheim, the 'White General', who, during Finland's civil war of 1917–18, succeeded in defeating the Finnish 'Red Guards'.

Once again, he urged a Nordic mutual assistance pact, but Sweden would not be drawn. And when Stalin began pressing for border adjustments to strengthen Russia's naval defences in the eastern Baltic, Mannerheim advocated compromise: an exchange of territory, and leasing key islands. The government refused, but neither would it increase the defence budget. The field marshal was on the point of resigning when the Russians declared war, on 29 November 1939. At the age of 72, Mannerheim again took command of the country's forces, and moved to the headquarters at Mikkeli, from where he had directed the closing moves of the war of independence twenty years before. His first general order was of a Napoleonic grandeur and Churchillian insight:

> Brave soldiers of Finland!
> I enter on this task at a time when our hereditary enemy is once again attacking our country. Confidence in one's commander is the first condition for success. You know me, and I know you ...

No other nation's commander-in-chief at that time could have made so simple an assertion of mutual confidence: Mannerheim was an undisputed war hero, a general of proven ability, a patriot and a household name.

The Winter War

The Russians attacked through the Karelian isthmus, but with neither the strength nor the skill expected. After a precipitate withdrawal by the Finnish covering force – which

Carl Gustaf Mannerheim

Mannerheim checked by sheer force of personality – the army fought hard and effectively along the line of fixed defences. The Soviet advance ground to a halt, like that of the French before Wellington's Lines of Torres Vedras. But unlike Wellington's great defensive position, the Mannerheim Line was not anchored on impassable natural obstacles (the lakes were frozen): the field marshal knew the defences could be breached if the Soviets concentrated their force.

A second axis of advance north of Lake Ladoga fared no better at first. The Finns' mastery of movement in the snow-covered wilderness, and their *motti* tactics (encirclement and later destruction; see opposite), inflicted huge casualties. But in January 1940 a new Russian commander, Timoshenko, was able to reopen the offensive on both axes with greater concentration of effort. With no practical help forthcoming from Sweden or the Allies, Mannerheim pressed the government to sue for peace.

Stalin was only too willing to negotiate: he had gained his immediate object – control of the isthmus and a zone of Karelia north of Lake Ladoga, safeguarding the strategically vital Leningrad–Murmansk railway. But it was at a prodigious cost in men, material and prestige – at least 120,000 dead. The cost to the Finns had been great, too: 27,000 dead, and, under the terms of the Moscow peace treaty, more territory than the Russians had originally demanded. But the moral effect of fighting the invader to a standstill was considerable. Mannerheim knew that although the country was now more vulnerable than before (the new Russian frontiers allowed little space to be traded in a covering action), paradoxically Finland's strategic position was improved.

Improved, but extraordinarily tricky. The peace was fundamentally unstable: half a million Finns had been displaced by the peace treaty, whose terms also allowed the rail transit of Russian troops. This would soon be paralleled – almost literally in places – by the rights given to German troops to pass through Finland to occupied northern Norway. Finnish sovereignty was therefore highly fragile, and without help from the Allies or Sweden, the only source of military matériel and economic aid (grain especially, a critical factor in any future mobilization) was in supping with Hitler, if with the longest possible spoon. Germany was certainly keen to help.

Finnish soldiers preparing to attack a Red Army unit, early February 1940. With their camouflaged snowsuits and skis, the Finns were masters of the severe winter conditions, while the Soviets were poorly equipped and suffered terribly from the cold.

(Left) **An entire Soviet division** was trapped and wiped out at Suomussalmi by the Finns, using their *motti* tactics – and aided by their great ally, General Winter, which froze thousands of Russian troops to death.

FINNISH MOTTI TACTICS

MOTTI LITERALLY IS A CUBIC METRE of cut timber; traditionally in Finland, *motti* were cut and stacked throughout the forests for later collection. During the Winter War the Finns called encircled Soviet troops *Mottiryssä* or *Motti-Russki* – a gruesome analogy with firewood just waiting to be burned.

The Red Army's November 1939 offensive, in the wilderness of Karelia especially, was tied to narrow, single-track roads through snowbound forests. Unlike the Finns, the Russians were dependent on motor transport, and their rate of advance inevitably slowed; in places the long columns became bogged down and strung out over long distances, with small groups of vehicles becoming isolated, even more vulnerable to attack. The Russians were strangely uncomfortable in this environment – jumpy even: when the head of the advancing column was attacked, the rest of the vehicles would stop and adopt static defensive positions rather than attempting to counter-attack.

Once the column had been halted, Finnish infantry – ski troops especially – would begin a series of envelopments, and it was the enveloped forces that became known as *motti*. Initially the tactic was opportunistic, but one *motti*, at Suomussalmi, was fully planned from the outset, and on a much larger scale than hitherto: it succeeded in trapping the entire Soviet 44th and 163rd Divisions, cutting the line of supply and making numerous smaller *mottis* of the line of communication troops.

As a rule, the Finns attacked the weakest *motti* first, further isolating the stronger and less vulnerable pockets. Where the *motti* were too strong to overrun, Finnish ski troops, armed with sub-machine-guns, grenades, Molotov cocktails, satchel charges and smoke grenades, kept up pin-prick attacks, often infiltrating the defences, to harass the Russians and keep them off-balance. The severe winter did the rest. Thousands of Russian troops simply froze to death at their posts. Meanwhile the warmly clad and well-camouflaged Finns moved from one *motti* to another, attacking them at will and then disappearing into the forest. Soviet officers said they never actually saw a Finnish soldier, only their handiwork.

Attempts to break out of the *motti* were usually blocked successfully, for the Soviet troops were reluctant to abandon their vehicles. Re-supply by the Red Air Force was often their only salvation.

Attack on the 163rd Division
11–28 December 1939

163rd Div.

25 December

Attack on the 44th Division
5–8 January 1940

N

Suomussalmi

SOVIET FORCES

U S S R

FINNISH FORCES

44th Div.

0   5 km

0   5 miles

Position
22 December–8 January

Assembly area 30 December
after defeat of 163rd Division

Trace of road ploughed
through snow by Finns

F I N L A N D

Carl Gustaf Mannerheim

The unstable peace and the Continuation War

Through the rest of 1940 and the early months of 1941, Mannerheim prepared for war as best he could. When Hitler confirmed his intention to attack the Soviet Union, and his wish for a co-offensive with the Finns, Mannerheim recognized both a degree of inevitability (Stalin would regard them as de facto allies) and opportunity – perhaps the only opportunity – to re-establish secure borders. What followed in terms of campaign planning, with its Clausewitzian linkage to the ends of grand strategy, was really quite remarkable.

It all hinged on the fate of Leningrad. Mannerheim's object was the restoration of the 1939 borders, not the capture of Leningrad or German conquest of the Soviet Union. On the other hand, the German General Staff wished to tie down as many Soviet troops as possible in Finland. They calculated the Stavka (the Soviet High Command) would be prepared to withdraw troops north of Lake Ladoga for the defence of Leningrad, but not from the isthmus, for that would allow a rapid and easy advance to the city. Accordingly, OKW (the German High Command) pressed the Finns to mount their major offensive in the north. Mannerheim argued instead that he needed to concentrate his forces on the isthmus: it was there that the greatest threat lay, the 1940 frontier being so far west. He calculated that Stalin would recognize this as a move to restore the 1939 frontier rather than a move against Leningrad, which would not be the case with an offensive in the north.

Operation Barbarossa – the German attack on the Soviet Union – took Stalin wholly by surprise, despite Anglo-US warnings. The Finns were able to recover ground in the isthmus, but poor initial advances by the Germans allowed Mannerheim to launch a secondary offensive north of Lake Ladoga. He could now recover the 1939 border without

(Below right)
Mannerheim shakes hands with Hitler, 27 June 1942, as Field Marshal Wilhelm Keitel looks on. In his efforts to secure Finnish territorial integrity, Mannerheim was obliged to enter into a marriage of convenience with Nazi Germany.

(Below) **THE FINNISH ARMY DEPLOYMENT TO FACE TIMOSHENKO'S OFFENSIVE,** 6 February 1940.

the Soviets believing the Finns were part of a combined operation to take Leningrad. Indeed, the Finnish government was at pains to proclaim 'co-belligerency' and not alliance with Germany. Finnish troops advanced rapidly to the old frontier, but Mannerheim then took the decision to press on to the Svir river to secure a line of defence against the inevitable counter-offensive. The move was not without cost: Britain formally declared war on Finland on 6 December 1941 (a rare case of one democracy declaring war on another), though the British took only limited military action – principally air cover for the Red Army supplied by RAF Hurricanes based at Murmansk.

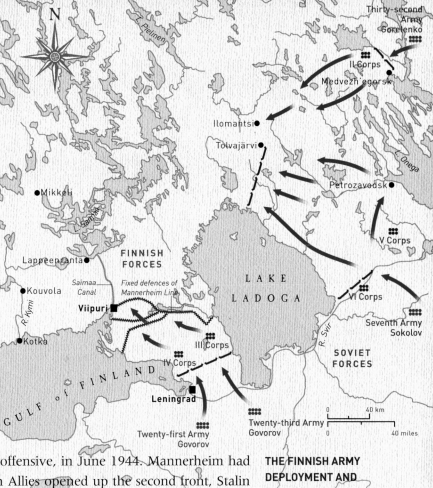

THE FINNISH ARMY DEPLOYMENT AND THE RED ARMY OFFENSIVES, 1944.

Fighting on the Finnish front eventually died down with the Soviets' need to strengthen the defences of Leningrad and beyond; but German reverses, especially Stalingrad, brought the anticipated counter-offensive, in June 1944. Mannerheim had calculated, however, that when the Western Allies opened up the second front, Stalin would withdraw troops from the northern front for the race to Berlin. His dilemma was how long to fight alongside the Germans before making peace. Hitler suspected this, and demanded a pact: no separate peace with Stalin, in return for continued, crucial, support.

Mannerheim and Risto Ryiti, the Finnish president, dealt with this by a desperate *ruse de guerre*. Ryiti sent Hitler a personal undertaking not to begin independent peace negotiations with Moscow. Military aid therefore continued, and the Red Army's advance was slowed. But after a month's fighting it was clear the pressure was irresistible. As planned, therefore, President Ryiti resigned, appointing Mannerheim in his place, who at once repudiated Ryiti's 'personal' undertaking to Hitler, and opened negotiations with Moscow.

 The terms imposed by Stalin were severe: a return to 1940 borders, with other territorial appropriations and substantial reparations. They were also thorny: German troops were to be evicted. The alternative, however, was occupation. With this second treaty, President Mannerheim, Marshal of Finland (the rank had been created for him in 1942 for his 75th birthday), would at least achieve his grand strategic objective: an independent Finland.

The expulsion of Finland's former de facto ally was not without bloodshed, but it was achieved by a subtle use of force, ruse and the sheer power of Mannerheim's personality. And Finland was spared occupation by the Red Army, unlike the Baltic States and eastern Europe. Ill health forced Mannerheim's resignation in 1946, and he died five years later. But modern Finland is his legacy, and today he is still honoured throughout the country. His strategic grasp – clear-sighted, brave, yet pragmatic – deserves, however, a far wider appreciation. Perhaps his true genius in war, as Goethe famously said of writing, consisted in knowing when to stop.

Carl Gustaf Mannerheim

307

'I used to think that Rommel was good, but my opinion is that Rundstedt would have hit him for six. Rundstedt is the best German general I have come up against.' FIELD MARSHAL BERNARD MONTGOMERY

GERD VON RUNDSTEDT

1875–1953

MICHAEL BURLEIGH

GERD VON RUNDSTEDT was 64 when the Second World War broke out, so with the exception of active service during 1914–18, most of his career was spent in peacetime. A quintessential Prussian army officer, his chief claim to fame was to have preserved and translated much of the ethos and spirit of the old imperial-Prussian army across the Weimar Republic into the Nazi era.

Yet this was illusory. He was a traditional Prussian military potentate, in his carmine striped trousers and much-decorated tunic, disdaining the new creed of leading from the front, and preferring to use large-scale 1:1,000,000 maps to get the grand strategic overview. But much of the genius even his enemies ascribed to him was not his: although he had the external symbols of military power, the rank and titles, in fact the real thing was invariably wielded by others. Behind the easy grand manner and the diplomatic expertise, it could be argued that Rundstedt was a successful sham. Liddell Hart was not alone in being taken in by Rundstedt's gentlemanly manner, imagining there was more than met the beholder's charmed eye. What Rundstedt actually presided over was the progressive nazification of the German armed forces, the final capitulation by the old elites that the conservative dissident Ewald von Kleist-Schmenzin had foreseen in 1934.

The long apprenticeship of a Prussian warrior

Rundstedt came from a distinguished Junker family with a history of military service to the Prussian crown. After graduating from the cadet academy at Gross Lichterfelde, in 1893 he became a lieutenant in the 83rd Royal Prussian Infantry Regiment. After a decade as an adjutant, he entered Berlin's prestigious War Academy in 1902. Only one in five of those who took the three-year course survived to embark on an eighteen-month probationary period on the General Staff. He succeeded in becoming a captain on the Troop General Staff. In that capacity he served as operations officer to the 22nd Reserve Infantry Division within the First Army, and participated in the invasion of Belgium and France in August 1914. The following year Rundstedt, now a major, was transferred to the more mobile Eastern Front, before being assigned to help rebuild

Gerd von Rundstedt

the army of Austria-Hungary after its shattering defeat during the Russian Brusilov offensive. In 1917 he became chief of staff of LIII Corps, which advanced towards Petrograd so as to pressure the Bolsheviks into accepting the onerous Treaty of Brest-Litovsk. From March 1918 onwards he was chief of staff to XV Corps, which took part in the last major German offensive on the Western Front.

Given his connections and experience it was unsurprising that after the war Rundstedt should be chosen by General von Seeckt to join the Truppenamt, the Weimar Republic's disguised substitute for the General Staff, which the Versailles Treaty had abolished. He joined a distinguished group of newly minted lieutenant colonels, including Werner von Blomberg, Fedor von Bock, Kurt von Hammerstein-Equord and Wilhelm von Leeb, who dominated the Reichswehr under Weimar. During that period, Rundstedt advanced to the rank of major-general. By now in his fifties, he proved an adroit operator in the authoritarian reconstruction of the later Weimar Republic associated with the names of Hindenburg, Schleicher and Papen, emerging as the general commanding the Berlin-based First Army Group, the six divisions that defended Germany's eastern frontier.

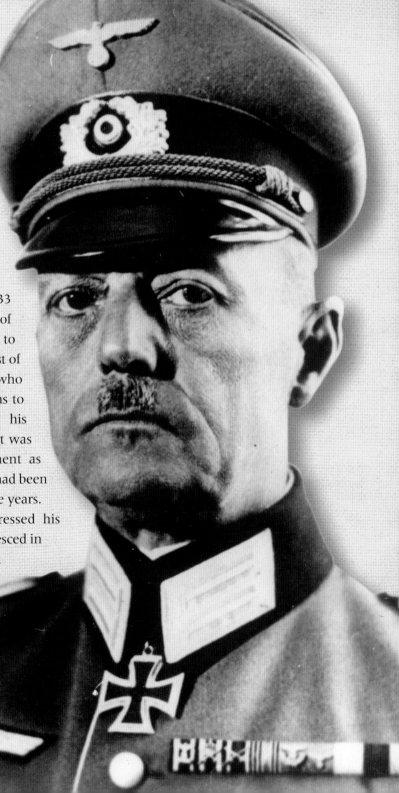

Operating under the Nazis

The advent of Hitler's chancellorship in January 1933 resulted in the appointment as minister of defence of Werner von Blomberg, who in turn attempted to promote General Walter von Reichenau to the post of army commander-in-chief. Leeb and Rundstedt, who objected as much to Reichenau's relative youth as to his pronounced Nazi sympathies, stymied his appointment by threatening to resign. Rundstedt was only marginally less satisfied by the appointment as commander-in-chief of Werner von Fritsch, who had been a former subordinate and was also younger by five years.

Although Rundstedt often privately expressed his disdain for the Nazis, he and his colleagues acquiesced in the Night of the Long Knives in June 1934, in which Hitler ordered the murder of his rival, Ernst Röhm, and the other leaders of the Sturmabteilung (SA), which was threatening to become more than a paramilitary formation. Rundstedt and his colleagues also, apparently, acquiesced in the cold-blooded murder of General Schleicher and his wife, and Major-General Ferdinand Eduard von Bredow, who were all gunned down in the same SS mafia-style operation, which was logistically facilitated by the regular army. Rundstedt further demonstrated his loyalty by personally administering the oath that senior officers were obliged to swear to the Führer. In the same year as the Night of the Long Knives, Blomberg, Fritsch and Rundstedt took prominent positions in the Nazi Party's annual Nuremberg rally. Rundstedt also undertook many of the social functions that fell upon General Fritsch, who as a bachelor workaholic had no time for such things as a courtesy appearance at the funeral of King George V.

Rundstedt managed to preserve the framework of the military old guard as Hitler expanded the German armed forces, even managing to tolerate such daring innovations as Guderian's infatuation with tanks. He saw himself as the embodiment of the army, saying 'we' think or want this or that in the first person plural. In early 1938 Rundstedt was afforded another glimpse into the mindset of his political masters. Blomberg was ruined after he had been encouraged to marry a woman who turned out to have a police record, while General Fritsch was simultaneously exposed as a closet homosexual. This last charge was trumped up and involved deliberately mistaking Fritsch for someone else. In a late-night interview with Hitler, Rundstedt demanded a court of inquiry to exonerate Fritsch, while refusing to countenance Reichenau as Fritsch's replacement. In the end, he agreed on General Walter von Brauchitsch. Fritsch was subsequently exonerated, insisting via Rundstedt on fighting a duel with Heinrich Himmler, whose subordinate Reinhard Heydrich had orchestrated the charges against him. The challenge was never delivered.

During the Munich crisis of late summer 1938 Rundstedt joined other senior generals in warning Hitler that the armed forces were not ready for a European war, although he coldly declined to join in their plans for a coup to overthrow him, describing the plot as 'base, bare-faced treachery'. After helping to occupy the Sudetenland in October 1938, Rundstedt retired with the honorary rank of colonel-in-chief of the 18th Infantry Regiment. But when Hitler set his sights on Poland in 1939, Rundstedt was recalled to undertake the military planning (see opposite).

The attack in the west

After the spectacular success of the Polish campaign, Rundstedt spent a brief spell as military governor of Poland. But after the northwestern 'Warthegau' province and West Prussia were incorporated into Germany and the remnant turned into the 'General Government', Rundstedt was reassigned to the headquarters of Army Group A, one of the commands in the west. Like his colleagues, notably Brauchitsch and Halder, Rundstedt had little enthusiasm for the proposed western offensive against what they took to be formidable Anglo-French forces. He nevertheless silently acquiesced in Hitler's desire to have a war at all costs and his megalomaniac confusion of his own nihilistic destiny with that of the German people. Rundstedt was thus no more than a professional hireling whose job was to turn these fantasies into reality. In the existing version of the war-plan, Case Yellow, little more than a stalemate would ensue after the Germans had ploughed across Holland and Belgium to face British and French

(Opposite) **A German column advances** into Poland, September 1939, the old border marking having been removed.

Gerd von Rundstedt

310

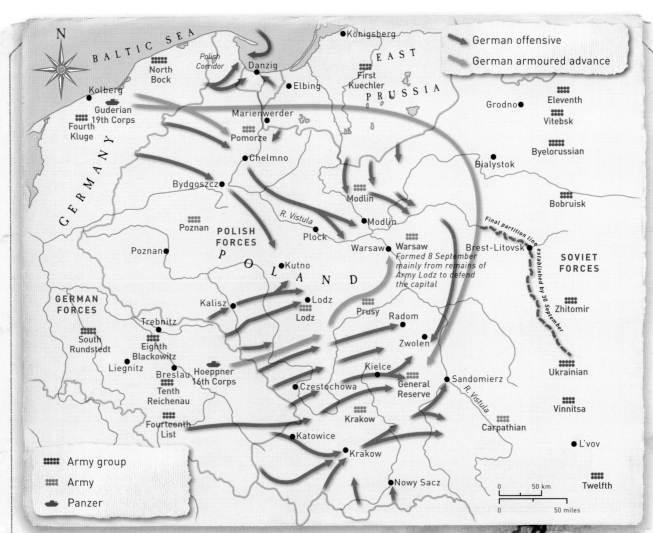

BALTIC SEA

German offensive
German armoured advance

Königsberg

EAST PRUSSIA

Polish Corridor

Danzig • Elbing

North Bock

First Kuechler

Kolberg •

Guderian 19th Corps

Fourth Kluge

Marienwerder

Grodno •

Eleventh

Vitebsk

GERMANY

Pomorze

Chelmno

Byelorussian

Bydgoszcz •

Bialystok

Modlin

Bobruisk

Poznan

R. Vistula

Plock •

Modlin

Final partition line established by 30 September

POLISH FORCES

Poznan •

Warsaw •

Warsaw
Formed 8 September mainly from remains of Army Lodz to defend the capital

Brest-Litovsk •

SOVIET FORCES

P

Kutno •

Zhitomir

O

L

Kalisz •

Lodz •

Lodz

Prusy

Radom •

GERMAN FORCES

Trebnitz •

A

N

D

Zwolen •

Ukrainian

South Rundstedt

Eighth Blackowitz

Liegnitz •

Breslau •

Hoeppner 16th Corps

Czestochowa •

Kielce •

Sandomierz •

General Reserve

R. Vistula

Vinnitsa

Tenth Reichenau

Fourteenth List

Krakow

Krakow •

Katowice •

Carpathian

L'vov •

▦ Army group

▦ Army

🚂 Panzer

Nowy Sacz •

0   50 km

0   50 miles

Twelfth

CASE WHITE:
THE INVASION OF POLAND

IN APRIL 1939 RUNDSTEDT, then aged 64 and officially retired, was given his own 'Working Staff Rundstedt', which operated from his home in Kassel. He was joined in this by Erich von Manstein and Gunther Blumentritt to prepare Case White for the invasion of Poland. By August Rundstedt's little group had mutated into a much larger operational headquarters for Army Group South, then massed on Poland's border. Rundstedt seems to have imagined that this was another example of Hitler's penchant for gambling for high stakes – another bluff or double-bluff like the one a year earlier when the German army had been poised to invade Czechoslovakia before the Munich agreement. But this time it was no bluff. Poland was rapidly enveloped as two armies, one moving southwards from East Prussia and the other northwards from Silesia, thrust towards Warsaw, the aim being to trap the main Polish force west of the Vistula. With a few brilliant modifications necessary to combat unexpected Polish resistance, Rundstedt and Bock's army groups invested Warsaw. After Soviet forces had invaded the country from the east on 17 September, Hitler decided to bring the capital quickly to its knees by launching a savage artillery and aerial bombardment. Warsaw surrendered on 28 September, the Polish government having already fled.

Gerd von Rundstedt

forces dug in along the line of the Aisne and Somme. This struck both Hitler and Manstein, who reappeared at Rundstedt's side, as both woefully unambitious and liable to result in high numbers of unnecessary casualties. Rundstedt backed Manstein's more ambitious scheme for a huge armoured thrust through the Ardennes, plans that gave substance to the Führer's own vision. However, Rundstedt also acted as a break on the more headstrong Manstein and Guderian by factoring in more armour and appointing an old-style cavalry commander, Ewald von Kleist, to command the armoured group.

As the invasion of France got under way in May 1940, Rundstedt was a constant cautious presence, insisting that the armour should not advance too rapidly, while always conscious of the need to secure the German flanks against the French commander Gamelin's possible counter-attacks. Hitler was sufficiently impressed to let him have his way. The Luftwaffe, rather than Rundstedt's armour, would take on the task of obliterating the British evacuating Dunkirk, while Rundstedt and Bock would concentrate on pushing ahead towards Paris. By 17 June Philippe Pétain was ready for an armistice. A couple of days later an exhilarated Hitler announced the promotion of twelve generals, including Rundstedt and his rival Reichenau, to the rank of field marshal. From their headquarters at Fontainebleau, the German General Staff turned its collective imagination to Operation Sealion, the invasion of Britain, it being envisaged that Rundstedt's Army Group A would seize a 100-mile bridgehead along the marshes and levels of Kent and Sussex. This was dropped in favour of seeing what Goering's Luftwaffe could achieve in the skies of Britain. In the event, the German Few fell like flies to the larger Few of the Royal Air Force in the Battle of Britain (July–September 1940).

Barbarossa and Army Group South

While other senior colleagues were relocated east, Rundstedt was made commander-in-chief in the west, in charge of all Wehrmacht forces in Belgium, France and Holland. He may have savoured the fact that Field Marshal Reichenau was now his subordinate. On 31 January 1941 Brauchitsch informed Bock, Leeb and Rundstedt that they were the

Gerd von Rundstedt

designated group commanders for Operation Barbarossa, the greatest land invasion the world has ever seen. Rundstedt was to lead Army Group South, operating between the Pripet Marshes and the Crimea. The aim was to encircle and destroy Russian forces near the border, where neither new post-1939 defences had been built nor the old 1918 ones dismantled. Rundtstedt began marshalling his enormous forces on the Polish border. At a meeting of senior officers on 30 March 1941 Hitler made it clear that they would be waging a war to exterminate a political system, and that their 'quaint' notions of chivalry no longer applied. Rundstedt's reaction to this was unrecorded, as was his response to the matrix of 'criminal orders' that set the moral parameters for this campaign. Soviet political officers were to be summarily executed, while German troops were absolved of any responsibilities towards the Soviet civilian population. The army was to extend full cooperation to the SS *Einsatzgruppen*, which flitted about with the sole purpose of killing Jews. There is no evidence that Rundstedt demurred.

Barbarossa commenced in the early hours of Sunday 22 June, after Rundstedt and his two colleagues had signalled the codeword 'Dortmund' to the three army groups. Forty-three German and fourteen Romanian divisions jumped off as Army Group South; their opponents comprised eighty-nine Soviet divisions in two army groups. Since Stalin imagined that Hitler would concentrate on the economic resources of the Ukraine, rather than the political target of Moscow, he had focused his forces in the south and sent General Georgi Zhukov, one of his top commanders, to oversee them. A direct result of this was that Rundstedt had to scale down plans for a vast

German soldiers round up Polish Jews for forced labour, 1939. The war in the east, in which Rundstedt played such a leading role, was to see the German military abandon the humane treatment of civilians.

encirclement of Soviet forces in favour of the rapid seizure of Kiev and the trapping of a relatively small Soviet force after the main one had escaped. The surrender of 100,000 Russian troops was small beer in comparison with what took place elsewhere during Operation Barbarossa.

After Hitler had decided to concentrate on economic goals in the north and south, Rundstedt's southern army group pressed southwards towards the Crimea and into the area between Kharkov in the north and Rostov-on-Don in the south, the gateway to the oil of the Caucasus. Hitler's SS bodyguard, the SS-Leibstandarte, took Rostov on 21 November, although they were forced out by a Russian counter-attack and the Germans had to fight their way back in once more. When Rundstedt expressly contemplated withdrawal, Hitler replaced him as army group commander with the more biddable Reichenau. Ill after a heart attack, Rundstedt experienced that rare thing, an apology from Hitler, after Sepp Dietrich, commander of the SS-Leibstandarte, admitted to Hitler that the only alternative to retreat from Rostov would have been the annihilation of its four divisions. Rundstedt declined to spend the large cash sum that accompanied the apology. In January 1942 he had the satisfaction of representing Hitler at Reichenau's funeral after his rival had suffered a fatal stroke.

Defending Fortress Europe

In the summer of 1942 Rundstedt was appointed to command Army Group D, based in the occupied zone of northern France, and also given overall command of the whole of the western theatre. Rundstedt managed to sustain good relations with Pétain – he spoke good French – even as he carried out Operation Anton (November 1942) in which the Germans occupied the whole of Vichy France as a precaution against an Allied landing on the Mediterranean coast.

He also oversaw the construction of the vast Atlantic Wall, designed to repel invaders from the west, while at the same time suffering from a constant depletion of his own forces to sustain Germany's flagging efforts on the Eastern Front, a process he warned would result in a worrying inferiority vis-à-vis the Allied forces massing in England for a cross-Channel invasion. In return for men sent east to fight the Soviets he received low-grade 'eastern troops' – Ukrainian and Russian conscripts and collaborators who made up one in six of 'German' forces in France. Many German units also consisted of men aged over 30 or with similar categories of wound or ailment, so that entire battalions had men with stomach problems. The size of a German division had also shrunk from an average of 17,000–18,000 men earlier in the war to a notional 13,000. To correct all this, in November 1943 Hitler despatched the dynamic Erwin Rommel, at 51 the youngest German field marshal and eighteen years Rundstedt's junior –

A German soldier stands guard on the Atlantic Wall. In 1942 Rundstedt assumed overall command of the western theatre, and oversaw the construction of this great line of coastal defences.

Rundstedt referred to him as 'Marschall Bubi', roughly meaning 'Marshal Laddie'. The two men fundamentally disagreed as to whether it would be better to mass German armour near the beaches, so as to wipe out the Allies while their boots were still wet, or to keep armour in reserve to be deployed in a major engagement should the Allies break out from their beachheads. This last strategy left the tank forces vulnerable to Allied air attack should they seek to move any distance. Rundstedt was then effectively made Hitler's cipher when the dictator assumed overall command of the army in the west.

When the invasion came in June 1944, the German defences were overstretched, having been deceived by the Allies into thinking that the landing would take place further north. After losing the argument with Hitler about how to regroup to combat the invasion, Rundstedt received a letter regretfully accepting his (spurious) resignation on health grounds. The addition of Oak Leaf Clusters to his Knight's Cross was supposed to soothe the sting of this rude dismissal.

> 'In future the word will be "as characterless as a German bureaucrat, as godless as a Protestant minister, as unprincipled as a Prussian officer".'
>
> EWALD VON KLEIST-SCHMENZIN, IN 1934

Within weeks, in the wake of the failed July bomb plot, Rundstedt was back in harness, presiding over the court of honour that discharged fifty-five senior officers allegedly involved in the conspiracy so that they would be liable to a degrading execution after 'trial' before Roland Friesler's People's Court. Many of his colleagues never forgave Rundstedt for playing this part in Hitler's gruesome revenge, and there was more than a whiff of hypocrisy as Rundstedt delivered the eulogy after the enforced suicide of his colleague Erwin Rommel, who had also been implicated in the plot. In September, in return for these political services, Rundstedt was reinstated as commander-in-chief in the west, not at Fontainebleau, but at Arensberg outside Koblenz, a dismal reminder of the pass to which Hitler had brought Germany. Although exhaustion and overextended supply lines accounted for the Allies' sudden halt in October 1944, even the Allies' own popular press attributed this to Rundstedt's skills as a generalissimo, greatly exaggerating the one undoubted German victory achieved by Model at Arnhem, when he temporarily routed a combined airborne operation. The Allies also attributed to Rundstedt the initially devastating Ardennes offensive (16 December 1944 – 25 January 1945), although he had little or nothing to do with its conception. By March 1945, with US forces pouring across the Rhine at Remagen, Hitler decided that Rundstedt was too old for the job and replaced him with Field Marshal Albert Kesselring.

Rundstedt was captured by US troops on 1 May 1945 while recuperating in a hospital based at the SS training school of Bad Tolz in Bavaria. He claimed that only lack of fuel and airpower had stopped him repelling Operation Overlord, the Allied invasion of northwest Europe. Rundstedt was imprisoned in the 'Ashcan' holding centre for key captives near Spa in Belgium before being transferred, with his English-speaking son Gerd for company, to Camp 11 at Bridgend, near Swansea, in Wales. He was able to convince the Allies that, despite his rank, he was not a key player in the decision to go to war or in deciding how that war was conducted. Although he avoided the tribunal for major war criminals, he was kept in captivity for four years as the Allies pondered lesser charges. He was freed on health grounds in 1949 and settled in a flat above a shoe shop in Celle. He died on 24 February 1953; the officiating cleric spoke of 'the burial of the last great Prussian'.

Gerd von Rundstedt

ERICH VON MANSTEIN

MICHAEL BURLEIGH

1887–1973

ERICH VON MANSTEIN was one of Nazi Germany's leading generals. He was the architect of Hitler's lightning victory in the west in the summer of 1940, and responsible for a number of brilliant holding operations on the Eastern Front, operations that have received less attention than the more dashing offensives of other generals. Although Manstein did more than most, through his memoirs, to shape the image of the decent Wehrmacht's studious non-involvement in Nazi war crimes and crimes against humanity, nowadays he is thought to have been heavily implicated in both. The new Manstein is a grim figure, far removed from the much-decorated noble knight of his own imagining.

(Opposite) **Erich von Manstein,** although not one of the most dashing generals of the Second World War, was the architect of Hitler's lightning victory in the west in 1940, and in 1943–4 oversaw the first stages of the German retreat in the east.

Manstein was born to command. Fritz Erich von Lewinski was the tenth child of a Prussian artillery general who died during a training accident. Thereafter he was brought up by an uncle, General Georg von Manstein, and his wife Hélène, who were childless. Erich von Manstein, as the boy became, had soldiering in his blood; some sixteen of his ancestors had been generals. One of his uncles was Field Marshal (and future president) Erich von Hindenburg. Manstein progressed swiftly from the prestigious Prussian Cadet Academy to the Imperial War Academy, before serving as a guards officer during the First World War. After being badly wounded, he spent the rest of the war as a General Staff officer on both the Eastern and Western Fronts. By this time he had fully imbibed the ethos and values of the Prusso-German military caste.

Manstein's political views

Generals are never impervious to the politics and prejudices of their age and class, least of all in unsteady democracies or dictatorships. Manstein's military career continued unabated as a Reichswehr officer under the Weimar Republic and then, after January 1933, as an officer in Hitler's Wehrmacht. As a former royal page, Manstein regarded the abdication in 1918 of the Kaiser as the 'collapse of his world' and the Versailles Treaty as an 'act of dishonour'. He detested the party politics of Weimar and welcomed the authoritarian turn that Hitler represented. Although he disliked the purging of

Erich von Manstein

316

officers of Jewish ancestry, since for him caste was everything, Manstein welcomed the broader anti-Semitic thrust of the Law for the Protection of the Professional Civil Service that these measures came under.

By 1936 Manstein had become quartermaster general, traditionally the stepping-stone to becoming Chief of the General Staff, in this case in order to follow Ludwig Beck, and such distant luminaries as Moltke and Schlieffen. Perhaps because of his closeness to disgraced General Werner von Fritsch, Manstein was abruptly posted to command the 18th Infantry Division based in Silesia, although he was careful to maintain his General Staff connections. There he delivered a speech celebrating Hitler's fiftieth birthday, which expressed approval of all the measures the Führer had taken since 1933 and the aggressive revision of Versailles that Hitler envisaged. Manstein fully subscribed to the view that Germany had been deliberately 'encircled' by the Allies, and eagerly supported Hitler's intention to break out of this encirclement with a more robust foreign and security policy.

Manstein played a major role in the illegal German annexation of Austria and the incorporation into the Wehrmacht of its armed forces, and then in the occupation of the Sudetenland in the wake of the Munich agreement of September 1938. During the invasion of Poland, Manstein served as chief of staff under Field Marshal Gerd von Rundstedt, the commander of Army Group South.

The planner

Manstein played a major part in overhauling the outmoded plans for the invasion of France in the summer of 1940 after he was posted to Koblenz in late October 1939. The existing plan, Case Yellow, was a degraded version of the elaborate First World War Schlieffen Plan. Instead of seeking the enemy's encirclement on a vast scale, Case Yellow projected losing up to half a million men in a broad and crude frontal attack designed to hurl the Allies across the Somme. After these losses it would take a further two years for Germany to recover sufficiently to launch an onslaught against France. The strategic pessimism reflected in this plan may have

Erich von Manstein

reflected the desire of key generals to postpone the western invasion at a time when they felt Hitler was leading Germany to disaster. By contrast, Rundstedt's thought was more in line with Hitler's own love of the decisive gesture. To that end he commissioned Manstein to introduce more movement and surprise into projected operations. In this, he succeeded magnificently.

The Fall of France

Backed by Rundstedt, but opposed by Army Chief of Staff Halder, Manstein proposed a plan that Churchill subsequently dubbed the 'Sickle Cut'. Its crucial innovation, which may have been due to a chance intervention by the tank expert Heinz Guderian (see pp. 324–31), was to push armoured formations through the inhospitable terrain of the Ardennes and Eifel, so as to encircle and destroy the main Allied forces on the Channel coast. There were three major thrusts, launched during a spell of such fine weather that Hitler rewarded his chief meteorologist with a gold watch.

In the north Fedor von Bock's Army Group B 'waved its matador's cloak' so as to lure the British Expeditionary Force and the French army in Flanders northeastwards into Belgium, thereby leaving them vulnerable in the rear. To the south, General Leeb's Army Group C would pin down French forces defending the Maginot Line. Lastly, in the centre the forty-four divisions of Rundstedt's Army Group A would traverse the Ardennes, which the French had lightly garrisoned with poor-quality troops, with a view to emerging behind the Allies in the region of Boulogne. Among the factors leading to Allied defeat were the presence of such generals as Guderian and Rommel, and the Luftwaffe's successful coordination of bombers and Stukas with the advancing armoured formations. As a result of these operations, the British were forced to evacuate through Dunkirk, while German forces ploughed forwards and took an undefended Paris on 14 June. Contrary to Halder's gloomy prognostications, it had taken Germany only six weeks and the loss of nearly 30,000 men to take France. Notwithstanding the monumental traffic jams and the reliance on infantry and horses rather than the armoured blitzkrieg of legend, Manstein had been largely responsible for planning this brilliant operation.

> # 'Prussian field marshals do not mutiny!'
> ERICH VON MANSTEIN

Fearing that Manstein was part of a ploy by Rundstedt to achieve operational autonomy, Halder engineered Manstein's posting as commander of the 38th Infantry Corps, even as Hitler approved Manstein's modified version of the plans for the invasion. Halder was given the task of working Manstein's ideas into a fresh master-plan. Three million German troops were subsequently deployed for the invasion, a quarter of them veterans of the First World War aged over 40. Shortly after this victory, Manstein was

Erich von Manstein

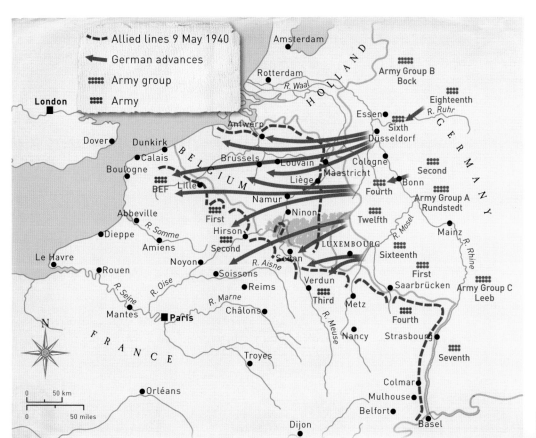

(Below) **German tanks break through French lines** near Sedan, having traversed the rugged terrain of the Ardennes during the German invasion of France, 10 May – 25 June 1940. Manstein was responsible for the bold plan by which German armoured formations pushed through the lightly defended Ardennes, while the main Allied forces were distracted in Belgium and along the German frontier.

made an infantry general and awarded the Knight's Cross to add to his Iron Cross. Even his opponents began to refer to him as a 'military genius', partly so as to cover up their own egregious errors.

Thereafter, Manstein was involved in the planning for Operation Sealion, the proposed German invasion of Great Britain, and the occupation of northern France.

Manstein and Operation Barbarossa

Plans to invade Britain petered out as Hitler convinced himself that the solution to Britain lay in the plains of Russia. In February 1941 Manstein was transferred to command the 56th Motorized Armoured Corps, operating on the Leningrad front. In that capacity his tanks ventured as far as Lake Ilmen, leaving their supply train some 90 miles behind. This led him to be considered a master of wars of movement. What received less attention was that his Operation Northern Light was unsuccessful in taking and destroying Leningrad. Instead, he recommended investing the city and starving its defenders and inhabitants to death. The total absence of moral scruple is noteworthy in a man whose self-image was that of an apolitical soldier – unlike the dastardly ideologues of the SS.

Although he had no direct role in establishing the wider ideological framework for the conduct of the war on the Eastern Front, Manstein was responsible for implementing the various orders that contributed to the barbarous behaviour of German operations in this vast theatre. Following the death of General von Schobert in a plane crash in September 1941, Manstein was appointed commander-in-chief of the

Erich von Manstein

Eleventh Army, which was the most southerly part of Army Group South. Manstein's role was to conquer the Crimean peninsula. In this capacity, he relayed the 'Reichenau Order', which enjoined the Wehrmacht to collaborate in crimes against the Soviet civilian population. This especially applied to the Jews: 'The Jewish-Bolshevik system must be annihilated once and for all. It must never be allowed to interfere in our European living space.' The practical result of this was that Manstein's Eleventh Army fully cooperated with the mass murderers under SS Gruppenführer Otto Ohlendorf of *Einsatzgruppe D*, who slaughtered approximately 90,000 Jews, Gypsies and psychiatric inmates in the course of their operations in the Crimea, relying on the Eleventh Army for both intelligence and logistics. Regular soldiers set up perimeter cordons and were occasionally also involved in the shooting of victims. Ohlendorf would subsequently testify at Nuremberg that relations between the *Einsatzgruppen* and the Wehrmacht were excellent. One document shows how Manstein personally ordered the distribution to his men of wrist-watches looted from 10,000 Jews murdered by Ohlendorf's men in Simferopol. He also vainly tried to reconcile insistence that his troops live from local resources with the political imperative of rallying all non-Bolshevik forces, arguably the single greatest blunder of the entire campaign on the Eastern Front.

From Sebastopol to Stalingrad

Ably assisted by the Romanians, in 1942 Manstein launched a second assault on the harbour fortress at Sebastopol, after he had connived at the downfall of General Count Sponeck by refusing to permit him to withdraw to evade a counter-attacking Soviet pincer movement. In this respect, Manstein behaved exactly like Hitler, who wanted Sponeck shot. In the event, he was tried by court martial and sentenced to six years in jail. Using heavy 60 cm and 80 cm mortars, and heavy bombing raids by the Luftwaffe, in July 1942 the Eleventh Army succeeded in expelling the Soviets from Sebastopol. Manstein was promoted to field marshal. In August he was transferred north to command the ongoing siege of Leningrad: his role, to repulse Soviet attempts to relieve the besieged city.

Against the background of the developing crisis at Stalingrad, in November 1942 Manstein was given command of a new Army Group Don, which included General Paulus's beleaguered Sixth Army, surrounded at Stalingrad by the Soviets and with its supply lines too extended. A relief operation (Winter Storm) was designed to come to the aid of the hapless Paulus, who had never commanded such large formations, let alone under such atrocious conditions. General Hoth would drive his armoured column to within 20 miles of the city, linking up with a force that had managed to break out. In the event, Hitler refused to countenance the break-out until it was too late for it to succeed, and Hoth remained stuck some 30 miles from Stalingrad. The fate of Paulus's Sixth Army was sealed, and the survivors were marched off to camps in Siberia.

Manstein had long sought to introduce more movement into the campaigns on the Eastern Front, while seeking to consolidate the army's command structure under a Chief of General Staff and a commander-in-chief for the Eastern Front, a role he envisaged for himself. This was intended to reduce the role of Hitler in day-to-day military decision-making and led to growing tensions between the two men. Manstein

Erich von Manstein

was also furious that while half the German army was scattered across western Europe waiting for invasions that failed to come, the other half was being hard pressed by the Soviets. Frustrated with Hitler's continuing interference, Manstein trained his pet dachshund Knirps to do the 'Hitler Greeting' with his right paw whenever the dog heard 'Heil Hitler'.

Managing insoluble positions

Great commanders are not always the hard-chargers who dash in to destroy their enemy or occupy his territory. During early 1943 Manstein played a distinguished part in counter-offensives to retake Kharkov and Belgorod, for which he was awarded oak leaves to his Knight's Cross. Although his relations with Hitler were increasingly fraught, especially after Hitler promised and then failed to deliver reinforcements, Manstein took no part in the military conspiracy to assassinate the Führer in the summer of 1944, finding it impossible to reconcile this deed with his soldierly conception of honour. When Claus-Schenk von Stauffenberg elliptically broached his discontent with the Führer, Manstein offered to transfer him to the front in order 'to clear his head'. He also rebuffed an offer to become the conspirators' future Chief of Army General Staff, an offer made by Rudolf-Christian Freiherr von Gersdorff of Army Group Centre, with the riposte: 'Prussian field marshals do not mutiny!'

Strategic withdrawal after Kursk

In the summer of 1943, Manstein led Army Group South in an attempt to pinch off the heavily defended Kursk salient, an operation so vast in scale that Hitler said it made his

Erich von Manstein

German soldiers advancing through burning streets during the recapture of Zhitomir, part of Manstein's counter-attack following his brilliant strategic withdrawal of Army Group South across the Dnepr in late 1943.

stomach turn even thinking about it. Four million troops were involved, along with 13,000 armoured vehicles and 12,000 planes. Manstein clashed with Hitler over the timing of Operation Citadel, as the German attack was codenamed. Hitler wanted it delayed to incorporate new weapons systems, but this merely enabled the Red Army to fortify the salient in prodigious depth. After the Kursk offensive was abandoned, and ignoring Hitler's orders to stay put, in September 1943 Manstein effected a brilliant strategic withdrawal of three of his armies across a 450-mile front. This involved using six bridges to cross the Dnepr, the largest river in Europe. Having executed this manoeuvre, he then counter-attacked around Zhitomir to stabilize the shortened front.

Withdrawal and stabilization were not what Hitler sought. On 30 March 1944 Hitler relieved Manstein of his command of Army Group South, fobbing him off by promising him command of a future western offensive should it come. A more concrete consolation was the gift of a large landed estate, although that could not compensate him for the loss of his eldest son on the Eastern Front. Manstein was relieved of his post and never received another command. He was arrested and interned by British forces in August 1945. Allied courts and the general himself raced to shape the immediate past with a view to how posterity would remember it.

Erich von Manstein

On trial

Manstein was initially summoned as a witness for the Allied prosecution at Nuremberg. He was one of the senior German generals who were required to produce a memorandum clarifying the role of the military under the Nazi dictatorship. The memorandum managed to dispense with such vulgar notions as guilt or responsibility for crimes that by then were well known. Old mentalities were unshakeable. Writing to his wife, Manstein highlighted his own part in ensuring that the Wehrmacht was not condemned as a criminal organization like the SS. This left unexplored the question of who had issued the complex of so-called 'criminal orders' that set the moral parameters on the Eastern Front by licensing mass murder. Manstein's memorandum set in motion the legend that the Wehrmacht had fought a clean and honourable war, despite the worst efforts of the SS to besmirch the image of the German fighting man. This myth largely took hold, despite the fact that between 24 August and 19 October 1949 Manstein himself faced seventeen counts of war crimes before a British military tribunal. Manstein's defence was helped by Soviet efforts to extradite him to face similar charges in Russia, and by Basil Liddell Hart's book *On the Other Side of the Hill*, which included a number of German generals' accounts of the war.

Manstein skilfully played to Western apprehensions in the early Cold War by talking up how the 'Asiatic' character of the fighting affected both sides. He claimed to have identified this as early as 1931 when he observed Red Army manoeuvres under the terms of military cooperation between the USSR and Weimar Republic. Manstein had much public sympathy in Great Britain, Churchill himself feeling sufficiently moved by the general's plight personally to contribute money to his defence fund. Manstein was sentenced to eighteen years in prison for ordering the shooting of Soviet political commissars and prisoners of war, and the abduction and killing of civilians. There was no mention of his role in facilitating *Einsatzgruppen* operations against Jews, Gypsies and the mentally ill. The sentence was reduced to twelve years on appeal; he was released on health grounds on 7 May 1953.

Post-war role

During the 1950s Manstein played a prominent role in advising on the formation of the West German Bundeswehr, while issuing a stream of letters and publications designed to exonerate the wartime Wehrmacht from charges of organized criminality. He died in 1973, having successfully shaped how future generations would think about the war, a feat he achieved through calculated amnesia regarding some of its most horrendous features and by narrowing notions of war down to the conduct of individual commanders and operational issues.

Manstein's role as a planner of the brilliantly successful invasion of France in the summer of 1940 continues to eclipse his indifferent conduct during the defeat at Stalingrad and the defeat of the German offensive at Kursk. Not only did he not stand up to Hitler, but he was clearly involved in facilitating Nazi war crimes, as well as barbarous behaviour towards Soviet civilians. An earlier enthusiasm for the field marshal on the part of his former foes seems remarkably unfortunate. Basil Liddell Hart thought that 'The ablest of all the German generals was probably Field Marshal Erich von Manstein. That was the verdict of most of those with whom I discussed the war, from Rundstedt downwards.' Rundstedt was probably being characteristically modest.

HEINZ GUDERIAN
1888–1954

MICHAEL BURLEIGH

HEINZ GUDERIAN IS CHIEFLY REMEMBERED as one of the great practitioners, and theorists, of armoured warfare, in which tanks, motorized artillery and infantry with close supporting aircraft deliver swift crushing blows to enemy forces. As he once remarked with characteristic bluntness: 'You hit somebody with your fist, and not with your fingers spread!' Guderian first put this doctrine into practice in a remarkably executed motorized dash from Sedan to Abbeville and Calais during the invasion of France in the summer of 1940, an exercise he repeated on a vaster scale during the opening thrusts of Operation Barbarossa into the Soviet Union a year later. Less often remarked is that Guderian was a leading advocate of anti-tank warfare, attaching such dedicated units to his own formidable panzer divisions. He was also one of the few commanders who stood up to Hitler, and almost alone in being dismissed and recalled by the Führer.

(Opposite) **Heinz Guderian,** one of the chief proponents of armoured warfare. He put his ideas into practice with considerable success during the invasion of France in 1940 and during Operation Barbarossa the following year.

Guderian admired the British military historian Basil Liddell Hart (see p. 295), and the latter admired him back. But against Liddell Hart's laudatory view of 'Hurricane Heinz' or 'Speedy Heinz' must be mentioned Guderian's political involvements, the secret gifts and payments he received from Hitler, his alleged ignorance of the 'criminal orders' issued before Barbarossa, his involvements in an arms industry reliant on foreign forced labour, and a number of his own strategic decisions that resulted in disaster. These things have so far not overshadowed his image in the popular imagination as a dashing panzer general.

Heinz Wilhelm Guderian was born in 1888 at Kulm in West Prussia (now Chełmno in Poland), the son of a lieutenant general. He served in the cadets at Karlsruhe before joining Berlin's prestigious War Academy, and during the First World War he served as a signals officer on the Western Front, having taken specialized courses in radio communications. His belief in wars of rapid movement was largely an instinctive response to the paralysed war of attrition he witnessed among the trenches of Flanders. He experienced Germany's collapse in northern Italy, and saw demoralized and bolshevized soldiers in Berlin and Munich first hand. In January 1919 he was posted to a newly

Heinz Guderian

minted 'Eastern Frontier Force', intended to stop Russian and Polish incursions into his Prussian homeland. He was finally posted as a liaison officer between the paramilitary Freikorp's Iron Division and the General Staff.

Views on armoured warfare

After the abandonment of the Baltic States to a precarious independence, Guderian entered the Reichswehr, becoming part of its covert General Staff, an institution proscribed by the Treaty of Versailles. Successive Reichswehr leaders sought to circumvent this and other restrictions on Germany's armed forces by modernizing them instead. In 1922 Guderian was appointed to investigate the possibilities of motorized warfare, to which end he studied the available technical literature, and (being able to read English and French fluently) monitored British experiments in using massed tank formations controlled by radio telephony – the British were pioneers of linking radios through a common frequency into what was called a 'net' work. By 1933 Guderian was a full colonel, convinced that in future conflicts rapid thrusts by independent armoured formations, commanded aggressively by leaders linked to tanks by radio, would be able to win the day by attacking the flanks and rear of the enemy or by chasing them when they fled. The fate of the formation's own flanks was an irrelevance given the mobility of these formations. His superiors had other ideas. When told that Guderian wished to lead 'from the front by wireless', General Ludwig Beck replied, 'Nonsense! A divisional commander sits back with maps and a telephone. Anything else is utopian.'

Legend has it that during an exercise involving Mark 1 tanks at Kummersdorf Guderian so impressed Hitler that he exclaimed 'That's what I need! That's what I want to have!' In fact, it is doubtful whether Hitler would have seen much potential in the glorified tractors or lorries with fake wooden turrets he saw that day. When it came to rebuilding the armed forces, Hitler favoured the Luftwaffe, and continued to think in conventional terms of artillery, infantry and cavalry, with armour only there in support.

Through sheer persistence, Guderian was able to force through building programmes that delivered light and medium tanks in sufficient numbers to make a plausible case for armoured warfare. He conducted the first exercise involving controlling tanks by radio telephony in 1935. In October of that year Hitler commissioned him to establish three tank divisions. A year later Guderian was promoted to major-general, and in 1937 published *Achtung – Panzer! The Development of Armoured Forces, Their Tactics and Operational Potential*, a book that propagated his theories of armoured warfare. Tanks, Guderian wrote, would be the spearheads of armoured battle groups. These would take pivotal positions, using anti-tank guns to ward off counter-attacking armour, before moving on for another thrust. The following year he was promoted to chief of mobile troops, commanding all tanks and motorized forces in the Wehrmacht, a mixed blessing since it was part of a ploy by the more senior 'Gunners', Commander-in-Chief of the Army Walther von Brauchitsch and General Ludwig Beck, to sideline him.

Field commander in Poland and France

In September 1939 Guderian commanded the 19th Panzer Corps in the invasion of Poland, his field of operations including his birthplace at Kulm. Fighting in difficult country, his tanks rapidly took their objectives, and Guderian was politically astute enough to advertise these triumphs when Hitler arrived on a tour of inspection. In eight days Guderian had advanced 100 miles to Brest-Litovsk.

Already distinguished by his role in Poland, Guderian played a crucial part in the reformulation of Case Yellow, the plan for the invasion of France, since he confirmed to his relative Wilhelm Keitel, head of the Wehrmacht High Command, that it was possible to take tanks through the intractable terrain of the Ardennes, where roads were few and of poor quality. At a final planning session, Hitler asked Guderian what he intended to do after he had crossed the Meuse. Guderian replied: 'I intend to advance westwards ... In my opinion the correct course is to drive past Amiens to the English Channel.' When the invasion came in May 1940, Guderian commanded a lead armoured formation in the thrust performed by Army Group B into France. There were constant rows as his more cautious superiors kept halting his forward advance in fear that such extended lines might be subject to attack on the flanks. One row led to his resigning on the spot, only to resume his command a few hours later when a compromise was reached, by which his tanks were allowed to carry out probing reconnaissance. Similar equivocations at the highest level prevented Guderian from delivering a killer blow to the Allied forces that had fallen back at Dunkirk. He blamed his senior rival, the mediocre Günther von Kluge, rather than Hitler for this fateful decision to spare the British from annihilation.

By way of reward, Hitler created a special Panzer Group Guderian, enabling the general to have giant 'Gs' painted on the vehicles of this two-corps armoured formation. He was promoted to colonel general, becoming one of the licensed idols in Goebbels's propaganda campaigns. A tough-looking man in a leather coat, Guderian was a master of pithy sayings, like 'Kick them, don't spatter them' or, as his tanks surged forward, 'Anyone for a ticket to the final station?' It was at this crucial juncture that Guderian claimed to have favoured a German Mediterranean strategy rather than an attack on Russia. According to this view, Germany should have concentrated on driving the British from Gibraltar, Malta, North Africa and Suez, thereby perhaps forcing Churchill's resignation and the appointment of a government more amenable to a peace deal. After picking off the British, the Germans could then have turned on Russia while the USA stood by. But Hitler was intent on opening a war on two fronts, and, despite his reservations, Guderian ended up playing a key role in the overwhelmingly successful early stages of Operation Barbarossa in the summer of 1941.

Operation Barbarossa

Ironically, the master of fast-paced mechanized warfare was initially deeply sceptical about the advisability of Germany fighting a two-front war by invading the USSR. Guderian later recalled that 'When they spread a map of Russia before me I could scarcely believe my eyes.' He thought his superiors were mad in thinking they could defeat Russia in a couple of months, especially by relocating captured French tanks to conditions for which they were unsuitable. He went so far as to express his reservations in writing to the chief of staff, Brauchitsch, who ignored him. When he realized that Hitler was hell-bent on this strategy, Guderian immediately began an intensified training programme for his own armoured divisions, while pressing the armaments minister, Fritz Todt, for enhanced production of mechanized vehicles. Guderian demanded monthly tank production be raised from 125 to 800, then to 1,000 vehicles. This was impossible to fulfil in the light of Germany's other commitments.

When Operation Barbarossa began, on 22 June 1941, Guderian commanded his own independent panzer group, consisting of three panzer corps, within Field Marshal Fedor von Bock's vast Army Group Centre. Guderian's formation had some 850 tanks when it set off from Brest-Litovsk on its fifteen-day journey to the Dnepr in the heat and dust of Russia's endless plains. Beyond lay further rivers to cross, including the Desna and the Oka. The strategy of leading from the front meant that Guderian was almost captured by the Russians on the third day of the attack. Throughout the advance, Guderian and his superior Kluge constantly bickered, with Kluge flying in to Guderian's HQ to insist that he halt on the Dnepr so that the infantry could catch up. This time Guderian got his way, and his forces crossed the river, destroying Soviet forces around Mogilev and taking Smolensk on 15 July. (It was there that they seized the entire archives of the local Communist Party, which when eventually captured by the Americans, would shed unique light on the inner workings of the Soviet Union.)

Guderian forged ahead towards Gomel, encircling and destroying some ten Russian divisions along the way. However, by mid August, although millions of prisoners had been taken, there was no sign of an end to the millions of replacements that the Soviets were putting into the field. At this point Hitler made the fateful decision to abandon the political objective of Moscow in favour of concentrating on Leningrad, the Crimea and the Ukraine.

After mid August, when Hitler abandoned his plan to advance on Moscow, German momentum in the centre was halted in favour of a defensive posture, while all efforts were concentrated on the wings. Guderian endeavoured to remonstrate with Hitler to stick with the original objective, but found himself alone in a room with more senior generals nodding in agreement with their Führer.

Operation Barbarossa, 22 June – 17 July 1941. Grenadiers of the 3rd Tank Division 'Totenkopf' ('death's head') during a break in the fighting near Smolensk.

Heinz Guderian

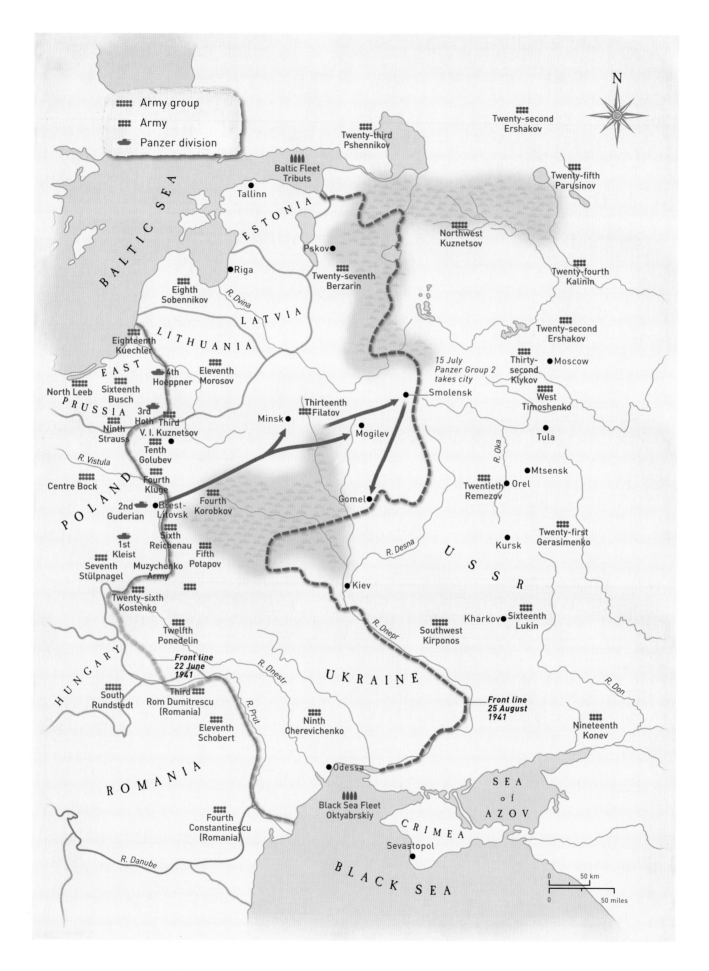

Army group

Army

Panzer division

N

BALTIC SEA

Twenty-second
Ershakov

Twenty-third
Pshennikov

Baltic Fleet
Tributs

Tallinn

ESTONIA

Twenty-fifth
Parusinov

Pskov

Northwest
Kuznetsov

Riga

Eighth
Sobennikov

R. Dvina

LATVIA

Twenty-seventh
Berzarin

Twenty-fourth
Kalinin

LITHUANIA

Eighteenth
Kuechler

Twenty-second
Ershakov

EAST

4th
Hoeppner

Eleventh
Morosov

Thirteenth
Filatov

15 July
Panzer Group 2
takes city

Smolensk

Thirty-
second
Klykov

Moscow

North Leeb

Sixteenth
Busch

PRUSSIA

3rd
Hoth

Third
V. I. Kuznetsov

Minsk

Mogilev

West
Timoshenko

R. Oka

Tula

Ninth
Strauss

Tenth
Golubev

R. Vistula

POLAND

Fourth
Kluge

Mtsensk

Twentieth
Remezov

Orel

Centre Bock

2nd
Guderian

Brest-
Litovsk

Fourth
Korobkov

Gomel

R. Desna

U S S R

1st
Kleist

Sixth
Reichenau

Fifth
Potapov

Kursk

Twenty-first
Gerasimenko

Seventh
Stülpnagel

Muzychenko
Army

Kiev

Southwest
Kirponos

Kharkov

Sixteenth
Lukin

Twenty-sixth
Kostenko

R. Dnepr

Twelfth
Ponedelin

*Front line
22 June
1941*

HUNGARY

South
Rundstedt

Third
Rom Dumitrescu
(Romania)

R. Dnestr

UKRAINE

*Front line
25 August
1941*

R. Don

Nineteenth
Konev

Eleventh
Schobert

R. Prut

Ninth
Cherevichenko

ROMANIA

Fourth
Constantinescu
(Romania)

Odessa

SEA
of
AZOV

R. Danube

Black Sea Fleet
Oktyabrskiy

CRIMEA

Sevastopol

BLACK SEA

0   50 km

0   50 miles

Heinz Guderian

328

In September, Guderian took his tank forces southwards to encircle Russian forces defending Kiev. They captured 660,000 men. The ease with which that was accomplished persuaded Hitler to resume the thrust to Moscow, fatally underestimating the reserves he would need to bring up to accomplish this. Despite having only a quarter of the tanks that he had started off with in June, Guderian was a firm supporter of this renewed thrust. In October Hitler duly ordered the resumption of the attack on Moscow, at a time when the weather was already inauspicious and Stalin was bringing fresh troops from Siberia more than able to cope with the freezing temperatures descending on western Russia. For a time the Germans benefited from the element of surprise; when Guderian's tanks attacked Orel, the trams were still crawling along its streets.

But the seemingly unstoppable advance encountered stiff resistance at Mtsensk. There Guderian's formations were hard pressed by new T-34 Russian tanks, which outclassed his panzers on poor ground. He immediately ordered studies of captured T-34s and demanded anti-tank guns capable of destroying them. At Tula, Guderian again encountered fierce resistance. In letters to his wife he wrote of the atrocious weather, the inadequate denim clothing worn by his men, and the paralysing lack of fuel, as his logistics lines stretched further and further.

By the opening days of December Guderian was forced to withdraw as the 1st Guards Cavalry Corps counter-attacked. Flying back to Hitler's headquarters at Rastenburg in East Prussia, Guderian pleaded for a tactical withdrawal. 'Positional warfare in this unsuitable terrain will lead to battles as material as in the First World War,' he explained. 'We shall lose the flower of our officer and NCO corps. We shall suffer huge losses without gaining any advantage. And these losses will be irreplaceable.' Having earlier praised Guderian's hands-on approach to leading from the front, Hitler now said his angle of vision was too restricted to the front. German troops came within 18 miles of central Moscow before the attack petered out through lack of reserves and matériel. At minus 34 degrees Centigrade it was so cold it was impossible to dig in, while motor oil congealed.

Germany had suffered its worse setback since 1918, and a defeat of such magnitude that it permanently crippled its prospects of victory in Russia. Guderian was partly responsible for that fateful decision. He imagined that the Soviets were at the end of their capacities and were scraping the barrel to put new forces together. In fact they had an almost infinite supply of fresh manpower, and had relocated their industries

(Opposite)
THE EASTERN FRONT,
22 June – 25 August 1941.

Guderian's panzers advance on Moscow as the bitter Russian winter sets in. Stiff resistance from superior Russian T-34 tanks, combined with the freezing conditions and a lack of reserves and matériel, meant that the attack petered out in December 1941.

eastwards beyond the Urals to churn out sturdy no-nonsense weaponry to fight the more fancily equipped Germans – who would soon suffer critical shortages of spare parts as well as of men and fuel.

Dismissal and return

On 24 December 1941 Guderian's arch foe Kluge accused him of an unauthorized withdrawal that had inadvertently left a gap of 25 miles between German positions. The following day – Christmas Day – Hitler dismissed Guderian from his command. By January 1942 the Wehrmacht had suffered nearly a million losses – wounded, captured, missing or dead – or about 29 per cent of the 3.2 million men involved in the opening phase of Barbarossa. By then the Wehrmacht had been pushed back nearly 200 miles west of Moscow, and the Soviet leadership had quietly returned from whence they had fled.

After recovering from a heart attack, Guderian spent the next fourteen months inactive. In October 1942, Hitler gave Guderian a sum of money sufficient for him to purchase Dneipenhof, an estate in the so-called Warthegau area of occupied Poland from which the original Polish owners were evicted. This was in addition to the 2,000 Reichsmarks a month Guderian received from Hitler to top up his officer's pay, not to mention the family estate at Gross-Klonia, also in the Warthegau, which the Guderians had retrieved in 1939.

Guderian (middle) examines a new Tiger tank during a visit to the SS Tank Grenadier Division 'Adolf Hitler' on the Eastern Front, April 1943. Guderian's withdrawal before Moscow in December 1941 had led to his dismissal by Hitler, but he was recalled in March 1943 as inspector general of armoured troops.

Guderian was recalled on 1 March 1943 as inspector general of armoured troops, reporting directly to Hitler. Within a month of his appointment he had raised the monthly production target from 600 to 1,955 tanks. Together with Speer he raced against the clock to take new tanks like the Tiger through their teething troubles or to 'up-gun' existing vehicles. He spent much time touring arms factories, making informed suggestions as to how to improve design from the point of view of the tank crews – he knew how to drive a tank and to fire its guns. During none of these tours of arms factories did Guderian appear to notice their mounting dependence on foreign forced labour. Simultaneously he tried to dissuade Hitler from such follies as prematurely attacking entrenched Soviet defences at Kursk.

Chief of the General Staff

Having rebuffed one set of military conspirators in 1942–3, Guderian declined to take part in the July 1944 attempt to assassinate Hitler. He spent 20 July, the day Stauffenberg's bomb failed to kill the Führer, shooting roebuck on his estate, ensuring that he remained incommunicado. In the gruesome aftermath, he was appointed to the Court of Honour that cashiered the surviving plotters prior to their trial before a

People's Court. In return for his loyalty, Hitler appointed Guderian Chief of the General Staff, although the status of the position had been much degraded. In his new role Guderian gave a radio broadcast in which he called for a National Socialist officer corps led by General Staff officers who should 'exhibit the thoughts of the Führer'.

Despite this public loyalty, there were epic clashes between Guderian and Hitler, under the silent gaze of the ambient sycophants at Hitler's headquarters. Again and again Guderian told Hitler to evacuate troops trapped in the Courland pocket, and to deploy them elsewhere. Hitler refused, claiming they were holding up larger Russian forces. Guderian also realized that the Ardennes offensive – an attempted re-run of his own earlier triumphs – was misconceived, and tried to have it broken off when it failed, so as to reinforce the crumbling Eastern Front. There were endless rows about the appointment, performance, dismissal or promotion of various generals – questions of personality that frittered away valuable time amidst gossip and innuendo.

Things came to a head on 28 March 1945, when Hitler insisted on dismissing General Theodor Busse for failing to defend Kustrin. He inveighed against the army, the General Staff, the officer corps and the generals. Guderian responded by criticizing Hitler's military leadership and his heartless abandonment of the inhabitants of eastern Germany to the invading Red Army. He insisted that a senior army figure be appointed to Himmler's incompetent SS staff. Hitler was so incandescent with rage that onlookers thought he might physically hit the general. After being restrained, Hitler said 'Colonel General Guderian, your physical health requires that you immediately take six weeks' leave.' By the time that period had elapsed, Hitler had committed suicide. At the end of the war Guderian was taken into captivity by the Americans. The Poles tried to extradite him, but he never faced war crimes trials. He was released from US custody in 1948. Guderian died on 14 May 1954 at the age of 65.

> **'Your operations always hang by a thread.'**
> FIELD MARSHAL GÜNTHER VON KLUGE

Assessment

Guderian was one of the most important advocates of armoured mechanized warfare, and a distinguished commander of such forces in the field. Whereas Hitler initially regarded such formations as part of a gigantic bluff to convey the impression of huge armed might, Guderian wanted to build them up into the real thing – a formidable fighting force capable of smashing through the enemy's weak points. With dash and flair bordering on recklessness, he was one of the commanders responsible for Germany's victory in the west in the summer of 1940. A year later he essayed similar rapid advances over the much greater expanses of Russia, despite fully realizing the likelihood that these would simply peter out as the bitter Russian winter set in and the enemy's enormous potential resources came into play.

Guderian was certainly not afraid to speak his mind to Hitler, let alone to his own commanders, but this sits curiously with the fact that he was happy to accept covert bribes and pay-offs, which more honourable figures like Rommel declined. There is also the disturbing detachment in his memoirs regarding unspeakable atrocities committed within areas where his forces were operational. Conversations overheard during his captivity indicate that Guderian thought that National Socialism was a fine idea misapplied.

Heinz Guderian

'In the absence of orders, go find something and kill it.'

ERWIN ROMMEL

ERWIN ROMMEL

1891–1944

MICHAEL BURLEIGH

IN THE 1951 FILM *The Desert Fox*, Erwin Rommel was portrayed by the British actor James Mason as a noble knight in armour, disdainful of Nazi fanaticism. Ironically, Rommel was himself a bit of a film star, having figured prominently in Goebbels's film *Victory in the West*, and subsequently had one of the limping propaganda minister's experts permanently attached to his staff to keep his image well burnished. The real Rommel – the youngest German field marshal of the Second World War – was undoubtedly one of the most charismatic figures of that conflict, and even his most prominent opponents, including Churchill, Montgomery and Patton, became transfixed by him, to the point of obsession. Among the qualities of a great general that Rommel possessed was the ability to colonize the mind of his enemy – to the extent that Churchill grew tired of hearing his name.

During the First World War Rommel had achieved a highly distinguished record as a combat commander, demonstrating enormous initiative and courage even after being wounded. Although he was the author of a book on infantry warfare – studied by General Patton among others – during the invasion of Poland in 1939 he quickly appreciated the importance of tanks, and went on to reveal as much skill in strategic retreat as in offensive operations. His mystique was further enhanced by his relative youth and by the nobility of his death in 1944 in the wake of a failed attempt to kill Hitler.

But how much of this stands up to critical scrutiny? Was it possible for any senior member of the German armed forces to insulate themselves from Nazi criminality? Did the war in the desert simply involve the British, Germans and Italians, with no reference to the surrounding Arabs? Despite the glamorous image of a man of action – the sunburned face, the dusty cracked lips, the crow's feet from screwing up his eyes in blinding light, the penchant for shooting gazelle with a sub-machine-gun from his staff car – Rommel was a prematurely sick man, suffering from depression, headaches, insomnia, low blood pressure, rheumatism and stomach trouble. A complex figure then, if not the matinée idol set up with the collusion of his former enemies.

Erwin Rommel

The birth of a legend

Rommel was not a scion of the Prussian Junker caste used to the carmine stripe down their generals' trouser legs, but rather the son of two Swabian schoolteachers from a small town near Ulm in Württemberg. He was a short, shy boy, who just managed to pass the secondary-school leaving certificate or *Abitur*, without which it was impossible to become an officer in the German army. He joined the 124th Infantry Regiment as a cadet in 1910, and a year later was promoted from NCO to lieutenant. Rommel was a brave and physically tough soldier rather than a military bureaucrat. Upon the outbreak of the First World War he took part in the advance to the Marne, where he led his men into a fire-fight with French troops in the hamlet of Bleid. He was wounded in the thigh in September 1914 after taking on three French soldiers, despite having run out of ammunition. For this he received the Iron Cross second class. In early 1915 he stormed a French position and repulsed a counter-attack, for which he received the Iron Cross first class.

Erwin Rommel, the Desert Fox, during the siege of Tobruk, 1941. Even Rommel's enemies found him a charismatic figure: General Bernard Montgomery, commander of the British Eighth Army in North Africa, kept a portrait of him on his wall.

Rommel's future genius is partly attributable to the fact that he did not spend the entire war grimly stuck in the trenches of the Western Front. His war was more mobile and varied. Wounded again in the leg, Rommel was transferred to a newly formed mountain unit, which was deployed in the Vosges and then sent to Romania. In two separate operations, he captured 400 prisoners, moving on to take heavily defended enemy lines, while personally sustaining a wound in the arm. Transferred to the Isonzo front, he played a key role in the Austrian victory at Caporetto (1917). Constantly active for fifty hours non-stop as he took Monte Matajur with a single battalion, Rommel captured a total of 150 Italian officers, 9,000 soldiers and 81 artillery pieces. For this he received the *Pour le Mérite* decoration and promotion to captain. His next exploit involved swimming the River Piave with six men in order to surprise an Italian garrison in the village of Longarone. The garrison duly surrendered.

In view of this remarkable war record, Rommel was selected as one of the 4,000 German officers kept on after the Treaty of Versailles in the drastically scaled-down Reichswehr. By October 1929 he was an instructor at the infantry school in Dresden, where a book based on his combat experiences became a Weimar bestseller. By 1937 he was a full colonel, director of the war college at Wiener-Neustadt, the army's liaison officer to the Hitler Youth and from time to time head of Hitler's military security battalion. In August 1939 he became a major-general, attached to Hitler's field headquarters and in charge of the dictator's safety. This should give us pause regarding Rommel's alleged anti-Nazi sympathies, which did not extend to the miracle-working Führer. For although

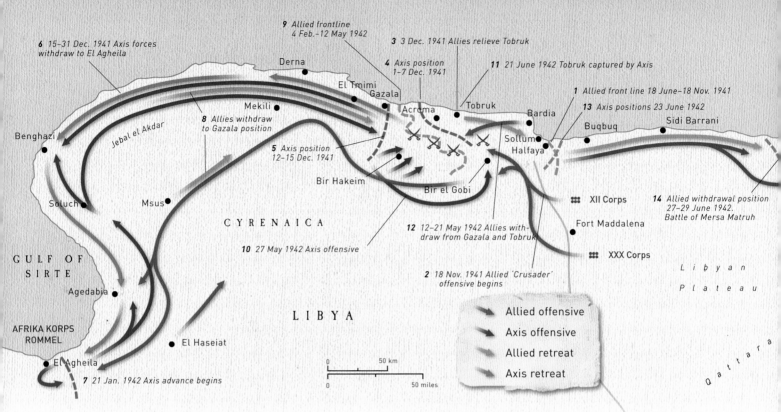

THE AXIS CAMPAIGNS IN NORTH AFRICA, June 1941 – August 1942.

Rommel had reservations about Nazism, this was counter-balanced by admiration for the dynamic dictator, especially since the latter had evaded the military restrictions of Versailles and rebuilt the armed forces as a pillar of restored German might. Hitler admired Rommel in turn as a brave combat soldier and a man whose background was almost as modest as Hitler's own.

After participating in the Polish campaign, in February 1940 Rommel was appointed commander of the 7th Panzer Division based at Godesberg. After rapidly mastering the techniques of armoured warfare, Rommel commanded his men in battle during the invasion of France, always leading from the front regardless of the dangers, and receiving two wounds in the process. Rommel's forte was speed and surprise, so much so that his division was nicknamed the 'Ghost Division': moving at 20–30 miles per hour, his troops captured tens of thousands of prisoners and took Lille within a few days. After an enforced rest and refit, his tanks crossed the Seine near Rouen and pushed the enemy back to Cherbourg, where 30,000 French troops followed Marshal Pétain's order to surrender. In six weeks, Rommel's armoured formation had taken over 100,000 prisoners as well as 450 enemy tanks, in return for modest losses.

Lord of the desert

While the RAF and the Luftwaffe contested the skies over Britain in the late summer of 1940, Hitler's partner in crime, the Italian dictator Benito Mussolini, set about realizing his dream of recreating the Roman Empire in the Mediterranean by attacking the British in Egypt, and later by invading Albania, Yugoslavia and Greece. On 13 September 1940 the Italian army advanced from Libya into Egypt in order to capture the Suez Canal, a vital artery for imperial British interests. Five poorly equipped Italian divisions under General Mario Berti forced the British to retreat until, reinforced, the latter counter-attacked. When the Italians fell back into Tripolitania (northwestern coastal Libya), Hitler rushed in his 5th Light Division to thwart the British; this was the advance guard of the

Erwin Rommel

Map

MEDITERRANEAN SEA

Abu Qir

Mersa Matruh

El Daba
Alexandria
El Alamein
Burg el Arab
El Hammam
Alam Halfa

15 30 June 1942 limit
of Axis advance

16 14–16 and 21–22 July 1942:
Ruweisat battles indecisive.
Front lines stabilize
until 30 Aug. 1942

BRITISH
EIGHTH ARMY
AUCHINLECK

Depression

N   EGYPT

legendary Afrika Korps, the formation that Rommel commanded in a theatre where the Italians were notionally in ultimate charge. Rommel's orders were to prevent the British from expelling the Italians from North Africa entirely. He arrived in the middle of a rout: the British had taken several major centres, including Tobruk, and much of Cyrenaica (eastern Libya), together with 130,000 prisoners. An attack on Tripoli was only averted because General Wavell had to divert a corps to participate in the Allied effort to eject the Germans from Greece.

Rommel's limited remit, established at a meeting with Hitler in March 1941, was to recapture Cyrenaica, with a force that was predominantly Italian. Despite the modesty of this initial aim, Rommel went on to turn North Africa into a theatre that occupied most of the energies of the British. They in turn became obsessed with their wily opponent, nicknaming him 'the Desert Fox'. Without waiting for adequate supplies, Rommel attacked at the end of March, capturing El Agheila, Benghazi, and all of Cyrenaica except Tobruk itself.

Desert warfare had certain unique features. Compared with the vast forces engaged on the Eastern Front, both Allied and Axis armies in North Africa were modest in size. The harsh terrain had its own problems, notably the constant need for water for both men and machines, while the few roads were long and dusty. It is usually claimed that the absence of the SS in this theatre meant that with some exceptions the war was conducted according to the Geneva Conventions, under the curious gaze of the indigenous population. That was not so. The SS *were* present, in the form of the mass murderer SS-Obersturmführer Walther Rauff, a gas expert, and some 2,500 Tunisian Jews died in camps over a six-month period. Moreover, at a political level, the Nazis were heavily involved with Arab nationalists and Islamists, notably the Palestinian Grand Mufti of Jerusalem, whose anti-Semitic exterminatory zeal matched that of Hitler. Had Rommel succeeded in taking the Afrika Korps through Egypt into British-mandated Palestine, it is not difficult to imagine the fate of the 80,000 Jews settled there, since even without such a campaign Jewish population centres were subject to Luftwaffe bombing.

Germany's youngest field marshal

The war in North Africa moved to and fro over vast distances. In late 1941 and early 1942 Claude Auchinleck's Operation Crusader forced Rommel to retreat from Benghazi to Mersa

Rommel (front left) with his officers after a failed British advance near Sollum, May 1941. For eighteen months after his appointment as commander of the Afrika Korps in March 1941, Rommel retained the upper hand over ever-growing Allied forces in North Africa.

A German tank surrenders at the Second Battle of El Alamein, October 1942, the decisive battle that ended Rommel's dreams of linking up with German forces in southern Russia, or even of pushing east to India.

el Brega, where he waited on developments elsewhere that might improve his fortunes. After Field Marshal Albert Kesselring, commander-in-chief of German forces in the Mediterranean theatre, had achieved air superiority off Italy, Rommel's supply lines were more secure: convoys could now cross the Mediterranean carrying heavy armour and anti-tank guns. In January 1942 Rommel launched an attack along the coastal road from El Agheila, taking Benghazi, Derna and the western half of Cyrenaica. While the British geared themselves up for a counter-attack, Rommel struck first with Operation Venezia, destroying the Free French at Bir Hacheim, and then hit the British Eighth Army at Tobruk. The latter lost 260 tanks in one engagement, and 30,000 men were taken prisoner. Hitler promoted the 49-year-old Rommel to field marshal, the youngest in the German army. Instead of pausing to recuperate and waiting for the Axis to seize Malta so as further to secure his supply routes against British air assault, Rommel felt emboldened to push into Egypt in pursuit of the wild dreams of linking up with German forces in southern Russia, or even of conquering India.

These dreams encountered reality at a minor railway stop in the Qattara Depression called El Alamein. There, in July 1942, Rommel's tanks were routed by Auchinleck's guns. Using 'Ultra' intelligence gleaned from Bletchley Park, where teams of British code-breakers had succeeded in unscrambling the German Enigma cipher, Auchinleck directed his counter-attacks at the Afrika Korps's Italian elements, which were thought less resilient than the German units. After an attack at Alam Halfa failed, Rommel dug the Afrika Korps in, anticipating a counter-attack by the man who in August 1942 had replaced Auchinleck as the new commander of the Eighth Army, Lieutenant General Bernard Montgomery. Wracked with illness and despairing about his extended supply lines, his reliance on captured enemy equipment and his Italian allies, Rommel went home on convalescent leave in September 1942. His efforts to persuade Hitler and Mussolini of the gravity of the situation in North Africa came to nought. He began to intimate to his wife his disillusionment with Hitler.

Erwin Rommel

336

The 'panzer graveyard'

On 23 October Montgomery and General Alexander, the new commander-in-chief Middle East, launched the Second Battle of El Alamein, fortified by the addition of 40,000 extra troops from Australia, India and New Zealand and 300 US Sherman tanks (see also p. 343). In all, 200,000 men and 1,000 tanks moved against the Afrika Korps's 100,000 troops and 500 tanks. When Rommel's replacement, General Georg Stumme, died of a heart attack on 24 October, Hitler telephoned Rommel to urge him to resume his earlier command. Rommel anxiously looked on as the Battle of Stalingrad unfolded, aware that only a German victory on the Volga would free sufficient manpower to mount an invasion of Persia, forcing the British to call off the Eighth Army's attack at El Alamein by redeploying their main forces there. His gloom deepened as Allied aircraft succeeded in sinking one after another of his precious supply ships.

On returning to North Africa on 25 October, Rommel found chaos, with his men on half rations and only enough fuel for three more days. The Italian army had been bled white at Stalingrad, and its troops in North Africa were exhausted. They sometimes fought bravely, despite being equipped with rifles of 1890s vintage and grenades that were often lethal to the user; some of the simpler souls wore ribbons on their sleeves to help them distinguish left from right. By the time the Second Battle of El Alamein had come to a close on 5 November, virtually all of Rommel's armour had been wiped out; the battle became known as the 'panzer graveyard'. Hitler had ordered Rommel to 'stand fast'. Instead, Rommel ordered withdrawal.

From El Alamein to the Kasserine Pass

Rommel pulled out of western Egypt in early November 1942 just as US, British and Free French forces landed 1,400 miles to his west in French Morocco and Algeria. Rommel went on to conduct a brilliant fighting retreat to Mersa el Brega. His new orders were to defend Libya at all costs, prior to expelling the Allies from Tunisia. He flew to Hitler's Rastenburg headquarters to remonstrate that this was pointless and

German transports head for the front past a burning US truck during the Battle of the Kasserine Pass, January–February 1943. In the course of the fighting Rommel inflicted a bloody blow to American forces new to North Africa.

Erwin Rommel

that the North African campaign was effectively over. A furious Hitler ignored him.

Back in North Africa, Rommel extricated himself from Libya with a view to linking up with Italo-German forces under Colonel General Jürgen von Arnim installed in a bridgehead in northern Tunisia. Arnim set about securing the passes through the Dorsale mountains in order to effect a junction with Rommel's more southerly forces. This set the scene for what became known as the Battle of the Kasserine Pass, which commenced in January 1943.

Rommel completed moving his Panzerarmee from Libya into Tunisia, where he was to be replaced by the Italian commander General Giovani Messe. With Montgomery paused at the Mareth Line just over the Libyan–Tunisian border, Arnim and Rommel were encouraged by Kesselring to strike in a pincer movement through the Kasserine Pass and on towards the Allies' main supply dump in eastern Algeria. This would kill the Allied presence in Tunisia. Partly because of a lack of coordination with Arnim, in late February Rommel called off his attacks amidst the carnage of the Kasserine Pass.

Although Rommel had given the relatively inexperienced and poorly led Americans a nasty shock, the wider goals of the battle were unrealized. Rommel was briefly appointed commander of the entire Army Group Africa, but this was too late to halt the momentum of Montgomery's Eighth Army. After vainly pleading with Hitler to wind up the entire campaign, Rommel had to watch from the sidelines on sick leave as Montgomery destroyed the Axis forces in Tunisia, taking nearly a quarter of a million prisoners in operations that had a similar effect on Allied morale as Stalingrad.

Defender of Fortress Europe

As the Axis forces in North Africa faced final defeat in May 1943, Rommel was posted to a secret planning group to deal with the contingency of Italy dropping out of the war. After the Allied landings in Sicily in July, Rommel was tasked with the occupation of key nodal points in northern Italy to cover Kesselring's withdrawal from the south. From September 1943 onwards Rommel was based at a headquarters on Lake Garda. He and Kesselring differed as to whether Italy should be defended south of Rome or from Rommel's northern bastion. Hitler supported the overly optimistic Kesselring and appointed him supreme commander in Italy, while assigning Rommel to inspect the coastal defences on the Atlantic in anticipation of further seaborne invasions.

Although Gerd von Rundstedt was the western theatre commander (see p. 314), Rommel was the de facto commander of German forces in the west. In early 1944 he desperately tried to improve the Normandy defences, adding 5 or 6 million mines, together with concrete gun emplacements and clusters of 'Rommel asparagus', high poles designed to impede gliders, while the coastal shallows were covered with underwater obstacles and booby-trap devices. Rundstedt paradoxically became the main advocate of mobile warfare, holding fire-fighting forces in reserve to hit the Allies after they had got a toehold on shore; in contrast, Rommel wanted to spread his forces along the coast so as to massacre the Allies while they were up to their waists in sea water or pinned down on the open beaches. This made greater sense, as total Allied air supremacy meant that all German movements were lethally interdicted. With one field marshal distinguished by age and authority and the other by youthful charisma, Hitler found it impossible to go for one strategy or the other, so the German forces in France ended up labouring under a synthesis of both. Rommel was at home in Germany when, on the morning of 6 June

1944, the Allied invasion of Normandy started. It quickly became evident to him that the Allies were too strong to be dislodged and that it would be best to write off Normandy so as to defend their likely routes into Germany. Hitler refused to countenance this and urged Rundstedt and Rommel to counter-attack. They duly did so, but achieved little apart from losing more men and matériel. Hitler then replaced Rundstedt with Kluge, who rapidly came to the same gloomy conclusions as Rommel.

Death of the Desert Fox

On 17 July 1944 Rommel was badly wounded when two Allied planes attacked his staff car, leaving him with a skull fracture and other injuries. It was while he was recovering from this incident that his name was dropped into the vengeful atmosphere immediately following the 20 July attempt on Hitler's life: Rommel had been spoken of as a substitute head of government who would immediately broker a peace deal with the Western Allies.

While recuperating at home, Rommel received a visit from two generals, who presented him with a stark choice: face a treason trial, or commit suicide. If he killed himself, his wife and son would be left unharmed – a serious threat since the Nazis were murdering the families of many of the plotters. Rommel got into a car with the generals and swallowed a cyanide capsule; his body was incinerated to prevent a post-mortem. With characteristic cynicism, Hitler decreed that the young field marshal, only 53 years old when he died, should be given a state funeral, and insisted that an imposing memorial should be erected over Rommel's grave.

German prisoners captured during the Battle of Falaise, Normandy, August 1944. Rommel was the de facto commander of German forces in the west at the time of the Allied invasion, but his recommended strategy of concentrating forces on the coast was diluted by Hitler.

> '**Casualties are inevitable in war, but unnecessary casualties are unforgivable.**' BERNARD MONTGOMERY

BERNARD MONTGOMERY

1887–1976

ALISTAIR HORNE

FIELD MARSHAL MONTGOMERY has been hailed as the greatest British field commander since Wellington, not a title for which there can be much competition. On the other hand, various details of his career, and particularly his personality, have rendered him one of the most controversial leaders of the Second World War. Over the years his reputation has ebbed and flowed, suffering most of all in the United States – as much through media-oriented criticism as from serious military studies.

Bernard Law Montgomery ('Monty' to detractors and fans alike) was born on 17 November 1887, into a Victorian-Irish family of slender means. His father was a churchman who became Bishop of Tasmania shortly after Monty's birth. His mother, Maud, seems to have been a harsh woman; Monty grew up with little affection from her. He decided on an army career, claiming that he did it to annoy his mother. He could not afford his first choice, the Indian Army, joining instead the less 'posh' Warwickshire Regiment.

When the First World War broke out, Monty was 26, a full lieutenant. In action near Ypres he was shot through the lung by a sniper. Narrowly surviving, he was left short of breath for the rest of his life, hating tobacco smoke. He was awarded the DSO (Distinguished Service Order) and spent the remainder of the war on various staffs. He never forgot what he saw of the incompetence of the British army leaders and their wasteful expenditure of soldiers' lives. Monty ended the war a lieutenant colonel, a rank in which he stuck for two deadening decades. Among the polo-playing officer corps with private means, he came across as a boring misfit, with his single-minded professionalism and pursuit of higher standards. He became friends with another brilliant 'misfit' – the military historian and strategic thinker, Basil Liddell Hart.

In the 'wilderness years' of the 1920s and 1930s, Monty was described as having the 'self-abnegation of a monk'. In 1927, love struck the 40-year-old bachelor. He married Betty Carver; they had one son, David. Betty opened a wider world of culture, affection and fun to Monty, with a softening effect on his austere personality. Then tragedy struck; in 1937, an insect bite turned to septicaemia and Betty died. Monty was inconsolable. With war on the horizon, he once more devoted himself to soldiering, more single-mindedly than ever before. He was now a 50-year-old brigadier, on the verge of retirement. Then, in April 1939, after serving as commander of the 8th Division in Palestine for a year, he was summoned home to take command of the 3rd (Infantry) Division.

The early years of the war

Nicknamed the 'Iron Division', the 3rd was one of the handful of elite British units sent to France in the British Expeditionary Force (BEF) at the outbreak of war. The corps commander was Monty's fellow Irishman and long-time supporter, Lieutenant General Alan Brooke. Monty's self-confidence was immeasurable; he was going to command the most effective division – and he was going to win the war. But the BEF proved dismally unfitted for modern warfare. Monty brought the Iron Division through the retreat from Dun-kirk in excellent fighting order. Back in England, it became the only div-ision with sufficient heavy arms to equip it.

Monty was put in charge of the new V Corps, defending a denuded south of England, and was promoted lieutenant general. His first priority was fitness, 'physical and mental'. Officers had to be 'full of binge'; meaning that 'they must look forward to a good fight'.

Montgomery at a press conference shortly after D-Day. His willingness to speak his mind publicly at all times, and to ignore the niceties of tact and diplomacy, was both a strength and a major weakness throughout his career.

When inspecting troops, he asked them to remove their helmets so that he could see whether or not their eyes showed 'binge', the light of battle. Woe betide the commanding officer if they did not. To a stout colonel whose doctor had warned that an early-morning run would kill him, he observed that he should get it over with, so that he 'could be replaced easily and smoothly'. This robust approach gained Monty the respect of rank-and-file and junior commanders, but it tended to alienate his peers. When command of the battered Eighth Army in North Africa came up in August 1942, he was not Brooke's first choice.

Monty's victory at El Alamein (see opposite and p. 337) was the first turning point in the war. Churchill, however, recognized that it was only the 'end of the beginning'; compared with the titanic battles on the Russian front, it was but a sideshow. Now followed Sicily and the long slog up through Italy, where for a variety of reasons, Monty did not shine. But Alamein had put him on the map as the general who could win. At the end of 1943 he was set in charge of Operation Overlord, the operation to take the Allied armies into northern France in June 1944.

THE BATTLE OF EL ALAMEIN

of his colleagues. He imposed clarity in his battle orders. He built up a massive weight of artillery and – for the first time on the Allied conduct of the war – moved the tactical airforce HQ alongside him. Above all he imbued the whole army, down to the lowliest private, with a sense of 'binge', that they were going to 'hit the enemy for six out of Africa'.

With his stonewall defence at Alam Halfa (30 August – 5 September), Monty blunted Rommel's final bid for Cairo and the Suez Canal. Yet the costly thirteen-day 'rough-house' of Alamein itself (23 October – 5 November), the heavy casualties breaking through the German minefields, were the antithesis of everything Monty stood for. It was 'an untidy battle', but it brought the narrow margin of success. After Alamein, though, Monty's armoured *corps-de-chasse* failed to pursue the success cohesively: an over-cautious pursuit to Tripoli permitted the bulk of Rommel's army to escape. For this failure Monty has been criticized, but as he had admitted in his diary as late as October: '... the training was not good and it was beginning to become clear to me that I would have to be very careful ... that formations and units were not given tasks which were likely to end in failure because of their low standard of training ... I must not be too ambitious in my demands.'

Map

'Trieste' MoT. Div.

Sidi Abd el Rahman

M E D I T E R R A N E A N S E A

28 October

90th Div.

15th Pz. and 'Littorio' Divs.

28-29 October

'Trento' and 164th Divs.

9th Aust. Div.

51st (H) Div.

El Alamein

23 October

1st Arm'd Div.

XXX Corps

27 October

N.Z. Div.

10th Arm'd Div.

Alexandria (65 miles)

4 November
1st, 7th and 10th Armoured Divisions pass through breach

'Bologna' Div.

1st S.A. Div.

X Corps

Minefields

Ramcke Bde

4th Ind. Div.

Ruweisat Ridge

AFRIKA KORPS ROMMEL

Alam Halfa

N

21st Pz. Div.

'Brescia' Div.

BRITISH EIGHTH ARMY MONTGOMERY

XIII Corps

26 October

'Folgore' Div.

50th Div.

0   3 km
0   3 miles

Minefields

Greek Bde

44th Div.

'Ariete' Div.

25 October

7th Arm'd Div.

El Taqa Plateau

'Pavia' Div.

1st F.F. Bde

Qattara Depression

Qaret el Himeimat

ITS MORALE THOROUGHLY SHAKEN, the Eighth Army had been steadily retreating before Rommel since January 1942, and now had its back to the Suez Canal at El Alamein, little more than 100 miles away. Monty was to take over command under General Alexander. The British army as a whole had hardly won one encounter with Hitler's Wehrmacht. Its equipment was inferior, and Eighth Army armoured tactics were not much better: during one terrible Balaklava-style charge in July 1942, the British had lost 118 tanks to three of the enemy.

Churchill persuaded Roosevelt to rush 300 Sherman tanks round the Cape to replace the heavy losses inflicted by Rommel's panzers, and by late October, Monty would have a powerful superiority in weaponry. But more important than matériel was turning around a beaten army. Within three months, Monty's sharp features, like those of an aggressive Jack Russell, were to become the most celebrated in the Western world – to the amazement

Bernard Montgomery

343

Preparations for Overlord

Monty's overall boss was to be General 'Ike' Eisenhower, now nominated Allied Supreme Commander. Ike, a staff officer, had never seen 'the face of battle'. The two did not start off well. At their first meeting, Monty (then still senior in rank) had barked at Ike for lighting up in one of his conferences. Ike, a chain-smoker with a low boiling point, never forgave Monty. Monty's first move was to scrap the existing plans for the invasion with brutal bluntness. He increased the original three-division front to five. Even this was to leave an uncomfortably small margin of elbow-room from which to punch out of the beachheads. What set the limit was the shortage of landing-craft, which were being held back for a subsequent invasion of Mediterranean France, a dispersal of effort pressed upon Churchill by Washington.

An essential ingredient of Overlord was the brilliant deception plan – pushed by Monty – which persuaded German intelligence that the main invasion would take place across the Pas de Calais. It pinned down the powerful Fifteenth German Army, which could otherwise have intervened decisively in Normandy. Apart from overseeing every meticulous detail of the biggest landing operation in history, Monty was responsible for the relentless bombing which would impede German movement of reinforcements across France. Meanwhile, he tirelessly raised 'binge', visiting a division a day, seven a week. Monty got it over to every man of the nervously waiting troops that they would only go in with immense supporting fire, and that they would win.

Montgomery with Allied commander-in-chief Eisenhower before D-Day. Tensions between the two men began prior to D-Day and continued beyond the end of the war, typically expressed by Montgomery thus: 'His ignorance as to how to run a war is absolute and complete.'

More controversial was Monty's presentation of a map of 'phase lines'. To Monty, geographical lines were unimportant; what counted was the destruction of enemy forces within that area. But what would hang like a millstone round his neck was a boastful assumption that Caen, the critical hub on the east of the British/Canadian sector, would be taken on D-Day itself.

Overlord

On 6 June 1944, D-Day, the Allied invasion of Normandy, began (see also p. 368). Five out of eight assault brigades were British and Canadian; two out of the three airborne divisions were American. Of the aircraft deployed that day, 6,080 were American and 5,510 were from the RAF or other Allied contingents; but of the naval force, only 16.5 per cent were American (because of the demands of the Pacific War). The Americans landing on Omaha Beach had the misfortune to encounter a newly arrived German division and suffered horrendous losses. On the British sector, a major success was the capture of Bayeux on D-Day itself. But the failure to secure Caen for another two months was to prove costly; but what, for Monty, proved most disastrous – certainly in the eyes of his US critics – was his boast that 'everything had gone according to plan'.

Montgomery set up his HQ only 3 miles from the German lines. This may have seemed rash but it was a symbol that D-Day had succeeded, the Allies were firmly established – and the war in effect won. Monty exercised a personal and hands-on style of

Bernard Montgomery

command. His use of forward HQs put him supremely in touch with the fighting formations under him, but it left him out of touch with senior staffs back in England. With every setback, the murmurings of Montgomery's many enemies – British as well as American – rose unchecked, and Montgomery was never there to explain his strategy to Eisenhower.

The conquest of Normandy

Events, however, vindicated his strategy of drawing the panzers on to the British front on the east end of the line and wearing them down, preparatory for the American break-out from the west by Patton's fresh US Third Army (see p. 378). Eight out of Rommel's nine panzer divisions were pinned down by British and Canadian armies in the Caen sector. If the Germans could have shifted just one towards Bradley, who had undergone a costly battle to secure Saint-Lô, it would have made his break-out more difficult – perhaps even impossible before August. Holding the 'hinge' aggressively at Caen also prevented any likelihood of intervention from the German Fifteenth Army locked in the Pas de Calais.

Monty fought three hard battles around Caen. Heavy bombers destroyed the medieval city, but the rubble made it difficult for British armour to advance. When he tried to break through the third time, lack of elbow-room – the narrow width of the bridgehead – meant Monty had no room for the massed armour to deploy in the east – also led to failure with brutal tank losses as the thin-skinned Shermans came up against dug-in lines of German '88s. For a while, it seemed there might be a stalemate in Normandy. Under extreme pressure from both the US and the British press, Churchill came close to sacking Montgomery.

At the end of July, however, Patton swung relentlessly towards Paris, and the fleeing remnants of the German armies were smashed in the trap at Falaise. Montgomery has been criticized for not closing the jaws of the trap, allowing a large number of the enemy to escape (though without most of their heavy equipment). Patton claimed that he could have closed the gap from the south, but this is not sustained by his chief Bradley: Patton's forces were simply not strong enough to take such a risk. Nevertheless, Falaise meant the end of the Normandy campaign. The Germans were reckoned to have lost 450,000 men including 210,000 PoWs, more than 20 generals, 1,500 tanks and 3,500 guns. Allied casualties had by no means been light: 209,672, of whom 36,976 had been killed (roughly in a ratio of two British and Canadian casualties to three American), a testimony to how hard the Wehrmacht had fought, despite almost total lack of air support.

'In defeat, unbeatable;
in victory, unbearable.'

WINSTON CHURCHILL ON MONTGOMERY

In strategic terms, the Battle of Normandy was a decisive victory to rank with Stalingrad. And no one can deny the key role Montgomery played in it. As one of his severest critics, Eisenhower's chief of staff Bedell Smith, was to remark of D-Day: 'I don't know if we could have done it without Monty. It was his sort of battle. Whatever they say about him, he got us there.'

The advance on Germany

On 25 August Paris was liberated; on 3 September Brussels. Abruptly, the whole tenor of the war changed. Now the falling-out between Eisenhower and Montgomery began in earnest. Both American and British armies felt that the Germans would collapse as

Bernard Montgomery

A British soldier helps an elderly inhabitant of the shattered city of Caen, close to the British D-Day landing beaches. Allied forces reached the city centre on 9 July, but did not eliminate German resistance in the town until August.

they had in 1918. But the Combined Chiefs of Staff, at a level above Montgomery and Eisenhower, had no contingency plan for the next stage if the Germans did not collapse.

After D-Day, proportions in Allied forces had swiftly changed until by May 1945 the US predominance was to become of the order of three to one. It was inevitable that American public opinion would now insist on Eisenhower as overall land commander, the role Monty had held since Overlord. Great coalition leader though he was, Ike was no strategist. His plans were to advance all the Allied armies to the German frontier, then await opportunity. Montgomery thought this 'broad front' strategy represented a dangerous dispersal of effort. He besieged Eisenhower with his scheme of a 'single thrust' towards the Ruhr and then Berlin, spearheaded by the British armies in the north. Meanwhile Ike was under pressure from Patton for the go-ahead for a single thrust into central Germany across the Saar. History was to prove that Patton and Monty were both right, and wrong: logistically, as well as politically, there were not sufficient supplies even for one 'single thrust'.

Antwerp, Arnhem and the Battle of the Bulge

The disaster at Arnhem in mid September – for which Montgomery was held largely responsible – has been regarded as the key to the disappointing end of 1944. Possibly Eisenhower was at fault in permitting Monty to carry out this uncharacteristically risky operation – while at the same time letting Patton press on at Metz and the Saar far to the south. Yet, strategically, of far greater consequence was the earlier failure to clear the approaches to Antwerp, the largest (and still largely undamaged) port in northwest Europe, straddling the River Scheldt.

To use the port, the approaches on both the Belgian and Dutch sides of the Scheldt estuary would have to be cleared of the enemy. After a lightning advance, Major General 'Pip' Roberts's British 11th Armoured Division had captured most of Antwerp itself by 4 September. Then, running out of fuel and with no further orders, Roberts halted. He claimed later that he could easily have covered the vital 20 miles to secure the Scheldt approaches. For vital weeks, while Hitler's armies regrouped, the Allies were deprived of Europe's biggest port, at a time when most of their supplies were still arriving via the beaches of Normandy 300 miles to the rear. Moreover, the German Fifteenth Army was permitted to escape across the Scheldt, its evacuation across the 3-mile wide estuary in the teeth of Allied air and sea supremacy a feat little

Bernard Montgomery

less remarkable than that from Dunkirk in 1940. These troops would be in position when Montgomery launched his airborne attack on Arnhem on 17 September.

Amazingly, neither Monty nor Ike appreciated the significance of Antwerp. But Alan Brooke also appears to have been blind to it; so too was Churchill. The failure at Antwerp constitutes the single biggest error of the Northwest Europe campaign. Success would have made Arnhem unnecessary.

The gamble of Arnhem had much to do with Montgomery's determination to prove that his strategy of the 'narrow thrust' into Germany from the north was right. As an undertaking, Arnhem had many planning defects; not least, it was a fundamental error to land the British 1st Airborne so far from the vital bridge. But Ike should surely have ordered Monty, after the Liberation of Paris, to go flat out for Antwerp. As it was, the failure at Arnhem left the Allied line stretched northwards, inviting a German counter-thrust. There were not enough reserves available, and Hitler had obtained a breather to create two new panzer armies.

The 'Battle of the Bulge' in the winter of 1944/5, victory wrested out of defeat at appalling cost – 80,000 US casualties for the cost of 120,000 Germans – remains an epic of American heroism (see p. 369). It opened the door to the invasion of Germany. But could it have been avoided through a better-conceived strategy back in September 1944? Montgomery always thought so. It was, though, appallingly maladroit when, on 7 January 1945, he held a disastrous press conference in which he could not resist a note of 'I told you so'. He paid high tribute to the American troops and to Eisenhower, but his reference to 'the Bulge' as 'a most interesting little battle' was insufferable to US pride.

Bradley never forgave him, and Eisenhower claimed it caused him 'more distress and worry' than anything else in the entire war. For the remainder of the campaign, Eisenhower paid minimal attention to Montgomery's strategic pleas; the two armies largely did their own thing.

Assessment

The discord in the last months of the war provided a sad ending to the brilliant display of Anglo-American amity that preceded Overlord – and it was compounded by the post-war 'Battle of Memoirs' that flooded out on both sides of the Atlantic. Montgomery's, in which he persisted in his smug claims that everything had 'gone according to plan', was bitterly criticized in America. He deserved better. But Monty's claim to fame was not just having 'got us there' on D-Day. It lay also in orchestrating the decisive defeat of Hitler's armies in France. Perhaps a last word should go to Winston Churchill, the man who appointed Monty in the first place, who often found himself infuriated by his arrogant intractability – yet recognized his surpassing qualities of generalship. When, after the war, members of his entourage were passing snide comments on Monty, Churchill bit back. 'I know why you all hate him. You are jealous: he is better than you are. Ask yourselves these questions. What is a general for? Answer: to win battles. Did he win them without much slaughter? Yes. So what are you grumbling about?'

In summary, five factors diminished the brilliant coup of 'Overlord', prolonging the war into 1945: 1. Failure at Arnhem; 2. The dispersal of landing-craft to the Mediterranean for the Anvil landings in the south of France; 3. Failure to seize Antwerp and its approaches; 4. The 'Battle of the Bulge'; and 5. Eisenhower's strategy to 'Bull ahead on all fronts' in 1945. Only the first came under Montgomery's jurisdiction.

Bernard Montgomery

> 'If we come to a minefield, our infantry attacks exactly as if it were not there.' MARSHAL GEORGI ZHUKOV TO GENERAL EISENHOWER AT THEIR MAY 1945 MEETING

GEORGI ZHUKOV
1896–1974

SIMON SEBAG MONTEFIORE

MARSHAL GEORGI KONSTANTINOVICH ZHUKOV was probably the greatest commander of the Second World War. Certainly, he played a leading role in all the decisive battles of the Eastern Front that decided the fate of the entire global conflict. He was either at the forefront of the planning, or in command, directly or indirectly, of the battles of Leningrad, Moscow, Stalingrad, Kursk, Operation Bagration, and Berlin – an astonishing record.

In the West, we celebrate the cults of British and American generals such as Montgomery and MacArthur, Bradley and Patton, while paying scant attention to the decisive Eastern Front. Zhukov is often ignored even though his achievements tower over our own military heroes in terms both of numerical scale and decisive importance. We should not overlook the much larger contribution of the Russian Front where the bulk of Hitler's army was ultimately destroyed. What is more, Zhukov is unusual in being the only Allied general to win victories against both the Japanese and the Germans.

Zhukov – who became the favourite general and Deputy Supreme Commander of the Soviet dictator, Josef Stalin – personifies the ruthlessness, brutality and crudity of the Stalinist system but also symbolizes the incredible courage and colossal sacrifices of the Russian people, who lost 27 million dead in what they call the Great Patriotic War. His triumphs and his failures always came at a terrible cost in casualties – indeed he prided himself on his ruthlessness. Arrogant, harsh, merciless, self-promoting, vain and unsubtle, he presided over costly disasters as well as remarkable victories. But he was neither sadistic nor devious but courageous, indefatigably energetic and drivingly optimistic in his campaigns against the Germans and the Japanese, often fearless in his dealings with Stalin, and brilliantly gifted as a battlefield commander.

From shoemaker's son to Soviet soldier

Zhukov was born on 1 December 1896, the son of a shoemaker peasant in Kaluga province, 124 miles south of Moscow. At 11, he was apprenticed to an uncle as a sub-master furrier but in 1915, during the First World War, he was conscripted by the Tsarist army and remained a soldier for the rest of his life. In 1916 he was wounded, awarded

Georgi Zhukov

two crosses of St George and promoted to NCO. In 1918, he volunteered to fight for the new Bolshevik government in the Civil War and served in the 1st Moscow Cavalry Division, fighting the Whites in the Urals and in the continuing battle for Tsaritsyn (later renamed Stalingrad), becoming a member of the Communist Party on 1 March 1919 and remaining in the Red Army after the Communist victory.

By 1931, aged 34, he was already known for his harsh competence and plain-spokenness. He was promoted to assistant to the legendary Inspector of Cavalry, Cossack commander in the Civil War, and Stalin's favourite general, Semyon Budyonny, who became Zhukov's protector and patron. Fortunately, he was not yet a senior officer when Stalin unleashed his savage purge of the Red Army officer corps in 1937, during which the tyrant shot three of the five Marshals of the Soviet Union and as many as 40,000 of his officer corps, devastating his command structure. Zhukov was vulnerable because of his rude and direct manner, his severity to seniors and subordinates alike. He was interrogated but ultimately his defiance – and the protection of Budyonny – saved him: he emerged from the bloodbath still tainted by the accusations against him but also as a respected young corps commander in a decimated army.

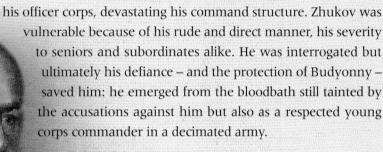

Georgi Zhukov, perhaps the key military figure of the Second World War.

Japanese threat

In June 1939, Zhukov was summoned by Marshal Klim Voroshilov, People's Commissar for Defence, Stalin's top political general, and, like Marshal Budyonny, a crony from the Battle of Tsaritsyn in the Civil War, Stalin's baptism of fire as a warlord. This notoriously ignorant and bungling mediocrity appointed him to command Soviet and Mongolian forces that were facing a Japanese incursion close to the Khalkin Gol River. Defying and pushing aside the Stalinist political cronies, and taking firm command, Zhukov demanded reinforcements, which he duly received. He then launched a costly but powerful offensive against the Japanese, winning a decisive victory. Around 60,000 Japanese were killed or captured while Zhukov lost around 18,500; the combination of high cost, forceful offensive and ultimate victory remained Zhukov's trademarks. The Japanese defeat undoubtedly discouraged them from intervening against the USSR in 1941 and thus in its

Georgi Zhukov

way was a decisive engagement. Had the Japanese been emboldened to intervene in 1941, Moscow would probably have been lost – and Russia may have fallen.

Summoned by Stalin, who immediately liked (as much he liked anyone) and respected (as much as he respected anyone) the plain-speaking general, Zhukov was promoted to General of the Army and Commander of Kiev District. There, he commanded the annexation of Bessarabia in the summer of 1940, one of the gains of Stalin's 1939 Molotov–Ribbentrop Pact with Hitler.

German threat

At the end of 1940, Zhukov distinguished himself in the tense war-games ordered by Stalin that revealed the embarrassing ineptitude of the Soviet High Command. A furious Stalin sacked his chief of staff Meretskov and appointed Zhukov, aged 45, to the post on 1 February 1941. As Stalin rejected the convincing and repeated intelligence warnings that Hitler was about to attack, Zhukov, always aware how close he had come to liquidation in 1937, cautiously and uncomfortably tried to push the dictator towards precautionary readiness, despite the threats of Stalin's vicious henchmen. He urged vigilance and mobilization but only so far: Stalin's 'dungeons', he later admitted, were never far from his thoughts.

When Hitler launched Operation Barbarossa against the USSR on 22 June 1941 (see also pp. 327–8), it was Zhukov who rang Stalin at his residence to give him the news. When he finally got through and the dictator came to the phone, Zhukov said the Germans were attacking. He could hear Stalin breathing. 'Did you understand me?' repeated Zhukov. Finally Stalin summoned commanders and Politburo to the Kremlin.

In the chaotic routs and retreat towards Moscow that followed, a floundering Stalin deployed the severe and blunt Zhukov as troubleshooter, first to the collapsing southwestern front. Zhukov managed to lead a counter-attack, using his favoured Stalinist methods: 'Arrest immediately!' he would say concerning any retreating officers. 'Bring them to trial urgently as traitors and cowards.' Stalin always appreciated Zhukov's talent and brutal honesty; as Marshal Timoshenko recalled: 'You know Zhukov was the only person who feared no one. He was not afraid of Stalin.'

Zhukov had repeatedly warned Stalin of the dangers of Nazi aggression. Now, as the Soviet armies collapsed and disintegrated, facing encirclement and retreat, Stalin recalled him to Moscow.

Outspoken general

On 28 June Minsk fell, opening the road to Smolensk and Moscow. Stalin realized that the USSR was in danger of defeat. When he visited the Defence Commissariat to confront the generals, his toughest commander, Zhukov, admitted he had lost control of the front but rudely demanded the right to get on with his work. A row broke out between Zhukov and Beria, Stalin's fearsome secret police boss. 'Excuse my outspo-

Georgi Zhukov

kenness,' Zhukov said to Stalin. But the dictator lost his temper, shouting at Zhukov, who burst into tears, being comforted by Stalin's chief henchman, Molotov. Stalin retired exhausted and demoralized to his mansion but emerged reinvigorated three days later to command the war as Supreme Commander-in-Chief.

Zhukov was henceforth his chief military adviser as the southern fronts now shattered. On 29 July, Zhukov recommended that Stalin avoid encirclement of more troops by abandoning Kiev. 'Why talk rubbish?' shouted Stalin, at which Zhukov lost his temper: 'If you think the chief of staff talks rubbish, then I request you relieve me of my post and send me to the front,' shouted Zhukov. Stalin was shocked – and impressed: 'Don't get heated,' he answered, 'but since you mention it, we'll get by without you. Calm down, calm down.' Zhukov was sacked as chief of staff – but Stalin kept him as a member of Headquarters, the Stavka, and almost uniquely admitted later that Zhukov had been right.

Leningrad and Moscow

Meanwhile Leningrad was in danger of falling to the Germans: on 8 September 1941, Stalin despatched Zhukov to save the city and remove the bungler Voroshilov. Displaying sang-froid, merciless Stalinist discipline (including the death penalty used liberally) and military skill, Zhukov stabilized the front, even counter-attacking. Hitler cancelled his assault and decided to starve, not storm, Leningrad into submission.

On 5 October, Stalin summoned Zhukov back to Moscow, which was increasingly in danger of falling to the Germans. Stalin was considering abandoning the capital, which would probably have heralded Soviet defeat and therefore Nazi hegemony over Europe. In one of the most brutal battles of human history, Zhukov took command and managed at a terrible cost to halt the German offensive. On 5 December, he launched an offensive that pushed the Germans back over a hundred miles. This was his most decisive victory (see pp. 352–3).

In the following months, Zhukov tried to restrain Stalin's craving for vast offensives and his lack of military comprehension that lost entire armies in German encirclements and cost many millions of Soviet troops. In May 1942, the Kharkov offensive ended in disaster, opening up the road to the city of Stalingrad and the Caucasian oilfields that Hitler needed to fuel his exhausted war machine.

Stalingrad

The Battle of Stalingrad became a savage struggle to save the city, but gradually Hitler's Sixth Army was sucked deeper and deeper into the ruined city until it became vulnerable to Soviet counter-attack and encirclement. On 27 August 1942, Stalin promoted Zhukov to Deputy Supremo. Zhukov refused: 'My character wouldn't let us work together.' Stalin replied: 'What of our characters? Let's subordinate them to the interests of the Motherland.'

On 12 September, Stalin called Zhukov and chief of staff Marshal Vasilevsky to the Kremlin. It was a historic meeting. All three stared at the map. 'There might be another solution,' muttered the generals. 'What other solution?' asked Stalin. Before they could answer, he ordered them to work out a plan. The three of them evolved the concept of Operation Uranus, the encirclement of the German Sixth Army. The next night, Stalin greeted the generals uniquely with a handshake and agreed the plan with the

Georgi Zhukov

(Below) **THE BATTLE OF MOSCOW.** The German offensive (left) and the Soviet counter-offensive (right), September 1941 – April 1942.

words: 'No one else knows what we three have discussed here.' Stalin, after losing 6 million men through his own follies, had finally started to take military advice and become a competent supreme commander. Zhukov and Vasilevsky worked out details of the plan, but just before it was launched Stalin appointed Zhukov to command a huge diversionary offensive, Operation Mars, on the Kalinin and western fronts further north. Operation Mars, with its brutal frontal assaults, was Zhukov's biggest and most costly defeat. He admitted later that, throughout the war, he sometimes cleared

ARMY GROUP NORTH

R. Medveditsa

R. Tvertsa

R. Nerl

R. Volga

Kalinin

Klin

Rzhev

R. Volga

Front line 30 September 1941

SOVIET FORCES

Moscow

Borodino

R. Moskva

Vyazma

GERMAN FORCES

Smolensk

R. Oka

Kaluga

Sukhinichi

Tula

Kirov

Roslavl

ARMY GROUP CENTRE

Bryansk

Front line 5 December 1941

Orel

R. Oka

R. Don

Front line 30 October 1941

R. Desna

Kursk

N

0   50 km

0   50 miles

Soviet troops in action during the Battle of Moscow. The German attack on the Soviet capital began on 30 September 1941; within a week, Stalin, near panic, put Zhukov in charge of the defence. It turned out to be the biggest and most decisive battle of the Second World War.

THE BATTLE OF
MOSCOW

THE BATTLE OF STALINGRAD is the most celebrated clash of the Eastern Front and rightly regarded as the turning point of the entire Second World War. The Battle of Kursk was the biggest tank battle; the Battle of Berlin was the colossal Wagnerian climax of the war; but truly the Battle of Moscow was the most decisive. Had Moscow fallen, the entire history of the world would be different. It was the biggest battle of the entire war, indeed the largest in human history. Seven million men fought and 926,000 Soviet soldiers died (more than combined British and American casualties in the entire war). In all, 2.5 million were killed or wounded, 2 million of them Russian. This was Zhukov's battle.

Leaving Leningrad to its siege in the autumn of 1941, Hitler switched his panzers to Operation Typhoon, the taking of Moscow. Battle started on 30 September. On 3 October, the panzer general Guderian took Orel and the Soviet fronts collapsed. Panicked, Stalin called Zhukov in Leningrad: 'I've got just one request. Can you get a plane and come to Moscow?' 'I'll be there,' said Zhukov. On 7 October, Stalin received Zhukov and ordered him to save Moscow. As the fronts on all sides of Moscow were collapsing, Zhukov had

Georgi Zhukov

minefields or took positions with savage frontal assaults regardless of the human cost: he was very much a Stalinist general. Uranus became the decisive victory of Stalingrad, which began the defeat of Hitler.

On the offensive

In January 1943, Zhukov was promoted to Marshal of the Soviet Union. A relationship of rough, guarded but mutual respect had grown up between Stalin and Zhukov; over

only 90,000 men. He nonetheless took control of the colossal conflict. Visitors to Stalin's office were amazed by Zhukov's 'commanding tones as if he was the superior officer, and Stalin accepted this'. But the advance continued. Law broke down on the Moscow streets. By 15 October, Stalin was considering whether to abandon the city. On the 16th, ministries and all the embassies were despatched to Kuybishev in the rear. But still Stalin refused to leave, demanding on the 17th that order be restored. By 18 October, Kalinin in the north and Kaluga in the south had fallen and there were panzers on the battlefield of Borodino. On the 19th, Stalin declared a state of siege and savage punishments for any defeatism or panic as Zhukov commanded the desperate struggle with dwindling reserves. In Berlin, the Reich Press Office declared 'Russia is finished'. But the Germans – convinced victory was theirs – rested a day as the temperatures sank to a deep freeze. Stalin, now convinced that Japan would not attack Russia, gave Zhukov his hidden reserve: the crack 700,000 troops of the Far Eastern Army. On 7 November, Stalin showed his defiance by holding the annual parade in Red Square. On the 13th, Zhukov reluctantly agreed to Stalin's insistence on a counter-attack but it wasted more troops and was subsumed in the last German push of 15 November. Stalin called Zhukov to ask: 'Tell me honestly as a Communist, can we hold Moscow?' 'We'll hold it without a doubt,' said Zhukov. On 5 December, having lost 155,000 men in twenty days, Zhukov fought the Germans to a standstill.

On 6 December, Stalin gave Zhukov three new armies. Zhukov planned a counter-offensive on the four nearest fronts. He managed to push the Germans back 200 miles. Moscow was saved. Zhukov was so exhausted that he slept for many hours. Even when Stalin called, his adjutants could not wake him. 'Don't wake him up until he wakes himself,' said Stalin, 'Let him sleep.' It was the first Soviet victory but a very limited one. German forces were not destroyed yet and could fight another day. But for now, Zhukov had saved Russia.

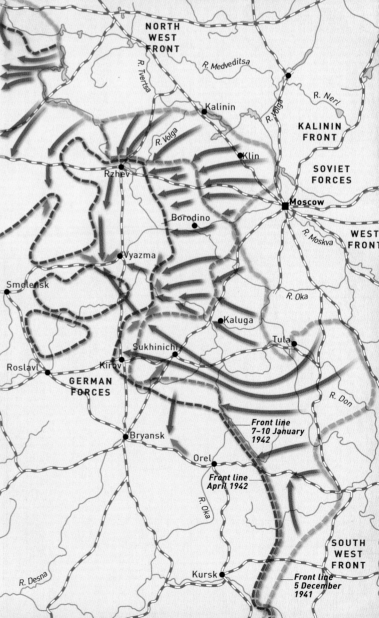

meals in the early hours, they sometimes discussed even personal matters such as Stalin's relationship with his mother and sons. Zhukov said Stalin was like a temperamental boxer who got excited and always wanted to give battle, even when he wasn't prepared.

On 5 July 1943, Hitler launched Operation Citadel – an attack of 900,000 men and 2,700 tanks on the vulnerable Soviet bulge at Kursk. Zhukov was at the forefront of the fortification of Kursk, which withstood the German attack, and then, on 12 July, of the launching of the Soviet offensive that became history's biggest ever tank battle and the defeat of Hitler's last big offensive on the Eastern Front. For the rest of 1943 – during the battle to retake the Ukraine, and during the colossal offensive in Belorussia, Operation Bagration, planned and overseen by Zhukov in 1944 – the Deputy Supremo remained the top Russian general as the Germans were chased off Soviet soil.

As Soviet forces halted outside Warsaw, Stalin retook personal command of the fronts from Deputy Supremo Zhukov, whom he now appointed to command of the 1st Belorussian Front. On 1 April 1945, Stalin ordered Zhukov and his rival, Marshal Konev, commander of the 1st Ukrainian Front, to race each other to take Berlin, whatever the costs. Zhukov was to take Berlin from the Oder bridgeheads over the Seelow Heights while Konev was to push through Dresden and Leipzig, with this northern flank thrusting towards southern Berlin. Between them they had 2.5 million men and 6,250 tanks.

On 16 April, Zhukov attacked the Seelow Heights outside Berlin with 14,600 guns, but on being repulsed and under the pressure of Stalin's irritation, he stormed the Heights at a terrible cost of 30,000 men. Stalin taunted Zhukov and then allowed Konev to push towards Berlin. Both marshals fought their way into the city. On 1 May Zhukov called to inform Stalin that Hitler had committed suicide: 'So that's the end of the bastard,' said Stalin. 'Too bad we couldn't take him alive.' Hitler's body was found by the secret police and taken back to Moscow, but Stalin pretended to Zhukov that he did not know this. Now the war was over, Zhukov was no longer Stalin's confidant.

Hounded hero

Zhukov was now Russia's greatest military hero. He dispatched planes of booty and art back to Moscow. His mistresses were top Russian singers and he travelled with a huge entourage, but he rashly implied in a press conference that he was the chief

architect of the Soviet victory. Stalin, who promoted himself to Generalissimo, was suspicious of Zhukov's fame and prestige. On 9 May 1945, Zhukov presided over the official German surrender, himself supervised by Stalin's henchman, Vyshinsky. When Zhukov met US General Eisenhower, he shocked the American by explaining that his method of clearing minefields was to send infantry running across them.

On 24 June, Stalin gave Zhukov the honour of reviewing Soviet forces on a white Arabian charger at the victory parade in Moscow. But Zhukov was now out of favour. The Western press actually cited him as a potential heir to Stalin and the dictator even probed this idea: 'I'm getting old,' he told Marshal Budyonny. 'What do you think of Zhukov as my successor?' The secret police were soon investigating Zhukov and raided his apartments to find a 'Museum' of war booty, art and furniture. In June 1946, at a meeting of the Supreme Military Council, Stalin orchestrated an attack on Zhukov who was then demoted to command the minor Odessa Military District. His officers were arrested and tortured, his houses searched, his booty confiscated and he suffered a heart attack, though Stalin refused to order his arrest. When the secret police presented evidence of conspiracy against him, Stalin replied: 'I don't trust anyone who says Zhukov could do this. He's a straightforward, sharp person able to speak plainly to anyone but he'll never go against the Central Committee.' Politically he had to destroy Zhukov, but personally he respected him.

Zhukov, on a white Arabian charger, reviews Soviet forces during the victory parade in Moscow, 24 June 1945. After the war, Zhukov fell out of favour with Stalin, who feared his popularity.

After Stalin

On Stalin's death on 5 March 1953, Zhukov was recalled to become Deputy Defence Minister. In June he assisted the rising Nikita Khrushchev in the arrest and later liquidation of Lavrenti Beria, the secret police chief and temporary Soviet strongman for three months after Stalin's death. Khrushchev became the all-powerful Soviet leader – though he was no Stalin, either in terms of statesmanship or cruelty. In 1955 Zhukov was appointed Defence Minister. In 1957 he joined the ruling Presidium (Politburo) and when Khrushchev was almost overthrown by Molotov and Stalin's old henchmen, Zhukov helped Khrushchev defeat them. But Khrushchev was, like Stalin before him, jealous of Zhukov's power and suspicious of his ambition. Soon afterwards that same year, he accused Zhukov of 'Bonapartism', and sacked him. Zhukov remained in retirement under his death in 1974.

'The war in Europe has been won and to no one man do the United Nations owe a greater debt than to Marshal Zhukov.'
GENERAL EISENHOWER

A statue of Zhukov on horseback has recently been raised on Red Square in Moscow. He was truly the greatest military hero of the Soviet Union. His monstrous faults, remarkable gifts and colossal achievements earn him a special place in the pantheon of Russian heroes with Prince Alexander Nevsky of Novgorod, Prince Alexander Suvorov, who served Catherine the Great and Paul I, and Prince Mikhail Kutuzov, Alexander I's commander of 1812. In 1942, Stalin created the Orders of Suvorov and Kutuzov to reward courage and victory, medals that are still awarded in the Russian army today. One day, there will be an Order of Zhukov.

Georgi Zhukov

> 'The main fighting qualities of a military leader are his ability to control troops and a constant readiness to assume full responsibility for what he has already done and what he is planning to do.' IVAN KONEV

IVAN KONEV
1897–1973

RICHARD OVERY

THERE ARE AMONG THE RED ARMY COMMANDERS of the Second World War perhaps a dozen who are known in the West among those with an interest in military history, but as household names there are only two: Marshal Zhukov and Marshal Ivan Konev. Konev won his reputation in four years of gruelling combat on the Eastern Front. His capacity to hold together large forces and to manage a complex and fluid battlefield for the conquest of much of central Europe in 1944 and 1945 marks him as a commander of exceptional quality. He was not a strategic thinker, but under the duress of war he acquired a firm grasp of operational realities.

Konev, like any other senior Soviet commander, operated as part of a large team, dominated by supreme headquarters and the General Staff, and above all by Stalin. It is difficult for the historian to decide how much independence of action any Soviet commander had, but it was essential once a task had been set that the operational commander fulfilled what was required of him. Konev, like all other Soviet military leaders, was measured on performance in the field. Since the campaigns from 1943 were almost continuous, operational capacity was constantly tested. Survival of the fittest was built in to Red Army performance. This, too, says much about Konev's qualities as a military commander.

The early years

Ivan Stepanovich Konev was born on 28 December 1897. This is one of the few facts from his early life about which there is agreement. Konev is usually described as coming from a village near Podosinovsky in central Russia, but his records show that he was born in the village of Lodeino, near Nikolsk in northwestern Russia. His family were poor peasants, though a later attempt to blacken Konev's name in the 1930s produced evidence that his father had been a *kulak*, a well-to-do peasant, hiring labour and owning livestock. Konev had an elementary education, worked on the farmstead until he was 12 and then became a lumberjack before being called up into the tsarist army in April 1916.

Ivan Konev

He immediately attracted attention and was sent on a course for NCOs. He had seen no fighting by the time he was posted to an artillery division, and when the Revolution came he returned to Nikolsk, where he became a local Bolshevik military commissar and a lifelong and committed communist. He helped to suppress the Kronstadt rebellion in 1921, staged by disgruntled sailors near Leningrad, and during the Russian Civil War became first commissar of an armoured train, then commissar of the 17th Maritime Corps in Nikolsk. He was posted to the Ukraine in 1924, and in 1926 attended staff courses at the newly founded Frunze Military Academy. He commanded the 17th Rifle Division from 1926 to 1932, and then attended further staff courses. When Stalin's purges started to sweep through the armed forces in 1937, Konev was fortunate to survive, since he had been serving under General Uborevich, one of those executed. He was posted in 1938 to command the 57th Special Corps in Mongolia, most of whose officers had already been purged, and rose rapidly thereafter. In May 1941 he was made commander of the Nineteenth Army in the Ukraine, which is where he was when Germany invaded on 22 June 1941.

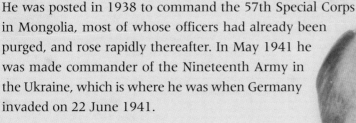

Ivan Konev, after Marshal Zhukov the best-known Soviet commander of the Second World War, celebrated for his role in managing the massive campaigns on the Eastern Front in 1944–5.

Konev and the defence of Moscow

The next four months were the most difficult of Konev's career. He was unfortunate to be in command of an army right in the path of the German attack, exposed like other commanders to Stalin's wrath when the Soviet front caved in. But Konev's early battles marked him out as distinctive. Personally brave, a tough commander who fought alongside his men, Konev was among those who imposed temporary reverses on the German attacker. His Nineteenth Army drove the Germans out of Vitebsk before being forced to retreat towards Smolensk. It was here that Konev's army took part in the Red Army offensive

to try to dislodge the German hold on the town, though it failed. On 12 September Konev was promoted to head the Western Army Group of six armies to prepare for the defence of Moscow, but the losses sustained at Smolensk and the strengthening of the German Army Group Centre led to disasters around the small town of Vyazma, where his long front line was based. German armoured thrusts cut through the weak Soviet forces and linked up behind Vyazma, ensnaring several of Konev's armies, which were forced to surrender. German armies netted 690,000 prisoners during the operation.

The disaster was scarcely Konev's fault, since the strength of the two sides was so unbalanced, but he had also been exposed to a major operation after just two weeks in high command. Nor had Soviet intelligence understood the nature of the German attack. Stalin thought about punishing Konev, and an investigation was begun into the Vyazma disaster, but General Zhukov, according to his own account, successfully interceded with Stalin, took Konev on as his direct deputy for the battle in front of Moscow, and placed him as commander of the Kalinin Army Group northwest of the capital, with the new rank of colonel general. Here he was able to prove himself as a commander at last. He stabilized the northern part of the Moscow Front around Kalinin, absorbing the German attack before launching a counter-offensive on 5 December, along with the rest of the Moscow Front, which led to the recapture of Kalinin. In January Konev's army group was strengthened and he was ordered together with Zhukov to try to encircle the bulk of German Army Group Centre around the Vyazma–Smolensk axis; but although Konev's forces succeeded in penetrating German lines, the operation was too ambitious in mid winter with limited resources, and Smolensk remained in German hands.

Konev was fortunate to have survived the crisis of autumn 1941, but thereafter he remained one of the favoured inner circle of senior generals, commanding the Western Front in August 1942, the Northwestern Front in March 1943 and finally the reserve Steppe Front, created behind the Kursk salient in June 1943 to lead the planned counter-offensive after the German attack (Operation Citadel) had faltered. On 3 August 1943, directed personally by Zhukov, his army group, together with the Voronezh Army Group under General Vatutin, drove the German army rapidly back, liberating Belgorod and finally Kharkov, the Soviet Union's fourth largest city, which had changed hands between the two sides so often in early 1943 that the urban area

Ivan Konev

was completely destroyed. The success of the Kursk counter-offensive opened the way for a Red Army drive across the Ukraine to the River Dnepr. Konev's army group was renamed the Second Ukrainian Army Group, one of four responsible for driving back the whole of the centre and south of the German front. Between August 1943 and April 1944, when Konev's army group entered Romanian territory at Botosani, his forces were in almost continuous combat, driving the retreating German army back across the Dnepr and then on to the frontiers of eastern Europe. It was during this advance that Konev coordinated the encirclement at Korsun that earned him the rank of marshal of the Soviet Union (see pp. 360–61).

Konev brought a number of operational priorities of his own in commanding enormous numbers of men on complex and fluid battlefields. He adopted the Red Army tactic of concealment and deception, and generally used it successfully. Time and again the German side was caught out by uncertainty as to Soviet intentions. Konev also placed a top priority on learning about the enemy's dispositions as closely as possible, using a number of forms of reconnaissance and relying on infiltration and scouting. He saw this as one of the principal aims of any divisional commander. The main object was to find out where the enemy artillery was concentrated so as to direct fire without waste and in a sudden devastating barrage. The short, sharp artillery attack was then followed by rapid movement forward before the enemy forces had time to recover or re-establish communication. Rather than large numbers of infantry, Konev later wrote that 'the decisive factor in combat is fire'. Konev also favoured the use of tanks, strongly supported by aircraft, which he sent forward in numerous small penetration operations, breaking through into the enemy rear and creating confusion, rather than massing them for one major attack. The effect was to create panic among the defending troops and speed their withdrawal or surrender. The very great numerical superiority enjoyed by the Red Army and Air Force by 1944 and 1945 made this use of tanks a realistic tactic, and it explains the alarm felt by German soldiers when they faced an enemy who seemed capable of moving forward remorselessly, like a swollen river.

Soviet troops of Konev's **First Ukrainian Army Group** taking cover under a bridge during the fighting on the Vistula, August 1944. Their next major operation was to be the advance on Berlin.

Konev's greatest campaigns

The first of Konev's major offensives in 1944 was the operation launched on 13 July 1944 in western Ukraine, which brought his forces to the Carpathian Mountains and the River Vistula in Poland. He was now the commander of the First Ukrainian Army Group, following the death of General Vatutin; it was the largest single Soviet

THE BATTLE FOR WHICH KONEV was made a marshal of the Soviet Union, and which he came to regard as a model operation, took place from 24 January to 17 February 1944 in the southern Ukraine, after Konev's Second Ukrainian Army Group had pushed German forces back from the River Dnepr around Dnepropetrovsk. German forces held on to their positions on the river further north around Korsun, creating a large salient that Konev tried to eliminate by a strategy of encirclement. The battle that followed led to the destruction of what became known as the 'Korsun–Shevchenkovsky pocket' (sometimes known as the Cherkassy pocket) and the elimination, according to Soviet estimates, of 77,000 men.

Although Konev later claimed that he had directed and won the battle around Korsun, it was, like most Soviet

THE KORSUN–SHEVCHENKOVSKY POCKET

offensives, in part a joint effort. Marshal Zhukov, who was the Soviet headquarters representative in the Ukraine, recommended trying to pinch off the salient, along the same lines that had been used to encircle General Paulus at Stalingrad. South of Korsun, Konev's Second Ukrainian Army Group was to strike northeastwards behind the salient, while General Nikolai Vatutin's First Ukrainian Army Group struck southeast. The plan was to make a wide corridor defended on both sides against enemy counter-attacks while the pocket was reduced by sustained air and ground attack. Konev set up a complex deception plan to mislead German defenders about the true destination of his attack, although unusually it failed to work this time. The attack, launched on 18 January and fought in bitter weather and atrocious ground conditions,

force, comprising seven infantry and three tank armies, and four mobile corps, a testament to his growing stature as an operational leader. His force occupied the southeastern part of Poland in little more than two weeks, reaching the Vistula by 29 July. The all-important rail city of L'vov was the major target, and Konev's forces not only encircled and captured the city on 27 July, but succeeded in surrounding a force of 40,000 Germans at Brody, in another classic encirclement operation. Konev's army group then rested after months of combat while the Red Army further south moved into Romania and Bulgaria.

The second major operation was the so-called Vistula–Oder operation. This once again paired Zhukov and Konev as army group commanders, after Stalin decided that Zhukov should personally command the operations into Germany. Konev and Zhukov both now led army groups vastly larger in size and equipment than the German enemy

Ivan Konev

brought ten days of hard fighting before the two Soviet army groups met at the village of Zvenigorodka, trapping the German XI and XLII Army Corps, with six divisions (including the SS Wiking Division), inside the pocket.

The German Army Group South under Field Marshal Erich von Manstein was short of tanks and aircraft, but he attacked the whole Soviet circle, on Hitler's instructions, rather than trying to break through to the pocket at one particular juncture. Konev proved able to control a difficult and dispersed battlefield, and prevented any serious penetration of the line. By 8 February he felt confident enough to invite the German commander in the pocket, Lieutenant General Wilhelm Stemmermann, to surrender. He refused, and Stalin began to fear that a breakout was planned. On 12 February Konev was given unitary control of the whole operation, and once again a more concentrated German effort to reach the south side of the pocket was blunted by Konev's redeployments, and only got to within 6 miles of the trapped German divisions. But on 15 February Stemmermann was ordered to do anything to try to break out, and over the next two days an estimated 35,000 escaped by filtering through Soviet lines, leaving almost all their equipment behind.

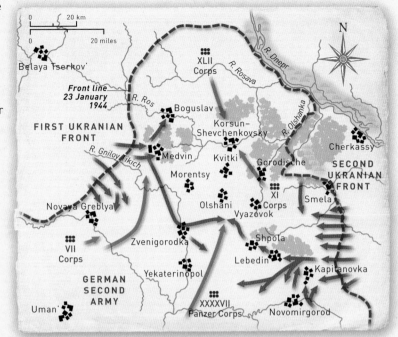

(Left) **Soviet cavalrymen** come across a column of abandoned vehicles in the Korsun–Shevchenkovsky pocket. It was here, early in 1944, that Konev's forces destroyed a force of more than 66,000 Germans.

Konev ordered attacks on the escaping garrison with tanks and cavalry, but only the rearguard was caught and slaughtered, including Stemmermann, whose body was found on the battlefield. Out of an original trapped force of a little under 60,000, around 19,000 were killed or captured (and not the 77,000 claimed), but this does not include the substantial casualties inflicted on Manstein's divisions trying to reach the pocket. The news of the escapes was not revealed to Stalin, but Konev's operation, in difficult fighting conditions against a desperate enemy, inflicted a major operational defeat, with heavy losses of men and equipment, and opened the way to the broad Soviet advance across the southern Ukraine that began a few weeks later.

they faced. Nevertheless the last two major operations, to the River Oder and then to Berlin in May 1945, were carried out with great speed and completeness. Konev's army group began its operations on 12 January, and crossed most of Poland to reach the Oder and Silesia in only two weeks. Both Konev and Zhukov, who had also crossed Poland, wanted to press on further, and Konev moved another 75 miles nearer Berlin to the banks of the River Neisse. But determined German resistance and supply problems slowed down the whirlwind advance, and Konev and Zhukov had to wait until April before the high command in Moscow was satisfied that Berlin could be seized with certainty.

The 'race for Berlin' was perhaps Konev's most famous operation. In March 1945 Stalin ordered firm operational preparation for the capture of the German capital

Ivan Konev

employing Konev's First Ukrainian and Zhukov's First Belorussian Army Groups as the major players. Plans and redeployment had to take place very quickly, but Konev succeeded in extricating his armies from the conquest of Upper Silesia and had them prepared for attack by mid April. On 16 April he and Zhukov began their attacks, Zhukov directly opposite Berlin, Konev to the south. Although Konev was supposed to use his force to push south and southwest, Stalin deliberately left open the demarcation line between the two army groups in case Konev might be needed to help capture Berlin. As Zhukov's attack stalled, Konev's succeeded rapidly and on 17 April Stalin telephoned Konev to find another solution. Konev told him that he could easily swing his armour northwards towards the German capital, and Stalin gave him the go-ahead. By 21 April Konev's advance guard had reached the outskirts of Berlin, and by the 24th had made contact with Zhukov's armies, which had now moved forward as well. In the end Konev's forces held back while Zhukov took the glory of the capitulation of Berlin, but it was now evident that the apprentice Konev had become a major rival, as capable of mastering a vast battlefield and destroying enemy formations at speed as his one-time mentor. Konev had the distinction of overseeing the last fighting

A Soviet tank in Berlin. Konev's advance guard reached the outskirts of the city on 21 April 1945, but in the end it was Zhukov who took the glory of receiving the German surrender.

Ivan Konev

in Europe. His forces moved south as well as north in late April, reaching the Czech border. Here German resistance continued, and on 9 May Konev's forces occupied Prague; two days later he took the surrender of the remnants of General Schörner's Army Group Centre, three days after VE-day was celebrated in western Europe.

Konev's post-war career

On 5 May 1945 Konev was appointed commander-in-chief of the Central Group of Forces in Austria and part of Hungary. In April 1946 he was made commander of land forces in the Soviet Union. Unlike many other leading Soviet commanders, Konev kept Stalin's confidence after the war, perhaps because of his mounting rivalry with Zhukov. When Stalin summoned Zhukov before the Central Committee in 1946 and accused him of conspiracy, self-glorification and corruption, Konev was present. Although he denied that Zhukov could have been disloyal, he did agree openly that he was a difficult and temperamental personality. Zhukov was demoted, while Konev took his place as Red Army commander-in-chief. It is tempting to see in Konev's behaviour mere political opportunism, but his relationship with Zhukov was difficult even during the war years,

> 'His primary gift as a military leader, which had emerged gradually and was confirmed on the field of battle, was his careful study of the enemy.'
>
> OLEG RZHESHEVSKY

perhaps because Konev himself sensed that as an operational commander he had grown at least to be Zhukov's equal, but got little of the credit.

Konev, a popular and well-respected Red Army leader and the most important figure in the post-war military establishment, went on to become commander-in-chief of Warsaw Pact forces, and in this role oversaw the ruthless suppression of the Hungarian Revolution in 1956. Five years later he was posted to be commander of Soviet forces in East Germany during the crisis over the Berlin Wall. In 1963 he went into retirement, and eight years later died of cancer. As a twice-decorated Hero of the Soviet Union he was buried in the Kremlin Wall.

DWIGHT D. EISENHOWER

1890–1969

CARLO D'ESTE

DWIGHT EISENHOWER gained a place in military history on 6 June 1944, the day the Western Allies invaded Normandy and thereby changed the course of the Second World War. As Supreme Allied Commander, the responsibility for carrying out the campaign to defeat Germany was his and his alone. Eisenhower was called upon to make one of the most difficult and courageous decisions ever required of a military commander: to launch the Allied invasion of Normandy despite bad weather which threatened to wreck the invasion. Few commanders have ever faced such extraordinary responsibilities, and that decision in itself, with its awesome potential for failure, changed the course of history.

The third of the seven sons of David and Ida Eisenhower, members of a strict, pacifist Mennonite religious sect called the River Brethren, Dwight David Eisenhower was born in Denison, Texas, on 14 October 1890, during a violent thunderstorm. Shortly thereafter the family moved to Abilene, Kansas. Although the Eisenhowers were so impoverished that wearing shoes was deemed a luxury, Dwight, known by the nickname 'Ike', grew to manhood in a happy home. He and his brothers were taught the values of honesty, hard work, independence and responsibility from an early age.

Ike at West Point

Eisenhower never aspired to become a professional army officer but, too poor to advance beyond high school yet determined to earn a college degree and eventually escape poverty, he passed a competitive examination and entered the United States Military Academy at West Point in 1911. A popular but undistinguished cadet, Eisenhower never took West Point seriously. He never pushed himself to excel, managed to accumulate a high number of demerits, walked numerous punishment tours and was fortunate not to have been expelled for his frequent violations of regulations. An inveterate prankster, his antics and irresponsibility ranged from inattention to his studies, smoking (an expulsion offence), leaving West Point without permission (another expulsion offence), and high jinks such as pouring water from buckets on unsuspecting cadets in the barracks.

Dwight D. Eisenhower

364

Ike was a superb athlete and a promising football player, but his knee was severely damaged early in his cadet days and further injured when he fell from a mean-spirited pony during a dangerous equestrian drill. He was very nearly not commissioned because of it. He also had back and stomach trouble and a host of other ailments that late in his life led to ileitis (an intestinal complaint) and heart disease. These health problems were exacerbated by an addiction to cigarettes begun at West Point, which by the Second World War had escalated to four or more packs a day.

His West Point class became the most famous in Academy history and was later known as 'The class the stars fell on'. During the Second World War it produced two five-star generals (Eisenhower and Omar N. Bradley) and more than a dozen division commanders, most of whom served under their classmate Eisenhower in the Mediterranean and European theatres.

Early military career

Eisenhower entered the army in 1915 a second lieutenant of infantry with few career aspirations and a happy-go-lucky attitude that soon changed into one of professional seriousness. In 1916, he married Mamie Doud whom he had met shortly after arriving at his first duty station in San Antonio, Texas. Their remarkable marriage lasted until Ike's death in 1969.

Eisenhower made his mark as a superb trainer of troops, a duty he came to detest as one training assignment followed another during the months leading up to American participation in the Great War. He desperately wanted a combat assignment in France in Pershing's American Expeditionary Force (AEF). Instead, he was assigned to the new tank corps and sent to command Camp Colt at Gettysburg, Pennsylvania, where he trained men destined for service in the AEF tank corps commanded by a young officer named Patton. When the armistice ended the war on 11 November 1918, Ike was devastated at not having seen combat and perceived his career a failure. 'I will make up for this,' he declared in anger and frustration.

Dwight D. Eisenhower during the Second World War. An important reason for his swift rise to command was his ability to get along with others and be trusted, a result of his friendliness, humility and optimism.

The inter-war years

In 1919, the age of the motor vehicle was in its infancy. Eisenhower was offered a chance to escape the routine of the peacetime army life by becoming a member of what was called the Transcontinental Motor Convoy. In an amazing feat, a US Army convoy of trucks and assorted vehicles travelled from Washington DC to San Francisco in an epic seventy-nine-day journey across a virtually roadless America.

In the United States, the terrible bloodshed in Europe bred a revulsion for future war. By the early 1920s, the great patriotism of the First World War had turned into a national aversion to all things military and to the symbol of war – the military establishment. A militant pacifism took seriously the notion that America had indeed fought 'the war to end all wars'. Common symbols of the times in the 1930s were signs proclaiming: 'Dogs and soldiers, stay off the grass.' The army consisted of only a little over 100,000 men. During those years Ike served in a series of staff assignments, all the while wishing for but not getting troop assignments, and believing his career would end in his retirement as a relatively junior officer.

He served sixteen years as a major, studied tank tactics with his friend George S. Patton, learned to fly, studied war with his mentor General Fox Conner, served on the American Battle Monuments Commission under General John J. Pershing, and in the 1930s toiled for nearly nine years as an aide and staff officer to General Douglas MacArthur in Washington and the Philippines.

THE NORMANDY LANDINGS, 6 June 1944, showing the Allied beachheads.

Pearl Harbor to Overlord

With the advent of the Second World War, chief of staff General George Marshall purged the army of its many aging officers. Those over 50 were unceremoniously

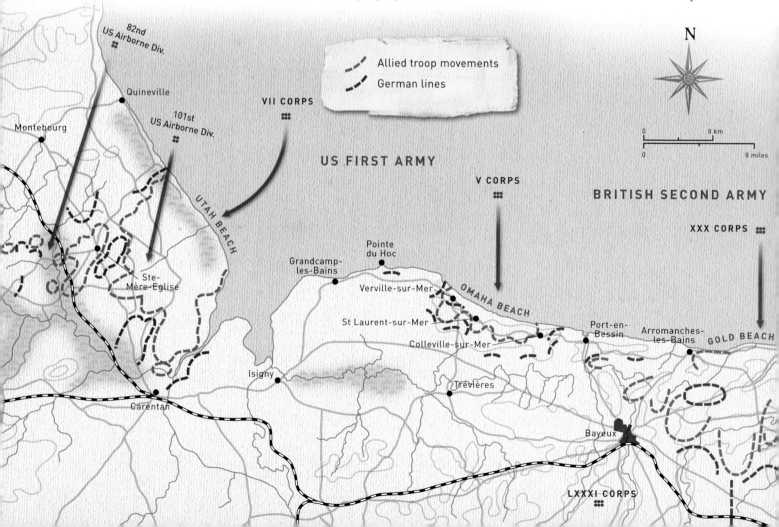

retired. Two notable exceptions were Eisenhower and Patton, each of whom had become too valuable to retire on the grounds of age alone. In 1941, as America was being drawn into war with Japan, Italy and Nazi Germany, Eisenhower's aspirations were modest. He would have considered himself successful merely to serve as a colonel in an armoured division under the command of his long-time friend, the flamboyant Patton. Instead, his star rose dramatically that year as a result of the Louisiana Manoeuvres – the largest peacetime military training exercises ever conducted in the United States. As the chief of staff of the Third Army, Eisenhower's brilliance as a planner was on full display and resulted in his promotion to brigadier general.

After Pearl Harbor (7 December 1941), he was summoned to Washington to become the army's chief war plans officer. His efforts won the approval of Marshall who sent him to Britain in the summer of 1942 in command of US forces. In London, he passed the most demanding test of all by impressing Winston Churchill, who approved of his appointment to command Allied forces for Operation Torch, the joint Anglo-American invasion of French North Africa in November. In 1942 and 1943, Eisenhower commanded Allied forces in the Mediterranean. The campaigns in Tunisia, Sicily and Italy were all testing but valuable experiences that led to his appointment in December 1943 as supreme Allied commander for the invasion of northwest Europe in 1944.

On 6 June (D-Day) Allied forces crossed the English Channel to seize beachheads on the Normandy coast (see also pp. 344–5). Although the fighting in the close hedgerow country (*bocage*) was difficult, the Allies

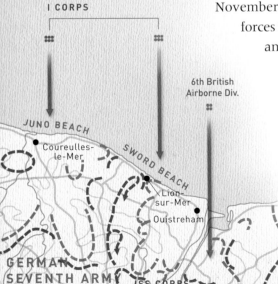

Dwight D. Eisenhower

OPERATION OVERLORD

IN 1944, EISENHOWER came of age as the commander responsible for the planning and execution of the largest amphibious invasion ever mounted, Operation Overlord, the invasion of Normandy, originally scheduled for 5 June. The Allies had massed nearly 6,000 ships and 150,000 men when a full-blown gale not only rendered any hope of launching the invasion on the morning of 5 June unthinkable, but also threatened to wreck the entire invasion timetable.

Eisenhower was compelled to order a postponement while the armada trod water, its thousands of participants virtual prisoners in their encampments and aboard naval vessels; final briefings were postponed and sealed instructions revealing their target remained unopened. A mood of pessimism prevailed among many senior Allied commanders that in spite of the extensive preparations and training the invasion might still fail on the beaches of Normandy. The atmosphere was not lightened by updates from Allied intelligence that the German commander, Field Marshal Erwin Rommel, had strengthened the Normandy front by several new divisions, with more possibly on the way.

At the late evening briefing on 4 June the assembled generals, admirals and air marshals could distinctly hear the sounds of pounding rain and the wind howling outside. Nevertheless, the senior Allied meteorologist, RAF Group Captain J. M. Stagg, reported to the tense commanders that there was a glimmer of hope for 6 June. While the weather would remain poor, visibility would improve and the winds decrease, though barely enough to risk launching the invasion. This was arguably the most important weather prediction in history: a mistaken forecast for D-Day could turn the entire tide of the war in Europe against the Allies. Eisenhower swiftly learned that time had run out. He had to make a crucial decision for or against, then and there. He was obliged to weigh not only the decision itself but its longer-term impact. There was utter silence in the room except for the sound of the wind and rain as Eisenhower pondered whether or not to permit the invasion to go forward. Any delay beyond 6 June meant postponement of Overlord until the next full moon in July, further risking its compromise by the Germans.

In preparation for this eventuality, Eisenhower and his weather team had practised such a scenario for some weeks. Finally, he announced his decision: 'OK,' he said. 'We'll go.' With that simple declaration, Eisenhower had made his historic decision. Once unleashed, the Allies were irrevocably committed and it took considerable courage to set into motion the operation that would decide the victor and the vanquished of the war. Had any been present, Eisenhower's critics, who have painted him in unflattering terms as a chairman of the board, beholden to many and in command of none, would have witnessed his finest hour.

Rommel's naval deputy, Vice Admiral Friedrich Ruge, later marvelled that Eisenhower made such an important decision without recourse to higher authority, noting that no one in the German chain of command would have dared. It was, Ruge believed, 'one of the truly great decisions in military history'.

Landing craft on Omaha Beach, D-Day, 6 June 1944. The heavy American casualties here contrasted with the relative straightforwardness of the landings in other areas, and emphasized the great dangers associated with embarking on a massive invasion in poor weather conditions.

Dwight D. Eisenhower

succeeded in breaking out in August. Paris was liberated on 25 August. Most of France, Belgium, Luxembourg and the southern Netherlands quickly fell into Allied hands, but the advance ground to a virtual halt in mid September with the failure of Montgomery's attempt to seize bridgeheads at Arnhem on the lower Rhine (Operation Market Garden; see pp. 346–7).

The Battle of the Bulge

On 16 December 1944, with the Allies stalled on the border of Germany, Hitler, in an all-out gamble to compel the Allies to sue for peace, launched the largest German counter-offensive of the war in the West, with three armies, more than a quarter of a million troops. Its objective was to split the Allied armies by means of a surprise blitzkrieg thrust through the rugged, heavily forested but lightly defended Ardennes, a planned repeat of what they had done twice previously – in August 1914 and May 1940.

American units were caught flat-footed and fought desperate battles to stem the German advance. The US 101st Airborne Division was surrounded at Bastogne, its commander issuing a one-word refusal to surrender that has become a symbol of defiance: 'Nuts!' As the German armies drove deeper into the Ardennes in an attempt quickly to secure vital bridgeheads west of the River Meuse, the line defining the Allied front on the map took on the appearance of a large protrusion or 'bulge', the name by which the battle would forever be known.

The Battle of the Bulge, the German counter-attack in the Ardennes region of southern Belgium in the winter of 1944/5, led to bitter fighting in appalling conditions. It resulted in almost 20,000 American deaths, the worst US casualties of the entire war.

Dwight D. Eisenhower

Eisenhower made another courageous and controversial decision, this one to appoint British field marshal Bernard Montgomery to take command of the northern half of the 'Bulge' and restore order over what was a predominantly American sector. The decision proved far-reaching and at the height of the battle Eisenhower was promoted to the five-star rank of General of the Army. Although the Battle of the Bulge (16 December 1944 – 25 January 1945) earned the dubious distinction of being the costliest engagement ever fought by the US Army, which suffered over 100,000 casualties, the gallantry of American troops fighting in the frozen Ardennes proved fatal to Hitler's ambition somehow to snatch, if not victory, at least a draw with the Allies. *Time* magazine named Eisenhower its 'man of the year' for 1944.

At 2.41 a.m., 7 May 1945, Germany surrendered unconditionally at Supreme Headquarters Allied Expeditionary Force (SHAEF) in Reims, France. As Colonel General Alfred Jodl signed the documents of surrender for Germany, conspicuously missing was the man who had orchestrated the events leading to this historic moment. The death of soldiers in the cause of peace was close to Dwight Eisenhower's heart and soul. He was not unique as a professional soldier who hated war; but few hated their enemy with greater passion than did Eisenhower, who regarded his adversaries with nothing short of loathing. At Reims, he declined to attend the surrender ceremony and instead delegated to his chief of staff, Lieutenant General Walter Bedell Smith, the task of signing the surrender documents.

As a soldier, Eisenhower understood that it was not his place to announce the end of the war in Europe, but a function of the heads of state who would make the formal announcement the following day. It was typical of Eisenhower that he would not take credit for the Allied victory. Instead his message to his bosses – the combined chiefs of staff – was utterly devoid of self-congratulation, and as unpretentious as the man himself. Only a single sentence long, it read simply: 'The mission of this Allied force was fulfilled at 0241 hours local time, May 7, 1945. [signed] Eisenhower.'

Only after the Germans had departed did Eisenhower finally unbend and relax. As a horde of photographers were admitted to his office and scrambled to record the scene, his famous grin reappeared and he signaled a 'V' for Victory by holding aloft the two gold pens with which the German surrender documents had been signed.

For all his military experience, Ike ultimately came to detest war and everything it stood for. He once said, 'I hate war as only a soldier who has lived it can, only as one who has seen its brutality, its futility, its stupidity.' That Eisenhower well understood that sometimes war is inevitable is beyond question. Yet so profound was his experience that – as president of the United States – he was moved to remark in 1953: 'Every gun that is made, every warship launched, every rocket fired signifies, in the final sense, a theft from those who hunger and are not fed, those who are cold and are not clothed.'

The post-war years and the Eisenhower presidency

Eisenhower emerged from the war a national hero. He served as US Army chief of staff from 1945 to 1948, when he became the president of Columbia University. His memoir of the war, *Crusade in Europe*, became an international bestseller and greatly enhanced his public image. In December 1950 he was recalled to active duty and appointed the first supreme commander of the North Atlantic Treaty Organization (NATO), where he served until May 1952 when his military service ended. His great national popularity led to his drafting as the Republican party candidate for president and his election in November 1952, and his re-election by a landslide margin in 1956.

Dwight Eisenhower's trademark grin was perhaps the best known of any public figure in American history. *Time* magazine said of him in 1952: 'They saw Ike, and they liked what they saw ... They liked him in a way they could scarcely explain. They liked Ike because, when they saw him and heard him talk, he made them proud of themselves and all the half-forgotten best that was in them and in the nation.'

His two terms as one of the most popular presidents in American history were marked by passage of the first civil rights acts since the end of the Civil War, intervention in Arkansas to enforce desegregation of the Little Rock public schools, and the promulgation of the Eisenhower Doctrine of American intervention against any nation that used armed force to promote international communism. One of Eisenhower's enduring achievements as president was the creation of the Interstate Highway System in 1956. Its enabling legislation came about as a result of his experience during the Transcontinental Motor Convoy of 1919.

Eisenhower's legacy

Dwight Eisenhower may not have fitted the mould of the warrior hero or of a battlefield general in the tradition of Robert E. Lee, 'Stonewall' Jackson or George S. Patton, yet he was every inch a soldier. His legacy is based on effectively shaping an alliance of Britain and America, two prickly, independent-minded countries with fundamentally disparate philosophies of waging war.

> 'They liked Ike because . . . he made [Americans] proud of themselves and all the half-forgotten best that was in them and in the nation.'
>
> *TIME* MAGAZINE, 1952

History has unfairly stereotyped Eisenhower as a lightweight and a bumbling orator, famous for mangling his syntax, who spent his lifetime concealing his intellect and intelligence behind the image of the 'country bumpkin from Kansas'. But the famous grin masked a man of great intelligence, whose hidden-hand leadership was that of a master craftsman and a thoughtful, caring human being. Eisenhower did far more than make Americans proud. As a soldier and a commander, his place in history was indisputably earned as the supreme commander who guided the Allies to victory in the Mediterranean and in Europe during the most destructive war in history.

Whether in war or peace, Eisenhower always insisted there was no such thing as an indispensable man. Twenty years after the war he was aboard the liner *Queen Elizabeth* for a nostalgic return to Normandy, the scene of his greatest triumph. One night over dinner he said he had read a poem that summed up his attitude about indispensability. It ended this way:

The moral of this quaint example
Is to do just the best that you can.
Be proud of yourself, but remember,
There is no indispensable man.

Perhaps. But it can be safely argued that in the Second World War, Dwight David Eisenhower was indispensable to the victory of the Allies.

Dwight D. Eisenhower

GEORGE S. PATTON

TREVOR ROYLE

1885–1945

GEORGE SMITH PATTON was the outstanding exponent of armoured warfare produced by the Allies in the Second World War. During the fighting in Europe in 1944 and 1945 he demonstrated a mastery of handling large armoured formations, deploying them in mobile, high-speed operations, and thereby winning the admiration of German opponents such as General Günther Blumentritt, who called him 'the most aggressive panzer-general of the Allies'. An inspired leader who possessed physical and mental energy in abundance, Patton was blessed with courage and boundless self-confidence, virtues that made him a spirited and highly effective military commander who always encouraged his soldiers to embrace the will to win. But for a moment of madness in Sicily in August 1943, when he struck two private soldiers suffering from shell shock and was duly reprimanded, he would have commanded the US ground forces following the D-Day landings instead of his great rival, General Omar N. Bradley.

Very much a product of his times, Patton was imbued with his country's military doctrine of speed, manoeuvre and surprise, followed by the deployment of overwhelming force to crush the opposition. It was simple and effective, and the philosophy is best summed up by Patton in his own words: 'The only way you can win a war is to attack and keep on attacking, and after you've done that, keep attacking some more.' He was also a larger-than-life character whose flamboyance made him an unmistakable figure in an increasingly dull and monotonous age. At a time when many commanders dressed in the same style as their soldiers and were prone to disguise trappings of rank, Patton sported a smart uniform complete with stars, riding boots and ivory-handled revolvers, and his flashy motorcades always made sure that he was the centre of attention.

Early training
Patton was born on 11 November 1885 and received his military training at the Virginia Military Institute in Lexington and at West Point. In 1909 he was commissioned in the

George S. Patton

15th Cavalry Regiment, and three years later represented the USA in the modern pentathlon event at the Olympic Games in Stockholm. His first chance to test himself as a soldier came in a frontier war that broke out along the border with Mexico in the summer of 1916. It was a minor conflagration involving rival gangs of Mexican bandits and there were no set-piece battles, but the experience was not lost on Patton. Not only did it provide him with his first opportunity of coming under fire, but having been appointed to the staff of General John J. Pershing, he also learned about the importance of good staff work. In most respects the Mexican campaign was a series of low-intensity operations against a mobile enemy who used the vast reaches of the border area to good advantage by mounting attacks on US positions and then disappearing into thin air. Matters came to a head in March 1916 when Pancho Villa, a Robin Hood-like desperado, attacked the town of Columbus in New Mexico and killed eighteen Americans, including six soldiers.

To prevent further incursions a punitive expedition consisting of 10,000 soldiers was mounted under Pershing's command. Although it failed to crush Villa, it marked the beginning of a new phase in US military operations – the force was motorized and accompanied by eight army biplanes for reconnaissance. The expedition also added lustre to Patton's name. In a daring raid at San Miguelito in May 1916 Patton's patrol ambushed Villa's principal lieutenant, Julio Cárdenas, who was killed along with two other Mexicans in a shoot-out that could have come straight out of a Western movie.

First World War service

The US decision to declare war on Germany in the spring of 1917 gave Patton his first opportunity to experience modern industrialized warfare. Initially Patton served on the staff of the American Expeditionary Force (AEF), but on 10 November he was ordered to take command of a training school for tank crews as part of the AEF's initiative to create a tank corps of 200 heavy and 1,000 light tanks.

The main drawback was that the AEF was reliant on the French for its supplies of Renault

George S. Patton

373

FT-17 tanks, and it was not until the spring of 1918 that they began arriving. In April Patton was promoted to lieutenant colonel and given command of the US army's first two light-tank battalions, which he quickly welded into a coherent and well-disciplined force. Because the tank crews would be fighting on a battlefield in which split-second decisions would have to be taken and they would be operating vehicles without any means of communication, Patton insisted that they maintain high standards of discipline. His message was simple: if his tank commanders assimilated close-order drill and if it became second nature to them they would produce 'instant, cheerful, unhesitating obedience' in the chaos of the battlefield.

In the late summer of 1918 Patton's tank force, the 1st US Tank Brigade (344th and 345th Tank Battalions), saw its first action in the Battle for the St Mihiel salient, a triangular bulge in the German lines that reached as far as the River Meuse south of Verdun. The feature had been in German hands since the first months of the war, producing a threat to the French forces in Champagne, and it was agreed by the French that it represented a good objective for an independent American action on 12 September. Patton's tank brigade was ordered to support the attack on the southern salient by two American infantry divisions, the 1st and the 42nd. As the tanks did not start arriving until 24 August Patton had little time to arrange the supporting fuel and ammunition dumps, and it was not until two hours before the attack began that he was able to get his last tanks into position. He had also reconnoitred the ground over which his men would fight, a requirement that he would impose on all of his commanders later in his career.

Compared to many other battles fought on the Western Front, the offensive at the St Mihiel salient was a minor affair. It only lasted two days, and the US success was as much due to the German decision to withdraw as to the skill of the AEF, but the attack boosted the morale of those who took part in it. The US Tank Brigade also came of age. The two battalions led the attack; of the 174 tanks that took part in the fighting only three received hits and, remarkably, only forty-three broke down. Some got too far ahead of the infantry while others foundered in the heavy-going ground, but the tanks showed that they were capable of winning and holding terrain. In one attack, a section of tanks broke the German line, thereby proving Patton's point that they could be used as a mobile penetration force capable of smashing into the enemy's rear.

Armoured warfare

Although the AEF came back to a hero's welcome, the huge expeditionary force was quickly disbanded, and by the beginning of 1920 the army was once more small in number, having reduced its size to just 130,000 soldiers. Patton stayed with the Tank Corps until the autumn of 1920, when he returned to the cavalry, serving twice in Hawaii and in Washington between 1928 and 1934, when he worked on the staff of the chief of cavalry. During the 1920s and 1930s he wrote and published extensively, producing a wide variety of papers on mechanized warfare, manoeuvre in battle, sport as training for war and, above all, the need for personal leadership. In 1923 he completed the field officers course at Fort Riley, Kansas, and the following year he graduated from the Command and General Staff College at Fort Leavenworth, also in Kansas. This was followed in the winter of 1931/2 by a spell at the Army War College at Fort McNair, Washington DC.

By 1938 Patton had been restored to his wartime rank of full colonel; with it came command, first of the 5th Cavalry Regiment and then the 3rd Cavalry Regiment. By then, too, another war seemed probable, and for the next three years the US army underwent a period of rapid modernization. New armoured forces were raised and Patton was given command of the 2nd Armoured Division, which quickly became a byword for its skills and efficiency. During a series of war games played out in Tennessee, Louisiana and South Carolina in 1941 his division excelled, and shortly after the USA declared war on Japan and Germany at the end of the year Patton was given command of I Armoured Corps.

During this period of intensive training a pattern had begun to emerge in Patton's style of leadership. He insisted on speed and aggression in making attacks, and tried to gain the upper hand by relying on surprise, using reconnaissance to good advantage – he was a stickler for gathering intelligence about his opponents' movements. He also inculcated discipline in his commanders so that their standards would be passed on to the men, and made sure that he was known to all his soldiers, devoting considerable time to addressing them in person. On the technical side he was an innovator, flying a light aircraft to tour the operational areas and using wireless to keep in touch with forward positions. In short, by the time the USA went to war, Patton had proved himself to be an inspirational commander capable of leading large numbers of men in battle.

Patton addresses officers of a US airborne division prior to the invasion of Sicily, summer 1943. A very competitive character, Patton felt his Seventh Army was being sidelined during the Sicilian campaign, and went all out to capture Palermo to show its worth.

North Africa and Sicily

Following the US declaration of war it was agreed that US forces should lend their weight to the Allied campaign in North Africa. Known as Operation Torch, its object was to gain complete control of North Africa from the Atlantic to the Red Sea, starting with landings in Algeria and French Morocco before rolling up the Axis forces in Libya,

George S. Patton

where the British Eighth Army was engaging the Axis forces. Patton was given command of the task force that landed at Casablanca unopposed on 8 November 1942. Thereafter matters did not run so smoothly, and just two months later Major General Lloyd Fredendall's US II Corps suffered ignominious defeats at Sidi-Bou-Zid and the Kasserine Pass in February 1943 (see pp. 337–8). As a result Fredendall was sacked and replaced in March by Patton, who quickly set about the essential task of restoring discipline and rebuilding morale.

Within ten days of taking command Patton was leading his men in the Allies' first joint offensive to crush Axis resistance in North Africa. The plan was to use the British Eighth Army to attack Tunis through the Mareth Line from the south while a New Zealand army corps made a diversionary attack inland to outflank the Axis defensive positions. If the assault succeeded the Italians would be driven north along the coastal plain towards Tunis, where they and the German forces would be crushed by the Allies. Patton's role in the operation was to attack enemy positions along the eastern flank – running through the hills known as the Eastern Dorsale – and to capture the hill towns of Gafsa, Sened and Maknassy, together with the associated air strips that would otherwise threaten the Eighth Army as it drove towards Tunis. All the objectives were taken with an élan that would have been impossible in the immediate aftermath of the débâcle at the Kasserine Pass.

George S. Patton

376

On 13 May 1943 Tunis fell, and the war in North Africa came to an end with a resounding victory that did much to restore Allied self-respect. The next stage involved the capture of Sicily as a precursor to the invasion of Italy. The Sicilian operation called for a seaborne assault by the British Eighth Army between Syracuse and the Pachino peninsula on the island's southeastern coast on 10 July, while the US I and II Armoured Corps under Patton's command would land on a 40-mile front along the southern coast between Gela and Scoglitti and Licata on the left flank. British and US forces also staged an airborne assault to capture key points. The general plan was that the British would push north on the right flank while Patton's US forces shielded the left.

This was a difficult time for Patton, who believed that US forces were being given a subsidiary role – a symptom of the friction then prevalent in the Allied command structure. Patton's solution was to give a demonstration of his army's capability by rushing northwestwards to take possession of the capital, Palermo. In itself the city was not a vital strategic objective – the main aim was to take Messina in the northeast corner – but Patton knew that a successful operation would increase the status of the US army. On 21 July Palermo duly fell, and this allowed Patton to use it as a spring-board for attacking Messina, which was entered by triumphant US forces on the evening of 16 August.

France and northwest Europe

Patton's successes in North Africa and Sicily should have been followed by promotion to command the US forces for the invasion of Europe (see pp. 344–5 and 368), but following the incidents in which he slapped two privates he was sidelined and given command of the US Third Army. It was not until the end of July 1944, almost two months after the D-Day landings, that Patton joined the battle in Normandy – but he immediately made his mark. His leadership in the break-out battle towards Avranches, in which he used blitzkrieg tactics with devastating effectiveness, showed Patton at his aggressive best and allowed the US forces to push rapidly towards the Seine valley (see pp. 378–9). By 30 August Patton had moved the Third Army across the River Marne and was within reach of Metz when their petrol reserves began to run dry. Only the lack of regular supplies – the logistic tail stretched over 400 miles back to Cherbourg – prevented Patton from pressing home his advantage, and for a time the Allied advance stalled.

It was at this stage of the battle, when the Allies were still confident that the end of the war was in sight, that the Germans decided to counter-attack in the Ardennes. The plan was the brain-child of Adolf Hitler, who reasoned that the winter weather – 'night, fog and snow' – would give the Germans the opportunity to hit back at the Allies through the dense Ardennes forest, with its narrow steep-sided valleys, and then turn rapidly north to recapture Brussels and Antwerp. It did not turn out that way, but the Battle of the Bulge, as it came to be known, almost allowed the Germans to achieve their aims by creating a huge salient or 'bulge' in the Allied lines. During the battle, in one of the best-executed manoeuvres of the war, Patton realigned his Third Army, turning its three divisions to attack northwards out of Luxembourg to dent the German assault. Owing

'I want you men to remember that no bastard ever won a war by dying for his country. He won it by making the other dumb bastard die for his country.'

GEORGE S. PATTON, ADDRESSING US TROOPS BEFORE D-DAY, 1944

George S. Patton

(Below) **Heavy armour of Patton's US Third Army** moves south through Bolleville on 29 July 1944, during Operation Cobra, the break-out from the Normandy beachheads.

to Patton's foresight – he had already anticipated the move and had plans in place to execute it – the entire operation was completed within four days. Once the bulge had been blocked German resistance in the Ardennes came to an end.

Ahead lay the drive into Germany and the crossing of the River Rhine, as the Allies pushed into the enemy heartlands. Patton's Third Army raced into southern Bavaria and ended the war close to the border with Czechoslovakia, but its commander

NORMANDY
BLITZKRIEG

FOLLOWING THE SUCCESSFUL Allied landings in Normandy in June 1944, the next phase of the operation involved the Allies fighting to consolidate their beachhead before attempting a break-out, while the Germans made every effort to drive them back into the sea. This gave Patton, who arrived in Normandy in late July, his chance to exploit the situation by leading a rapid armoured assault to move US forces into open country before the Germans had the chance to regroup. It was to be the only example of the use of blitzkrieg by the Allies during the Second World War – the rapid and ruthless penetration of the enemy's lines using overwhelming force to encircle and destroy the opposition. Air support was integral to this style of warfare, with strike aircraft acting as airborne artillery in advance of the main tank assault.

The Normandy stalemate was broken by Operation Cobra, mounted on 25 July by the US First Army, which pushed as far south as Avranches and the pivotal neighbouring town of Pontaubault. Suddenly the possibility opened of invading Brittany in the west and racing eastwards towards Le Mans and the River Seine. The task was given to seven divisions of Patton's US Third Army, which moved with exemplary speed into Brittany, frequently running ahead of their lines of communication as they sped into the open countryside. Bottlenecks and traffic jams were overcome by the simple expedient of dispatching staff officers to forward positions with instructions to get the units through, regardless of their sequence in the battle-plans. Within three days Patton's divisions were through the Avranches–Pontaubault gap; it was not a manoeuvre that would have been recognized at staff college, but it worked.

While this breakthrough was gratifying it was obvious that Brittany had become a backwater and that there was better employment for Patton's forces. They had shown what could be accomplished by a mobile army

George S. Patton

did not live long to relish the triumph or to take his military career into the post-war world. It is one of the many ironies in his life that Patton did not die, as he wished, 'with the last bullet in the last battle of the war', but as the result of a needless car crash near Mannheim in Germany. He died on 21 December 1945 in a hospital in Heidelberg, and was buried at the US military cemetery in Luxembourg, his grave lying alongside other Third Army soldiers who had died under his command a year earlier.

using speed and aggression backed up by air power; now was the time to deploy those assets eastward against the bulk of the German forces guarding the Paris–Orléans gap. It was there, argued Patton, that 'the decisive battle of the European war would obviously be fought'. Backed by fighter-bombers of the US XIX Tactical Air Command, the US Third Army pushed through the southern Normandy countryside, advancing rapidly without worrying about the need to protect their flanks.

Once engaged in the break-out, Patton's armoured divisions had shown that they had taken their general's philosophy to heart. What began at Avranches continued in the race to the Seine, and the operation was to demonstrate everything that was good about Patton's leadership in the pursuit phase of a battle. With the fall of Dreux, Chartres and Orléans, all the objectives had been achieved by mid August, leaving Patton to exult that the operation was 'probably the fastest and biggest pursuit in history'.

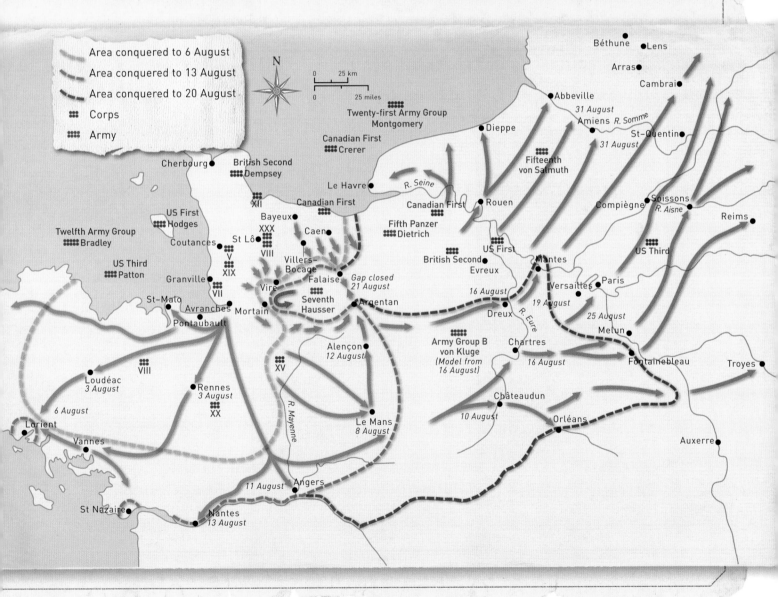

George S. Patton

TOMOYUKI YAMASHITA
1885–1946

ALAN WARREN

LIEUTENANT GENERAL TOMOYUKI YAMASHITA'S seventy-day campaign to capture Singapore on 15 February 1942 was one of the most spectacular in modern history, earning him the nickname 'the Tiger of Malaya'. At Singapore, the British Empire's illusion of permanence and strength was brought crashing down in a matter of weeks. A rational strategic thinker, Yamashita was not a man obsessed with spiritual values at the expense of practical considerations. With a large, shaven head and broad neck, he was tall by Japanese standards, a dignified man noted for his stoicism and lack of public emotion. Behind the mask, however, he was energetic, ambitious and possessed of a high level of imagination. A senior staff officer shrewdly described Yamashita as a 'clear-headed type of politician'.

War in Asia had broken out in July 1937 as a consequence of Japanese encroachments on northern China. By 1939 the conflict between Japan and the Chinese Nationalists had reached stalemate. Yet in the wake of Germany's stunning triumph over France, in September 1940 the Japanese government opportunistically joined the Axis and became an ally of Nazi Germany. The situation was transformed again when the Germans invaded the Soviet Union in June 1941. With the Russians, Japan's traditional enemy, fully occupied, Japan's imperialist leaders saw chances for conquest at the expense of poorly defended European colonies in Southeast Asia. When the Japanese were drawing up plans to overrun the region, the best available army formation – the Twenty-fifth Army – was set aside to attempt the capture of Singapore, the most important Allied base in the region.

Early career

The general appointed to command the vital Twenty-fifth Army was Lieutenant General Tomoyuki Yamashita. The second son of a doctor, Yamashita had been born in November 1885 in an isolated mountain village on the Japanese home island of Shikoku. He attended the Central Military Academy in Tokyo, and was commissioned at the end of 1905.

Tomoyuki Yamashita

In 1918, after graduation from the War College, Yamashita arrived at the Japanese embassy in Switzerland as assistant military attaché. Captain Hideki Tojo, Japan's future wartime prime minister, was also posted to the Berne embassy at that time. The two men struck up a friendship and, after the end of the First World War, toured Germany and the silent battlefields of the Western Front. Yamashita returned to Tokyo and the War Ministry, but he later spent a further three years in Europe as military attaché in Vienna, leaving his estranged wife behind in Japan. While in Vienna, Yamashita had an extended and passionate affair with a German woman; he later said that his Vienna posting was the best period of his life.

By 1936 Yamashita was a major-general and chief of military affairs at imperial Headquarters in Tokyo. An attempted military coup that year badly damaged his political position within the army, and drew the ire of the emperor. Henceforward Yamashita was keenly aware of that disapproval and the consequent need to demonstrate his loyalty publicly. A spell in Korea as a brigade commander was followed by service as a divisional commander in China after war broke out in 1937. Yamashita, on active service for the first time, earned a fine reputation for bravery and leadership.

After Japan had joined the Axis, Yamashita led a military mission to Europe to investigate Germany's crushing victory over France. He met Hitler in Berlin and said privately that he was 'an unimpressive little man'. Yamashita was exposed to German concepts of armoured warfare that emphasized speed and mobility. After returning to Japan, he was posted to Manchuria as part of the build-up in that region in preparation for possible war with the Soviets. Early in November 1941 he was recalled to take command of the Twenty-fifth Army for the invasion of Southeast Asia.

The invasion of Malaya

In 1941 Singapore, the greatest port between India and China, was part of the British colony of Malaya. The British had built a naval base at this 'Gibraltar of the East', and emplaced large-calibre naval guns on the south coast of the island to deter an attack from the sea. There was, however, no British fleet there prior to the

Tomoyuki Yamashita, 'the Tiger of Malaya'. Given a hundred days by the Japanese High Command to take Singapore, he completed the task in seventy.

Tomoyuki Yamashita

Second World War. Owing to the demands of the war in Europe, only two British capital ships – *Prince of Wales* and *Repulse* – could be spared for the Far East.

The British Empire's army garrison in Malaya had been strongly reinforced during 1941 to over 90,000 men, yet there was no British tank force in the colony. The army commander in Malaya was Lieutenant General A. E. Percival, a mild-mannered man who had spent much of the previous decade as a desk-bound staff officer.

At Southern Army's Saigon headquarters, General Count Hisaichi Terauchi gave the Twenty-fifth Army his best divisions. Japanese officers of the Taiwan Army Research Section had been working on preparations for the campaign in Southeast Asia for months. Amphibious landings had been practised in southern China and on Hainan Island, and exercises undertaken using bicycles to convey combat units long distances.

General Yamashita left Saigon for Hainan Island on 25 November 1941, where a part of the Twenty-fifth Army was assembling at the port of Samah. On 4 December, as his forces set out from Hainan, Yamashita wrote a poem:

> *On the day the sun shines with the moon*
> *Our arrow leaves the bow*
> *It carries my spirit towards the enemy*
> *With me are a hundred million souls*
> *My people from the East*
> *On this day when the moon*
> *And the sun both shine.*

Japanese troops march through Singapore, 27 February 1942. The fall of Britain's great naval base in the Far East not only had major strategic consequences, it also showed the peoples of Asia that the Europeans were not invincible.

The finalized Twenty-fifth Army plan was to land the 5th Division at Singora and Patani in southern Thailand, whilst a regiment of the 18th Division landed at Kota Bharu in northeast Malaya to seize nearby aerodromes. The Imperial Guards Division was to take part in the invasion of Thailand, and then move down into Malaya by road.

A brigade-strength tank unit was available to support the Twenty-fifth Army's infantry. Japanese troops were experienced, obedient and possessed an indestructible morale that drew inspiration from *bushido*, the Spartan creed of the Samurai.

On 7 December 1941 Japan's daring plan to attack the United States fleet at Pearl Harbor came to fruition, together with the invasion of Thailand and Malaya. Yamashita and his headquarters were aboard the transport ship *Ryujo Maru*, and he intended to go ashore at Singora, close behind the first wave of invaders. The convoys were only briefly sighted as they closed on their destinations. The landings in southern Thailand were almost unopposed, and the Thai government soon capitulated. The landing on the northeast coast of Malaya at Kota Bharu was timed to start at the same moment as the raid on Pearl Harbor, though by accident it actually began an hour or two early. At the outset of the campaign, the under-strength RAF was quickly shot out of the skies of northern Malaya, while *Prince of Wales* and *Repulse*, attempting a delayed foray in the South China Sea, were swiftly sunk by modern Japanese torpedo-bombers.

On land, the well-balanced Japanese expeditionary force advanced south from Thailand. At Jitra, in northwest Malaya, the Anglo-Indian defenders were swept aside, and Yamashita sensed that he already had the British on the run. Japanese troops used bicycles to keep moving forward along good local roads. General Percival had retained half of his force at Singapore and southern Malaya as he feared a direct amphibious attack on those places. Penang was abandoned, and the Japanese used small boats to 'hook' troops down the west coast of Malaya. The dazed 11th Indian Division was shattered by Japanese tanks at Slim river on 7 January 1942, and Kuala Lumpur, the capital of the Federated Malay States, fell to the invaders a few days later. In southern Malaya the enterprising Japanese broke through a weakly held flank and the British retreated to Singapore Island. The Japanese had advanced over 500 miles in less than eight weeks, and had suffered fewer than 5,000 casualties.

> 'No one can ever dispute Yamashita executed one of the most effective delaying actions in the whole history of warfare.'
>
> ROBERT ROSS SMITH, IN THE US ARMY'S OFFICIAL HISTORY, *TRIUMPH IN THE PHILIPPINES* (1963)

Towards the close of January, several Japanese air force units were transferred from Malaya to support operations in the Dutch East Indies. An angry Yamashita had responded: 'All right, in that case we shall not rely upon the cooperation of the air force. The army will now capture Singapore single-handed.' British reinforcement convoys continued to sail into Singapore at the eleventh hour, bringing the garrison to over 100,000 men. A vast pillar of dark smoke billowed skywards from the burning fuel dumps of the evacuated naval base. The Battle of Singapore was about to begin (see pp. 384–5).

The capitulation of Singapore

Yamashita insisted on a face-to-face meeting with Percival to conclude the week-long battle for Singapore, and on 15 February 1942 the British commander led a small party bearing the Union Jack and a large white flag to parley with the Japanese. The conference, which began at 5.15 p.m., took place at the Ford Motor Factory near Bukit Timah village. Percival looked haggard; Yamashita presented a bullet-headed, stocky figure in his khaki field uniform. When discussions bogged down, Yamashita impatiently banged the table with his fist: 'The time for the night attack is drawing near. Is the British army going to surrender or not? Answer YES or NO?' (He used the

Tomoyuki Yamashita

THE BATTLE OF SINGAPORE

GENERAL YAMASHITA RESOLVED TO ATTACK SINGAPORE in February 1942 after only a week's preparation. The Twenty-fifth Army's advanced headquarters was sited in the sultan of Johore's Green Palace, the Istana Hijau, on the bank of the Malayan mainland facing Singapore. Yamashita sent a message to his divisional commanders telling them that he would directly observe their efforts from his new command post. He assured his adjutant: 'The enemy won't fire on this place. They would never dream I would come so near in such a prominent position.' Yamashita's leadership was, as always, energetically driving his army forward.

The strait separating Singapore from the Malayan mainland is narrow, only half a mile to a couple of miles across. Yet, rather than concentrate a large part of his force opposite where the strait was narrowest, the British commander, General Percival, spread his garrison right around Singapore's coast. By use of various decoys Percival's attention was diverted to the northeast coast of Singapore, and on the evening of 8 February 1942 Yamashita threw just about his entire force against the northwest coast in 300 small boats. The force deployed by Percival along that stretch of coast consisted of just one Australian brigade. By morning the thin line of defenders had collapsed and retreated several miles to the rear in disorder. The following night the Imperial Guards attacked between the Kranji river and the causeway linking Singapore Island to the mainland. The assault of the Imperial Guards came close to failure, but Yamashita refused to be panicked and the attack was pushed onward successfully.

Percival was still worrying about fresh landings on other parts of the Singaporean coast, unaware that almost the entire Japanese force was already ashore. Yamashita's aggressive handling of his forces made them seem numerically stronger than was in fact the case. On the night of 10/11 February the Bukit Timah heights, in the centre of Singapore Island, were seized in a bayonet assault. After the

Royal Engineers prepare to blow up a bridge in Malaya during the British retreat to Singapore. During the Malayan campaign, the Japanese – many riding bicycles – advanced over 500 miles in less than eight weeks, and suffered fewer than 5,000 casualties.

(Opposite) **Women and children being herded together by Japanese soldiers** after the fall of Singapore, February 1942. The first weeks following the surrender saw the summary execution of possibly as many as 30,000 Chinese by the occupiers.

English words.) Japanese newspapers reported exaggerated accounts of Yamashita bullying Percival into surrender with his bulk and glaring eyes.

Yamashita wrote that Percival 'was good on paper but timid and hesitant in making command decisions', and said of the final stage of the campaign: 'I knew if I had to fight long for Singapore I would be beaten. That is why the surrender had to be at once. I was very frightened all the time that the British would discover our numerical weakness and lack of supplies and force me into disastrous street fighting.' Throughout the campaign Percival had failed to concentrate his forces, whereas the Twenty-fifth Army had massed force on a narrow front, and made full use of surprise and manoeuvre to punch through its enemy's line. Yamashita's plan for the assault on Singapore Island, whereby the bulk of the Twenty-fifth Army was thrown against a small part of the defending force, repeated the formula that had worked so well on the mainland.

Tomoyuki Yamashita

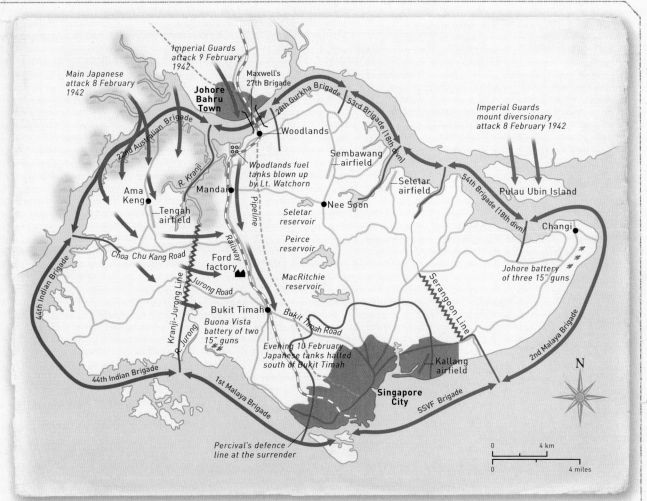

Japanese managed to land tanks they consolidated their hold on the central part of Singapore Island, including the reservoir catchment area.

From 12 February, constant Japanese attacks slowly contracted the British perimeter. As Japanese ammunition ran short, Yamashita visited his units to apologize for the shortage and to urge continued advance relying on the bayonet. Yamashita told his staff: 'The enemy is also going through a hard time. If we halt now, we will lose the initiative over the battle and the enemy will discover our shortage of supplies and counter-attack us!' When Percival finally agreed to negotiate a surrender on 15 February, the beaten garrison had been backed into a narrow perimeter surrounding the town and waterfront.

A ceasefire came into effect at 8.30 p.m. on 15 February. The following day a vast army of British, Indian and Australian servicemen went into grim and often fatal captivity. For the British, the shame of the manner of Singapore's fall demonstrated, in no uncertain terms, that the days of empire and world power were drawing to a close. At dawn on 16 February, the day after the capitulation, Yamashita rose from his bed and went outdoors. He stood at the edge of a wood and bowed to pray, facing in the direction of the emperor's palace in Tokyo. The Japanese High Command had allotted a hundred days to take Singapore. The task had been successfully completed in seventy.

General Arthur
Percival, commander
of Allied forces in
Singapore, goes to
parley with the Japanese,
15 February 1942.
Yamashita later con-
fessed that if he had not
persuaded Percival to
surrender promptly, the
Japanese might not have
succeeded in taking
Singapore. (Percival is to
the left of the Japanese
officers, holding the
Union flag.)

One of the more immediate consequences of the fall of Singapore was the summary execution of thousands of Chinese by Japanese forces in the first weeks after the surrender. The Singapore garrison commander, Major-General Kawamura, subsequently claimed Yamashita gave the order on 18 February for mopping-up operations against 'hostile' Chinese, or what became known as the *Sook Ching*, 'purification by elimination'. Senior Japanese officers later conceded that 5,000 Chinese had been executed by military police (*Kempaitai*) and detachments from all three of the 25th Army's divisions. Leaders of Singapore's Chinese community have estimated that over 30,000 people were killed.

The battle for the Philippines, 1944–5

Yamashita did not entirely approve of his popular sobriquet, 'the Tiger of Malaya', and once told a German military attaché: 'The tiger attacks its prey in stealth but I attack the enemy in a fair play.' Surprisingly, Yamashita did not play a prominent part in the war in the period following his capture of Singapore. In July 1942 he was sent from Singapore to command one of the two army groups stationed in Manchuria along the frontier with the Soviet Union. This was a command of importance, but within the army it was felt that Yamashita had been kept away from Japan by Prime Minister Tojo for political reasons. Yamashita had not been permitted to stop off in Japan en route to Manchuria for the audience with the emperor that a victorious military commander had reason to expect.

Only after Tojo's resignation as prime minister in July 1944 was Yamashita recalled from Manchuria. He finally had an audience with Emperor Hirohito on 30 September 1944 and was told that 'the fate of the empire rests upon your shoulders'. Yamashita was swiftly dispatched to lead Japanese forces in the Philippines. He assumed command of over 400,000 men on 9 October 1944, just as the Americans were poised to attack. The situation for Japan had changed dramatically for the worse since the fall of Singapore.

The first American landings were made on the island of Leyte on 20 October 1944 amid a great series of naval battles. By the end of 1944 Japanese forces on Leyte had been destroyed by the massive firepower the Americans were able to deploy. Luzon, the

Tomoyuki Yamashita

main Philippine island, was invaded on 8 January 1945. Yamashita had no intention of defending Manila, the capital of the Philippines, and ordered his local army commander to conduct demolitions ahead of the advancing Americans and then evacuate the city. At Manila, however, Rear Admiral Sanji Iwabuchi decided that it was his duty to deny Manila's harbour installations for as long as possible. In the battle that followed (February–March 1945), the Japanese force was annihilated, but parts of the city were demolished, an estimated 100,000 civilians died, and there was widespread murder, rape and torture of civilians by Japanese troops within the confined space of the shrinking perimeter.

In north Luzon, Yamashita's main force tenaciously held its ground until crippling losses drove it deep into the mountainous interior. After Japan's final capitulation, a thin Yamashita gave himself up to the Americans on 2 September. He did not commit hara-kiri and was reported to have said: 'If I kill myself someone else will have to take the blame.' There is no doubt that Yamashita's defence of Luzon displayed generalship of the highest standard.

Trial and execution

Yamashita was put on trial as a war criminal by the Americans. The trial in Manila began on 29 October 1945. The main charges against the general related to his responsibility for the massacres that had undoubtedly taken place in Manila. Senior Japanese officers

Yamashita leads his troops out of the mountains of Luzon in the Philippines to surrender to American forces, 2 September 1945. He was hanged for war crimes on 23 February 1946.

testified that Yamashita had ordered that Manila was not to be defended. Nonetheless, the general's death sentence was pronounced on 7 December, the anniversary of the bombing of Pearl Harbor. Yamashita told an interviewer:

> My command was as big as MacArthur's or Lord Louis Mountbatten's. How could I tell if some of my soldiers misbehaved themselves? It was impossible for any man in my position to control every action of his subordinate commanders, let alone the deeds of individual soldiers ... What I am really being charged with is losing the war. It could have happened to General MacArthur, you know.

Yamashita was hanged on 23 February 1946. The dubious legal circumstances of his conviction have garnered for him a degree of sympathy, and were seen in some quarters as an official lynching. Yet if the general had not been tried as a war criminal in Manila, he would very likely have been tried and executed by the British in Singapore for the organized massacre of the Chinese carried out by Japanese troops after their capture of the island.

Tomoyuki Yamashita

387

'Old soldiers never die, they just fade away.'
DOUGLAS MACARTHUR

DOUGLAS MACARTHUR
1880–1964

CARLO D'ESTE

ONE OF THE GREATEST SOLDIERS ever to wear the US Army uniform and one of the most enigmatic, MacArthur's flamboyance and brilliance were matched by a towering ego and a penchant for the dramatic. His star-studded career spanned half a century: first in his class at West Point, most decorated combat commander of 1917–18, superintendent and reformer of West Point, chief of staff of the interwar army, military proconsul both in the Philippines and in Japan, Medal of Honor winner, commander of Allied forces in the South Pacific, commander of UN forces during the first critical months of the Korean War, and one of only five men to be accorded the five-star rank of General of the Army.

General Douglas MacArthur, photographed in Manila in 1945, enjoying his famous corn-cob pipe.

Douglas MacArthur was born in Little Rock, Arkansas, in 1880, the son of a career army officer, Lieutenant General Arthur Mac-Arthur, who won the Medal of Honor at Missionary Ridge, Tennessee, in 1863 as a Union officer. Douglas grew up on military posts with a single aim in life: to emulate his famous father by also winning the Medal of Honor, the nation's highest decoration for bravery. 'My first memory was the sound of bugles,' he would later recall. 'I learned to ride and shoot even before I could read or write – indeed, almost before I could walk or talk.'

MacArthur entered West Point in 1898 and not only achieved the distinction of first captain of the corps of cadets but also graduated first in the class of 1903, a

Douglas MacArthur

388

glittering academic record only surpassed by two other graduates, one of whom was Robert E. Lee.

After commissioning as an engineer officer, he was posted to the Philippines where he soon had the first of many brushes with death, waylaid by two desperadoes while on a surveying mission in the jungle. MacArthur later wrote, 'Like all frontiersmen, I was expert with a pistol. I dropped them both dead in their tracks.'

Back in the United States, MacArthur served as an aide in the White House to President Theodore Roosevelt and in 1914 participated in the expedition to Vera Cruz, Mexico, where he was nominated for, but not awarded, the Medal of Honor for his exploits while on a reconnaissance mission. He had gone behind Mexican lines and daringly managed to purloin three locomotives before returning with them to friendly lines through a hail of gunfire.

First World War service

By the time the US entered the First World War in 1917, MacArthur had achieved the rank of full colonel. Sent to France as chief of staff of the 42nd 'Rainbow ' Division, a New York National Guard unit, he served in the front lines as a brigade commander. Utterly fearless and constantly exposing himself to enemy fire, MacArthur earned exceptional distinction as the most highly decorated American soldier of the war, winning two Distinguished Service Crosses (the second highest decoration awarded for bravery), seven Silver Stars, the Distinguished Service Medal and two Purple Hearts for wounds received in battle. MacArthur was also recommended for the Medal of Honor for leading his brigade during the battle for the Côte de Châtillon in the Meuse–Argonne campaign in October 1918. However, the commander-in-chief of the American Expeditionary Force (AEF), General John J. Pershing, inexplicably denied it. By the end of the war, MacArthur was a brigadier general in command of the division during the Sedan offensive. Secretary of War Newton D. Baker called MacArthur 'the greatest American field commander produced by the war'.

The inter-war years

MacArthur emerged from the First World War with an impressive service record and eight rows of ribbons on his uniform. Whereas most other officers were demoted in the peacetime army, not only did MacArthur keep his rank of brigadier general, but his reputation as one of the army's most brilliant officers earned him the prestigious appointment of superintendent of West Point. During his tenure from 1919 to 1922, he overcame the entrenched status quo by instituting badly needed reforms that modernized the academy's archaic academic curriculum and put the brakes on its lax discipline and notorious 'hazing' practices of ritualized abuse of new recruits.

During the 1920s MacArthur served two tours of duty in the Philippines, one of them in command of the Philippine Department, and in 1925 he became the army's youngest major general. His reputation for supporting amateur athletics led to his appointment to chair the US committee for the 1928 Olympic Games.

In 1930, President Herbert Hoover appointed MacArthur army chief of staff. His most difficult undertaking was merely to hold the small peacetime army together during the Great Depression and stave off repeated attempts to decimate its annual

Douglas MacArthur

parsimonious budget appropriations. He also reformed the army education system and the results paid off handsomely when war came and men who had benefited from MacArthur's initiatives were given important commands; they uniformly succeeded.

In 1932, MacArthur was at the centre of the controversy over the infamous Bonus March on Washington by thousands of destitute First World War veterans who were protesting the government's failure to make good on its promise of bonus money. With the full support of MacArthur, who acted with unseemly relish, the army was ordered to disperse the marchers and the resulting violence – which included the use of tear gas, sabres and bayonets – marked one of the most shameful episodes of American history.

He imprudently claimed to have saved the nation from 'incipient revolution' by a mob of 'insurrectionists'; the long-term damage from the Bonus March was incalculable in an era where the military was already weakened and under fire, and facing still more budgetary cutbacks. MacArthur and the army became the public exemplars of an ungrateful nation that rewarded its veterans by gassing, bayoneting and shooting them. During his long and distinguished military career Douglas MacArthur was at the heart of numerous controversies but none did more to tarnish his reputation permanently, and that of the army he headed, than his actions over the Bonus March.

Although he embraced President Franklin D. Roosevelt's New Deal, MacArthur became unpopular with the president for his vocal opposition to pacifism and America's rampant isolationism. When his term as chief of staff ended in October 1935, Philippine president Manuel Quezon, an old friend from his earlier duty, persuaded MacArthur to come to Manila to help form and train the Philippine army. Offered the opportunity to return to a place he dearly loved, he accepted at once. It never seems to have dawned on the politically naïve MacArthur, who was thought to be considering a run for president, that it suited both Roosevelt and his many other enemies to have him 11,000 miles from Washington.

Those who knew or served under MacArthur either admired his genius or despised his narcissism. One of his principal assistants in Washington and the Philippines in the 1930s was Dwight Eisenhower, who has said of him that: 'He did have a hell of an intellect! My God, but he was smart. He had a brain.'

In Manila, MacArthur's ego was on full display. He officially retired from the army in 1937 in order to accept an appointment as a field marshal in the Philippine army, the only American officer ever to hold such a rank. The appointment was widely seen as dubious and was derided by Eisenhower, who was far from alone in his belief that not only was MacArthur being disloyal to the army, but that it was absurd for him to be the field marshal of a virtually non-existent force.

In large part, MacArthur was a victim of the Great Depression during his tenure in Manila. His constant feuds with Washington over funding and equipment for the fledgling Philippine army were equally harmful. Grossly inadequate funds and insufficient military equipment left MacArthur unable to fulfil his mission of creating a viable Philippine army. But he would spend much of the Second World World preoccupied with the Philippines, albeit as commander of US Far East forces.

The Philippines in the Second World War

With war clouds gathering in the Pacific, Roosevelt recalled MacArthur to active duty in the summer of 1941 and named him commander of US Far East forces, sending him

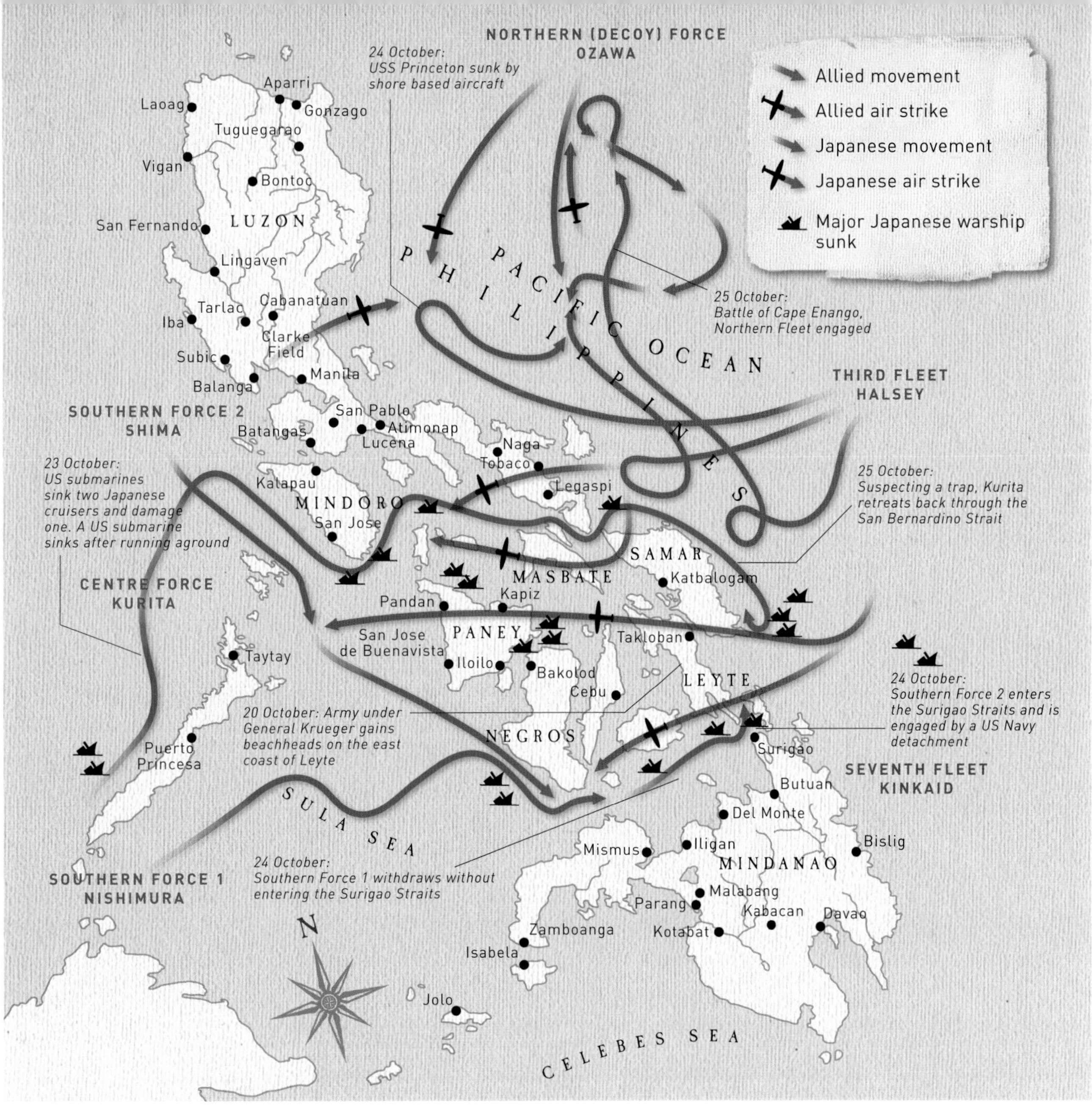
NORTHERN (DECOY) FORCE
OZAWA
24 October:
USS Princeton sunk by shore based aircraft
Allied movement
Allied air strike
Japanese movement
Japanese air strike
Major Japanese warship sunk
25 October:
Battle of Cape Enango, Northern Fleet engaged
THIRD FLEET
HALSEY
PACIFIC OCEAN
PHILIPPINES
LUZON
Aparri
Laoag
Gonzago
Tuguegarao
Vigan
Bontoc
San Fernando
Lingaven
Tarlac
Cabanatuan
Iba
Clarke Field
Subic
Manila
Balanga
SOUTHERN FORCE 2
SHIMA
San Pablo
Atimonap
Batangas
Lucena
Naga
Tobaco
23 October:
US submarines sink two Japanese cruisers and damage one. A US submarine sinks after running aground
Katapau
Legaspi
MINDORO
San Jose
25 October:
Suspecting a trap, Kurita retreats back through the San Bernardino Strait
SAMAR
Katbalogam
CENTRE FORCE
KURITA
MASBATE
Kapiz
Pandan
PANEY
San Jose de Buenavista
Takloban
Taytay
Iloilo
Bakolod
Cebu
LEYTE
24 October:
Southern Force 2 enters the Surigao Straits and is engaged by a US Navy detachment
20 October: Army under General Krueger gains beachheads on the east coast of Leyte
NEGROS
Puerto Princesa
Surigao
SEVENTH FLEET
KINKAID
Butuan
SULA SEA
Del Monte
Mismus
Iligan
Bislig
MINDANAO
24 October:
Southern Force 1 withdraws without entering the Surigao Straits
SOUTHERN FORCE 1
NISHIMURA
Malabang
Parang
Kabacan
Davao
N
Zamboanga
Kotabat
Isabela
Jolo
CELEBES SEA

THE BATTLE OF THE PHILIPPINES, 20–27 October 1944.

back to the Philippines. When Japan attacked Pearl Harbor on 7 December 1941, MacArthur again became a four-star general. His years of attempting to forge a defence of the Philippines came to naught in the succeeding days, the islands being indefensible and the Philippine army no match for the better-trained and far more powerful Japanese.

Japanese aircraft attacked Clark Field near Manila on 8 December, where the US B-17 bomber fleet was caught on the ground and severely mauled. This was followed by Japanese landings on the island of Luzon that, by the end of December, proved unstoppable. Manila was evacuated and by early January 1942 US and Philippine forces retreated to the Bataan peninsula and the island fortress of Corregidor. During the first desperate months of 1942, the fate of MacArthur's force was sealed and by early March, with surrender only a matter of time, Roosevelt ordered MacArthur to Australia. He was secretly evacuated from Corregidor by PT boat on 11 March and after a harrowing escape vowed, 'I shall return'. Despite the loss of the Philippines MacArthur was awarded the Medal of Honor, largely to help boost morale at home

> 'I shall return.'
>
> DOUGLAS MACARTHUR ON HIS EVACUATION FROM THE PHILIPPINES, MARCH 1942

MacArthur strides ashore on his return to Leyte on 20 October 1944. In defiance of protocol, to his right, and a step behind, is Philippine President Sergio Osmeña.

and to counter Axis propaganda that portrayed him as a coward who had deserted his troops.

Indeed, many never forgave him for leaving behind his embattled force led by Lieutenant General Jonathan Wainwright, which held out until 7 May before surrendering. The survivors became part of the infamous Bataan Death March. The loss of his Philippine force was anguish for MacArthur, who declared that: 'Through the bloody haze of its last reverberating shot I shall always seem to see a vision of grim, gaunt, ghastly men still unafraid.' Although unwarranted, the derisive term 'Dug-out Doug' forever tainted MacArthur's reputation.

Although it was impossible to have reinforced the Philippines, MacArthur was unforgiving and bitterly blamed Washington for the loss of his force there. His relations with Roosevelt ranged from the frosty to the downright disrespectful.

Appointed supreme commander of Allied forces in the Southwest Pacific (SWPA), MacArthur established his headquarters in Australia and initiated campaigns to recapture key islands, beginning with New Guinea in 1943. He also fought a bitter turf battle with the US Navy over control of the war in the Pacific. MacArthur wanted to focus on recapturing New Guinea and the Philippines, while the admirals favoured a strategy of island-hopping across the central Pacific in a manner that made better use of the US carrier fleet. In the end, both strategies were carried out. MacArthur was especially effective in his employment of air power in support of ground operations.

On 20 October 1944, MacArthur carried out his promise to return when he waded ashore on the island of Leyte during the successful campaign to recapture the Philippines (see also pp. 386–7). After retaking the islands, and as the war neared its end, he began to plan for the invasion of Japan in late 1945. However, the employment of the atomic bomb on Hiroshima and Nagasaki brought about Japan's unconditional surrender, which was taken by a triumphant MacArthur on the deck of the battleship USS *Missouri* on 2 September 1945.

Proconsul of Japan

Designated the Supreme Commander of Allied Powers, MacArthur now took on perhaps his most demanding assignment yet: the governance of a defeated, shattered nation. Determined to bring about a peaceful and orderly transition to eventual independence, he became an administrator and under his even-handed tutelage Japan not only recovered but made the transition from dictatorship to democracy and, eventually, to the status of a world economic power. For five and a half years MacArthur was literally the governor of Japan, a benevolent but firm-handed leader who guided, cajoled, and where necessary compelled a series of actions that brought about reforms, massive reconstruction, and the formation of a democratic state.

MacArthur also believed that it was essential for the morale and the future of the nation that Emperor Hirohito be kept as Japan's spiritual leader and not punished or forced to abdicate for the acts of the militarists who brought about the war.

Douglas MacArthur

MacArthur's enduring legacy in Japan was the creation of a constitution that is still the basis of a modern democratic nation.

War in Korea

On 25 June 1950, in the divided Korean peninsula, the army of North Korea crossed the border, soon overran Seoul and was on the verge of conquering all of South Korea. US occupation forces were unprepared, largely untrained, and in disarray from the surprise invasion. The United Nations Security Council authorized the creation of a UN armed force to aid South Korea. MacArthur was named supreme commander and immediately began planning an amphibious invasion behind enemy lines at Inchon that was brilliantly carried out on 15 September 1950.

The Inchon landings were a masterstroke. MacArthur's daring gambit caught the North Koreans by surprise and within a matter of days the capital of Seoul was liberated and the North Korean Army was in full retreat, pursued by UN forces deep into North Korea.

MacArthur, watched by Britain's General Arthur Percival and Lieutenant General Jonathan Wainwright, prepares to receive the Japanese surrender, signed by foreign minister Shigemitsu and General Umezu, aboard USS *Missouri* on 4 September 1945.

Macarthur ignored warnings from Beijing that such an advance was deemed provocative and would bring China into the war. In November 1950, he committed the greatest blunder of his career when he boldly announced that the war was won and his troops would be home by Christmas, recklessly dismissing the mounting, incontrovertible intelligence that the Chinese People's Liberation Army was massed in North Korea. By pursuing the North Korean army to the Yalu River on the Manchurian border, his UN force became dangerously exposed. The result was a humiliating and costly fighting retreat from 'the frozen Chosin' and an emergency evacuation from the port of Hungnam.

MacArthur publicly and privately disagreed with the American policy of limiting the war in Korea and avoiding a possible larger conflict with China. His blatant challenge to civilian authority and his insolent behaviour toward his commander-in-chief led President Harry S. Truman to relieve him of command for insubordination on 11 April 1951. MacArthur's sacking was enormously controversial, with Truman cast as a villain for removing one of America's greatest military heroes from command. When MacArthur returned to the United States he was greeted by an outpouring of public adulation and invited to address a joint session of Congress.

His compelling speech was broadcast to the nation on both radio and television. MacArthur insisted that in the twilight of his life he was only doing his duty and that from the time he first entered West Point he had served his country for fifty-two years. He concluded by quoting an old barrack-room ballad: '"Old soldiers never die, they just fade away." And like the old soldier of that ballad, I now close my military career and just fade away – an old soldier who tried to do his duty as God gave him the light to see that duty.' The enormous controversy notwithstanding, Macarthur had indeed not only mishandled the war but also violated the principle that soldiers do not dictate foreign policy. Truman's courageous decision was wholly

The United Nations forces landing at Inchon on 15 September 1950, a masterstroke by MacArthur that began the fightback against the North Korean army.

justified and eventually vindicated by a Congressional investigation. MacArthur's strong defence of his actions in testimony before Congress was discredited by a parade of distinguished witnesses, including Secretary of State George C. Marshall and General Omar N. Bradley, the chairman of the joint chiefs of staff, both of whom persuasively argued that his actions would have pushed the United States into a ruinous and unnecessary war with Red China, and possibly with the Soviet Union as well.

MacArthur's legacy

MacArthur was a man of many contradictions. As one of his biographers has written: 'MacArthur's life was shaped by the nineteenth-century belief that history is created by the actions of great men ... His only goal in life was to be remembered with the great.'

One who knew him well in the Philippines offered this thoughtful assessment: 'There was never any middle ground; people either idolized this man or hated him, while all the time he dwelt on another mental plane, and was probably seldom aware of either the worship or the hate.' His career-long penchant for surrounding himself with sycophants who told him only what he wanted to hear was his undoing in Korea. The deliberate suppression of the incontrovertible fact of the Red Army's presence in Korea by his chief intelligence officer, Major General Charles A. Willoughby, was the most costly example.

MacArthur was thought to have political ambitions in the 1930s, which is a principal reason why Roosevelt orchestrated his exile to the Philippines. In 1952, it was widely believed that he might attempt to run for president, but public adulation quickly faded and he did not challenge his former subordinate, Dwight Eisenhower, who won the Republican nomination – and the election.

Throughout his life, MacArthur never forgot what West Point had taught him. His most famous and moving speech occurred when he returned in 1962 to address the Corps of Cadets. He reminded them that: 'The soldier, above all other people, prays for peace, for he must suffer and bear the deepest wounds and scars of war. But always in our ears ring the ominous words of Plato, that wisest of all philosophers, "Only the dead have seen the end of war" ... in the evening of my memory, always I come back to West Point.' Always there were echoes and re-echoes of Duty, Honour, Country. 'Today marks my final roll call with you, but I want you to know that when I cross the river my last conscious thought will be the Corps – and the Corps – and the Corps. I bid you farewell.'

To his detriment, MacArthur's legendary vanity and penchant for self-promotion has left him just as controversial today as he was at the time of his relief from command by Truman in 1951. It has also tended to obscure his exceptional accomplishments. He was perhaps the most dynamic general in modern American history, and while his legacy and his reputation continue to be contentious, what can never be taken away from Douglas MacArthur was a life of great and courageous adventure. As he had predicted, MacArthur did fade away and his death in April 1964 at the age of 84 ended a brilliant but flawed military career.

MacArthur with President Truman
on 16 October 1950, when the United Nations forces were pursuing the North Koreans and shortly before they took Pyongyang. The implications of the offensive for US relations with China led to serious disagreement between the two men.

Douglas MacArthur

'When you cannot make up your mind which of two evenly balanced courses of action you should take – choose the bolder.'
WILLIAM SLIM

WILLIAM SLIM
1891–1970

HUGO SLIM

BILL SLIM was one of history's best all-round commanders. He had a genius for planning, strategy, logistics, manoeuvre and morale, all of which he combined to extraordinary effect against Japanese forces in one of the hardest theatres of modern war – the mountains, plains and jungles of eastern India and Burma. Learning fast from his initial defeat during the Japanese invasion of Burma in January 1942, Slim pioneered much of the modern practice of warfare by combining mobility and concentration of force on the ground with sophisticated air supply over an enormous area – one that had few roads and which was drenched by torrential monsoon rains.

Slim's army of 1 million men was the biggest army fielded by Britain and its empire during the Second World War. It was a truly multiracial army. Only 12 per cent of Slim's troops were British. The great majority were from India, Nepal and East and West Africa. Slim's rapport with his troops – to whom he was affectionately known as 'Uncle Bill' – was unique among the commanders of the 1939–45 war. Always dressed in his Indian army battle dress, with Gurkha hat, binoculars and a machine-gun slung over his shoulder, Slim spent much of his time visiting and encouraging his men in the terrible conditions in which they fought. As their leader, he was calm, direct, humorous and determined to give them what they needed to do the job. Slim's striking confidence, clear thinking and sense of purpose were embodied in his jutting chin; but he was also personally modest, and possessed of a genuine capacity for self-criticism – a rare quality in the egos of great men. He claimed little for himself, but always recognized the brilliance of his staff and the skill and courage of his men.

From Birmingham to Burma

William Slim was born in Bristol in 1891, the younger of two sons in a struggling middle-class family. In 1903 his father's business failed and the family moved to Birmingham, where Slim's devout mother ensured him a good Catholic education at St Phillip's Grammar School, followed briefly by entry into Birmingham's famous King Edward's School. But his education was cut short at 16 when his father's business failed

William Slim

again, and all the family's resources were put towards his brother's medical degree. Slim now had to earn his living. He worked first as a primary-school teacher in a poor part of Birmingham for two years, and then for four years as a clerk in an ironworks. Here he got to know factory life and working people.

Slim had always dreamt of a military career, but a commission was never within his means. He did, however, somehow manage to join the Officer Training Corps at Birmingham University, even though he was not a student there. When war broke out in 1914 he was gazetted as a second lieutenant in the Royal Warwicks, with whom he served at Gallipoli – where he was badly wounded – and then in Mesopotamia, where he was awarded the Military Cross and wounded once more.

Transferred to the Indian army in 1919 – where commissions were cheaper – Slim joined the Gurkhas in 1920. He managed to support his military career with lucrative short-story writing for London magazines, using the pen name William Mils (Slim backwards). In the Indian army Slim stood out as the leading intellectual soldier of his generation – first as a pupil and then as a teacher at staff colleges in Quetta, Camberley and Belgaum – while also seeing regular active service on the North-West Frontier.

With the outbreak of the Second World War, Slim was given his first brigade command, in Sudan and Eritrea, where he was wounded again fighting the Italians. This was followed by his first divisional command, in Iraq, where he fought the Vichy French and their allies before going on to invade Persia. In March 1942 Slim was chosen as the commander of Burma Corps, under General Alexander. His task was to stop the Japanese, who had invaded Burma, and were set on advancing on India.

More with less

In the three years of the Burma campaign (1942–5) Slim was tested, and proved himself a master, in all four of the great challenges of command – retreat, regrouping, defence and offence – usually with less equipment and resources than his peers in other theatres.

In his leadership of Burma Corps, Slim oversaw the longest retreat in British military history, some 900 miles. Poorly trained, ill-equipped and constantly compromised by Alexander's political efforts to keep on good terms with the Chinese, Burma Corps was defeated and retreated out of Burma in May 1942. During the retreat Slim

William Slim, complete with Gurkha hat. One of Britain's finest but least celebrated generals, Slim had an unconventional background for an army officer, having worked as a young man as a primary-school teacher and as a clerk in an ironworks.

kept looking for any chance to attack, while gradually withdrawing his beaten forces and avoiding a rout. Arriving defeated, emaciated but in order in India, his men cheered him at his farewell address to them. Slim later commented that 'To be cheered by troops whom you have led to victory is grand and exhilarating. To be cheered by the gaunt remnants of those whom you have led only in defeat, withdrawal and disaster is infinitely moving – and humbling.'

In June 1942 Slim was made commander of XV Corps, part of General Noel Irwin's Eastern Army focused on the Arakan in the south. It was in XV Corps that Slim began to implement his new tactics and training for beating the Japanese. Irwin sidelined Slim, however, rejecting his strategy and insisting on taking operational control of the first Arakan campaign himself. Irwin's conventional and unimaginative offensive tactics in the Arakan produced disaster. Irwin tried to blame these new defeats on Slim, who once again had to save the situation by resuming command for an orderly retreat. At the end of May 1943 Irwin was relieved of his command and replaced by General George Giffard, with whom Slim had an excellent working relationship.

Giffard ordered Slim to prepare for a new offensive in the Arakan. This time Slim had the monsoon season to train XV Corps properly and the freedom to design his own strategy and tactics. In October 1943, with the arrival of Lord Louis Mountbatten as Supreme Allied Commander Southeast Asia, Giffard was made commander of land forces and Slim was appointed as commander of the new Fourteenth Army to replace Eastern Army. Slim's training and organization of the Fourteenth Army (whose badge he designed himself) is the classic example of the making of an army. In forging this new force, Slim shaped the spirit and confidence needed to win, while developing the tactics and training necessary to fight in extreme and often isolated surroundings. He also procured or improvised the right equipment, and built up a winning morale throughout his diverse force. The results were spectacular.

In late 1943 Slim asked XV Corps, now under General Philip Christison, to deliver Operation Cudgel in the Arakan. After a slow start, XV Corps began to use Slim's new approach – treating Japanese tactics of encirclement and infiltration as an opportunity not a threat. Aggressive patrolling was combined with Slim's famous 'boxes'. Whenever units were encircled or attacked, they were to stand firm and fight aggressively. Supplied by air, and with all non-combatant support staff trained to fight as well, they could then defeat relentless waves of Japanese attacks. Learning from the Japanese 'hooks', Slim also encouraged XV Corps to avoid frontal assaults, infiltrate behind Japanese positions and attack them in their rear or on their flanks, so turning the Japanese out of heavily defended positions to ground of the Fourteenth Army's choosing. XV Corps did all this and won. It was the first defeat of Japanese forces and was a tonic for the confidence of the Fourteenth Army. But it was only the beginning.

Slim was now making ready for the major Japanese offensive against India, which, he guessed rightly, would come further north, in Assam. In his planning, preparations and mobility, Slim showed himself to be a master of aggressive defence. Ignoring the advice of others to take the battle to the Japanese by moving into Burma, Slim preferred to wait for them where he was strongest and they would be weakest. As he expected, Mutaguchi's Fifteenth Army came at him in Assam in Operation U-Go (March 1944), which was intended to spearhead the invasion of India. Slim's plan was to lure Mutaguchi on to the plain around Imphal and to smash his army there.

Imphal and Kohima

Between March and July 1944 Slim led one of the fiercest and most complex battles of the war around Imphal and Kohima. The fighting lasted for five months. Much of it was face-to-face, reminiscent of the Somme in the First World War, as the Japanese continuously fought to the death. Slim's approach was subtle and involved deliberate fighting withdrawals by two divisions to pull the Japanese army on to the plain. His plan involved the anticipated siege of Imphal and the pre-arranged and superbly organized movement of two divisions by air across a vast and difficult front.

But there were also misjudgements, to which Slim typically confessed. He got his timing wrong on the withdrawal from Tiddim, so that the 17th Division had to fight for their lives as they withdrew. He was also surprised when Mutaguchi attacked with a division at Kohima when Slim had expected him to strike instead at the Fourteenth Army's main supply base at Dimapur. Extraordinary courage in the defence of Kohima saved the day, and famously involved repeated hand-to-hand fighting across the district commissioner's tennis court – the white lines of which remain marked out in cement today as the centrepiece of the Allied cemetery in this beautiful mountain town.

But Slim's plan worked. Mutaguchi met ferocity, professionalism and mobility he had never expected. As Slim anticipated, this infuriated him and he refused to give up, repeatedly throwing his troops at Slim's forces, whose new confidence now saw every Japanese attack as an opportunity to kill more of the enemy. When the Japanese did eventually retreat, the Fourteenth Army were aggressive and thorough in their pursuit. Mutaguchi's army was decimated. From 105,000 men, the Japanese suffered 90,000 casualties, of whom 65,000 were killed. Only 600 surrendered. Imphal was the biggest ever defeat in Japanese military history, and it turned the tide. After the battle, Slim and his three corps commanders, Christison, Geoffrey Scoones and Montagu Stopford, were all knighted by Viscount Wavell, viceroy of India, on a dusty bulldozed field at Imphal.

Viscount Wavell, viceroy of India, knights Slim in December 1944 at Imphal, the site of the biggest ever defeat in Japanese military history. Having saved India from Japanese invasion, Slim went on to lead the re-conquest of Burma.

The reconquest of Burma

Slim now led the Fourteenth Army in a dashing reconquest of Burma itself (January–May 1945). Although sea- and airborne operations were ruled out – the invasion of France had taken all available resources – Slim was convinced that his men could do it. But first he had to ensure that they trained for a more open fighting style suited to the plains of central Burma, which gave good opportunities for massed armour, long-range artillery and mechanized infantry. The reconquest also meant still more demanding preparations in logistics and engineering, as the advance involved ever longer lines of communications, the crossing of the Irrawaddy, one of the world's biggest rivers, and the usual race against the monsoon. But it would be made easier by the Allies' complete aerial superiority. Even as he went full tilt on the offensive, Slim still remained thoughtful and well prepared.

As a strategist, Slim was always cunning – reading, luring and deceiving his enemy while manoeuvring himself into a position where he could beat him outright. In so doing, he frequently turned the tactics of the Japanese against themselves. In the offensive to retake Burma – Operation Capital – Slim brought this approach to a crescendo by secretly moving a whole corps in a 320-mile silent march down dirt tracks to attack the Japanese rear at Meiktila – a move that his defeated opponent, General Kimura, later described as Slim's 'masterpiece' (see opposite).

Slim as a leader

The Fourteenth Army was mainly Indian; only one in eight of its men were British. Other vital contingents came from Nepal, East and West Africa, Australia, New Zealand and the USA, plus Chinese divisions under General Stilwell's command in northern Burma. Fluent in Hindi, Urdu and Ghurkali, Slim was able to communicate intimately in the three common languages of his troops. He was a master of morale, with a natural, relaxed and unaffected genius for relating and communicating with his men. He understood their fears, their needs and their hopes, realizing instinctively that fighting and leadership are emotional as well as physical and intellectual endeavours. He held his army in great affection, an affection that his army returned in equal measure. Robert Lyman and others who have written about Slim see this emotional connection as the hallmark of Slim's generalship – that he was truly loved by his men in a way that had not been seen in the British military since Nelson and Wellington.

But there was more to Slim than just charisma. He was also a rigorous and imaginative planner. His men loved him because he also delivered. Slim's genius for logistical and administrative organization, together with the exceptional abilities of his senior administrative and engineering staff like Alf Snelling and William Hasted, meant that the Fourteenth Army could

Slim is cheered by his troops as he leaves Mandalay, March 1945, after the successful conclusion of Operation Extended Capital. The campaign involved not only sophisticated coordination of simultaneous advances by three separate corps, but also a masterstroke of deception.

William Slim

MEIKTILA
OPERATION EXTENDED CAPITAL

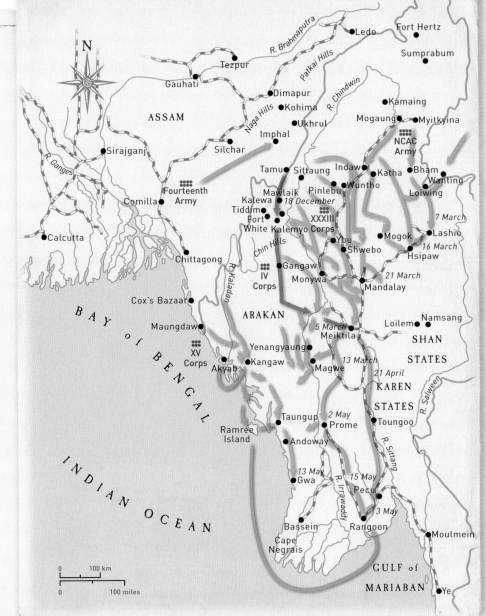

S LIM'S INITIAL PLAN for the decisive battle in central Burma was to meet the Japanese after crossing the Irrawaddy and defeat them across a broad mobile front. This too was what his opponent expected and for which he also began to prepare. But when Slim realized that he and his enemy were both preparing for the same thing, he typically decided to surprise him by luring him one way and then also hitting him hard somewhere unexpected. So Slim added Operation Extended Capital to his original plan.

Extended Capital was a necessarily covert, high-risk and daring plan, which set out to surpass the Japanese at their own game by launching a long and powerful hook south behind their main lines to strike and take the main Japanese supply and administrative base at Meiktila. At a stroke, this would cripple Japanese supplies, force their army to turn and fight in two directions at once and also provide Slim with a classic hammer-and-anvil situation – crushing Japanese forces between Fourteenth Army divisions fighting from both north and south.

Slim entrusted the 320-mile silent march south to IV Corps under Messervy, and while it moved, he effectively deceived his opponent by setting up a false IV Corps HQ, which sent and received fake radio signals for the weeks necessary for Messervy to outflank the Japanese. Meanwhile, Stopford led XXXIII Corps in the attack on Mandalay and Christison led XV Corps in amphibious assaults along the Arakan coast, capturing the airfields needed to supply the Fourteenth Army as it moved south.

The attack on Meiktila by IV Corps began on 1 March 1945, and the town was taken four days later. Cowan and others went on to conduct aggressive defensive fighting

for a further month as the Japanese, who had been totally surprised, fought hard to regain and secure their rear. But it worked. Slim had lured General Honda, the Japanese army commander, into a battle of destruction around Meiktila simultaneous with that around Mandalay, while the amphibious operations in the south had made possible constant air supply.

Slim's extraordinary deception, together with the simultaneous and interlinked advances of the three corps with their air and naval support, are widely recognized as one of the finest feats of combined arms during the Second World War. The Japanese army was steadily crushed and dispersed, while the Fourteenth Army raced on towards Rangoon, which was initially taken from the sea, after all, on 3 May after IV Corps had been held up by the early arrival of the monsoon.

support divisions on the move in the most difficult of terrain, even during the monsoon. This was done by extraordinary and well-planned feats of engineering, medical care and air support. Slim was sometimes irritated by comments that his army was famous for 'improvising'. Yes, it constantly innovated and made use of whatever was available, but it was always, he insisted, working to detailed plans and objectives that were well prepared in advance. To cross the Irrawaddy – a river three times as wide as the Rhine – Slim's engineers had to build the ships and the bridges they needed themselves, using teams of 3,000 elephants to haul the thousands of trees required. Where there was no parachute silk for air supply, they used local jute to make 'parajutes'. They grew their own food in massive farms, and baked millions of bricks to make their own roads. They also pioneered treatments for malaria, dysentery, typhus and other diseases, with considerable success: in 1943, for every man evacuated wounded 120 were evacuated sick; astonishingly, by 1944, in the unhealthiest theatre, the Fourteenth Army was the healthiest army in the world, with only one soldier in every thousand sick each day.

Much of this planning and efficiency involved intimate combined land–air operations. With Slim's vision, and gifted colleagues like Jack Baldwin and Stanley Vincent in the RAF and George E. Stratemeyer in the US Air Force, the battle for Burma was won by unprecedented cooperation between army and air forces, a relationship that Slim described as 'a close brotherhood'. By 1945, nearly 90 per cent of the Fourteenth Army's supplies were provided by air, in some 7,000 sorties each day. The gradual

A US plane makes an airdrop in Burma. Slim was a pioneer of air support, and by 1945 nearly 90 per cent of his multiracial Fourteenth Army's supplies were provided by air.

increase of this air support – which was years ahead of its time – was made possible by the energetic endorsement of the Supreme Allied Commander, Mountbatten, with whom Slim shared a common vision and enjoyed a highly creative working relationship.

Slim's relationships with senior officers were either very good or strangely problematic. His own corps and divisional commanders respected him enormously for his relaxed style and his calm ability to delegate, empower, discuss and actively support. Many, but not all, were long-standing Indian army friends and colleagues. With Mountbatten, Giffard and the famously difficult American, General Stilwell, Slim got on extremely well. With Irwin and Oliver Leese things were difficult. Some of these difficulties may have turned on the old British hang-up about class. Slim, the grammar-school boy from the Indian army, may have been looked down upon or unconsciously underrated by some from the smart upper-class set of the British army. This, in turn, may well have raised Slim's hackles and elicited a bit of Brummie scorn. Yet, in any clash with senior officers, it was Slim who was vindicated and twice (with Irwin and Leese) he famously took the jobs of those who tried to sack him. With the maverick Orde Wingate, Slim was patient but firm, always rightly convinced that only a whole-army approach would defeat the Japanese. Slim realized that while Wingate's behind-the-lines guerrilla operations with his Chindits could be useful, their effect was overblown in the imagination of their leader and his prime ministerial patron in far off Downing Street.

> 'Slim was the finest General that the Second World War produced.'
> EARL MOUNTBATTEN OF BURMA

The battles in which Slim led his troops were fierce, fought in the harshest climate with disease ever present, and against an unrelenting enemy who always fought to the death. The campaign saw great bravery: the Fourteenth Army numbered among its men twenty-nine recipients of the Victoria Cross. In these extreme conditions, Slim forged an extraordinary multiracial force, made daring plans, overcame huge logistical obstacles and called forth immense willpower, courage, talent and good spirit in his troops. Slim always knew that it was his men who 'did it', but many of them felt that his leadership had carried them beyond themselves and that, even if they had made the victory, Slim had somehow made them.

Later life

After the war, Slim initially retired from the army and became vice chairman of the newly nationalized British Railways. But he was soon recalled from civilian life, made a field marshal and served as chief of the Imperial General Staff from 1948 to 1952, the first Indian army officer to be appointed to the top job in the British armed forces. From 1952 to 1960 Slim was a highly successful governor-general of Australia. During this time, he wrote his famous book about the war in Burma, *Defeat into Victory*, which is probably the finest commander's account of a campaign since Julius Caesar's *Gallic Wars*. *Defeat into Victory* is still studied in military academies all around the world, a beautifully written and modest masterclass in leadership and military command. In 1963, towards the end of his life, Slim was made governor of Windsor Castle. Finally, in 1970, he retired to London and died in December the same year.

In the many busy years of his life, Slim was supported throughout by a remarkable woman from Scotland, Aileen Robertson. They had met on a ship to India in 1924 and married the following year.

GERALD TEMPLER

JOHN HUGHES-WILSON

1898–1979

FIELD MARSHAL TEMPLER was one of the most successful British military commanders of the twentieth century. Most soldiers spend their careers awaiting the call to arms, but Templer was an exception. He joined the army in the middle of the Great War, fought to put down colonial rebellions in the inter-war years, saw the Second World War out from start to finish and then went on to fight and defeat the communist insurgency in Malaya in the twilight of the British Empire. He could with justification claim to be one of Britain's most successful generals; his Malayan campaign is a model for counter-insurgency operations.

Gerald Walter Robert Templer was one of the remarkable crop of soldiers grown out of the martial soil of Ulster during the twentieth century, along with Alexander, Alanbrooke, Auchinleck, Dill and Montgomery. Born in 1898 as the son of a serving officer, the combination of Wellington College and Sandhurst seems almost pre-ordained. In November 1917 he joined his father's old regiment, the Royal Irish Fusiliers, on the Western Front, taking part in the retreat from the Somme in spring 1918 and then advancing as part of Haig's victorious last offensive in the autumn.

In 1919 he was in the Caucasus as part of the Allies' abortive attempt to overthrow the Bolshevik revolution in Russia. 'All great fun,' he wrote, 'but pretty unsatisfactory from the political point of view.' Later, during the Cold War, he claimed that he was the only serving senior officer who had actually fought the Red Army. By 1922 Lieutenant Templer was back in England to become bayonet-fighting champion of the army and part of the British Olympic hurdling team of 1924.

In 1927 he went to the army's staff college at Camberley. His first staff job, at HQ 3rd Division, was a disaster. He clashed with his senior staff officer who gave him an adverse report and even recommended that he be dismissed from the army. Templer protested, and appealed to his general who ripped up the offending report and saved his career by packing him off to Northern Command. By 1935, Captain Templer was hunting down terrorists in Palestine as a company commander in the Loyal Regiment. For his efforts Templer was awarded a DSO (Distinguished Service Order), an unusual honour for a junior commander. Like his contemporary Orde Wingate, Templer learned a lot about his trade among the rocky hills of Judea and later admitted to actually weeping over the tragedy of the Arab–Jewish problem. But he always claimed that it was 'Palestine that taught [me] the mind and method of the guerrillas'.

The outbreak of Hitler's war saw him as a staff officer in the Directorate of Military Intelligence where he helped to lay the foundations of two successful organizations, MI Special Operations (later to become SOE) and the Army's Intelligence Corps. This experience gained him the post of GSO 1 (Int) in the British Expeditionary Force (BEF) in France in 1939 and later as chief of staff to the ill-fated 'MacForce' which tried to keep the western corridor of the retreat to Dunkirk open before the Wehrmacht's rampaging panzers. On 27 May 1940 Lieutenant Colonel Templer was evacuated from Dunkirk; one of the many British officers who discovered that defeat is the hardest school of all.

From soldier to general

If his career until then had made him a competent soldier, the next five years saw the making of Templer as a general. From a brevet lieutenant colonel in 1939 he rose to a general in 1945. He was appointed brigadier commanding 210 Brigade in November 1940, went as the chief of staff to V Corps in May 1941, and by April 1942 was a major-general commanding 47th London Division. This was meteoric, and his appointment as corps commander of Second Corps at Newmarket in the autumn of 1942 astonished many. He was, at 44, the youngest lieutenant general in the army. He was renowned as a martinet with high standards and drove himself and his men hard.

Like Wellington before him, he had an eagle-eye for sloppiness, inefficiency and slackness, and would not tolerate those who failed to share his commitment and drive. Perhaps his greatest quality as a general was his ability to focus on the mission: that rare ability of great leaders to distil the selection and maintenance of the aim. Templer always knew what he wanted and he always knew how best to get it.

Templer then did an extraordinary thing: he demanded a reduction in rank and a posting to the battlefront – anywhere. With a true soldier's instinct he knew that he had to head for the sound of the guns. A bemused War Office granted his wish and by the summer of 1943 *Major*-General Templer was in the North African theatre commanding the 1st Division. By October he had been switched to lead 56th Division in Italy as the Allies struggled across winter mountains and rivers in the face of determined German resistance. In November his division assaulted across the River Garigliano to evict the Germans from Monte Cassino. The attack failed with heavy casualties.

In January 1944 the Allies tried again, this time with an overwhelming array of firepower and blew the Germans – and Monte Cassino – off the hill for good. Hardly had Templer's division settled in for an advance on Rome when they were whipped away to reinforce the hard-pressed Anzio beachhead. At one point he personally ordered every staff officer, cook and sanitary orderly into the firing line to beat off a German assault. In March 1944 his exhausted division was pulled back to Egypt to refit, but by 26 July Templer was again back in Italy, this time to command 6th Armoured Division.

An unusual wound

Templer was a hands-on, front-line general, and blacked-up infantry patrols would get back to their lines to find an impatient GOC himself leading their debriefing. 'He was like a red-hot poker,' said one officer. The fiery general's war ended when he joined the ranks of his soldiers wounded in action. On 10 August he was driving up to the front when a truck pulled off the road and hit a landmine on the verge. The vehicle exploded and a looted grand piano fell on to Templer's vehicle, breaking his back. Seriously injured, he was taken back to Britain and was not ready for action again until the spring of 1945. He would say ruefully that he 'was the only British officer to be wounded by a piano'.

In the last months of the war he was seconded to convalesce at SOE where he was one of the architects of Operation Foxley, a plan to assassinate Hitler with a sniper at his mountain retreat, the Berghof. Other counsels prevailed, however. Churchill decided that Hitler alive as a rotten strategist was much more useful to the Allies than Hitler as a dead Nazi martyr.

The post-war years

The war's end saw Templer take over a challenging appointment as military governor of the British zone of occupied Germany. He announced his policy with brutal clarity: 'I intend to be firm to the point of ruthlessness ... I still have to meet a German who says he is sorry.' In late 1945 he sacked the post-war mayor of Cologne for laziness and incompetence. This was typical Templer and certainly galvanized the other builders of the new West Germany. However, as the mayor in question was Konrad Adenauer, who went on to become the first chancellor of the new Bundesrepublik Deutschland. The decision came back to haunt him. To his credit, Adenauer never bore Templer a grudge and sent him a present of a crate of wine every time he came to London.

War Office appointments in cash-strapped Whitehall taught Templer the need to get along with politicians. Finally in 1950 he was put out to grass as GOC Eastern Command. There he might have remained if terrorists in Malaya had not ambushed and shot the governor-general, Sir Henry Gurney. Whitehall suddenly realized that the insurgency and civil war 'emergency' (so-called for insurance reasons) was getting out of hand, and decided to appoint a senior soldier with, unusually, both civil and military powers.

At the Rideau Hall conference in Ottawa in January 1952, discussing the weakness of Commonwealth defences, Winston Churchill looked down the dinner table. 'Templer,' the great man growled through the cigar smoke, waving a brandy glass. 'Malaya!' he bellowed. 'Full powers, now, Templer. Full powers,' he added. About ten minutes later, after a whispered confab with his startled advisers, Churchill broke through the conversation again. 'Full power, Templer. Very heady stuff. Make sure you use it sparingly.' Thus was Sir Gerald Templer appointed governor-general of strife-torn Malaya, with greater military and political powers than any British soldier since Cromwell.

A battalion of Australian Imperial Forces marches through a Malayan village during operations in Singapore. Ultimately about 40,000 British and Commonwealth forces were deployed, against fewer than 10,000 insurgents.

Gerald Templer

A high commissioner at war

Templer arrived in Malaya in February 1952, by which time it looked as if he might be too late. The post-war communist uprising against British rule was succeeding. Over 250,000 soldiers and policemen were combing the jungle fruitlessly trying to locate and destroy a few thousand terrorists led by Chin Peng. Ironically it was the British who had armed and trained the guerrillas in the first place and used them in their undercover war against the occupying Japanese; they had even given Chin Peng an OBE. Now the 'CTs' ('Communist Terrorists') had turned on their colonial masters. Templer's orders from Churchill were clear: smash the communists and turn Malaya into a single, self-governing democratic state.

The political challenge would take time but Templer quickly saw that the real problem was a lack of coordination at every level. The army and the police did not work together; the colonial planters and civil service acted as if the insurgency was the military's problem; and there was deep suspicion between the Chinese and the Malay populations. Morale was low. With characteristic energy Templer decided to shake up the situation from the start. He travelled by armoured car or helicopter and suddenly the spare figure of the sharp-eyed boss was everywhere. Suddenly he, and not the CTs, was driving events. The sleepy civil service was shaken to its core. On one occasion the new governor general asked a startled civil servant what he did, to be told, 'Nuclear emergency planning, sir'. Templer considered this and said, 'What's the likelihood of a nuclear strike on Malaya?' The bureaucrat laughed, 'Zero, I would say.' 'Good,' rasped Templer. 'I agree. You're fired.'

The whiplash of Templer's tongue and his eagle-eye settled on the slack, the ineffi-cient and the lazy. Even colonial rubber-plantation managers in the middle of the

Gerald Templer

jungle suddenly realized that they were part of the war. Templer listened to one planter moaning about inadequate army and police protection. 'Do you ever go down and talk to the troops or the police?' he demanded. 'Of course not, it's not my job,' replied the planter. Templer exploded. 'Well, it's true we've got some bloody bad soldiers and bad police in Malaya, but we've got some bloody bad planters as well – and you're the worst of the lot! Now get the hell out of here!'

Hearts and minds

From the outset the British realized that the real battle in Malaya was not for a military objective but for the popular support. Templer said that with two-thirds of the population on his side he could end the emergency in three months. He also saw that the key to winning the people over was to make them understand that the rule of law had to be observed and the government was going to win.

His secretary of defence and right-hand man, Robert Thompson, emphasized the need for government credibility. The whole policy was summed up as, 'winning the hearts and minds of the people'. In this Templer was helped by two important advantages: a well-thought-out plan and a political ace card.

The four-point plan laid the foundations for victory: to dominate the populated areas to give a feeling of security and government control; to isolate and disrupt the communist organization within those populated areas; to cut the bandits off from their food supplies; and finally to destroy the bandits by forcing them to attack the security

Templer visits a unit of the Home Guard of the Muala Krai area of Kelantan in September 1952. His unique combination of exerting relentless pressure on the insurgents while winning over the hearts and minds of the general population paid huge dividends.

forces on their own ground. Templer inherited this plan from the previous director of operations, but he made it work spectacularly successfully.

The key to this strategy was the 'new village programme', where nearly half a million Chinese squatters were moved out of the jungle and rehoused in new government-built protected villages. These were secured by a police force expanded to five times its 1948 level and included large areas for private cultivation. The Chinese settlers were then encouraged to become land-owners and offered citizenship. This was a masterstroke, as it effectively 'drained the sea in which the guerrillas swam' while holding out the hope of a brighter future by incorporating the Chinese into Malayan society and giving them a stake in its success.

Not everyone agreed with this forced resettlement. After one ambush in which twelve British soldiers were killed, Templer personally swooped on the village and demanded the names of those responsible. On receiving no answer, he locked down the village, restricted its food supplies and told the elders that the restrictions would stay until they gave up those responsible. These tough measures were greeted with a chorus of

FIGHTING AN INSURGENCY

THIRTY-FIVE YEARS EXPERIENCE of soldiering had taught Templer some invaluable professional lessons, all of which came to the fore in Malaya. First and foremost was his understanding that without a clear political goal, there can be no military victory. Second, once he had a clear aim, he stuck to it tenaciously; he even re-read his own list of goals every morning while he shaved. Third, he believed passionately in the unity of command. Others might consider his methods high-handed, but no-one was ever in doubt as to who was in charge and what they were trying to achieve. Reluctant

policemen, civil servants and soldiers were all forced to work together from joint command centres and share their information, whether they liked it or not.

Above all, Templer believed in the importance of intelligence. Not for nothing had he chased elusive guerrillas in the Judean hills and gone on to head up branches of military intelligence and SOE. 'Better a well-targeted ambush than endless jungle-bashing,' was his motto. Templer placed military intelligence officers in every static police headquarters and fused military and Special Branch intelligence into a single asset to be used to identify, track and attack the 'Communist Terrorists' (CTs) in their safe retreats. This policy allowed the army to concentrate on offensive tasks, leaving the police and local defence forces as area defence. The result was that gradually the hunters became the hunted. By the time Templer was through, every CT in Malaya was looking over his shoulder, wherever he was hiding.

This blend of politics, good intelligence and taking well-targeted operations to the enemy was highly successful. However, the key to that victory lay not just in the fighting in the jungle and the villages: Templer's real victory was that he managed to win the hearts and minds of the indigenous people. The CTs withered away, either surrendering in droves or retreating into the jungle to flee across the border.

Nevertheless, although Templer is rightly credited with turning the campaign round, this kind of war will always be a slow business. It would take another seven years before Malaya could be declared free from communist insurgents and final victory declared.

When Templer left Malaya, the road to the airport was lined with cheering crowds of Malays and Chinese in a sponta-neous demonstration of gratitude for the only commander to have crushed a full-blown communist-inspired insurgency. Templer's victory, and his methods, have much to teach us still.

Templer warns elders of a village committee in Lower Perak in April 1953 that, if their village does not quickly take a firmer line against the insurgents, they can expect serious consequences.

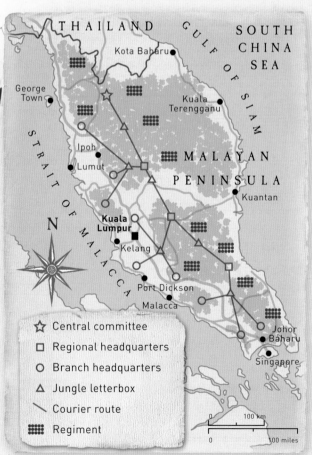

THAILAND — GULF OF SIAM — SOUTH CHINA SEA

Kota Bharu

George Town

Kuala Terengganu

STRAIT OF MALACCA

Ipoh
Lumut

MALAYAN PENINSULA

Kuantan

N

Kuala Lumpur

Kelang

Port Dickson

Malacca

Johor Baharu

Singapore

☆ Central committee
□ Regional headquarters
○ Branch headquarters
△ Jungle letterbox
＼ Courier route
▦ Regiment

0   100 km
0   100 miles

outrage from newspapers in Britain. Nevertheless, Templer's grim measures worked. Gradually the locals realized that it was safer to be on Templer's side – and uncomfortable if they were not.

Templer's trump cards

These measures were backed by a revitalized intelligence service with the police and the army working together in joint operations rooms. Well-targeted special forces raids, air strikes and ambushes began to put the bandits at risk in what they thought of as 'their' jungle: but the jungle is neutral and the re-trained Commonwealth Forces learned to use it to turn the tables to hunt the CTs. Soon military casualties went down by 30 per cent and communist casualties mounted. The first trickle of surrendering bandits began to emerge from the jungle, eventually to turn into a flood.

In all this military effort Templer was helped by his political ace: nationhood. His appointment as governor-general was a civilian one and he never forgot it. His favourite theme was the new Malaya – but only when the communists were defeated. Crucially he ensured that the new Malaya would have common citizenship and independence. When he gave the Chinese the vote, the Malays called him 'pro-Chinese'; when he later brought in a modern tax structure that hit the wealthy Chinese hard, they denounced him as being 'pro-Malay'. The truth was Templer was focused on building a common new Malaysian identity and nation. His brusque military common sense told him that the days of old-style colonialism were gone and he blew away all the remnants of segregation and imperialism. He was not called the 'Tiger of Malaya' for nothing. On hearing that the Sultan of Selangor had been refused entry into the smart 'Lake Club' because of the colour of his skin, Templer reacted with fury, pointing out that there was no colour bar among his security forces risking their lives to defend the club members. The committee resigned en masse and segregation ended.

The man behind the mask

Despite his manner Gerald Templer was a man of great humanity. He genuinely cared about people: he would suddenly turn up at Malayan weddings, sing raucous army songs with the sergeants' mess and spend as much time organizing a wide-ranging and liberal programme of social legislation as on winning the fight in the jungle. Even the lowliest administrator learned to feel that Templer cared about him personally.

By the time he left Malaya in the summer of 1954 Templer had effectively broken the back of the insurgency. As he drove to the airport through cheering crowds of Malay and Chinese he genuinely could claim, 'Mission Accomplished'. His remarkable blend of intelligence, training, strategy and leadership, allied to his deft political skills and his sheer force of personality, ranks him as a commander of the highest stature. He won a crucial victory for his country and perhaps a greater one in the emergence of a new united Malaysia.

Although he may be one of Britain's least recognized generals, it is no exaggeration to say that Field Marshal Sir Gerald Templer ranks with Marlborough and Wellington as one of its most successful soldiers. The truth is that, without Templer's victory, Southeast Asia – and the post-war world – would be a very different place.

(Opposite)
ORGANIZATION OF COMMUNIST GUERRILLA FORCES during the Malayan insurgency, 1952–3.

Gerald Templer

MOSHE DAYAN
1915–81

MARTIN VAN CREVELD

MOSHE DAYAN called most of his subordinates by their nicknames: 'Dado' (David Elazar), 'Arik' (Ariel Sharon), 'Talik' (Israel Tal), 'Mota' (Mordehai Gur), 'Raful' (Rafael Eytan) or 'Gandhi' (Rehavam Zeevi). The only person who dared give Dayan himself a nickname was his mother who called him 'Musik' as a child, though later even she referred to him by his given name. From an early age he carried heavy responsibilities, yet he was a master at avoiding responsibility. He was a born leader of men, but he rarely returned the devotion those men felt for him. Affecting to be a plain-speaking soldier, he was a master of back-biting and intrigue. When circumstances demanded he could be completely ruthless, yet he enjoyed and wrote poetry like few other commanders. It was to him and others like him that the state of Israel owes its existence.

Moshe Dayan was the first child born, in 1915, to the members of the first kibbutz, Degania, on the southeastern shore of Lake Galilee. He grew up at Nahalal, a settlement not far from Haifa. It was there he went to school, though he never took his high school diploma. Most of his free time was taken up by working on the family farm. From time to time there were clashes with Arab youths from the neighbourhood; but they did not lead to any lasting resentment on Dayan's part, and he ended up by learning Arabic fairly well.

His military career started during the Arab revolt of 1936–9. The British forces were operating in the Valley of Esdraelon, trying to protect the oil pipeline that ran from Iraq to Haifa and to maintain order in general. They needed guides who knew the area, and the young Dayan qualified. One British officer in particular, Captain Orde Wingate, taught him a lot: how to make a silent approach so as to take one's enemy by surprise; how to mount an ambush; how to make prisoners talk; and, most important of all, how to kill, see one's own comrades killed, and find it within oneself to keep going.

In October 1939 he and some others were arrested by the British authorities for carrying weapons. By that time Wingate had left the country, the Arab revolt had died down and British need for Jewish allies diminished. He was sentenced to ten years in prison, later commuted to five. Apparently it was in prison that the leadership qualities of this darkly brooding personality, who was clever, crafty and possessed of a sarcastic sense of humour, were first noticed, causing him to end up as a spokesmen for his comrades.

Young commander

He was unexpectedly released in April 1941. The British were about to invade Syria and Lebanon. Once again, they needed local Arabic-speaking guides whom they could trust. Dayan was in charge of a squad whose mission was to capture and hold a bridge on the way to Beirut. They carried out their task, but Dayan was badly wounded in the face. It was several months before he came out of hospital, minus his left eye but plus the eye-patch that was to become his trademark.

Just what he did during the next six years is not very clear. Perhaps because he was older and more experienced than most of them, the commanders of PALMACH, the pre-1948 Jewish striking force, did not want him. Apparently he worked for the intelligence branch of Hagana, PALMACH's parent organization, setting up networks of Arab informants. At one point he went to Baghdad on an intelligence mission; in 1944–5, he was in charge of arresting members of the right-wing ETZEL terrorist organization who refused to obey the Jewish community's elected leadership. Probably it was at this time that he first caught the attention of the head of the Zionist Agency and future prime minister, David Ben-Gurion, as a man who would carry out orders. To his very great credit, he did so without creating lasting enmity between himself and the men he arrested.

When Israel's War of Independence broke out in 1948, he was a major. He seems to have served as a one-man fire brigade, showing up now here, now there. In April 1948

Moshe Dayan peers with his one good eye into huge binoculars, Golan Heights, 18 October 1973. During the Yom Kippur War Syrian forces occupied much of the southern area of the Golan Heights, but by the end of the war had been pushed back by an Israeli counter-attack.

he was instrumental in making a battalion of Druze troops that had invaded Israel from Syria change sides. Later in the same month he commanded an artillery battery that helped save his birthplace, Degania, from a Syrian offensive. May found him commanding a mechanized battalion against ETZEL, preventing them from landing an unauthorized shipment of arms at Kfar Vitkin, north of Tel Aviv. Later that month the battalion took part in fighting the Jordanians and the Egyptians. It also helped conquer the then purely Arab towns of Ramleh and Lydda, resulting in perhaps 50,000 refugees.

In June Dayan was transferred to Jerusalem where he became city commander. By that time the fighting in the city had almost died down; two minor attacks he launched against the opposing Jordanians failed. Apparently Ben-Gurion put him in this post not because of his military abilities but mainly because of his political and diplomatic skills. The prime minister wanted somebody who could negotiate – which Dayan did, forcing the Jordanians to give up a strip of territory in the West Bank. Even more important, the prime minister needed somebody who would carry out orders and agree to leave half of Jerusalem to the enemy.

Top gun

Dayan was now recognized as a top gun, and Ben-Gurion gave him a series of appointments clearly designed to prepare him for taking over the highest post of all. First he became commander-in-chief, South, then commander-in-chief, North, and finally deputy chief of staff. In the first of these roles he used fairly brutal methods to drive out Arabs whom the state claimed should not be there, across the border into Jordan and Gaza. In the last one he had a hand in organizing raids in retaliation for the killing and wounding of Israelis by Arab 'infiltrators'. Some of the raids resulted in dozens of civilians killed. In 1955, having taken over as chief of staff, he expanded the raids into Gaza and the Sinai as well.

His military masterpiece was the Sinai campaign of October–November 1956 (see opposite). Not long after, at the beginning of 1958, he left the army. A year later he joined the Cabinet as minister of agriculture, a post he held until 1963 and in which he was not a great success.

Israeli operations during the Sinai campaign, 1956. Lieutenant Colonel Ariel Sharon (left) with his troops during the costly attack on the Mitla Pass during the Sinai campaign, 30 October 1956, the only hiccup in an otherwise triumphant campaign for Dayan.

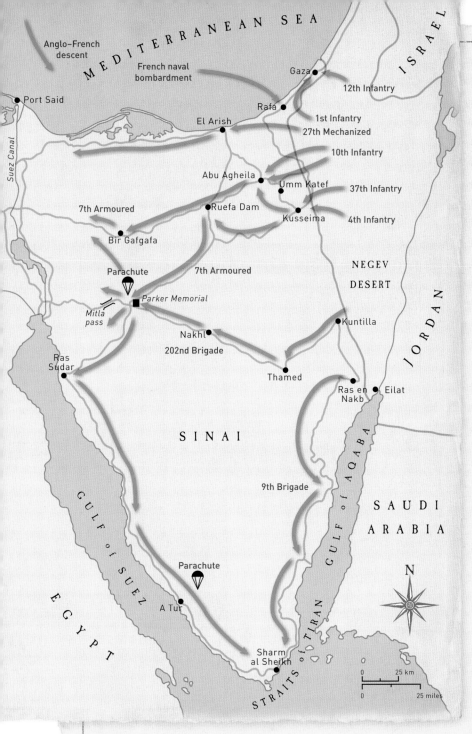

Anglo-French
descent

MEDITERRANEAN SEA

French naval
bombardment

Port Said

Gaza

12th Infantry

Rafa

El Arish

1st Infantry
27th Mechanized

10th Infantry

Abu Agheila

Umm Katef

37th Infantry

Ruefa Dam

7th Armoured

Kusseima

4th Infantry

Bir Gafgafa

NEGEV
DESERT

Parachute

7th Armoured

Parker Memorial

Mitla
pass

Kuntilla

Nakhl

202nd Brigade

Ras
Sudar

Thamed

Ras en
Nakb

Eilat

SINAI

9th Brigade

SAUDI
ARABIA

Parachute

A Tur

Sharm
al Sheikh

N

0   25 km

0   25 miles

GULF of SUEZ

GULF of AQABA

STRAITS of TIRAN

EGYPT

Suez Canal

ISRAEL

JORDAN

THE SINAI CAMPAIGN

ISRAELI PLANNING FOR THE SINAI CAMPAIGN started in
October 1955, when Egypt announced a large arms deal
with Czechoslovakia (in reality, the Soviet Union). From
the beginning, it was hoped to involve Britain and France
as well. Half of the Egyptian army was deployed west of
the Suez Canal in anticipation of a Franco-British
offensive, and the forces that Israel could muster were
about equal to the Egyptian ones. Each side had approximately 45,000 men.

Considering how devious and
unreliable Israel's allies were, designing a
campaign that would make military sense
while still taking account of political realities
was extremely difficult. Dayan, sketching his
ideas on the back of cigarette box, only
needed about five minutes to do so.
However, convincing prime minister
Ben-Gurion and making the necessary
preparations took longer.

By the end of October 1956, everything
was ready. First, by concentrating some of his
elite units on Israel's eastern border, Dayan
convinced the enemy that he was about to
attack Jordan. Next, a daring air force
operation cut Egyptian communications in
the Sinai, preventing the enemy forces from
coordinating their defence.

The offensive, when it came, was
launched from a totally unexpected direction.
A battalion of paratroopers was dropped deep
into the Sinai, confronting the enemy with a
surprise from which he never recovered;
next, the rest of the paratroop brigade,
commanded by Lieutenant Colonel Ariel
Sharon, linked up with it. First the Egyptian
fortifications in central Sinai, then those in
the northeastern corner of the peninsula
near Rafa, were attacked and occupied.
Except for one unauthorized operation which
Ariel Sharon launched into the Mitla Pass
and which, though ultimately successful,
carried a heavy cost in casualties, the rest
was merely mopping up.

Dayan himself was 41 years old. An
impetuous commander who hated meetings,
he spent the campaign driving and flying all
over the theatre of operations; some of the
time he was out of touch with the general
staff in Tel Aviv. He pushed his commanders,
encouraged them, and, as happened at Abu Agheila where
the initial Israeli attack failed, fired them when he felt they
deserved it. Characteristically, the end of the campaign
found him at the Straits of Tiran, about as far from
headquarters as he could be.

The Sinai campaign was much the smallest of the
four in which Dayan played a part or which he commanded. Judging by the fact that for each of the 170
soldiers killed, three Egyptian divisions were destroyed, it
was also the most successful by far. It gave the country
ten years of almost uninterrupted peace.

Moshe Dayan

Though he remained a member of a splinter party in the Knesset, politically he was barely active. Apparently he warned the prime minister, Levi Eshkol, and the chief of staff, Yitzhak Rabin, that their aggressive policy towards Syria was 'madness' and would lead to war. Though married and the father of three, he entertained an endless series of mistresses.

His country's saviour: the Six Day War

Salvation came from an unexpected quarter. In April 1967 hostilities along the Israeli-Syrian border escalated. At one point, Egyptian president Gamal Abdel Nasser decided he could no longer stand aside and watch; he mobilized, re-occupied the Sinai peninsula (which had been demilitarized in 1957), and closed the Straits of Tiran to Israeli shipping. To make the crisis worse, Jordan, Syria and Iraq joined hands in declaring their intention to fight the Zionist enemy.

After three weeks of political manoeuvring, Dayan was appointed minister of defence. As he assumed the post, the entire country heaved a sigh of relief; here, at last, was a man who seemed to know what he wanted and had what it took to carry it out. Three days later, on 5 June 1967, Israel went to war.

First a devastating air strike – the plans had been prepared and rehearsed long before he took office – demolished most of the Egyptian air force on the ground. Next, three armoured divisions crashed into the Sinai, overrunning or bypassing the fortifications in their way and scattering the enemy in front of them. Eight Egyptian divisions, totalling about 100,000 men, were smashed; only a single brigade succeeded in getting away intact. Within four days, the Israelis were standing on the Suez Canal.

When the Jordanians intervened, their little air force, too, was destroyed. Israeli ground forces moved into the West Bank from three directions, north, south, and west. Those operating at the centre of the front, in and around Jerusalem, quickly surrounded the city; by so doing, they cut the West Bank in half. Though the Jordanians fought bravely, they were helpless against the Israeli air force. Within three days the entire area was occupied. Meanwhile the Israel air force also found time and aircraft with which to strike at the westernmost Iraqi air base from which attacks had been launched on Tel Aviv.

Throughout the four days these operations lasted, the Syrians, from their fortified positions on the Golan Heights, rained down artillery shells on the Israeli settlements below. The general staff, as well as members of the Cabinet, demanded that

June 1967: Dayan (centre) and Yitzhak Rabin (right) enter the Old City of Jerusalem to pray at the Western Wall, the first Israelis to be able to do so since 1948. Taking the Old City had not been part of the original Israeli plan, but Dayan authorized Uzi Narkiss (left) to complete the takeover before the ceasefire.

Moshe Dayan

Dayan authorize an attack on the Heights; fearing Soviet intervention, he refused repeatedly. Once Egypt agreed to a ceasefire during the night of 8 June, however, he changed his mind, ordering the assault without bothering to inform the prime minister. Later, he was often blamed for this.

As in 1956, he took the most important decisions as to which enemy to fight, where to fight him, and, perhaps most important of all, where to stop. As in 1956, he spent as much time as he could away from headquarters. He toured the fronts and gave directives on the spot; one result of this was that, when Israeli aircraft mistakenly attacked the USS *Liberty*, he could not be reached. Some of the decisions he made, such as leaving the Temple Mount under the control of the Muslim Waqf (religious endowment) were to have consequences that last to the present day.

Towards the Day of Judgment

In 1967–73, Dayan presided over a great expansion of the Israel Defense Force (IDF), whose order of battle grew by about 60 per cent. Many new weapons were purchased, and qualitative improvements introduced. The result was to turn a force which, until then, had been very well motivated and trained but poor and technologically somewhat backward, into a regional juggernaut.

The years 1967–70 in particular were anything but quiet. A military administration had to be put in place in the occupied territories. There were numerous

Moshe Dayan

Dayan in a bunker on the Golan Heights, 11 October 1973, during the Yom Kippur War. He was politically embattled as well at this juncture, having failed to anticipate the Arab attack; and had offered his resignation as minister of defence the previous day.

skirmishes with Jordanian and Syrian forces as well as, increasingly, Palestinian guerrillas operating first from Jordan and then from Lebanon.

The largest and most dangerous clashes took place along the Suez Canal from March 1969 to August 1970. Relatively small Israeli forces, hunkering in their bunkers, confronted an enormous Egyptian force equipped with as many as 1,000 artillery pieces. To restore the balance, Dayan ordered the Israeli air force into action. This in turn caused the Soviets to intervene – they already had 'advisers' at every level of the Egyptian army. In April 1970 several Soviet fighters were shot down. For a time, it looked as if the mighty Soviet Union would be drawn into a war against tiny Israel.

The pressure on Dayan during those years was enormous. To make things worse, in 1968 he was nearly buried alive during an archaeological dig, receiving injuries from which he never quite recovered. Once a ceasefire was agreed on along the Suez Canal in August 1970, things became somewhat easier. Too easy perhaps; when a quarter of a million Arab troops with 5,000 tanks between them attacked in October 1973, they found Israel unprepared.

The Yom Kippur War

Dayan, in fact, had suspected there might be a war. In the spring he repeatedly warned the General Staff to prepare; however, later in the summer, when no Arab attack materialized, he calmed down. During the last few days before the Egyptian–Syrian attack he held frantic consultations with the prime minister as well as his main military advisers, but in the end no decision to mobilize was made. As a result, on 6 October 1973, Yom Kippur or the Jewish Day of Judgment, the Egyptians and the Syrians took Israel by surprise just as Israel had surprised them six years earlier.

Moshe Dayan

Early in the war, it was Dayan who had to make the most critical decisions. Which front, the Egyptian or the Syrian one, to give priority; whether to try to hold ground or retreat to a line further in the rear; whether to use the air force to attack the enemy's anti-aircraft systems, as planned, or sacrifice it in a desperate attempt to stop the enemy's advance; and so on. As was his habit, he preferred to make these and similar decisions not in the comfort of general headquarters but on the basis of visits to the front. Later Ariel Sharon, who commanded a division in the south, recalled that Dayan had been the only senior commander to visit him.

Seen in retrospect, some of the decisions he made during those days may not have been correct. It seems that there was a moment on Sunday 7 October or Monday 8 October, when things looked so bad that Dayan suggested threatening Syria with Israel's nuclear weapons. Whether the threat was made, and what effect it had, remains shrouded in secrecy to the present day.

From Wednesday 10 October the fronts stabilized. Dayan offered Prime Minister Golda Meir his resignation, but was told to stay at his post. While he went on visiting the fronts, others, including above all chief of staff General David Elazar, now made the most important decisions. When the war ended on 24 October, the Syrians had been thrown back, about a third of the Egyptian army was surrounded, and Israeli troops stood west of the Suez Canal, just over 60 miles from Cairo.

Final years

When the commission set up to investigate the war published its findings, it did not condemn Dayan – the supreme example of his ability to evade responsibility. Public opinion nonetheless forced him to resign. In June 1974, though still a

'From Moshe [Moses] to Moshe [Dayan] there was none like Moshe.'
ISRAELI POPULAR SAYING

member of the Knesset, he returned home and spent the next eighteen months writing his memoirs, a fascinating account by a difficult and complex man.

In May 1977 Israel's new prime minister Menahem Begin asked Dayan to serve as foreign minister. In this capacity, he played a critical part in negotiating peace with Egypt at Camp David (September 1978). Soon thereafter, realizing that Begin had no intention of continuing the peace process so a solution might be found that would rid Israel of its 'hump' – the occupied West Bank – he resigned. By that time he was a sick man, suffering from colon cancer. He tried to warn Begin against launching a war in Lebanon, but did not live to see the failure of his efforts. On 16 October 1981, he died. He was buried in Nahalal, close to his parents and other relatives. Proud to the last, he had asked that no eulogies be held on his grave, and his wish was respected.

VO NGUYEN GIAP

GEOFFREY PERRET

1911–

GIAP STUDIED THE ACHIEVEMENTS of such great commanders as Napoleon and Mao, and applied the lessons to the anti-colonial struggle in Vietnam. Taking advantage of the huge loyalty and enthusiasm of the Vietnamese peasantry whom he adulated, Giap built up an army from nothing, and with it he defeated two great powers, France and the United States.

Vo Nguyen Giap was born in August 1911 in An Xa, a small coastal town in the province of Quang Binh, in the narrow waist of Vietnam. His father was a minor civil servant and land owner.

The youthful Giap's course in life was shaped largely by the French occupation. For much of the nineteenth century France had struggled to bring Indochina into its empire. By 1885 France controlled Indochina, which consisted mainly of French protectorates, plus the colony of Cochinchina. Although they justified their rule as *'une mission civilatrice'*, spreading the values of the Enlightenment to inferior peoples, the true pillars of French rule were systematic torture, harsh prison sentences and Madame Guillotine. Seeking a cowed population, what they got instead was resistance movements.

Given the region's history, warrior motifs had ineluctably worked their way into the names of people and places. Giap's family name of Vo, for example, can be read as 'military force,' while Giap means both 'first' and 'intact armour'. Some Vietnamese even claim that his name in its entirety means 'commander-in-chief'.

The making of a revolutionary

More important than the symbolic references contained within his names were the fervently anti-French sentiments of Giap's father. He recited patriotic poems to his son, taught him songs of sacrifice and courage and talked about the many wars of Vietnam, fought mainly against the Chinese. Throughout his life Giap would remain wary of the great neighbour to the north.

Even so, the collapse of imperial China in the same year that Giap was born brought more than thirty years of civil strife that wracked every major Chinese province, city and large town. China's internal struggles inflamed patriotic and nation-

Vo Nguyen Giap

alistic movements of every variety, from anarchism to Marxism to crypto-fascism. Sparks cast out from these struggles had incendiary effects in neighbouring Vietnam.

As childhood gave way to adolescence the young Giap was not so much pushed into anti-French politics as rushing to embrace it. Exceptionally intelligent and hard-working, at the age of 14 he won admission to one of the most prestigious secondary schools in the country, the Lycée Quoc Hoc in Hué. The school's graduates included Ho Chi Minh and Ngo Dinh Diem.

One day a fellow student handed him a proscribed pamphlet entitled 'French Colonialism on Trial'. Giap climbed into a tree to read it undisturbed. He descended filled with rage, but thrilled to his patriotic core. The author was Ho Chi Minh, although Giap did not know that then as it had been published under one of Ho's many aliases.

In 1930 the French arrested seven teachers at Giap's school and a number of students were rounded up, including Giap. He was sentenced to two years' hard labour. When he left prison, however, he was offered a second chance. A senior French official encouraged him to apply to the Lycée Albert Sarraut in Hanoi, the Vietnamese equivalent of Eton. The French routinely attempted to co-opt the future leaders and opinion-shapers among their colonial subjects while they were still at a formative stage, with careers to make.

Vive l'Empereur!

In 1934, having gained his baccalaureate, Giap taught history and French at a *lycée* while studying law at the University of Hanoi. By now, he was a dedicated communist,

although as with most Vietnamese communists, his was a communism that was grafted on to nationalistic rootstock.

Meanwhile he was cultivating intellectual interests that had little or no connection with the legal profession. At the start of the history course he taught, he informed his students, 'I'm going to tell you about two things – the French Revolution and Napoleon.' Throughout his long life, every one of the emperor's battles and campaigns fascinated Giap and inspired him. After all, Napoleon was a great revolutionary as well as being a great soldier.

'The Red Napoleon.'

TIME MAGAZINE ON GIAP, 1966

In 1938, as the number one student in his law school class, Giap was offered a full scholarship to attend any of the *grandes écoles* or universities of France. There he would be free to study whatever he desired. He rejected the offer as a matter of course. By this time, Giap knew just what his life's work would be: to get the French out of Indochina. He turned his talents to waging a propaganda offensive. With a group of like-minded friends Giap bought a failing newspaper and devoted its pages to tales of French perfidy and Vietnamese courage. Although his prose style was larded with the mind-numbing jargon of Marxism-Leninism he saw himself as a writer by vocation and introduced himself to people as a journalist.

Giap also travelled to China, where he finally met the author of 'French Colonialism on Trial.' Ho Chi Minh – meaning 'the enlightened one' – was by this time the best-known figure in the growing resistance to French rule. Ho and Giap became so close they might as well have been father and son. During this Chinese journey Giap also came into contact with one of the most famous military formations of all time, the Eighth Route Army, the creation of Mao Zedong and a professional soldier, Zhu De. Following a failed attempt to engineer a peasant uprising in his home province of Hunan in 1926, Mao had concluded that for the Chinese Communist Party to survive it must build its own army. Zhu was ready to help, but where would they find troops?

Peasant power

Mao had the answer: the despised peasants of China constituted the most powerful revolutionary force imaginable. Organize them, mobilize them, inspire them, and these peasants, the truly wretched of the Earth, could defeat anyone. They had little to lose but their lives, but under most Chinese governments, those lives were hardly worth living anyway. Mao taught his soldiers that their mission in life was to protect the peasantry against both the rapacious Nationalist forces of Jiang Jieshi (Chiang Kai-shek) and the invading armies of imperial Japan.

Mao's soldiers were taught to take nothing from the people, not even a needle and thread. In learning to respect others, they began to respect themselves. There will always be men who are willing die for an idea, and Mao gave them one. He also gave them a military education that any illiterate peasant could understand:

> *Enemy advances, we retreat.*
> *Enemy halts, we harass.*
> *Enemy tires, we attack.*
> *Enemy retreats, we pursue.*

Giap was also influenced by Napoleon's approach to battle. Strategically, this meant a belief that only the offensive is decisive in war. Tactically, it meant, as Napoleon expressed it, 'Get stuck in and see what follows'. It was risky, opportunistic and only someone able to read the fog of war like a map could ever hope to master it.

Meanwhile, in 1939, Giap married and the next year his wife Quang Thai had a child, a baby girl. With the fall of France in June 1940 the French hold on Indochina became increasingly tenuous. They began to mount large-scale roundups of known and suspected critics of their rule. They seized Quang Thai but Giap escaped his pursuers. Quang Thai's sister was seized, tortured and shot. Quang Thai herself was tortured in prison and perished there.

In 1941 the Japanese arrived in Vietnam but Giap did not believe they would be there long. The Axis countries – Germany, Italy and Japan – could never hope to prevail against an alliance based on the United States, the British Empire and the Soviet Union. From a rudimentary camp only a few miles into China, Giap prepared himself for the coming struggle. Yet he was taught how to organize and wage a guerrilla struggle by veterans of the Eighth Route Army. He also studied Mao's extensive writings on protracted war, including such classic texts as *A Single Spark Can Start a Prairie Fire*.

The traditional Marxist theory of armed struggle called for organizing the industrial workers. China had virtually no industrial workers. Nor had Vietnam. However, Mao had already demonstrated that in a peasant-based society it was the peasants who held the keys to power. It was impossible, though, for Giap to acknowledge his debt to Mao Zedong. Instead, he claimed that the doctrine of protracted war and the crucial role of the peasant were ideas that originated in Vietnam, with an obscure revolutionary named Bac Ho, whom very few have ever heard of.

Unable to organize in areas under French or Japanese control, Giap established himself in remote and mountainous border regions populated mainly by non-Vietnamese people who spoke their own tribal languages. Giap learned two of these languages, won their trust and set up military training camps on both sides of the border with China. Meanwhile Ho Chi Minh was creating a revolutionary political arm, the Viet Minh. Ho believed it would be possible to negotiate the French out of Vietnam. There did not have to be a war.

Ho Chi Minh photographed in July 1946 by Laure Albin-Guillot.

Armed propaganda brigades

The compromise between Ho's views and Giap's was the formation of 'Armed Propaganda Brigades'. These would wage a propaganda offensive and, when the opportunity arose, mount military attacks on isolated French police posts. Giap chose thirty-one men and three women to form the first brigade. It boasted a single light machine-gun, seventeen rifles, two handguns and some ancient shotguns and pistols.

By December 1944 Giap was ready to mount his first military assault, striking a regional French police headquarters on Christmas Eve, when the French were likely to be inebriated and easy to surprise. The headquarters was captured and the French commander perished in its defence. An almost laughably small force of thirty-four lightly armed volunteers thus became

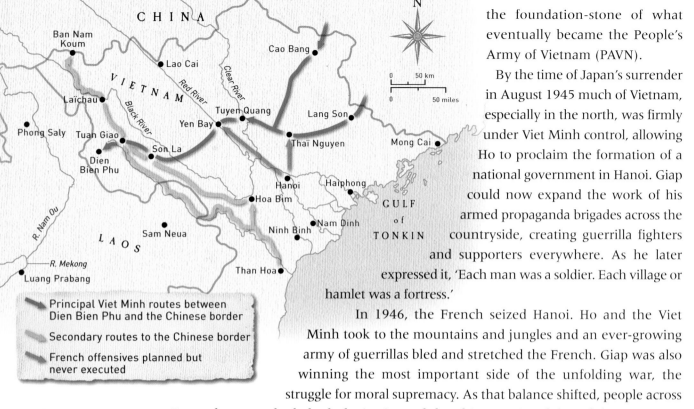

Principal Viet Minh routes between Dien Bien Phu and the Chinese border

Secondary routes to the Chinese border

French offensives planned but never executed

THE VIET MINH'S LINKS across Vietnam to Dien Bien Phu, 1954.

the foundation-stone of what eventually became the People's Army of Vietnam (PAVN).

By the time of Japan's surrender in August 1945 much of Vietnam, especially in the north, was firmly under Viet Minh control, allowing Ho to proclaim the formation of a national government in Hanoi. Giap could now expand the work of his armed propaganda brigades across the countryside, creating guerrilla fighters and supporters everywhere. As he later expressed it, 'Each man was a soldier. Each village or hamlet was a fortress.'

In 1946, the French seized Hanoi. Ho and the Viet Minh took to the mountains and jungles and an ever-growing army of guerrillas bled and stretched the French. Giap was also winning the most important side of the unfolding war, the struggle for moral supremacy. As that balance shifted, people across France began to doubt both the justice and the ultimate winnability of the war.

Red River campaign

The army he had crafted possessed what commanders down the ages have prized most – an indomitable fighting spirit, sustained by high morale. In January 1951 Giap launched a frontal assault to take Hanoi back from the French.

Impatient and inexperienced, he accepted the advice of Chinese military advisers and mounted a human-wave attack in broad daylight, thrusting 20,000 soldiers into a killing-ground that the French had prepared. In a matter of days Giap suffered at least 10,000 men killed, wounded or captured. He had also failed to recognize that during the battle the French commander had made a serious mistake, one that could have put victory within Giap's reach.

Refusing to admit defeat, two months later he tried again, with a three-division attack. This time he called it off after losing 3,000 troops. Undeterred, Giap mounted yet another major attack, albeit from a different direction, and lost another 10,000 soldiers to death, wounds and captivity. When he did the same again, for a fourth time, some 9,000 PAVN soldiers perished.

Morale crumbled and desertions rose. Had it not been for Ho Chi Minh, Giap would have been removed from his command. By this time, however, he had learned how to move his army, how to conceal it, how to supply it and how to use it. Without his failed Red River campaign of 1951–2, Giap would never have been able to pull off his masterstroke, the capture of Dien Bien Phu. He had also learned at last the wisdom of the military adage that says, 'Amateurs talk tactics, professionals talk logistics'.

For France, the Indochinese struggle had become a political disaster at home and abroad. They were almost desperate to hand the bulk of the fighting over to a Vietnamese army that was French-trained and French-equipped. That would allow

(Opposite) **Viet Minh troops attack at Dien Bien Phu, 1954.**
The 56-day battle brought to an end the French presence in Indochina.

Vo Nguyen Giap

Paris to withdraw most of its troops but still dominate Vietnam politically.

In 1953, the new French commander in Indochina, Henri Navarre, proposed to defend northern Laos. He would spend 1954 building up a cordon of mutually supporting bases. Then, in 1955, he would thrust into the areas that Giap controlled and destroy the PAVN's main force units. Like other French generals before him and American generals after him, Navarre liked to think that he held both the tactical and strategic initiative. In a conventional war, this might have been true. In the kind of war that Giap was waging, it was he, not Navarre, who held the initiative, always.

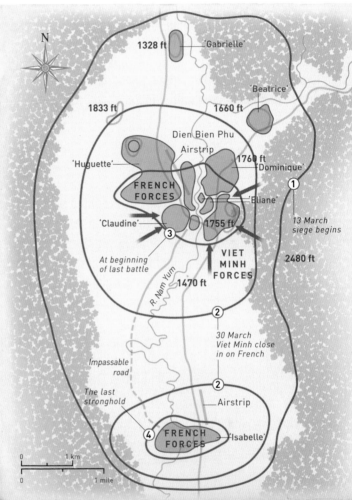

Dien Bien Phu

The key to Navarre's strategy was the large base he was building at Dien Bien Phu, close to the northern Vietnamese border with Laos. With insouciance verging on contempt, Navarre and other senior officers convinced themselves that they did not have to occupy the high ground.

Mao meanwhile offered Giap twenty-four of the 105mm howitzers captured by Chinese troops from American units in Korea. He also offered hundreds of tons of 105mm ammunition. But how would Giap get these heavy pieces up on those jungle-clad hills? How would he move all that ammunition? Giap appealed to the peasants and nearly 1 million volunteered to serve as porters.

The Viet Minh meanwhile were mounting so many ambushes that the French tried to avoid using the roads. Giap was turning Dien Bien Phu into a virtual island, one that could be reached only by air.

When the fight opened on 13 March 1954, Giap

had 49,000 soldiers to pit against Navarre's 11,000 at Dien Bien Phu, plus 2,000 French reinforcements who arrived in the course of the fight. The Chinese advisers at Giap's headquarters, who included Zhu De, urged him to mount human-wave attacks, but he had learned the cost of their advice during the Red River campaign. Despite angry lectures from Chinese generals, he held fast.

Giap knew his men would fight to the death, but he wanted them to fight to victory. He would take Dien Bien Phu by classic siege tactics, including digging trenches ever closer to the objective. He had millions of rounds of small-arms ammunition, nearly 200 artillery pieces, 60,000 rounds for his artillery, and a small mountain of rice. He was also going to need 4,000 tons of supplies to reach his army every day, much of it only after being carried for hundreds of miles on bicycles.

Giap concentrated overwhelming forces at each of the strong-points that ringed Dien Bien Phu, seized one then moved on to the next. He was also sending men to make attacks on French installations deep in the enemy's rear, striking airfields and barracks, pinning the French down not only at Dien Bien Phu but across Indochina.

Meanwhile the 105s fired day and night. The French wounded were flown out and reinforcements were flown in – some even parachuted in – until the Chinese provided anti-aircraft guns. After that there were few flights in either direction. Casualties among the defenders were comparatively light but their food, water and medical supplies were running out, just as a conference on the future of Indochina was about to be convened in Geneva. Giap attacked with all that he had. The French broke first. Dien Bien Phu surrendered on 7 May 1954, the day before the Geneva Conference convened. Giap had incurred around 23,000 casualties; the French, approximately 8,000.

French prisoners-of-war march, defeated, from Dien Bien Phu, under the guard of the victorious Communist Viet Minh, July 1954.

The aftermath

After Giap's triumph at Dien Bien Phu the French quickly departed from Indochina, but the victory did not yet lead to the unification of Vietnam and, within the Viet Minh elite Giap had accumulated powerful rivals and critics.

Communist governments are always fearful of 'Bonapartism' – the glamorous, popular general who stages a coup. Giap was the kind of great captain that the grey politicians needed but sought to limit once victory was won. His preference for the Soviets over the Chinese also carried a price.

Giap was consulted on future operations, but he was no longer commander-in-chief. He was, for example, extremely dubious about the Tet Offensive against the Americans in 1968. The plan was predicated on a popular uprising in support of the opening round of attacks, something Giap doubted would happen. All the same, once the decision was made, he loyally did all he could to make the offensive a success.

Wounded US troops at Khe Sanh, during the North Vietnamese Tet Offensive, April 1968. Although the offensive ended in victory for US and South Vietnamese forces, the bitter fighting it entailed ultimately eroded US commitment to the Vietnam War.

He fooled the American commander General William C. Westmoreland into pushing troops and air assets into a major fight at Khe Sanh, but the offensive was aimed at the cities and major towns of South Vietnam; Khe Sanh was just a diversion to pull American troops away from heavily populated areas. The base depended on a small river that flowed down from the north for its water supplies. Giap could have made the base untenable by poisoning the river. The fact that he did not do so revealed his true intentions, but Westmoreland never realized that.

In his book *People's War, People's Army* (1962) Giap had explained his strategy for victory: 'Military action was necessary, but propaganda was much more important.' Westmoreland never understood that, nor did Navarre, but Tet proved Giap's point, for a second time. In 1975 the army and the guerrilla forces that Giap had created destroyed the American-backed government in Saigon. Vietnam was finally united, and in the manner that Giap had preached from the beginning. His was the strategy, ultimately, of the greatest of all military thinkers – Sun Tzu: defeat your enemy in his mind first, the rest will follow.

In the end, Giap could claim to have defeated eight French generals, of whom Navarre was only the last. After that he defeated four American generals. And now, in his 98th year, he is honoured around the world. In 1966, as an American army deployed across South Vietnam, *Time* magazine warned what they were up against. Giap, it declared, was 'the Red Napoleon'. For him, there could be no greater accolade.

FURTHER READING

MAURICE OF NASSAU

Marco van der Hoeven (ed.), *The Exercise of Arms: Warfare in the Netherlands, 1568–1648* (Brill, Leiden, 1998).

B. H. Nickle, *The Military Reforms of Prince Maurice of Orange* (Ann Arbor, MI, 1981).

Jan den Tex, *Oldenbarneveldt* (2 vols, Cambridge University Press, Cambridge, 1973).

GUSTAVUS ADOLPHUS

Michael Roberts, *Gustavus Adophus: A History of Sweden 1611–1632* (2 vols, Longman, London, 1953–8).

Geoffrey Parker (ed.), *The Thirty Years War* (second edition, Routledge, London, 1997).

COUNT TILLY

Michael Kaiser, *Politik und Kriegführung: Maximilian von Bayern, Tilly und die Katholische Liga im Dreißigjährigen Krieg* (Aschendorff, Münster, 1999).

C. V. Wedgwood, *The Thirty Years War* (London, 1938).

Georg Gilardone, *Tilly, der Heilige in Harnisch* (Kosel und Pustet, Munich, 1932).

Onno Klopp, *Tilly im Dreißigjährigen Kriege* (2 vols, Stuttgart, 1861).

OLIVER CROMWELL

Micheál Ó Siochrú, *God's Executioner: Oliver Cromwell and the Conquest of Ireland* (Faber, London, 2008).

Barry Coward, *Oliver Cromwell* (Longman, Harlow, 2000).

Tom Reilly, *Cromwell: An Honourable Enemy* (Brandon, Dingle, 1999).

Christopher Hill, *God's Englishman* (Penguin, London, 1990).

VICOMTE DE TURENNE

Jean Bérenger, *Turenne* (Fayard, Paris, 1987).

Max Weygand, *Turenne* (George G. Harrap & Co., London, 1930).

DUKE OF MARLBOROUGH

Winston S. Churchill, *Marlborough: His Life and Times* (George G. Harrap & Co., London, 1947).

David Chandler, *Marlborough as Military Commander* (The History Press, Stroud, 2003).

PRINCE EUGÈNE OF SAVOY

Nicholas Henderson, *Prince Eugen of Savoy* (Weidenfeld & Nicolson, London, 1964).

Derek McKay, *Prince Eugène of Savoy* (Thames & Hudson, London, 1977).

CHARLES XII

Ragnhild Hatton, *Charles XII of Sweden* (Weidenfeld & Nicolson, London, 1968).

Robert I. Frost, *The Northern Wars, 1558–1721* (Longman, Harlow, Essex, 2000).

Peter Englund, *The Battle of Poltava: The Birth of the Russian Empire* (Gollancz, London, 1992).

MAURICE, COMTE DE SAXE

Comte Maurice de Saxe, *My Reveries upon the Art of War*, in T. R. Phillips (ed.), *The Roots of Strategy* (Stackpole Books, Harrisburg, PA, 1985), pp. 189–257.

J. E. M. White, *Marshal of France: The Life and Times of Maurice, Comte de Saxe, 1696–1750* (Hamish Hamilton, London, 1962).

FREDERICK THE GREAT

Giles MacDonogh, *Frederick the Great: A Life in Deed and Letters* (Weidenfeld & Nicolson, London, 1999).

David Fraser, *Frederick the Great* (Allen Lane, London, 2000).

Christopher Duffy, *Frederick the Great – A Military Life* (Emperor's Press, London, 1995).

Dennis E. Showalter, *The Wars of Frederick the Great* (Longman, London, 1996).

ROBERT CLIVE

Michael Edwardes, *The Battle of Plassey* (Batsford, London, 1963).

Mark Bence-Jones, *Clive of India* (Constable, London, 1974).

Robert Harvey, *Clive: The Life and Death of a British Emperor* (Hodder & Stoughton, London, 1998).

Thomas Babington Macaulay, *Essay on Clive* (London, 1840).

JAMES WOLFE

Stephen Brumwell, *Paths of Glory: The Life and Death of General James Wolfe* (Continuum, London, 2006).

C. P. Stacey, *Quebec: The Siege and the Battle* (Macmillan, Toronto, 1959).

NATHANAEL GREENE

Terry Golway, *Washington's General: Nathanael Greene and the Triumph of the American Revolution* (Holt, New York, 2005).

John Ferling, *Almost a Miracle: The American Victory in the War of Independence* (Oxford University Press, New York, 2007).

NAPOLEON BONAPARTE

David Chandler, *The Campaigns of Napoleon* (Weidenfeld & Nicolson, London, 1966).

Philip Dwyer, *Napoleon: The Path to Power, 1769–1799* (Bloomsbury, London, 2007).

Charles Esdaile, *The Wars of Napoleon* (Longman, London, 1995).

Charles Esdaile, *Napoleon's Wars: An International History, 1803–1815* (Allen Lane, London, 2007).

DUKE WELLINGTON

Elizabeth Longford, *Wellington: The Years of the Sword* (Weidenfeld & Nicolson, London, 1969).

Richard Holmes, *Wellington* (HarperCollins, London, 2002).

Gordon Corrigan, *Wellington: A Military Life* (Hambledon Continuum, London, 2001).

Alessandro Barbero, *The Battle: A New History of the Battle of Waterloo* (Atlantic Books, London, 2005).

LOUIS-NICOLAS DAVOUT

John G. Gallagher, *The Iron Marshal: A biography of Louis N. Davout* (1976; reissued by Greenhill Books, London, 2000).

Daniel Reichel, *Davout et l'art de la guerre: recherches sur la formation, l'action pendant la Révolution et les commandements du maréchal Davout, duc d'Auerstaedt, prince d'Eckmühl, 1770–1823* (Centre d'Histoire et de Prospective Militaires, Neuchâtel, 1975).

Joseph, Comte Vigier, *Davout: maréchal d'empire, duc d'Auerstädt, prince d'Eckmühl, 1770–1823* (2 vols, Paul Ollendorff, Paris, 1898).

MIKHAIL KUTUZOV

Roger Parkinson, *The Fox of the North* (Purnell, London, 1976).

Christopher Duffy, *Borodino* (Sphere, London, 1972).

L. G. Beskrovny, *The Patriotic War and Kutuzov's Counter-Offensive* (Moscow, 1951).

A. Brett James, *1812, Eyewitness Accounts of Napoleon's Defeat in Russia* (Macmillan, London, 1966).

Adam Zamoyski, *1812: Napoleon's Fatal March on Moscow* (HarperCollins, London, 2004).

Alan Palmer, *Napoleon in Russia* (Deutsch, London, 1967; revised edition, London, 1999).

Alan Palmer, *Russia in War and Peace* (Weidenfeld & Nicolson, London, 1972).

Alan Palmer, *Alexander I: Tsar of War and Peace* (Weidenfeld & Nicolson, London, 1974).

CARL VON CLAUSEWITZ

Michael Howard and Peter Paret (eds), *Carl von Clausewitz: On War* (Princeton University Press, Princeton, NJ, 1989).

Raymond Aron, *Clausewitz*, translated by Christine Booker and Norman Stone (Routledge, London, 1983).

Christopher Clark, *Iron Kingdom: The Rise and Downfall of Prussia 1600–1947* (Allen Lane, London, 2006).

SIMÓN BOLÍVAR

John Lynch, *Simón Bolívar: A Life* (Yale University Press, New Haven and London, 2006).

David Bushnell, *Simón Bolívar: Liberation and Disappointment* (Prentice Hall, New York, 2004).

David Bushnell (ed.), *El Libertador: Writings of Simón Bolívar* (Oxford University Press, Oxford, 2003).

Daniel Florencio O'Leary, *Bolívar and the War of Independence*, translated and edited by R. F. McNerney, Jr (University of Texas Press, Austin, TX, 1970).

R. A. Humphreys (ed.), *The 'Detached Recollections' of General D. F. O'Leary* (Athlone Press, London, 1969).

SHAKA ZULU

Ián Knight, *The Anatomy of the Zulu Army: From Shaka to Cetshwayo 1818–1879* (Greenhill Books, London, 1995).

John Laband, *The Rise and Fall of the Zulu Nation* (Arms and Armour, 1997).

Donald Morris, *The Washing of the Spears* (Simon and Schuster, New York, 1966).

Alan Mountain, *The Rise and Fall of the Zulu Empire* (kwaNtaba, 1999).

GIUSEPPE GARIBALDI

L. Riall, Garibaldi, *Invention of a Hero* (Yale University Press, London & New Haven, 2007).

D. Mack Smith, *Garibaldi: A Great Life in Brief* (Hutchinson, London, 1957).

G. M. Trevelyan, *Garibaldi* (3 vols, Longman, London, 1907–11).

ROBERT E. LEE

Edward H. Bonekemper III, *How Robert E. Lee Lost the Civil War* (Sergeant Kirkland's Press, San Diego, CA, 1998).

J. F. C. Fuller, *Grant and Lee: A Study in Personality and Generalship* (Indiana University Press, Bloomington, IN, 1982).

Gary W. Gallagher (ed.), *Lee the Soldier* (University of Nebraska Press, Lincoln, NE, 1996).

Alan T. Nolan, *Lee Considered: Gen. Robert E. Lee and Civil War History* (University of North Carolina Press, Chapel Hill, NC, 1996).

Emory M. Thomas, *Robert E. Lee: A Biography* (W. W. Norton & Co., New York, 1997).

'STONEWALL' JACKSON

George F. R. Henderson, *Stonewall Jackson and the American Civil War* (Longmans, Green and Co., London and New York, 1898).

James A. Kegel, *North with Lee and Jackson* (Stackpole Books, Mechanicsburg, PA, 1996).

James I. Robertson, *'Stonewall' Jackson: The Man, the Soldier, the Legend* (Macmillan, New York, NY, 1997).

Frank E. Vandiver, *Mighty Stonewall* (McGraw-Hill Book Company, New York, NY, 1957).

GEORGE MEADE

Freeman Cleaves, *Meade of Gettysburg* (University of Oklahoma Press, Norman, OK, 1960).

Edwin B. Coddington, *The Gettysburg Campaign: A Study in Command* (Charles Scribner's Sons, New York, 1968).

David W. Lowe (ed.), *Meade's Army: the Private Notebooks of Lt. Col. Theodore Lyman* (Kent State University Press, Kent, OH, 2007).

George Meade, *The Life and Letters of George Gordon Meade* (Charles Scribner's Sons, New York, 1913).

ULYSSES S. GRANT

Edward H. Bonekemper III, *A Victor Not a Butcher: Ulysses S. Grant's Overlooked Military Genius* (Regnery Books, Washington, DC, 2004).

Josiah Bunting, *Ulysses S. Grant* (The American Presidents Series, Times Books, New York, 2004).

Ulysses S. Grant, *Memoirs and Selected Letters, 1839–1865* (Library of America, New York, 1990).

Michael Korda, *Ulysses S. Grant: The Unlikely Hero* (Eminent Lives series, HarperCollins, New York, 2004).

Brooks Simpson, *Ulysses S. Grant: Triumph Over Adversity, 1822–1865* (Houghton Mifflin, Boston, 2000).

WILLIAM T. SHERMAN

Lloyd Lewis, *Sherman: Fighting Prophet* (Harcourt, Brace and Company, New York, 1932).

John F. Marszalek, *Sherman: A Soldier's Passion for Order* (The Free Press, New York, 1993).

William T. Sherman, *Memoirs of General William T. Sherman by Himself* (D. Appleton and Company, New York, 1885).

Brooks D. Simpson and Jean Berlin (eds), *Sherman's Civil War: Selected Correspondence of William T. Sherman, 1860–1865* (University of North Carolina Press, Chapel Hill, NC, 1999).

HELMUTH VON MOLTKE

Lieutenant Colonel F. E. Whitton, *Moltke* (Constable, London, 1921).

Peter Paret (ed.), *Makers of Modern Strategy* (Oxford University Press, Oxford, 1986).

Michael Howard, *The Franco-Prussian War* (Hart-Davis, London, 1962).

GARNET WOLSELEY

Brian Bond (ed.), *Victorian Military Campaigns* (Hutchinson, London, 1967).

Halik Kochanski, *Sir Garnet Wolseley: Victorian Hero* (Hambledon Continuum, London, 1999).

Joseph Lehmann, *All Sir Garnet: A Life of Field Marshal Lord Wolseley* (Jonathan Cape, London, 1964).

ERICH LUDENDORFF

John Lee, *The Warlords: Hindenburg and Ludendorff* (Weidenfeld & Nicolson, London, 2005).

Correlli Barnett, *The Swordbearers* (Cassell, London, 2000).

Peter Paret (ed.), *Makers of Modern Strategy* (Oxford University Press, Oxford, 1986).

FERDINAND FOCH

Ferdinand Foch, *The Principles of War* (Kessinger Publishing, Whitefish, MT, 2007).

Michael S. Neiberg, *Foch: Supreme Allied Commander in the Great War* (Brassey's US, Washington, DC, 2004).

Basil Liddell Hart, *Foch: Man of Orleans* (Kessinger Publishing, Whitefish, MT, 2008).

PHILIPPE PÉTAIN

C. Williams, *Pétain* (Little, Brown, London, 2005).

G. Pedroncini, *Pétain, le soldat et la gloire, 1856–1918* (Perrin, Paris, 1989).

S. Ryan, *Pétain the Soldier* (A.S. Barnes & Co., New York, 1969).

EDMUND ALLENBY

M. Hughes, *Allenby and British Strategy in the Middle East, 1917–1919* (Routledge, London, 1999).

L. James, *Imperial Warrior: The Life and Times of Field-Marshal Viscount Allenby, 1861–1936* (Weidenfeld & Nicolson, London, 1993).

JOHN PERSHING

Frank E. Vandiver, *Black Jack: The Life and Times of John J. Pershing* (2 vols, Texas A & M University Press, College Station, Texas and London, 1977).

John J. Pershing, *My Experiences in the World War* (2 vols, Frederick A. Stokes, New York, 1931).

Donald Smythe, *Pershing: General of the Armies* (Indiana University Press, Bloomington, 1986).

Thomas Fleming, *'Iron General'*, *Military History Quarterly*, vol. 7, no. 2 (Winter 1994).

KEMAL ATATÜRK
Lord-Kinross, *Atatürk: The Rebirth of a Nation* (Weidenfeld & Nicolson, London, 1964).
A. L. Macfie, *Atatürk* (Longman, Harlow, 1994).
Andrew Mango, *Atatürk* (John Murray, London, 1999).

BASIL LIDDELL HART
Alex Danchev, *Alchemist of War: The Life of Basil Liddell Hart* (Weidenfeld & Nicolson, London, 1998).
Sir Basil Liddell Hart, *The Memoirs of Captain Liddell Hart* (Cassell, London, 1965).
Sir Basil Liddell Hart, *Great Captains Unveiled* (Presidio Press, Novato, CA, 1990).
John J. Mearsheimer, *Liddell Hart and the Weight of History* (Cornell University Press, Ithaca, NY, 1993).

CARL GUSTAF MANNERHEIM
H. M. Tillotson, *Finland at Peace and War* (Michael Russell, London, 1993).
J. E. O. Screen, *Mannerheim: the Years of Preparation* (Hurst, London, 1970).
Oliver Warner, *Marshal Mannerheim and the Finns* (Weidenfeld & Nicolson, London, 1967).
Stig Jägerskiöld, *Mannerheim: Marshal of Finland* (Hurst, London, 1986).

GERD VON RUNDSTEDT
Charles Messenger, *The Last Prussian: A Biography of Field Marshal Gerd von Rundstedt 1875–1953* (Elsevier, London, 1991).
Earl F. Ziemke, 'Field Marshal Gerd von Rundstedt', in Correlli Barnett (ed.), *Hitler's Generals* (Grove Press, London, 1989), pp. 175–207.

ERICH VON MANSTEIN
Enrico Syring and Ronald Smelser (eds), *Die Militarelite des Dritten Reiches*, 'Erich von Manstein – Das Operative Genie' (Ullstein, Berlin, 1995), pp. 325–48.
Oliver von Wrochem, *Erich von Manstein. Vernichtungskrieg und Geschichtspolitik* (Schöningh, Paderborn, 2006).

HEINZ GUDERIAN
Heinz Guderian, *Panzer Leader* (Michael Joseph, London, 1952).
Kenneth Macksey, *Guderian* (Greenhill, London, 1992).

ERWIN ROMMEL
Charles Douglas-Home, 'Field Marshal Erwin Rommel', in Michael Carver (ed), *The War Lords* (Weidenfeld & Nicolson, London, 1976).
Rick Atkinson, *An Army at Dawn: The War in North Africa 1942–1943* (Little, Brown, London, 2003).
David Fraser, *Knight's Cross: The Life of Field Marshal Erwin Rommel* (HarperCollins, London, 1993).

Samuel Mitcham, *The Desert Fox in Normandy: Rommel's Defence of Fortress Europe* (Cooper Square Press, London, 2001).

BERNARD MONTGOMERY
Bernard Montgomery, *The Memoirs of Field-Marshal the Viscount Montgomery of Alamein* (William Collins, Glasgow, 1958).
Nigel Hamilton, *Monty, The Life of Montgomery of Alamein: 1887–1942* (Hamish Hamilton, London, 1981).
Nigel Hamilton, *Monty, The Life of Montgomery of Alamein: 1942–44* (Hamish Hamilton, London, 1983).
Nigel Hamilton, *Monty, The Life of Montgomery of Alamein: 1944–76* (Hamish Hamilton, London, 1986).

GEORGI ZHUKOV
Robert Service, *Stalin* (Macmillan, London, 2004).
G. K. Zhukov, *The Memoirs of Marshal Zhukov* (Jonathan Cape, London, 1971).
Andrew Nagorski, *The Greatest Battle: The Battle of Moscow 1941–2* (Aurum Press, London, 2007).
Chris Bellamy, *Absolute War: Soviet Russia in the Second World War* (Macmillan, London, 2007).
William J. Spahr, *Zhukov: The Rise and Fall of a Great Captain* (Presidio Press, Novato, CA, 1993).
Antony Beevor, *Stalingrad* (Viking, London, 1999).
David M. Glantz, *Zhukov's Greatest Defeat: The Red Army's Epic Disaster in Operation Mars* (University Press of Kansan, Lawrence, KS, 1999).

IVAN KONEV
Ivan Konev, *Year of Victory* (Progress Publishers, Moscow, 1969).
Ivan Konev, 'The Korsun–Shevchenkovsky Pocket', in *Battles Hitler Lost* (Richardson and Steirman, New York, 1986), pp. 111–26.
Evan Mawdsley, *Thunder in the East: The Nazi–Soviet War 1941–1945* (Hodder Arnold, London, 2005).
Harold Shukman (ed.), *Stalin's Generals* (Weidenfeld & Nicolson, London, 1993).
David Glantz, Jonathan House, *When Titans Clashed: How the Red Army Stopped Hitler* (University Press of Kansas, Lawrence, KS, 1995).

DWIGHT D. EISENHOWER
Carlo D'Este, *Eisenhower: Allied Supreme Commander* (Weidenfeld & Nicolson, London, 2002).
Geoffrey Perret, *Eisenhower* (Random House, New York, 1999).

GEORGE S. PATTON
Martin Blumenson, *Patton: The Man Behind the Legend* (Jonathan Cape, London, 1986).
Carlo D'Este, *A Genius for War: A Life of George S. Patton* (HarperCollins, London, 1995).

Trevor Royle, *Patton: Old Blood and Guts* (Weidenfeld & Nicolson, London, 2005).

TOMOYUKI YAMASHITA
J.D. Potter, *A Soldier Must Hang* (Muller, London, 1963).
Akashi Yoji, 'General Yamashita Tomoyuki: Commander of the 25th Army', in Brian P. Farrell and Sandy Hunter (eds), *Sixty Years On: The Fall of Singapore Revisited* (Times Academic Press, Singapore, 2002).

DOUGLAS MACARTHUR
D. Clayton James, *The Years of MacArthur* (2 vols, Houghton Mifflin, Boston, 1970 and 1975).
Geoffrey Perret, *Old Soldiers Never Die: The Life of Douglas MacArthur* (Random House, New York, 1996).

WILLIAM SLIM
Field Marshal Viscount Slim, *Defeat into Victory: Battling Japan in Burma and India 1942–45* (Cooper Square Press, London, 2000).
Robert Lyman, *Slim: Master of War, Burma and the Birth of Modern Warfare* (Constable, London, 2005).
Ronald Lewin, *Slim: The Standardbearer, A Biography of Field-Marshal The Viscount Slim* (Leo Cooper, London, 1976).

GERALD TEMPLER
John Cloake, *Templer, Tiger of Malaya: The Life of Field Marshal Sir Gerald Templer* (Harrap, London, 1985).
Robin Neillands, *A Fighting Retreat: The British Empire 1947–97* (Hodder & Stoughton, London, 1997).
Brian Lapping, *End of Empire* (St Martin's Press, New York, 1985).
Anthony Heathcote, *The British Field Marshals 1736–1997* (Pen & Sword Books Ltd, Barnsley, 1999).
Kumar Ramakrishna, *Emergency Propaganda: The Winning of Malayan Hearts and Minds 1948–1958* (Curzon Press, Richmond, 2002).

MOSHE DAYAN
Moshe Dayan, *Story of My Life* (Weidenfeld & Nicolson, London, 1976).
Martin van Creveld, *Moshe Dayan* (Cassell, London, 2002).

VO NGUYEN GIAP
Cecil B. Currey, *Victory at Any Cost: The Genius of Vietnam's Vo Nguyen Giap* (Potomac Books, Washington, DC, 1997).
Robert J. O'Neill, *General Giap: Politician and Strategist* (Praeger, New York, 1969).
Vo Nguyen Giap, *People's War, People's Army* (Praeger, New York, 1962).

INDEX

Figures in italics refer to illustrations

PICTURE CREDITS

Quercus Publishing has made every effort to trace copyright holders of the pictures used in this book.
Anyone having claims to ownership not identified below is invited to contact Quercus Publishing.

AKG Images Page 12, 21, 24, 29, 30, 32, 34, 38, 45, 49, 53, 61, 63, 94, 98, 99, 125, 131, 144, 153, 157, 159, 186, 232, 245, 247, 248, 263, 264, 288, 294, 301, 304, 306, 309, 311, 312, 313, 314, 318, 327, 329, 330, 333, 335, 339, 349, 350, 355, 358, 359, 362, 382.
Private Collection 22, 397, 399.
Topfoto 26, 104, 172, 180, 228, 235, 293, 303, 319, 321, 322, 336, 337, 367, 378, 381, 386, 409, 410.
Bridgeman Art Library / Museo Nacional, Bogota / Archives Charmet 1, 167, The Detroit Institute of Arts, USA/ Founders Society purchase, Mr and Mrs Edgar B. Whitcomb fund 2, 142, Private Collection 8–9, 46, 62, 134, 135, 138, 193, 197, Deutsches Historisches Museum, Berlin 37, Christie's Images 42, National Army Museum, London 48, 66, 101, 242, Harris Museum and Art Gallery, Preston, Lancashire 50, Louvre, Paris / Lauros / Giraudon 55, 145, Bibliothèque Nationale, Paris 65, Heeresgeschichtliches Museum, Vienna 69, 75, Kunsthistorisches Museum, Vienna 70, Royal Palace, Drottningholm, Stockholm 78, Rafael Valls Gallery, London 81, Pushkin Museum, Moscow 82, Musée de la Ville de Paris, Musée Carnavalet /Giraudon 85, Château de Versailles, France/ Giraudon 87, Château de Versailles, France/ Lauros / Giraudon 89, 234, Kurpfalzisches Museum, Heidelberg / Lauros / Giraudon 93, Fine Art Auctioneers, New York 115, Fitzwilliam Museum, University of Cambridge 121, Musée de l'Armée, Brussels, Château de Versailles, France 128, 233, Private Collection/ Mark Fiennes 133, 428, Patrick Lorette 127, Private Collection / The Stapleton Collection 143, 158, State Historical Museum, Moscow / RIA Novosti 148, Hermitage, St. Petersburg 151, Musée des Beaux-Arts, Caen / Giraudon 154, Manchester Art Gallery 155, Private Collection / Archives Charmet 161, 168, 169, 183, 261, 272, Atwater Kent Museum of Philadelphia 192, Private Collection / Peter Newark Military Pictures 204, 217, Chicago History Museum 213, 215, Private Collection / Ken Welsh 246, Archives de Gaulle, Paris / Giraudon 423.
Scala 72, 73, 91, 97, 171, 185, 187.
The Art Archive / Musée du Château de Versailles / Gianni Dagli Orti 40, 56, 77, 141, India Office Library 103, 107, AA 352, 376.
RMN Musée de l'Armée / Alain Argentin 59.
The British Library, London 102.
Mary Evans Picture Library 176, 239, 240.
Library and Archives, Canada 109, 111, 112.
New Brunswick Museum Archives & Research Library 113.
Independence National Historical Park Library, Philadelphia 117.
Corbis / Francis G. Mayer 118, Hulton-Deutsch Collection 162, 286, 290; Bettmann 165, 177, 189, 191, 199, 200, 207, 219, 221, 223, 224, 227, 250-251, 267, 269, 282, 283, 298, 305, 325, 365, 368, 369, 373, 375, 388, 392, 393, 394, 395, 402, 413, 421, 425, 426, 427, Underwood & Underwood 178-179, 277, Medford Society Historical Collection 208, 210, 218, Austrian Archives 299, David Rubinger 417, Dien Bien Phu Museum/Reuters 425,
US Army Center of Military History 122.
Rex Features 266.
Greenwich National Maritime Museum, London 126.
The Museum of the Confederacy, Richmond, Virginia 203.
Getty Images / Hulton Archive 237, 270, 273, 280, 342, 354, 357, Keystone 285, 317, 385, Mansell / Time Life Pictures 287, Topical Press 296, Frank Scherschel / Time Life Pictures 344, Time Life Pictures/US Army 387, Three Lions 407, Popperfoto 408, 418, Ministry of Defense 414, Israeli GPO/Newsmakers 416.
Imperial War Museum, London 252 (Q48178), 255 (Q7629), 258, 259 (Q949),(Q9271), 271 (Q15562), 274 (Q12364), 341 (B5337), 343 (E18542), 346 (B6794), 384 (KF89), 400 (SE3530).
Library of Congress, USA 279.
PA / Associated Press 360, 405.

Dedicated to Alex Coulson and Alec Foster-Brown

First published in Great Britain in 2009
Quercus Publishing Plc
21 Bloomsbury Square
London
WC1A 2NS

A CIP catalogue record for this book is available from
the British Library

Printed and bound in China

10 9 8 7 6 5 4 3 2 1

Cloth case edition: ISBN 978 1 84724 260 0

Printed case edition: ISBN 978 1 84724 516 8

PUBLISHING DIRECTOR Richard Milbank
PROJECT EDITOR Penny Gardiner
DESIGNER Austin Taylor
PICTURE RESEARCH Elaine Willis
CARTOGRAPHY The Maltings Partnership
    and William Donohoe